Nino Pirrotta
An Intellectual Biography

Nino Pirrotta (1908–98), *Licenza, Dipl. di magistero, Dott. in Lettere*, A.M., D.F.A., L.H.D., Mus.D. (Cantab.), Laurea «Ad Honorem.»

NINO PIRROTTA
An Intellectual Biography

Anthony M. Cummings

American Philosophical Society
Philadelphia • 2013

Transactions of the
American Philosophical Society
Held at Philadelphia
For Promoting Useful Knowledge
Volume 103, Part 1

Copyright © 2013 by the American Philosophical Society for its Transactions series.

All rights reserved.

ISBN: 978-1-60618-031-0
US ISSN: 0065-9746

Library of Congress Cataloging-in-Publication Data
Cummings, Anthony M.
  Nino Pirrotta : an intellectual biography / Anthony M. Cummings.
    pages ; cm — (Transactions of the American Philosophical Society ; Volume 103, Number 1)
  Includes bibliographical references and index.
  ISBN 978-1-60618-031-0
  1. Pirrotta, Nino. 2. Musicologists—Italy—Biography. I. American Philosophical Society II. Title.
  ML423.P566C85 2013
  780.92—dc23
                    [B] 2013014518

In Memory of Pierluigi Petrobelli

Dottore in Lettere, Università degli Studi di Roma, «La Sapienza»
M.F.A., Princeton University
Professore Ordinario di Storia della Musica, «La Sapienza»

and of Harold S. Powers

M.F.A., Ph.D., Princeton University
Scheide Professor of Music History, Princeton

Books by Anthony M. Cummings

The Politicized Muse: Music for Medici Festivals, 1512–1537 (1992)

co-authored with William G. Bowen et al., *University Libraries and Scholarly Communication: A Study Prepared for the Andrew W. Mellon Foundation* (1993)

co-edited with Jessie Ann Owens, *Music in Renaissance Cities and Courts: Studies in Honor of Lewis Lockwood* (1996)

The Maecenas and the Madrigalist: Patrons, Patronage, and the Origins of the Italian Madrigal, Memoirs of the American Philosophical Society CCLIII (2004)

MS Florence, Biblioteca Nazionale Centrale, Magl. XIX, 164–167 (2006)

The Lion's Ear: Pope Leo X, the Renaissance Papacy, and Music (2012)

co-edited with John J. Joyce Jr. and Bruce Boyd Raeburn, Sam Morgan's Jazz Band, *Complete Recorded Works in Transcription* (2012)

co-edited with Linda L. Carroll, Zachary W. Jones, and Philip Weller, Antonio Molino, *Delightful Madrigals for Four Voices . . ., Newly . . . Composed and Brought to Light . . . . First Book . . . . 1568* [*I DILETTEVOLI MADRIGALI A QUATTRO VOCI . . ., NUOVAMENTE . . . COMPOSTI ET DATI IN LUCE . . . . LIBRO PRIMO . . . . MDLXVIII.*] (2012)

Contents

A Note on Bibliographic Citations	ix
Prologo	xi
Excursus	xxiii
Acknowledgments	xxv
Principal Dates in Pirrotta's Life and Career	xxix

Atto I.^{mo}
Studente   1

Scena 1.^a	**Famiglia** (1908–24)	3
Scena 2.^a	**Student Days** (1924–31): The R. Conservatori di Musica «Vincenzo Bellini» di Palermo and «Luigi Cherubini» di Firenze and the R. Università degli Studi di Palermo and Firenze	23
Scena 3.^a	**Palermo** (1931–36): *Il Sacchetti e la tecnica musicale del trecento italiano*	53

Intermedio I.^{mo} ["non apparente"]   73
Pirrotta's Intellectual and Musical Formation

Atto II.^{ndo}   125
Bibliotecario

Scena 4.^a	**The Conservatory of Palermo** (1936–48): *Il Trecento*	127
Scena 5.^a	**The Conservatorio di Musica «Santa Cecilia» di Roma** (1948–56): *Opera Seicentesca*	155
Scena 6.^a	**Princeton, California, and Columbia** (1954–55)	193

	Intermedio II.^{ndo} *["apparente"]* **Images**	201
	Atto III.^{tio} **Professore**	241
Scena 7.^a	**Harvard University** (1956–71): *Rinascimento* (or: "Rome Fumbles, and Harvard Recovers")	243
Scena 8.^a	**The Università degli Studi di Roma, «La Sapienza»** (1972–78)	295
Scena 9.^a	***Il Principe*** (1978–98): *Opera Settecentesca ed Ottocentesca*	309
	Epilogo **Pirrotta's Narrative of the History of Italian Music: Music and "Cultural Fashion"**	337
Appendix:	*Documents of Pirrotta's Formal Education*	355
Bibliography: The Publications of Nino Pirrotta		359
Index		385

A Note on Bibliographic Citations

References in the footnotes to Pirrotta's publications are formatted as follows: the year of publication (in **bold**), followed by a short title. For the complete reference, the reader is referred to the "Bibliography: The Publications of Nino Pirrotta." Thus the following title:

Antonino Pirrotta, "Fonti iconografiche e stilistiche della pittura su maioliche del Rinascimento," 2 vols. (*Tesi di Laurea* [*Dottore in Lettere*], Facoltà di Lettere e Filosofia, Regia Università degli studi di Firenze, ["Presentata il 31-X."] 1931).

will hereafter be cited as:

1931: "Fonti iconografiche e stilistiche della pittura su maioliche del Rinascimento."

Prologo

In a memorial tribute to Antonino ("Nino") Pirrotta (1908–98),[1] Lewis Lockwood reported that he could "remember a graduate student in the 1970s in Princeton who had never met...Pirrotta or heard him speak, but...was so taken by the quality of Pirrotta's work that he kept a portrait poster of him on the wall of his carrel."[2] Professor Lockwood discreetly refrained from naming the student, considering it the latter's prerogative to disclose his identity, which I am now pleased to do. When Pirrotta lectured at Princeton later in the 1970s, I had the good fortune to meet the subject of the portrait poster that had been hanging in my study carrel. And, in 1996, I took the opportunity to express my regard for him publicly:

> It is impossible for me to express adequately the extent of my personal and intellectual indebtedness to Professor Nino Pirrotta, and my regard for him. I still remember vividly the extreme intellectual excitement I experienced when I first read his work as a graduate student. I believe that his writings are in a class by themselves, for their knowledge of and sensitivity toward the historical background and for their quality as examples of humanistic research and expression. In my view, no one has practiced the art of music history better than he, and most of us have not come close; his work is representative of the very best our discipline has to offer.[3]

---

[1] *Licenza in storia della musica, Diploma di magistero in organo e composizione organistica, Dottore in Lettere* (history of art), A.M., D.F.A., L.H.D., Mus.D. (Cantab.), *Laurea «Ad Honorem»*; Docente in Storia della Musica, Professore di Storia della Musica, and Bibliotecario at the R. Conservatorio di Musica «Vincenzo Bellini» di Palermo (1936–48); Direttore of the Biblioteche dell'Accademia e del Conservatorio di Musica «Santa Cecilia» di Roma (1948–56); Walter W. Naumburg '89 Professor of Music and Head of the Eda Kuhn Loeb Music Library, Faculty of Arts and Sciences, Harvard University (1956–71); and Professore Ordinario di Storia della Musica, Facoltà di Lettere e Filosofia, Università degli Studi di Roma, «La Sapienza» (1972–78).

[2] Lockwood, "In Memory of Nino Pirrotta," *Studi musicali* 28 (1999): 21–23.

[3] Anthony M. Cummings, "The Company of the Cazzuola and the Early Madrigal," in "Essays in Memory of Nino Pirrotta," special issue, *Musica disciplina* 50 (1996): 203–38, especially 203 n. *

In my esteem for Nino Pirrotta, I am honored by the company I keep. As early as 1948, François Lesure, reviewing Pirrotta's essay on the Modena manuscript,[4] acclaimed it as a model of descriptive musicology:

> Sans parler de la nouveauté de cette étude, on peut la considérer comme un modèle de musicologie descriptive, moins peut-être par l'étendue des compétences— paléographiques, historiques et musicales —que l'auteur met en jeu, que par l'intelligente comprehension des problèmes qu'il soulève.[5]

Pirrotta's study of music in the Italian theater during the fifteenth, sixteenth, and seventeenth centuries[6] drew praise from Stuart Reiner,[7] Howard Mayer Brown,[8] John Walter Hill,[9] Denis Arnold,[10] George J. Buelow,[11] Iain Fenlon,[12] and Denis Stevens.[13] Anthony Newcomb wrote:

> Pirrotta's . . . method is to try to understand the functions and the ways of communication . . . of theatrical music between c. 1475 and 1600— much of which has not come down to us. . . . Pirrotta brings to the difficult task of reconstructing an unwritten tradition from written documents not only an imposing mass of detail but also more than the usual scholarly daring and imagination in interpreting what this detail might mean.[14]

Pirrotta's edition of the music of fourteenth-century Italy elicited a scholar's appreciation from W. Thomas Marrocco[15] and David G. Hughes.[16] Pirrotta's facsimile editions of the original manuscript sources transmitting that repertory were favorably reviewed by Richard H. Hoppin[17] and David Fallows.[18]

---

[4]**1944/45**: "Il codice estense." Throughout this study, I refer to titles in Pirrotta's bibliography of writings in abbreviated form, as here: the year of publication, in **bold**, followed by a brief identifying title. See my Bibliography for the complete reference.

[5]*Revue de musicologie* 30 (1948): 100. Charles van den Borren wrote similarly positively of the same publication: *Revue belge de Musicologie* 2 (1948).

[6]**1969**: *Music and Theatre.*

[7]*Notes*, 2nd ser., 28 (1972): 423–35.

[8]*Musical Quarterly* 57 (1971): 671–77.

[9]*Journal of the American Musicological Society* 36 (1983): 519–26.

[10]*Music & Letters* 58 (1977): 475–77.

[11]*Musical Quarterly* 69 (1983): 607–11.

[12]*Musical Times* 117 (1976): 742–43.

[13]*Musical Times* 123 (1982): 479.

[14]*Renaissance Quarterly* 37 (1984): 109–13.

[15]*Musical Quarterly* 41 (1955): 115-17.

[16]*Journal of the American Musicological Society* 10 (1957): 47–49.

[17]*Musical Quarterly* 48 (1962): 129–31.

[18]*Early Music* 24 (1996): 345–46. See also Margaret Bent, *Early Music History* 15 (1996): 251–69: "Pirrotta provides an elegant introductory essay for the volume. . . . More recently, and here, he makes an elegant and subtle case for placing the manuscript in the Veronese circle of the author Gidino da Sommacampagna. . . . [H]is essay is filled with humane and perceptive observations"; and James Haar, *Journal of the American Musicological Society* 49 (1996): 145–55, 150.

Finally, anthologies of his essays have been positively received by James Haar,[19] David Fallows,[20] Maria Rika Maniates,[21] Leeman Perkins,[22] W.T. Atcherson,[23] F.W. Sternfeld,[24] Janet Palumbo,[25] and Iain Fenlon.[26] Ellen Rosand writes:

> Nino Pirrotta's stature as perhaps the most profoundly humane musical scholar of our time has long been appreciated by those who have followed his research and meditations over the past three decades. In Italy he is recognized as the doyen of modern musicological studies: "il principe elettorale della musicologia italiana".... Although his history of music encompasses the widest cultural perspective, Pirrotta pieces together that perspective from the smallest details, his lens shifting back and forth from close to far, from single observation to general theory, and then back again.... His music history is cultural history in the largest sense, but it is also a history of individuals. He always remembers that the creators of music were living men.... Pirrotta's career is an affirmation of the humanity of musicology.[27]

In my experience, the tributes to Pirrotta are unsurpassed and perhaps even unequaled. The cumulative effect of reading them is to be reminded that their dedicatee was a singular figure indeed.

*****

What was it about Nino Pirrotta—the man and the scholar—that elicited such expressions of regard? What in his formation explains how he became the scholar he became? And most important—given that this is an intellectual biography[28]—what is it in his scholarly writings that evoked such responses?

---

[19]*Early Music History* 5 (1985): 269–74.
[20]*Early Music* 13 (1985): 578–79.
[21]*Musical Quarterly* 70 (1984): 567–72.
[22]*Renaissance Quarterly* 38 (1985): 529–32.
[23]*Sixteenth Century Journal* 16 (1985): 155–56.
[24]*Music & Letters* 66 (1985): 397–99.
[25]*Notes*, 2nd ser., 42 (1985): 281–83.
[26]*Musical Times* 126 (1985): 411.
[27]*Journal of the American Musicological Society* 39 (1986): 389–95:
[28]Among the many models for my biography, one has proved to be especially useful: E.H. Gombrich, *Aby Warburg: An Intellectual Biography* (London: Warburg Institute, 1970). See also Spyros Papapetros, "The Eternal Seesaw: Oscillations in Warburg's Revival," *Oxford Art Journal* 26 (2003): 169–76; for this reference, I am grateful to Professor William Tronzo. I also profited from *The Intellectual Migration: Europe and America, 1930–1960*, ed. Donald Fleming and Bernard Bailyn (Cambridge, MA: Belknap Press of Harvard University Press, 1969), especially the Introduction, Harry Levin's entry "Two *Romanisten* in America: Spitzer and Auerbach," and Colin Eisler's, "*Kunstgeschichte* American Style: A Study in Migration." This latter title was illuminating in describing the role European scholars have played in American academic life. Predictably helpful and stimulating was also Anthony Grafton, "Momigliano's Method and the Warburg Institute: Studies in His Middle Period," in *Worlds Made by Words. Scholarship and Community in the Modern West* (Cambridge, MA: Harvard University Press, 2009), 231–54 and 402–11.

For many years, historical musicologists have had repeated recourse to Pirrotta's writings, and re-readings have often yielded rich new returns. When I first read his writings, I was immediately impressed by their *quality*, in two senses of that word: (1) their *excellence;* and (2) their distinctive *character,* so unlike that of other examples of musicological discourse.

Many of Pirrotta's admirers have invoked the term "interdisciplinarity" to describe his intellectual distinctiveness. And at first, I, too, would have used that term. As an undergraduate, I had read Erwin Panofsky's classic *Gothic Architecture and Scholasticism*,[29] and it was a revelation: a particular aesthetic or intellectual sensibility may be traceable in more than one expression of human creativity at a given moment, in this instance the scholastic method in theology and a simultaneous architectural style, the "Gothic." Then when I entered graduate school, Professor Kenneth Levy urged that I read Pirrotta's "Dante *Musicus:* Gothicism, Scholasticism, and Music,"[30] which by Pirrotta's account is indebted to Panofsky's essay. At the time, I would have attributed the effect of these essays to their "interdisciplinarity": their transcendence of traditional disciplinary boundaries. But eventually I came to believe that explaining Pirrotta's achievement (or Panofsky's, for that matter) in terms of its "interdisciplinarity" is not altogether satisfactory.

In my opinion, "interdisciplinary" is one of the most loosely scrutinized and misapplied terms in the modern academic lexicon. In some instances, it is used in a way that suggests that there is an insufficient appreciation for the highly constructed nature of many disciplines.[31] Sander Gilman, one of the most acute observers and practitioners of "inter-" or "transdisciplinarity," has written:

> By the end of the nineteenth century the universities had become centers for research and teaching in the natural sciences as well as in the humanities. Central to this model was the belief that knowledge was present in the universe and only needed to be uncovered. This process of "uncovering" was undertaken through human agency, but it was independent of the vagaries of human difference and individual bias. By the close of the nineteenth century, positivism defined the role of the investigator as well as the teacher. . . . Teaching and research; research and

---

[29]Erwin Panofsky, *Gothic Architecture and Scholasticism* (New York: World Publishing Co., 1957).
[30]**1965**: "Dante *musicus.*"
[31]Some elements in the construction of the disciplines are expressions of unalterable "givens" that are dictated by nature. The distinction between organic and inorganic chemistry is one such case, but the same situation obtains within the humanistic disciplines: To a considerable extent, the disciplines of art and music history are expressions of the senses of sight and sound, both biological givens (on this very matter, see the quotation from Leonardo da Vinci at the conclusion of Pirrotta's **1966**: "Despres, Josquin"); the history of literature is text-based discourse, the history of art is sight-based discourse, and the history of music is sound-based discourse. In many other cases, however, the disciplines are constructed through a series of conscious or unconscious choices and assumptions, and they are altogether mutable. On this matter, see Benedetto Croce, *The Aesthetic as the Science of Expression and of the Linguistic in General*, trans. Colin Lyas (Cambridge: Cambridge University Press, 1992), 128 and n. 8.

teaching—these involve asking new questions, creating new disciplines, restructuring older fields, exploring and experimenting. Nevertheless, all along, the myth has been maintained that this knowledge (and its means of presentation) was simply to be found in nature.... [T]he academic has argued that the uncovering of knowledge was simply a natural act, a revealing of that which was present.... Assuming that the division of knowledge is not the reflex of some natural law, I argue that restructuring disciplines and rethinking their goals is a natural and regular procedure in the university.[32]

The emergence of a new discipline is often followed by aftereffects: a department in academic institutions, a professional society, a journal dedicated to scholarship by practitioners of the new discipline, specialized methodologies and knowledge bases that are the preserve of the initiate. Later, when questions arise that cannot be answered satisfactorily by that particular existing discipline, we deploy the materials and methodologies of multiple disciplines in the attempt to provide answers. There is thus a temporal element to the emergence of "interdisciplinarity": it may follow chronologically upon the establishment of a recognized discipline.

The celebration of interdisciplinarity seems an ironic enterprise: the academic world first constructs its disciplines and establishes their boundaries; it then celebrates those whose interests transcend the classification. Inadvertently, the very term "interdisciplinary" may unduly legitimize the boundaries separating the established disciplines from one another and thus celebrate "interdisciplinarity" more than is warranted. The term suggests that we may have uncritically accepted disciplinary distinctions at the outset, and thereafter, in response to a perceived need, we construct a concept—"interdisciplinarity"—that also uncritically legitimizes the meta-discourse and was required by the unthinking acceptance of disciplinary boundaries in the first place.

Nino Pirrotta's principal concern was to situate the musical fact[33] within the broadest contexts, which assumed that existing disciplinary boundaries would not constrain his act of contextualization. He was not restricted by the limitations imposed by the construction of the disciplines—the potentially clumsy classification, within the academy's fields of knowledge, of various intersecting realms of human activity—and he did not operate within them. The distinctions among disciplines that governed much of the scholarly activity of his time were not part of his constitution.

---

[32]Sander L. Gilman, *The Fortunes of the Humanities: Thoughts for After the Year 2000* (Stanford, CA: Stanford University Press, 2000), 26, 31–32.

[33]See Pierluigi Petrobelli's observations in his "Introduzione" in *Musicologia fra due continenti. L'eredità di Nino Pirrotta. Convegno internazionale (Roma, 4–6 giugno 2008)*, Accademia Nazionale dei Lincei (Rome: Scienze e lettere, 2010), 7–8.

It is partly this quality that makes his writings vivid, evocative, and atmospheric. And it is precisely this quality that gives them their explanatory power, because in elucidating the music, he demonstrates its relationship to the broader cultural sensibilities and material conditions that shaped its setting.

Moreover, the disciplines are, to some extent, expressions of cultural differences. What is interdisciplinary in the American context may not be so when the practitioner is the legatee of a different intellectual tradition. In Pirrotta's case, his interdisciplinarity was the product of a different set of a priori assumptions, a different construction of knowledge and the interrelatedness of its various realms.

There is another respect in which Pirrotta's biography is important to his intellectual profile and an understanding of the phenomena of disciplinarity and his interdisciplinarity.[34] The subject matter of his writings, almost without exception, was Italian music, which is only one element in the whole of Italian culture and history. And because Pirrotta was an Italian, he was elucidating his own national tradition, perceived as an organic integrity. The academy's penchant for parsing the elements of that organic culture—for segmenting it into painting, sculpture, architecture, language and literature, music, history, philosophy, and other expressions of human experience—would not have been as operative in his case. Non-Italian scholars, representatives of the academy's various disciplines, would perhaps be more inclined than he to extract these expressions of human experience from the cultural context and remove them to their "scientific laboratories," as "samples" to be studied in isolation. Dissatisfaction with the result might then lead to an ex post facto reassembling of the culture, a reconstitution of the context: in short, to interdisciplinary activity.[35]

An appreciation of Pirrotta's interdisciplinarity is thus to be understood within a particular context. And, more important, the characterization of his work in such terms demands careful scrutiny. Given the construction of the disciplines in the American university of the 1950s and '60s, a representative of another heritage could invoke seemingly atypical intellectual assets, which Pirrotta did. The distinctiveness of his intellectual style was in part a function of his experiences: he had not been subject to the same influences as his American colleagues.

This is not to minimize his achievement. On the contrary, few beneficiaries of the experiences he enjoyed would have profited from them as he did. Pirrotta's intellectual sensitivity, when applied to the material mastered as a

---

[34] Sabine Eiche suggested the following to me, which I am developing from her suggestions.

[35] Moreover, there may also have been contrasting theories of knowledge operative, as well as cultural differences: at least according to its opponents, one philosophy of history—the Positivist—abstracts historical data from their context and removes them to the "laboratory" for antiseptic examination; another—the Idealist—advocates their (re)contextualization.

result of his educational and professional experiences, produced the results that are the subject of this study.

It is also worth observing that interdisciplinarity in teaching—especially at the undergraduate level, where students are less conversant with the practices of the established disciplines—occasions less debate, and in some respects is more readily accepted. On the other hand, authoritative interdisciplinarity in scholarship demands a professional's competence in the several disciplines invoked in attempts to solve the problems encountered. Pirrotta's expertise in multiple established disciplines— music, literature, history, art history—facilitated a legitimate exercise of scholarly interdisciplinarity.[36] Thus an irony of Pirrotta's scholarship is that, despite his close identification with the mission of graduate education as supported at some of the world's great research universities—Princeton, Columbia, Harvard, the University of Rome—his writings often overcame that excessive specialization that is sometimes characteristic of institutions that offer the doctorate.[37] Rather, his scholarship manifested the transdisciplinarity, organicism, synthetic quality, and tendency toward contextualization that is often more characteristic of undergraduate liberal arts education (not to mention the liberal arts tradition of *belles lettres*, which distinguishes his elegant style of expression and mode of presentation).

*****

There is, I believe, a further aspect to the quality that Pirrotta's admirers have sought to describe. His profile resists the usual attempts at classification not so much in the narrower sense that his interests transcended the established American disciplines of the day, as in the broader sense that his experiences —and resultant skills, methodologies, and profile—were multiform and unusual.

---

[36]Pirrotta's Italian pupil Fabrizio Della Seta has observed that with respect to a conversance with the texts, Pirrotta possessed a professional's competence in the history of Italian literature from its origins to the seventeenth century; see Della Seta, "Appunti per un ritratto intellettuale di Nino Pirrotta," *Recercare* 10 (1998): 9–15, especially 10. In 1995, when the Facoltà di Lettere e Filosofia of the Università degli Studi di Urbino requested of the University rector that Pirrotta be granted the *Laurea «Ad Honorem»*, the accompanying justification observed that Pirrotta had pioneered in introducing Italian scholars—of music and literature—to the systematic study of the aesthetic interconnections between the text-based and sound-based arts; see "Laurea 'honoris causa' a Nino Pirrotta," *Studi urbinati. B: Scienze umane e sociali* 68 (1997/98): 9–16, especially 10. For providing me with a copy of this text, I am grateful to Professor Agostino Ziino. For further reflections on that scholarly versatility, see *"Per un regale evento": Spettacoli nuziali e opera in musica alla corte dei Medici*, ed. Maria Adelaide Bartoli Bacherini, exh. cat. (Florence: Centro Di, 2000), 190–91, no. 126.

[37]For an expression of one research-university president's concern with such specialization, see William G. Bowen, "Graduate Education in the Arts and Sciences: Prospects for the Future. Report of the President, April 1981," in *Ever the Teacher: William G. Bowen's Writings as President of Princeton* (Princeton, NJ: Princeton University Press, 1987), 189–237, especially 219–21, "National Trends Threatening Graduate Education: The Problem of Specialization."

Pirrotta was not the exclusive product of either the conservatory or the university. As he recounted on several occasions, comprehensive training in music history was unavailable at the Italian university when he was a student, and neither the university nor the conservatory alone provided would-be music historians with the range of skills required to embark on a career in the field. Pirrotta thus created his own methodology and unfettered vision of the discipline, which was fresh and unpredictable.

Moreover, Pirrotta's style was fully beholden to neither of two principal tendencies shaping Italian intellectual life when he was undergoing his formation: Positivism, whose principal Italian exponent was Roberto Ardigò, and various twentieth-century spiritualist responses to it, among them the Idealism of Benedetto Croce and Giovanni Gentile. With respect to his personal theory of epistemology and his methodology—what we can characterize as his intellectual profile—Pirrotta positioned himself between (or above) these various tendencies, and his independence of them was distinctive. His Positivistic respect for the authority of the verifiable historical datum was gently tempered and colored by the Idealist's imaginative and intuitive apprehension and vivid representation thereof.

In Pirrotta's work, we also hear resonances of another important Italian intellectual tradition of his time: economic Materialism (whose principal Italian exponent was Antonio Labriola), which further distinguishes his writings from those of other American musicologists of the 1950s and '60s. The music he studied was the compositional output of living, breathing human beings, who were subject to material circumstances that he elucidates vividly.

And most obviously, Pirrotta was exclusively neither Italian nor American in his formation and development. His Italianate sensibilities are refreshing when apprehended against the backdrop of the predominant intellectual tendency of American musicology of the postwar era, the neo-Positivism that has been described by Joseph Kerman.[38] On the other hand, on his return to Italy in 1972, his Italian disciples found his approach a revelation in its more Germanic, Positivistic emphasis on the sources.[39]

In each of these instances, Pirrotta operated at the interstices of the sometimes clumsily dualistic constructs of his time: the oppositions of conservatory versus university, as embodying contrasting modes of engagement with the arts and their history; of Positivism versus the various spiritualist reactions thereto, as embodying contrasting intellectual sensibilities and theories of epistemology; of the Germanic versus the Italianate. In my view, this is

---

[38] Joseph Kerman, *Contemplating Music: Challenges to Musicology* (Cambridge, MA: Harvard University Press, 1985).

[39] For this observation, I am indebted to, among others, Pirrotta's pupil Franco Piperno, who is now the incumbent of the chair Pirrotta once held at the University of Rome, and who made such observations during a private meeting generously granted me on 20 December 2007.

precisely what explains the distinctiveness of his scholarly persona, that seeming unpredictability of the substance and style of his writings. More so than most, Pirrotta cannot be typed or classified.

*****

What in Nino Pirrotta's formation and career experiences explains these results? To some extent, they were caused by individual temperament and character, which may in part have been inherited from his parents and grandparents. Pirrotta's pupil James Haar observed that his teacher was "typified" by an "openness,"[40] and, indeed, throughout his career, Pirrotta responded to opportunities afforded him. He noted that his decision to withdraw from the conservatory and university in his native Palermo in 1927 and enroll instead at the conservatory and university in Florence was unusual for the time. His decision to avail himself of the opportunity of a career in the United States—especially when, by his own admission, he did not yet command the English language—is also notable and not to be underestimated. To relocate one's family at age 48 to embark on a career in another country is a mark of uncommon "openness," and, indeed, of courage, especially since it occurred in 1956, when international travel was more complicated than today.[41]

The distinctiveness of his profile is also partly the result of the influence of key figures in his professional development:

1. Luigi Amadio, his private piano teacher, Professor of Organ at the Conservatory of Palermo, who was called to Florence in 1927, and whom Pirrotta followed there;
2. Mario Salmi, his thesis adviser in art history at the University of Florence;
3. Ettore Li Gotti, his close friend and collaborator on a 1935 book on the Trecento poet Franco Sacchetti and the musical settings of his verse, which launched Pirrotta's formal musicological career; and, finally,
4. Oliver Strunk, another of Pirrotta's closest friends, who invited him to teach at Princeton University in 1954/55 and thus helped inaugurate the consequential American phase of his career.

The characteristics of the scholar are thus extensions of those of the man. Pirrotta's varied experiences, atypical for an Italian scholar of his time, allowed

---

[40]See Haar's contribution to the volume of recollections of Pirrotta in *Studi musicali* 28 (1999).

[41]But as was observed by Sabine Eiche, who emigrated with her family from Europe to Canada in 1956, the difficulties of the 1950s were more logistical than legal; it was the period of substantial, post-World War II emigration from Europe.

him to transcend inherited perspectives, both personal and intellectual. Notwithstanding an innate personal reserve, he took advantage of the unusual opportunities afforded him, in which the important contribution of his wife was undeniable.

The imaginativeness that characterizes his writings may thus be a reflection of that openness, that sensitivity to "Otherness," that proclivity toward travel, whether literal (the relocation to Cambridge, Massachusetts) or metaphoric (the imaginative, vivid re-situating of himself and his readers within the Italian Renaissance court, for example). Pirrotta's decision to reside and pursue professional opportunities outside his native land seems to have had the effect of liberating him from the limitations of quotidian life, so that he was free to give reign to his imagination's capacity for metaphoric "time travel." And his literal relocation to Massachusetts had another effect: It enabled him to study his own musical culture from without as well as within; his trans-Atlantic experiences permitted him to gain some distance on Italian musical tradition, unlike Italian scholars who spent their entire professional lives in Italy, so that he could perceive it more dispassionately. The clarity and disinterestedness of his discourse are partly the results of such life and professional choices.

*****

My biography is, above all, about the ongoing making of the discipline of historical musicology, about the special vision of the discipline embodied in the writings of one of its distinguished practitioners.

As a scientific university profession, historical musicology is now more than a century old and therefore mature enough to sustain regular systematic scrutiny. This biography is offered as a compelling case study. Pirrotta's influence—especially because his career had both Italian and American phases—has been considerable, and his practice of the discipline constitutes a fascinating example for anyone with an interest in the scholarly study of European music.

Our understanding of the European musical past is in good part a function of the questions we pose and the methodologies we adopt in attempting to answer them, and in those respects Pirrotta's writings are exemplary. I mean no disrespect to the many other esteemed members of my profession when I express the opinion that there are no finer models of humanistic discourse than Pirrotta's writings and state my belief that he is one of the few musicologists deserving at this juncture of the kind of biography I have attempted.

With respect to my regard for him as one of the makers of our discipline, I quote here what two colleagues have said:

> [W]e . . . come up against . . . the question of the place of the scholar *her-* or *himself* in the work of scholarship. I think that is ultimately the question that [Joseph]

Kerman has raised about musical scholarship. We would do well to take up the challenge, not only to discuss it, but to pursue our work with a consciousness that it is a central question. [Oliver] Strunk's attitude about this is thrown into relief by the rather different one of his good friend, Nino Pirrotta (I am surprised to find this name missing from the index of [Kerman's] *Contemplating Music*, not only because of the importance of its bearer for American musicology, but especially because his work would seem to exemplify Kerman's ideal in such high measure.... The title of his essay "*Ricercari* and Variations on *O rosa bella*"... reveals Pirrotta's attitude. Through it he identified his work as an invention, and himself as the inventor. It is a creative act performed with historical material.[42]

Portrayals of born-again musicology variously describe it as innovative, contextual, interdisciplinary, politically progressive, aware of historical situatedness, human, and humane.... [O]ne can only hope that students will not feel exempted from reading the work of the likes of Nino Pirrotta—from judging by themselves whether that work is fairly described as an accumulation of verifiable data.[43]

Is the "new musicology"[44] really so new?

---

[42]See Treitler's review of Kerman's book in *Journal of the American Musicological Society* 42 (1989): 375–402.
[43]See the quotation from Stefano Castelvecchi in Della Seta, "Appunti per un ritratto intellettuale di Nino Pirrotta."
[44]For a consideration of the elements of the "new musicology" from the perspective of one of Pirrotta's pupils, see the "Preface" to Fabrizio Della Seta's collection of his essays *Not Without Madness: Perspectives on Opera*, trans. M.W. Weir (Chicago: University of Chicago Press, forthcoming); I am grateful to Professor Della Seta for sharing this text prior to publication.

Excursus: What This Biography Aims to Do, and What It Does Not

I think it important to specify the limits to what I intended to accomplish in this study. This is an intellectual biography, based above all on Nino Pirrotta's writings, the principal evidence for his thought. I have sought to reconstruct his biography only insofar as it was essential to understanding his intellectual profile and development. I have not sought to recover many of his letters; he was a prolific correspondent, and it would have required a Herculean effort to collect his correspondence. However, I availed myself of offers from many who knew him well to see his letters to them. They were a valuable source of information.

After his wife's death in 1996, Pirrotta disposed of many papers of a personal nature and of correspondence to him. A few remaining private letters from various periods of his life concern matters of a personal character, not germane to a study of this nature. Other remaining papers, collected from the Pirrotta's home in Rome after his death, pertain principally to scholarly projects then underway and left incomplete, and I have limited the evidence of his thought to those writings actually brought to fruition, as constituting the best testimony to his finished, fully articulated ideas.

Acknowledgments

I am grateful to many individuals whose assistance was indispensable to the writing of this biography.

I could neither have undertaken nor completed this biography without the assistance of Nino Pirrotta's four children and their spouses and families: Adelaide M. Pirrotta-Bahr, M.D.; her husband, Professor Donald M. Bahr, Ph.D.; and their children Paolo Bahr, M.D., and Maria Pia Bahr, J.D.; Professor Vincenzo Pirrotta, Ph.D., and his wife, Donna; Dott.ssa Silvia Pirrotta-Giuffré and her children, especially her son Dott. Mario Giuffré; and Sergio Pirrotta, Ed.D.; his wife, Eileen, and their children, Alexander and Catrina. All were generous with their recollections and wisdom; all shared unpublished material in their possession and reminiscences of their parents.

Members of the larger Pirrotta family also offered invaluable assistance, principally among them Nino Pirrotta's nephew, Professore Agostino Ziino; Agostino's wife, Dott.ssa Paola Granata-Ziino; and their children, especially Ottavio Ziino and Francesca Ziino-Zonta; and Francesca's husband, Professore Mauro Zonta.

In drafting the chapter on Pirrotta's childhood and *liceo* training, I benefited from the assistance of Dott.ssa Fiorella Superbi of Villa I Tatti, The Harvard University Center for Italian Renaissance Studies, Florence; and Dott. Valerio Pacini, Dott. Giovanni Pagliarulo, and Dott.ssa Ilaria Della Monica of the Biblioteca Berenson at I Tatti; Professor Susann Lusnia of Tulane University; Professor Adolfo Scotto di Luzio of the Università degli Studi di Bergamo; and Professors Paul Cefalu and David Sunderlin of Lafayette College.

In drafting the chapter on the Conservatory and University of Florence, I benefited from the assistance of Professore Paolo Biordi and Professore Gianni Ciabbatini of the Conservatorio di Musica «Luigi Cherubini» di Firenze, and Dott.ssa Kathryn Bosi and Dott. Pacini of the Biblioteca Berenson.

Professor Alessandro Giovannelli and Dott.ssa Gisella Gisolo of Lafayette College proofread my transcriptions of the texts of Pirrotta's journalistic writings, produced during his post-Conservatory and post-University years

(1931–36), and saved me from error. Professor Linda L. Carroll of Tulane University also reviewed my transcriptions and translations of the journalistic writings and read a draft text of the article devoted to them; as always, Linda provided wise criticism, from which I profited greatly. The "*Intermedio I.^{mo}*" proved especially challenging to write, and I could not have done so without the counsel of Professore Fabrizio Della Seta of the Facoltà di musicologia, Cremona, of the Università degli Studi di Pavia; Professors Giovannelli, Joseph Shieber, Peter Gildenhuys, and Meghan Masto of the Department of Philosophy at Lafayette College; Professor Emeritus Paul Benacerraf of the Department of Philosophy at Princeton University; and Professor Emeritus Philip Gossett of the Department of Music at the University of Chicago.

The chapter on the years at the Conservatory of Rome owes much to Dott. Francesco Zimei, Professore Roberto Giuliani of the Conservatory of Rome, Professore Andrea Coen, and Signora Maria Vèrnole-Blazer, who sang the title role in the 1951 broadcast performance of Jacopo Peri's *Euridice*, and Maria's children—David Blazer, M.D., and Judith Blazer. Dr. Beth Glixon, a specialist in early Seicento opera, read a draft of the chapter and offered many useful suggestions regarding my presentation of the scholarship in a field in which I am no expert. For the same reason, I am grateful to Professor Tim Carter of the University of North Carolina, Chapel Hill, who corrected several of my earlier incorrect formulations in the sections on Jacopo Peri.

For assistance with the chapter on the visiting year at Princeton, I am grateful to my teachers Professors Lewis Lockwood and Kenneth Levy. But my debt to Lewis is greater still: He was one of Pirrotta's good friends; I consulted with him regularly and frequently throughout the research for and writing of this biography, and he was invariably helpful and generous with wise counsel. Lewis's advice and encouragement were indispensable to my completing this work.

Farris G. Wahbeh of Columbia University assisted with documentation concerning Pirrotta's visiting appointment at Columbia.

Many individuals assisted in the research for the chapter on the Harvard years. Professor Anthony Newcomb, who was Pirrotta's colleague at Harvard during part of that time, had invaluable recollections. Professor Anne Shreffler, former Chair of the Department of Music at Harvard, granted and facilitated access to documents not yet in the University Archives but housed instead in the Departmental offices, documents that proved indispensable in reconstructing Harvard's offer to Pirrotta and the terms of his appointment. So, too, did Nancy Shafman, the Department's efficient administrator. Kyle P. DeCicco-Carey and Robin Carlaw assisted with documentation held centrally at Harvard in University archives and collections of materials. Professors James Haar and Frank D'Accone, probably the two Harvard graduate alumni most closely associated with Pirrotta, had invaluable reminiscences and advice, for which I thank them sincerely. So, too, did Professor Carl Schmidt, another of Pirrotta's doctoral advisees. Professor Claudia Wiener, University of Munich, assisted with the translation of a neo-Latin text critical to my presentation, as did my colleague Professor Markus Dubischar of Lafayette College. Another Lafayette colleague, Nancy Ball, assisted with information about Stephen Davidson Tuttle, a promising Harvard faculty member whose tragic early death created one of the vacancies in the Department's staffing that resulted in Pirrotta's appointment. Professor Joshua Rifkin read an early version of a portion of the Harvard chapter, and made invaluable comments, as did historian of science Craig Martin, Associate Professor of History at Oakland University, and Professor Curtis Cacioppo of Haverford College.

Professore Della Seta and Professore Franco Piperno (the two Italian pupils of Pirrotta especially closely associated with him) and Professore Pierluigi Petrobelli were helpful particularly with information on Pirrotta's years at the «Sapienza». They all contributed in many important ways, with advice, recollections, and assistance.

Professor Daniel Heartz read an early draft of the chapter on Settecento opera and had wise and thoughtful counsel.

Four colleagues and friends deserve special mention. Dr. Sabine Eiche read the entire typescript for presentation, in a way that few authors today have their work read and edited. Dr. Eiche is an art historian, not a music historian, but she *is* a specialist in the art of the Italian Renaissance, and her editorial interventions improved the presentation more than I can say. Both Professore Della Seta and Professor Iain Fenlon (perhaps the English musicologist most closely associated with Pirrotta) read the entire manuscript for content, and had so many valuable suggestions that I could not possibly enumerate them adequately. Professor Della Seta was probably my most important adviser throughout the research for and writing of this book. I consulted with him regularly, asked him to review draft chapters, and profited immeasurably from his understanding of Pirrotta's intellectual profile and achievement, based on his deep acquaintanceship and friendship with Pirrotta. Alexandra Hayley Trowbridge, Lafayette College '12, my able research assistant at Lafayette, was the first to read draft chapters and made the initial effort at streamlining and clarifying my presentation.

Finally, many colleagues and friends and several institutions contributed in general ways. Professor Franz Birgel of Muhlenberg College translated most of Pirrotta's entries for *Die Musik in Geschichte und Gegenwart* into a clear, idiomatic English. Kevin McKenna of the University of Chicago helped me obtain valuable material. Professor Lino Pertile and Anna Bensted of Villa I Tatti and the I Tatti staff made my stay there as Robert Lehman

Visiting Professor in Residence during the fall semester of 2011 the remarkable experience that an appointment at I Tatti invariably is. My time there permitted me to complete a draft of the book, and I must record a special debt to Professor Pertile, who read the chapters on Pirrotta's formal schooling and intellectual formation: Matters that he, as an Italian, understands better than most non-Italians ever can. The American Academy in Rome, which appointed me American Academy in Rome Scholar in Residence for the spring semester of 2012, similarly made it possible for me to revise and edit the manuscript and consult materials available only in Rome. I am grateful to the Academy's president, Adele Chatfield-Taylor, and its director, Professor Christopher Celenza, for the honor and privilege of an appointment at the Academy, and to Professor Anna Harwell Celenza for her "musicological companionship." Lafayette College has many times made considerable resources available to me: for travel, for research assistance, for the purchase of services and materials, and especially in the form of sabbatical time that could be dedicated to this work. Teaching at Lafayette has many wonderful advantages, and I am thankful that I am there. Professor Wendy Hill, Lafayette's most excellent provost, is especially to be thanked, as is my friend Professor John Meier, Associate Provost. Among colleagues at the American Philosophical Society, I am grateful to Pamela Lankas for her expert editorial work. Last, but by no means least, I am deeply grateful to Mary McDonald, Director of Publications at the American Philosophical Society, who has twice been so gracious as to accept one of my books for publication in the distinguished series of which she is editor; I cannot sufficiently express my appreciation to her.

Authors typically absolve those who assisted them in their writing of responsibility for errors of fact and interpretation that remain, and never was such absolution more necessary than in this case. What virtues this book has are due to the inspiration provided by its subject and the wise counsel and generous assistance of those identified here; what defects it has are due to its author's inadequacies. But my hope is that those defects are relatively few, because Pirrotta deserves better.

Principal Dates in Pirrotta's Life and Career

PALERMO (1908–27):

1908: Born in Palermo to Vincenzo and Adele Restivo-Pirrotta (13 June); tutored privately at home until he enrolls at the *ginnasio*

1917: Enrolls in the five-year course at the Regio Ginnasio «Giuseppe Garibaldi» di Palermo

1922: Enrolls in the three-year course at the Liceo «Giuseppe Garibaldi»

1924: Enrolls in the Scuola d'Organo e di Composizione Organistica of the Regio Conservatorio di Musica «Vincenzo Bellini» di Palermo to study with Maestro Luigi Amadio, Professore d'Organo e di Composizione Organistica; is tutored privately at home to complete the obligatory final year of the *liceo*

1925: Passes the *esame di maturità classica* (June), qualifying to register—and registering (4 November)—in the Facoltà di Lettere e Filosofia of the Regia Università degli Studi di Palermo, intending to study philosophy

1926: Officially awarded the *diploma di maturità classica* (26 January)

FLORENCE (1927–31):

1927: Withdraws from the Conservatory and University of Palermo (12 November) and enrolls (22 October) in the Scuola d'Organo e di Composizione Organistica and Scuola di Storia della Musica of the Regio Conservatorio di Musica «Luigi Cherubini» di Firenze (to continue studying with Maestro Amadio) and (30 November) in the "Philosophy section" of the Facoltà di Lettere e Filosofia of the Regia Università degli Studi di Firenze

1929: Receives the Licenza in Storia Della Musica and the Diploma di Magistero in Organo e Composizione Organistica at the Conservatory of Florence under Maestro Amadio's tutelage (June)

1929–31: Continues study at the Conservatory: in composition (with Maestro Vito Frazzi); harmony, counterpoint, and fugue; and violin

1930: Receives the *laurea* in history of art at the University of Florence under the tutelage of Dott. Mario Salmi, Professore Straordinario di Storia dell'Arte, and is named Dottore in Lettere (13 November)

1931: Withdraws from the Conservatory of Florence (October); consigns a copy of his *tesi di laurea* to the University of Florence (31 October); returns to Palermo

PALERMO (1931–48):

1931–33: Concertizes in Palermo; completes obligatory military service

1933–35: Studies composition privately with Maestro Antonio Savasta; serves as music critic for the Palermitan daily *L'Ora;* participates in the activities of the Palermitan "Amici della Musica"; serves "fuori l'elenco principale" (i.e., as a visiting faculty member) at the Conservatory of Palermo, where he teaches and has responsibilities in the library

1934–35: Coauthors *Il Sacchetti* . . . (Florence: Sansoni, 1935) with Ettore Li Gotti

1936: Appointed to the "elenco principale" (the roster of full-time tenured/tenure-track faculty members) at the Conservatory of Palermo, initially on a "non-stabile" (nontenured) basis, as Docente in Storia della Musica and Bibliotecario

1937: Wins the *concorso* to identify a permanent occupant for the chair in music history at the Conservatory of Palermo and the post of Bibliotecario

1938: Named "titolare di cattedra" (chair-holder) in music history at the Conservatory of Palermo and awarded "stabile" (tenured) status as Professore di Storia della Musica and Bibliotecario

1939: Marries Lea Paternostro (27 December)

1941: Recalled to military service and serves until 1942
Adelaide Maria ("Dilli") Pirrotta born (15 May)

1942: Vincenzo Pirrotta born (1 December)

1945: Silvia Pirrotta born (29 June)

ROME (1948–56):

1948: Sergio Pirrotta born (11 October)
Pirrotta is appointed Direttore delle Biblioteche of the Accademia and Conservatorio «Santa Cecilia» di Roma (November)
1954–55: Serves as Visiting Professor of Music at Princeton University, Princeton, New Jersey (academic year)
1955: Serves as Visiting Professor of Music at Columbia University, New York (fall semester)
1956: Named a member of the Accademia «Santa Cecilia» (15 January)

CAMBRIDGE, MASSACHUSETTS (1956–71):

1956: Appointed Professor of Music and Head of the Eda Kuhn Loeb Music Library in the Faculty of Arts and Sciences at Harvard University, Cambridge, Massachusetts (1 July)
1956–57: Awarded the Harvard degree of A.M.
1958: Formally resigns his post as Direttore delle Biblioteche of the Academy and Conservatory of Rome
1961: Named Walter W. Naumburg '89 Professor of Music at Harvard, succeeding composer and music theorist Walter Piston (1 July)
1965: Appointed chairman of the music department at Harvard (1 July)
1967: Named a member of the American Academy of Arts and Sciences
1968: Concludes his term as chairman of the music department at Harvard
1969: Concludes his term as Head of the Eda Kuhn Loeb Music Library (30 June)
1970: Awarded the degree of Doctor of Fine Arts "Honoris Causa" by The College of the Holy Cross, Worcester, Massachusetts
1971: Retires from teaching at Harvard (31 December)

ROME (1972–98):

1972: Appointed Professore Ordinario di Storia della Musica in the Facoltà di Lettere e Filosofia of the Università degli Studi di Roma, «La Sapienza» (1 January)
1975: Awarded the degree of L.H.D. "Honoris Causa" by the University of Chicago

1978: Retires from full-time teaching at the University of Rome (31 October); named an honorary member of the Royal Musical Association
1980: Named an honorary member of the American Musicological Society
1983: Awarded the Premio «Antonio Feltrinelli» by the Accademia Nazionale dei Lincei
1985: Awarded the degree of Mus.D. "Honoris Causa" (Cantab.) by the University of Cambridge
1987: Awarded the Premio «Viareggio»
1988: Awarded the degree of L.H.D. "Honoris Causa" by Princeton University
1996: Awarded the *Laurea «Ad Honorem»* by the Università degli Studi di Urbino
Lea Paternostro-Pirrotta dies in Rome (18 February)
1998: Pirrotta dies in Palermo (22 January)

Atto I.^{mo}

Studente

Scena 1.ᵃ

Famiglia (1908–24)

An accurate and illuminating word picture of Nino Pirrotta would be a complex and richly colored one. He was dignified and aristocratic in manner and on occasion could appear severe, but was never actually so. On the contrary, he was warm, gracious, humane, generous spirited, modest to the point of self-deprecation, whimsical, verbally playful, and appreciative of life's ironies. His manner was serene and reserved, and he seemed continually absorbed in reflection. But he was also adventurous, courageous, and open to opportunity, both personal and professional. Deeply and broadly learned, he was exacting in his mastery of the pertinent source data and impressively in command of the findings and methodologies of more than one established discipline. Yet with respect to his own personal theory of epistemology, he also inclined toward the judicious exercise of insight and intuition; he was intellectually refined and Apollonian in his sensibilities, and his historical imagination was vivid and fertile.

How did Nino Pirrotta come by such qualities of intellect and character?

The answer is in part to be sought in his childhood, as his human characteristics were inherited to some degree from his forebears, and his intellectual sensibilities were a consequence to some degree of his early family life. Pirrotta's parents and grandparents were members of the Palermitan upper middle class, which afforded him material advantages; he benefited from his family's cultural interests and activities; and he profited from the vital artistic and intellectual life of early-twentieth-century Palermo.

*****

Pirrotta's paternal grandmother, Giulia, was the daughter of Felice Pirandello. Her first cousin Stefano was the father of Luigi Pirandello, the 1934 Nobel laureate in literature and one of the most celebrated literary figures of the twentieth century. Pirrotta's father, Vincenzo, was thus the Nobel Laureate's second cousin, and Nino Pirrotta his second cousin once removed (see Figure 1).¹

The relationship between the Pirrotta and Pirandello families[2] was only one in a network of such relationships that linked the Pirrottas to other prominent members of contemporary Palermitan society. Nino Pirrotta's younger sister Giulia Pirrotta-Ziino recalled that, with so vast a web of interrelationships, she would often make the acquaintance of a distinguished gentleman or lady whom she had never met, but with whom she then discovered a great-grandparent or great-aunt or -uncle in common.[3]

Giulia Pirandello-Pirrotta's father, Felice, was the first of 23 children of Andrea Pirandello, the son of Ligurians who emigrated to Sicily in the mid-eighteenth century. When Andrea died in the cholera epidemic of 1837, Felice inherited the patrimony, including the family business, which exported citrus fruit and sulphur.[4] His daughter Giulia, Nino Pirrotta's paternal grandmother, possessed that austere dignity characteristic of many Sicilian women of her time and status: when seeing her grandchildren, she would utter not one word, but only extend her hand for them to kiss.[5]

In contrast, her husband, Antonino Pirrotta, was warm and affectionate with his grandchildren.[6] Ottavio Ziino, who would marry Nino Pirrotta's sister Giulia, recalled that Antonino was one of the wealthiest men in Palermo.[7] He and his wife lived in an elegant palazzina in Via Libertà, a beautiful street lined with villette in a variety of architectural styles.[8] When Antonino died in 1916, his widow and family moved to an apartment in another palazzo, also in Via Libertà, which was even grander than the one previously occupied.[9]

Nino Pirrotta's father, Vincenzo, was Antonino and Giulia's eldest son, affording him significant status in Sicilian and European society of earlier

---

[1] On the Pirandello family history, see Gaspare Giudice, *Pirandello: A Biography*, trans. Alastair Hamilton (London: Oxford University Press, 1975), 4–5. However, Giudice accepts the conventional understanding of Luigi Pirandello's lineage, which is different from what I provide in the family tree, which follows more recent scholarship. See, for example, Elio Providenti, *Colloqui con Pirandello* (Florence: Polistampa, 2005); for useful exchanges on this matter, I am grateful to Professor Mauro Zonta of the University of Rome, who is married to Giulia Pirandello-Pirrotta's great-great granddaughter, Francesca Ziino, and is thus a Pirandello family in-law.

[2] Although the Pirrotta family was understandably proud of its relationship to the Nobel Laureate, there was little, if any, ongoing personal interaction between the two families; correspondence with Adelaide M. Pirrotta-Bahr, M.D.

[3] Indispensable to my reconstruction of Nino Pirrotta's childhood are the "Appunti per una breve storia di famiglia e nipoti," an unpublished manuscript written by Pirrotta's sister Giulia Pirrotta-Ziino (Erice, 1984) and then typed by Pirrotta himself. For furnishing me with a copy of this invaluable document, and permitting me to make use of it, I am grateful to his four children: Adelaide M. Pirrotta-Bahr, M.D.; Professor Vincenzo Pirrotta, Ph.D.; Dott.ssa Silvia Pirrotta-Giuffré; and Sergio Pirrotta, Ed.D. See Pirrotta-Ziino, "Appunti," 6.

[4] Giudice, *Pirandello*, 4-5.
[5] Pirrotta-Ziino, "Appunti," 8.
[6] Pirrotta-Ziino, "Appunti," 8.
[7] Ottavio Ziino, *Ricordi di un musicista* (Palermo: Flaccovio, 1994), 27.
[8] Pirrotta-Ziino, "Appunti," 6.
[9] Pirrotta-Ziino, "Appunti," 8.

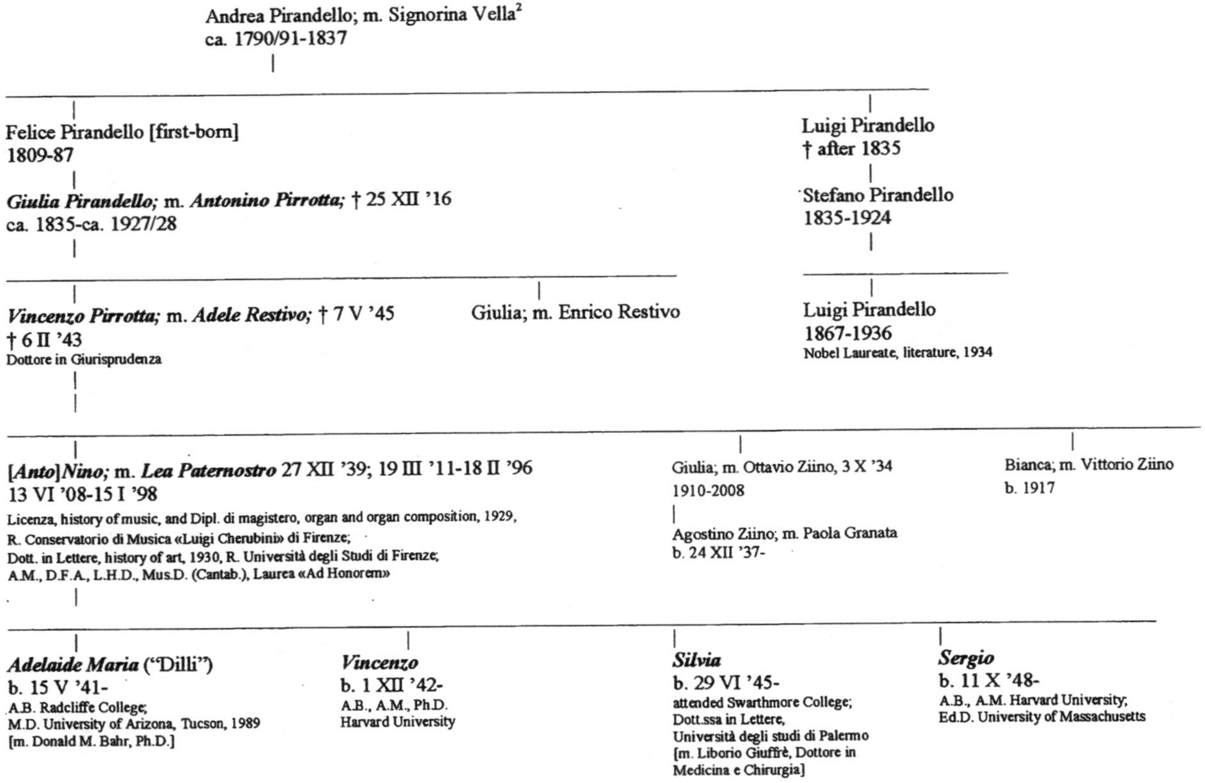

FAMIGLIA (1908–24)

Andrea Pirandello; m. Signorina Vella[2]
ca. 1790/91-1837

Felice Pirandello [first-born]
1809-87

Giulia Pirandello; m. *Antonino Pirrotta*; † 25 XII '16
ca. 1835-ca. 1927/28

Luigi Pirandello
† after 1835

Stefano Pirandello
1835-1924

Vincenzo Pirrotta; m. *Adele Restivo*; † 7 V '45
† 6 II '43
Dottore in Giurisprudenza

Giulia; m. Enrico Restivo

Luigi Pirandello
1867-1936
Nobel Laureate, literature, 1934

[*Anto*]*Nino*; m. *Lea Paternostro* 27 XII '39; 19 III '11-18 II '96
13 VI '08-15 I '98
Licenza, history of music, and Dipl. di magistero, organ and organ composition, 1929;
R. Conservatorio di Musica «Luigi Cherubini» di Firenze;
Dott. in Lettere, history of art, 1930, R. Università degli Studi di Firenze;
A.M., D.F.A., L.H.D., Mus.D. (Cantab.), Laurea «Ad Honorem»

Giulia; m. Ottavio Ziino, 3 X '34
1910-2008

Agostino Ziino; m. Paola Granata
b. 24 XII '37-

Bianca; m. Vittorio Ziino
b. 1917

Adelaide Maria ("Dilli")
b. 15 V '41-
A.B. Radcliffe College;
M.D. University of Arizona, Tucson, 1989
[m. Donald M. Bahr, Ph.D.]

Vincenzo
b. 1 XII '42-
A.B., A.M., Ph.D.
Harvard University

Silvia
b. 29 VI '45-
attended Swarthmore College;
Dott.ssa in Lettere,
Università degli studi di Palermo
[m. Liborio Giuffrè, Dottore in
Medicina e Chirurgia]

Sergio
b. 11 X '48-
A.B., A.M. Harvard University;
Ed.D. University of Massachusetts

Figure 1. Partial genealogy of Nino Pirrotta's family.

Sources: [1] Giulia Pirrotta-Ziino, "Appunti per una breve storia di famiglia e nipoti" (unpublished typescript, Erice, 1984); [2] Elio Providenti, *Colloqui con Pirandello* (Florence: Polistampa, 2005).

† Date of death.

times, entailing the parallel responsibilities and benefits of primogeniture. Ottavio Ziino described Vincenzo Pirrotta as "definitely a gentleman in the old mold," "a great gentleman, truly noble."[10] When Nino Pirrotta died, an Italian newspaper used similar terms, describing him as "a man from a bygone era, sensitive and with an aristocratic manner."[11]

Although Vincenzo rarely spoke of himself, his children came to understand that he had had an extraordinary young adulthood, stimulating and privileged. He traveled extensively, on one occasion on one of his father's cargo ships named the *Vincenzo Pirrotta*, which called at several ports in the Black Sea, including Odessa—his were not the usual experiences of a Sicilian of the late-nineteenth century, even of the upper middle class.

Vincenzo Pirrotta earned the degree of Dottore in Giurisprudenza at the University of Palermo, but he chose not to practice law. Instead, in partnership with one of his brothers, he acquired and managed a manufacturing firm that produced fine, small containers of tin, decorated in the so-called "Liberty" (*art nouveau*) style then current in Italian art. The containers served various purposes, such as to store biscuits and other confections, Egyptian cigarettes, and olive oil.

Significantly, both Vincenzo Pirrotta and his sister Annina were interested in music, and Vincenzo—without regular instruction—set about to master compositions in the operatic repertory and perform them on the piano.[12] His musical talents were imparted not only to his son, Nino, but also his youngest daughter, Bianca, who proved herself a gifted pianist.

Bianca's older sister, Giulia, shared the family's passion for music: She studied piano at the same time as Bianca and developed an acute musical sensibility, which was an important element in her relationship with her future husband, Ottavio.[13]

*****

When he was 35,[14] Vincenzo married Adele Restivo, a member of an accomplished Palermitan family. Whereas many marriages of that time were initiated by the interests of the parents or an understanding between the families, theirs was the result of free choice.[15] In the words of her son-in-law Ottavio,

---

[10]Ziino, *Ricordi*, 27, 64.
[11]Alfredo Gasponi in *Il Messaggero* (24 January 1998).
[12]See Nino Pirrotta, "Ricordi—ai miei figli carissimi," an unpublished memoir authored by Pirrotta for his children. For furnishing me with a copy, I am grateful to his four children.
[13]Correspondence with Dr. Adelaide M. Pirrotta-Bahr.
[14]Pirrotta-Ziino, "Appunti," 18.
[15]Pirrotta-Ziino, "Appunti," 18.

Adele Restivo was "a superior kind of woman, highly cultivated and of great moral stature."[16] Like many Palermitan women of her rank and time, Adele had studied at a "college"—a kind of finishing school—in Palermo. There, young women were taught foreign languages and literature; some "home economics"; needlepoint; and music or painting, according to the inclination of the pupil. In short, the education was limited to the kind of knowledge and accomplishments deemed sufficient for an alumna to enter society in search of a husband.

However, Adele—intellectually curious and desirous of broadening her horizons—would not accept such restrictions: during vacations, she would read widely in the library of her older brother Empedocle.[17]

Like his brother-in-law Vincenzo Pirrotta, Empedocle Restivo held the degree of Dottore in Giurisprudenza from the University of Palermo. A successful attorney, he entered politics, first at the municipal, then at the national level. After serving as a deputy in several legislatures, he resumed his legal career. Despite not being a member of the Fascist party, he secured an appointment as visitor ("incarico di insegnamenti" or "libero docente") at the University of Palermo, in both the Facoltà di Economia e Commercio[18] and Giurisprudenza, in this latter as instructor in banking law ("Diritto bancario") and philosophy of law ("Filosofia del Diritto").[19]

Empedocle also played an important role in the cultural life of the Palermo of his time. He founded the Municipal Gallery of Modern Art (Civica Galleria d'Arte Moderna) at the aula Rossa del Politeama in 1910, and in the following decade worked to establish and stabilize a tradition of concert life in Palermo.[20] A Palermitan daily reported that during the 1933 celebration of Richard Wagner, the audience heard a "moving speech by the Honorable [Empedocle] Restivo."[21]

In 1937, Empedocle became president of the Conservatory of Palermo, two years after that position had been restored following an experiment with an alternative administration, a Consiglio d'Amministrazione.[22]

Empedocle's sister Adele was also involved in the cultural life of Palermo: in 1932, a meeting of "the Honorable Patronage Committee of the Association

---

[16]Ziino, *Ricordi*, 27.
[17]Pirrotta-Ziino, "Appunti," 1–3.
[18]Pirrotta-Ziino, "Appunti," 3–4.
[19]*Annuario della R. Università degli studi di Palermo*. Anno accademico 1928–29 (anno VII) (Palermo: Tipografia Michele Montaina, 1929): 53–54.
[20]Consuelo Giglio, *La musica nell'età dei Florio* (Palermo: L'Epos, 2006), 88, 96 n. 2.
[21]The notice is in the 9–10 January 1933 issue of the Palermitan daily *L'Ora*, in the "Cronaca di Palermo."
[22]Federico de Maria, *Il R. Conservatorio di musica di Palermo* (Florence: Le Monnier, 1941), 37–38.

'The Friends of Music'" "in the noble salons of the Palazzo Niscemi . . . under the presidency of the Noble Duchess of Arenella" counted the "Signore Ziino-Caravella" and "Pirrotta-Restivo" among those present.[23] Nino Pirrotta's mother was an avid concertgoer and discerning critic of the performances she attended.[24]

In contrast, Enrico Restivo, another brother of Adele, chose a career in the military. Enrico later married Vincenzo Pirrotta's sister Giulia; thus two siblings (Vincenzo and Giulia Pirrotta) married two siblings (Adele and Enrico Restivo), a common enough occurrence in the complex marriage practices of Palermo's upper middle class of the time.[25]

*****

Both Pirrotta's parents were lovers of art, and over the course of some time they assembled a small but interesting collection, which they displayed in their home.[26] Adele also often hosted gatherings of art historians and connoisseurs of art then resident or visiting in Palermo,[27] which had to have had important consequences in Pirrotta's formation. Among those who frequented Adele's informal salon was Ettore Gàbrici,[28] Dottore in Lettere, formerly superintendent of the Museums of Naples and Rome, director of the Museo Nazionale di Palermo, and Reale Sovrintendente agli Scavi e Galleria (1914–26), and from 1927 professore ordinario of archaeology and history of ancient art at the University of Palermo. Gàbrici was responsible, most notably, for the resumption of the excavations in 1915 of the Greek city and sanctuary of Selinunte in Sicily, which were especially directed toward the sanctuary of Malaphoros.

Other frequent guests were Luigi Biagi, professor at the Accademia di Belle Arti in Palermo, and Maria Accascina, a *professoressa* at the Palermitano Regio Liceo «Umberto I» and a close Pirrotta family friend.[29] Adolfo Venturi and his son Lionello—the former the first incumbent of a professorship in art history at an Italian university and, importantly, the teacher of Pirrotta's thesis adviser at the University of Florence, Mario Salmi—also took part in

---

[23] See the brief report entitled "Riunione del Comitato di Patronato degli 'Amici della Musica'" in the 9–10 December 1932 issue of *L'Ora*, in the "Cronaca di Palermo."
[24] Correspondence with Dr. Adelaide M. Pirrotta-Bahr.
[25] Pirrotta-Ziino, "Appunti," 4–5.
[26] Pirrotta-Ziino, "Appunti," 19.
[27] On Adele Restivo-Pirrotta's *salon*, see Pirrotta-Ziino, "Appunti," 20–21.
[28] Born Naples 20 November 1868; died 1962.
[29] Ziino, *Ricordi*, 20.

FAMIGLIA (1908-24)

the discussions, as did reportedly—on one occasion—the American art historian and connoisseur Bernard Berenson.[30]

The mention of this last prompts fuller discussion. There was a complex network of associations among these figures, documented in a considerable correspondence between Adolfo Venturi and Bernard Berenson and also between Venturi's son and Berenson and in letters from Biagi to both Berenson and his wife, Mary. Pirrotta quotes from Berenson's writings in one of his most important publications,[31] and many years later he will accept an appointment at Berenson's Alma Mater, Harvard University. Later still, Bernard Berenson will bequeath his property outside Florence—Villa I Tatti—to Harvard to serve as a Center for Italian Renaissance Studies, to which Pirrotta will thereafter be devoted for the remainder of his days.[32] One can only assume that the early network of relationships among his parents, Biagi, the Venturis,[33] and Berenson was a factor in Pirrotta's lifelong association with these figures and in his devotion to the research institute established by Berenson in 1959.

*****

Antonino ("Nino") Pirrotta was born on 13 June 1908. His two sisters—Giulia and Bianca—followed in 1910 and 1917.

During their early childhood, the Pirrotta children—like other upper-middle-class children in Palermo—were privately tutored at home, the instruction designed to permit them to meet the requirements for admission to the

---

[30]Berenson's attendance at meetings of Adele Restivo-Pirrotta's *salon* is reported by Pirrotta's younger sister Giulia in Pirrotta-Ziino, "Appunti." I consulted published extracts of Berenson's diaries and letters for substantiating documentation, but without success. My search, however, was not exhaustive. See such sources as *The Bernard Berenson Treasury: A Selection from the Works, Unpublished Writings, Letters, Diaries, and Journals of the Most Celebrated Humanist and Art Historian of Our Times, 1887–1958*, ed. Hanna Kiel, intro. John Walker, pref. Nicky Mariano (New York: Simon and Schuster, 1962); *Rumour and Reflection* (New York: Simon and Schuster, 1952); *The Passionate Sightseer; from the Diaries, 1947 to 1956*, pref. Raymond Mortimer (New York: Simon and Schuster [1960]); and *Sunset and Twilight; from the Diaries of 1947–1958*, ed. with epilogue Nicky Mariano, intro. Iris Origo, 1st ed. (New York: Harcourt, Brace & World [1963]).

In his *Viaggio in Sicilia*, versione dal manoscritto originale di Arturo Loria (Milan: Electa, 1955), Berenson recounts trips to Sicily ("vari viaggi da me compiuti in Sicilia"; see p. 13), specifically in 1888, 1908, and 1927; the 1908 visit in particular might have occasioned the relevant visit to the Pirrotta home.

I am grateful for assistance on this matter to Dott. Valerio Pacini, Dott.ssa Ilaria della Monica, Dott. Giovanni Pagliarulo, and Dott.ssa Fiorella Superbi, all of Villa I Tatti, The Harvard University Center for Italian Renaissance Studies, Florence, where this correspondence is preserved.

[31] See my "*Scena 4.ᵃ* The Conservatory of Palermo (1936–48): *Il Trecento*."

[32]For testimony to Pirrotta's devotion to I Tatti, I am grateful to Agostino Ziino, interview with A.M. Cummings. Pirrotta's status as a member of the I Tatti Advisory Committee is documented, of course, in the Center's newsletters, available at the I Tatti website.

[33]Lionello Venturi later figures in a letter that Pirrotta writes after his first semester at Harvard, when he learns the results of the first *concorso* organized to identify incumbents of newly established professorships in music history in the Italian universities: see my "*Scena 7.ᵃ* Harvard University (1956–71): *Rinascimento*."

ginnasio.³⁴ At age nine, Nino Pirrotta enrolled in the Regio Ginnasio «Giuseppe Garibaldi» di Palermo, which he attended for five years, from 1917 to 1922. Thereafter he studied for two years, from 1922 to 1924, at the R. Liceo «Giuseppe Garibaldi» di Palermo.³⁵ In the fall of 1924, he registered at the Conservatory of Palermo; simultaneously, he completed the prescribed third and final year of *liceo* privately at home³⁶ in order to qualify for admission to the Faculty of Letters and Philosophy of the University of Palermo.

Admission to both the *ginnasio* and *liceo* was by entrance examination, and a commission appointed by the Minister for Public Instruction examined all students at the conclusion of their *liceo* studies. Successful performance on this final examination—the *esame di maturità classica*—was a prerequisite for admission to the faculty of letters and philosophy at the university.

Once at the *ginnasio* and *liceo*, the student enrolled in a course of study celebrated for its rigor and classicizing tendencies; it consisted largely of training in Latin and Greek languages and literatures, Italian language and literature, and history. During the five-year course at the *ginnasio*, students became versed in the Italian, Greek, and Latin languages, Greek and Roman antiquities, a modern foreign language, and the elements of rhetoric; they received more limited instruction in geography, history, and mathematics. During the three-year course at the *liceo*, Italian, Greek, Latin literature, and history were emphasized, though less so than at the *ginnasio*, complemented with mathematics, and, for the first time in the entire eight-year course, the history of art, philosophy, political economy, chemistry, physics, and natural history.³⁷ It was very much an education designed for a tiny social, economic, cultural, and intellectual elite, at a moment in Italian history when almost 100% of Sicilians and some 95% of Italians generally were effectively illiterate.³⁸

---

³⁴For the evidence concerning proficiency in the Italian language, mathematics, and knowledge of general culture—required for admission to the *ginnasio*—see Lorenzo Minio-Paluello, *Education in Fascist Italy* (London: Oxford University Press, 1946), on which I drew extensively for what follows. The syllabus for the entrance examination to the *ginnasio* legislated by the Fascist reforms of 1923 suggests continuity with what had been required before.

³⁵On Pirrotta's *liceo* education, and its importance for his intellectual formation, see such sources as "Antonino Pirrotta," *Premi "Antonio Feltrinelli" 1983* (Accademia Nazionale dei Lincei), 69; *Die Musik in Geschichte und Gegenwart*, ed. Friedrich Blume (Kassel: Bärenreiter Verlag, 1949–73), 10:1296–97; and *Dizionario enciclopedico universale della musica e dei musicisti. Le biografie* (Turin: UTET, 1988), 6:29–30. On the «Garibaldi», see http://www.liceogaribaldi.it. Pirrotta's education at the *ginnasio* and *liceo* was a legacy of the unification of Italy in the mid-nineteenth century. The legislative act establishing the national educational system—13 November 1859—is remembered to this day as the *legge Casati*, in honor of Count Gabrio Casati, Minister for Public Instruction at the time. It was the *legge Casati* that stipulated that the course of study at the *ginnasio* (gymnasium) be five years, and that at the *liceo* (lyceum) three.

³⁶Pirrotta, "Ricordi."

³⁷It was also a tradition marked by extreme conservatism: one student has remarked that "No type of school was subjected to fewer changes between 1859 and 1923" than the *ginnasio-liceo*. Minio-Paluello, *Education*.

³⁸For indispensable exchanges on these matters, I am grateful to Professor Lino Pertile.

Table 1 Curriculum of the Classical *Ginnasio* and *Liceo*

NUMBER OF PERIODS ALLOTTED EACH WEEK TO EACH SUBJECT:	*ginnasio* 1	2	3	4	5	*liceo* 1	2	3
ANCIENT AND MODERN LANGUAGES: Italian language and literature	7	7	7	5	5	4	4	3
Latin language and literature	8	7	7	6	6	4	4	3
Greek language and literature				4	4	4	4	3
foreign language		3	4	4	4			
SOCIAL SCIENCES: history and geography	5	5	4	3	3			
history						3	3	3
philosophy and political economy						3	3	3
MATHEMATICS AND SCIENCES: mathematics	1	2	2	2	2			
mathematics and physics						4	4	5
nature, chemistry, and geography						3	2	3
HISTORY OF ART							2	2

It is impossible to understand Nino Pirrotta's intellectual profile and personal intellectual sensibilities without an understanding of the educational practices and traditions of the "classical" *liceo;* we consider them in some detail.

The numbers of periods allotted each week to the different subjects are shown in Table 1. The significance attached to the humanistic disciplines—ancient and modern languages, history, and philosophy—is clear.

What was such training intended to produce? The *esame di maturità classica* that Pirrotta took at the conclusion of his studies at the *liceo* was rigorous and comprehensive: for the examination in history, candidates for the *diploma di maturità classica* were responsible for no fewer than forty-nine subject areas, ranging from "Christianity and the organization of the Church in the first centuries A.D." to "the World War; economic and moral forces; ideologies; the new organization of the civilized world."

In Latin and Greek languages and literatures, the candidate—during the three years of his study in Greek at the *liceo*—was expected to translate one or two books of Homer, one Greek tragedy, one book of Herodotus or another Greek historian, and a few hundred lines of Greek lyric poetry. Although not much more was expected in Latin, the texts were to be understood within their historical context and assessed as to their artistic and philosophical merit. An understanding of the history of literature, both Latin and Greek, was essential, the relevant historical time period beginning with the earliest Greek and Latin literature and concluding with Christian writers of the fourth and fifth centuries C.E. and later, because the Latin "classics" subsumed the neo-Latin literature of the Renaissance humanists and modern Latin poets. The principal elements of Greek and Roman institutions, customs, religion, and art were to be mastered.[39]

In other subjects—Italian literature,[40] epistemology[41] and ethics,[42] history of art,[43] and mathematics, physics, chemistry, biology, mineralogy, physical geography, and political economy[44]—the coverage was similarly comprehensive, especially in the first four of these.

However, accompanying such comprehensiveness in coverage were some obvious deficiencies, as veterans of the *ginnasio–liceo* system have suggested. Such deficiencies were largely pedagogical in nature. The schedule of classes devoted to each subject—reproduced in Table 1—was followed inflexibly, as were the pedagogical methods employed. From 8:30 a.m., let us say, until 12:30 p.m., young Pirrotta had four lessons of about one hour each, during which he was expected to sit quietly in place, listening to the instructors' lectures and undergoing questioning and evaluation on the answers given.[45] What few texts were read in the later "forms" of the *ginnasio* and in the *liceo*—Homer, Horace, Xenophon and Herodotus, Livy and Tacitus, Sophocles and Virgil—were fragments,[46] construed principally as material for the study of syntax or to test the pupils' knowledge of irregular verbs or Greek dialectical forms. The poetic meters were mastered by rote. The Italian language was dissected into sentences, clauses, and parts of clauses, which were classified according to established categories of Latin grammar and syntax.

These methods were intended to discipline pupils to develop the habit of clear expression; Latin and Greek were thought to have a formative value

---

[39] Minio-Paluello, *Education*.

[40] See Minio-Paluello, *Education*, for an enumeration of the expectations for the *esame di maturità* concerning demonstration of mastery of Italian literature.

[41] Minio-Paluello, *Education*.

[42] Minio-Paluello, *Education*.

[43] Minio-Paluello, *Education*.

[44] Minio-Paluello, *Education*.

[45] Minio-Paluello, *Education*.

[46] One book of Homer, one of Virgil, a few *Odes*.

because their study demanded training in analyzing speech. Symptomatic of the limitations of such a tradition is the fact that, for the typical *ginnasio-liceo* student, the texts he would recall were not editions of primary texts by classical authors, but, rather, the canonical grammars and dictionaries, the majority of which were either translations or adaptations from the German or imitations of standard German schoolbooks.[47] According to one alumnus of the *liceo classico*, such training "resulted in mental gymnastics in language."[48]

*****

How is one to understand the durability of such practices? And what was their utility for Nino Pirrotta? The prestige accorded the classics by the educational institutions of Europe (and the larger Europeanized world) was a legacy of the Italian Renaissance. As two scholars of Renaissance humanism recently wrote, "the skills . . . inculcated had an established practical value in fifteenth-century Italy. . . . [A]lthough the programme was strictly literary and non-vocational, it . . . opened the way to a number of careers."[49]

However, humanistic training was thought to have other, less obviously vocational benefits as well. Close analysis of classical texts was thought to enhance the student's ability to reason critically, his capacity for informed intellectual exchange, and his powers of judgment. The arts curriculum of the Italian Renaissance assumed that literary studies developed such powers of reasoning through a process of simplification of language and refinement of oratorical technique.[50]

Above all, the curriculum was valued as a system of discipline, "an essential requirement of a self-sufficient programme of education" based upon "the impeccable . . . example of . . . mature Roman education."[51]

Such was the prestige of the classical tradition that it was exported more or less wholesale to much of the Europeanized world. But whereas there was an authentic relationship between neoclassical learning and the social order in fifteenth-century Italy, in the New World that relationship was contrived, if it existed at all. The learned tongues had limited usefulness in the American colonies of the mid-eighteenth century, but that did not diminish their prestige.[52] As recently as the mid-1950s, James Bryant Conant—who retired from the Harvard presidency just before Pirrotta accepted his position there—could

---

[47]See Minio-Paluello, *Education*, for a full listing of the titles in question.
[48]Minio-Paluello, *Education*.
[49]Anthony Grafton and Lisa Jardine, *From Humanism to the Humanities* (Cambridge, MA: Harvard University Press, 1986), 23–24.
[50]Grafton and Jardine, *From Humanism*, 73.
[51]Grafton and Jardine, *From Humanism*.
[52]Bernard Bailyn, *The Ideological Origins of the American Revolution* (Cambridge, MA: Belknap Press of Harvard University Press, 1967), 24, 26.

write that in "Europe west of the Iron Curtain, the literary tradition in education still prevails. An educated man or woman is a person who has acquired a mastery of several tongues and retained a working knowledge of the art and literature of Europe."[53]

And the Europeanized world imported not only the substance of the classical curriculum but also its pedagogy.[54] In the nineteenth century, students at American liberal arts colleges were lectured on ancient texts, modern languages, mathematics, and other subjects. They undertook exercises in writing English, Latin, and Greek. They translated texts in the ancient and modern languages and analyzed their grammar. They declaimed in English, French, and the classical languages. And after having heard lectures in mathematics, they were expected to undertake "demonstrations" and respond to "questions propounded."

However, if the classical curriculum and its pedagogy had limited application in the nineteenth and twentieth centuries in America and elsewhere in the Europeanized world, it continued to have significance for Italy in the early twentieth century, notwithstanding the criticisms it received even there; and for Nino Pirrotta, it was a great advantage as well. Twentieth-century Italians trod the very ground once trod by Republican and Imperial Romans. They were surrounded by the remnants of structures once inhabited by their Roman forebears. For learned Italians, the classical tradition had—and has—a resonance that it cannot have in the larger European and Europeanized world. And, after all, Pirrotta was to make his career decoding the very intellectual traditions that had bequeathed their educational practices to him as a candidate for the *diploma di maturità classica*. For Pirrotta the study of Latin, Greek, Italian, history, philosophy, and art history was not only useful, it was indispensable.

If the methods employed in teaching language "resulted in mental gymnastics," they served Pirrotta well when he undertook to render the complex neo-Ciceronian Latin of Paolo Cortese's *De cardinaltu* into a fluent vernacular. If the poetic meters were learned by rote, such discipline facilitated his mastery of poetic verse forms, exemplified in such studies as "On Text Forms from Ciconia to Dufay" and numerous others. If the *liceo*'s demands for a conversance with Dante and Compagni were more "formalistic"[55] than might be ideal, they enhanced his command of texts that later served him in such studies as "Dante *musicus*" and in his reconstruction of the biography of Paolo *tenorista*, whose madrigal *Godi Firenze* celebrates the Florentine conquest of

---

[53]Conant, introduction to Thomas S. Kuhn, *The Copernican Revolution. Planetary Astronomy in the Development of Western Thought* (Cambridge, MA: Harvard University Press, 1957).

[54]Frederick Rudolph, *The American College and University. A History* (New York: Knopf, 1962), 131–53.

[55]The characterization is Minio-Paluello's; see *Education*, 42.

Pisa, described in Compagni's chronicle. If the engagement with literary texts by Sacchetti, Poliziano, Pulci, Ariosto, Tasso, Machiavelli, Metastasio, Goldoni, and Carducci and philosophical texts by Plato, Aristotle, and Seneca was also inordinately "formalistic," an early familiarity with them was helpful to Pirrotta, as anyone who knows his scholarly writings will appreciate: the elucidation of neo-Platonic elements in Giovanni Bardi's thought, the conversance with the poetry of Ariosto and Tasso that underlies the studies of the sixteenth-century madrigal, the explication of Metastasio's aesthetic doctrines—these features of Pirrotta's writings, and many others, are in part legacies of the training he received in the *ginnasio* and *liceo*.[56]

Finally, the texts by Berkeley, Fichte, Hegel, and Spaventa exposed him to the philosophical tenets and vivid presentation of the Idealists, which was to serve him in the development of his authorial voice.

Above all, the comprehensiveness of the *liceo*'s curriculum instilled in Pirrotta a sense of the organicism of the humanistic disciplines (which may be one explanation for that "interdisciplinarity" in his scholarly methodology), and the rigor of its pedagogical practices instilled in him a discipline that proved essential to his formation.

*****

Notwithstanding these virtues, the *ginnasio–liceo* tradition was thought by the Fascist régime to warrant reform, which occurred precisely during Pirrotta's final years as a *liceo* student (academic years 1922/23 and 1923/24). The reform was directed not so much toward the substance of the curriculum as the methods of delivering it. The agent of reform was the Italian Idealist philosopher Giovanni Gentile, who had developed an elaborate philosophy of education that his appointment as Benito Mussolini's Minister of Public Instruction permitted him to actuate. We can detect traces of these educational practices in Pirrotta's development.

However, even before the Fascist initiative, the *ginnasio–liceo* had been reformed by a number of Gentile's predecessors, principally Alfredo Baccelli, who, like his Fascist successors, focused particular attention on pedagogy. Baccelli believed that

> [n]o subject must be taught as if it were a quantum of science to be learnt by heart; it would become a dead weight in the memory of students, engendering nothing but boredom and a desire to get rid of it as soon as possible.... Teaching must

---

[56] I suspect, too, that the sensitivity to literary history in Pirrotta's writings was a consequence of the nature of his introduction to musicology, the study of the polyphonic settings of the poetry of Francesco Sacchetti (**1935**: *Il Sacchetti e la tecnica musicale del Trecento italiano*); had Pirrotta's introduction to the discipline had a different impetus, he may not have featured literary concerns so prominently in his later scholarship.

be ruled not by the catchwords of an encyclopaedia, but by the laws of mental development.... [T]he pupils ... will study not in order to pass an examination but to acquire a perpetual treasure for the intellect.... Latin and Greek grammar must be the means to a deep understanding of the authors one has to read in those languages.[57]

In these words we already sense the influence of that same Idealist philosophy that will color the Gentilean reforms: the barely concealed antipathy toward science (characterized by one historian of twentieth-century Italian thought as Idealism's "witch-hunt for 'scientism'") and the call for an approach to the study of language that would shift the balance from an unreflective emphasis on grammar toward an involvement with the ancient and modern languages and literatures per se, which were "the means to a deep understanding of the authors one has to read in those languages."[58] The reforms demanded that the pupils engage independently with the sources, which was to become a distinguishing feature of Pirrotta's intellectual style.

Between December 1922 and October 1923, Gentile issued a series of decrees that were the basis for his reforms, which nonetheless continued to be faithful to tradition.[59] Gentile believed that the syllabus must not be permitted to intervene between the master who "lives" his truth and his pupil. Like Baccelli, he believed that the study of the "sterile rules of grammar" ought to be abolished, although he acknowledged that a knowledge of them was required if one were to attain an understanding of the value of literary and historical works.[60]

Substantively, as contrasted with pedagogically, "[t]he Gentilean school is essentially a school of philology, history, literature, philosophy; ancient literature, but also Italian literature: Dante, Petrarch, Boccaccio, and for

---

[57]Minio-Paluello, *Education*.

[58]The Italian Idealists—Benedetto Croce, Giovanni Gentile, and their disciples—had clearly defined philosophical positions on language, and there are some correspondences between their philosophy and Pirrotta's scholarly method. The Idealists rejected as misguided the attempts of linguists to apprehend language in scientific terms, as divorcing language from its social and cultural contexts and making of it a complex of abstractions; see Benedetto Croce's formulation in *The Aesthetic as the Science of Expression and of the Linguistic in General*, trans. Colin Lyas (Cambridge: Cambridge University Press, 1992), 156–64. My argument is that Pirrotta's habitual contextualizing of music—his disinclination to make of *music* an abstraction divorced from *its* social and cultural contexts—is consistent with the Idealist philosophy of language.

[59]Adolfo Scotto di Luzio, *Il liceo classico* (Bologna: Il Mulino, 1999), 144.

[60]Minio-Paluello, *Education*. I have also benefited from correspondence with Professor Adolfo Scotto di Luzio of the Università degli Studi di Bergamo, who (in private correspondence of 16 June 2008) suggested that the thesis of the Idealist educational reformers (and their Fascist benefactors) was that it was "upon the conviction of an historicistic type—not upon the linguistic-rhetoric exercises—that in order to penetrate a culture it is necessary to read its written testimonies directly."

FAMIGLIA (1908-24)

the nineteenth century Alfieri, Foscolo, Leopardi, Manzoni."[61] There was a decidedly Nationalist cast to the curriculum.[62]

The Gentilean reforms took effect immediately, and among those responsible for implementing them was Francesco Ercole, Fascist Minister of Education from 1931–34, who was *rettore* (president) of the University of Palermo during Pirrotta's years there.[63]

*****

Pirrotta passed the *esame di maturità classica* at the conclusion of academic year 1924/25[64] and was certified to enter the university. On 26 January 1926 he was awarded the *diploma di maturità classica*[65] as the result of his studies at the R. Ginnasio-Liceo «Giuseppe Garibaldi» and his performance on the examination.

*****

Pirrotta's formal schooling was complemented with experiences later to prove very important to him. He and his cousins were afforded the opportunity to study French, which in Sicily was then more widely diffused than English. French was the language of polite society, and one's ability in it was deemed a social accomplishment; indeed, in many homes of the socioeconomic status of the Pirrotta home, where a governess would typically have been present, the children were required to speak French, with the governess in particular.[66]

Pirrotta and five of his cousins had lessons together from an elderly woman, Mademoiselle Longoni, who was succeeded by a professor remembered only as "Minet-minet." The lessons ceased after about a year, and Pirrotta and

---

[61] Private e-mail correspondence of 16 June 2008 with Professor Scotto di Luzio.

[62] Minio-Paluello, *Education*. One of the Idealist reformers' "heroes" was Giosuè Carducci (private correspondence with Professor Scotto di Luzio, 16 June 2008), whose writings were to figure so prominently in Pirrotta's early scholarship (see, for example, **1935:** *Il Sacchetti;* and **1946** and **1947:** "Per l'origine e la storia della «caccia» e del «madrigale» trecentesco").

[63] *Regia Università degli studi di Palermo* (Rome: Casa Editrice Mediterranea, 1940), 15, and Leonello Paoloni, *Storia politica dell'Università di Palermo dal 1860 al 1943* (Palermo: Sellerio, 2005), 406.

[64] See the text of the formal documentation in my Appendix. I suspect that the results were affected by the fact that Pirrotta completed the crucial third and final year of the *liceo* privately, under the direction of a tutor, and also because he was simultaneously enrolled at the Conservatory, absorbed in the initial stages of the studies for the *Diploma di Magistero*.

[65] See the text of the formal documentation in my Appendix. This document is in the archives of the University of Florence. Pirrotta would have to have furnished it to secure admission to the Faculty of Letters and Philosophy. For assistance in procuring a copy, I am grateful to Dott. Valerio Pacini of the Biblioteca Berenson at Villa I Tatti, The Harvard University Center for Italian Renaissance Studies, Florence.

[66] For assistance on this matter, I am grateful to Iain Fenlon.

his sister Giulia continued their lessons with an Alsatian priest, Monsieur l'Abbé Auguste Ronsard.

*****

While Nino Pirrotta was still very young, his family also began to introduce him to the European operatic tradition. During the 1914 Carnival season, when he was not yet six years old, he saw his first opera performed at the Teatro Massimo, of which he retained a clear memory until the very end of his life: It was Wagner's *Parsifal*, followed the Sunday thereafter by Verdi's *Aida*.[67]

Indeed, opera was fundamental to Italian bourgeois cultural experience at that time, in ways that are now difficult to comprehend, especially for non-Italians. The Teatro Massimo, designed by G.B.F. Basile and opened in May 1897, is one of the largest theaters in the world, with five tiers of boxes and 3200 seats.[68] Pirrotta's exposure to its offerings, which generally were of great importance to the *ambiente* within which he and his family lived, had the most significant effect on his fundamental cultural formation, as his journalistic writings[69] and lifelong scholarly engagement with the Italian operatic tradition (including the "great tradition" of the nineteenth century) suggest.

*****

During Nino Pirrotta's years at the *ginnasio* and *liceo*, his parents provided him with another opportunity that had profound consequences for his formation: They arranged for him to have piano lessons with Maestro Luigi Amadio, then Professor of Organ at the Conservatory of Palermo.[70] In entrusting their son's early musical education to Amadio, Vincenzo and Adele Restivo-Pirrotta made him the beneficiary of a distinguished tradition. And Amadio was the first of a small number of individuals who had a significant influence on Pirrotta's development.

Amadio, born in Chiarano (Treviso) in 1881, had been a favorite organ pupil of M. Enrico Bossi, one of the most celebrated organists and composers

---

[67]**1997**: "Dalla favola pastorale all'opera," especially 9.

[68]Paolo Emilio Carapezza and Giuseppe Collisani, "Palermo," *Grove Music Online. Oxford Music Online*, http://0-www.oxfordmusiconline.com.libcat.lafayette.edu/subscriber/article/grove/music/20745 (accessed 3 October 2011). On the Teatro Massimo, see also Ente autonomo del Teatro Massimo, Palermo, *I cinquant'anni del Teatro Massimo (1897-1947)* (Palermo: I.R.E.S., 1947) and Luigi Maniscalco Basile, *Storia del Teatro massimo di Palermo* (Florence: L. S. Olschki, 1984). For assistance on this general matter, I am grateful to Iain Fenlon.

[69]On Pirrotta's journalistic writings, and their documentation of the activities of the Teatro Massimo, see my "*Scena 3.ᵃ* Palermo (1931-36)" and Anthony M. Cummings and Sabine Eiche, "Nino Pirrotta's Early Music-Critical Writings," *Studi musicali* 37 (2008): 253–337.

[70]Pirrotta, "Ricordi."

of Italy in the late-nineteenth/early-twentieth century;[71] his place in Italian music history may be likened to that of Camille Saint-Saëns or Cesar Franck in the history of French music. Bossi was founder of an Italian "school" of organ performance, and his *Metodo di studio per l'organo moderno* (Milan, 1893)—coauthored with Giovanni Tebaldini—served as a reference work in Italy until well into the twentieth century. In the words of one student, his compositions for organ are characterized by a "fine contrapuntal fabric." Another suggested that Bossi, "probably more than any other," "may be credited with bringing Italian Romantic organ music to full flower"; German critics regarded him as the "Brahms of Italy."[72]

It was during Bossi's tenure as director of the Liceo Musicale di Venezia (1895–1902) that Luigi Amadio studied organ, counterpoint, and fugue with the great Italian master,[73] who, besides discharging his administrative responsibilities at the Liceo, also taught composition and organ. Following his studies with Bossi at the Liceo Musicale in Venice, Amadio became organist at the Duomo of Vercelli. Thereafter he held the position of *titolare* (tenured professor) in organ at the Conservatory of Palermo,[74] where he succeeded Antonino Mauro.

A 1913 prospectus of the Conservatory[75] furnishes glimpses of Amadio's activities there and suggests something about his pedagogical practices and the demands made of his students, the young Pirrotta boy among them. In 1911, Amadio collaborated with his colleague Maestro Franco Tufari, Professor of Violin, on a recital[76] that included such compositions as Tartini's *Sonata in g minor* (which featured Amadio's accompaniment on the organ), Bach's *Fugue in D Major*,[77] two works by Bossi, and Vieuxtemps' *Concerto in d minor*, with the reduction of the orchestral accompaniment performed on the

---

[71]On Bossi, see Harvey B. Gaul, "Bonnet—Bossi—Karg-Elert: Three *Aperçus*," *Musical Quarterly* 4 (1918): 353–64, especially 357–60; Bea Friedland, "Italy's *Ottocento*: Notes from the Musical Underground," *Musical Quarterly* 56 (1970): 27–53, especially 48–50; Barbara Owen: "Keyboard Music," *Grove Music Online*, ed. L. Macy (accessed 6 October 2007), http://www.grovemusic.com; Elvidio Surian/Graziano Ballerini: "Bologna," *Grove Music Online*, ed. L. Macy (accessed 6 October 2007), http://www.grovemusic.com; and, most important, Federico Mompellio, *Marco Enrico Bossi* (Milan: Hoepli, 1952), 118–19, 121, 132, and 216–48 (list of compositions).

[72]Interestingly, Pirrotta was later to review a performance of one of Bossi's compositions by "Il Quintetto femminile," in the Palermitan daily *L'Ora*, 9 June 1935.

[73]Mompellio, *Bossi*; Adelmo Damerini, *Il R. Conservatorio di Musica "Luigi Cherubini" di Firenze* (Florence: Le Monnier, 1941).

[74]Damerini, *Il R. Conservatorio*.

[75]Benedetto Morasca, *Raccolta di Programmi, audizioni e concerti Vocali e Strumentali tenuti Nel R. Conservatorio di Musica "V. Bellini,, di Palermo dal 1893 al 1911* (Palermo: Stabilimento Tipografico Lao, 1913). See also Giglio, *La musica nell'età dei Florio*, 29.

[76]Morasca, *Raccolta di Programmi*, 92.

[77]This is presumably the fugue of the *Prelude and Fugue* in D, BWV 532, which dates from before 1712–13 (see Ellwood S. Derr, Walter Emery, Eugene Helm, Richard Jones, Ernest Warburton, and Christoph Wolff, *The New Grove Bach Family* [London and New York: W.W. Norton, 1980, 1983], 199); it therefore gives some sense of Amadio's organistic abilities.

piano by Amadio. Later that year, Amadio prepared the chorus for a performance of one of the Cherubini requiem masses;[78] and in 1912 Conservatory student Ignazio Alfano, who was then completing the "Corso 8° del Prof. L. Amadio," performed Mendelssohn's "Adagio in Do minore"[79] and Bach's "Preludio e fuga in Do minore; per Organo."[80] These works convey some sense of the kind of repertory Amadio would have introduced to Nino Pirrotta. In 1911, "M.° Luigi Amadio" is listed as "Prof. di Organo" under the rubric "Organico del Conservatorio."

Nino Pirrotta esteemed Amadio so highly that he enrolled at the Conservatory in 1924, even before having completed the *liceo*, and followed him to Florence in 1927, when Amadio was appointed *titolare* in organ at the Regio Conservatorio di Musica «Luigi Cherubini» di Firenze. Indeed, Pirrotta's decision to specialize in organ performance and composition at the conservatory is attributable in good part to Amadio's influence.

*****

What effects did these varied experiences have on Nino Pirrotta's character and development?

Later in life, Pirrotta regularly invoked his *sicilianità*, which not only shaped his qualities of character and personal and professional sensibilities but also informed his understanding of musical traditions he was seeking to elucidate.

Sicily's status as an island in the center of the Mediterranean is such that its identity has been formed by that fragile combination of insularity on the one hand with a susceptibility—even a vulnerability—to an extraordinary array of external influences on the other. The pre- and early-modern Mediterranean world—the world that predated air travel—functioned as an organic system precisely because it was centered on a navigable body of water bounded by land on all sides, the indispensable material basis of any cultural system in the premodern world; and interactions among the inhabitants were facilitated because of their access to the Mediterranean: Greeks, Arabs, Turks, Italians,

---

[78]Morasca, *Raccolta di Programmi*, 92.

[79]Presumably none other than the "Adagio" from the *Sonata Opus 65 n. 2 in c minor*; see *Six Sonatas* (1845), c/C, 21 December 1844, in *Felix Mendelssohn Bartholdy's Werke: kritisch durchgesehene Ausgabe*, ed. J. Rietz (Leipzig, 1874–77), xii/2.

[80]Either BWV 546, composed in Leipzig in 1723-29, or BWV 549, composed in Leipzig after 1723; see Derr et al., *New Grove Bach*, 200.

Spaniards, and French all traded with one another and imparted elements of their identities to one another, not always peacefully.[81]

Throughout the millennia, each successive wave of immigration to Sicily—each "invasion"—left traces of the identity and practices of its place of origin, and the indigenous peoples of Sicily forged a synthesis of the new influences with the old, with those already existing "on a site that held ... older and differing memories," to invoke the words of novelist James Hilton.[82]

Pirrotta will make reference throughout his career to Sicily's cultural identity as the expression of its susceptibility to pan-Mediterranean influences, and, more specifically, reference to pan-Mediterranean musical culture. As early as the mid-1930s, during his career as a journalist, Pirrotta interpreted Giuseppe Mulè's music as follows:

> In Mulè—even more so than in any other Sicilian artist—there is a spark of that pagan sensibility for which myth is not an arid literary notion, for which the vision of a Taorminian afternoon or a sunset among the papyruses of Cyane is animated by a spontaneous vibrating of ductile spectres to the sound of Theocritan, Hellenic reed-pipes.

In his earliest scholarly writing, Pirrotta returned to the matter of the "Hellenic" in Sicilian culture.[83]

Pirrotta later wrote of the *greghesche*—"polyphonic pieces ... of comical character on texts in the *lingua greghesca* or *stradiotesca*, a mixture of Venetian dialect and modern Greek words, which was supposed to imitate the parlance of the Stradioti (... Greek mercenaries in the service of the Venetian Republic)"[84]—that they "owe their name to the use of a half-Venetian, half-Oriental *lingua franca*, which was widely used in the Mediterranean ports."[85]

---

[81]On the Mediterranean world as cultural system, and as it has been supplanted by the Atlantic world, see the classic by Fernand Braudel, *The Mediterranean and the Mediterranean World in the Age of Philip II*, trans. Siân Reynolds, 2 vols. (New York: Harper & Row, 1972, 1973); Bernard Bailyn, *Atlantic History: Concept and Contours* (Cambridge, MA: Harvard University Press, 2005), especially 4–5; Terence K. Hopkins, Immanuel Wallerstein, Robert L. Bach et al., *World-Systems Analysis: Theory and Methodology* (Beverly Hills, CA: Sage Publications, 1982); and, among the titles Bailyn cites, J. G. A. Pocock, *The Machiavellian Moment: Florentine Political Thought and the Atlantic Republican Tradition* (Princeton, NJ: Princeton University Press, 1975). For useful discussion on this matter, I am grateful to my colleague Professor Paul A. Cefalu of the Department of English at Lafayette College.

[82]*Lost Horizon* (New York: Pocket Books, 1939), 100.

[83]**1936-37**: review of Federico Mompellio, *Pietro Vinci madrigalista siciliano*. For other examples in Pirrotta's journalistic writings of his addressing the Hellenic qualities of Sicilian music, see Cummings and Eiche, "Nino Pirrotta's Early Music-Critical Writings."

[84]**1956**: "Greghesca."

[85]**1954**: "Commedia dell'Arte e Melodramma."

Later still, he wrote of the canzone villanesca alla napolitana:

> I may ... be biased because I myself am from southern Italy, but I feel the ring of a southern, maybe also Mediterranean ethnic lore in the humorous delivery of the dialectal texts, in the spirited truncations and repetitions of words, in the sudden slowing and brisk acceleration of tempi, resulting as a whole in a remarkable variety and directness of rhythmic accentuation and expression.

In 1992, Pirrotta wrote that

> Even in relatively more recent centuries, one encounters not a few echoes of the song of "ciciliane" (and I am Sicilian), of songs characteristic not only of the island but perhaps also of all the more properly Mediterranean regions of our peninsula (the "kingdom" of Sicily).[86]

Pirrotta's sensitivity to the character of these pan-Mediterranean practices was a consequence of his own experience.

The formation of any young upper-middle-class Palermitan was also influenced by those elements of Sicilian society resulting from its political experience: the traces in one's comportment of an almost feudal political–economic system, based on possession of property; an inherent formality; the imposition of custom by the community on the individual.[87]

Nino Pirrotta derived his "polite, almost courtly" bearing—his formality and "modi aristocratici"—from his father; paternal grandmother, Giulia Pirandello-Pirrotta; and other progenitors. He synthesized such qualities with the warmth of his paternal grandfather, Antonino, whose name he was given.

Pirrotta inherited both his father's and maternal uncle Enrico's adventurousness and his maternal uncle Empedocle's calmness and serenity. From both his parents, he derived a reverence for the arts, an appreciation for the aesthetic, and a refined visual sense, which served him throughout his musicological career. From his studies at the *ginnasio* and *liceo*, he acquired the intellectual skills and initial conversance with languages and texts that will facilitate his scholarly work, as well as that command of history, history of art, literature, and philosophy, which is in evidence in his writings. From Luigi Amadio, he received the encouragement that stimulated his passion for music.

With these influences of family, school, and community having guided his boyhood formation, Pirrotta embarked on his formal career as a conservatory and university student: first at the Conservatory of Palermo (academic years 1924/25–1926/27), and then concurrently at the University of Palermo (academic years 1925/26–1926/27).

---

[86]**1992**: "Contemplando la musa assente."
[87]Giudice, *Pirandello*, 26–27. As Iain Fenlon reminds me, this is the world evoked in Giuseppe Tomasi di Lampedusa's novel *Il Gattopardo*, later made into a motion picture directed by Luchino Visconti.

Scena 2.ᵃ

Student Days (1924–31)

Il Conservatorio «Vincenzo Bellini» Di Palermo: 1924–27
The University of Palermo: 1925–27
Il Conservatorio «Luigi Cherubini» Di Firenze: 1927–31
The University of Florence: 1927–30

IL CONSERVATORIO «VINCENZO BELLINI» DI PALERMO: 1924–27

The Conservatory of Palermo, where Nino Pirrotta registered at the beginning of academic year 1924/25, originated in an institution founded by the Neapolitan viceroy in the early seventeenth century. With the Risorgimento and unification of Italy, it passed to the Italian state in 1861 and in 1889 became the Regio Conservatorio. The institution's administrative structure was reformed several times in the late nineteenth and early twentieth centuries: an ecclesiastical rectorate, abolished in 1884, was replaced by a presidency, which in turn was abolished and supplanted by a Consiglio d'Amminstrazione (Administrative Council). In 1935 the presidency was restored, and two years later Pirrotta's uncle Empedocle began a brief term as president.

However, the more significant administrative position was that of director. The directorship of composer Guglielmo Zuelli was extremely important to the evolution of the institution that Pirrotta knew, first as student and later as faculty member. Zuelli[1] became director in 1894 and served until 1911, when he assumed the analogous position in Parma. It was because of Zuelli that the Conservatory was named for Vincenzo Bellini. It was during Zuelli's tenure that Pirrotta's teacher Amadio was appointed to the faculty. And among the composition students whom Zuelli taught were Gino Marinuzzi

---

[1] Zuelli (1859–1941) had won the Sonzogno competition, the same competition that Mascagni had earlier won for *Cavalleria Rusticana*.

(1882–1945) and Giuseppe Mulè (1885–1951), both of whom figured prominently in Pirrotta's career: Marinuzzi as dedicatee of one of Pirrotta's important articles on seventeenth-century opera;[2] both Marinuzzi and Mulè as subjects of his journalistic writings of the early to mid-1930s.[3]

In 1922, Mulè became director of the «Bellini», where he remained until the end of the first of Pirrotta's three years as student (1924/25). Then, from 1925 to 1943 he served as director of the Conservatory of Rome, where Pirrotta was later to serve as *Bibliotecario*. Notwithstanding the brevity of his tenure in Palermo, Mulè initiated important artistic and administrative reforms.

In 1926, Antonio Savasta (1874–1959), another important figure in Pirrotta's formation, succeeded Mulè.[4] Pirrotta studied composition privately with Savasta after completing his formal studies at the Conservatory and University of Florence,[5] and among Savasta's other composition students was Mario Pilati, who—like Marinuzzi and Mulè—was a subject of Pirrotta's music-critical writings for the Palermitan daily *L'Ora*. Savasta was director of the Conservatory throughout the early to mid-1930s when Pirrotta began his professional activities there as docent in music history and librarian. And he was the institution's chief administrative officer when Pirrotta won the *concorso* (competition) in 1937 for the positions of *titolare* (tenured professor) *in Storia della musica* and *Bibliotecario*, which he assumed in 1938, the year Savasta resigned from the directorship.

During the second decade of the twentieth century, shortly before Pirrotta was to enroll there, the Conservatory of Palermo had a faculty of some thirty, including the "Prof[.] di Organo," "M.° Luigi Amadio," and Pirrotta's predecessor as librarian, Emanuele Paolo Morello.

THE UNIVERSITY OF PALERMO: 1925–27

Having completed the final year of *liceo* privately during his first year at the Conservatory of Palermo (1924/25) and passed the *esame di maturità*, Pirrotta

---

[2]1954: "Le prime opere di Antonio Cesti."

[3]Cummings and Eiche, "Nino Pirrotta's Early Music-Critical Writings" (see "Scena 1.$^{\underline{a}}$," n. 69).

[4]Savasta studied composition at the Conservatory of Naples with Nicola D'Arienzo (who also instructed Leoncavallo). At seventeen, Savasta had won the competition for the *cattedra* (chair) in harmony at the Conservatory of Florence, and in 1915 he succeeded D'Arienzo as incumbent of the chair in *alta composizione* and counterpoint in Naples, the position he resigned to assume the directorship in Palermo. On Savasta, see Agostino Ziino, "Antonio Savasta e i suoi allievi tra Napoli e Palermo: le ragioni di una 'scuola,'" in *Alfredo Sangiorgi*, ed. Riccardo Insolia and Antonino Marcellino, *Quaderni dell'Istituto Musicale Vincenzo Bellini di Catania* 3 (2003): 5–23.

[5]See such sources as Pierluigi Petrobelli, "Nino Pirrotta 1908–1998," in Antonio Delfino and Maria Teresa Rosa-Barezzani, eds., *Col dolce suon che da te piove: Studi su Francesco Landini e la musica del suo tempo: In memoria di Nino Pirrotta* (Florence: SISMEL – Edizioni del Galluzzo, 1999), and *Dizionario enciclopedico universale della musica*, 6:29-30 (see "Scena 1.$^{\underline{a}}$," n. 35).

STUDENT DAYS (1924-31)

was qualified to enter university, and in the fall of 1925 he registered in the Faculty of Letters and Philosophy at the University of Palermo, intending to pursue the doctorate (laurea) in philosophy.[6]

It was exceptional for a Sicilian to pursue the laurea, let alone anywhere other than in Sicily.[7] Pirrotta's decision to enroll in letters and philosophy and pursue the doctorate in philosophy rather than letters was also uncommon; of the 161 students enrolled in letters and philosophy for the academic year 1928/29, 158 were enrolled in letters.[8] Pirrotta's choice suggests something not only about his personal tastes but also about the influences of family and environment: He was motivated by intellectual interest, by a passion for the study of the humanistic disciplines irrespective of potential professional outcomes. Training at the *ginnasio/liceo* yielded no practical qualification prior to the completion of university studies, and sending a boy of ten to the *ginnasio* implied that his parents expected him to remain a student until about his twenty-second or twenty-third year.[9]

*****

Pirrotta's years at the University commenced on 4 November 1925 with the customary inaugural lecture. University President Francesco Ercole called on Professor Giovanni Alfredo Cesareo (1877–1937)—Senator of the Kingdom of Italy since 1924 and senior member of the Faculty of Letters and Philosophy—to address the assembly.[10] It is one of the ironies of Pirrotta's career that Cesareo delivered the opening lecture that day, since Cesareo's work on Salvator Rosa[11] would later serve Pirrotta in his studies of seventeenth-century opera. Some of Cesareo's other scholarly writings—on the *pasquinate* of Leo X's Rome, for example[12]—suggest an interest in the literary manifestations of popular culture, whose *musical* manifestations were of great interest to

---

[6]In 1860 the "Facoltà filosofica e letteraria" had been authorized to confer the laurea in the two fields under its jurisdiction, philosophy and letters. There were ten members of the Faculty of Letters and Philosophy in academic year 1928/29; among the members of the Faculty of Letters and Philosophy (see *Annuario della R. Università degli studi di Palermo. Anno accademico 1925–26* [n.d.]) was Ettore Gàbrici, *professore non stabile* ("assistant professor") of archaeology and a close Pirrotta family friend; and in academic year 1923/24—just before Pirrotta enrolled—some 200 to 250 students were registered in the Faculty.

[7]A. Di Pasquale, "La popolazione studentesca universitaria di Palermo dalle origini ai giorni nostri," *Statistica* 8, no. 4 (1948): 468–82; 9, no. 1 (1949): 27–56.

[8]Di Pasquale, "La popolazione studentesca."

[9]See also Minio-Paluello, *Education*, 40 (see "Scena 1.ª," n. 34).

[10]He spoke on "The Poetry of Action" ("La poesia dell'azione")—*Annuario della R. Università degli studi di Palermo. Anno accademico 1925-26* (n.d.): 9–30—a theme with Idealist resonances.

[11]Giovanni Alfredo Cesareo, *Poesie e lettere edite e inedite di Salvator Rosa*, 2 vols. (Naples: Tipografia della Regia Università, 1892).

[12]Cesareo, "Papa Leone e Maestro Pasquino," *Nuova antologia di scienze, lettere ed arti*, 4th ser., 75, Della Raccolta, 115 (1898); Cesareo, *Pasquino e pasquinate nella Roma di Leone X* (Rome: Società romana di storia patria, 1938).

Pirrotta throughout his career: the practices of "famous popular singers" who belonged to one of his favorite categories, namely, "that of musicians very much admired in their time, whose activities are beyond the scope of musical history because they had no use for musical notation." It was perhaps inevitable that Cesareo's interest in such elusive, nonelite phenomena would influence Pirrotta's formation and intellectual tastes.

The disciplinary expertise of the Faculty of Letters and Philosophy reveals a curricular vision that undeniably had an effect on its enrollees; the statutes[13] document a premium on breadth during the first two years of study, as well as a fair degree of prescription:[14]

> Registrants in the Philosophical section are held to pursuing the following sequence of studies:
>
> In the first year:
>
> 1. Philosophy (1st course);
> 2. History of ancient philosophy (1st course);
> 3. History of medieval and modern philosophy (1st course);
> 4. Pedagogy (1st course);
> 5. Latin language and literature (1st course);
> 6. Greek language and literature (1st course);
> 7. Ancient history (1st course);
> 8. German and English.
>
> In the second year:
>
> 1. Philosophy (2nd course);
> 2. History of ancient philosophy (2nd course);
> 3. History of medieval and modern philosophy (2nd course);
> 4. Pedagogy (2nd course);
> 5. Greek language and literature (2nd course);
> 6. Latin language and literature (2nd course);
> 7. Ancient history (2nd course).

Pirrotta thus settled into his rigorous, broadly gauged literary and philosophical studies in the fall of academic year 1925/26.

At that moment in the history of Italian university education, the critical exercises were the culminating examinations and the writing of the *tesi di laurea* (doctoral thesis); the individual lecture courses were intended largely as preparatory to the completion of those exercises, and were otherwise less

---

[13]Ministero della Pubblica Istruzione. Direzione Generale Istruzione Superiore. Regia Università di Palermo, "Statuto approvato con ordinanza ministeriale del 10 novembre 1921," *Bollettino Ufficiale* 1, no. 50 (9 December 1924 [1925]): 32.

[14]See the series of "annuari" for the University of Palermo, as, for example, *Annuario della R. Università degli studi di Palermo. Anno accademico 1928–29* (anno VII) (Palermo: Tipografia Michele Montaina, 1929).

significant. The two professors of philosophy whose lectures Pirrotta would have attended—both *professori di ruolo stabili* (tenured professors)—were Drs. Pantaleo Carabellese and Vito Fazio-Allmayer,[15] both distinguished philosophers, both adherents of Idealism. The significance of this latter circumstance for Pirrotta's development is immeasurable, because the manner in which he negotiated his own personal relationship to the tenets of the Idealist "school" was of great consequence for his formation.

In the years just before and during Pirrotta's time at the University, Carabellese (1877–1948) wrote several works that document his Idealist sympathies, among them a general account of "the problem of philosophy from Kant to Fichte"[16]—two of the great figures of European Idealism—and a translation of Kant's "minor writings."[17]

Fazio-Allmayer (1885–1958) was an even more celebrated and devoted Italian proponent of Idealism, if for no other reason than that he enjoyed a close personal relationship with Giovanni Gentile. Fazio-Allmayer had first earned the laurea in jurisprudence. Then, having made Gentile's acquaintance, he began attending Gentile's university lectures in philosophy and earned a second laurea. He thereafter embarked on a teaching career, first in the *liceo* and then, after 1918, when he attained the appropriate qualification, at the university level. In 1922, Gentile—having been named Fascist Minister of Public Instruction—invited Fazio-Allmayer to Rome to collaborate with him on a reform of the *scuola media* (middle school). Fazio-Allmayer remained in Rome until 1924. The following year he won the *concorso* that earned him appointment to the Faculty of Letters and Philosophy of the University of Palermo.

Although Fazio-Allmayer had historical interests, especially in the history of science—which might otherwise suggest a sympathy with Positivism[18]—his Idealist sensibilities are documented by his studies of "matter and sensation" and "the theory of liberty in the philosophy of Hegel,"[19] to whom the Italian Idealists owed a debt in constructing their own national variant of Idealism—indeed, their greatest debt.

Although one can detect resonances of Idealism in Pirrotta's profile, it is important to emphasize that he was celebrated for his independence from both Idealism and Positivism. In 1995, when the Faculty of Letters and

---

[15] *Annuario della R. · Università degli studi di Palermo. Anno accademico 1925–26* (n.d.): 49–50. Note, however, that when this particular annual circular went to press Fazio-Allmayer was not yet on the *ruolo stabile*.

[16] Carabellese, *Il problema della filosofia da Kant a Fichte (1781–1801)* (Palermo: Trimarchi, 1929).

[17] Emmanuele Kant, *Scritti minori*, trans. P. Carabellese (Bari: G. Laterza, 1923).

[18] As documented by studies of Bacon and Galileo and an edition of Aristotle's *De anima:* Fazio-Allmayer, *Saggio su Francesco Bacone* (Palermo: Trimarchi, 1928); *Galileo Galilei* (Milan: R. Sandron, n.d. [1911?]); and Aristotle, *Dell'anima*, ed. Vito Fazio-Allmayer (Bari: G. Laterza, 1912).

[19] Fazio-Allmayer, *Materia e sensazione* (Milan: R. Sandron, n.d. [1911]); *La teoria della libertà nella filosofia di Hegel* (Messina: Principato, 1920).

Philosophy of the University of Urbino requested that Pirrotta be granted the *Laurea «Ad Honorem»*, it was observed that the style of his writings

> in fact appeared entirely new: distant, indeed, whether from the positivistic historiography still dominant outside Italy, or the idealistic historiography much in vogue within.[20]

Indeed, Pirrotta used to recount that when he enrolled at Palermo to study philosophy, his growing awareness of the prevailing Idealist direction in the teaching of the discipline there was critical to his decision to abandon it and concentrate instead on the history of art.[21]

IL CONSERVATORIO «LUIGI CHERUBINI» DI FIRENZE: 1927–31

In 1925, Maestro Alberto Franchetti (1860–1942), a celebrated Italian composer, was appointed director of the Conservatory of Florence and president of its associated Accademia. Under his direction, which lasted four years, the institution enhanced the quality of its faculty through the appointment of several exceptional instructors, among them Pirrotta's organ teacher, Luigi Amadio, who resigned from the «Bellini» to accept appointment at the «Cherubini» as *titolare di Organo e Composizione organistica*.[22]

Pirrotta's decision to leave Palermo and follow his teacher to Florence was the first of several crucial decisions that reveal an openness to opportunities in life, a receptivity to potential experiences of great consequence, which were—in some cases—occasioned almost by happenstance. Later in life, he suggested that

> in an era in which one had not yet been accustomed from childhood to reach faraway places with ease, for me it was already a notable fact, going to complete my humanistic and musical studies at the University and Conservatory of Florence.[23]

If the «Cherubini» students' demographic profiles[24] were anything like that of the University of Florence students at that time, Pirrotta was indeed one of only trace numbers of Sicilians.[25] His ability to operate at the boundaries,

---

[20]See "Laurea 'honoris causa' a Nino Pirrotta," 9 (see "*Prologo*," n. 36).

[21]Fabrizio Della Seta, "Appunti per un ritratto intellettuale di Nino Pirrotta" (see "*Prologo*," n. 36).

[22]Adelmo Damerini, *Il R. Conservatorio* (see "*Scena 1.ª*," n. 73).

[23]See "Laurea 'honoris causa' a Nino Pirrotta" (see "*Prologo*," n. 36).

[24]*Annuario del R. Istituto musicale "Luigi Cherubini . . . di Firenze* X—Anno Scolastico 1913–1914 (1915): 7, 10-11.

[25]Of the 184 first-year students enrolled at the University in 1928/29, four were from Catania, three each from Messina and Agrigento, and one from Palermo. See the series of "annuari" of the University, as, for example, R. Università degli studi di Firenze, *Annuario per l'anno accademico 1928–1929* (Anno VII) (1929).

his oft-attested "noble" detachment—which permitted him to disagree with colleagues without engaging in polemic[26]—are in part the result of life and career choices that enabled him to understand his own experiences within a larger context and acquire an appreciation for human difference, as well as difference of scholarly opinion. Pirrotta's time at the «Cherubini» also provided him with the opportunity to observe the Florentines firsthand, which permitted him to make such ironic observations as the following:

> It would be as wrong to classify [Giovanni] Bardi as a conservative as to call him a progressive. It would appear that he was open to the ideas of his own time, while being, as is often the case with Florentines, stubbornly attached to certain traditions.[27]

Elsewhere, he makes reference to the Florentines' "keen sense of reality."[28]

At the same time, Pirrotta's decision to complete his university-level education in Florence was by no means unheard of, in particular for a member of a privileged family from the south of Italy: at that moment in history, as at other moments, Florence, culturally, was the most active and innovative center in Italy.[29] The importance of the city's status in this respect for Pirrotta's general formation cannot be exaggerated.

*****

Any number of «Cherubini» appointees influenced Nino Pirrotta's development. When Franchetti left the directorship in 1929, he was succeeded by Guido Guerrini (1890–1965), another figure whose career was closely intertwined with Pirrotta's. Guerrini's first year as director coincided with Pirrotta's third year as student, and he was later to serve as director of the «S.ᵗᵃ Cecilia» in Rome for ten years (1950–60), during six of which (1950–56) Pirrotta was his colleague as librarian.

Among the «Cherubini»'s faculty members per se who had a particular influence on Pirrotta's formation—other than Amadio—was Vito Frazzi (1888–1975), *titolare di Composizione* from 1912–58. Another of Frazzi's composition students during the period when Pirrotta was enrolled was the

---

[26]See, for example, Fabrizio Della Seta, "Appunti per un ritratto intellettuale di Nino Pirrotta" (see "Prologo," n. 36). Also, Pierluigi Petrobelli, in his "Introduzione" *Musicologia fra due continenti*, 7–8 (see "Prologo," n. 36), made reference to Pirrotta's "signorile distanza." See also *"Per un regale evento,"* 190–91, no. 126 (see "Prologo," n. 36).

[27]**1969**: *Music and Theatre*, 211. See also **1997**: "Francesco Landini: i lumi della mente," especially 6. Further such characterizations of the Florentines occur in **1983**: "Rhapsodic Elements in North-Italian Polyphony of the 14th Century," especially 84, and in **1997**: "Francesco Landini: i lumi della mente."

[28]**1969**: *Music and Theatre*, 129.

[29]For useful advice on this matter, I am grateful to Professor Lino Pertile.

legendary Luigi Dallapiccola. Those years must have been stimulating ones, professionally and personally, for the future musicologist.[30]

And the young organ student's association with Frazzi was to develop in ways that he could not then have imagined: in 1953, Frazzi undertook a "Trascrizione e realizzazione" of Antonio Cesti's *Orontea*, performed in Siena "in occasione della X Settimana Musicale Senese,"[31] a performance for which Pirrotta was responsible, and which occasioned the writing of several of his early studies of seventeenth-century opera.[32]

Pirrotta also offered warm reminiscences of his "dear master" Arnaldo Bonaventura, Professor of the History and Aesthetics of Music.[33] Bonaventura's directorship of the institution's library offered a model for how one might combine responsibilities as conservatory librarian with teaching and scholarly activity.[34] The catalog of the Conservatory library[35]—its "INTRODUZIONE" signed "a.b."—was published during Pirrotta's time as a student, and it documents the sorts of scholarly resources that an emerging bibliophile like

---

[30]Pirrotta's regard for Dallapiccola is suggested by comments that appear many years later in **1994**: *Don Giovanni's Progress:* 189 n. 21 and 196 n. 24. One of the obituaries issued when Pirrotta died (*La Nazione* [24 January 1998]) explicitly documented a friendship between Pirrotta and Dallapiccola. For a brief biography of Dallapiccola, with reference to his studies with Vito Frazzi at the «Cherubini», see Pierluigi Petrobelli, "Luigi Dallapiccola," *Musical Times* 116 (1975): 337–38.

[31]*Orontea. Dramma giocoso per musica di Giacinto Andrea Cicognini. Musica di Antonio Cesti. Trascrizione e realizzazione di Vito Frazzi. Da rappresentarsi al Teatro dei Rinnuovati in Siena il 16 e il 19 Settembre 1953 in occasione della X Settimana Musicale Senese* (Siena: Accademia Chigiana, 1953).

[32]**1956:** "Cesti, Antonio o Marco Antonio"; **1953:** "Nella biblioteca di Santa Cecilia; **1954:** "Le prime opere di Antonio Cesti"; and **1953:** "Tre capitoli su Cesti."

[33]See **1975**: "Le tre corone e la musica." On Bonaventura, see "Bonaventura, Arnaldo" in *The New Grove Dictionary of Opera*, ed. Stanley Sadie. Grove Music Online. Oxford Music Online, http://0-www. oxfordmusiconline.com.libcat.lafayette.edu:80/subscriber/article/grove/music/O002217 (accessed July 13, 2009); and Frank A. D'Accone et al., "Florence," in *Grove Music Online*. Oxford Music Online, http://0-www. oxfordmusiconline.com.libcat.lafayette.edu:80/subscriber/article/grove/music/09847 (accessed July 13, 2009). See also *Annuario del R. Istituto musicale "Luigi Cherubini,, di Firenze* X—Anno Scolastico 1913–1914 (1915): 5; the list there gives the name of Pirrotta's teacher "Frazzi Vito, id.—*Pianoforte complementare.*" In **1986:** "Historiae Musicae Cultores," Pirrotta reminds the reader that Bonaventura was the first to describe the famed Medici codex, a collection of motets compiled in 1518 for Lorenzo di Piero di Lorenzo de' Medici, which has elicited much scholarly attention.

[34]The following is a sampling of Bonaventura's own academic publications, and they convey a sense of the sorts of scholarly interests he had, which he evidently communicated to Pirrotta: Bonaventura, *Manuale di storia della musica*, 6th ed. (Livorno: Raffaello Giusti, 1921); Orazio Vecchi, *L'Amfiparnaso. Comedia harmonica. Cenni illustrativi e libretto*, eds. la Sezione fiorentina dell'Associazione dei musicologi italiani and Arnaldo Bonaventura (Florence: Tipografia Domenicana, 1914); Vincenzo Galilei, *Dal secondo libro de madrigali*, pref. Arnaldo Bonaventura (n.p. [Florence]: A cura della Sezione fiorentina dell'Associazione musicologi italiani, 1930); Girolamo Frescobaldi, *Primo libro d'Arie musicali: per cantarsi nel gravicembalo e tiorba, a una, a dua, e a tre voci* (n.p. [Florence]: A cura della Sezione fiorentina dell'Associazione musicologi italiani, 1933).

[35]A. Bonaventura, C. Cordara, R. Gandolfi, *Catalogo delle opere musicali teoriche e pratiche di autori vissuti sino ai primi decenni del secolo XIX. Biblioteca del Conservatorio di musica di Firenze*, (n.p. [Bologna]: Forni, 1977).

Pirrotta had at his disposal. And because Bonaventura was responsible for what little formal instruction Pirrotta ever received in the history of music, his role in Pirrotta's formation was critical.

Luigi Amadio's appointment at the Conservatory had attendant consequences for his career and professional activities, which they may have had for Pirrotta's, too. Soon after his appointment as *titolare*, Amadio was named "accademico onorario"[36] of the Conservatory's associated Academy (or learned society), in the company of Adelmo Damerini, who was later to write a history of the «Cherubini» and—more important still—serve as its director.[37] Another of Amadio's fellow *accademici onorari* was the renowned art historian Aby Warburg, whose celebrated article on the 1589 Florentine *intermedij*[38] had appeared in the *Atti dell'Accademia del Regio Istituto Musicale di Firenze*. The *intermedio* was a subject of great significance in Pirrotta's scholarly career,[39] given its importance to the Renaissance era's understanding of the potential for theatrical uses of music.

*****

On the basis of prior study at the «Bellini» and an assessment of his proficiency, Pirrotta was admitted to level 8 of the organ major at the Conservatory of Florence on 22 October 1927; the following month, he registered in both level 8 of the organ major and level 1 of the minor in history of music (obligatory for prospective composition majors), and at the end of that academic year (June 1928) he was promoted without examination to level 9 in organ and level 2 in history of music.

After three years at the Conservatory of Palermo (1924/25–1926/27) and two at the Conservatory of Florence (1927/28–1928/29), Pirrotta was awarded the *licenza in storia della musica* and the *diploma di magistero in organo e composizione organistica* by the «Cherubini», in June of 1929. He thereafter pursued additional study in composition (with Maestro Frazzi); in harmony,

---

[36] See the series of "atti" of the Conservatory, as in, for example, *ATTI DELL'ACCADEMIA DEL R. CONSERVATORIO DI MUSICA "LUIGI CHERUBINI,, FIRENZE. Anno LVIII* (Florence: LA STAMPERIA, 1934).

[37] In 1953, while Pirrotta was "direttore della Biblioteca Musicale S. Cecilia," Damerini collaborated with him on an exhibition on the 300th anniversary of Arcangelo Corelli's birth, which resulted in a catalog that the two men coedited: **1953**: *Catalogo della mostra corelliana*. On Damerini, see Federico Ghisi, "Adelmo Damerini nel suo Ottantesimo Compleanno," *Acta musicologica* 32 (1960): 158.

[38] Aby M. Warburg, "I costumi teatrali per gli intermezzi del 1589: I disegni di Bernardo Buontalenti e il libro di conti di Emilio de' Cavalieri," *Commemorazione della riforma melodrammatica*, Atti dell'Accademia del Regio Istituto Musicale di Firenze, 33 (1895): 133–46.

[39] See the relevant chapter in **1969**: *Music and Theatre*; **1960**: "Intermezzo, I.1."; and **1957**: "Intermedium."

counterpoint, and fugue; and in violin. In October of 1931, he withdrew from the Conservatory.

*****

Nino Pirrotta's intellectual profile is to be understood as a synthesis of the practices and traditions of the conservatory and the university. The absence of an opportunity to study music history at the university when he was a student[40] compelled—indeed, liberated—him to develop a personal vision of the discipline based directly on his experiences as conservatory licentiate in history of music and diplomate in organ and organ composition, and university laureate in art history: he applied the rigorous scholarly methods of art history as practiced at Florence to the primary materials of music history. Yet in many respects his approach to the music always revealed the effects of his conservatory training.

What professional skills were imparted to Nino Pirrotta during study for the organ diploma at the «Cherubini»?

The program was impressively demanding of aspiring diplomates. The requirements are presented in Table 2; I shall then discuss some of their elements in more detail.

However, before doing so, I briefly state the simpler requirements for the *licenza* in history of music, which Pirrotta also earned: for admission to the Scuola di Storia della Musica, he had to be certified by the Scuola di Grammatica, Storia e Geografia, a requirement easily fulfilled by virtue of his having earned the *licenza liceale* in Palermo; in addition, he was expected to take three one-hour lessons per week. When Pirrotta was awarded the *licenza in storia della musica* in June 1929, he received the maximum possible grade of 10. Demonstrably, he possessed a talent for the study of music history.

The requirements for the *Diploma* in organ are more complex: The requirements for the organ major ("Scuola d'Organo") interlock with those for several others: organ majors were simultaneously enrolled in the major in figured-bass accompaniment ("Scuola d'Accompagnamento numerico," "Obbligatoria per gli alunni d'Organo"); they were expected to attain proficiency equivalent to that of harmony, counterpoint, and fugue majors who had completed their second year, and piano minors ("Scuola Complementare di Pianoforte") who had completed *their* second year; in turn, the major in figured-bass accompani-

---

[40]For a brief but informative account of this phase of the history of musicology in Italy as a formal intellectual enterprise, see the "Preface" to Fabrizio Della Seta's collection of his essays *Not Without Madness* (see "*Prologo*," n. 44); I am grateful to Professor Della Seta for sharing this text prior to publication.

Table 2 Requirements for the Various Majors, Minors, and Programs at the Conservatory of Florence

Organ Major*	
ENTRANCE REQUIREMENTS:	• minimum age, 14 years; maximum age, 16 years • attainments equivalent to those of the [1] second year of the major in harmony, counterpoint, and fugue; [2] and of the second year of the piano minor
COURSE OF STUDY:	• normal course, 5 years; superior course, 2 years; total, 7 years • three lessons per week, of three hours' duration each
*Admittees to the organ major have to be enrolled simultaneously in the major in figured-bass accompaniment.	
Major in Harmony, Counterpoint, and Fugue**	
ENTRANCE REQUIREMENTS:	• minimum age, 12 years; maximum age, 15 years • attainments equivalent to those of the [second year of the program in *solfège*], and of the [second year of the piano minor]
COURSE OF STUDY:	• 6 years • three lessons each week, of three hours' duration each
**Obligatory for organ students; optional for the others.	
Piano Minor ¶	
ENTRANCE REQUIREMENTS:	• minimum age, 10 years; maximum age, 22 • attainments equivalent to those of the [first year of the program in elements of music]
COURSE OF STUDY:	• for organ students, 3 years • six lessons per week of three hours' duration each, alternating one day for classes in organ, figured-bass accompaniment, and counterpoint, and one day for voice classes
¶ Obligatory for organ students.	

continued

Table 2 *(continued)*

Major in Figured-Bass Accompaniment †	
ENTRANCE REQUIREMENTS:	• minimum age, 14 years; maximum age, 16 years • attainments equivalent to the [3] certificate of the program in *solfège* and to those of the [second year of the piano minor]
COURSE OF STUDY:	• 4 years • three lessons per week, of three hours' duration each
† Obligatory for organ students.	
Program in *Solfège* §	
ENTRANCE REQUIREMENTS:	• minimum age, 10 years • attainments equivalent to those of the [first year of the program in elements of music‡]
COURSE OF STUDY:	• 3 years • three lessons per week, of three hours' duration each
§ When the professor perceives the beginning of the voice's maturation in the student, he must inform the director, who withdraws the student from the study of *solfège* for a year. At the conclusion of the suspension, the student retakes the interrupted course, repeating it with the faculty member with whom he was studying when the suspension began. During the above-said period, students are required to attend the program regularly as an auditor.	‡ The first year of the program in elements of music having been concluded, the students have to be enrolled in the program in *solfège*.

continued

Table 2 *(continued)*

Program in Elements of Music††	
ENTRANCE REQUIREMENTS:	• knowledge of reading and writing in Italian and performing elementary arithmetical calculations • demonstrating an aptitude for the study of music, and, above all, possessing a sense of pitch and rhythm
COURSE OF STUDY:	• 3 years • three lessons per week, of three hours' duration each
†† The first year of the program in elements of music having been concluded, the students have to be enrolled in the program in *solfège*.	

ment demanded the same level of proficiency as that of students who earned the certificate in *solfège*.[41]

The nominal duration of the program for the organ major is notable: five years for the normal course, an additional two for the superior course. The student met with the instructor three times weekly for three-hour lessons.[42] And these were solely the requirements for the organ major; the obligatory cross-enrollment in related majors entailed additional hours of instruction.[43]

Thus in addition to the skills required to perform on the major instrument, diplomates in organ had mastered realization of figured bass and figured-bass accompaniment; harmony, counterpoint, and fugue; and *solfège*.

Such training was intended to develop the following abilities in those who completed the course and sat for the examinations for the diploma:[44]

Program of examinations for the License and Diploma . . . 79th Article—Organ:

---

[41] Although there were other prerequisites for the organ major, they were met by completing requirements already specified: harmony, counterpoint, and fugue majors were expected to attain proficiency equivalent to that of students who had completed the second year of *solfège;* but because the certificate in *solfège* was stipulated for majors in figured-bass accompaniment, the second requirement supersedes the first. That majors in harmony, counterpoint, and fugue and in figured-bass accompaniment complete the second year of the piano minor replicates the identical requirement for organ majors. Similarly, the condition that piano minors and candidates for the certificate in *solfège* complete the first year of the program in elements of music is superseded for organ majors by the requirement that they possess the certificate in *solfège*, by virtue of their obligatory cross-enrollment in the major in figured-bass accompaniment.

[42] The earlier annual circular, *Annuario del R. Istituto musicale "Luigi Cherubini,, di Firenze* X—Anno Scolastico 1913–1914 (1915): 10–11, specifies 12 hours of lessons per week.

[43] The program in elements of music also entailed mastering the fundamentals of the Italian language and arithmetic, but Pirrotta's attainments as a graduate of the *liceo* and concurrent enrollee in the Faculty of Letters and Philosophy at the Universities of Palermo and Florence would have superseded what was expected.

[44] *Annuario del R. Istituto musicale di Firenze (Anno I) e Atti dell'Accademia (Anni XXXI–XXXV)* (1899): 78–79.

First test: Performance of a *Prelude and Fugue* for organ by [J.] S. Bach and of a *tempo di Sonata*, or other *pezzo di concerto*, selected by the candidate from among those of the best modern authors.

Second test: Improvisation on the organ of a little *Prelude*, on a given theme.

Third test: Indicating a Gregorian melody with the voice and then accompanying it on the organ, having it followed by an analogous *Postlude*.

Fourth test: Sight-reading a brief piece for organ and a piece in vocal score for 4 voices in the respective clefs. Transposition of a little piece for organ.

Fifth test: Interpretation on the organ of a piece of medium difficulty assigned by the Examining Commission, prior study for four hours, closed room.

Sixth test: Composition of a *Fughetta* for three or four parts for the organ.

Seventh test: Responding to questions on the method of instruction, history, technology, construction, and registration of the organ, and the theory of Gregorian chant. Giving proof of knowing the best composers and didactic authors. License examination of complementary technical subjects, according to the programs of the Institute, or presentation of qualifications equivalent in the judgment of the Commission. Presentation of qualification of literary culture not inferior to the certificate of promotion from the 3rd to the 4th, Gymnasium, or to the license of the Technical School, or corresponding examination, according to the program of the Institute.

The third and seventh examinations, which tested mastery of Gregorian chant, merit special comment. Many diplomates in organ would have been aspiring church organists—indeed, Pirrotta's own teacher Luigi Amadio had begun his career as a cathedral organist—and many years later, Pirrotta reflected on the importance of what he had learned from Amadio about the Gregorian chant.[45]

One also notes the emphasis on the aspiring diplomate's skills in improvisation. Does the instruction preparatory to the examination help to explain Pirrotta's lifelong interest in orality, in the dialectic between oral and written traditions, and in improvisation?

Pirrotta acquitted himself admirably on his examinations: the seven scores averaged a highly creditable 8.6 out of a possible 10, and, notably, his highest score—9.5—was on examination 7. The historical character of this examination is obvious, and—like the perfect score of 10 earned when Pirrotta

---

[45]"I can make comparisons from personal experience, having myself studied organ with Luigi Amadio . . . a pupil of Bossi at the Venetian *liceo*. . . . Bossi . . . was led as organist to seek a repertory and models 'upstream' from romanticism, in Bach and in the Italian organists of the sixteenth/seventeenth centuries. From his method for organ and his transcriptions, I learned to become acquainted with Frescobaldi, and, from his pupil and my teacher, the Gregorian chant, then an indispensable introduction to the church responsibilities of an organist." **1982**: "Malipiero e il filo d'Arianna."

was awarded the license in history of music—so his score of 9.5 on examination 7 documents a particular aptitude for music-historical studies.[46]

Pirrotta's musicianship—illustrated above all in his edition of the music of fourteenth-century Italy, but also in the journalistic writings from the early 1930s and innumerable other publications—conveys a sense of what musical talent could produce when an enterprising young student undertook demanding study for the diploma.

THE UNIVERSITY OF FLORENCE: 1927–30

Once Pirrotta resolved to accompany Luigi Amadio to Florence and pursue the Diploma at the «Cherubini», he withdrew from the University of Palermo (on 12 November 1927), took up residence "presso Tito Travaglia / Via di Pepoli 224" in Florence,[47] and matriculated on 30 November in the Faculty of Letters and Philosophy at the University, "Philosophy section," "3rd year."[48] What he experienced there was to have the most profound consequences for his development.

If Pirrotta's academic responsibilities as a conservatory student in Florence were exacting and time-consuming, his enrollment at the university there facilitated entrée to a vital world beyond the institution. From time immemorial, universities have uneasily countenanced an "extracurriculum," and Florence in the late 1920s was especially rich in extracurricular stimuli.[49] On 15 October 1927, during the very time Pirrotta was registering at the «Cherubini» and sitting for his Conservatory entrance examinations, the eminent German art historian Aby Warburg delivered the inaugural lecture celebrating the return of the German Art Historical Institute in Florence (the Kunsthistorisches Institut in Florenz) to its former seat in Palazzo Guadagni.[50] Warburg spoke on a subject that would have appealed greatly to Pirrotta's developing

---

[46] Much of the information of this section is drawn from an important document provided by Professors Paolo Biordi and Gianni Ciabbatini of the «Cherubini» and obtained by Dott.ssa Kathryn Bosi and Dott. Valerio Pacini of the Biblioteca Berenson at Villa I Tatti, The Harvard University Center for Italian Renaissance Studies, Florence; it is reproduced in my "*Intermedio II.$\underline{ndo}$*" and transcribed in my Appendix. The Conservatory maintained a handwritten register with a separate page of entries for each matriculant, and I reproduce in the Appendix the entire page devoted to Pirrotta, which contains valuable information about subjects studied, dates for the License and Diploma, etc.

[47] See the document from the archives of the University of Florence in the Appendix.

[48] See the document in the archives of the University of Florence in the Appendix.

[49] For suggesting that I consider more fully the extracurricular intellectual world beyond the University and its possible influences on Pirrotta's development, I am grateful to Dr. Sabine Eiche, a longtime resident of Florence.

[50] See Gombrich, *Aby Warburg*, 264–66, 341 no. 37, and 345 no. 20 (see "*Prologo*," n. 28).

historical imagination: "Medicean Pageantry at the Valois Court in the Flemish Tapestries of the Galleria degli Uffizi"[51] and the 1565 Bayonne festivities depicted in the tapestries' background. More interestingly still, Warburg "was linking his study of the Bayonne festival with the results of his earlier paper on the *Costumi teatrali*,[52] which had also been connected with a Medicean pageant of the second half of the Cinquecento"; there was an "increasing emphasis on music on these occasions," Warburg observed in his lecture, and such

> festivals ... bore in themselves the roots of a new kind of art, of Italian opera.... From here it is but one step to Monteverdi's new art form: "The humanization of the ancient pathos formula through *recitativo* opera."[53]

There were also less formal venues for one's extracurricular intellectual development, such as the renowned "Giubbe Rosse" café in Piazza della Repubblica 13–14/r, which took its name from the waiters' distinctive red jackets.[54] In 1913, one of the rooms in the café became the office of the *letterati* associated with the journal *Lacerba*, at the very moment when its editors—Giovanni Papini among them—were developing an interest in the Futurist aesthetic program of Filippo Tommaso Marinetti; that same year there was an exhibit of Futurist paintings in the café itself. Important literary journals like *La Voce*, founded by Giuseppe Prezzolini[55] in 1908, were envisioned and created on the tables of the Giubbe Rosse and effectively flourished there. Avant-garde artists—who counted Papini among their most active benefactors—read Marinetti's Futurist manifesto at the café as soon as it was published.[56]

*****

It is an irony of the history of education that, notwithstanding Florence's status as one of the greatest centers of learning in European history, its

---

[51] For the text of Warburg's lecture, see Gombrich, *Aby Warburg*, 341 no. 37 and 345 no. 20 (see "*Prologo*," n. 28); it is now available in English translation in Warburg, *The Renewal of Pagan Antiquity: Contributions to the Cultural History of the European Renaissance*, intro. Kurt W. Forster; trans. David Britt (Los Angeles, CA: Getty Research Institute for the History of Art and the Humanities, 1999), 343–49.

[52] Aby M. Warburg, "I costumi teatrali per gli intermezzi del 1589: I disegni di Bernardo Buontalenti e il libro di conti di Emilio de' Cavalieri."

[53] Gombrich, *Aby Warburg*, 265–66.

[54] For the material in this paragraph, I am heavily dependent on Ernesto Livorni, "The Giubbe Rosse Café in Florence. A Literary and Political Alcove from Futurism to Anti-Fascist Resistance," *Italica: Journal of the American Association of Teachers of Italian* 86 no. 4 (2009): 602–22. The developments recounted here predate Pirrotta's arrival in Florence; my aim is simply to convey something of the informal intellectual *ambiente* that Florence provided, as illustrated by the Giubbe Rosse, whose vestigial influences lingered after the period of its most vital activity.

[55] Prezzolini was later to have a brilliant career at Columbia University (Livorni, *Giubbe Rosse*, 608).

[56] For an English translation of Marinetti's text, see http://www.cscs.umich.edu/~crshalizi/T4PM/futurist-manifesto.html. The Giubbe Rosse later became a locus of anti-Fascist sentiment.

university is of relatively recent foundation. The institution from which it evolved—the Regio Istituto di Studi Superiori, Pratici e di Perfezionamento—was raised to university grade only shortly before Pirrotta enrolled. All the same, the institution's curriculum was a legacy of the Italian Renaissance.

The Regio Istituto was established at the time of the Risorgimento. An institution of five faculties (including Letters), it was envisioned as having not merely vocational but also scientific purposes. (In that respect it seems to have drawn inspiration for its fundamental characteristics from similar institutions, such as the Collège de France.) There was also a political motivation to its founding: the Florentines were anxious to have their city (re)emerge as the intellectual capital of the peninsula, profiting from their prodigious cultural assets to counteract the political "Piedmonticization" of the newly unified country.

In 1923, during the tenure of Giovanni Gentile as Minister of Public Instruction, the Istituto was granted university status, and in its first year of operation (1924/25) it comprised four faculties, including the Faculty of Letters and Philosophy, which had been the Sezione di "Studi Legali, di Filosofia e Filologia" of the old Regio Istituto.

A recent student of the Faculty has justly characterized it as offering "probably . . . the most formidable complex of humanistic studies that Italy could then claim."[57] Among its legendary members were the medievalist historian Gaetano Salvemini and the medievalist art historian Pietro Toesca, who came to Florence from Turin in 1915.

Notwithstanding its excellence in other disciplines, the Faculty of Letters and Philosophy at Florence always manifested a particular dedication to the kind of philosophical and philological studies characteristic of the humanistic culture of the Florentine Renaissance. The principal feature of the entire enterprise—the most important element in the Florentine "school" of humanistic scholarship—was the interpenetration of philology and languages, on the one hand, and of classical and Romance philology on the other.

The University also enjoyed particular distinction in paleography, especially Latin paleography, exemplified by the presence of Luigi Schiaparelli,[58] the foremost Italian paleographer of the first half of the twentieth century. Symptomatic of such a profile is that, even during its incarnation as the Sezione di "Studi Legali, di Filosofia e Filologia" of the Regio Istituto, the Faculty had established institutes indicative of such interests; most important was a "Scuola di paleografia e diplomatica." In 1925, the Scuola was absorbed

---

[57]Paolo Marrassini, "Una facoltà improduttiva: Lettere fra cultura e politica," in *L'Università degli studi di Firenze, 1924-2004*, (Florence: L. S. Olschki, 2004), 1:49–164, especially 59.

[58]R. Università degli studi di Firenze, *Annuario per l'anno accademico 1928-1929* (Anno VII) (1929): 56–57, 64.

into the newly established University of Florence as the "Scuola speciale per bibliotecari e archivisti paleografici."[59]

The importance of this institute for Pirrotta's formation is suggested by the fact that in 1944/45, Mario Salmi, Pirrotta's thesis adviser, was named to the roster of the Scuola's instructors, as specialist in the history of manuscript illumination. Anyone familiar with Pirrotta's scholarship—with its grounding in languages, literatures, and paleography—will recognize the congruence of his scholarly sensibilities with those of the Florentine "school": the Positivistic side of his intellectual constitution had found more congenial intellectual terrain. In the words of Fabrizio Della Seta,

> [i]t is certain that Pirrotta could not *not* adopt the language and intellectual style of Idealism . . ., but in his *forma mentis* he was very much closer to scholarship of positivistic influence. Certainly his mentality was not idealistic, and in Florence—perhaps more so than in Palermo—he was able to find favorable terrain, with philologists like Giorgio Pasquali and art historians like Mario Salmi (with whom he wrote the *tesi di laurea*).[60]

*****

What did Pirrotta's formal experiences at the University of Florence entail?[61] Just before he enrolled, it was stipulated that study for the laurea in letters be of four years' duration, comprising two subsidiary biennia.[62] He had completed the first biennium in philosophy at Palermo and been admitted to the second biennium of the "Philosophy section" at Florence.

---

[59]Only students who had completed the first biennium of the four-year course in Jurisprudence or Letters and Philosophy were eligible to enroll, and the school thereafter offered instruction at two levels: specialized instruction during the second biennium, for students who had not yet completed the laurea; and a "scuola di perfezionamento" for students who already possessed the laurea in *Lettere, Giurisprudenza,* or *Scienze politiche*.

[60]Private e-mail communication with Professor Della Seta, 7 October 2007.

[61]The annual circulars (*annuari*) published during his tenure at the University furnish detail about the specific course he pursued..

[62]"During the [first] Biennium, each student is required to frequent—for at least one year—all thirteen of the institutional courses that compose the two clusters of subjects.

[cluster I]	[cluster II]
[1] Latin	[7] Ancient history
[2] Italian	[8] Modern history
[3] French	[9] Geography
[4] Greek	[10] History of philosophy
[5] German (theoretical and applied)	[11] Political economy
[6] English	[12] Philosophy
[13] Pedagogy	

In order to be admitted to the II. Biennium, the student will have to have passed the examination in a group of four subjects included in one of the two clusters—about which above—at his discretion." "Institutional courses" are more general in content; in American parlance, they are "survey courses."

But then came the consequential decision to abandon philosophy for art history, which required that he transfer within the Faculty from Philosophy to Letters. Moreover, he was concurrently at the Conservatory of Florence, fulfilling the demanding obligations there for the license in music history and diploma in organ, both attained in 1929. Therefore, rectifying the inevitable deficiencies resulting from the transfer from Philosophy to Letters and only thereafter undertaking study at the second-biennial level in Letters meant that completing the second biennium in Letters and drafting and defending the doctoral thesis—which otherwise would have occurred at the end of academic year 1928/29 or the beginning of 1929/30—were delayed, occurring instead at the beginning of 1930/31.

The first biennium at Florence, like that at Palermo—whether in Letters or Philosophy—was characterized by breadth, the second by depth:

> During the [second] Biennium, the student is required to frequent eight annual monographic courses, in no fewer than six subjects, four of which are required, the others elective. The required subjects are determined by Faculty Statute, according to the 'curriculum' of studies pre-selected by the student at the beginning of the III.rd Year of the Course.[63]

The second-biennial courses offered during 1929/30 were as shown in Table 3. "[A] t the beginning of the III.rd Year of the Course," Pirrotta would have "pre-selected" the " 'curriculum' of studies" in art history, and that decision would have governed the further selection of "eight annual monographic courses...in no fewer than six subjects, four...required, the others elective."

In the second biennium (as in the first), general course titles were accompanied by more specific descriptions of content; thus the course offered by Pirrotta's thesis adviser Mario Salmi—"History of Medieval and Modern Art"; Tuesday, Thursday, Saturday, 3-4 p.m.—treated "Florentine Painting of the Fourteenth century" and "Gothic architecture in Italy (with visits to Florentine Galleries and monuments)."[64]

Finally, the doctoral thesis:

> For the conferring of the title of doctor in letters or philosophy, the aspiring Laureate will have to have sustained the test of an "oral examination" on two themes, selected from among four proposed by the Adjudicating Commission—themes concerning

---

[63] See the series of University *annuari*. "Monographic courses" are more specialized in content; in American parlance, such courses are specialized upper-level electives.

[64] See the University *annuari*.

Table 3 Third- and Fourth-Year Courses in Letters at the University of Florence

COURSES	TEACHERS	MONDAY	TUESDAY	WEDNESDAY	THURSDAY	FRIDAY	SATURDAY
Italian literature	Prof. Guido Mazzoni						
Classical philology (I)	Prof. Giorgio Pasquali						
Classical philology (II)	Prof. Ettore Bignone						
Latin paleography, and diplomatics	Prof. Luigi Schipiarelli						
Greek paleography	Prof. Enrico Rostagno						
Classical antiquities	Prof. Ugo Enrico Paoli						
Archaeology	Prof. Luigi Pernier						
Comparative history Indo-European languages	Prof. Giacomo Devoto						

continued

Table 3 (continued)

COURSES	TEACHERS	MONDAY	TUESDAY	WEDNESDAY	THURSDAY	FRIDAY	SATURDAY
Comparative history Romance languages	Prof. Carlo Battisti						
Neo-Latin languages and literatures	Prof. Mario Casella						
French literature	Prof. L. Fosc. Benedetto						
Spanish language and literature	Prof. Mario Casella						
Ancient and medieval English literature	Prof. Aldo Ricci						
Modern English literature	Prof. Guido Ferrando						
German literature	Prof. Guido Manacorda						
Slavic languages and literatures	Prof. Nicola Ottokar						

continued

Table 3 (*continued*)

COURSES	TEACHERS	MONDAY	TUESDAY	WEDNESDAY	THURSDAY	FRIDAY	SATURDAY
Ancient history	Prof. Luigi Pareti						
Medieval history	Prof. Nicola Ottokar						
Modern history	Prof. Nicolò Rodolico						
History of medieval and modern art	Prof. Mario Salmi		15-16		15-16		15-16
Geography	Prof. Renato Biasutti						
Sanskrit and civilization of ancient India	Prof. P. Emilio Pavolini						
Semitic philology and classical Oriental civilization	Prof. Giuseppe Furlani						
Assyrian-Babylonian	Prof. Giuseppe Furlani						

continued

Table 3 *(continued)*

COURSES	TEACHERS	MONDAY	TUESDAY	WEDNESDAY	THURSDAY	FRIDAY	SATURDAY
Hebrew language and literature	Prof. Umberto Cassuto						
Literature and Civilization of the East Orient	Prof. Alberto Castellani						
History of religions	Prof. Umb. Fracassini						
History of philosophy	Prof. E.P. Lamanna						
Theoretical philosophy	Prof. Franc. De Sarlo						
Moral philosophy	Prof. Ludov. Limentani						
Psychology	Prof. Enzo Bonaventura						
Pedagogy	Prof. Giovanni Calò						
Applied political economy	Prof. Giovanni Lorenzoni	SEE THE FACULTY OF JURISPRUDENCE					

important scientific questions on the required subjects of the preselected 'curriculum'—and the discussion of the thesis for the Laurea.[65]

*****

The broad scope of history of art as taught at Florence, encompassing not only medieval and modern art but also archaeology and classical antiquities, was particularly important for Pirrotta's development. Indeed, the program in Letters as a whole aimed for comprehensiveness, for which the students were well prepared by their training at the *liceo classico*.

Of the members of the Faculty of Letters and Philosophy whose lectures Pirrotta would have attended—or whose influence would have been felt in other ways, directly or indirectly—one of the most important was the historian Gaetano Salvemini (1873–1957). Although dismissed from the faculty for his anti-Fascist activities shortly before Pirrotta enrolled, Salvemini nonetheless had a profound effect on the course of Italian intellectual life of the early twentieth century. Interestingly, Salvemini had been a docent at Pirrotta's Palermo *liceo* prior to securing his first university-level appointment.[66]

Salvemini practiced a Materialist history that reflected the influence of Antonio Labriola, the great Italian exponent of Materialism, and similar resonances of Materialism are characteristic of Pirrotta's writings.[67] However, Salvemini also inclined toward an Idealism of the sort practiced by Croce and Gentile. He subscribed to the traditional Idealist distinction between history and the sciences (which for Salvemini embraced the social sciences), in that history comprised "all investigations aiming at re-creating the past without pretense at determining laws," whereas the social sciences embraced "attempts to determine the laws of human behavior."[68]

---

[65]See the University *annuari*.

[66]See http://www.liceogaribaldi.it.

[67]In Salvemini's case, that sensibility is reflected in his *Magnati e popolani in Firenze dal 1280 al 1295* (Florence: Carnesecchi, 1899). Croce identified Salvemini as belonging to a "school" of writing that comprehended the historical process in economic–legal terms; most of its exponents, Croce suggested, had socialist sympathies and were influenced by intellectual positions articulated by the historical Materialists, an influence that, in Croce's words, "remained determinative in their intellectual life." Throughout this section, I am dependent on Norberto Bobbio's *Ideological Profile of Twentieth-Century Italy*, trans. Lydia G. Cochrane (Princeton, NJ: Princeton University Press, 1995).

[68]Bobbio. The congruence of Salvemini's position and Croce's is clear, as will presently be substantiated. Moreover, Salvemini possessed some of the Idealist's impatience with Positivism's obsession with the verifiable fact: Many historians, he observed, were almost paralyzed by concerns about the possibility of bias and accordingly did little more than collect data deemed susceptible to substantiation; others pursued an illusory objectivity. However, one must not overinterpret Salvemini in this manner. Bobbio (pp. 81, 83, 89–90) rightly suggests that those who had learned the lessons of the Positivistic method when Positivism was in vogue (that *facts* must be taken into account) did not surrender to Idealism. Salvemini was one of the empiricists of this history and manifested an empiricism and a passion for well-reasoned argument substantiated by data. His own philosophy of history divided philosophers into the "eagles of idealistic theology" and the "sparrows of empiricism," and he contentedly located himself among the latter, by which he meant that—unlike the Idealists—he did not presume to know that all that *had* happened, had happened necessarily, and that all that *was* to happen was already hidden in the womb of what had already taken place.

Like Salvemini, Pietro Toesca, professor of medieval and modern art, left the Faculty of Letters and Philosophy at Florence shortly before Pirrotta enrolled there (1926); but his influence, like Salvemini's, persisted. Pirrotta's intellectual profile had much in common with that of Toesca. Both combined "vast philological learning" with an approach that situated the work of art within the broadest possible historical–cultural context. In his *I precetti d'arte italiani* (1900),[69] Toesca argued that the analysis of the work be based, not on the abstract nineteenth-century Positivist concept of "progress," but—and here he, too, reveals the influence of Idealism and Materialism—on the concrete, particular historical conditions that determined the work's originality and value.

But unquestionably the faculty member who had the most profound influence on Pirrotta was his thesis adviser, Mario Salmi. He is the second of those key figures in Pirrotta's development whose own formation and achievements warrant detailed description.

Salmi had come to Florence from the University of Pisa as *professore straordinario* (*nonstabile*, or untenured)[70] of the history of medieval and modern art, beneficiary of an initiative to enhance teaching in art history, which occurred just prior to and during the time Pirrotta was writing his thesis.[71] Salmi had a brilliant career, both at Florence (where he was later to serve as *preside*—dean—of the Faculty of Letters and Philosophy[72]) and elsewhere.

Salmi had studied law and earned his *dottorato in giurisprudenza* (1910) at Pisa. However, his doctoral thesis, "La tutela giuridica del patrimonio artistico nazionale" ("Juridical Protection of the National Artistic Patrimony"), suggests that his true interests already lay elsewhere. Rather than practicing law, he enrolled at Adolfo Venturi's Scuola di Perfezionamento negli Studi di Storia dell'Arte Medioevale e Moderna in Rome. Salmi, therefore—and, indirectly, Pirrotta—was Venturi's intellectual spawn.

The network of interrelationships among those who exercised an influence on Pirrotta's development thus becomes more complex and interesting still, since Adolfo Venturi and his son Lionello had attended Adele Restivo-Pirrotta's Palermitan "salon." A brief excursus, therefore, on Venturi follows.

Venturi[73] had begun his tenure at the University of Rome in 1890, lecturing in the history of art. In 1901, the University named him to the first professorship in that discipline at an Italian university. His Scuola di Perfezionamento,

---

[69]*Precetti d'arte italiani: saggio sulle variazioni dell'estetica nella pittura dal XIV al XVI sec.* (Livorno: Belforte, 1900).

[70]R. Università degli studi di Firenze, *Annuario per l'anno accademico 1929-1930* (Anno VIII) (1930): 51, 57, 62: 51.

[71]In 1928/29–1930/31.

[72]R. Università degli studi di Firenze, *Annuario per l'anno accademico 1937-1938* (Anno XVI) (n.d.): 29. Salmi's tenure as dean began on 29 October 1935; ibid., 53.

[73]After study at the Istituto di Belle Arti in Modena, Adolfo Venturi was appointed to the Ministry of Public Instruction in Rome in 1888. That same year he founded the *Archivio storico dell'arte*, which he later renamed *L'Arte*, the first journal in the Italian language devoted to scholarship on Italian art.

founded in 1896, trained many of Italy's most accomplished scholars and administrators in the discipline, not only Salmi but also Pietro Toesca.[74] Venturi's principal publication was his monumental *Storia dell'arte italiana*,[75] which was extremely well received. A review by Finnish art historian Tancred Borenius identified the defining elements of its method, which were imparted to Salmi and, through him, to Nino Pirrotta. It was marked by a "grasp of the intricate geographical subdivisions of" the subject matter—"the currents of influence and ties of affinity between the various regions of Italy"—as well as comprehensive mastery of primary materials combined with a command of the secondary literature, including rare local publications little known outside Italy.[76] These are hallmarks of the writings of the author's intellectual grandson, Nino Pirrotta, who was ever sensitive to regional "dialectical" distinctions within the pan-Italian musical traditions of the late-medieval and early-modern periods and to the interactions among them. And they were hallmarks of Mario Salmi's writings, too.

After his studies with Venturi in Rome, Salmi won the competition for the chair in medieval and modern art at Pisa, where, as first incumbent, he founded the Institute of Art History. In 1929, he accepted the position at Florence, which he resigned two decades later to accept appointment as *professore ordinario* at the University of Rome, first as professor of medieval art, and then, as Venturi's successor, as professor of Renaissance and modern art.

By the time Nino Pirrotta arrived in Florence, Salmi had already published over sixty studies, and he encouraged Pirrotta in his developing passion for scholarship.

Salmi's method was based on scrupulous philological practices in service of a particular objective: the definition—historical and aesthetic—of the personality of the artist being investigated, as expressed in the artist's contribution to the development of the artistic culture of the early Renaissance. The combination of rigorous philological method with a dedication to biography was also to distinguish the work of Pirrotta, whose capacity for vivid depiction of the lives of the composers has been signaled by Ellen Rosand.[77]

*****

After having "sustained the test of an 'oral examination' on two themes . . . concerning important scientific questions on the required subjects of the

---

[74]Toesca later wrote an account of Venturi's career and achievements: *Adolfo Venturi* (Rome: Reale Istituto d'Archeologia e Storia dell'Arte, 1942).

[75]Originally planned as a compendium in seven volumes, later expanded to eleven: *Storia dell'arte italiana*, 11 vols. (Milan: Hoepli, 1901–40, 1967).

[76]See Borenius, "Professor Venturi on Quattrocento Painting," *Burlington Magazine for Connoisseurs* 29 (1916): 161–65.

[77]See the "*Prologo*," where I quote extensively from Rosand's review of the collection of Pirrotta's essays published by Harvard University Press in 1984.

STUDENT DAYS (1924-31)

preselected 'curriculum'" in art history, Pirrotta also "sustained the discussion of the thesis for the Laurea," which was thereupon granted (13 November 1930).[78] The following year, on 31 October 1931, he deposited his thesis with the secretary of the Faculty of Letters and Philosophy: a two-volume work entitled "Fonti iconografiche e stilistiche della pittura su maioliche del Rinascimento" ("Iconographic and Stylistic Sources of the Painting on Renaissance Maiolica").[79]

The text proper (Volume I) is accompanied by an album of photographs (Volume II), which illustrate the works discussed and substantiate Pirrotta's arguments concerning them. Among the "iconographic ... sources of the painting on Renaissance maiolica" is the imagery of mythological musicians (Apollo, Orpheus) accompanying their own singing on the *viola da braccio*,[80] and it is worthwhile noting that one of Volume II's illustrative figures[81] is used again more than three decades later in *Li due Orfei* to support and document Pirrotta's thesis about the practice of "singing ... *ad citharam*."[82] Throughout his life, Pirrotta was systematically accumulating a rich store of historical material—literary, visual, musical—that he subsequently invoked as necessary to substantiate a thesis then being advanced.

*****

Between late 1930, when the thesis was successfully defended and Pirrotta was *laureato* and named *Dottore in Lettere*, and late 1931, when the thesis was deposited with the secretary of the Faculty of Letters and Philosophy, Pirrotta was engaged in continuing, private, post-license and diploma studies

---

[78]The date of 1930 is given on the page devoted to Pirrotta in the handwritten register of University matriculants: "Laureato il 13 Novembre 1930, ... Titolo della tesi di laurea "Fonti iconografiche e stilistiche della pittu=ra su maioliche umbro-marchigiana durante il Rinascimento." Note, however, that this entry reflects a state of affairs that *postdates* the "discussion of the thesis" (Pirrotta was "Laureato" as of 13 November 1930) but *predates* the deposit of the copy with the secretary of the Faculty, since the title it gives for the thesis is slightly at variance from that on Pirrotta's title page.

[79]Page 1 of the thesis reads "TESI DI LAUREA di ANTONINO PIRROTTA / FONTI ICONOGRAFICHE E STILISTICHE DELLA PITTURA SU MAIOLICHE DEL RINASCIMENTO / Firenze, ottobre 1931-IX." (The Roman numeral "IX" signifies that 1931 was year 9 of the Fascist era.) The preceding page records the date when the thesis was consigned to the Faculty of Letters and Philosophy: "Presentata il 31-X.31.X [sic] / Il Segretario.... / [stamp] FACOLTA DI LETTERE E FILOSOFIA UNIVERSITA DEGLI STUDI DI FIRENZE."

Notice of Pirrotta's having officially been awarded the diploma is published in the *Annuario* of the University of Florence for academic year 1931-32, in the list of laureates in Letters in the Facoltà di Lettere e Filosofia, at no. 29 in the list: *Annuario [della] r. Università degli studi di Firenze per l'anno accademico 1931-1932*, anno X (1932), "29. Pirrotta Antonino, 'Fonti iconografiche e stilistiche della pittura su maioliche del Rinascimento.'"

[80]Volume II, figs. 42–50.

[81]Volume II, fig. 43: Venice, Civico Correr, Fabbrica d'Urbino, Anderson 14056.

[82]**1969:** *Music and Theatre*, vi and 23, and Illus. 5; Volume II, fig. 46 of the doctoral thesis depicts the Bacchæ dismembering Orpheus, an iconic moment in the myth also treated extensively in *Music and Theatre*, 19, 21, 28–29 and Ex. I on p. 30.

at the Conservatory. He withdrew from the Conservatory the same month he deposited the thesis (October 1931) and returned to Palermo.

*****

The influences on Pirrotta's development during his years in Florence were not exclusively the formal influences of teacher on pupil, however. He often recalled that one of his close friends there was Eugenio Garin. A year younger than Pirrotta, Garin had enrolled at the University of Florence two years before him (1925) and was awarded the laurea in moral philosophy in 1929.[83]

Upon graduating from the University of Florence, he taught for a time at the *liceo scientifico* of Palermo, which would have afforded further opportunity for him to deepen his relationship with Pirrotta.

Garin is generally considered one of the three most celebrated twentieth-century historians of Italian Renaissance thought, the others being Hans Baron and Paul Oskar Kristeller.[84] Garin had had a classical, Positivist training, and whatever truth there may be to an argument that his thought reveals an early Idealist, Gentilean phase, the Second World War precipitated a crisis in the Italian Idealist tradition, in that Idealism became associated with Italian Fascism and discredited German culture. During the 1950s, Garin and a pupil undertook a reinterpretation of the history of Italian philosophy, ridding it of its Idealist associations and investing it instead with a "neohistoricist" orientation. Garin's fundamental instincts as a scholar and his Positivist training limited overt politicizing tendencies in his scholarly discourse.

These developments postdate the period of his personal association with Nino Pirrotta.[85] But one of the defining characteristics of Garin's scholarly profile, as it existed before the war and was developed thereafter, was "his ... interest in the biographical and contextual approach to the interpretation of humanists, best seen in his famous series of *ritratti*,"[86] and such an interest in biography and contextualization was characteristic of Pirrotta's scholarly persona as well.[87]

---

[83]R. Università degli studi di Firenze, *Annuario per l'anno accademico 1929–1930* (Anno VIII) (1930): 172.

[84]See James Hankins, "Garin and Paul Oskar Kristeller: Existentialism, Neo-Kantianism, and the Post-War Interpretation of Renaissance Humanism," in the proceedings of the conference *Eugenio Garin: Dal Rinascimento all'Illuminismo, Firenze, 6–8 marzo 2009* (Florence: L. S. Olschki, forthcoming). I am very grateful to Professor Hankins for sharing his study prior to publication.

[85]Hankins, "Two Twentieth-Century Interpreters of Renaissance Humanism: Eugenio Garin and Paul Oskar Kristeller," in Hankins, *Humanism and Platonism in the Italian Renaissance*, 2 vols. (Rome: Edizioni di storia e letteratura, 2003–04),1:573–90.

[86]Hankins, "Two Twentieth-Century Interpreters"; the *ritratti* are translated as *Portraits from the Quattrocento* (New York: Harper & Row, 1972).

[87]However, for all that there are such correspondences in the two men's thought, I believe that Pirrotta's understanding of the Italian Renaissance as a phenomenon in European history is more aligned with Kristeller's. See my "*Scena 7.ª* Harvard University (1956–71): *Rinascimento*."

*****

Nino Pirrotta's principal achievements after his years of study in Florence were of two types. There were, first, the musico-performative skills attained during demanding training at the Conservatory: mastery of organ performance and composition; figured bass and figured-bass accompaniment; harmony, counterpoint, and fugue; and *solfège;* and, more specifically, the conversance with the Gregorian chant repertory and improvisatory techniques. Second, he acquired broad and deep classical learning and humanistic sensibilities, the result of his comprehensive training at the University: the command of languages, literatures, and history; the mastery of paleography as a scholarly methodology; the refined visual sense.

In particular, Pirrotta's university education was critical to his development as a music historian. Music history as then taught at the Italian conservatory was not only limited in scale, but also designed with an applied objective in mind: to provide composers and performers with a (rudimentary) understanding of historical context. Pirrotta's studies in art history at the University helped him develop a more intellectually refined sensibility. He came to appreciate that besides its utilitarian, applied value, the history of the arts was also intrinsically meritorious, in intellectual terms, in its own right. Understanding the innate intellectual viability of the history of the arts was critical to the development of his authorial voice and vision of music history as a fully legitimate university discipline.

Finally, it was during the Florence years that Pirrotta began to avail himself of uncommon life opportunities: to travel, to experience other geographic regions and peoples different from his own familiar fellow Palermitans. This "openness"—to borrow the term used by James Haar—was to serve him well in the decades to come.

Scena 3.ᵃ

Palermo (1931–36)

After depositing his thesis with the secretary of the Faculty of Letters and Philosophy (October 1931), Nino Pirrotta returned to Palermo and began concertizing. In the 26–27 December 1931 issue of *L'Ora* he was praised for a concert inaugurating the new organ at the Church of S. Maria di Gesù:

> A musician of broad and sound culture who knows every secret of his complex instrument, Nino Pirrotta Restivo possesses a remarkable sense of style as well as an impeccable technique. He is able to express the essential characteristics, to find the right interpretive approach ... for each piece of music. ... Thus in the *Pastorale* of [Domenico] Zipoli,[1] the *Petit Poncet* [sic; recte: *Poucet*] of Ravel,[2] and the *Vecchio Castello* of Monssorgsky [sic; recte: "Moussorgsky"],[3] he attains a singular delicateness of touch, while in the *Toccata* of Palasuti, the *Preludio e fuga* in mi min. by Bach,[4] and the *III Corale* of Franck[5] he demonstrates to perfection his gifts of execution and style.

These are demanding compositions, exemplifying a range of styles and high expectations concerning technical proficiency and sensitivity to stylistic interpretation.

A pressing obligation awaited him, however: his military service. Pirrotta's status in Italian society was such that he could enlist as an officer. He therefore trained at officer candidate school, and given his tall and slender frame—he was affectionately nicknamed "sfilatino" (*"baguette"*)—he was

---

[1] The *Pastorale* in part 1 of *Sonate d'intavolatura per organo e cimbalo: Orgel- und Cembalowerke (1716)*, ed. Luigi Ferdinando Tagliavini, 2 vols., (Heidelberg: W. Müller, Süddeutscher Musikverlag: 1959).

[2] A transcription for organ of the so-named second movement from the piano/four-hand composition *Ma mère l'oye* (1908-10): "Pavane de la belle au bois dormant," "Petit poucet," "Laideronnette, impératrice des pagodes," "Les entretiens de la belle et de la bête," and "Le jardin féerique."

[3] A transcription for organ of the so-named movement from the original piano version of the composer's *Pictures at an Exhibition*.

[4] Either BWV 533, *Prelude and fugue*, e (?before 1705); or BWV 548, *Prelude and fugue*, e (revised 1727–31).

[5] The third of the *Trois chorals* in E major, B minor, and A minor for organ (1890).

detailed to the cavalry and served as lieutenant. Upon being discharged,[6] and finally free of all previous obligations, he was able to contemplate his career more purposefully.[7]

*****

Many years later, Pirrotta recalled wanting to devote himself to the history of music but was having difficulty realizing his ambition. Ottavio Ziino, his boyhood friend and future brother-in-law, was a music critic from 1929 to 1931 and wrote on Wagner's *Tristan und Isolde*, Moussorgsky's *Boris Godunov*, Boïto's *Nerone*, and similar subjects for the Palermitan daily *L'Ora*. Ziino's journalistic activities suggested a means for Pirrotta to establish himself professionally, an outlet for his developing musical and music-historical interests.[8] Between December 1933 and October 1935, he wrote at least 26 journalistic pieces for the same daily that had published Ziino's music criticism. These critical writings were long neglected, but they have recently been republished and are illuminating documents of Pirrotta's earliest activities as essayist and aspiring music historian.[9]

*****

While writing for *L'Ora*, and even earlier, Pirrotta was also deeply involved with the Palermitan "Friends of Music" ("Amici della Musica"), serving as secretary in August of 1933.[10] Throughout the early to mid-'30s, he was also establishing himself—initially on an *incaricato* (visiting or adjunct) basis—at his Alma Mater, the Conservatory of Palermo:[11] in early 1935, his father

---

[6]The earliest mention of public activity after his service dates from August 1933, concerning his involvement with the Palermitan "Amici della Musica."

[7]Various secondary sources report that after completing the *diploma* in Florence, Pirrotta also pursued private study in composition with his old teacher at the Bellini, Antonio Savasta: *Dizionario enciclopedico universale della musica*, 6:29–30 (see "Scena 1.ª," n. 35); Pierluigi Petrobelli, "Nino Pirrotta 1908-1998" (see "Scena 2.ª," n. 5); Accademia di Santa Cecilia, *Annuario 1955–1956 (CCCLXXI-CCCLXXII)* (n.d.): 158–59.

[8]Ottavio Ziino, *Ricordi*, 29 (see "Scena 1.ª," n. 7).

[9]I say "at least" because one of the reviews that is demonstrably Pirrotta's is unsigned, and thus there might be others of this kind. See Cummings and Eiche, "Nino Pirrotta's Early Music-Critical Writings" (see "Scena 1.ª," n. 69), where we contextualize the writings and offer a preliminary analysis of their content and significance. On Pirrotta's journalistic career, see also Accademia di Santa Cecilia, *Annuario 1955–1956*: 158–59.

[10]"The Special Commissions have remained constituted thusly: Musical Commission . . . *Maestro* Nino Pirrotta-Restivo, Secretary." *L'Ora di Palermo*, 5–6 August 1933.

[11]Another of the reports of Pirrotta's involvement with the *Amici della Musica* (October 1933) records that "work has been going on for some time now to prepare the poster for the coming Season, a . . . task entrusted to the Special Musical Commission, under the enlightened direction of the illustrious *Maestro* comm. Savasta (preëminent director of our Royal Conservatory) with the collaboration of *Signora* Ester Mazzoleni and *Maestri* Franz Tantillo, Alfredo Sangiorgi, Terenzio Gargiulo, and Nino Pirrotta of our Conservatory." *L'Ora* 25–26 October 1933.

Vincenzo reported to Pirrotta's sister Giulia that "[b]y now, Nino has made himself at home at the Conservatory."[12] Thus even before his formal appointment in 1936 to the Conservatory's roster of full-time faculty, as docent in music history and librarian, Pirrotta was employed there on a temporary basis, *fuori ruolo*, which suggests his developing professional dedication to that institution and to music librarianship.

*****

In 1934, while he was concertizing,[13] writing critical pieces for *L'Ora*, teaching part time at the Conservatory, and contributing his time and energies to the "Amici della Musica," Pirrotta was approached by a close friend, Ettore Li Gotti (1910–56), Romance philologist and docent at a local *liceo*, who invited him to collaborate on a study of the verse of Trecento Florentine poet Franco Sacchetti and its musical settings.

Pirrotta's acceptance of the invitation was among the most consequential developments of his career, as he would later recount. Li Gotti immediately became an important figure in his professional formation. Giulia Pirrotta-Ziino recounted that her brother's musicological career had "begun almost by chance." Li Gotti afforded him the means he sought[14] and was in part responsible for that almost chance beginning to his decades-long absorption in the scholarly study of Italian music. We will consider Pirrotta's relationship with Ettore Li Gotti in some detail here, focusing especially on their collaboration on *Il Sacchetti e la tecnica musicale del Trecento italiano*.

---

[12]"Nino si è ormai ambientato nel Conservatorio— . . . Pal. 30/1/35." Further, "Nino continues his study as usual, interspersed with lessons at the Conservatory and his duties as librarian" ("Nino continua al solito il suo studio, interpolato con le lezioni al conservatorio e le sue mansioni di bibliotecario— . . . Palermo 27/2/35"). For providing me with copies of these letters, I am grateful to Professor Agostino Ziino.

[13]Pirrotta's concertizing in Palermo actually began in 1930, before he withdrew from the «Cherubini» ("ottobre 1931") and deposited his doctoral thesis with the secretary of the faculty at the University of Florence ("Presentata il 31-X.31. . . . "): the 26–27 December 1931 article in the Palermitan daily *L'Ora* ("I concerti. Nino Pirrotta inaugura il nuovo organo in S. Maria di Gesù") states that "[i]l maestro Nino Pirrotta Restivo si era imposto lo scorso anno all'attenzione e all'ammirazione del pubblico palermitano in un riuscitissimo concerto degli «Amici della Musica»" ("Maestro Nino Pirrotta had commanded the attention and admiration of the Palermitan public last year in a most successful concert of the 'Amici della Musica'"), but gives no further information.

Several secondary sources (at least one authored by Pirrotta) also suggest that he performed organ recitals during this period, in some instances stating that they were for broadcast over Italian radio—*Die Musik in Geschichte und Gegenwart*, 10:1296-97 (see "Scena 1.ª," n. 35); *Dizionario enciclopedico universale della musica*, 6: 29–30 ("Dopo aver svolto per breve tempo attività concertistica. . . . ") (see "Scena 1.ª," n. 35); Carolyn Gianturco, "Nino Pirrotta," *Rivista italiana di musicologia* 33 (1998): 3–6; Accademia di Santa Cecilia, *Annuario 1955–1956 (CCCLXXI-CCCLXXII)* (n.d.): 158–59 ("svolse attività concertistica")—but I have been unable to locate any substantiating primary documentation on such broadcasts.

[14]Pirrotta, *Musica tra Medioevo e Rinascimento* (Turin: Einaudi, 1984), x. On Li Gotti's role in the inception of Pirrotta's musicological career, see Pierluigi Petrobelli, "Nino Pirrotta e Diego Carpitella: due maestri," *L'eredità di Diego Carpitella: etnomusicologia, antropologia e ricerca storica nel Salento e nell'area mediterranea: atti del convegno, Galatina, 21, 22 e 23 giugno 2002*, ed. Maurizio Agamennone and Gino Leonardo Di Mitri (Nardò: BESA, 2003), 53–58, especially 53.

*****

Ettore Li Gotti was born in Palermo, where he earned the doctorate in letters in 1931. In 1933, he enrolled in the advanced course in Romance philology at the University of Rome, offered by the celebrated though controversial Giulio Bertoni. Li Gotti then won the *concorso* for the chair in Italian and Latin literatures in the *licei*, and in 1934—when he and Pirrotta began collaborating on their book—he was teaching at the Liceo «Umberto I» di Palermo. He attained qualification for university teaching in 1936, the same year that Pirrotta began teaching full time at the Conservatory of Palermo. (The publication of *Il Sacchetti* provided both men with the professional certification that justified their advancement.) As of 1943, Li Gotti was teaching Romance philology at the University of Palermo, and in 1952—following the customary *concorso*—he was appointed to the chair in that discipline. Li Gotti died suddenly and unexpectedly in December 1956, during a meeting of the faculty council of the Faculty of Letters and Philosophy.

Li Gotti enjoyed an international reputation, counting among his non-Italian colleagues the Spanish philologist Ramón Menéndez Pidal. Pirrotta and Li Gotti collaborated on a study for Menéndez Pidal's Festschrift of the fourteenth-century Italian composer Paolo *tenorista*, whose life and œuvre were among Pirrotta's principal scholarly concerns.[15]

The year before he succeeded to the chair at Palermo, Li Gotti had cofounded the "Centro di Studi Filologici e Linguistici Siciliani," described as the "point of departure for modern Sicilian philology." The Center was divided into a linguistic section, responsible for the preparation, compilation, and publication of a Sicilian dictionary, and a philological section (the "Commission for Texts"), responsible for publishing ancient Sicilian literary monuments. Li Gotti served as editor of the Center's *Bollettino* and *Collezione di testi siciliani dei secoli XIV e XV*.[16]

Both Pirrotta and Li Gotti identified strongly with their *sicilianità*. A few years before his death, Li Gotti lamented the lack of a "coordination of scientific work and a systematic investigation of the ancient language of the Island (Sicily), from the earliest documents until the 'triumph' of Tuscan," which had prompted the establishment of the Centro di Studi Filologici e Linguistici Siciliani. Li Gotti's identity as Sicilian was manifested in pioneering work as cofounder of the Centro and editor of its *Bollettino* and collection

---

[15]**1949**: "Paolo Tenorista, fiorentino «extra moenia»." Pirrotta was later to dedicate his **1961**: *Paolo Tenorista in a new fragment of the Italian Ars Nova* to the memory of Li Gotti.

[16]He understood that the Center's success depended ultimately on the quality of its administrative as well as intellectual leadership and secured the participation of the University's *rettore*, Lauro Chiazzese, first president of the Center, and of Pirrotta's politically prominent first cousin Franco Restivo, son of his maternal uncle Empedocle and *Presidente della Regione Siciliana*, who succeeded Chiazzese as president.

of texts.[17] Pirrotta's *sicilianità* inspired a series of articles in which he sought to recapture elusive Sicilian elements in Italian music of the medieval and early-modern eras.[18]

Li Gotti's final work, published posthumously, was on the celebrated Sicilian tradition of the puppet theater.[19] Li Gotti and Pirrotta thus also shared an interest in the popular cultural practices of early-modern Italy, which they presumably inherited from their teacher at the University of Palermo, Giovanni Alfredo Cesareo.[20]

*****

But that was not all that Nino Pirrotta and Ettore Li Gotti had in common: much more important were their similar attitudes toward Italian Idealism and their similar scholarly profiles, suggesting a similar conclusion to the intellectual odyssey that resulted in their relationship to Idealism's tenets. It is one of the reasons that Li Gotti was such an important figure in Pirrotta's formation, and Pirrotta in Li Gotti's.

Li Gotti's teacher in Rome, Giulio Bertoni (1878–1942), was one of the great students of Italian language and literature and one of the great figures of Italian Idealism. Bertoni subscribed to Crocean and Gentilean Idealism's understanding of language.[21] In his *Brevario di neolinguistica* of 1925, cowritten with Matteo Bàrtoli, the authors "demolish the ... *harmful prejudice of phonetic laws* [emphasis added]."[22] The *Neolinguistica* advanced a theory of linguistic change, and on the basis of that theory, which was aligned with Croce's philosophy (above all in *The Aesthetic*), the authors developed their methodology of "neo-linguistics." The indebtedness to Crocean Idealism is

---

[17]By 1957, Li Gotti's *Collezione di testi siciliani* comprised eight volumes.

[18]See, for example, **1936-37:** review of Federico Mompellio, *Pietro Vinci madrigalista siciliano;* **1938:** review of Ottavio Tiby, *La musica bizantina;* **1979:** "I poeti della scuola siciliana e la musica"; and **1981:** "La siciliana trecentesca"

[19]Li Gotti, *Il teatro dei pupi* (Florence: Sansoni, 1957), 1–2, contain a synoptic biography of Li Gotti and 179-82, a select bibliography of his writings.

[20]See the preceding chapter.

[21]One of his apologists, Giuliano Bonfante, wrote that, "[a]s in his literary scholarship, so in linguistics, [Bertoni] followed, sometimes perhaps with excessive zeal, the Idealist direction. But without doubt his great merit was having sought to integrate linguistic phenomena ... together with those of civilization.... His works ... had the ... merit of reacting vitally to the *mechanistic conception and mental constrictions* of the Positivist direction, placing into light the importance of the individual creative and *aesthetic elements of language,* which is *not a mere inventory of sounds* [emphases added] but part of the culture of a people." Giuliano Bonfante, "Giulio Bertoni 1878–1942," *Italica* 20, no. 4 (1943): 216–17. The Crocean lineage of such a philosophy is apparent in passages like that in Croce, *Logic as the Science of the Pure Concept*, trans. Douglas Ainslie (London: Macmillan, 1917), translation of *Logica: come scienza del concetto puro*, 2nd ed. (Bari: G. Laterza, 1909), 4–5. See also Croce, *The Aesthetic as the Science of Expression and of the Linguistic in General*, trans. Colin Lyas (Cambridge: Cambridge University Press, 1992), 154–64, and Croce, *Teoria e storia della storiografia* (Bari: G. Laterza, 1917); trans. as *History: Its Theory and Practice*, trans. Douglas Ainslie (New York: Russell & Russell, 1960), 131.

[22]Bonfante, "Giulio Bertoni."

particularly obvious in the belief that the "spiritual" dimension of language (an Idealist preoccupation) is located largely in syntax and style and only insignificantly in phonology, which was instead a principal concern of the scientific linguists of Positivist inclination.[23] Bertoni—and Croce and Gentile—resisted the efforts of Positivist linguists to reduce language to a science: to a series of laws that, in Idealism's view, were abstractions, "mechanistic ... constrictions" revealing that "harmful prejudice of phonetic laws."[24]

Predictably, the scientific linguists reacted sharply. In a review of Bertoni's publications, Robert A. Hall, Jr. voiced the scientific linguist's impatience with Idealism's linguistic theories. Concepts such as "the spirit," "creativity," and "spiritual energy" belong to the realm of metaphysics, where verification is not required; scientifically, they are meaningless and their introduction into putative scientific discourse "short-circuits inquiry."[25] When Bertoni asserted that "the history of poetry belongs to linguistics" ("la storia della poesia appartiene alla linguistica"), he was rendering Positivistic understanding of "science" meaningless, and obliterating the distinction between the Idealists' definition of linguistics and the kind of cautious, objective study that linguists critical of Croce sought to make the basis of the scientific study of language, independent of aesthetico-literary study.

In the Positivists' estimation, Idealism's understanding of the science of linguistics failed to distinguish between language itself—a signal that elicits observable reactions in other people—and its meaning. As a science, linguistics considers language more or less exclusively in its external manifestations and "meaning" not within its purview, not susceptible to definition in physical terms. Concepts like "culture" and the "soul," which resist exact definition, are not matters for fruitful scientific discussion.[26]

Finally, operating beneath Bertoni's linguistic theories and adherence to Crocean and Gentilean Idealist philosophies of language were larger, transcendent forces: Simon Gaunt and Julian Weiss identified the "distinctly nationalist" character of Bertoni's endeavor and observed that his "discourse is shot through with the ideology of the mid-twentieth-century nation state."[27]

---

[23]Phonetic change, in their view, must not be accorded any particular significance as a determining factor in linguistic change; rather, it was subordinate to other, more "spiritual" varieties of linguistic change.

[24]Bonfante, "Giulio Bertoni."

[25]Robert A. Hall, Jr., review of Giulio Bertoni, *Lingua e Pensiero. Studî e saggî linguistici* (Florence: L. S. Olschki, 1932); *Lingua e Poesia. Saggî di critica letteraria* (Florence: L. S. Olschki, 1937), in *Italica* 15, no. 4 (1938): 239–42.

[26]Croce, in the words of Niels Helsloot, imposed a "subjectivist stamp" on Italian linguistic thought, which countered the inclination of Ferdinand de Saussure—the Swiss linguist who first attempted to establish linguistics as an independent discipline—to privilege the objectivism of language-system, as contrasted with the subjectivism of the practical and political uses of language. Helsloot further regarded Bertoni's and Gentile's elaborations of Croce's subjectivism as "excesses." Niels Helsloot, "Linguists of All Countries ... ! On Gramsci's Premise of Coherence," *Journal of Pragmatics* 13 (1989): 547–66, especially 553–56.

[27]Simon Gaunt and Julian Weiss, "Cultural Traffic in the Medieval Romance World," *Journal of Romance Studies* 4, no. 3 (2004): 1–11.

From his writings on historical and literary subjects, one gains some understanding of how these sensibilities shaped Bertoni's historical imagination. In a review of Bertoni's book on Ariosto's *Orlando furioso* and the Ferrarese Renaissance, Edmund G. Gardner observed that the author demonstrated how *Orlando* represents the spirit of its time: the first and second parts of the book are entitled "The Constituent Elements of Lodovico Ariosto's Mentality and Art" ("Gli elementi costitutivi della mentalità e dell'arte di Lodovico Ariosto") and "Traditional Forms and the New Spirit of Ariosto's Classical and Romance Culture in the *Orlando Furioso*" ("Forme tradizionali e spiriti nuovi della coltura classica e romanzesca dell'Ariosto nell'*Orlando Furioso*").[28]

But by no means did Li Gotti's studies with Bertoni result in an uncritical absorption of Idealist sensibilities. On the contrary, Li Gotti's intellectual self-confidence permitted him to establish his independence from Bertoni. The same Robert Hall who was so sharply critical of Bertoni's theories lauded Li Gotti's *Volgare Nostro Siculo: Crestomazia dei testi siciliani del sec. XIV* (*Our Sicilian Vernacular: Collection of Sicilian Texts of the Fourteenth Century*).[29] And Li Gotti's more Positivistic temperament is revealed in other of his publications as well. His biography of Giovanni Berchet was described as "detailed, well informed[,] and studiously fair."[30] Isabel Pope—who earned the Ph.D in Romance philology at Radcliffe College, and whose name is well known to musicologists—wrote sympathetically of Li Gotti's theory about the Arabic origins of the Romance lyric, of his "thoughtful analysis of the attendant controversies" and "careful analysis and objective evaluation of the most recent works related to the subject."[31]

However, one should not assume that Idealism left no traces whatever on Li Gotti's intellectual style, nor on Pirrotta's, for that matter. Both Li Gotti and Pirrotta successfully navigated the potentially perilous straits between these two tendencies in Italian intellectual life. Giuliano Bonfante wrote that Bertoni's

> great merit was having sought to integrate linguistic phenomena...together with those of civilization. ... His works ... had the ... merit of ... placing into light

---

[28]Edmund G. Gardner, review of Giulio Bertoni, *L'"Orlando Furioso" e la Rinascenza a Ferrara* (Modena: Umberto Orlandini, 1919), and Bertoni, *Studi su vecchie e nuove poesie e prose d'amore e di romanzi* (Modena: Umberto Orlandini, 1921), in *Modern Language Review* 17, no. 1 (January 1922): 99–100.

[29]Robert A. Hall, Jr., review of Ettore Li Gotti, ed., *Volgare Nostro Siculo: Crestomazia dei testi siciliani del sec. XIV. Parte I: Testi non letterari* (Florence: La Nuova Italia, 1951), in *Italica* 29, no. 2 (June 1952): 144–45.

[30]Positivist sensibilities in the work are suggested by Li Gotti's full and objective citations of the sources and secondary literature, and the careful, exhaustive bibliographic apparatus to which the reviewer makes reference.

[31]Isabel Pope, review of Ettore Li Gotti, *La "Tesi Araba" sulle "Origini" della Lirica Romanza*, Biblioteca del Centro di Studi Filologica e Linguistici Siciliani 7 (Florence: Sansoni, 1955), in *Speculum* 34, no. 3 (July 1959): 477–81.

the importance of the individual creative and aesthetic elements of language, which is ... part of the culture of a people.³²

Li Gotti and Pirrotta shared with Idealism that component of its program: the concern to nest language (or works of literature, or art, or music) within a context, rather than remove them from their setting and make abstractions of them, and reduce them to a series of "mechanistic" laws.

And both Pirrotta and Li Gotti subscribed to the Idealist view that history entailed vivid narration. In his review of the *Storia di Milano*, Li Gotti signaled his interest in the promised publication³³ of a celebrated manuscript source of fourteenth-century Italian music, the Squarcialupi codex, and similarly revealed his interdisciplinary, contextual sensitivities when he lauded the contributions of Pirrotta's teacher Mario Salmi (who discussed "with a particularly fine clarity the frescoes of the great hall of the Rocca di Angera") and Monsignor Enrico Cattaneo (whose entry on the Ambrosian chant is characterized as "outstanding"). He twice stated his understanding of history's "basic ... character" as "narrative," which was consonant with Idealism's similar understanding: the *Storia di Milano* is said to exemplify "civic history in the broadest sense (political, economic, institutional, and social)," which is "set forth in an admirable narrative manner."³⁴

*****

As a Romance philologist, Li Gotti was principally interested in Sacchetti as poet. But, knowing that Sacchetti's verse was frequently set to music by contemporary composers, he recognized that he needed the expertise of a musician or music historian. He turned with hope and expectation to his good friend Nino Pirrotta.

In the tradition of the autodidact, Pirrotta set out to master the intricacies of Trecento musical notation so that he might fulfill his obligations as Li Gotti's musicological collaborator. Even before the book on Sacchetti was published, there was evidence of Pirrotta's achievement in an article by P. Raffaele M. Taucci on the Trecento Florentine composer Andrea de' Servi: the article was accompanied by a five-page appendix of musical examples, the "Transcription by Maestro Nino Pirrotta" ("Trascrizione del M.º Nino Pirrotta") prepared from the redactions in the Squarcialupi codex.³⁵

---

³²Bonfante, "Giulio Bertoni."
³³By the Istituto di Cultura.
³⁴Li Gotti's review appears in *Speculum* 31, no. 1 (January 1956): 203–08.
³⁵**1934–35:** "Fra Andrea dei Servi, organista e compositore del trecento," especially 104–08. The article was subsequently cited in *Il Sacchetti*. Pirrotta was later to edit the entirety of Andrea's compositional output and publish it in the fifth volume of his unfinished edition of fourteenth-century Italian music.

*****

Nino Pirrotta's *Il Sacchetti e la tecnica musicale del Trecento italiano* is the curtain-raising on a storied scholarly career, and remarkable for the extent to which it adumbrates many of the principal themes, intellectual assumptions, and methodological approaches that will inform much of Pirrotta's later scholarship.[36] The invitation to collaborate on *Il Sacchetti* was, in its way, an implicit challenge to Pirrotta to make an inaugural statement about who he was as an intellectual and—specifically—as a musicologist (especially a self-taught musicologist), and in that respect it is a subtle and sophisticated achievement.

Pirrotta and Li Gotti begin by expressing their gratitude to their teachers Giovanni Alfredo Cesareo and Giulio Bertoni ("masters of philological studies") and to Heinrich Besseler ("who was generous with counsel and help on the musical part"[37]) and Johannes Wolf. That Pirrotta acknowledged the assistance of Besseler and Wolf is itself significant, because the fact that he was even conversant with their work—let alone consulted directly with them—distinguishes him from the majority of his Italian musicological contemporaries (what few there were), who were not necessarily disposed toward mastering German scholarly writing. Pirrotta's familiarity with the professional literature of his nascent discipline, regardless of the language in which it was written, is established as a feature of his method.[38] And, of course, his appeal to the expertise of Besseler and Wolf situates his contribution within the tradition of rigorous, scientific, university-level musicological scholarship, exemplified by the nineteenth/early-twentieth-century German pioneers of the discipline.

In one sense, Pirrotta's task was simply to elucidate annotations in the autograph manuscript of Sacchetti's *rime*[39] that pertain to musical settings of his verse, several of which are extant, and in that respect he fulfilled his obligations admirably. He described the principal forms of Italian verse typically set in Trecento musical compositions (madrigal, caccia, and ballata), and his section of the book includes transcriptions of twelve polyphonic settings of Sacchetti's poetry, accompanied by an exhaustive, meticulous,

---

[36]In my synopsis and analysis of this publication, I have benefitted greatly from Fabrizio Della Seta's "Storia, filologia e gusto musicale: rileggendo i primi scritti di Pirrotta," *Musicologia fra due continenti. L'eredità di Nino Pirrotta. Convegno internazionale (Roma, 4–6 giugno 2008)*, Accademia Nazionale dei Lincei (Rome: Scienze e lettere, 2010), 37–54.

[37]*1935: Il Sacchetti*, 4. Also, see 71, where Pirrotta recounts having submitted several of his transcriptions to Besseler for his comment.

[38]This matter was repeatedly referenced in my conversations with Professors Fabrizio Della Seta and Franco Piperno. On the limited nature of earlier German musicological engagement with the music of the Italian Trecento, see Petrobelli, "Nino Pirrotta e Diego Carpitella," 54.

[39]In the Biblioteca Mediceo–Laurenziana, Florence.

Musikwissenschaftlich statement of editorial principles and detailed notes to the transcriptions.[40]

However, Pirrotta capitalizes on the opportunity presented him to advance a fully developed view of the musical culture of fourteenth-century Florence. Within a few pages of the opening of his section,[41] we encounter the first statement of a thesis that recurs like a leitmotif throughout his later writings. He argues that the written musical record—the "written tradition," as he was later to call it[42]—can distort our historical understanding, that its very richness can inadvertently result in an insufficient awareness of other species of musical activity, which may escape our notice because they are incompletely recorded in the extant written documents (or even entirely unrecorded). If judiciously interpreted, unwritten practices[43]—typically illuminated by nonmusical evidence—can illuminate more precisely the contours of that better-known written tradition, and vice versa.[44]

Pirrotta elaborates, explaining the interconnection between a particular kind of musico-compositional technique—polyphony—and that technique's inevitable dependence on the "technology" associated with it: musical notation.

> It will not seem strange that the manuscripts of the Ars nova, which are guardians of an almost exclusively polyphonic repertory (as that which—because of its greater technical complexity—demands a precise written tradition with more pressing need), have preserved settings of ballate for us only from the moment at which it was thought to apply a contrapuntal technique to them, until that point the exclusive prerogative of the madrigal and caccia.[45]

But the existence of an ample extant repertory of *polyphonic* ballate must not blind us to the likelihood of the earlier production of *monophonic* ballate, certainly more numerous than the polyphonic settings, to judge from the

---

[40]**1935:** *Il Sacchetti*, 69–104. The edition presented, for the first time, transcriptions into modern notation of the 12 extant musical settings of Sacchetti's verse accompanied in his autograph by indications that they were so set to music by fourteenth-century polyphonists (with the exception of a single work, which had earlier been published by Johannes Wolf). These 12 are the sole extant settings of the 34 texts accompanied by such annotations in Sacchetti's autograph; see *Il Sacchetti*, 70.

[41]**1935:** *Il Sacchetti*, 35–65.

[42]On Pirrotta's invocation of the concept, see Petrobelli, "Nino Pirrotta e Diego Carpitella," 54.

[43]Pirrotta's pupil at the University of Rome and his successor in the chair of music history, Franco Piperno, described Pirrotta's life long consideration of the unwritten tradition as "il primo grande contributo di metodo e di mentalità (le intersezioni fra tradizione orale e scritta) che Pirrotta fornì alla musicologia internazionale." See Piperno, "Omaggio a Nino Pirrotta. Ricordo di un nobile studioso," *Amadeus. Il mensile della grande musica* 10 (1998): 48–49.

[44]**1935:** *Il Sacchetti*, 39. Pirrotta's use of the verb "rappresentare" (past participle: "rappresentata") in this passage to describe the "correct historical consideration of artistic activity" that is fashioned from the "rich tradition of musical monuments" is Idealist and Crocean.

[45]**1935:** *Il Sacchetti*, 50.

proportions among madrigals, cacce, and ballate in Sacchetti's literary output.[46]

Pirrotta also contrasts some of the fundamental characteristics of fourteenth-century Italian vocal polyphony with those of the contemporary French musical repertory and recapitulates the themes of a journalistic piece of April 1935.[47] There, the polarity suggested by the references to "the resources of counterpoint" and the "*baggage* and *apparatus* of *learned elaborations*," on the one hand, and to "the *eminently lyric nature* of Bellini [emphases added]," on the other, is not unlike a polarity invoked in *Il Sacchetti*, where Pirrotta writes of the *"airy melodic naturalness"* of the upper voice of Trecento madrigals and a rhythmic sense that "flows quietly," "renouncing the *subtleties and finenesses*... that *serrate* and *torture* the melodic norms of contemporary French art [emphases added]."[48] Pirrotta was drafting the two texts—one journalistic, the other scholarly—simultaneously, and his use of similar language in analyzing such seemingly disparate repertories is thereby explicable. In both instances, the contrast he draws is between the "subtle," "learned" contrapuntal traditions of northern Europe and the "airy," "eminently lyric" melodicity of Italian composition, whether of the fourteenth century or the nineteenth.

This contrast between northern and southern compositional aesthetics is elaborated throughout the remainder of *Il Sacchetti*, and, indeed, throughout the remainder of Pirrotta's career. It is the expression of a "musical" (or "musicological") "nationalism" (which is also reflected in the journalistic writings[49]). Pirrotta says of the madrigal and caccia—"the oldest forms of the Italian Ars nova"—that they are "generally considered as typical, and most jealously guarded, of the features of national musical expression." And he accepts the established view attributing the subsequent, sudden cultivation of the polyphonic ballata "to the influence of French art,"[50] which he qualifies,

---

[46]Pirrotta will return to these arguments in **1949–51**: "Ballata." See also **1954**: *The Music of Fourteenth Century Italy*, vol. I (1954), p. II, for another instance.

[47]Cummings and Eiche, "Nino Pirrotta's Early Music-Critical Writings," 263–65, 317–21, 329–31 (see "Scena 1.ª," n. 69).

[48]The Idealist patrimony of such diction is, I believe, proved by the very close congruence of this passage with one in Luigi Ronga's *The Meeting of Poetry and Music*, trans. Elio Gianturco and Cara Rosanti (New York: Merlin Press, n.d.), 24–25. For a similar means of drawing the contrast between the French and Italian musical aesthetics, see **1949–51**: "Ballata," **1973**: "Bartholomaeus de Bononia," and **1984**: "Echi di arie veneziane del primo Quattrocento?" See also **1963**: "Bartolino da Padova," 196: "the broken and uneven melodic line and minutely opposed and syncopated rhythm—exacerbating tendencies already existing in the polyphony of northern Italy—draw it closer, whether it be indeed externally, to contemporary manneristic French style, and they merit the definition of musical «shining Gothic»."

[49]See the introductory comment to Cummings and Eiche, "Nino Pirrotta's Early Music-Critical Writings" (see "Scena 1.ª," n. 69).

[50]**1935**: *Il Sacchetti*, 43-45. In **1954**: *The Music of Fourteenth Century Italy*, vol. III, p. II, Pirrotta, similarly, observes that the fact that Donatus de Florentia also set one piece in the analogous form of the *virelai* is confirmation that the impulse for the polyphonic setting of the *ballata* must have come from the example of French polyphony. See also **1949–51**: "Ballata."

however, with the suggestion that so rapid a change was due to a more ramified set of circumstances. Indeed, a tradition of polyphonic musical settings of ballate cannot be said to be due exclusively to French influence. Written documentation for the Italian monophonic ballata is deceptively limited, because it did not depend on musical notation for its dissemination and performance. Rather, as a "fundamental form of the Italian lyric," the ballata—"more than . . . formal scheme"—is to be considered

> an *instinctive canon* of musical proportion, *ingrained in the collective sentiment* from the remotest of origins [emphases added], which Carducci wished to have traced back to the *ballistea* of Roman children. "Spontaneous and welcome guide to singable poetry"—[Fernando] Liuzzi acutely defines it—"by reason of the double poetic and musical harmony that the lyric assumes in that first phase."[51]

The Idealist and Nationalist patrimonies of such an argument are evident.

How, then, did Italian composers and audiences of the fourteenth century arrive at a tradition of *polyphonic* ballate? The proposed answer to that question is developed by means of a kind of argument familiar to anyone conversant with Pirrotta's later writings.

Carducci had identified the polyphonic madrigal and caccia as the musical expressions of what he termed the *mondo elegante*, that "refined, worldly, and elegant bourgeois society"[52] of fourteenth-century Florence, but Pirrotta suggests instead that the favored musical genre of the *mondo elegante* was far likelier at first to have been the monophonic ballata, substantiation for which is found in such representative texts as Boccaccio's *The Decameron*. There, Boccaccio offers no evidence—even incidental—for the performance of musical settings of madrigal verse (though he himself actually composed such verse, as did his great contemporary Petrarch). Subsequently, the polyphonic ballata furnished the means by which "polyphonic effects finally found a way to enter the cultural patrimony of the *mondo elegante* and become an essential part of musical recreation":[53]

> it was much more subject to fashion and therefore induced to imitation of well-accepted models, among which (in the general intrusion of French customs, several times lamented by Sacchetti, too) had to be—in the first place—those of trans-Alpine polyphonic art.[54]

---

[51]**1935:** *Il Sacchetti*, 50-51. For an evocation of this observation (and of the entire book on Sacchetti) in later scholarship, see the article by Howard Mayer Brown, "Fantasia on a Theme by Boccaccio," *Early Music* 5 (1977): 324–39.
[52]**1935:** *Il Sacchetti*, 51.
[53]**1935:** *Il Sacchetti*, 53–54.
[54]Pirrotta restates this argument in **1949–51:** "Ballata," 1161.

But notwithstanding its later polyphonic refashioning under the influence of French musico-compositional techniques, "the Italian ballata ... will never cease to demonstrate the profundity of its roots in a purely national tradition":

> whether for the typical structure of the national form; whether for the melodic style, which—even in some ballate that more deliberately set the French model for themselves—conserves a plasticity of line and harmonious sense of proportion, indicating a felicitous tempering of stylistic characteristics; whether for the preference given to the exclusively-vocal polyphonic "set-up," with the recitation of the text or texts in all voices.[55]

Moreover, despite the French influences clearly evident at the end of the fourteenth century and thereafter, singers retained the "Italianate" option of performing polyphonic compositions as vocal solos, with the lower voice(s) executed instrumentally, an option supported by the evidence of the sources, which in some instances transmit "in monodic form, with instrumental accompaniment" compositions elsewhere transmitted as vocal polyphony.[56]

Pace Carducci's theory, the polyphonic madrigal and caccia—"far, far from being the musical delight of the *mondo elegante*"—were much likelier to have been the expressions of a more restricted sector within fourteenth-century Florentine society: the religious community, which was better equipped for the performance and appreciation of compositions exemplifying the virtuosic singing and complex contrapuntal elaborations of those two genres. Notwithstanding the paucity of evidence, there can be little question of the existence of a widespread Italian practice of liturgical polyphony, and more generally of "a *refined technical culture* ... of which *the ecclesiastical world and religious orders were the guardians* [emphases added]." The German historian Robert Davidsohn—whose monumental, multivolume *Geschichte von Florenz*[57] Li Gotti and Pirrotta had carefully digested—testified "to the frequency with which members of various orders were acquiring renown"[58] for their technical ability as singers.

Here, then, Pirrotta articulates another theory that will recur often in his subsequent work, concerning the relationship between the composition and performance of polyphony and the cultural circumstances that these assume: an ecclesiastical environment was especially suited to the cultivation of polyphony, given that its members were the heirs of a particular educational tradition, which we can metaphorically characterize as "scholastic."

---

[55]**1935:** *Il Sacchetti,* 54.
[56]**1935:** *Il Sacchetti,* 54–55.
[57]*Geschichte von Florenz* (Berlin: E.S. Mittler und Sohn, 1896–1927).
[58]**1935:** *Il Sacchetti,* 63.

Therefore, the unwritten tradition furnished Carducci's *mondo elegante* with its principal initial musical manifestation, the monophonic ballata, which was the expression of an age-old Italian literary and musical sensibility. Simultaneously, the ecclesiastical ambience instead favored contrapuntally complex settings of madrigal and caccia verse. When polyphonic practice was then absorbed by the *mondo elegante*, under the influence of the prestigious French compositional tradition, the seeming suddenness of the absorption was due to the preexistence of a robust monophonic ballata tradition, which was rapidly refashioned by Italian composers—who had already acquired the necessary compositional skills—to embrace polyphonic technique.

In the final pages of his section of the book, Pirrotta advances an argument that will underlie much of his later writing, including "Music and Cultural Tendencies in 15th-Century Italy." He contrasts the "cognitive attitude" of the "French cultural world" ("impregnated with scholastic doctrines")—which "leads to the conceptual symbolistic of the motet of [Philippe de] Vitry and his contemporaries"—with "the different nature and manner of living and thinking of *our* people"—which "leads musicians, more than to the musical interpretation of *concepts*, to the translation of *images*."

He concludes with a Crocean rhetorical flourish, laced with vivid Idealist diction ("innate," "intuition," "instinctive," "self-governing," "purely spiritual need, "purest laws of aesthetic intuition").[59] The distinguishing characteristics of scholasticism as an intellectual tradition, as the "cognitive attitude" of medieval France—its "subtleties," its "conceptual symbolistic," its dictum-laden technicality—are contrasted with the instinctiveness, intuitiveness, and spontaneity characteristic of the contemporary Italian aesthetic, the "airy" "melodicity" of the music being an expression of the "different nature and manner of living and thinking" of Italians.[60]

*****

Il Sacchetti was well received; Salvatore Castiglione of Yale University characterized it as "useful" and "encouraging . . . , for it points to a novel and more comprehensive interpretation of . . . Sacchetti, derived from examination of all his writings, rather than from the limited field represented by his *Novelle*."[61] Pirrotta was fully aware that the book established his reputation, both within

---

[59]Della Seta also quotes and interprets this revealing language in "Appunti per un ritratto intellettuale di Nino Pirrotta" (see "*Prologo*," n. 36), and returns to a consideration of it in "Storia, filologia e gusto musicale: rileggendo i primi scritti di Pirrotta," where he analyses the significance of such vocabulary.

[60]**1935**: *Il Sacchetti*, 63–64.

[61]*Italica* 14 (1937): 139–41.

Italy and abroad, as an authority on the music of the Trecento; it launched his career as specialist in a field of study that he essentially created, notwithstanding the earlier scholarship—German and Italian—devoted to it. And he took great pride in the fact that Giulio Bertoni lavished praise on the book.[62]

Most important, Pirrotta's appointment at the Conservatory of Palermo was regularized as a consequence of *Il Sacchetti*'s publication. He had been teaching there on a temporary basis, as an "adjunct" or "visitor," and also working in the library. At the beginning of the 1936 academic year (*Il Sacchetti* was published in 1935), he was appointed to the *elenco principale* (roster of regular tenured/tenure-track faculty), initially as a *non-stabile* docent in music history (untenured "assistant professor") and *bibliotecario* (librarian); but within two years—after the publication of his first scholarly article, which further developed material from the book on Sacchetti[63]—he won a *concorso* and was granted *stabile* (tenured) status as *titolare di cattedra* in music history (*Professore di Storia della Musica* and incumbent of the chair in music history) and *bibliotecario*.

There is another important inference to be drawn from the achievement that *Il Sacchetti* represents. Pirrotta had studied musical performance and composition, both formally and informally; he had concertized; he had practiced music criticism. Yet there was clearly something about the writing of *Il Sacchetti* that elicited a particular response in him, in that it suggested a kind of engagement with music—a variety of professional activity—that he had not experienced before. There was an elemental, almost visceral sense of satisfaction in the substantive scholarly research and academic writing, evident in the summoning of the fullness of his talents, expertise, and achievements, as musician, historian, and essayist, and the research and writing manifestly appealed to the cerebral, reflective elements of Pirrotta's character.

The nascent music historian in Nino Pirrotta was thus awakened. For him, the first sip of the drink called "musicological scholarship" had an almost addictive effect. From that time forward, he essentially abandoned his concertizing and music criticism and devoted almost the whole of his professional energies to his responsibilities as librarian and to his musicological scholarship. More so than many musicologists, Pirrotta successfully managed what in the popular imagination is understood as "right-brain/left-brain" oppositions, the kinds of contrasting sensibilities typically entailed in engaging with music: the more performative, creative, intuitive sensibilities of the organist;

---

[62]Della Seta, "Appunti per un ritratto intellettuale di Nino Pirrotta" (see "*Prologo*," n. 36) and "Storia, filologia e gusto musicale: rileggendo i primi scritti di Pirrotta."

[63]**1936:** "Lirica monodica trecentesca."

and the more intellective, scholarly, scientific sensibilities of the emerging musicologist.[64] But in Pirrotta, the "left-brain" mode of engagement ultimately prevailed.

*****

Two final observations:

1. There is a Nationalist strain in Pirrotta's earliest writings, in both *Il Sacchetti* and the journalistic writings of the early to mid-1930s,[65] and one could identify similar sensibilities in the writings of many Italian scholars of the time. Such sensibilities surely had a nonintellectual origin, as well as intellectual ones. They are comparatively absent in Pirrotta's writings on Italian opera from the late 1940s and the '50s, which leads me to conclude that the chronological context is relevant.

Were it not for Fascism's (mis)appropriation of such otherwise benign sensibilities—continuing expressions of the nineteenth-century fervor that led to the unification of Italy—a consideration of the Nationalist strain in the writings of Pirrotta and his contemporaries would not be so delicate a matter. As it is, it demands sensitive, though direct and honest, treatment.

Il Sacchetti was published in 1935, and its cover bears the date of publication "1935–XIII," the Roman numerals signifying that it was thirteen years since the Fascists had taken control of the Italian government. Time began with Mussolini's coming to power; the nation's collective clock had been reset to synchronize with the beginnings of Fascism. In such an environment, either because such societal sensibilities directly or indirectly influenced one's own, or because of an anxiety about failing to show due respect for the powerful new political order, almost all Italians felt moved to manifest appropriate Nationalist enthusiasm.

Other than what is suggested about such generalized Nationalist sensibilities, here and elsewhere in my biography, I know of little evidence of Pirrotta's political sentiments. James Haar reported to me that Nino and Lea Pirrotta voted for the preservation of the Italian monarchy in the postwar referendum;

---

[64]For a systematic consideration of what Lewis Lockwood calls these "two basic modes of perception," see Lockwood's "The Study of Music at University—6. The University and Musical Thought," *Musical Times* 114 (1973): 783, 785–87. Lockwood writes that music, "on the one hand . . . may be taken as a form of direct, immediate and essentially irrational experience. On the other hand, it may be taken as a more nearly cognitive form of experience, for which the pure perception of aesthetic events would remain incomplete without some sort of explanation or rationalization of the musical phenomenon . . . , as an experience that seems insufficient in the absence of any mode of thought that might arise . . . if only one were willing to take music 'hard.'" The second of these "basic modes of perception" is partially the preserve of "professional scholars" who have a particular set of "special interests, modes of thought, vocabularies, and to some extent constituencies. . . . What ultimately connects them . . . is a sense of identification with an approach to music that is emphatically cognitive." A musical performance can therefore be regarded by some listeners as "a re-enactment of the thought behind the composition and thus in the best sense an act of historical reconstruction."

[65]On the Nationalist references in the journalistic writings, see Cummings and Eiche, "Nino Pirrotta's Early Music-Critical Writings" (see "*Scena 1.ª*, n. 69).

but in this respect they were like millions of other Italians (indeed, the decision to abolish the monarchy was supported by only a slim majority). Italy had had no recent national experience with republicanism, and the monarchy symbolized the familiar and the stable, though support for the institution of monarchy tells us nothing whatever about one's posture toward Mussolini and Fascism. My sense is that Pirrotta was essentially apolitical.

Important in this context is the potential effect of Nationalism on Pirrotta's musicological discourse. For example, it may be that his keen interest in the lyric, melodic qualities of the music of the Trecento (and Italian music more generally) is attributable to Nationalist influences. On the other hand, it may also be attributable to the nature of the instruction in the Italian conservatory, where courses in the composition and analysis of melody were distinguished from those in harmony.[66] But perhaps the Italian curricular tradition was itself an expression of a Nationalist interest in a quintessentially Italianate melodicity?

One of the most influential exponents of Nationalist sentiment in early-twentieth-century Italy was Gabriele D'Annunzio,[67] champion of German philosopher Friedrich Nietzsche and a figure with pronounced musical interests and an understanding of lyricism as a manifestation of the distinctiveness of Italian cultural identity. In this, D'Annunzio's sentiments were consonant with those of Idelbrando Pizzetti, whose celebration of Vincenzo Bellini's melodic expression Pirrotta seems to echo in his journalistic writings.[68] Mussolini himself saw a political advantage in expropriating the Italian musical past: Adelmo Damerini[69] reported in 1943 that

> [t]he Maggio Musicale, ordered by the Duce, supported by the Fascist Government, and begun in 1933, ties directly into the old customs of Renaissance Florence.... This is why the Florentine Maggio Musicale ... has come to signify the symbol of musical Italian-ness and the celebration of our genius which has come to the fore in every century.[70]

In Andrew Dell'Antonio's words, the "Italian artistic heritage" was portrayed "as unbroken, genetically innate and reflective of the unity of the Italian spirit,"[71] a formulation consistent with Pirrotta's characterization of the ballata

---

[66]On this matter, see also my "Scena 4.ª," n. 11.

[67]For much of the following paragraphs, I am indebted to an interesting article by Andrew Dell'Antonio: "Il divino Claudio: Monteverdi and Lyric Nostalgia in Fascist Italy," *Cambridge Opera Journal* 8, no. 3 (November 1996): 271–84.

[68]See Cummings and Eiche, "Nino Pirrotta's Early Music-Critical Writings," 263–65 and especially n. 33 (see "Scena 1.ª," n. 69).

[69]Damerini was an "accademico onorario" of the Accademia del R. Conservatorio di Musica «Luigi Cherubini» di Firenze while Pirrotta was a student there, later served as the Cherubini's director, and collaborated with Pirrotta on one of his publications. See my "Scena 2.ª."

[70]Damerini, "Aspetti dell'VIII Maggio musicale fiorentino," *La Musica* 2 (Florence, 1943): 207–13, especially 207, as quoted in Dell'Antonio, "Il divino Claudio," 281.

[71]Dell'Antonio, "Il divino Claudio," 276.

as "an instinctive canon of musical proportion, ingrained in the collective sentiment from the remotest of origins."

However, identifying a Nationalist motivation for the distinctions Pirrotta draws between French and Italian musical aesthetics, for example, does not necessarily invalidate such distinctions. I believe that there is warrant for them, that they are supported by revealing details of the musical "text"; it is simply that one rationale for his identifying them in the first instance may have been Nationalist in origin.

Moreover, there is evidence that Pirrotta did not uncritically embrace D'Annunzio's (and the Fascist era's) Nationalist celebration of Italian melodicity. Whereas D'Annunzio vilified Puccini and other representatives of verist opera,[72] Pirrotta's position in his journalistic writings was more qualified.[73] Whereas Salvino Chieregin writes in 1943 that "Monteverdi... gradually moves from polyphonic intertwining and harmonic motion to the conquest of a pure melodic line,"[74] Pirrotta will later see as absurd the sharp contraposition of Monteverdi, the monodist and cantata composer, and Monteverdi, the polyphonist and madrigalist of the preceding period: the polyphony and monody of the time were parallel rather than contrasting expressions of analogous needs.[75] Whereas Federico Ghisi writes (shortly after the end of the Fascist era) that "[t]he *recitar cantando* of the Florentines was, in fact, an end to itself and the progress of the *melodramma* would have come to a halt had not the limp figure of the early 17th-century dramatic monody received a transfusion from the life-giving stream of Monteverdi,"[76] Pirrotta—although invariably skeptical himself about the true importance of the Florentine camerata[77]—will also be so bold as to subscribe to what he characterizes as "Monteverdian Heresies":

> [i]t is a heresy not to believe in [Monteverdi's] infallibility... [I]t is heretical of me to explore three moments in Monteverdi's operatic activity in order to see how that activity was rooted in his time.[78]

In this, he distinguished himself somewhat from those Fascist-era apologists for Monteverdi who made a hero of him.

---

[72] Dell'Antonio, "Il divino Claudio," 271 and 273.

[73] Cummings and Eiche, "Nino Pirrotta's Early Music-Critical Writings," 276–77, 306–07 (see "Scena 1.ª," n. 69).

[74] Chieregin, "Claudio Monteverdi," *Rivista musicale italiana* 47 (1943): 212–29, especially 214–15, quoted in Dell'Antonio, "Il divino Claudio," 277.

[75] See my "Scena 7.ª."

[76] Ghisi, "Ballet Entertainments in Pitti Palace, Florence, 1608–1625," *Musical Quarterly* 35 (1949): 421–36, especially 436; see Dell'Antonio, "Il divino Claudio," 282.

[77] **1953**: "Temperamenti e tendenze nella Camerata fiorentina," and regularly thereafter.

[78] **1963**: "Monteverdi e i problemi dell'opera."

In short, notwithstanding the clear, undeniable evidence of a Nationalist sensibility in Pirrotta's discourse, as substantiated previously, the full political dimension of the various positions adopted on these matters may have had less effect on Pirrotta than his fellow Italian musicologists of the time; his analysis and conclusions appear to have been governed by a somewhat more detached scholarly attitude.

2. As early as *Il Sacchetti*, Pirrotta reveals what will become his signature approach as an historical musicologist. While fulfilling his obligations as a "Positivist" paleographer—he accompanies transcriptions of the music and musical analyses with a detailed critical apparatus—he declines to limit his engagement with the material in that way, to abstract the music from its setting(s). Rather, the paleography is merely preparatory to the ultimate objective: a full and revealing re-situating of the music, its re-location within ramified contexts, whether philosophical, literary, social, or intellectual.[79] His writings leave his readers with an enhanced understanding of the place of music in the culture of which it is an oft-elusive expression.

Pirrotta's experiences as a conservatory student prepared him for the specifically musical and music-historical tasks associated with drafting *Il Sacchetti;* his experiences as a *liceo classico* and university student furnished him with an understanding of the cultural and social contexts for the music. From these varied, nonoverlapping experiences, he created his own independent vision of the fledgling discipline of historical musicology, one that relinquished pride of place to neither of the two underlying academic traditions, but, rather, amalgamated the musical microcosmic and the historical/contextual macrocosmic into an illuminating synthesis.

---

[79]On Pirrotta's practice of considering "le connessioni storiche e culturali," see Petrobelli, "Nino Pirrotta e Diego Carpitella," 54.

Intermedio I.^{mo}
["non apparente"]

Pirrotta's Intellectual and Musical Formation

Pirrotta's Intellectual Profile, I
>   **Visual Sensitivity: The Study of Art History**
>   **The Study of Musical Performance and Composition at the Conservatory**
>   **Pirrotta and European Academic Culture: Philology**
>   **Pirrotta's Reading in the Musicological Literature: Visions of the Discipline**

Philosophical Tendencies in Twentieth-Century Italy
>   **Science and Positivism**
>>   Roberto Ardigò
>
>   **Spiritualist Reactions: Henri Bergson**
>
>   **Spiritualist Reactions: Italian Idealism**
>>   Benedetto Croce
>>   Giovanni Gentile
>>   Idealism and Pedagogy
>>   Idealism and Nationalism
>
>   **Spiritualist Reactions: Giovanni Vailati and Pragmatism in Italy**
>
>   **Spiritualist Reactions: "The Forces of the Irrational"**
>>   Giuseppe Prezzolini and Giovanni Papini
>
>   **Economic Materialism**
>>   Antonio Labriola
>>   Hippolyte Taine

American Musicology in the 1950s, '60s, and '70s: History as Science?

Pirrotta's Intellectual Profile, II
>   **The Influences of Positivism**
>
>   **The Influences of Italian Spiritualist Philosophies**
>>   Philosophy of History
>>   Diction
>>   The Intuitive Mode of Apprehension
>>   The Narrative Rhetorical Mode
>>   The Refutation of Genre
>>   Auto-didacticism
>>   Idealism and Nationalism: *Italianità* and *Sicilianità*
>
>   **The Influences of Economic Materialism**

This chapter was the most challenging to write and may well be the most challenging to read.[1] My ambition is to define Pirrotta's intellectual profile

---

[1] My indebtedness to many colleagues will be obvious in what follows, but here I must immediately acknowledge the thoughtful and knowledgeable assistance of Professor Fabrizio Della Seta, who read an earlier version of this chapter and suggested many ways in which it could be improved.

or sensibility, as revealed in his diction, methodology, and other oft-oblique phenomena, and identify determinative influences.

Pirrotta's formation occurred at a time when two principal tendencies were shaping Italian intellectual life: Positivism and Idealism. In his work we find the Idealist's imaginative and intuitive apprehension and vivid representation of the historical datum tempering and coloring his Positivistic respect for the authority of the verifiable.

Yet another Italian intellectual tradition expressed in his writings was Economic Materialism. Pirrotta was habitually cognizant that he was concerned with music created by living human beings, affected by Material circumstances.

First, some other matters.

PIRROTTA'S INTELLECTUAL PROFILE, I

Visual Sensitivity: The Study of Art History

One of the explanations for the "imaginative feel"[2] to Pirrotta's work was a visual sensitivity awakened in part by his training in art history at the University of Florence. This is most obvious when the subject matter directly concerns art: in the analysis of "Andrea Mantegna's frescoes in the so-called Wedding Chamber in the Gonzaga castle of San Giorgio in Mantua,"[3] for example; or in "Teatro, scene e musica nelle opere di Monteverdi," where Pirrotta—to assist his readers in envisioning the sets for *L'incoronazione di Poppea*—writes that

> [t]o visualize the . . . scenes we can make use of . . . sets conceived by . . . Torelli . . . . For Seneca's villa, the villa in *Deidamia* . . . can be of help . . . ; for Poppea's garden, the . . . *giardino* from *Bellerofonte* . . . may be pictured. . . . For Nero's imperial palace we can make use of the *tempio di Bacco* in *La Venere gelosa*.

We might also refer to "The Orchestra and Stage in Renaissance *Intermedi* and Early Opera" and "Commedia dell'arte e Melodramma," the latter an example of how Pirrotta uses iconographic material to complement the fragmentary musical evidence of a vital musical-theatrical tradition.

The training in art history, specifically as taught at Florence, is also evident in the paleographical techniques of the articles on the Modena and Lucca manuscripts, the facsimile edition of the fragmentary manuscript of Paolo Tenorista's works, and elsewhere.

---

[2]This characterization is Lewis Lockwood's, suggested to A.M. Cummings in a private interview.
[3]**1969**: *Music and Theatre*, 5–6.

Thus when Pirrotta was awarded the *Laurea «Ad Honorem»* by the University of Urbino, the citation read:

> What distinguishes Pirrotta the scholar is not only the great attention ... paid to the scenography and iconography of the musical theater (subjects that had barely merited consideration previously) but also—even more so—his "paleographical eye," with which he "gave voice" to the illuminations and decorations of musical books that were extremely difficult to date and decipher (the pages dedicated to the parchment fragments in the Biblioteca Comunale of Foligno are stupendous). And among the many examples of Pirrotta's fertile capacity for interweaving diverse cultural sectors, we would like to mention only one: the "dialogue" that he sets in motion between Mantegna's *Camera degli Sposi* and Poliziano's *Orfeo*.[4]

However, for me, Pirrotta's visual acumen is most evocatively revealed in less predictable ways. In his lectures, he frequently employs a visual metaphor that renders tangible the oft-intangible point he is making.[5] At the opening of "Temperamenti e tendenze nella Camerata fiorentina," he writes, "If by chance we come across the source of a mountain stream, we find it difficult to decide whether it is the beginning of a great river or just the modest trickling of a brooklet." At the opening of "Commedia dell'Arte e Melodramma," he opts for a similarly resonant metaphor to illustrate the relationship between the two traditions:

> I would prefer that what I am going to say about the two most typical forms of the Italian theater—*commedia dell'arte* and opera—should not take the form of a parallel. ... If I may be permitted to make a comparison, I would choose ... that of two branches growing from a common trunk—two branches not quite opposite and divergent, but near each other in their origin, then sometimes separated, sometimes brought nearer by the imponderable factors of air, of light, of the juices running through them and nourishing them.

"Marchettus of Padua and the Italian Ars Nova" opens with an atmospheric image:

> That period of music history which ... is generally referred to as the Italian Ars Nova may be compared to an island ... appearing on the horizon after a long voyage through centuries of silence and obscurity. The sudden and brilliant rise of this island delights us, but as we near it and are able to make out the configuration of its shore line, we see that after it there is another expanse of silence and obscurity separating it from the larger and more solid continent, the music of the Italian Renaissance.

---

[4] "Laurea 'honoris causa' a Nino Pirrotta," 10 (see "*Prologo*," n. 36).
[5] This point has also been made by Ellen Rosand in her review of the anthology of Pirrotta's essays in the *Journal of the American Musicological Society* 39 (1986): 389–95, especially 394.

The visual metaphor need not be so fully developed; often it is no more than a single word or phrase. A personal favorite appears in Pirrotta's analysis of Gesualdo's madrigal *Ecco morirò dunque* (Book IV), where he writes of the "delicate *sfumature* in the prevalent mother-of-pearl sonority of the female voices."[6]

The Study of Musical Performance and Composition at the Conservatory

Pirrotta often observed that neither the Italian university nor the Italian conservatory of the 1920s and early '30s facilitated the development of the entire range of skills required by an aspiring music historian.[7] Therefore, he forged his own vision of the discipline of historical musicology: he applied the literary, paleographical, and historical and historiographical skills acquired in the arts curriculum at the Universities of Palermo and Florence to the primary materials of music history.[8]

However—and this is crucially important—Pirrotta's formal training in music was that of a conservatory licentiate and diplomate, not that of a laureate in letters and philosophy from the university. Many historical musicologists—certainly many American historical musicologists—come to the discipline by way of university rather than conservatory training, for historical reasons. Pirrotta's formation within the two not fully compatible traditions is fundamental to his profile.

Pirrotta's understanding of the differences is expressed not only in the reflections cited here, but also in a report he issued as head of the Eda Kuhn Loeb Music Library at Harvard, in which he writes of the library as a "practical and effective ... instrument for a humanistic approach to music," where "books on musical subjects equaled, or even slightly exceeded, the scores," as

> might be expected in a university such as Harvard, where the accent must naturally fall on broad coverage of all aspects of the general field of music rather than on exhaustive coverage of the needs of practical performance.[9]

Pirrotta routinely makes his position explicit on the editing of medieval, Renaissance, and Baroque music, regarding transcription, that is: translating

---

[6] **1961**: "Gesualdo da Venosa nel IV centenario della nascita." Echoes of Pirrotta's conversance with art history could be documented with numerous other texts; see, for example, the opening paragraphs of **1992**: "Contemplando la musa assente."

[7] **1952**: "Le biblioteche," **1982**: "Malipiero," **1954**: "Compiti."

[8] This is also the formulation of Franco Piperno; see "Omaggio a Nino Pirrotta" (see "*Scena 3.ª*," n. 43).

[9] **1958**: "The Eda Kuhn Loeb Music Library." See also Lewis Lockwood's "The Study of Music at University," 783, 785–87 (see "*Scena 3.ª*," n. 64), especially 786, where Lockwood writes of "the difference between a university music department and a conservatory or ... school of music within a university."

the period musical notation into modern notation so that the compositions can be studied and performed by those not conversant with the period notation and musical style. He asserts the right to exercise discretion, according to his understanding of the music.[10] That sensibility was partly due to the influence of Idealism; it was also partly due to Pirrotta's status as a conservatory diplomate.

For Pirrotta, the music of Gherardellus de Florentia, Carlo Gesualdo da Venosa, and Jacopo Peri was living music, experienced "from the inside out," so to speak, with the sensibilities of a performer and composer. He regarded it as his obligation to interpret the music and employ whatever means he deemed appropriate and necessary in apprehending the essence of the music and communicating it to his readership. Anthony Newcomb has described this quality:

> Pirrotta's boldness in taking a personal stand ... is matched by his lightly touched but stylistically sensitive discussions of the musical examples, and by his openly reconstructed modern editions of those same examples, with their irregular barring, their rich fund of added accidentals (above the staff of course), and their speculative division of voices and instruments. Pirrotta clearly feels that he is better qualified to speak on these editorial matters than most performers, and that he would abdicate his responsibility in not doing so. This refusal to take refuge behind an untouched Urtext is particularly convincing here, since in much of the music involved, the quest for a definitive, authoritative Urtext is vain.

Pirrotta asserts the need for interpretive discretion in representing rhythm.[11] As early as 1954, in the first volume of the edition of the *Trecento* repertory, he writes that

> [i]n many cases the use of the equivalent modern measure and rhythmic figures has seemed inadequate for a faithful reproduction of the rhythmical sense in the music transcribed. This is because in music of the Italian *ars nova* each measure with its rhythmic organization is but a unit in a larger rhythmic movement.... Theoretically the placing of bar lines according to the measure of the notation does not prevent us from perceiving the largest rhythmic movement on the melodic line. In practice such is not the case. The present writer is not the only one to sense an acute discomfort in the face of certain transcriptions that seem to be *imprisoned* and *suffocated* in too frequently drawn bar lines [emphases added]. He has therefore decided to free the full flow of the melody, writing, when necessary, measures that group those in the original. He is aware that the good in this principle does not

---

[10]This quality of Pirrotta's was referred to by Franco Piperno. He suggested—in an interview with A.M. Cummings, 20 December 2007—that Pirrotta's approach to transcription "was as much musical as philological," that "the music he studied was a living thing," and that "he had musical abilities, acumen, and sensibilities."

[11]For an explicit statement attesting Pirrotta's understanding of the challenges in apprehending the rhythmic characteristics in particular of the music he studies, see the concluding paragraphs of **1986**: "Problemi di una storia della musica."

necessarily avoid the possibility that its application may in some cases apparently or even actually be open to discussion. But this danger is less than that which it forestalls.[12]

Here Pirrotta reveals not only a musical sensitivity but also an openness to disagreement. He was willing to adopt positions not susceptible to Positivistic demonstration, because the consequence of avoiding such positions would be considerably more "dangerous." Above all, his method is characterized by an exercise of "intuition," in the tradition of Crocean Idealism.[13]

Pirrotta thus declines to be paralyzed by excessive Positivistic restraint. A passage in the article on *O rosa bella* reads:

> I do not hesitate to admit that one element on which my version is based is musical sensitivity. It has always been my conviction that an editor must give the reader, besides his skill as a musical paleographer, his ampler experience and familiarity with the style of the music presented; he must offer his own personal interpretation of it, of course as a suggestion that does not exclude other possible interpretations.[14]

In the article on Monteverdi's poetic choices, Pirrotta writes: "The actual rhythmic substance of the *Scherzi* should be extricated from the purely metrical data of the notation."[15] In his contribution to the panel discussion "Problems in Editing the Music of Josquin des Prez," he writes

> I feel we insist too much on the idea that an edition be "scientific." Of course, every edition has to be scientific in the sense that it should be done in the best possible way. But I strongly feel that the aim should not be to show how scientific we are, but how good and ... worthwhile the music is. Our attention should be focussed on how best to bring out the quality, the essence of the music.[16]

---

[12]**1954:** *The Music of Fourteenth Century Italy*, vol. 1, pp. II–III. My understanding of Pirrotta's position has greatly benefitted from Fabrizio Della Seta's "Storia, filologia e gusto musicale: rileggendo i primi scritti di Pirrotta" (see "*Scena 3.ª*," n. 36). Della Seta observes that Pirrotta's approach of departing from others' practice of a rigid adherence to the notation was first evident in the monograph on Sacchetti, and then applied consistently in the CMM edition, most vividly, for example, in the transcriptions of compositions by Laurentius de Florentia; more generally, Della Seta and I agree that these matters of rhythmic interpretation reveal the effects of Pirrotta's training as a musician, within the conservatory tradition.

[13]The statement of "Editorial Principles" in the edition of Andrea Gabrieli's choruses for Sophocles' *Oedipus* is similar (**1995:** *Chori in musica composti sopra li chori della tragedia di Edippo Tiranno*, 19), as is a revealing footnote in *Li due Orfei* (**1969:** *Music and Theatre*, 258 n. 76).

[14]**1972:** "Ricercari e variazioni su 'O rosa bella,'" 157. This passage in particular has received repeated comment, as emblematic of Pirrotta's practices with respect to transcription. In particular, see Della Seta's "Storia, filologia e gusto musicale: rileggendo i primi scritti di Pirrotta" (see "*Scena 3.ª*," n. 36).

[15]**1968:** "Scelte poetiche di Monteverdi," 292 n. 52.

[16]**1971:** contributions to the panel discussion, "Problems in Editing the Music of Josquin des Prez," 737–38.

In each instance, Pirrotta asserts the prerogatives of the editors (or readers): they are free to enliven exacting, Positivistic paleographical activity with musical insight.[17] (At the same time, it must be acknowledged that Pirrotta's advocacy of irregular barring has not gained many adherents.)

Pirrotta's musical acumen is exemplified by another instance of edition making, in which the challenges were of a different kind. When the first edition of *Li due Orfei* was published, the missing partbook of the set at the Newberry Library had not yet been recovered. Accordingly, both Pirrotta and his American pupil H. Colin Slim composed the missing voice of a number of the madrigals, based on a conversance with the general style of the music and parallels with compositional procedures in the extant voices. When the missing partbook was located at Sutton Coldfield, near Birmingham, readers were permitted to compare Pirrotta's and Slim's reconstructions to Philippe Verdelot's originals. Pirrotta said simply, "We can now compare our results with the original." Slim reported that in one instance Pirrotta's

> reconstruction . . . comes closer than mine to the original. . . . He even correctly arrived at a full triad at m. 22 with "c" sharp in the altus, whereas I, relying on Barberiis, opted for an open fifth with "e."

Pirrotta's engagement with the music thus lay at the intersection of two traditional modes of apprehension, the "practical" and the "cognitive."[18] I have first explained it from the vantage point of the cognitive: his status as editor. But he also acknowledged and respected the *practitioner's* cognitive mode: when conductor Arturo Toscanini died in 1957, the *Harvard Crimson* solicited Pirrotta's comment, and he

> praised Toscanini for his high standards of perfection, citing the many instances in which he searched for the original manuscript of a composition in order to find the true interpretation as intended by the composer.[19]

Just as Pirrotta the musicologist approached the music with a performer's sensibilities, so Toscanini the performer approached it with a musicologist's.

---

[17] See also **1963**: "Monteverdi and the Problems of Opera," 421 n. 1. Consider how different Pirrotta's engagement with edition making is from the mode of engagement described in Kerman, *Contemplating Music*, 49 (see "*Prologo*," n. 38). For an explicit statement of Pirrotta's understanding of the challenges inherent in edition making, of his convictions, that is, as to the limitations of philology and the consequent need for an intuitive approach, especially with respect to the transcription of rhythmic notation, see **1993**: "Natura e problemi del testo musicale."

[18] I am borrowing the terms of the contrast employed by Lewis Lockwood in "The Study of Music at University" (see "*Scena 3.ª*," n. 64)

[19] *Harvard Crimson*, 17 January 1957, http://www.thecrimson.com/article/1957/1/17/toscanini-dies-of-stroke-at-89/.

Pirrotta and European Academic Culture: Philology

As a scientific undertaking, university-supported scholarship was the creation in great part of German scholars of the late eighteenth and early nineteenth centuries, among them, notably, Friedrich August Wolf. And their preferred scholarly method was philology.[20] Wolf's 1795 study of Homer has been characterized by Anthony Grafton as "the charter of classical scholarship as an independent discipline."[21] Wolf understood that the virtue of the philological method was due especially to its power "to instil self-discipline": access to the sensibilities and mentalities of past cultures resulted principally from rigorous linguistic, grammatical, and orthographical analysis.[22]

These principles spread throughout the European and Europeanized educational world like a contagion.[23] The American higher educational system, which before the second half of the nineteenth century had been dominated by the undergraduate liberal arts college, now subsumed graduate education and the scholarly mission within its redefined institutional *raison d'être*.[24]

The relevance of these developments to Pirrotta's formation is obvious. We recall the emphasis at the *liceo* on exacting grammatical study, based on the conviction that such training enhanced intellectual discipline. Pirrotta analyzed fragments of classical texts for what they revealed about grammar and syntax, dialectical forms, and the correct conjugation of irregular verbs. The texts, significantly, were textbooks, translated or adapted from German models.

More important, the fundamental character of the Florentine "school," as expressed in the offerings of the Faculty of Letters and Philosophy at the University of Florence, owed much to these pan-European tendencies in scholarship. There was an emphasis—which Pirrotta thereafter privileged—on languages, philology, and paleography (which in this case were also legacies of the Florentine Renaissance). Such an emphasis was symbolized by the "Scuola di paleografia e diplomatica," and Pirrotta's thesis adviser was a member of the faculty of the Scuola.

---

[20]See Peter Watson, *The German Genius: Europe's Third Renaissance, the Second Scientific Revolution, and the Twentieth Century* (New York: Harper, 2010), the chapter "Winckelmann, Wolf, and Lessing: The Third Greek Revival and the Origins of Modern Scholarship," the subsection "The Origins of Modern Scholarship"; Watson's book, though "popularizing," is nonetheless a useful synthesis.

[21]Watson, *The German Genius*; see also F.A. Wolf, *Prolegomena to Homer [1795]*, trans. with intro. and nn. Anthony Grafton, Glenn W. Most, James E.G. Zetzel (Princeton, NJ: Princeton University Press, 1985).

[22]Watson, *The German Genius*.

[23]For an interesting recent consideration of the philological method and its history, see Sheldon Pollock, "Future Philology? The Fate of a Soft Science in a Hard World," *Critical Inquiry* 35 (summer 2009): 931–61. For this reference, I am grateful to Dr. Herman Tull.

[24]See the chapter "The University Movement" in Frederick Rudolph, *The American College and University. A History*. New York: Knopf, 1962.

Pirrotta's Reading in the Musicological Literature: Visions of the Discipline

Bibliographical citations in Pirrotta's earlier writings (before the move to Harvard in 1956) document a conversance with these pan-European sensibilities.[25] He was thoroughly familiar with the scholarship of pioneering German musicologists Heinrich Besseler and Johannes Wolf. But the alignment of his temperament with the scholarly traditions identified here is more fully demonstrable. References to particular scholars and titles recur repeatedly, and a picture emerges that suggests sympathy for certain methodologies and scholarly sensitivities and a conviction about the authority of particular authors, titles, and approaches.

In *Il Sacchetti*, Pirrotta cites, in addition to those by Heinrich Besseler and Johannes Wolf, many titles by the German musicologist Friedrich Ludwig, whose work has been characterized as distinguished by a "passion for philological accuracy and mastery of the sources."[26] And the literary scholarship Pirrotta cites there[27] also decisively documents a Positivistic sensibility: the writings of Giosuè Carducci, Emilio Lovarini, Francesco Novati, and Natalino Sapegno.[28]

Other writings on the music of the Italian and European Middle Ages published during the Palermo and Rome years[29] cite the findings of many of the same German and Italian scholars, as well as Guido Adler, Franz Xaver

---

[25]For suggesting that I pay particular attention to Pirrotta's "letture musicologiche," as documented by his citations, I am grateful to Fabrizio Della Seta.

[26]Edward E. Lowinsky, "Obituaries. Heinrich Besseler (1900–1969)," *Journal of the American Musicological Society* 24 (1971): 499–502, especially 499. Pirrotta also cites Ludwig in, for example, **1955**: "Florence [. . .] Codex Palatino Panciatichiano 26," and it would be an exceptionally easy matter to compile a long list of other writings where he does so. But on Ludwig's intellectual profile, see the qualifications in the important study by John Haines, "Friedrich Ludwig's 'Musicology of the Future': A Commentary and Translation," *Plainsong and Medieval Music* 12, no. 2 (2003): 129–64. The nationalist and Hegelian-Idealist characteristics of Ludwig's profile are therein elucidated; they suggest that Ludwig—like Pirrotta—was able to combine a Positivistic command of the sources with an overarching thesis as to the *meaning* of the primary data. In Ludwig's case, this is manifested above all in his Hegelian thesis of the existence of a modal rhythm inherent in medieval secular monophony, even where the notation makes no obvious attempt to represent it unambiguously.

[27]In engaging with this professional literature, he was presumably guided (at that time and subsequently) by his like-minded friend Li Gotti.

[28]I inquired of my friend and former colleague Linda L. Carroll, Professor of Italian at Tulane University—whose expertise in the matter is infinitely greater than mine—if she could characterize Pirrotta's habits of reading in the scholarship on medieval Italian literature, and she responded immediately and spontaneously as follows: "My very first impression is that he is reading superbly-grounded and cutting-edge positivist scholars, many of whom gathered large amounts of primary source material in archives and . . . revolutionized the excessively Romanticized notions of the Renaissance and Middle Ages"; and, further, "Pirrotta's excellent standards are immediately evident in his reading list."

[29]The articles on the Modena manuscript, the origins and history of the caccia and madrigal, "dulcedo" and "subtilitas," the Lucca manuscript, "Sumer is icumen in," Paolo *tenorista*, the ballata (in *Die Musik in Geschichte und Gegenwart* [*M.G.G.*]), Donatus de Florentia [*M.G.G.*], the Panciatichiano manuscript [*M.G.G.*], the "parody" mass, and Italian polyphonic schools of the fourteenth century, as well as the edition of the music of the Trecento.

Haberl, and Hugo Riemann, among others. In addition, the relatively scant scientific Italian musicological scholarship is cited, most notably the writings of Federico Ghisi.[30]

With the move to Rome in 1948, the access to primary sources documenting other phases of Italian music history, the commissions from the *Enciclopedia dello spettacolo*, and the corresponding expansion in the range of Pirrotta's intellectual interests come new habits of reading and different bibliographic citations. Now, in the publications on music in the Italian theater of the late-Renaissance period and on the beginnings of opera (the Florentine aristocratic phase and the operas of Antonio Cesti), in addition to references to the scholarship of Italian colleagues Giacomo Benvenuti and Oscar Chilesotti, submissions to the *Rivista musicale italiana*,[31] and other writings of Ghisi, there are references to Lionel de la Laurencie, Henri Prunières, Hugo Goldschmidt, Hermann Kretzschmar, Hellmuth Christian Wolff, and many others.

Pirrotta absorbed the findings of these fellow scholars, and their influence on his developing voice and scholarly persona can be traced. They furnished him with a methodological model and a vision of both the musicological and broader scholarly programs.

Adler[32] offered a systematic exposition of the program of the young discipline of *Musikwissenschaft*, and resonances of his Positivistic emphases are traceable in Pirrotta's profile.[33] Adler asserted that "a work of art . . . must first of all be defined palaeologically," and after identifying other "objects of investigation in musicological research," he suggested that "[f]rom this the system of this science is to be constructed," which "consequently subdivides into an historic and a systematic section"; among the subjects of the former are "the investigation of the laws of art of different periods, which takes the highest precedence." The tools and methodologies available to the historical musicologist are enumerated:

> [a] great number of auxiliary sciences are affiliated to this section of musicology: . . . general history, with its ancillary sciences, palaeography, chronology, diplomatics, bibliography, library and archival knowledge.

In Adler's vision, there is thus an emphasis on science and the scientific character of the discipline; palaeography, diplomatics, bibliography, archival

---

[30]For example, Federico Ghisi, "Italian Ars-Nova Music: The Perugia and Pistoia Fragments of the Lucca Musical Codex and Other Unpublished Early 15th Century Sources," *Journal of Renaissance and Baroque Music* 1, no. 3 (1946): 173–91.

[31]Notably, for example, Vittorio Ricci, "Un melodramma ignoto della prima metà del '600. »Celio« di Baccio Baglioni a di Niccolò Sapiti," *Rivista musicale italiana* 32 (1925): 51–79, which Pirrotta cites in one of his essays on Cesti.

[32]As Joseph Kerman notes, one of Adler's pupils, significantly, was Egon Wellesz, whose writings on *Seicento* opera were utilized by Pirrotta. Kerman, *Contemplating Music*, 38 (see "*Prologo*," n. 38).

[33]Guido Adler, "Umfang, Methode[,] und Ziel der Musikwissenschaft," *Vierteljahresschrift für Musikwissenschaft* 1 (1885): 5–20 [trans. Erica Mugglestone in "Guido Adler's 'The Scope, Method, and Aim of Musicology' (1885): An English Translation with an Historico-Analytical Commentary," *Yearbook for Traditional Music* 13 (1981): 1–21].

research: these are the privileged tools of the Positivist music historian. Even more revealing of an alignment with Positivism is the assertion that "the investigation of the laws of art of different periods... takes the highest precedence," an element of the Positivist program to which Idealist historians will take especially sharp exception, given that their vision of history instead emphasized the concrete and particular and favored the narrative mode of presentation over the construction of abstract laws.

Any remaining ambiguity as to Adler's understanding of musicology and its Positivist, would-be scientific character is removed by further elaborations:

> To attain his main task, namely, the research of the laws of art of diverse periods and their organic combination and development, the historian of art utilises the same methodology as that of the investigator of nature; that is, by preference the inductive method. From several examples he extracts that which is common and separates those aspects which differ, and utilises also the method of abstraction in which, from given concrete conceptions, particular sections are neglected and others preferred.[34]

But Pirrotta's conversance with and absorption of German scholarship was not limited to its Positivistic expressions; in the work of Heinrich Besseler, there are reflections of the "*geistesgeschichtlicher* approach" of Besseler's teacher Willibald Gurlitt, of an "imaginative ability to reconstruct the sound of old music." For Besseler, as for Pirrotta, music was "the most eloquent symbol of an epoch, of a spiritual and intellectual climate, of a style of life."[35]

With the inception of the series of studies on Seicento opera, the tone of Pirrotta's presentation changes, expressing an expanded, altered scholarly sensibility. Most notably, the Materialist quality of the writings on Cesti may reveal the influence of Henri Prunières, who, as a Frenchman, would have been a natural beneficiary of that French scholarly interest in social and economic history culminating in the work of the "Annales" school. Prunière's Materialist predilections could be documented with dozens of examples.[36]

PHILOSOPHICAL TENDENCIES IN TWENTIETH-CENTURY ITALY

It bears repeating that there is little to no evidence that Pirrotta aligned himself decisively with any philosophical school, as the officials at the University of Urbino observed when they conferred the honorary laurea upon him. On the

---

[34] And for the continuing prestige of the German vision of "Musikwissenschaft," see also the Preface to Fabrizio Della Seta's collection of his essays *Not Without Madness* (see "*Prologo*," n. 44); I am grateful to Professor Della Seta for sharing this text prior to publication.

[35] Lowinsky, "Obituaries. Heinrich Besseler."

[36] See, for example, Prunières, "Opera in Venice in the XVIIth Century," trans. M.D. Herter Norton, *Musical Quarterly* 17 (1931): 1–13. Pirrotta writings on seventeenth-century opera cite title after title by Prunières, documenting his conversance with the literature and its underlying sensibilities and methodologies.

contrary, the defining characteristics of his approach—and its virtue, in my estimation—were its flexibility, eclecticism, and practicality. He implicitly asserted the right to be free of fixed methodologies that might otherwise have constrained him, had he subscribed to a particular philosophical tradition (with all of the accompanying potential "political" complications[37]).

Science and Positivism

Giacomo Rinaldi identified four main trends in nineteenth-century Italian philosophy, the first of which—Augustine's and Aquinas's *dualistic metaphysics*—need not concern us here. The remaining three were very important for Pirrotta's formation (and that of his contemporaries), and Rinaldi's taxonomy partly governs what follows: "[1] *methodological empiricism*, ... which found its most prominent exponent in the *positivist* thinker Roberto Ardigò (1828–1920); ... [2] the speculative German tradition of *Kantian–Hegelian idealism* ... ; and ... [3] Marx's and Engels's *historical materialism*, ... spread and fostered ... by Antonio Labriola (1843–1904)."[38]

Pirrotta was a university student at a time of sharp spiritualist responses to the achievements of nineteenth-century European science (especially those of Charles Darwin and his followers) and the resultant interest in extending the methods and defining attributes of science to neighboring disciplines. One of those responsible for popularizing Darwin's findings on the continent—Ernst Haeckel—characterized Darwin as a "cautious naturalist." But if Darwin himself was reluctant to pursue the full implications of his findings, Haeckel and others were not: and to its critics, the post-Darwinian universe was a troublingly Positivistic, Mechanistic, Scientific–Materialistic universe, where even human beings were the product of natural forces similar to those that

---

[37]The American Pragmatist philosopher William James wrote of the Italian philosophical tradition that "... [h]er sons still class the things of thought somewhat too politically, making partizan [sic] capital, clerical or positivist, of every conquest or concession." See James, "G. Papini and the Pragmatist Movement in Italy," *Journal of Philosophy, Psychology and Scientific Methods* 3 (1906): 337–41, especially 337.

[38]Several sources were especially useful to me in drafting this section: [1] Norberto Bobbio, *Ideological Profile of Twentieth-Century Italy* (see "Scena 2.ª," n. 67); [2] Randall Collins, *The Sociology of Philosophies: A Global Theory of Intellectual Change* (Cambridge, MA: Belknap Press of Harvard University Press, 1998) (for suggesting this title, I am grateful to Joseph H. Shieber); [3] James Hepokoski, "The Dahlhaus Project and Its Extra-Musicological Sources," *19th-Century Music* 14 (1991): 221–46, which suggested how one might apply the materials of general intellectual history in describing a musicologist's professional formation (for suggesting this title, I am grateful to Philip Gossett); [4] Philip Gossett, "Carl Dahlhaus and the 'Ideal Type,'" *19th-Century Music* 13 (1989): 49–56; and [5] Hayden White, *Metahistory: The Historical Imagination in Nineteenth-Century Europe* (Baltimore: Johns Hopkins University Press, 1973) (for suggesting this title, I am grateful to Paul Cefalu).

cause iron to rust and flowers to bloom. It was to this alleged diminution of the distinctively human that adherents of various European spiritualist movements objected.[39]

Nonetheless, for a considerable time, experimental science and its allied philosophy of Positivism enjoyed almost unchallenged prestige. Norberto Bobbio's brilliant *Ideological Profile of Twentieth-Century Italy* has characterized nineteenth-century Positivism as a philosophy of history that envisioned society's potential for improvement through a shift from a military to an industrialized society, from a stratified society controlled by the Church to one of free classes competing with one another, the whole regulated by scientific knowledge.[40] Even Giovanni Papini, who would become the most celebrated Italian spokesman for the forces of the "irrational" reacting to nineteenth-century Positivism, could nonetheless write of one phase of his own intellectual development that

> [i]t seemed to me that only science could offer certainty; and so, since it was philosophy I wanted, it had to be a philosophy deeply grounded on the sciences and born of them. Such a philosophy I found—a philosophy that everyone knows. In our day, in Italy, it goes under the name of Positivism. I set out, accordingly, to make a "positivistic" demonstration.[41]

The Italian sociologist and criminologist Enrico Ferri offered his own understanding of the reach of science:

> the profound scientific revolution caused by Darwinism and Spencerian evolution has reinvigorated . . . the physical, biological[,] and even psychological sciences. . . . It has led . . . through the initiative of Auguste Comte . . . to the creation of a new science, Sociology, which should be . . . the crowning glory of the new scientific edifice erected by the experimental method. . . . Marxian socialism is in harmony with modern science and is its logical continuation. That is exactly the reason why it has made the theory of evolution the basis of its inductions

---

[39] See, among the interpretive essays, Jacques Barzun, *Darwin, Marx, Wagner: Critique of a Heritage* (Garden City, NY: Doubleday, 1958); and among the primary texts, Charles Darwin, *The Descent of Man, and Selection in Relation to Sex*, intro. James Moore and Adrian Desmond (London: Penguin Books, 2004); Ernst Haeckel, *The History of Creation: or the Development of the Earth and its Inhabitants by the Action of Natural Causes*, trans. E. Ray Lankester, 2 vols. (New York: D. Appleton, 1880); and Haeckel, *The Riddle of the Universe* [*Die Welträthsel*]: *at the Close of the Nineteenth Century*, trans. Joseph McCabe (New York: Harper & Brothers, 1900).

[40] Bobbio, *Ideological Profile of Twentieth-Century Italy*, 3 (see "Scena 2.ᵃ," n. 67).

[41] Papini, *The Failure* [*Un Uomo Finito*], trans. Virginia Pope (New York: Harcourt, Brace, 1924), 81. For an account of other Italian Pragmatists' personal intellectual odyssey with respect to Positivism, especially Giovanni Vailati's, see the introduction to Giovanni Vailati, *Logic and Pragmatism: Selected Essays*, trans. Claudia Arrighi, ed. Claudia Arrighi, Paola Cantù, Mauro De Zan, and Patrick Suppes, (Stanford, CA: CSLI, 2010), xxi–lix and lxix–xcvii, especially xxii–xxiii, xxvii–xxviii, xxx–xxxi, xxxiv, xxxviii–xxxix, xlvii, and lxxiii.

and . . . marks the truly living and final phase . . . of socialism[,] which had theretofore remained floating in the nebulosities of sentiment[,] and why it has taken as its guide the unerring compass of scientific thought.[42]

With its inductive, experimental method, scientific thought seemed to furnish an "unerring compass" and means of countering the "nebulosities of sentiment"; the theory of evolution was deemed applicable to a range of disciplines and realms of human experience beyond science. These sensibilities secured a foothold in early twentieth-century Italy, as can be documented by the texts of Papini and Ferri, among many others.

Roberto Ardigò

The preeminent Italian proponent of Positivism was Roberto Ardigò,[43] whose studies of natural science and psychology during the 1860s and '70s and developing conversance with the writings of Herbert Spencer prompted his conversion to Positivism.[44] For the Positivist scientist, there was a certainty about the datum, matter, sensation, and Ardigò asserted the reality of matter, independent of human thought concerning it:

> If sound as such is essentially a thought and not a reality distinct from it, everything else that enters into the idea of matter is also essentially a thought.[45]

It was important for Ardigò—here his status as a psychologist is clear—to explain the interaction between the external phenomenon and the psyche's apprehension of it: between the "Not Me" (the external entity, the object), and the "Me" (the internal entity, the subject). Sensations have absolute cognitive value, and the distinction between external phenomena and internal understanding of them is made on the basis of the scientist's time-honored techniques of observation and experiment:

---

[42]Ferri, *Socialism and Modern Science (Darwin, Spencer, Marx)*, trans. Robert Rives La Monte, 3rd ed. (Chicago: Charles H. Kerr, 1912), 155–57.

[43]On Ardigò, see "Roberto Ardigò a Suicide. Famous Italian Philosopher Kills Himself at the Age of 90," *New York Times* (7 February 1920); Bobbio, *Ideological Profile of Twentieth-Century Italy*, 3 and 203 n. * (see "Scena 2.ª," n. 67); Preface, Ardigò, *An Inconsistent Preliminary Objection Against Positivism*, trans. Emilio Gavirati (Cambridge: W. Heffer, 1910), 3.

[44]On Ardigò's philosophy, see, in addition to Bobbio, Guglielmo Salvadori, "Positivism in Italy," *Journal of Philosophy, Psychology and Scientific Methods* 5 (1908): 449–53; Salvadori (451 and elsewhere) particularly traces the influence of Spencer. See also Giovanni Gentile, *Teoria generale dello spirito come atto puro* (Florence: Le lettere, 2003); trans. as *The Theory of Mind as Pure Act* with intro. by H. Wildon Carr (London: Macmillan, 1922), xvii.

[45]All translations are mine. I consulted the original Italian in Ardigò, *Opere filosofiche di Roberto Ardigò* (Padua: Angelo Draghi, 1898–12), vol. 10—Parte Seconda, which contains the text I quote extensively here, "Una pretesa pregiudiziale contro il positivismo"; see especially 308.

> For the knower, sugar is that external sweetness (or cause) that produces the internal sweetness (or effect). . . . Knowing is done by means of sensations.[46]

The external entity—the "that," the object, the block of external sensations—is thus set against the internal entity—the "this," the subject, the block of internal sensations.[47]

Ardigò was also intent on explaining the physiological basis for abstractions such as "sweetness" ("certain . . . genres of ideation"), and he sought organic explanations for cognitive processes. In organizing individual sense experiences into the intellectual abstractions constructed from them ("sweetness"), the role of language—the word, which fixes the idea—is all important. Notably, Ardigò extends his argument to the "historical sciences":

> Whether it be in the species and genera of the descriptive sciences, or the special and generic laws of the dynamic sciences, or the titles of the subsidiary and superior groups of the statistical and historical sciences, one finds commonality connecting the many subsidiaries, starting from a cognizance of the individuals and thence giving way to the verification—which one has in them—of that very commonality, such that they are associated either through likeness, coexistence, or succession. The association of many distinct [individuals], or the synthetic idea of them, is marked and fixed by a word, apt to return it to the mind in its virtuality each time it is wanted. . . . So that then, a very general idea having been obtained, marked, and fixed in a word . . . one can proceed inversely from this—deductively, that is—in order to recall the words (and indirectly the related ideas) that indicate the underlying generalities, and thus further on, then, until coming to the individuals from which the intuitive work, or of construction of the science, departed.[48]

The references to classification—to the "species and genera of the descriptive sciences" and the "subsidiary and superior groups of the . . . historical sciences"—are illustrative of Positivism's penchant for taxonomies and classification schemes, to which the Idealists will take vehement exception, as they will to the Mechanistic, Scientific–Materialist quality of the arguments in Ardigò's text and his emphasis on the physiological and the organic.

Both Scientific Positivism and Historical Positivism thus placed a premium on observation; both subscribed to convictions about the reality of matter (or the datum, including the historical datum) and the value and reliability of sense experience.

Spiritualist Reactions: Henri Bergson

The spiritualist reactions, pan-European in origin, were sharp and multiform. Among the most influential early critics was Henri Bergson, who had already

---
[46] Ardigò, *Opere filosofiche*, 346, 349.
[47] Ardigò, *Opere filosofiche*, 341–45.
[48] Ardigò, *Opere filosofiche*, 338.

published two of his most important works by the time Ardigò was honored by his disciples with a Festschrift in 1898.

Bergson's philosophy was vigorously debated by Italian intellectuals of the early-twentieth century. The nature of his critique of Herbert Spencer is evident:[49]

> [W]hen a philosopher arose who announced a doctrine of evolution... in which... correspondences between the external and... internal would be followed step by step... to him all eyes were turned.... Spencer is right in defining the intellect by this correspondence.... Nature.... is reflected in mind.

However,

> Spencer... believed that the intellect is sufficiently explained as the impression left on us by the general character of matter:[50] As if the order inherent in matter were not intelligence itself!... [H]ow can we fail to see that intelligence is supposed when we admit objects and facts?... [P]hilosophy... knows... that what is visible and tangible in things represents our possible action on them.... [I]nstead of saying that the relations between facts have generated the laws of thought, I can as well claim that it is the form of thought that has determined the shape of the facts perceived, and consequently their relations among themselves.

The debate thus turned on the question of emphasis, of where it was placed, of first principles: Spencer, Ardigò, and the Positivists in general began from matter, the datum, the external phenomenon, the object, to which Spencer assigned priority. Bergson, on the other hand, assigned it to the human intellect. In this critique lies the germ of the Idealist conviction that the activity of the intellect was indispensable to the construction of reality.

Spiritualist Reactions: Italian Idealism

The preeminent Italian spiritualist philosophy was the Idealism of Benedetto Croce and Giovanni Gentile. Gentile defined Idealism as "the negation of any reality... opposed to thought as its presupposition"[51] and Positivism as "the philosophy that conceptualizes reality as the reality of fact, independent

---

[49]Bergson, *Creative Evolution*, trans. Arthur Mitchell (London: Electric Book Company, 2001 ["Based on the First Edition,... 1911 / Macmillan and Co., Limited"]), 148, 182, 184, 350–51, 353–55.

[50]See also Bergson, *La pensée et le mouvant. Essais et conférences*, Bibliothèque de philosophie contemporaine (Paris: Les Presses universitaires de France, 1969): "La philosophie de Spencer visait à prendre l'empreinte des choses et à se modeler sur le détail des faits"; Bergson, "Introduction. I. Retrograde Movement of the True Growth of Truth," in *The Creative Mind*, trans. Mabelle L. Andison (New York: Philosophical Library, 1946), 10.

[51]Giovanni Gentile, *Teoria generale dello spirito come atto puro*, trans. by H. Wildon Carr as *The Theory of Mind as Pure Act*, 18. I have slightly altered Carr's translation on the basis of a rereading of the original Italian text.

of any relationship with the spirit that studies it."[52] In Gentile's understanding, matter (or a historical fact) is, for the Positivist, real, irrespective of whether it figures in a relationship to a human mind that apprehends it; for the Idealist, matter is made real only through the mind's apprehension of it. In Croce's words, "reality is spiritual, not mechanical."[53] As Fabrizio Della Seta suggested,[54] it was not necessary to have studied the writings of the principal Italian representatives of Idealism to be influenced by them. Their theories were very much in the intellectual air that Pirrotta and his contemporaries were breathing. The prestige enjoyed by both Croce and Gentile was so great—especially because of their relationship to the Fascist political order during the time Pirrotta was finishing the *liceo* and beginning the Conservatory[55]—that no sentient, inquisitive student could have escaped their influence. Christopher Celenza has written that Croce and Gentile were of "titanic importance in shaping the intellectual life of Italy in the twentieth century."[56]

The status that Positivism had enjoyed in nineteenth-century Italy was decisively challenged not only by Croce and Gentile, but also by Pantaleo Carabellese (Pirrotta's philosophy professor at the University of Palermo[57]) and other eminent early-twentieth-century Italian exponents of Idealism. Croce and his like-minded contemporaries were "[c]aught up in the general *fin de siècle* mistrust of (and boredom with) positivism, which seemed to have deprived humanity of its creativity and spontaneity."[58] But as Norberto Bobbio also explained,

[t]he reaction against positivism . . . widespread at the start of the 'new century' was more than a critique of philosophy; it was also a critique of politics. The campaign against an antihumanistic determinism, . . . arid naturalism, . . . ingenuous adoration of raw facts, and . . . reduction of humankind to its environment went along with polemics against the reformist ideas . . . shaking the old order.[59]

---

[52]Gentile, 49–51.

[53]Benedetto Croce, *Logic as the Science of the Pure Concept*, trans. Douglas Ainslie (London: Macmillan, 1917), translation of *Logica: come scienza del concetto puro* (Bari: G. Laterza, 1909 [2– ed.]), 48. For Rinaldi's felicitous summary, see his p. 355.

[54] Personal communication with A.M. Cummings.

[55]Croce was minister of education from 1920 until 1921, just before the Fascists seized control of the Italian government (1922); Gentile was minister in 1922–24, just as Pirrotta was completing the three-year program at the Liceo (academic years 1922/23–1924/25) and enrolling at the Conservatory of Palermo (academic year 1924/25).

[56]Christopher S. Celenza, *The Lost Italian Renaissance: Humanists, Historians, and Latin's Legacy* (Baltimore: Johns Hopkins University Press, 2004), 18.

[57]On Carabellese here, see Giacomo Rinaldi, "Italian Idealism and after: Gentile, Croce and others," *Twentieth-Century Continental Philosophy*, ed. Richard Kearney (London: Routledge, 1994), 350–89, especially 364–67, and an important primary text: Carabellese, *Critica del concreto* (1921; Rome: A Signorelli, 1940 [2– ed.]), 23.

[58]Edmund E. Jacobitti, "Labriola, Croce, and Italian Marxism (1895-1910)," *Journal of the History of Ideas* 36 (1975): 297–318, especially 305.

[59]Bobbio, *Ideological Profile of Twentieth-Century Italy*, 7 (see "Scena 2.ª," n. 67).

Positivism embodied the ideal of science, and of progress and freedom *through* science: scientific knowledge—not theological or metaphysical knowledge—was to govern the reform of postunification Italy. Conversely, to its opponents Positivism was a weapon of the reformist assault on the established political and cultural order, an assault that the Idealists sought to mitigate.

As Randall Collins suggested,[60] there were also geographic and religious oppositions in the debate: north/south and secular/Catholic oppositions. In the more secularized regions of northern Italy, where Positivism had a stronghold, universities rapidly became integrated into the international scientific community. However, because Catholic priests constituted a substantial proportion of the instructors in Italian schools (especially in the south), the task of staffing the new, secularized educational system of post-*Risorgimento* Italy developed into a conflict with the Church. Antonio Labriola sought a compromise: independence of the schools from the Church, but also an acknowledgment of the Idealist's respect for the "spirit" of religious sentiment.

To those concerned about the potentially destabilizing effects of the reform movement, Idealism's virtues were obvious: above all, there was a "spiritual" dimension to Idealism, and when Croce portrayed the "advance of culture" in the early twentieth century—suggesting that nothing could arrest the "inward decay of positivism"—he argued that among the causes of the crisis was "a certain widely diffused spirit . . . to which the crude simplifications of positivism, particularly in delicate matters of art, religion, and the moral consciousness, were intolerable."[61] "[P]ositivism was finished," writes Bobbio, "prompting a witch-hunt for 'scientism' on the part of a perennial spiritualism."[62] It is important to remember that Italian Idealism's intellectual center-of-gravity was the south, and that Nino Pirrotta was a Sicilian who made repeated reference to such status throughout his career.

Thus the Idealists' assault on Positivism altered not only the direction of Italian philosophy of the early twentieth century, but also the general style, affections, and disaffections of an entire epoch, as Bobbio argued.

When we read paradigmatic texts of Italian Idealism, especially after having read comparable texts by Ardigò, we are struck by the differences in the atmospherics of these two Italian schools of thought, revealed not only in the Idealists' vivid *linguaggio* but also in the contrasting epistemological positions

---

[60]Collins, *Sociology of Philosophies*, 684. Rinaldi also identifies the matter of the geographic component to the Idealist/Positivist debate; see 351.

[61]Bobbio, *Ideological Profile of Twentieth-Century Italy*, 71 (see "Scena 2.$^{\underline{a}}$," n. 67).

[62]"The Spirit" is an iconic Idealist term, to my knowledge never systematically defined by either Croce or Gentile. As I understand the term, it refers to that which the Idealists regarded as the quintessentially human, that which cannot be reduced to Scientific–Materialist explanations, however much the Scientific-Materialists and Positivists might have wished and attempted to do so. See also my previous chapter, on Ettore Li Gotti's independence from the Idealism of his teacher Bertoni.

staked out and contrasting techniques of presentation. The Italian Idealists dismissed natural science as traffic in generalities, favoring instead a vision of history as a "science" of the individual that resisted the natural scientist's abstract schemes. For Croce, the kind of intellectual program that was particularly useful exemplified historicity and a sense of the concrete and the individual.[63] Of all the Italian philosophies of the early twentieth century that may have left their traces in Pirrotta's thought, Crocean Idealism was among the most important.

Benedetto Croce[64]

In four volumes, published between 1902 and 1917, Croce outlined a systematic "philosophy of the spirit," as he subtitled the installments:

1) *Estetica come scienza dell'espressione e linguistica generale: teoria e storia* [The Aesthetic as the Science of Expression and the Linguistic in General: Theory and History] (Milan: R. Sandron, 1902);[65]

2) *Logica: come scienza del concetto puro* [Logic: as Science of the Pure Concept], Filosofia come scienza dello spirito [Philosophy as Science of the Spirit], vol. 2 (Bari: G. Laterza, 1909 [2nd. ed.]);[66]

3) *Filosofia della pratica, economica ed etica* [The Philosophy of Practice, Economics, and Ethics] Filosofia come scienza dello spirito, vol. 3 (Bari: G. Laterza, 1909); and

4) *Teoria e storia della storiografia* [Theory and History of Historiography], Filosofia come scienza dello spirito, vol. 4 (Bari: G. Laterza, 1917).[67]

For our purposes, the second and third of these are less relevant, the first and fourth critical. Croce systematically elaborated his philosophy of history in the fourth volume, as its title suggests. But in the first, equally important volume, Croce argues for subsuming history under the aesthetic, with all that such an argument signifies. We begin with a consideration of the theory of

---

[63]Bobbio, *Ideological Profile of Twentieth-Century Italy*, 70, 75 (see "Scena 2.ª," n. 67).

[64]In interpreting Croce's thought, I found useful George H. Douglas, "A Reconsideration of the Dewey-Croce Exchange," *Journal of Aesthetics and Art Criticism* 28 (1970): 497–504. But of the utmost importance was R.G. Collingwood's classic *The Idea of History*, rev. ed. with Lectures 1926–28, ed. and with an intro. W. Jan van der Dussen (Oxford: Oxford University Press, 1946/1993/1994), especially 190–204; however, I found the entirety of Collingwood's work useful for understanding the intellectual lineage of Croce's thought. See also my "Scena 3.ª Palermo (1931–36)" on Giulio Bertoni's philosophy of language, which reveals a profound relationship to Crocean and Gentilean Idealism.

[65]See also *Estetica come scienza dell'espressione e linguistica generale: teoria e storia*, ed. Giuseppe Galasso (Milan: Adelphi, 1990), which was the basis for the translation I used: Croce, *The Aesthetic as the Science of Expression and of the Linguistic in General*, trans. Colin Lyas (Cambridge: Cambridge University Press, 1992).

[66]Translated as Croce, *Logic as the Science of the Pure Concept*, trans. Douglas Ainslie (London: Macmillan, 1917).

[67]Translated as *History: Its Theory and Practice*, trans. Douglas Ainslie (New York: Russell & Russell, 1960).

epistemology underlying Crocean Idealism, which Croce terms "intuitive knowledge."

Whereas Ardigò wrote, "I have expressed myself with respect to the absolute cognitive value of sensation," Croce revealed his radically different view of the status of sensation—or of data (including historical data), or of matter—in several passages near the very beginning of *The Aesthetic*, which employ a telling diction to characterize sensation or the datum and the act of engaging with it: "unformed material," "merely material," "mechanism," "brute-like." Croce's objective is to argue for a different *kind* of knowledge: "intuitive" and "non-intellectualistic."[68] The spiritual dimension of Idealism is obvious, as is the different attitude concerning the status of "the material."

> Having . . . freed intuitive knowledge from any intellectualistic suggestion whatsoever ["da qualsiasi soggezione intellettualistica"] . . . , we must now . . . determine its boundaries . . . against a different kind of invasion ["invasione"]. . . . On the other side, below a lower limit ["limite inferiore"], there is sensation, there is unformed material ["materia informe"], which the spirit can never grasp in itself, insofar as it is mere matter ["mera materia"], and which it can possess only by giving form to it, ... This matter . . . is mechanism ["meccanismo"], it is passivity ["passività"], it is that which the spirit of man endures ["subisce"] but does not produce. Without it no human knowledge or activity is possible; but the merely material gives us our animal nature, what in man is brute-like and impulsive ["la mera materia ci dà l'animalità, ciò che nell'uomo è di brutale e d'impulsivo"], and not the spiritual realm in which being *human* consists [italics original].[69]

Italian Idealism shared with Idealism's other European manifestations a concern with the exercise of human rationality, of the intellect on matter (or upon the historical datum). Is there a reality independent of human rationality, and if we stipulate that there is, how does one apprehend it? For the Positivist, the method is to be sought in science. For the Idealist, it is pointless to speak of the "thing in itself" apart from rational apprehension of it, and the consequent question concerns the most efficacious approach or method to be adopted in apprehending reality, which cannot be separated from the apprehension itself.

Croce carefully defines intuition (or expression) and is equally careful to acknowledge that interpreting sense experience completely requires a nonintuitive kind of activity as well, the "intellectual" (or "conceptual"):

---

[68] Croce, *The Aesthetic*, trans. Lyas, 2. For purposes of our account of Pirrotta's formation, the most important of these terms are indeed "intuitive" and—or, rather, versus—"intellectualistic."

[69] Croce, *The Aesthetic*, trans. Lyas, 6, 11, 16–17, 23. I have slightly modified Lyas's translation of the opening phrase, after consulting the original Italian. Croce returns to this fundamental matter in vol. 2 of the series (Croce, *Logic*, trans. Ainslie, 6–7; 201): "We . . . have thus distinguished two fundamental forms of the Spirit: the representative or fantastic form, and the logical." Note the use of the word "representative" as equivalent to "intuitive," since it will be important to an understanding of Pirrotta's intellectual sensibility.

> Independent from and autonomous with respect to intellection ["l'intellezione"] . . . [,] an intuition ["l'intuizione"] or representation is to be distinguished from that which feels and endures ["subisce"], from the flood and flux ["onda e flusso"] of sensation, from psychic material, as *form* [italics original]; and this form, this taking possession, is expression.[70]

Croce then arrives at his thesis on the nature of history as an undertaking, which for our purposes is most important, given that historical musicology is, after all, a historical discipline:

> [K]nowledge divides between the disciplines that study nature, those that study history[,] and those that study art, leaving to the first the job of counting and measuring, to the second the representation of actual events[,] and to the third the representation of those which are possible; . . . What philosophy can study about history is the way in which it is constituted (by intuition, perception ["intuizione, percezione"], documents, probabilities, etc.); what it can study about the natural sciences are the forms of the concepts that constitute them (space, time, motion, number, experiment, observation ["tipi, classi"]).

Croce later explicitly subsumes history under art. But within the passage just quoted is the seed of a distinction between history ("the representation of actual events") and art ("the representation of those which are possible"), and the fuller elaboration will consider what distinguishes history from art as well as what similarities the two possess: history is an art, not a science; it possesses a kind of certainty, but not the certainty of science; rather, the historian is like the juror who has heard evidence, and his conviction is a nondemonstrable one. Clearly, we are no longer in the Positivistic world of Roberto Ardigò.

Having established a discrete space for history's program, Croce more fully describes it and its procedures. His definition of history is one to which Nino Pirrotta, I believe, partly subscribed. Unlike science, history does not seek to identify laws nor construct universals or abstractions. Rather, it posits intuitions (in the specific sense of that term as Croce uses it in the passages quoted above): intuitions of the "wholly determinate individual," "particular entities, with their individual physiognomy." And its rhetorical mode is narrative.

Nowhere is the Idealist conviction that history concerns itself with the concrete and individual rather than the abstract and universal more evident than in Idealism's refutation of "genre." For both Croce and Gentile, the Idealist historian rejects the generic for the particular, and this position, too, is important to Pirrotta's formation, since he had a similar suspicion of genre.[71]

---

[70]Croce, *The Aesthetic*, trans. Lyas, 6, 11, 16–17, 23. My word "intellection" is substituted for Lyas's "the intellectual."

[71]For Gentile's position on the same matter—wholly congruent with Croce's—see Giovanni Gentile, *Teoria generale dello spirito come atto puro*, trans. by H. Wildon Carr as *The Theory of Mind as Pure Act*, 224–25.

Croce offers a more detailed description of the nature of the historian's activity and its specific objectives, and the important distinction between true history and a series of related kinds of activity: paleography, "philologism." The intent is to free the historian of the Positivist's anxiety about the verifiable fact, to afford him a different relationship to the primary material he is seeking to explicate; in Celenza's formulation, "the historian-philosopher must be conscious of the fact (in the tradition of Vico) that he is himself *creating*, rather than *describing*, history."[72]

Croce's immediate concern is the work of art, but his argument extends to other vestiges of a past society—a text, a musical composition—especially since history has been subsumed under the aesthetic.[73] In their efforts to re-enter the world that produced the work of art—or the text, or the musical composition—historians are to surpass the work of the paleographers and philologues, whose contributions he minimizes. In contrast with the true historian, the researcher or incoherent chronicler is little better than a monkish eunuch. In Randall Collins's words, history is no positive science of fact gathering: since the past is dead, all that can be recovered is its spirit.[74]

We conclude our survey of the philosophy of history in *The Aesthetic* by citing further important terms in the Idealist's lexicon (in addition to "intellectualistic" and "intuitive"): "ratiocination" and "hedonistic."[75] Anyone familiar with Pirrotta's writings will recall his use of such terms and know of their importance to him.

The final installment in Croce's series of four volumes on "the philosophy of the spirit"—*Theory and History of Historiography*—elaborates themes already considered in *The Aesthetic*, although it contains formulations that merit further brief consideration.[76]

---

[72]Celenza, *Lost Italian Renaissance*, 27.

[73]Croce, *The Aesthetic*, 139–40: "[R]eproduction will . . . take place when we . . . put ourselves into the circumstances in which the stimulus (the physically beautiful) was produced. . . . As far as the physiological object goes[,] the paleographers ['paleografi'] and philologists ['filologi'], restorers of texts to their original character, . . . strive just ['appunto'] to conserve or give us again the physical object in all its original force. . . . To restore in us the psychological conditions ['condizioni psicologiche'] that have changed in the course of history is the work of historical interpretation, which revives the dead, completes the fragmentary ['ravviva il morto, compie il frammentario'], gives us a way of seeing a work of art (the physical object) as the author saw it in the act of creation." Lyas translates "paleografi" as "paleontologists"; I have substituted "paleographers." The memorable final sentence of this passage is quintessentially Crocean and will be deployed by Beardsley and Wimsatt in their classic article on the intentional fallacy, as emblematic of Croce's thought. Monroe C. Beardsley and William K. Wimsatt Jr., "The Intentional Fallacy," *Sewanee Review* 54 (1946): 468–88, especially 472.

[74]Collins, *Sociology of Philosophies*, 684.

[75]Another quintessential Idealist term—"representations"—is, for Croce, synonymous with "intuition[s]" and "representative" is synonymous with "intuitive" (and thus antonymous to "intellectualistic"). See the quotations from Croce, *Logic*, trans. Ainslie, 6-7 and 201, and Croce, *The Aesthetic*, trans. Lyas, 6, 11, 16–17, 23, above.

[76]However, as Professor Della Seta suggested to me (in private communication), this should by no means be understood to signify that Croce's philosophy of history as outlined in the fourth installment was identical to that outlined in the first, that it had achieved the status of a fully formed system from the outset. On the contrary, an ongoing elaboration of that philosophy led him to re-envision its conceptions continuously. Among other considerations, the *Aesthetic* was elaborated before he was familiar with Hegel's thought, which occurred immediately thereafter under Gentile's influence.

Croce offers additional distinctions between the historical and scientific programs and a refutation of Positivist historians' attempts to make a science of history. In place of the Positivists' definition of history, Croce offers an alternative, in which he once more invokes the Idealists' assumption about the indispensability of human thought to the status of "reality." Croce again refers to the interaction of the intuitive (or representative) and intellective (or conceptual) processes as fundamental to his theory of epistemology. The initial apprehension of matter or the datum is intuitive; the intellect then organizes the apprehended material into a concept.[77]

The one issue addressed in some detail in *Theory and History of Historiography* that I wish to consider more fully here is Croce's thesis concerning philologistic activity as an enterprise different from "true" history.

Once more, Croce's nuanced word usage is all important. Croce was by no means a stranger to Positivist methodology. His initial activity as a scholar lay entirely within the realm of documentary research, and even after the inception of his philosophical activity—with the *Aesthetic*—he continued to produce learned studies in which he always demonstrated the greatest mastery of the historical–philological method.

His diction reveals the subtle distinction he was intending. He disdained, not philology, but what he termed "philologism": a misguided tendency to make philology an end in itself rather than an instrument of historical knowledge, to which it was indispensable.

Giovanni Gentile[78]

Giovanni Gentile was born in Sicily and educated at Pisa. There he became conversant with the philosophy of Croce's uncle Bernardo Spaventa, a Hegelian and professor at the University of Naples, whose pupil Donato Jaja was Gentile's teacher at Pisa. In 1917 Gentile was appointed to a professorship at Rome, and in 1922 became minister of education in the new Fascist regime.[79]

The distinguishing characteristic of Gentilean Idealism, as contrasted with that of Croce, is its emphasis on dynamic process: on the act of thinking.

---

[77]Note the terms "brute" and "coarse," deployed repeatedly throughout this entire section of the book (pp. 65, 69, 72–73, 75, 80); note, too, the distinction drawn once more between the sciences and history; finally, with respect to the status of the "thing in itself," note the distinction between Croce's Idealism and Ardigò's Positivism, as expressed in the following passage from Ardigò: "Metaphysical . . . —and scientifically unsustainable—are the monistic data of . . . Idealism, . . . the Here-after [of E. Littré], the Noumenon [of Kant], . . . because considered as many transcendent entities in themselves, whereas they are instead nothing other than as many distinguishable moments of the knowable scientific datum of which we have told: that is, of that which one thinks of and understands as 'that which is'" Ardigò, *Opere filosofiche*, 351–52.

[78]On Gentile, see J.A. Smith, "IV.—The Philosophy of Giovanni Gentile," *Proceedings of the Aristotelian Society* 20 (1920): 63–78; and Warner Fite, review, *The Theory of Mind as Pure Act*, *Philosophical Review* 32 (1923): 548–51. The latter has proved to be of exceptional value.

[79]On Gentile's biography, see Celenza, *Lost Italian Renaissance*, 19–20; Smith, "The Philosophy of Giovanni Gentile," especially 67; and my "*Scena 1.ª Famiglia* (1908–24)."

Gentile is indebted to Hegel, like the Italian Idealists generally, whose "Spirito" is Hegel's "Geist," though transformed.[80] Like the other Idealists, Gentile aspired to a philosophy that transcended the subject–object dichotomy. In this respect he is indebted to Kant, in that there was a synthesis in Kant's philosophy between the thinking subject and the objective world, a synthesis that thought represented.

However, Gentile's philosophy extended Kant's: it is a philosophy of "actual idealism" ("actual" in the sense of "present" or "current," deriving from the root verb "to act"), wherein the act of thinking does not simply create reality; rather, it *is* reality, the *sole* reality.[81] In Randall Collins's formulation, Gentile's Actual Idealism takes the identification of reality with action to an extreme: not only is there no separation of thought from an external world, but no separation of thought from practice. "The true is what is in the making."[82]

The paradigmatic text of Gentilean Idealism, comparable in influence to Croce's series on the "philosophy of the spirit," is his *Teoria generale dello spirito come atto puro* [*General Theory of the Spirit as Pure Act*].[83] Therein, there are analogous characterizations of Scientific Positivism as it contrasts with Idealism, and analogous refutations of Ardigò's Positivism. There is a similar emphasis on the value of intuition and an identical skepticism concerning the theory of genre. Finally, there is a common understanding of history. Unlike Croce, Gentile was a philosopher, not a historian, and his consideration of the question cannot be expected to be as systematic or comprehensive as Croce's. All the same, his philosophy of history was essentially Croce's. There is a comparable emphasis on the role of the historian, colorful Idealist speech ("brute nature," "representations"), an explicit contrast drawn with the Positivist historian's understanding of history, and a skepticism about the status of the "skeletal objectivity" that putatively remains when "a history" has been "despoiled" of the historian's reconstruction of it. In Gentile's view, "there's no *there* there"; only the historian's intuitive and intellective activity creates historical reality.

Idealism and Pedagogy[84]

Consonant with the greater Gentilean emphasis on the dynamic act of thinking, there are attendant implications for pedagogy, consistent with the distinction

---

[80]For assistance on this point, I am indebted to Professor Della Seta.

[81]Celenza, *Lost Italian Renaissance*, 20–21.

[82]Collins, *Sociology of Philosophies*, 684, quoting Gentile, *The Theory of Mind as Pure Act*, trans. by H. Wildon Carr, 10.

[83]Gentile, *Teoria generale dello spirito come atto puro*, trans. by H. Wildon Carr as *The Theory of Mind as Pure Act*.

[84]For more on Idealist theories of pedagogy, see my "*Scena 1.ª Famiglia* (1908–24)," where I summarize some of the Gentilean reforms of secondary education. See also Renzo Titone, "The Development of Italian Educational Philosophy in the 20th Century," *International Review of Education / Internationale Zeitschrift für Erziehungswissenschaft / Revue Internationale de l'Education* 4 (1958): 313–26.

between the more "kinetic" (Gentilean) and "static" (Crocean) constructions of Idealism.

Gentile's relationship to the Fascist political order afforded him the opportunity to translate his philosophy into concrete initiatives, precisely during Pirrotta's student days, and in Giacomo Rinaldi's words "an undeniably original, creative development of Gentile's thought with respect to Hegel's is . . . to be found in his pedagogical theory." In 1922, the Italian Parliament authorized the Fascist government to undertake educational reforms, which were put into effect the following year. Some had been anticipated by Gentile's immediate predecessor,[85] but there were others introduced by Gentile: the study of Latin was to receive increased prominence, not only in the *liceo*—whose curriculum was already decidedly classicistic—but also in the technical schools.

The range of pedagogical techniques was extended and modified: Latin was to be taught in such a way as to reveal what lay behind the text, not simply according to the particularities of grammatical rules.[86] Norberto Bobbio has described this sensibility as reflective of Gentile's "critique of the moribund, bookish" instructional methodologies previously employed in the Italian secondary school.[87]

Moreover, whereas Positivism had stimulated scientific experimentation in educational practice, Idealism eliminated scientific influences as incompatible with principles that celebrated the dignity of pure thought. In Gentile's view, true cultural "formation" consisted solely of that which the human mind creates, and it was therefore humanistic in nature. Thus even in the grammar schools, pupils were fed a substantial diet of art and religion, and in the *liceo* they were encouraged to undertake their own "philosophizing"; there, history, philosophy, and the history of philosophy were synthesized, and the curriculum characterized above all by the study of the development of human thought and culture throughout history.[88] Scientific or technological cognition were thought to possess value only insofar as they constituted a useful means to spiritual formation.

We should bear this last, quintessentially Gentilean position in mind, which I believe is congruent with Pirrotta's own; such Idealist sensibilities are even expressed in one of Pirrotta's most vivid, most resonant metaphors:

> No human rational process can ever be totally free of emotional elements—not even the computer's, for the monster "feeds" on human blood.[89]

But there was considerably more to the nexus of Idealism and pedagogy. Gentile supplemented his defense of nontechnical, "universalist" curricular

---

[85]As suggested in my "*Scena 1.ª*"; see, in addition, Celenza, *Lost Italian Renaissance*, 22.
[86]Celenza, *Lost Italian Renaissance*, 22.
[87]Bobbio, *Ideological Profile of Twentieth-Century Italy*, 125 (see "*Scena 2.ª*," n. 67).
[88]Titone, "Development of Italian Educational Philosophy," 317.
[89]**1965**: "Dante *musicus*," 19.

content with a spiritualistic conception of the teacher–pupil relationship,[90] Idealist in inspiration and character. In Renzo Titone's words, education was understood as the inner unfolding of the self, by and in the self: education was self-education. Accordingly, and most important, the duality of the teacher–pupil relationship was obliterated. In Rinaldi's formulation, the dialectical oppositions traditionally assumed as characteristic of educational activity are the pupil's subjectivity and science's objectivity, embodied in the person of the teacher. So long as these two terms of the relation remained in the form of mutual exclusion, no real progress in the pupil's spiritual development can occur. Rather, it was necessary that the pupil convert the teacher's objectivity into his or her own self-consciousness, becoming his or her own teacher. In Gentile's words, the pupil learns "and throbs and lives in the teacher's word, as if he heard a voice sound in it that bursts out from the inwardness of his own being." Genuine knowing is never mere passive learning but the pupil's free spiritual creation of knowledge.

Anyone familiar with Pirrotta's career will know of his autodidacticism, which I relate in part to the influence of Gentile's theories of pedagogy, gaining currency when Pirrotta was at a critical juncture in his own development, as he was completing secondary school and beginning university education. He writes of autodidacticism more than once, in terms that suggest his admiration for the autodidact.[91]

Idealism and Nationalism[92]

Finally, there are resonances of nationalism in the Idealist program, again not surprisingly, given the relationship of the two greatest figures of twentieth-century Italian Idealism to their nation's political order.

However, the relationship of nationalist sentiment and Italian philosophy has a longer history still. As one of the consequences of nineteenth-century

---

[90]Bobbio, *Ideological Profile of Twentieth-Century Italy*, 125 (see "Scena 2.$\underline{\text{a}}$," n. 67).

[91]**1982:** "Malipiero," **1954:** "Compiti," **1952:** "Biblioteche." The celebration of autodidacticism seems to have had a pan-European dimension in the early-twentieth century. See, for example, "Children's Reading. I–II," in Sir Arthur Quiller-Couch, *On the Art of Reading* (Cambridge: University Press, 1920), where Quiller-Couch writes that "The meaning of 'education' is a leading-out, a drawing forth; not an *imposition* of something on somebody . . . upon the child; but the eliciting of what is within him." Quiller-Couch seems to have derived his ideas from Edmond Holmes, whom he references in his lectures: see Holmes, *What Is and What Might Be. A Study of Education in General and Elementary Education in Particular* (London: Constable & Co., 1911), especially his Preface and Chapter 1. For these observations and references, I am very grateful to Dr. Sabine Eiche.

[92]On the relationship between Idealism and the early twentieth-century Italian political order, see Randall Collins, *Sociology of Philosophies*, 685, as well as the other texts cited here. See also James Hankins, "Two Twentieth-Century Interpreters" (see "Scena 2.$\underline{\text{a}}$," n. 85), where Hankins writes that the "nationalistic bias in the Italian study of humanism continued under Benedetto Croce and Giovanni Gentile." See also my "Scena 3.$\underline{\text{a}}$ Palermo (1931–36)" on Bertoni's Idealist philosophy of language, where the nationalist cast of his philosophy is discussed.

nationalist fervor, both Germany and Italy—significantly, the two European nations most recently unified—perceived a role for philosophical activity in constructing national identity.[93] Indeed, the very notion that philosophy as an enterprise was not universal (as, for example, is geometry) but could have a national character is to some extent a product of that moment in European history. Bernardo Spaventa, Croce's uncle, wrote that, "it is a natural phenomenon that a free people should find its fullest self-expression in the thought of its philosophers."

For Gentile, the state was an ethical entity, a doctrine derived from Hegel, for whom the state was a global expression of "the Spirit." The congruence with Gentile's "Actual Idealism" more generally is obvious: "[t]he state . . . is a reality, a real, ethical activity, which does not *discourse* about itself, but affirms itself, *realizes* itself perennially";[94] nations were considered tangible manifestations of the Spirit.[95]

Croce, too, argued that, "the struggles of states—wars—are *divine actions*" and that "we individuals must accept . . . and submit to them."

None of this is to suggest an identity of Idealism and Nationalism, by any means. Historical writings (including music-historical writings) that were Positivistic in tone and method could just as easily contain pronounced nationalist elements. My objective here was simply to elucidate some interconnections between Idealism and Nationalism, without implying that there was anything more to the relationship between them.

Spiritualist Reactions: Giovanni Vailati and Pragmatism in Italy

There were other spiritualist reactions to the philosophical debates of early-twentieth-century Italy. The American philosophy of Pragmatism, identified above all with William James, had its Italian iteration, represented by the important work of Giovanni Vailati and Mario Calderoni, among others.[96] James wrote of the Italian Pragmatist movement:

---

[93]On this entire subject, see Marcel Grilli, "The Nationality of Philosophy and Bertrando Spaventa," *Journal of the History of Ideas* 2 (1941): 339–71. Also, see Hankins, "Two Twentieth-Century Interpreters" (see "*Scena 2.ª*," n. 85), where Hankins writes of Spaventa's "concern . . . to defend the honor of Italy by establishing the priority and genetic relationship of Italian philosophy to modern thought."

[94]Bobbio, *Ideological Profile of Twentieth-Century Italy*, 126–28 (see "*Scena 2.ª*," n. 67).

[95]Celenza, *Lost Italian Renaissance*, 23.

[96]See the very important collection of essays: Giovanni Vailati, *Logic and Pragmatism*. A synopsis of Vailati's species of Pragmatism is on p. lxxiii; for fuller treatments, see essay no. 18 and essay no. 19 in the collection. One of the ways in which the Pragmatism of Vailati in particular is expressive of the assault on Positivism is Vailati's thesis that not only can history not be subsumed under science, but that science itself does not proceed as it purports to proceed, and does not attain what it purports to attain; even science is historically contingent. Rather than history being a science, therefore, science is itself to be subject to historicist interpretation. See Vailati, *Logic and Pragmatism*, xxxi and especially xxxix.

> Pragmatism, according to Papini, is . . . only a collection of attitudes and methods, and its chief characterisic is its armed neutrality in the midst of doctrines. . . . [W]hat pragmatism has always meant to him is the necessity of enlarging our means of action, the vanity of the universal as such, the bringing of our spiritual powers into use, and the need of making the world over instead of merely standing by and contemplating it. It *inspires human activity*, in short, differently from other philosophies. . . . Instead of affirming with the positivists that we must render the ideal world as similar as possible to the actual, . . . Papini emphasizes our duty of turning the actual world into as close a copy of the ideal as it will let us.[97]

Even this abbreviated consideration of Italian Pragmatism suggests its relationship to Pirrotta's intellectual constitution: His impatience with excessive philosophizing, his own "pragmatism" and eclecticism in the methodologies adopted, his penchant for action and corresponding refusal to be paralyzed by the fragilities and uncertainties of Positivistic scholarship.

Spiritualist Reactions: "The Forces of the Irrational"[98]

Giuseppe Prezzolini and Giovanni Papini

In Italian intellectual life at the beginning of the twentieth century, the opposition to Positivism was common to all the various spiritualist strains. They were characterized by a call for a return to the inner life and an appeal to the profundity of the soul over the presumptions of the intellect.[99] The most exaggerated spiritualist reaction—and for that reason, the most colorful and clearly presented and apprehended—was the philosophy of Giovanni Papini.[100]

Papini's prose portrays the contrasts and oppositions in contemporary Italian philosophical life. The privileged philosophy of the moment—Positivism—was deemed a philosophy "of . . . spineless dullards," the Positivists pretending "to be . . . registrars of a reality duly witnessed," as if reality were not an active construction of the mind but a phenomenon merely to be registered: dispassionately witnessed and disinterestedly attested. Idealism, on the contrary, questioned the very existence of matter and asserted the absolute priority of the mind. And Papini acknowledges his allegiance to American Pragmatist philosophy:

> A philosophy of action, a philosophy of doing, of rebuilding, transforming, creating! . . . The *true* is the *useful*. To *know* is to *do*. . . . If something is not true but

---

[97]James, "G. Papini and the Pragmatist Movement in Italy," 339.
[98]My subtitle for this section is borrowed from Bobbio.
[99]Bobbio, *Ideological Profile of Twentieth-Century Italy*, 33–34 (see "Scena 2.$\underline{a}$," n. 67).
[100]See also my chapter on Pirrotta's student days, specifically the sections on his years at the University of Florence and on the "Giubbe Rosse" café.

we wish it were true, we will *make* it true: by *faith*. A gospel of power, a gospel of courage, a practical, an optimistic, an *American* gospel!.... Away with metaphysics!... We must have a tool-philosophy, a hammer-and-anvil idea, a theory that produces, a practical promotion and exploitation of spirit! Taken in this way in a somewhat lyrical tone, and duly exaggerated, of course, pragmatism was an inspiration to me.[101]

Irrationalism's assault on Positivism was a consequence of the latter's abstract intellectualism and its unexamined faith in reform through science.[102]

Fabrizio Della Seta has suggested that these "irrationalist" forces may be a source for particular passages in Pirrotta's writings where he manifests "an immediate, almost instinctive, relationship to the sonorous material." Della Seta asks: "An intuitive, almost mystic Pirrotta? I do not want to be pushed very far in that direction," although Pirrotta himself makes reference to a tension within him between two opposing tendencies, experienced when first studying the Gregorian chant: between the mystical mode of apprehension and the philological.[103]

Economic Materialism

Antonio Labriola

Antonio Labriola was the foremost Italian exponent of a Marxist theory of history. The Marxist patrimony of Labriola's variant of Economic Materialism is acknowledged by Labriola himself in any number of representative texts.

In this matter, as in all others thus far, it is important to qualify that Labriola's thought, which represents a well-delineated historical–philosophical position, need not have influenced Pirrotta directly. Indeed, in this instance particularly, Pirrotta's references to the relationship between the arts and the social–economic context are more generic, owing as much to the arguments of Hippolyte Taine, for example. In quoting from Labriola, I intend simply to convey something of the nature of the Materialist argument.

The paradigmatic text is Labriola's *La concezione materialistica della storia* (*The Materialistic Conception of History*).[104] The principal conclusions to be drawn from a reading pertain not only to the questions with which he concerns

---

[101]Papini, *The Failure*, 204–05.
[102]Bobbio, *Ideological Profile of Twentieth-Century Italy*, 69 (see "Scena 2.ª," n. 67).
[103]**1972**: "Ars musica." I return to a fuller consideration of this interesting article in my "Scena 8.ª. The Università degli Studi di Roma, «La Sapienza» (1972–78)." For Della Seta's remarks, see his "Storia, filologia e gusto musicale: rileggendo i primi scritti di Pirrotta" (see "Scena 3.ª," n. 36).
[104]Labriola, *Essays on the Materialistic Conception of History*, trans. Charles H. Kerr (New York: Cosimo, 2005); translation of *La concezione materialistica della storia*, which I consulted in the following edition: ed. and with an intro. by Eugenio Garin (Bari: G. Laterza, 1965).

himself but also (once more) to a revealing *linguaggio:* the all-important terms in the Materialist's lexicon, such as "conditions" ("material conditions," "social conditions," "historical conditions"), "circumstanced," and "environment." Pirrotta regularly uses these terms, and he regularly employs Materialist causal explanations for any number of music-historical phenomena.

In Norberto Bobbio's formulation, Labriola

> attacked both idealist historians, who thought history could be written by approaching historical events from . . . men's ideas, not from their socioeconomic relations . . . , and positivist historians, who had chosen the right approach—facts—but had failed to find the right compass to guide them through the thickets. . . . That compass was historical materialism. . . . [M]aterialism made possible an objective comprehension of facts . . . —a comprehension . . . made possible by tearing away the wrappings that men's ideas had put around facts.[105]

Note the relationship of Materialism to Positivism: the attempt to extend putatively scientific explanations to matters that lay outside the purview of science per se.

Labriola's fundamental theory in his *Materialistic Conception of History* is stated in a few epigrammatic passages; I draw attention especially to the emphasis on "conditions," "circumstances," and "environment":

> Ideas do not fall from heaven; . . . like the other products of human activity, they are formed in given circumstances ["date circonstanze"], in the . . . fullness of time, through the action of definite needs, thanks to . . . repeated attempts at their satisfaction . . . and by the discovery of such . . . means of proof which are . . . the instruments of their production and . . . elaboration. Even ideas involve a basis of social conditions ["condizioni sociali"]; they have their technique; thought also is a form of work. To rob the one and the other, ideas and thought, of the conditions and environment ["dalle condizioni e dall'ambito"] of their birth and . . . development . . . is to disfigure their nature and . . . meaning. . . . To transport ideas arbitrarily from the basis and . . . historic conditions ["condizioni storiche"] in which they arise to any other basis whatever . . . is like taking the irrational for the basis of reasoning.[106]

This is the essential argument: Thought and ideas are products of Material conditions and circumstances. Labriola elaborates with a more detailed analysis of the dynamic process by which a society's economic substructure initially generates related "practical activity"—"facts of legal-political order," which

---

[105]Bobbio, *Ideological Profile of Twentieth-Century Italy*, 9 (see "Scena 2.ᵃ," n. 67).
[106]Labriola, *Essays on the Materialistic Conception of History*, 158–59.

is a first-order "projection of economic conditions"—and then, ultimately, "art, religion[,] and science."¹⁰⁷

Hippolyte Taine

One celebrated text in which Hyppolyte Taine systematically adumbrates his own stimulating though controversial Materialist theory is his *History of English Literature*, characterized by Alvin Kernan as entailing "[c]osmic theories of art and literature" that are "nominally materialistic," where "literary history" is represented as "turning on climate."¹⁰⁸ And in the *Philosophie de l'art*,¹⁰⁹ Taine writes:

---

¹⁰⁷Labriola, *Essays on the Materialistic Conception of History*, 201, 216-19. There has long been a pronounced Materialist strain in Italian academic discourse, exemplified for many American academics by Robert S. Lopez, who left his native Italy and taught for more than three decades at Yale University. Lopez observed that "in the mediocre Latin that humanists reproached to medieval writers, 'primum vivere, deinde philosophari'; that is, artists have to eat, buildings need foundations, and while any style can rest on any foundation, size and solidity depend largely on the economic groundwork" (Lopez, *The Three Ages of the Italian Renaissance* [Boston: Little, Brown, 1970], 3.) In a series of classic publications, Lopez and his pupils—especially Harry A. Miskimin—sought to explain the complicated, even counterintuitive nature of the relationship of economic circumstance and the Material infrastructure to the extraordinary artistic achievements of the Italian Renaissance. See, in addition to Lopez's *Three Ages*, his classic "Hard Times and Investment in Culture" in Roland H. Bainton et al., *The Renaissance: Six Essays* (New York: Harper & Row, 1953), 29–54; Miskimin's *The Economy of Later Renaissance Europe, 1400–1600* (New York: Cambridge University Press, 1977), his "Agenda for Early Modern Economic History," *Journal of Economic History* (1971): 172–83; and Lopez and Miskimin's classic, coauthored "The Economic Depression of the Renaissance," *Economic History Review* (1962): 408–25; Carlo M. Cipolla's response; Lopez's response to Cipolla, "Economic Depression of the Renaissance? II," and Miskimin's response to Cipolla, "Economic Depression of the Renaissance? III," these two last both in *Economic History Review* (1964): 525–27 and 528–29.

Art historians likeliest to be familiar with Pirrotta's writings and interested in them will know, of course, of one of their discipline's most stimulating essays, Michael Baxandall's *Painting and Experience in Fifteenth Century Italy* (London: Oxford University Press, 1972), whose Materialist sensibility is expressed in its subtitle (*A Primer in the Social History of Pictorial Style*) and opening paragraph (p. 1): "[a] fifteenth-century painting is the deposit of a *social* relationship. On one side there was a painter.... On the other... there was somebody else who asked him to make it, *provided funds for him to make it* and, after he had made it, reckoned on using it in some way or other. Both parties worked within institutions and conventions—*commercial*, religious, perceptual, *in the widest sense social*—that were different from ours and influenced the forms of what they together made [emphases added]."

Materialist explanations are even invoked in the work of scholars like Alvin Kernan, otherwise resolutely non-Materialist in his formation: *The Death of Literature* (New Haven: Yale University Press, 1990).

¹⁰⁸H.A. Taine, *History of English Literature*, trans. H. Van Laun, 2 vols. (Philadelphia: David McKay, 1908). See Kernan, *The Death of Literature*, 9. It is worth noting that Giovanni Papini, whom we have quoted extensively, makes reference in *The Failure* to his one-time esteem for Taine.

¹⁰⁹Taine, *Philosophie de l'art* (Paris: G. Baillière, 1865), 16–17: "De même qu'il y a une température physique qui, par ses variations, détermine l'apparition de telle ou telle espèce de plantes; de même il y a une température morale qui, par ses variations, détermine l'apparition de telle ou telle espèce d'art. Et de même qu'on étudie la température physique pour comprendre l'apparition de telle ou telle espèce de plantes, ... de même il faut étudier la température morale, pour comprendre l'apparition de telle espèce d'art, ... Les productions de l'esprit humain, comme celles de la nature vivante, ne s'expliquent que par leur milieu." Taine's *Philosophie* was translated by John Durand as *Lectures on Art* (New York: Henry Holt, 1875); the quoted passage is on pp. 34–35.

> Just as there is a physical temperature, which by its variations determines the appearance of this or that species of plant, so there is a moral temperature, which by its variations determines the appearance of this or that species of art. And as we study the physical temperature in order to comprehend the advent of this or that species of plants, . . . so is it necessary to study the moral temperature in order to comprehend the advent of various phases of art, . . . The productions of the human mind, like those of animated nature, can only be explained by their *milieu*.

That these theories had currency in Italy by the time Pirrotta was at the university is documented by such texts as the following:

> Every work of art . . . is in some way the product of subjective and objective elements, and in determining its nature . . . the mind and spirit of the artist, on the one hand, contribute, [and], on the other, that sum of external circumstances that we, with an entirely new word, shall call the "ambiente."[110]

However, Pirrotta's own invocation of the Materialists' explanations is not as indiscriminate; on the contrary, he applied Materialist explanations selectively, in a restrained, circumspect manner.

AMERICAN MUSICOLOGY IN THE 1950S, '60S, AND '70S: HISTORY AS SCIENCE?

One apprehends the distinctive character of Pirrotta's thought especially when juxtaposed against that of other musicologists active in American universities during the 1950s, '60s, and '70s, when many of Pirrotta's English-language publications appeared. Indeed, it was a result of reading Pirrotta's publications against that background that I first became aware of and interested in the distinctiveness of his thought and first (unconsciously) contemplated this attempt to explain it systematically. I now consider that background.

In chapter 2—"Musicology and Positivism: The Postwar Years"—of his important and provocative *Contemplating Music*, Joseph Kerman describes postwar "Anglo-Saxon musicology" and its general adherence to a distinctive sensibility.[111] Phrases invoked to characterize its program include "postwar

---

[110]"Ogni opera d'arte...è in qualche modo il prodotto di elementi soggettivi ed oggettivi, e a determinarne la natura . . . contribuiscono da una parte la mente e l'anima dell'artista, dall'altra quella somma di circostanze esterne che noi, con parola novissima, chiamiamo l'ambiente." Leo Spitzer, "Milieu and Ambiance: An Essay in Historical Semantics," *Philosophy and Phenomenological Research* 3, no. 1 (September 1942): 1–42; and 3, no. 2 (December 1942): 169–218, especially 3, no. 2, 201, quoting Foffano, *Il poema cavalleresco* II, 3 (1904). Spitzer's excellent article deserves the most careful reading.

[111]Kerman, *Contemplating Music* (see "*Prologo*," n. 38). For Pirrotta's own synopsis of Kerman's argument, see his **1992**: "Contemplando la musa assente."

neopositivism in musicology"[112] and "the neopositivistic theory of music history,"[113] and Kerman's phraseology—like one of the principal documents he cites to substantiate his argument[114]—link Anglo-American musicology of the 1950s and later to the larger tradition of twentieth-century logical Positivism, which sought to extend the epistemology and methodology of science to other realms of knowledge.

There is a relationship to the Positivist philosophy of the nineteenth century, as the identity of nomenclature itself suggests. The epistemology underlying the two iterations of Positivism was similar: Both were typified by what the Idealists ridiculed as the worship of fact, as "an . . . ingenuous adoration of raw facts"; and both made science the model for other forms of knowledge, including historical knowledge.[115] Both placed a premium on observation; both subscribed to convictions about the intrinsic reality of matter (or the datum, including the historical datum) and the value of sense experience; both rejected metaphysical Idealism, with its transcendent entities.

Kerman characterized "postwar neopositivism in musicology" as marked by an

> emphasis . . . heavily on fact. New manuscripts were discovered and described, archives were reported on, dates were established, *cantus firmi* traced from one work and one composer to another. Musicologists dealt mainly in the verifiable, the objective, the uncontroversial, and the positive.[116]

Its privileged methods were "philological,"[117] and the undertaking was "conspicuously long on 'hard' information and short on interpretation."[118] Note especially Kerman's invocation of the term "the verifiable."

An important document substantiating Kerman's argument was Arthur Mendel's influential address "Evidence and Explanation," delivered at the 1961 meeting of the International Musicological Society, which, according to Kerman, "became a sort of musicological credo for many in the 1960s."[119] Mendel's argument, as he himself acknowledged, was heavily dependent

---

[112] Kerman, *Contemplating Music*, 50 (see "*Prologo*," n. 38).

[113] Kerman, *Contemplating Music*, 55 (see "*Prologo*," n. 38).

[114] Arthur Mendel's "Evidence and Explanation."

[115] For these formulations, see the all-important work of Bobbio, *Ideological Profile of Twentieth-Century Italy*, 7, 70, 81 (see "*Scena 2.ª*," n. 67).

[116] Kerman, *Contemplating Music*, 42 (see "*Prologo*," n. 38).

[117] Kerman, *Contemplating Music*, 50 (see "*Prologo*," n. 38).

[118] Kerman, *Contemplating Music*, 44 (see "*Prologo*," n. 38).

[119] Mendel, "First Public Address. Evidence and Explanation," International Musicological Society/Internationale Gesellschaft für Musikwissenschaft/Société Internationale de Musicologie, *Report of the Eighth Congress. New York 1961*, ed. Jan LaRue, 2 vols. Published for the International Musicological Society by the American Musicological Society (Basel, London, New York: Bärenreiter Kassel, 1961), vol. 2—"Reports," 3–18. The quotation from Kerman is at p. 31.

on the writings of his Princeton University colleague, the philosopher Carl G. Hempel.[120]

Ultimately, the question is whether history can be subsumed under science, or, to state it differently, whether the epistemology and procedures of science can be extended successfully to other disciplines, specifically history. Hempel was one of the most prominent members of the so-called "Vienna school," a circle of logical positivists, many of whom had had formal scientific training and were keenly interested in the question of "demarcation": of delimiting what science is and what it is not, of defining its limits and determining the criteria for doing so. Hempel was one of the more liberal members of that school, in that he was more willing than others to subsume other disciplines under science. The principal criterion for doing so convincingly was the existence of laws: for a discipline to be justifiably classified as a science, one had to be able to postulate laws. Thus the importance to Hempel, and to Mendel, of "General Laws in History."

For the logical empiricists or logical positivists of the Vienna circle, scientific activity enjoyed the status of paragon of rational activity. Experience and empirical evidence were the bases on which to determine truth or falsity. The criterion was verifiability (note the alignment with Kerman's characterization of Anglo-American musicology of the 1950s, '60s, and '70s[121]); arguments were to be tested against evidence. In that respect, the position of the logical positivists contrasted clearly with that of Idealist metaphysicians.

For historical musicologists, the urgent question is the extent to which such an epistemology and such principles can also characterize the (music) historical enterprise. Is history simply too different to be subsumed under science? Do historical explanations, knowingly or not, privilege one a priori assumption or another and thus render the enterprise too unlike science to be subsumed under it? Hempel—and, to some extent, Mendel, following Hempel—argued for a relationship between the two. Alternatively, Michael Oakeshott, for example, argued that these are fundamentally different intellectual programs:[122]

> In scientific experience, . . . it is possible to circumscribe and analyse both the antecedent and . . . consequent situations and . . . determine which elements of the

---

[120]Especially "The Function of General Laws in History," *Journal of Philosophy* 39, no. 2 (15 January 1942): 35–48. For assistance on Hempel's philosophy, I am grateful to his pupil Paul Benacerraf, Professor Emeritus of Philosophy at Princeton University.

[121]See Sven Ove Hansson, "Science and Pseudo-Science," *Stanford Encyclopedia of Philosophy* (fall 2008 ed.), ed. Edward N. Zalta, URL = http://plato.stanford.edu/archives/fall2008/entries/pseudo-science on the "various verificationist approaches to science" of the "logical positivists of the Vienna Circle": "The basic idea was that a scientific statement could be distinguished from a metaphysical statement by being at least in principle possible to verify."

[122]Oakeshott, "Historical Continuity and Causal Analysis," in *Philosophical Analysis and History*, ed. William H. Dray (New York: Harper & Row, 1966), 193–212.

latter were caused by which elements of the former, but in history this is impossible—not . . . because the evidence is insufficient . . . but because the presuppositions of historical thought forbid it. . . . A cause in scientific experience is . . . a form of explanation foreign to historical experience; and it is possible in science only because the world of scientific experience is a world, not of events[,] but of instances.

Further, history is a construction of the historian, dependent on assumptions:

No course of historical events exists until it has been constructed by historical thought, and it cannot be constructed without some presupposition about the character of the relation between events.

And for that reason, and others, the invocation of cause-and-effect explanations, for example, though perhaps appropriate in science, are inapplicable in history:

the only explanation of change relevant or possible in history is simply a complete account of change. History accounts *for* change by means of a full account *of* change. The relation *between* events is always other events, and it is established in history by a full relation *of* the events. The conception of cause is thus replaced by the exhibition of a world of events intrinsically related to one another in which no *lacuna* is tolerated. To see all the degrees of change is to be in possession of a world of facts which calls for no further explanation. History, then, neither leaves change unexplained, nor attempts to explain it by an appeal to some external reason or universal cause: it is the narration of a course of events which, in so far as it is without serious interruption, explains itself. . . . And the method of the historian is never to explain by means of generalization but always by means of greater and more complete detail. . . . The historian . . . is like the novelist whose characters . . . are presented in such detail and with such coherence that additional explanation of their actions is superfluous.

Therefore, is there simply too great a difference between the primary material that is the object of scientific inquiry—"matter"—and that which is the basis of historical inquiry—"the historical datum"—for the latter to be subsumed under the former? Is the distinction between "natural" and "human kinds"[123] simply too great for there to be genuine similarities in how they are approached and in the most efficacious means of apprehending them?[124] Ultimately, is

---

[123]For this distinction, see Ian Hacking, *Rewriting the Soul: Multiple Personality and the Sciences of Memory* (Princeton, NJ: Princeton University Press, 1995).

[124]For the Italian Pragmatists' special understanding of the debate concerning the nature of history, see my discussion above, and also Giovanni Vailati, *Logic and Pragmatism*, xxxix and all of essay no. 6 in that collection. Vailati writes of "the ever re-emerging disagreements on the characteristics that distinguish the historical sciences . . . from the strictly physical or natural sciences. . . . These notes refer mainly to the restrictions and precautions which should accompany, in the historical and social sciences, the use of the concepts of 'law' and of 'cause and effect,' as they are used in the natural sciences. It is still frequently debated whether we can speak of 'historical laws' in the same sense as we speak, for example, of physical or chemical laws, and whether to research them is the task of the historian, or whether a historian should keep to simple description and documentation of facts and to the critique of the respective testimonies."

history simply more an art than a science? Is there anything that links these two intellectual programs other than that both are "part of the same human endeavour, namely systematic and critical investigations aimed at acquiring the best possible understanding of the workings of nature, man, and human society," anything more than "an intellectual environment of collective rationality and mutual criticism"?[125]

*****

Reduced to its essence, my argument is that Nino Pirrotta's scholarly persona and authorial voice began to be formed when reactions to nineteenth-century Positivism were especially sharp; to some extent, his formation reveals the effects of the contemporary debate, and specifically the various critical spiritualist responses to nineteenth-century Positivism. Then, especially when apprehended against the backdrop of twentieth-century Positivism (or a particular iteration of it, "the neopositivistic theory of music history"), his writings reveal the influences of that earlier debate, in the periodic invocation of a contrasting epistemology and intellectual sensibility, whose target was Positivism (and its alleged deficiencies), whether its nineteenth- or twentieth-century manifestation. In Pirrotta's practice of musicology, there is a gentle inflection of what is otherwise a Positivistic (or neo-Positivistic) undertaking with elements of Idealism: the intuitive theory of knowledge; a colorful, spiritual word-usage; the refutation of genre. Pirrotta's fundamental epistemology was Positivistic (although it cannot be described as unidimensionally so), whereas other matters such as the questions he poses and his capacity and proclivity for vivid narration are instead consonant with the traditions of Italian Idealism. He positioned himself between—or alongside, or above—these various traditions and capitulated fully to none of them.

PIRROTTA'S INTELLECTUAL PROFILE, II[126]

Already in his journalistic writings (1933–35), Pirrotta reveals a sensitivity to the varied moods and methodologies of contemporary Italian philosophical

---

[125]Sven Ove Hansson, "Science and Pseudo-Science."

[126]On the general question of the reflections in Pirrotta's intellectual profile of these various traditions within Italian thought, I have benefitted, once again, from the writings of Fabrizio Della Seta (*Dottore in lettere*, Università degli studi di Roma, «La Sapienza», 1975), in particular Della Seta's "Storia, filologia e gusto musicale: rileggendo i primi scritti di Pirrotta" (see "*Scena 3.ª*," n. 36). Specifically, Della Seta makes the important observation that the resonances of Idealism detected in Pirrotta's writings are best described as the result of "a generic influence on Pirrotta's thought ['un'influenza ... generica sul pensiero di Pirrotta']," a characterization with which I am in complete agreement. I am grateful to Professor Della Seta for having made the text of his contribution to the conference proceedings available to me prior to its publication. Also very useful were the writings of Ellen Rosand (A.M. Harvard University 1964), especially her review of the anthology of Pirrotta's essays in the *Journal of the American Musicological Society*.

discourse. In one of his critical pieces, he contrasts the approaches of two biographers of Gioachino Rossini[127] and discloses his preferences; he is impatient with would-be Scientific–Materialist explanations for Rossini's character and seeks explanations instead in the external environment:

> The other profile is the work of a critic [Giulio Fara] who refuted the first, seeking the blood and color of the man and the artist behind the golden appearance of the idol; however, he lapses into sin, abandoning himself to illusory objectivity in a materialist conception by means of an exercise in pseudoscientific method.... Under a halo of rigorous scientific spirit, Fara took his point of departure methodically from Gioacchino's father, Giuseppe Rossini.

For Pirrotta, the more compelling explanation identifies "[n]ot constitutional causes" but sees Rossini rather as "the product of a complex of determinative exterior circumstances."[128]

Not infrequently in his writings, Pirrotta reveals his self-positioning. When he becomes conversational and autobiographical, he shows his hand:

> Musicology... is modeled... after the... name of philology. But whoever invented the older name set the accent on love—love of beauty in speech; every subsequent derivation has emphasized instead the *logos* component, with inelegant verbosity and, in the name of objectivity, ... a detached, almost aggressive attitude toward its purported subject ["in nome di obiettività, un atteggiamento di distacco, o addirittura di aggressività verso l'oggetto prescelto"[129]].... I can think of Musicology only as a maiden, whose secret love for no lesser deity than Apollo will never have a chance until she gets rid of her heavy glasses, technical jargon, and businesslike approach and assumes a gentler, more humanistic manner ["i pesanti occhialoni, il gergo tecnico, il tono burocratico, e non assuma un contegno piú gentile e umanistico"].[130] To be fair to ... Musicology, ... the magnifying glasses, the analytical approach, even statistics, are at present indispensable tools to her work. She acquired her status among the historical disciplines as late as the second half of the last century, at which time ... euphoric generalizations and rationalizations were made, quite often on the basis of only scanty documentary evidence. Musicology and musicologists are still reacting to those generalizations,

---

[127]Giulio Fara, *Genio e ingegno musicale, Gioachino Rossini* (Turin: Fratelli Bocca, 1915); and Giuseppe Radiciotti, *Gioacchino Rossini: vita documentata, opere ed influenza su l'arte*, 3 vols. (Tivoli: Arti grafiche Majella di Aldo Chicca, 1927–29), 1: «Primi anni e studi»; 2: «Nel mondo dell'arte»; 3: «L'uomo».

[128]See Cummings and Eiche, "Nino Pirrotta's Early Music-Critical Writings" (see "*Scena 1.ª*," n. 69), the critical piece dated 14–25 September 1934 (No. XII).

[129]This particular sub-passage was quoted by Oliver Strunk as emblematic of Pirrotta's manner of presentation; see Strunk, "A Letter from a Friend," *Rivista italiana di musicologia* 10 (1975): 8–9. The entire passage has been quoted by Fabrizio Della Seta ("Appunti per un ritratto intellettuale di Nino Pirrotta" [see "*Prologo*," n. 36]) as expressive of Pirrotta's fundamental scholarly sensibility, and, as he suggested to me in private conversation, it is the key to understanding that sensibility.

[130]The *linguaggio* of the two preceding sentences is almost reminiscent of Prezzolini's "irrationalist" formulation: "Positivism, erudition, verist art, historical method.... —all this stink...; all this screeching of machines, this commercial busyness, this noise."

and that is why we are so strictly bound to the document, ... It is refreshing, then, to raise my head from the microfilm reader, ... Only through conjectural work ["un lavorio di congetture"], taking leave for a while from my lady Musicology's stern rule of objectivity ["norme severe"], is it possible for me to suggest[131] that a connection existed between the creative impulse of the stil novo and the quickening activity of the Ars nova.

Musicology is thus an Apollonian, humanistic undertaking, and its (misplaced) emphasis on the Greek word "logos" has inadvertently—and erroneously—located it among those scientific or social-scientific disciplines that employ the same Greek word (psychology, anthropology, sociology), a development that Pirrotta views wistfully. All the same, he recognizes that the "euphoric generalizations and rationalizations" of the first generation of musicologists demand qualification; and, so, the practitioners of our discipline spent (and spend) significant amounts of time at the microfilm reader, as a result of which we wear heavy glasses and have adopted technical jargon, an analytical approach, even statistical methods, all of which are currently indispensable to fulfilling the discipline's mission.[132] And yet, Pirrotta wishes there to be room for [Idealist] conjecture and occasional leave-taking from the discipline's "severe norms" of [Positivistic] objectivity.[133]

There is always an oscillation in Pirrotta's sensibilities, which he references in ironic language. In the Festschrift for A. Tillman Merritt, he writes:

> I have been indulging in a nostalgic feeling for one aspect of my native island's past that is in the process of being irretrievably erased by the wave of modernization. But my offering such an exotic bouquet may also have some less morbid and more scholarly reasons, which shall be presently indicated by a sudden plunge of my recording pen from the vibrations of open-air singing to the flat austerity of dusty bibliographical information.

That tension is the source of the difficulty in attempting to classify Pirrotta, who "breaks script." Pirrotta's identity has been differently perceived by different audiences, depending on their cultural formation: many American readers, like me, perceive the Idealist elements in his temperament, whereas on his return to Italy in 1972, his Italian colleagues and pupils perceived him as more Positivist (though they may not have used that term).

---

[131]For Pirrotta's original "mi è possibile suggerire," which his translator translated as "I can suggest," I offer the alternative translation given here.

[132]See also Lewis Lockwood's "The Study of Music at University," 783, 785–87 (see "*Scena 3.ª,*" n. 64), where Lockwood writes of "techniques" that "may seem extraneous and diversionary to those whose primary view of music is an immediate experience," but "are obviously essential if the study of music of the past is to consist not of myth and hearsay but of well documented and carefully structured expositions of the fabric of music history."

[133]For an evocation and critical consideration of Pirrotta's Apollonian metaphor, especially its gendered elements, and its echoes in the writings of Leo Treitler, see Susan McClary, "*Music and the Historical Imagination by Leo Treitler,*" *Notes*, 2nd ser., 48 (1992): 838–40.

Pirrotta's cognizance of the potential for careful self-positioning relative to these various philosophies of history is revealed in an atypically explicit reflection; the context is an assessment of Fausto Torrefranca's intellectual profile:

> faith in the richness of the musical gifts of the Italian nation[134] and the artists expressed by it animated him and had always animated him, as well as the conviction that «not so much documents as ideas are the soul of historiography.... True history seeks, without respite, secret propulsive connections between epoch and epoch, school and school, style and style; it seeks and discovers them because it has already thought them»[135]....»The fascinating ideas nonetheless did not impede him from having a profound respect and most notable "nose" for documents.[136]

The Influences of Positivism

By no means did Pirrotta share Idealism's general skepticism about the intrinsic status of the datum. Those conversant with his work will know of its grounding in historical fact, and, more important, of his obvious (though not explicitly referenced) convictions as to the "reality" and independent status of the fact.

Pirrotta affirms the legitimacy of philology as a scholarly methodology and offers such observations in papers he wrote as a librarian; his sensibility thus indeed seems to be partly an expression of his status as librarian, of his professional activity as custodian of the primary sources.

He writes of the launching of "a new inventory of music-historical sources," the "Répertoire international des sources musicales" (RISM), an unequivocally scientific endeavor, suggestive of "a science that has as its duty being exact: bibliography." His predilections are evident in the codicological analyses of the Modena, Lucca, and Panciatichiano manuscripts and the parchment fragment containing compositions of Paolo Tenorista. His fellow Italian academics recognized that "he was guided by an acute understanding of the critical rigor inherent in all serious historical and philological research, acquired by means of a solid secondary and university education."[137]

---

[134]Note the nationalist sensibility.

[135]The Crocean/Gentilean cast to the passage Pirrotta is quoting from Torrefranca is obvious, as is the possibility (though not necessarily the inevitability) of a relationship of such Idealist sensibilities to Nationalism, as is suggested in my previous note. On Torrefranca's complicated Nationalist sensibilities, see Alfred Einstein's review of his *Il segreto del quattrocento* in *Music and Letters* 21 (1940): 392–95, and Carolyn Gianturco's contribution ("2. Italy") to Vincent Duckles et al., "Musicology," *Grove Music Online. Oxford Music Online*, http://0-www.oxfordmusiconline.com.libcat.lafayette.edu/subscriber/article/grove/music/46710pg3 (accessed 2 September 2011).

[136]**1983**: "Introduzione ai lavori."

[137]"Laurea 'honoris causa' a Nino Pirrotta" (see *"Prologo,"* n. 36). See also *"Per un regale evento,"* (see *"Prologo,"* n. 36), which refers to "l'investigazione minuziosa e profonda di qualsiasi argomento gli si presentasse."

But note, too, that for Pirrotta, the value of philology was that "without a rigorous basis of philological verification," the "ultimate objective of aesthetic understanding and evaluation" "cannot be realized with complete legitimacy." Such a justification for philology is reminiscent of the Gentilean philosophy that regarded scientific cognition as valuable only in so far as it constituted a means of spiritual formation. We thus turn to a consideration of the influence of Idealism.[138]

The Influences of Italian Spiritualist Philosophies

Such Positivist predilections as documented here would have been familiar to American scholars of the 1950s and '60s and later. Less familiar were elements of Pirrotta's temperament that reveal the influence of Idealism. Ellen Rosand writes:

> It is not the raw data in his work, such as his discoveries of documents, that requires particularly sophisticated abilities of translation but rather the larger context developed for those discoveries, their place in Pirrotta's view of the past, his attitude toward facts, his way of formulating hypotheses, his process.... His method depends on intuition and conjecture set in to motion by keen observation, on his ability to reconstruct a fuller picture of the past from the meager indications of written signs.

How fully can we substantiate Rosand's observations?

Philosophy of History

In his review of Gentile's *Teoria generale dello spirito come atto puro*, Warner Fite wrote that

> the key to ... modern (Anglo-German) epistemology, from Locke through Kant, might be found by remembering that its typical example of knowing is always the knowing of inanimate things. Hence its characteristic philosophy is...natural science. To understand Croce and Gentile— ... to see why their philosophical *milieu* may seem to us exotic, and thus "mystical"—one must remember that their typical knowing is the knowing of men; ... [T]hat hostility to "intellectualism" ... is the

---

[138]Pirrotta's understanding of the optimal relationship between rigorous philological practices and the ultimate objective of aesthetic appreciation is also suggested by a passage at the opening of **1992:** "Contemplando la musa assente," where he cites Joseph Kerman's *Contemplating Music* (see "*Prologo*," n. 38), a title that had already become iconic in the debate about "positivism" versus "criticism."

The program of Economic Materialism might also be construed as an application and extension of scientific principles to realms of human experience lying beyond science, and Pirrotta's invocation of Materialist explanations might therefore be seen as the exercise of a kind of Positivism, though it is, as suggested, sparing and sensitive. On the Italian Pragmatists' subtler and more nuanced interpretation of the Materialist conception of history, with which Pirrotta's was in some respects aligned, see Giovanni Vailati, *Logic and Pragmatism*, xxxix.

prominent characteristic of philosophies so different as those of . . . Schiller . . . and Gentile. . . . For intellectualism the characteristic feature of mind, or spirit, is knowing; and knowing means in the end something cool, disinterested, passive, merely registrative of given fact, and representative—of something else which is not mind, or spirit; which then becomes the external basis, or condition, of spirit. . . . [I]n Gentile, . . . the typical knowing is . . . of my human fellows. In the larger range this is the task of history—if we regard history, not as a chronicle of events, but as an understanding of the lives of men. . . . How . . . do we know another person? By sympathetic imagination, according to Gentile; or according to Croce . . . , by putting yourself in his place. . . . Gentile . . . tells us that knowing another person means actually living his life.

In an interview in 1987 Pirrotta stated:

The fundamental thing is not to limit onself to connecting one document with another document, one date with another date, one work with another work, but seeking to understand the human reality . . . existing behind the two documents, the two dates, the two or more works. It is a matter of divining the actuality of the distant fact.[139]

The congruence of this sensibility with Idealism could not be clearer.

Pirrotta's sympathy for some elements of the Idealist program, if not its epistemology, is clear from such classic formulations as in the lecture on the commedia dell'arte. The elusive nature of the documentary record requires careful, painstaking, and (above all) imaginative interpretation to recapture the lost historical actuality that spawned it.[140]

But the sympathy for Idealism may be documented more precisely still. As Fite suggested, "this is the task of history— . . . an understanding of the lives of men. . . . How . . . do we know another person? By sympathetic imagination . . . , by putting yourself in his place. . . . Gentile . . . tells us that knowing another person means actually living his life."

In his essay on Malipiero, Pirrotta writes of Malipiero's "full-blown spiritualist ['medianiche'] faculties,[141] his receptivity to the influences of personalities of the past." In the same article, he writes of the Monteverdi correspondence as serving "to infuse all the biographical and critical studies of Monteverdi with a new human warmth."

---

[139]This uncommonly explicit statement, which Fabrizio Della Seta has characterized as "one of the rare occasions in which Pirrotta permitted himself to go to considerations 'of method,'" occurred in the context of an interview on the occasion of the conferring of the *Premio «Viareggio»;* see Duilio Courir, "Pirrotta, un gentilhuomo che smaschera le note," *Corriere della sera* (11 July 1987), 3, as quoted in Della Seta, "Storia, filologia e gusto musicale: rileggendo i primi scritti di Pirrotta" (see "Scena 3.ª," n. 36).

[140]1954: "Commedia dell'Arte e Melodramma."

[141]In this case, I am using the word "spiritualist" not in the Idealist sense, of course, but in an ordinary, familiar sense, as the adjectival form of the noun that is a synonym for "medium" or "psychic." Indeed, Pirrotta's original adjective "medianico" derives from the related Italian noun for "medium."

Pirrotta's own success in exercising that "sympathetic imagination" is documented by responses to his work like the following:

> It is not merely assembling facts that constitutes the goal of scholarship, but rather using facts as the basis for an imaginative re-creation of historical situations and persons. In this respect, Pirrotta's biography of Paolo is exemplary, for it explains the little that is known, while plausibly but undogmatically advancing whatever is 'problematic' or conjectural.[142]

Diction

That Idealist objective of "putting yourself in his place" is typically articulated by means of a particular word, which recurs throughout Gentile's writings—and throughout Pirrotta's. And when revealing choices in parlance align, they suggest a congruence of Pirrotta's Idealist sympathies with Croce's and Gentile's. Gentile wrote that

> whenever we want to understand something which has a spiritual value, . . . we have to regard it not as an object...but rather as something that is identified with our spiritual activity[143] ["anzi come a tal cosa che s'immedesimi con la nostra attività spirituale"]. . . . [W]ith all spiritual reality, you can only know it . . . by resolving it into your own spiritual activity, gradually establishing that self-sameness or unity ["medesimezza o unità"] in which knowledge consists.

Note the use of the reflexive verb "immedesimiarsi" ("to identify oneself with") and the noun "medesimezza" ("sameness, identicality"), both of which are related to the adjective and pronoun "medesimo" ("self, same; himself, herself, itself"). The objective of Idealist historical practice is to achieve a state of spiritual identity or sameness with one's subject. In the essay on Malipiero, Pirrotta writes: "So far did he identify himself with Monteverdi ['In Monteverdi si immedesimò'] as to make of him one of the missions of his life." More revealingly still, in the lecture on "Temperamenti e tendenze nella Camerata fiorentina," Pirrotta writes that "when we attempt to reconstruct a historical period and represent it to ourselves, it proves difficult for us to identify with it" ("quando tentiamo di riscostruire e di rappresentarci un periodo storico, ci riesce difficile immedesimarci in esso");[144] that is, it proves

---

[142]Richard Hoppin, review of **1961**: ed., *Paolo Tenorista in a New Fragment of the Italian Ars Nova*.

[143]For Carr's translation "as something immediately identical with our own spiritual activity," I have substituted the translation given above.

[144]Translated by Nigel Fortune as "Temperaments and Tendencies in the Florentine Camerata," in *Music and Culture in Italy from the Middle Ages to the Baroque. A Collection of Essays* (Cambridge, MA: Harvard University Press, 1984), 217–34 and 418–21. I have modified Fortune's translation considerably, because in employing the translation "to steep ourselves in it," his otherwise excellent translation does not entirely satisfactorily capture the Crocean/Gentilean resonances of the verb "immedesimarsi." Note, too, the use of the verb "to represent," which is also Crocean.

difficult for us to realize fully the Idealist objective of spiritual identity or sameness with the subject.

The imaginative quality of Pirrotta's writings—his success in transporting his readers back to the lost worlds he is imaginatively recreating—are consequences of his ability to identify himself with those worlds.

The Intuitive Mode of Apprehension

The more intuitive mode of apprehending the datum (or the historical fact) serves Idealist historians. Croce asserts in *The Aesthetic* that he was the first to offer a fully developed theory of intuitive knowledge, as contrasted with existing theories of intellectualistic knowledge, which possessed their own time-honored methodology: logic. In addition to demonstrating the character of Idealism, Croce's theory also has a kind of quintessentially Italianate quality to it.

Pirrotta's writings are laced with references to the intuitive (specifically as contrasted with the intellectualistic), and his own mode of inquiry had an intuitive quality to it. However, before proceeding, I introduce two important qualifications. First, Croce's understanding of the terms "intuition" and "intuitive" as employed in *The Aesthetic* is slightly different from the common understanding, though not unrelated to it. Second, their relevance to an analysis of Pirrotta's profile is multidimensional.

With respect to the first: for Croce, an intuition was a distinctive mode of apprehension of mechanistic material, a means of ordering sensation, to be distinguished from the contrasting mode of apprehension, the intellective (or conceptual), which exists on a different level. The special contribution of intuitive activity is in the giving of form, in the expression—or taking possession, or representation—of sensation or material. Therefore, to posit an intuition—which is the essence of Idealist history—is, first, to apprehend historical data intuitively, rather than by means of the scientist's more intellective, conceptual mode (in accordance with the Idealist conviction that the "certainty of history is different from the certainty of science"), and then, by means of the rhetorical mode of narration, to represent the "individual physiognomy" of "particular entities," not to construct the scientist's "concepts," "universals[,] and abstractions." In contrast, our common understanding of the word "intuition"—a special way of knowing; a sixth sense; an instinct or insight not necessarily fully evinced by data—is not unrelated to Croce's understanding, though not perfectly congruent with it.

Second: the intuitive/intellectualistic duality in Pirrotta's thought operates on two different levels. On the one hand, his own way of knowing includes the intuitive (in both the common understanding of that term and the more specific, Crocean understanding), and the duality thus operates on the level of his own epistemological activity. But it also operates on the level of his analysis and presentation of the subject matter per se. That is, the Idealist distinction between the intuitive and the intellectualistic provides Pirrotta with a parlance that he invokes to analyze musical repertories and advance an understanding of stylistic tendencies in the music.[145]

Throughout his career, Pirrotta does not hesitate to offer insights and intuitions, often when the documentary record does not permit (or did not then permit) decisive empirical substantiation; and his success will occasion delighted comment from those familiar with his work. "[W]e ... often ... marvel at how infrequently Pirrotta has been caught off base by the discovery of important new material," wrote one commentator. "[C]andor requires that I remark on the extraordinary consistency with which Pirrotta seems to have all the right answers," wrote another. According to Harold Powers

> [a]nyone working in Italian opera history, particularly though by no means exclusively in its early phases, will sooner or later have benefitted from Nino Pirrotta's work. It is fifteen years or more now since I first started following up suggestions that could only have come through his unique combination of experience, learning, and imagination. . . . In this instance I was launched by one of his suggestions that has also appeared in print.[146]

Powers then cites Pirrotta's conjecture that Alessandro Stradella's *Gare dell'amore* is "almost certainly to be identified with the *Oratio Cocle*," which Powers substantiates by means of empirical evidence: "it is possible to confirm Pirrotta's identification."

Even Pirrotta's signature interest in the unwritten tradition, and in nonmusical evidence of musical practices, is an expression of the intuitive mode of inquiry, since it acknowledges the existence and importance of musical practices even where there is no musical evidence, which it seeks nonetheless to recover and describe. Here traditional philological practices are of limited utility, as Madeleine Biardeau has suggested: "The approach of historical philology will never be suitable for an oral tradition, which has no essential reference to its historical origin."[147]

Concerning the intuitive/intellectualistic duality, Pirrotta will often deploy the terms "intuitive" and "intellectualistic" in his analyses of music, as a

---

[145]Concering the redolent terms "intellectualism" and "intellectualistic," see also what I wrote above when discussing Croce's use of the terms "philologism" and "philologistic."

[146]Powers, "Il «Mutio» tramutato, Part I: Sources and Libretto," in *Venezia e il melodramma nel Seicento*, ed. Maria Teresa Muraro (Florence: L. S. Olschki, 1976), 227–58, especially 228. Powers is referring to Pirrotta's entry on Stradella in the *Enciclopedia dello spettacolo*. Pirrotta returns to Stradella, and to this opera in particular and its identity, in **1966**: "*Alessandro* STRADELLA" and **1982**: "Discorso inaugurale," especially 11.

[147]See Biardeau, as quoted by Wendy Doniger O'Flaherty, *Siva: The Erotic Ascetic* (Oxford: Oxford University Press, 1981), 12. For this reference, I am grateful to my friend Dr. Herman W. Tull.

means of capturing differences between two repertories, for example, or two aesthetic sensibilities.

Already in his first scholarly publication, Pirrotta invokes the Crocean *linguaggio*. Notably, the intellectualistic/intuitive[148] opposition is overlaid on a similarly Crocean northern/southern opposition (although here the north is Pirrotta's France rather than Croce's Germany).[149]

We encounter such Idealist speech in Pirrotta's description of the alternation in the professional activities of fourteenth-century ecclesiastical musicians.[150] We encounter it in the distinction between Italian and French early-fifteenth-century music: between the Italians' "dulcedo" (a quality exemplifying a "hedonistic pleasure . . . connected to the satisfaction of the secret exigencies of musical instinct and above all . . . those of a melodic sensibility unwittingly governed by latent harmonic laws") and the northerners' "subtilitas" ("[t]hat which is evident above all in French polyphony of the Gothic period, in which the worship of construction—well ordered by means of an industrious craftsmanship of technique and the liveliness of the ratiocination—finally gives way to an intellectualism and—geometricizing and symbolizing abstraction"). We encounter it in the article on the Faenza codex.[151] And we encounter it in "Chronology and Denomination of the Italian Ars Nova."[152]

To complete this survey of a revealing use of distinctive Idealist nomenclature, we return to the term "hedonism." Croce distinguished carefully between aesthetic activity and "a hedonistic side" ("lato edonistico")—"the useful or the pleasing"—and he identified the stages of "aesthetic production," the third of which comprised "the hedonistic accompaniment or pleasure in the beautiful" ("accompagnamento edonistico o piacere del bello"). His use of the term "hedonistic" is therefore not appreciably different from ours: both usages suggest a kind of guilty pleasure, an indulgence in sheer sensual experience, a willingness to revel in it.

Pirrotta's prose is larded with the term. It occurs in the analyses of Gesualdo's madrigals, specifically to make tangible the distinction in poetic choices available to late-sixteenth-century madrigalists, one more "hedonistic"—exemplified by Guarino's idyllic, sensual poetics—the other exemplified by Tasso's psychologically unsettling verse.[153]

But the most significant instances of the use of the term occur in the articles on seventeenth-century opera. Pirrotta's objective there is to describe

---

[148] Substituting for Croce's "intellectualistic" is Pirrotta's "scholasticism."
[149] See the final paragraphs of Pirrotta's portion of **1935**: *Il Sacchetti*.
[150] **1946–47**: "Per l'origine e la storia della 'caccia' e del 'madrigale' trecentesco."
[151] **1954**: "Note su un codice di antiche musiche per tastiera."
[152] **1955**: "Cronologia e denominazione dell'ars nova italiana." See also **1954**: *The Music of Fourteenth Century Italy*, vol. 3, p. IV, where Pirrotta writes of the "intellectualistic experiments" of Laurentius de Florentia.
[153] **1961**: "Gesualdo da Venosa nel IV centenario della nascita."

the conditions that justified the use of tuneful, melodious closed pieces—arias—within a genre initially governed by an aesthetic of realism, of speech-like recitative. The emergence of the aria is explained as a response to the desire for "hedonistic" indulgence in sensuous melodicity. Essentially the same observation is made in "Tre capitoli su Cesti," "Le prime opere di Antonio Cesti," and "Commedia dell'arte e Melodramma."[154]

The Narrative Rhetorical Mode

Pirrotta's writings also manifest an alignment with the Idealist's emphasis on narration, as fundamental to fulfilling the imperatives of the Idealist philosophy of history. This, I believe, is the origin of Pirrotta's particular commitment to biography:

> [h]is music history is . . . a history of individuals. He always remembers that the creators of music were living men. Seeking connections between their work and their personalities, he acknowledges the motivating force of human emotions, of jealousy, respect, depression, and self-confidence, on artistic acts. He emphasizes the human qualities of the historical figure he studies.[155]

But the adherence to the Idealist definition of history is revealed not only in the commitment to biography. Narrative is often Pirrotta's favored rhetorical mode, whether or not the subject matter is biography; and his choice of such a mode is a felicitous one. As one example, I cite the encyclopedia entry "Italien B. 14.–16. Jahrhundert."[156] The mode of presentation—what Pierluigi Petrobelli has described as "that limpid, terse, captivating prose that characterizes all his writings"[157]—is all important to the character of Pirrotta's discourse. The "captivating" quality of Pirrotta's prose is, I suggest, a consequence of his regular adoption of the narrative mode, which affords him an opportunity to assemble evocative particulars in atmospheric, pointillist fashion, nested within a continuous narrative. And throughout his career, he regularly sought—and capitalized on—opportunities to offer comprehensive narrative accounts of particular large-scale problems that engaged him. It was almost as if—amidst his many brief essays on highly specific problems—he

---

[154]I especially cite the observation as formulated in the last of these titles.

[155]Rosand, review, *Journal of the American Musicological Society*.

[156]**1957**: "Italien B. 14.–16. Jahrhundert." Pirrotta's understanding of the challenges inherent in writing encyclopedia entries—for example, the temptation to lapse into an exposition of the isolated particular—is implicitly suggested in a passage at the opening of **1986**: "Problemi di una storia della musica," where he characterizes *The New Grove* and *M.G.G.* as the most conspicuous and successful editorial ventures of recent decades in the diffusion of music-historical knowledge; however, they do not undertake the "tentativo di comporre il quadro diacronico." This by no means characterizes Pirrotta's own contributions to *M.G.G.*; on the contrary, his entry on "Italy" supplies precisely that "diachronic frame" that is missing in most examples of the genre.

[157]"Introduzione" in *Musicologia fra due continenti* (see "*Prologo*," n. 33). See also "*Per un regale evento*" (see "*Prologo*," n. 36), where reference is made to "una grande capacità di communicazione."

episodically hungered for the opportunity to view the entire set of developments from 30,000 feet, to "see the forest for the trees." His contribution to the Festschrift for Kurt von Fischer is an example.[158]

The Refutation of Genre

The Idealists' refutation of the doctrine of genre as an expression of their emphasis on the particular and the atomistic, as opposed to the abstract, is also reflected in Pirrotta's philosophy of history. In "Cronologia e denominazione dell'ars nova italiana," in response to a question he himself posed about the legitimacy of the expression "Italian *ars nova*," he responds, in good Crocean fashion, that "we must renounce a demonstration of such a genre, because 'history'—that of music included—unfortunately does not belong to the domain of the exact sciences."

But the clearest, most fully articulated statement of his skepticism about the doctrine of genre appears in "Tre capitoli su Cesti."[159]

Autodidacticism

In observing that neither the Italian university nor the conservatory offered a course of study appropriate to the needs of the aspiring musicologist, Pirrotta signals the necessity of autodidacticism,[160] and his remarks have a clear autobiographical cast to them.[161] Elsewhere, he praises Malipiero as "tenacious auto-didact."[162]

Idealism and Nationalism:[163] Italianità and Sicilianità

Pirrotta was intent on achieving an accurate understanding in the collective music-historical imagination of Italian musical accomplishment, especially as it relates to that of other cultures. Early evidence can be found in his critical writings, where he suggests that "[n]ot only today are we pleased to

---

[158]**1973**: "Novelty and Renewal in Italy, 1300–1600."

[159]**1953**: "Tre capitoli," 27–28. Interestingly, Pirrotta's observations are echoed in Harold Powers "*Il «Mutio» tramutato.*" A further illustration of the Idealist's mistrust of genre is the discussion of the style of Josquin's motets (in the encyclopedia entry for *La Musica*: **1966**: "Despres, Josquin [Després, Desprez, Des Prez, ecc.; Josquinus o Jodocus Pratensis, a Prato, ecc.; Juschino, Josse, ecc.]").

[160]On Pirrotta's auto didacticism, see Della Seta, "Storia, filologia e gusto musicale: rileggendo i primi scritti di Pirrotta" (see "*Scena 3.ª*," n. 36), quoting the citation issued when Pirrotta was awarded the *Premio* "Antonio Feltrinelli" in 1983. See also Piperno, "Omaggio a Nino Pirrotta" (see "*Scena 3.ª*," n. 43).

[161]**1952**: "Le biblioteche musicali italiane"; **1954**: "Compiti regionali, nazionali ed internazionali delle biblioteche musicali."

[162]**1982**: "Malipiero e il filo d'Arianna."

[163]For more on the Nationalist strain in Pirrotta's writings, and its sources and manifestations, see also the concluding paragraphs of my "*Scena 3.ª*."

admire the inexhaustible felicity of a tremulous lyric vein that gave the most limpid melodic gems to Italian art."[164]

And in order

> [t]o have proof of Bellini's symphonic and contrapuntal experience, it suffices to look at the overture and quintet of *Pirata*, much more eloquent proof if one considers that it is the opera of a young man, still 26 years old. His having voluntarily renounced it—notwithstanding the success that favored *Pirata*—shows that within himself, Bellini doubtless felt the baggage and apparatus of learned elaborations not only unnecessary, but an obstruction of his musical nature.

Pirrotta here advances an argument that will recur repeatedly in his scholarly discourse: that an apparent simplicity can be a chosen effect, the result not of compositional incompetence or creative deficiency but of conscious calculation, and that the perceived simplicity may be the expression of nationalist prejudice in the eye of the beholder.[165]

Pirrotta's musicological nationalism (or even musicological regionalism) is evident, above all, in his more-or-less exclusive absorption in Italian, and often specifically Sicilian, musical traditions, at least in his scholarship if not necessarily in his teaching (although his doctoral advisees, almost without exception, wrote on Italian topics). His essays on the sixteenth-century Italian madrigal, notably, concentrate on the postorigins phase that had been dominated by non-Italians (Verdelot, Arcadelt, Willaert, etc.); that is, he concentrates on that phase when native Italians had wrested control of the genre from those who had created it: the Frenchmen and Netherlanders residing in Italy.

But by no means was Pirrotta's discourse uncritically nationalistic, as any number of references document.[166]

The Influences of Economic Materialism

As early as the book on Sacchetti, Pirrotta locates the cultivation of polyphony in the "ecclesiastical ambience." As early as the article on fourteenth-century

---

[164]Cummings and Eiche, "Nino Pirrotta's Early Music-Critical Writings," 287 (see "*Scena 1.ª*," n. 69). Pirrotta will make the same kind of observation even more explicitly in his journalistic piece No. XXII, 24 April 1935, published in Cummings and Eiche, "Nino Pirrotta's Early Music-Critical Writings," 329–31. For yet another, entirely different example of a critique of Italian music that may be motivated by nationalist (specifically French) preconceptions, see Marcello Conati, "Between Past and Future: The Dramatic World of Rossini in *Mosè in Egitto* and *Moïse et Pharaon*," *19th-Century Music* 4 (1980): 32–48.

[165]See Pirrotta's contribution to **1961**: contributions to panel discussion. See also **1955**: "Cronologia e denominazione dell'ars nova italiana."

[166]See, for example, **1982**: "Metastasio and the Demands of his Literary Environment," 202, where Pirrotta writes of the torpid, conservative society that was Italian society (or as it was more or less intentionally kept during most of the eighteenth century).

monophonic lyric, he identifies the pertinent locales as the seigneurial courts and (once again) the religious ambiences. The article on the Modena codex is replete with references to the material infrastructure underlying the creation and performance of the repertory it contains. In "Concerning the Origin and History of the 'Caccia' and the Fourteenth-Century 'Madrigal'" ("Per l'origine e la storia della «caccia» e del «madrigale» trecentesco"), Pirrotta uses classic Materialist diction to refer to "the particular material and spiritual conditions of the environment." The essential argument of "Marchettus of Padua" is captured epigrammatically in Materialist vocabulary.[167] The first of the "Tre capitoli su Cesti" is effectively an exercise in Materialist explanations for the character of the early history of opera. To some extent, Materialist causal explanations form the basis of the argument in Pirrotta's "Music and Cultural Tendencies in 15th-Century Italy." A Materialist sensibility is evident even in such passing references as the following: "The Florentine court had only recently asserted its political power and the Medici may have been eager for their backing and trading past to be forgotten"; thus Pirrotta explains the motivation for the series of lavish court *intermedij* subsidized by the Medici throughout the Cinquecento.[168]

The Materialist influences in Pirrotta's writings align with the emphasis on biography. As Rosand suggested, the figures in Pirrotta's history of music are living, breathing human beings, and one of the means available to a scholar intent on imaginatively revivifying historic men and women is to invoke the precise, "three-dimensional" material conditions in which they lived: the precise nature of their employment, their compensation, the systems of patronage that supported their artistic activity, and so on.

*****

In sum: coloring Pirrotta's Positivist temperament were influences from Crocean/Gentilean Idealism, that philosophical tendency characteristic of Italian thought when Pirrotta's sensibilities were undergoing formation, which gently inflects and tempers his discourse. The often thinly veiled Idealist disdain for Germanic philologism, the emphasis on the intuitive mode of apprehension, the resistance to the Positivist historians' attempts to make a science of

---

[167] **1955**: "Marchettus of Padua": "the problem of the origin of the Italian Ars Nova does not lie in the question of where it came from. It has to do rather with *the determination of the conditions which induced*...ecclesiastical musicians to leave their monasteries, gave them increased opportunity for self expression in secular music, and provided their works a certain publicity that has permitted them to be preserved for us [emphasis added]."

[168] Further such characterizations of the Material infrastructure of Florence, and its significance for the city's musical history, occur in **1983**: "Rhapsodic Elements in North-Italian Polyphony of the 14th Century," 88. And there are Materialist sensibilities even where one might not expect them, underlying **1994**: "Rossini eseguito ieri e oggi," for example.

history, and the commitment to the narrative rhetorical mode have multivalent resonances in Pirrotta's temperament: in his references to the contrapuntal artifices of a more intellectualistic compositional aesthetic (as contrasted with an Italianate predilection for a more spontaneous, nonchalant aesthetic), in the marked reliance in his own epistemology on intuition, and so on. A northern Italian (even Germanic) philologistic, Positivistic, fact-drenched epistemology is tempered with a southern Italian (even Sicilian) Spiritualist, Idealist, intuitive epistemology. If we were to attempt to capture the essence of Pirrotta's intellectual style in a single word, we would be tempted to invoke a truism that is so truistic as to risk trivialization. All the same, provided that that single word is invested with the requisite multivalence in meaning suggested by the entire foregoing discussion, we might identity the character of Pirrotta's scholarly profile as quintessentially Italianate.

Inevitably, Pirrotta's autodidacticism and pragmatism liberated him from a single-minded reliance on any one of these intellectual traditions, which is precisely what explains the distinctiveness of his profile: he cannot be placed, nor typed. He was neither exclusively the conservatory licentiate and diplomate, nor the university laureate; he was neither exclusively Positivist in his own epistemology, nor exclusively Idealist.

All the same, in Pirrotta's writings it is possible to detect oblique yet powerful resonances of the positions of all of the figures preeminent in Italian thought during his *liceo* and university years: evidence of a benign Nationalism, for example, or of an appreciation for the intuitive mode of apprehension. There are innumerable passages in his writings that document a sensibility aligned with the principal Italian philosophical developments of his era, echoes of these inescapable influences current at the time of his formation. They are the ultimate explanation for that recognizable authorial voice.

Atto II.ndo

Bibliotecario

Scena 4.ª

The Conservatory of Palermo (1936–48): *Il Trecento*

PIRROTTA'S FIRST ACADEMIC APPOINTMENT

"LIRICA MONODICA TRECENTESCA," 1936

REVIEWS OF MOMPELLIO, *PIETRO VINCI MADRIGALISTA SICILIANO*, 1937, AND TIBY, *LA MUSICA BIZANTINA*, 1938

MARRIAGE AND FAMILY

"IL CODICE ESTENSE LAT. 568 E LA MUSICA FRANCESE IN ITALIA AL PRINCIPIO DEL '400"

"PER L'ORIGINE E LA STORIA DELLA 'CACCIA' E DEL 'MADRIGALE' TRECENTESCO"

" 'DULCEDO' E 'SUBTILITAS' NELLA PRATICA POLIFONICA FRANCO-ITALIANA AL PRINCIPIO DEL '400"

PIRROTTA'S FIRST ACADEMIC APPOINTMENT

In Italy in the mid-1930s, the employment possibilities for someone interested in a career as a music historian were limited, since positions in music history in the faculties of letters and philosophy at the Italian universities did not exist.[1] As Pirrotta explained, the librarian at an Italian conservatory would usually serve as the professor of music history as well,[2] except at larger institutions whose ampler finances allowed them to support separate positions.

---

[1] On the history of the establishment of such positions, see Carolyn Gianturco's contribution ("2. Italy") to Vincent Duckles et al., "Musicology," *Grove Music Online. Oxford Music Online*, http://0-www.oxfordmusiconline.com.libcat.lafayette.edu/subscriber/article/grove/music/46710pg3 (accessed 2 September 2011).

[2] See **1952**: "Le biblioteche musicali italiane" ("Italian Music Libraries") and **1954**: "Compiti regionali, nazionali ed internazionali delle bilioteche musicali."

Such a distinction had implications for his own career, since the Conservatory of Palermo combined these responsibilities, while the Conservatory of Rome— where he served as *bibliotecario* from 1948–56— could afford to assign him the responsibilities of library director alone.

An appointment as librarian and docent in music history at one of the conservatories was therefore the most logical position to which a would-be music historian like Pirrotta could then aspire. His career exemplifies the venerable European tradition of the scholar-librarian. And his command of the primary sources is attributable in part to the expertise he gained as Conservatory librarian in Palermo and Rome, and director of the music library at Harvard.

Pirrotta's status as a conservatory licentiate and diplomate qualified him for appointment to the faculty of the Conservatory of Palermo. His status as university laureate in letters was his principal initial certification as a scholar; his status as conservatory licentiate in history of music (the only formal university-level certification of status as a music historian then attainable in Italy), authorship of the music-critical articles for *L'Ora*, and—above all—coauthorship of the scholarly study of Sacchetti's poetry and its musical settings further qualified him as worthy of appointment as librarian and docent in music history.

Thus Antonino Pirrotta, *Licenziato in Storia della Musica, Diplomato di Magistero in Organo e Composizione Organistica, Laureato in Lettere*, settled into his responsibilities as Bibliotecario and Docente in Storia della Musica at the Regio Conservatorio di Musica «Vincenzo Bellini» di Palermo (Professore di Storia della Musica and *titolare di cattedra* as of 1938, after his success in the 1937 *concorso*),[3] giving basic instruction in music history for students in composition, voice, harp, organ, piano, strings, winds, brass, and instrumentation for band, and more advanced instruction for what few aspiring licentiates there were in music history.[4]

In 1937, his uncle Empedocle Restivo became president of the Conservatory, and in 1938 Rito Selvaggi was named both president and artistic director, succeeding Pirrotta's teacher Antonio Savasta as director.

*****

"LIRICA MONODICA TRECENTESCA," 1936

At the same time, Pirrotta settled into sustained activity as a historical musicologist, profiting from the status associated with his appointments at

---

[3]These dates are provided in many sources, among them, for example, Accademia di Santa Cecilia, *Annuario 1955–1956* (*CCCLXXI–CCCLXXII*) (n.d.): 158–59.

[4]Pirrotta recounted that his teaching career began with his move to the United States, which suggests that he did not regard the teaching he did as Professor of Music History at Palermo as consequential; see his introductory remarks in the collection of his essays *Music and Culture in Italy from the Middle Ages to the Baroque. A Collection of Essays* (Cambridge, MA: Harvard University Press, 1984).

the Conservatory. In 1936, eager for advice and encouragement, he paid a call on the legendary Fausto Torrefranca, then librarian at the Conservatory of Milan.[5] And he continued with his own scholarly writing.

While working on *Il Sacchetti*, Pirrotta resolved to investigate further one of the subsidiary aspects of the argument advanced therein. In 1936—the year he was named to the Conservatory's *elenco principale* (roster of tenured/tenure-track faculty)—he published his first scholarly article, on fourteenth-century monophonic song.[6]

The monophonic ballate in the renowned Squarcialupi codex and the then newly discovered Vatican Rossi manuscript had fascinated Pirrotta from the moment of his engagement with the Trecento repertory. The fifteen or so examples extant are precious vestiges of a vital lost practice, greatly surpassing in richness the polyphonic repertory of the Italian fourteenth century.[7]

Pirrotta again observes that the literary sources of the time do not mention polyphonic music. He reiterates the suggestion that the composition and performance of madrigals and cacce were restricted to environments possessing the necessary conditions and an audience appreciative of such practices: namely, either religious communities (after all, the majority of Trecento polyphonists were either members of monastic orders or organists by trade, serving in ecclesiastical institutions) or the north-Italian aristocratic courts of the della Scala, Visconti, and da Carrara.

Although there are no references to polyphonic music in contemporary literary sources, there *are* descriptions of performances of monophonic ballate or canzoni or instrumental dances. The monophonic ballata, in particular, would have met the usual musical needs of a vast and diverse public. The singing of a solo vocalist, accompanied on the lute or keyboard (or accompanying him- or herself), would ordinarily have sufficed for most public popular festivals or aristocratic entertainments: to articulate the rhythm of a dance, for instance, or frame the episodes of a jester's performance.[8]

The extant monophonic ballate are from two regions: an earlier repertory from northern Italy and a later one from Florence. Initially of popular origin,

---

[5]See **1983**: "Introduzione ai lavori," 11. But on Torrefranca's complicated place in the discipline of musicology, see Alfred Einstein's review of his *Il segreto del quattrocento* (see "*Intermedio I.^{mo}*," n. 135), and Gianturco's contribution ("2. Italy") to Vincent Duckles, et al., "Musicology," *Grove Music Online*. Oxford Music Online, http://0-www.oxfordmusiconline.com.libcat.lafayette.edu/subscriber/ article/ grove/music/ 46710pg3 (accessed 2 September 2011).

[6]**1936**: "Lirica monodica trecentesca." In my synopsis and analysis of this paper, I have benefitted greatly from Fabrizio Della Seta's "Storia, filologia e gusto musicale: rileggendo i primi scritti di Pirrotta" (see "*Scena 3.^{a}*," n. 36). For other evidence of Pirrotta's early musicological activity (specifically in 1939), see Guillaume De Van, "A Recently Discovered Source of Early Fifteenth Century Polyphonic Music," *Musica Disciplina* II–1/2 (1948), pp. 5–74; especially p. 5.

[7]On this point, see also **1949–51**: "Ballata," and **1954**: *The Music of Fourteenth Century Italy*, vol. I, p. II.

[8]Indeed, in some extant monophonic ballate, the rhythm is precisely articulated by means of the repercussion of a single, unvarying note, sung to the same repeated syllable of text, an effect that—it is easy to imagine—was supported by the accompaniment of a plucked-string or percussion instrument.

they subsequently served to provide musical dress for a learned, curial lyric, whose authors included such figures as Niccolò Soldanieri and Giovanni Boccaccio. The popular character of the poetry of some of the northern monophonic ballate should not deceive us: it was a deliberate effect, self-consciously chosen by anonymous, learned poets, in the same way that—throughout European history—members of elite strata of society periodically emulate popular culture.

Toward the conclusion of his article, Pirrotta offers the earliest expression of a theme on which he will elaborate throughout the rest of his career. He implicitly (and explicitly) contrasts the compositional principles underlying the design of the melodies of a *polyphonic* composition with those underlying the single melody of *monophonic* ballate:

> While the polyphonic settings—*under the stimulus of divergent melodic impulses* [emphasis added]—were not always in a secure relationship to the tonality, here, notwithstanding the uncertain and insufficient use of chromatic alterations, we are clearly tending towards the major or minor tonalities, with the prevalence of the latter.... [T]he tonal and harmonic sentiment revealed by the monophonic settings implies conceptions that were so totally different from what was ... customary and familiar to polyphonic composers.

What is his meaning? I believe that this is nothing less than a first—though predictably still inchoate—articulation of the concept of "aria." Later memorably defined as the distinguishing characteristic of a melody exemplifying "the quality ... [of] being, as it were, precisely determined and inflected on an unavoidable course"—one that embodies "a sense of self-possessed determination," marked by an "unrestricted and undiverted naturalness"[9] —an aria, in Pirrotta's formulation, is the characteristic that confers a sense of inherent direction.

Moreover, the reference to the "divergent melodic impulses" of "the polyphonic settings"—and the characterization of the "tonal and harmonic sentiment revealed by the monophonic settings" as "totally different from those ... familiar to polyphonic composers"[10]—are first expressions of the related argument that the multiple vocal lines of a polyphonic composition lack the spontaneity and buoyancy of a monophonic composition. Instead, they manifest qualities perceived as somewhat contrived and artificial. In later polyphonic composition, each of the several voices is required on occasion to serve as backdrop for the others, the voices subordinated to one another in alternation in order to furnish a harmonic background for the prominent voice or voices of the moment. Rather than expressive of an innate, natural

---

[9]**1969:** *Music and Theatre*, 248–49.
[10]Decades later, Pirrotta will write similarly: **1992:** "The Music."

melodic cogency, the resulting melodic style is more the consequence of some degree of compositional artifice, because the contours of the voices serving momentarily as backdrop exemplify writing undertaken to provide the requisite harmonic foundation for those being highlighted.[11]

Pirrotta moves briskly to his conclusion, in which—as in so many of his later conclusions—he states the most consequential implications of his analysis. The melody of a monophonic ballata exemplifies a compositional aesthetic that is more "natural"—more "popular" or "popularizing"—than that governing the design of the several melodies of a polyphonic composition. It manifests a naturalness—a buoyancy, an "aria," a "sprezzatura" (or "nonchalance")—which seems less the product of compositional effort than the result of melodic, harmonic, and "tonal" "instincts" latent in "the collective musical sensibility." The relationship of such an argument to the roughly contemporary argument concerning Bellini's development as a melodist, summarized in the previous chapter, is obvious. So, too, is the relationship to contemporary Idealist, and nationalist, sensibilities. Pirrotta's distinctive scholarly voice is now emerging.

*****

REVIEWS OF MOMPELLIO, *PIETRO VINCI MADRIGALISTA SICILIANO*, 1937, AND TIBY, *LA MUSICA BIZANTINA*, 1938

In 1937 and 1938, Pirrotta published reviews of monographs by Italian colleagues, and these, too, reveal something of his personal and professional formation, since they are documents of his identification with *la sicilianità*.

Moreover, other than some brief encyclopedia entries and a few preliminary essays on music in the Cinquecento theater,[12] Pirrotta's review of Federico Mompellio's study of the sixteenth-century Sicilian madrigalist Pietro Vinci[13] is his only publication on the music of the Italian Renaissance until he assumes his professorship at Harvard and begins a series of articles on the

---

[11]Ibid., 247ff., from which I have drawn heavily. See also Anthony M. Cummings, *MS Florence, Biblioteca Nazionale Centrale, Magl. XIX, 164-167* (Aldershot, Hants: Ashgate, 2006), 76–77. On this entire point, see also Fabrizio Della Seta's "Storia, filologia e gusto musicale: rileggendo i primi scritti di Pirrotta" (see "*Scena 3.ª*," n. 36). There, Della Seta makes the important observation that Italian conservatories traditionally distinguished courses in melody from those in harmony, and he speculates that this practice may have left its traces in Pirrotta's musical formation, in that it sensitized him to the possibilities afforded composers with respect to melodic composition when the melody was *not* to be embedded within a polyphonic context and thus susceptible to the vertical demands of the composition.

[12]One of these is the celebrated **1954**: "Commedia dell'Arte e Melodramma"; the other is **1950**: "Il 'Festino' di Banchieri."

[13]**1936–37**: review of Mompellio, *Pietro Vinci madrigalista siciliano*.

poetic choices of the Cinquecento madrigalists Carlo Gesualdo, Luca Marenzio, and Claudio Monteverdi, and other studies of Italian music of the fifteenth and sixteenth centuries.

Although the tradition of Sicilian popular song was then generally recognized, few musicians or musicologists were aware of more artistically developed performance and creative activity. In Pirrotta's view, the importance of Mompellio's book was that it treated the figure whose publications are the earliest known printed works by a Sicilian polyphonist. The review constituted his first reflections on that most representative genre of the Italian musical Renaissance, the madrigal.

Although a principal interest of the review is that it considers the question of the "Sicilian" element in music, it also addresses a matter that for Pirrotta was becoming increasingly urgent: the contrast between northern and Italian aesthetic ideals and sensibilities.

> Mompellio resolutely argues against the thesis that sees the madrigal as a marriage between Flemish polyphony and Italian homophony. . . . [T]he apparent contradiction between horizontal contrapuntal tendencies and homophonic verticality is resolved in the madrigal through a synthesis that draws its greatest expressive power precisely from the contrast of the component elements.

He concludes with a reference to "a delicate and graceful polymodality that gives the music an archaic flavor":

> "Does Vinci owe these characteristics"— asks Mompellio—"only to himself? Or are they an echo of that Hellenic art that prospered in his beautiful native land not far from Nicosia?" In that question arises the entire problem of Sicilian music.

Similarly, the review of Tiby's book on Byzantine music[14] reveals Pirrotta's personal and professional identification with his *sicilianità*, as it focuses attention on the larger "Sicilian musical history and the formation of the ethnophonic patrimony of the Island."[15] The history of Sicilian music reveals instances of a musico-anthropological phenomenon that had previously interested Pirrotta and will continue to do so. His concern is with the relationship between "learned" and "popular" traditions, with the vestiges of the latter that one can occasionally detect in the former and recover—if at all—only as the result of a conversance with a full range of musical and nonmusical

---

[14]**1938**: review of Tiby, *La musica bizantina.*

[15]See also Tiby's "Il problema della 'siciliana' dal trecento al settecento," *Bollettino del Centro di Studi Filologici e Linguistici Siciliani* 2 (1954): 5–31

evidence. Throughout his career, Pirrotta will be committed to retrieving elusive vestiges of popular practices that are reflected in the learned tradition.

*****

MARRIAGE AND FAMILY

Though not published until 1944/45, Pirrotta's study of the *ars subtilior* Modena manuscript was begun years earlier. However, after the publication of the two reviews of the late 1930s and the drafting of the study of the Modena manuscript, Pirrotta's musicological activity was temporarily suspended, for understandable reasons, one local and private, the other global and public. First, he met and married the woman he described as "the great love of my life," Lea Paternostro (b. 19 March 1911 to Angelo Paternostro and Francesca Sangiorgi-Paternostro; †18 February 1996), and they began their family. And shortly thereafter, the cataclysmic events of the Second World War intervened in the lives of all Italians.

*****

Lea Paternostro's family was propertied. Although their lands were on the island's east coast, the family had settled in Palermo, which is where Lea and Nino Pirrotta met. They were married on 27 December 1939.

Ellen Rosand, Pirrotta's American pupil, has described Lea Pirrotta as "the most extraordinary of women." Underlying her charm and gentility, and to some extent masked by them, were other qualities: an almost preternatural strength, resilience, an independence, and resourcefulness. She was, in the words of one of her children, "fearless" and "adventuresome."[16]

By everyone's reckoning, Lea's personal characteristics were indispensable to her husband's professional successes.[17] When offered the opportunity to teach in the United States, Pirrotta was troubled, aware of the disruption that it would cause in the lives of his wife and children. He confided to his colleague and successor at the Conservatory of Rome, Emilia Zanetti, that he regarded it as a "beautiful dream," impossible to realize. Left to his own

---

[16]A.M. Cummings interview with Dr. Sergio Pirrotta, 11 July 2008.

[17]On the matter of Lea's sociability and support of her husband as critical to his professional successes, I am grateful to (among many others) Professor Frank D'Accone: A.M. Cummings interview at the 2009 national meeting of the American Musicological Society, Philadelphia. See also the recollections of Franco Piperno: "Omaggio a Nino Pirrotta" (see *"Scena 3.ᵃ,"* n. 43).

devices, he would have declined the invitation, believing that he simply could not take it into consideration, that he could not leave his wife and children.

But Lea's adventuresome nature prevailed. Having some sense of the promise that such an opportunity held for her husband's career, she unhesitatingly suggested that they go.[18]

Like her mother-in-law, Adele, and her sister-in-law, Giulia, Lea was a gifted woman with considerable executive abilities, who happened to be born at a moment in history when most European women were not encouraged to acquire an education commensurate with their latent abilities. Yet like Adele and Giulia, Lea valued professional achievement and knowledge, and all three understood their husbands' need to pursue their professional goals. Even Lea's skills as a hostess should be understood in that light: they were elements in a network binding together her family and her many friends and helping to construct her husband's professional world.[19]

Nino Pirrotta and Lea complemented each other supremely well. If he was serene and could be reserved and occasionally taciturn, and was perhaps even shy, she was lively and daring and conversed gracefully and effortlessly. And although not identical to each other in personal "style," they were nonetheless of one mind with respect to fundamental values and principles: neither was inordinately bound by convention; both favored freedom of thought; both possessed an openness to possibilities, ideas, people, and different ways of being and living.

Therefore, just as Pirrotta forged his own unfettered vision of his discipline—of its methodologies and the questions it engages—so, too, encouraged by his family, he forged an unfettered vision of what his career might comprise: appointments that led him far from the familiar Palermo (and Italy) of his childhood and early adulthood.

*****

After Fascist Italy's entry into the Second World War in 1940 as an ally of Nazi Germany, Pirrotta was called back into military service. He served as lieutenant in the army from May 1940, through November 1941, posted either in Palermo itself or in the immediate vicinity (Ficuzza, in the province of

---

[18]This episode is recounted by different people about different phases of Pirrotta's career. One account suggests that it pertains to the invitation to the visiting appointment at Princeton, the other that it pertains to the invitation to the permanent appointment at Harvard. But it must be the former rather than the latter, since an element in the account is that Pirrotta encountered his colleague Emilia Zanetti in the library at the «S.ta Cecilia» immediately after receiving the invitation. The negotiations concerning the appointment at Harvard occurred while he was visiting professor at Columbia University, during the fall of 1955, thus excluding the possibility of an encounter with Dott.ssa Zanetti.

[19]Correspondence with Dr. Adelaide Maria Pirrotta-Bahr.

Palermo[20]). Assigned responsibilities as a quartermaster in charge of billeting, Pirrotta would often consult with his wife about the quantities of food necessary to provision units of some 200 servicemen. In 1942, as a teacher occupying an official post, he was furloughed and promoted to captain in the reserves.

But by no means did his release from military service signal the end to his family's war-time tribulations. After reversing the Axis conquests in North Africa (beginning in 1942), the Allies envisioned reclaiming first Sicily and then the southern Italian mainland, which Prime Minister Winston Churchill characterized in exchanges with President Franklin D. Roosevelt as "the soft underbelly of Europe." Palermo was increasingly subjected to Allied bombardment.

When the severity of the bombardments increased, Nino and Lea Pirrotta took the precaution of evacuating the family: first to Villa Carella in Santa Flavia, then further inland to Campo Fiorito, and finally to Mondello on the coast of Sicily just north of Palermo.

The war in Sicily effectively ended in August/September of 1943. In 1945, while Palermo was still occupied by an American garrison, the Pirrottas moved once more, this time to a villetta in Via Simone Cuccia, after which they relocated to Pirrotta's parents' home in Via Libertà, where they lived until the move to Rome in 1948/49.

*****

Nino Pirrotta's difficulties were not solely personal. For obvious reasons, the Conservatory could not operate normally during wartime. After the building that housed the institution was almost entirely destroyed in an Allied bombardment, Pirrotta and a colleague went to pick through the rubble and retrieve what they could of the library holdings. They removed everything salvageable to two large rooms of Teatro Massimo, where years earlier Pirrotta had witnessed performances reviewed for *L'Ora*.

With the beginnings of a return to normal life, Pirrotta undertook the daunting task of restoring the library's working order, and more than a decade later his success would be mentioned in the citation issued when he was elected *accademico* of the prestigious Accademia di «Sta Cecilia».[21] The catalog of the holdings had been destroyed. The collection itself—damaged volumes included—had been hurriedly packed in no particular order, removed to the Massimo, and piled there in unorganized stacks on the floor. Pirrotta began reorganizing and recataloging the collection. As an American military

---

[20]Pirrotta's military service is recounted by, for example, William D. Gettel, "II. From Palermo," *Musical Quarterly* 3 (1944): 358–67.

[21]Accademia di Santa Cecilia, *Annuario 1955–1956 (CCCLXXI–CCCLXXII)* (n.d.): 158–59

officer with whom Pirrotta was acquainted observed, "[t]hat a man of Professor Pir[r]otta's caliber should have to spend his time in such a pedestrian pursuit ... suggests the extent of the personal adjustments called for by the rehabilitation program."[22]

To this same acquaintance Pirrotta lamented his ignorance of developments in his discipline that was the inevitable consequence of war. When this officer expressed his gratitude to him by means of a gift—a recent American publication on medieval music—Pirrotta noted wistfully that it was the first non-German/non-Italian musicological publication he had seen in five years.

The very governance of the Conservatory was uncertain. Pirrotta reported to Giulia and her husband in Rome that

> the situation at the Conservatory is unclear, with respect both to the direction and in composition. For now, Raccuglia[23] functions as director and President by virtue of an Allied decree, which—because of the flight of the professors [titolari]—named him in their stead. But the Ministry has not yet communicated anything about either Bebuzzo[24] or Selvaggi,[25] who is thus nominally still Director.[26]

Rito Selvaggi was a Fascist appointee. When the chair in composition and the directorship fell vacant at the conclusion of Savasta's tenure in 1938, the Ministry waived the customary *concorso* and summarily appointed Selvaggi to both posts. With the collapse of the Fascist régime and the Allied occupation, Filippo Ernesto Raccuglia's succession to the directorship as a consequence of the Allied degree afforded the possibility of a return to more stable conditions at the Conservatory.

*****

Nino and Lea Pirrotta began to try to restore their prewar family lives. There was comfort for them in the knowledge that they and their children had survived the war. There was comfort, too, in returning to familiar surroundings, when they took up residence in the Pirrotta family home in Via Libertà.

---

[22]Gettel, "II. From Palermo."

[23]Filippo Ernesto Raccuglia, 1895-1987. On him, see ARCHIVIO BIOGRAFICO COMUNALE, http://www.mariolinopapalia.it/Siciliani%20Illustri.pdf.

[24]Baron Pietro Emanuele Sgadari di Lo Monaco.

[25]Rito Selvaggi, from October 1938, both president and artistic director of the Conservatory.

[26]Letter from Pirrotta to Ottavio Ziino, "Palermo 18 luglio": "Al Conservatorio la situazione è pure nebulosa[,] sia nei riguardi della Direzione che della composizione. Per ora Raccuglia funge da direttore e Presidente in virtù di un decreto alleato che, vista la fuga dei titolari, lo nominava al loro posto. Ma il Ministero non ha ancora comunicato niente circa Selvaggi (nè circa Bebuzzo)[,] che quindi è nominalmente ancora il Direttore." In the same letter, he asks Ziino for confirmation that "è vero che [the Ministry] ha ripreso il suo funzionamento a Roma" ("it is true that the Ministry has resumed functioning in Rome"). For a copy of this letter, I am indebted to Professor Agostino Ziino.

For Nino Pirrotta, these reassurances were complemented by the serenity resulting from a return to familiar intellectual terrain: He sought and found refuge in his musicological scholarship.

*****

"IL CODICE ESTENSE LAT. 568 E LA MUSICA FRANCESE IN ITALIA AL PRINCIPIO DEL '400"

As early as 1944 and '45, Pirrotta was publishing again: in 1945, a brief note—a playful rejoinder to an earlier piece by Li Gotti[27]—and in 1944/45, his study of the early-fifteenth-century manuscript Modena, Biblioteca Estense, α.M.5.24, which had been drafted "in its essential lines by 1938."[28]

The article on the Modena manuscript is one of several substantial studies Pirrotta will write (or coauthor) that apply a traditional bibliographical/codicological methodology to the analysis of an individual manuscript.[29] It is his first systematic attempt at this kind of approach, and the results are notable.

Pirrotta's work reflects the Nationalist interest in achieving an accurate understanding of the relative importance of native Italian and exogenous French aesthetics in early-fifteenth-century Italian musical style. He immediately states that it is not possible to generalize from the repertory of the Modena manuscript, that the evidence it furnishes of the ease with which the Italian Trecento tradition appeared to cede to foreign influences is in fact referable only to a restricted environment.[30]

Much of the opening section of the study also reveals the influences of his training in art history at Florence, where paleographical analysis of the sources was a preferred methodology. Pirrotta subjects the Modena manuscript to exhaustive codicological analysis, discussing—among other physical characteristics—the gathering structure; the distinction between an earlier, interior section (comprising three fascicles) and a later, exterior section (comprising two); the corresponding differences between the earlier Gothic and later

---

[27] **1945:** "Note ad "Anna,, o dei dispetti amorosi."

[28] **1944/45:** "Il codice estense lat. 568 e la musica francese in Italia al principio del '400," especially 5.

[29] **1948/49–51:** "Il codice di Lucca"; **1955:** "Florence [. . .] Codex Palatino Panciatichiano 26," *Die Musik in Geschichte und Gegenwart* (Kassel: Bärenreiter Verlag, 1949–73), vol. 4 [1955]; **1961:** *Paolo Tenorista in a new fragment of the Italian Ars Nova*; and **1992:** *Il Codice Rossi 215*; and one or two others that might be classified in the same category.

[30] Among the bibliographic references Pirrotta cites is a pioneering article on the manuscript by Li Gotti's teacher Giulio Bertoni (Bertoni, "Poesie musicali francesi nel cod. Estense lat. 568," *Archivum Romanicum* 1 [1917]: 21–57, with a diplomatic transcription of all the French texts). The citation issued when Pirrotta was awarded the Premio "Antonio Feltrinelli" reports that Bertoni had suggested that Pirrotta study the Modena manuscript: "Antonino Pirrotta," *Premi "Antonio Feltrinelli"* 1983, Accademia Nazionale dei Lincei, 69–74, especially 70.

humanistic scripts; and the illuminated initials, decorated with Gothic vegetal motifs, a monk, birds, and other ornamentation (here the expertise and influence of Mario Salmi—an authority on manuscript decoration—are very much in evidence).

Pirrotta's preliminary considerations of the content of the manuscript reveal the influence of the Materialist strain in Italian thought. The observations have the explanatory power that will become characteristic of the many later instances in which he invokes similar Materialist interpretations.

For example, the increasing size of written collections of polyphony is said to coincide with a broader dissemination of polyphonic music and a transformation of the social image of the musician:

> after the isolated, independent, disinterested artist, working only to satisfy his need of self-expression and for a restricted circle of connoisseurs—which the fourteenth-century polyphonists essentially were—came the performer-composer who was partly, if not fully, professional.

And the relationship between the papacy and professional musicians in Avignon is contrasted with practices in Rome (of "Rome *before* Avignon," to borrow the title of Robert Brentano's excellent book[31]):

> Since the time of the Avignon papacy, it was common practice for members of the curia to keep one or two musicians in their retinue. A new musical body had been formed in the papal palace at Avignon as a substitute for the ancient *schola cantorum*, which traditionally provided the music during the papal mass and had remained in Rome. The new pontifical chapel was composed prevalently of French musicians, who lived collegially and had such a close relationship to the pope that they could properly be called his "familiari e commensali."

Soon, any cardinal who was sufficiently well positioned financially to emulate the pope was doing so.

Pirrotta distinguishes between the more permanent, scholarly impulses underlying the contemporary and later humanistic compilation of literary manuscripts, and those "occasional" impulses underlying sources like the Modena manuscript. On the basis of the compositions' places of origin, he discriminates among repertorial layers: Trecento Florence, northern Italy, Avignon (in this layer are motets, a genre described—in a characteristic Idealist turn of phrase—as "the most refined and intellectualistically-complex among those created by French polyphonic art"), and Naples and Padua. (The

---

[31]*Rome before Avignon. A Social History of Thirteenth-Century Rome* (New York: Basic Books, 1974).

identification of a repertory that is Neapolitan in origin occasions a later article in which the existence of a Neapolitan "school" is posited,[32] a thesis that Pirrotta himself will subsequently disclaim, but which—more recently still—a young Italian scholar has convincingly argued anew.[33])

The more recent, exterior layer of the manuscript is almost exclusively devoted to compositions by Matteo da Perugia, whose biography (the part relevant to the compilation of the Modena manuscript) Pirrotta reconstructs for the first time, using such fundamental sources as a collection of documents on the history of the Cathedral of Milan.[34] The excerpts Pirrotta chooses reveal a sensitivity to atmospheric detail; a manifestation of that Crocean concern for vivid narration and the revealing particular, which becomes characteristic of so much of his writing.

The reconstruction of Matteo's biography leads in turn to the conclusion that the more recent layer of the manuscript is of Milanese origin, whereas the older layer is said to have originated in Bologna (an inference also supported, in Bertoni's judgment, by the style of the miniatures) and to reflect the activity of a group of musicians in the retinue of two early-fifteenth-century schismatic popes in temporary residence there, Alexander V and John XXIII.[35] In both instances, Matteo is the active agent in the creation—or compilation and preservation—of the repertories.

The study was published separately, as a monographic extract from its parent source, and thus was reviewed in the scholarly literature. It was well received by two esteemed "trans-Alpine" colleagues, François Lesure and Charles van den Borren, the first of whom lamented the limited circulation of the study and described it "a model." Apart from its specific findings, the article's importance in the entire corpus of Pirrotta's writings is that it is the first to advance a hypothesis fundamental to "Music and Cultural Tendencies in 15th-Century Italy" and other later writings: that the polyphonic repertory preserved in the Modena manuscript (and in other Italian sources of the early Quattrocento) reflects the presence in Italy of the musical retinues of the popes and schismatic anti-popes and members of the Church councils assembled in an effort to end the Great Schism. Piece by piece, Pirrotta is assembling the

---

[32]**1951:** "Scuole polifoniche italiane durante il sec. XIV."

[33]Carla Vivarelli, " *'Di una pretesa scuola napoletana':* Sowing the Seeds of the *Ars nova* at the Court of Robert of Anjou," *Journal of Musicology* 24 (2007): 272–96.

[34]*Annali della fabbrica del duomo di Milano, dall'origine fino al presente*, 6 vols. (Milan: G. Brigola, 1877–85).

[35]But on the Modena manuscript, see now Anne Stone, *The Manuscript Modena, Biblioteca Estense, αM.5.24, Commentary* (Lucca: Libreria Musicale Italiana, 2005), and the literature Stone cites. See also Benjamin Brand, "*Viator ducens ad celestia:* Eucharistic Piety, Papal Politics, and an Early Fifteenth-Century Motet," *Journal of Musicology* 20 (2003): 250–84, especially 253 and nn. 12–14.

elements of a comprehensive thesis on the development of Italian music in the medieval and early modern periods.

*****

I conclude my account of the Palermitan phase of Pirrotta's career with an analysis of two studies that are among the most important he will write during his six decades of professional engagement with the music of fourteenth-century Italy and the so-called *Ars subtilior*.

The first of these, "Per l'origine e la storia della 'caccia' e del 'madrigale' trecentesco" ("On the Origin and History of the 'Caccia' and Fourteenth-Century 'Madrigal'"), is consequential in part because of its very scale—it is among the longest articles Pirrotta will write—and in part because of the fundamental nature of the subject matter. The second study, "'Dulcedo' e 'subtilitas' nella pratica polifonica franco-italiana al principio del '400" ("'Sweetness' and 'Refinement' in Franco-Italian Polyphonic Practice at the Beginning of the 1400s") continues to engage scholars because of the methodology Pirrotta employs to situate the music within its broadest aesthetic and philosophical contexts.[36]

*****

"PER L'ORIGINE E LA STORIA DELLA 'CACCIA' E DEL 'MADRIGALE' TRECENTESCO"[37]

The initial objective in the first study—already anticipated in the book on Sacchetti—is to evaluate two principal, contrasting theories about the origins of the caccia, that of the literary historians Giosuè Carducci and his adherents Emilio Lovarini and Santorre Debenedetti (who argued for the caccia's derivation from the madrigal), and that of Francesco Novati (who argued instead for the priority of the French chace).

But the problem of origins cannot be solved solely on the basis of literary evidence. Rather, as a genre, the caccia in essence exemplifies a fusion of

---

[36]As recently as the 2008 Rome conference on the centennial of Pirrotta's birth; but as Pedro Memelsdorf correctly observed on that occasion, Pirrotta's article has also occasioned critical responses; see, for example, Ursula Günther, "Das Ende der Ars Nova," *Die Musikforschung* 16 (1963): 105–20, especially 112 and n. 8. I intend to publish an English translation of Pirrotta's article, so as to increase its circulation. See Memelsdorf's "Echi d'influenze pirrottiane in sessent'anni di ricerca musicologica," *Musicologia fra due continenti. L'eredità di Nino Pirrotta (Rome, 4–6 giugno 2008)*, Accademia Nazionale dei Lincei (Rome: Scienze e lettere, 2010), 187–210.

[37]Interestingly, the offprint copy in the Biblioteca Berenson at Villa I Tatti in Florence of the first installment of this two-part article has many autograph corrections by Pirrotta (and in one instance a long typewritten pasteover).

the poetic and the musical, an interpenetration of verse and music. And the compositional characteristic that immediately distinguishes the caccia from other musical genres—the use of exact imitation ("canon")—is not exclusive to a single national tradition, an argument that has implications for Pirrotta's evaluation of Novati's view that the caccia derives from the chace.

Here, then, is another instance of a quasi-Nationalist concern for a correct balance in the collective music-historical imagination between the relative importance of French and Italian aesthetics, which in turn leads to a fuller consideration of a potential misapprehension. An acknowledgment of France's place as the "animating but not monopolizing center" of polyphonic musical practices of the Middle Ages should not obscure the fact there were such practices elsewhere. And we have yet another illustration of the Materialist sensibility, which leads to a description of the actual material infrastructure permitting the ready exchange of polyphonic expertise (and a taste for polyphonic performance) from one European locale to another: the transnational ecclesiastical state. Pirrotta invokes classic Materialist speech when he writes of "the particular material conditions . . . of environment."

The objective of ensuring due recognition of Italy's place in the polyphonic musical culture of the Middle Ages leads to an elaboration of the thesis, in which Pirrotta implicitly contests the view that the culture of medieval Italy was somnolent at a time when French culture was vigorous:[38]

> The best known histories would lead us to believe that from around 1320–30 almost to the end of the century, Italian polyphony seemed to exist in an airtight compartment, completely isolated from contemporary musical events in the rest of Europe; indeed, that almost because of this isolation it managed to develop elements independently that were belatedly drawn from French polyphony of the thirteenth century. To counter this way of representing the history of Italian polyphony, we should note . . . that the surviving documents, although scarce and not continuous, testify that at least from the first half of the thirteenth century there was polyphonic activity in Italy, which, even if contained within modest limits, participated effectively in the general course of European polyphon. . . . Furthermore, all indications concur in demonstrating that this activity was not divorced from the general tendencies of European polyphony.

Indeed, rather than existing within a hermetically sealed hothouse, Italian polyphony manifests continuous contacts with French polyphony:

---

[38]For a statement of the thesis that understands the dynamism of the Italian Renaissance largely in contrast to the putatively moribund character of medieval Italian culture, which purportedly contrasted with that of medieval France, see, for example, Paul Oskar Kristeller, "Music and Learning in the Early Italian Renaissance," *Journal of Renaissance and Baroque Music* [now *Musica disciplina*] 1 (1946–47): 255–69. See also Denys Hay, *The Italian Renaissance in its Historical Background* (Cambridge: Cambridge University Press, 1961), Chapter 2; Hay subscribes to a similar historiographic assumption.

> Even before the papacy returned to Rome from Avignon, the events of the Schism [and] the influx of trans-Alpine prelates and singers into Italy led to the excesses associated with the fashion for Gallicizing academicism and technicalism (which, by the way, are much more limited in historical importance than is commonly believed). Evidence of this is the Modena codex, the repertory of a small group of musicians connected with the singers of Alexander V during his very brief Bolognese pontificate.

(Note the deployment here of findings resulting from the earlier study of the Modena manuscript, as well as the characteristic, Crocean diction: "Gallicizing academicism and technicalism.")

The "artifice" of exact imitation fundamental to the caccia as a compositional genre is, in fact, more characteristic of *peripheral* musical practices: it occurs more frequently in compositions of Spanish, German, and English (and Italian) origin, which were created in environments less subject to the intellectual rigor and stylistic purity prevalent among French masters.

Further, Pirrotta here elaborates an argument that will underlie his presentation of the entire musical culture of the Italian fourteenth century as an organic phenomenon, namely, that the stylistic diversity in fourteenth-century Italian polyphonic musical practice writ large is the expression of an alternation—a "rhythm," so to speak—in the lives and professional activities of ecclesiastical musicians.

The article, which continued with a discussion of the origins of the madrigal, concludes with the customary rhetorical flourish. In this instance, Pirrotta returns to a consideration of Italian–French aesthetic contrasts and—by invoking the evidence of another, parallel, academic discipline, the history of art—seeks to explain fourteenth-century Italian musical aesthetics as the expression of transcendent, fundamental Italian sensibilities more generally:

> [T]he madrigal ... stands to testify to a perennial inclination of Italian polyphony in ... the vocality of the tenor. ... T]he two voices [of a polyphonic madrigal] *are no longer independent of each other and juxtaposed according to mathematical or intellectualistic criteria* [emphasis added], but come to be interpenetrated, ... to fuse into one coherent whole: a typically Italian phenomenon, since there is almost nothing like it in the contemporary compositions of other countries. ... [T]he harmonic functionality ... adumbrated here ... frames [the musical syllables] in a sonorous "line"; in short, it creates *that ready ductility of Italian musical language* [emphasis added] that will later lead to the "contrappunto arioso" of the end of the fifteenth century, sixteenth-century madrigalisms and expressive chromaticism, and (why not?) the dramatic recitative and virtuosic vocality of the early seventeenth century. ... As far as it is possible and legitimate to refer to another form of artistic expression, *the clarity and melodic plasticity* [emphasis added], at which the unknown Italian polyphonists who prepared the *ars nova* gradually and surely

arrived, can be compared to the almost contemporary conquest of what [Bernard] Berenson[39] loved to call the "tactile values": of relief, that is, and of the pictorial space, which are among the newest and most striking characteristics of the Italian pictorial art of the Trecento.[40]

Pirrotta's familiarity with findings in art history and his sensitivity to parallels and correspondences in art and music are expressions of that "multidisciplinarity" often identified in his writings. In this context, the invocation of the concept of "tactile values"—an element fundamental to Berenson's vision of art history and criticism—is revealing: It suggests a relationship between a novel "sensuality" in Italian painting, as contrasted with preceding phases,[41] and a similar such sensuality in the music. And Pirrotta's final observation in the article is thus that the music of the Italian Trecento was an early manifestation of this new, more sensual, more "Italianate" understanding of music, which until then had been understood almost exclusively as one of the Quadrivia, "a species of sonorous geometry, mirror of astral harmonies, '[musica] mundana'... made terrestrial and human." Pirrotta's locating of the specific musical fact within such ramified, contemporary neo-Boethian philosophical and aesthetic contexts, as well as his elucidation of the arcane and elusive philosophical abstractions shaping the intellectual discourse of the historical period at issue, are rapidly becoming signature features of his vision of musicology.[42]

*****

---

[39] "Giotto e i valori tattili," *I pittori italiani del rinascimento*, trans. E. Cecchi (Milan: Hoepli, 1936), 62–63.

[40] This passage is also quoted and analyzed by Fabrizio Della Seta in his excellent "Appunti per un ritratto intellettuale di Nino Pirrotta" (see "*Prologo*," n. 36).

[41] *The Concise Oxford Dictionary of Art Terms* defines "tactile values" as follows: "A term devised by the American art historian and connoisseur Bernard Berenson (1865–1959) in his *Florentine Painters of the Renaissance* (1896) to describe those qualities in a painting that stimulate the sense of touch and which he deemed 'life-enhancing.' The phrase became something of a catchword for a whole generation of art historians and critics. Great art, for Berenson, consisted of the ability to give three-dimensional qualities to our perception of images made on flat surfaces. Berenson claimed that the power to stimulate the tactile imagination was particularly strong in the school of Florentine painters." See "tactile values," *The Concise Oxford Dictionary of Art Terms. Oxford Art Online*, http://0-www.oxfordartonline.com.libcat.lafayette.edu/subscriber/article/opr/t4/e1647 (accessed November 9, 2011). For assistance on this point, I am grateful to Dr. Eve Borsook and Professor Christina Neilson.

[42] **1948:** "On the Problem of Sumer is icumen in"—which was Pirrotta's first English-language article (although he describes "Temperaments and Tendencies in the Florentine Camerata" as his first: see his Preface to *Music and Culture in Italy from the Middle Ages to the Baroque*)—elaborates on many of the points first made in "On the Origin and History of the 'Caccia' and Fourteenth-Century 'Madrigal'"; indeed, he remarks that the 1948 article was "originally planned as an additional note to a third part of" the study in *Rivisita musicale italiana* 48 (1946) and 49 (1947). Pirrotta returns to the matters of the "unity of... Western musical culture in the Middle Ages and the progressive attitude of the so-called «peripheral schools» in England and Italy, especially in secular practice."

"'DULCEDO' E 'SUBTILITAS' NELLA PRATICA POLIFONICA FRANCO-ITALIANA AL PRINCIPIO DEL '400"

"'Sweetness' and 'Refinement' in Franco–Italian Polyphonic Practice at the Beginning of the 1400s" returns to themes already adumbrated in several earlier writings. It will become characteristic of Pirrotta to revisit material considered previously and treat it more systematically, to develop it and pursue the implications of observations earlier offered provisionally.

Because the repertory under consideration is that of the so-called *Ars subtilior*, which comprises both French and Italian compositions and is the expression of intimate contact between polyphonists from both national traditions, Pirrotta is afforded an opportunity to draw a clear contrast between the two, in which his knowledge of the Modena manuscript, composed of this kind of mixed repertory, was essential. At the same time, there are also resonances of the earlier studies on Sacchetti, the monophonic ballata, and the origins of the caccia and madrigal, and even the journalistic writings and the review of Mompellio's study of Vinci.

The article is also suffused with a Crocean vocabulary. "Dulcedo" is first defined as a quality exemplifying a *"hedonistic* pleasure . . . connected to the satisfaction of the secret requirements of musical *instinct* and above all . . . those of a melodic sensibility *unwittingly governed by latent harmonic laws*," and "subtilitas" as

> [t]hat which is evident above all in French polyphony of the Gothic period, in which the worship of construction—well-ordered by means of scrupulous technical ability and lively *ratiocination*—finally gives way to an *intellectualism* and . . . *geometricizing and symbolizing abstraction* [emphases added].[43]

The terms of the contrast—"hedonistic pleasure," "secret requirements of musical instinct," and "melodic sensibility unwittingly governed by latent . . . laws," on the one hand, and "worship of construction," "scrupulous technical ability," "lively ratiocination," and "intellectualism" and "geometricizing and symbolizing abstraction," on the other—immediately reveal the Idealist patrimony of the sensibility shaping the discourse,[44] which is also suggested by Pirrotta's characterization of the repertory of the Modena manuscript:

---

[43]This distinction is later invoked in **1951**: "Scuole polifoniche italiane durante il sec. XIV." See also **1984**: "Echi di arie veneziane del primo Quattrocento?" Pirrotta will elsewhere, and later, define *subtilitas* as "the sophistication of music through symbolic or rationalizing devices"; see **1976**: " '*Musica de sono humano*' and the Musical Poetics of Guido of Arezzo," 12.

[44]Decades later, Pirrotta will return to this distinction between the two compositional aesthetics toward the conclusion of his **1984**: "Echi di arie veneziane del primo Quattrocento?"

> The overall impression is of a musical production . . . increasingly being abstracted from every expressive effect for the sake of strictly technical ends.

Having defined his terms, Pirrotta identifies reflections of the French compositional aesthetic in the music of early-fifteenth-century Italian composers (and also vestiges of an Italian aesthetic). And in analyzing compositions that illustrate the antithesis, he summons colorful rhetorical devices. Filippotto da Caserta's ballata *Par le bon Gedeon et Samson* manifests an "apparent *Gallicized* patina," but "the true nature and Italian education of the musician are revealed" in an "open madrigalesque melodizing, in svelte melismatic sequences, which appear like oases in *the dense forest of stubborn syncopations* [emphases added]." In compositions like Antonello da Caserta's *Tres nouble dame souverayne* and Johannes de Janua's *Une dame requis l'autrier*, "every now and then, in the aridity of *barren academism*, we encounter islands of freshness." This latter composition, especially, is marked by an "organic unity of harmonic concatenation and . . . *airy melodiousness* [emphases added] of the cantus."[45]

Pirrotta invokes a Materialist's interpretation to explain *how* such compositional practices as those of the French *Ars subtilior* composers gained favor in Italy. "Avignonese academicism" did not prevail where native Italian traditions were robust, as in Florence;[46]

> [b]ut where the traditions were less rooted, and above all where Italian musicians were . . . in close contact . . . with their foreign brethren—in Rome and Naples in 1377–80, in Padua and perhaps in Milan in the first years of the fifteenth century, in Bologna around 1409, to cite only the more certain examples—the undeniable superiority of the technical level of French polyphony, the refinement of its notation, the intricate "mobility" of its contrapuntal combinations . . . had the effect that Italian musicians, denying all previous artistic experience, were seduced into trying to prove to themselves and their competitors that they were capable of understanding every one of their secrets and . . . emulating and surpassing them on their own ground.

(In essence, he is tracing the effects in music of what has long been conceptualized as the "international Gothic" aesthetic of the late Middle Ages.)

Pirrotta's conclusion summarizes the differences in aesthetic temperament between these two traditions and characterizes the temporary Italian acceptance of the French aesthetic as a "fashion":

> The fundamental aspect of the aesthetics of this phase of Franco–Italian music (which is more correctly defined as "poetics") is fully revealed to us once more:

---

[45] Lest it be thought that Pirrotta's characterization of *Ars subtilior* style is unduly motivated by Nationalist sensibilities, I observe that a similar mode of characterization is employed by David Fallows in "The End of the Ars Subtilior," *Basler Jahrbuch für Musikpraxis* 20 (1996): 21–40.

[46] Pirrotta returns to this thesis in **1948/49–51**: "Il codice di Lucca."

it is one of absolute objectivity, free of every element . . . not of a technical–musical nature; an approach that yet again had to favor the exchange of substance for form in . . . musical expression, and, consequently, the transition to virtuosity and technical academism. But above all, from the considerations mentioned above . . . it seems evident to me that the introduction of French stylistic elements and techniques into Italian polyphonic practice around the turn of the fourteenth century has all the characteristics of a phenomenon of "fashion," that is, of voluntary acceptance dictated by suggestions of custom, which, even if they could have had limited influence on the manifestations of musical taste, are previous and extraneous to them.

*****

That conclusion contains an important passage concerning "the exchange of substance for form in the musical expression."[47] Elsewhere in the article, Pirrotta had drawn a distinction between the *ars contrapuncti* (the art of composing counterpoint) and the *ars musicae mensurabilis* (the art of notating mensural music)—notwithstanding the indissoluble linkage between the two—and suggested that the *subtilitas* of fin-de-siècle composers was directed more toward the latter than the former, because it could be explored almost without limit. In elaborating his principal, ramified observation, he quotes Charles van den Borren:

> [W]hat counts more is the preponderant weight that the *notation* comes to exercise at the moment of creation itself, as a kind of *musical nominalism that transfers the essence of the sounds into the notes that are sign and symbol of it* [emphases added]. "C'est qu'elle (la notation) est, de fait, le miroir même de l'esthéthique qu'elle sert: esthétique qui va, dans les cas extrêmes, jusqu'à se subordonner elle-même, par l'effet d'une sorte de virtuosité à rebours, aux possibilité presques paradoxales de la notation."[48]

What is Pirrotta's meaning?

First: elsewhere in his writings, Pirrotta distinguishes between *musical notation* and that which it only imperfectly represents, the *music* per se. In "Italian Music Libraries," he refers to the need "to recognize the spirit and human experience reawakened behind those signs [i.e., musical notation] and sounds." This is a Crocean concern. For Pirrotta, too, "musical works are

---

[47]This passage provoked much comment also at the "Convegno internazionale. Musicologia fra due Continenti: l'eredità di Nino Pirrotta, Roma, 4–6 giugno 2008, Accademia Nazionale dei Lincei." For an evocation of it in further scholarship, see Anne Stone, "Glimpses of the Unwritten Tradition in Some Ars Subtilior Works," *Musica disciplina* 50 (1996): 59–93.

[48]The van den Borren quotation is from "Considérations générales sur la conjonction de la polyphonie italienne et la polyph. du Nord," *Bulletin de l'Institut historique belge de Rome* 19 (1938): 177. Pirrotta returns to this formulation in **1980**: "Medieval," 19, where he writes of a pronounced interest in the aspects of notation, practically resulting in a kind of musical nominalism.

necessarily expressed" by means of "the usual peculiarities of each period's musical notation, relying in great part on the intuition and inspiration of the performers who complete the written signs."[49] His Idealist *linguaggio*—"complete the written signs," "recognize the spirit and human experience reawakened behind" them—leaves little doubt that for him, as for Croce, the notation—the "series of graphic signs"—is but a means to an end, "indications of what we have to do . . . to produce . . . physical things" "that directly arouse experiences corresponding to aesthetic expressions."[50]

Second: the distinction between "the essence of the sounds" and "the notes that are sign and symbol of it" leads us to another distinction. Many years later, Pirrotta will write systematically of the established ancient, medieval, and early-modern tripartition of music into *musica mundana, humana*, and *organica* (or *instrumentalis*).[51] *Musica mundana* was the music of the cosmos, the sounds produced by the planetary and stellar bodies in motion in their orbits and the consonant relationships among those sounds, which produce celestial harmony. *Musica humana* was the harmonious coexistence of the body and soul and their faculties, the accord of man's body and soul. *Musica organica* or *instrumentalis*, finally, was the actual material, terrestrial sounds produced by the human voice or various artificial means: strings, winds, percussion instruments.

Only the last of these would have been understood as requiring musical notation for its very existence, and then only sometimes: even *musica organica*—its composition, preservation, transmission, and performance—need not always have assumed notation, as Pirrotta argued throughout his career. *Musica mundana*, conversely, is forever free of dependence for *its* existence on so quotidian, even pedestrian, a phenomenon as notation.

Boethius had provided the "intellectualistic equipment" for this customary tripartition of music, and his distinctions were invoked in monuments of medieval European civilization: in Dante's *Comedy*, for example, Inferno is an "evil chorus" ("cattivo coro"), Purgatorio resounds with *musica instrumentalis*, and *musica mundana* is in evidence at the very opening of the Paradiso. In such an interpretive scheme, terrestrial *musica instrumentalis* is but a reflection of celestial harmony, and implicit in Boethius's cosmology are the convictions that harmony is universal and earthly harmony only one of its manifestations.

Third: Boethius's classification scheme intersects, though imperfectly, with another philosophical proposition concerning the relationship between form

---

[49] See also **1986**: "Problemi di una storia della musica."
[50] Croce, *Estetica come scienza dell'espressione e linguistica generale* (see "Intermedio I.$\underline{mo}$," n. 65); Croce, *The Aesthetic as the Science of Expression and of the Linguistic in General* (see "Intermedio I.$\underline{mo}$," n. 65).
[51] **1965**: "Dante *musicus*"; **1973**: "Ars musica"; **1975**: "Le tre corone e la musica"; **1976**: "'Musica de sono humano' and the Musical Poetics of Guido of Arezzo"; **1993**: notes to *O tu chara sciença*.

and matter (or between universals and individuals) and the mode of existence attributed to each, which was the subject of a millennia-old debate. Plato had posited the existence of eternally subsisting "Forms" or "Ideas" and asserted in the *Timaeus* that these served as patterns or blueprints in accord with which the World-Maker fashioned an intelligible world out of recalcitrant preexistent matter.[52] Underlying such a proposition were quintessentially Greek assumptions about the "unreality of matter."[53] In the *Timaeus* and similar paradigmatic texts, that which is "intelligible" (as contrasted with that which is "sensible") is what the ancient Greeks called "form" (as contrasted with what they called "matter"). Of the two elements—the formal and the material—of which all is composed, the material contributes no positive element to its being; the form is the essence. The object is nothing more than a realization of form; its materiality is the source of nothing beyond that which it derives from its form. Thus in the ancient Greek philosophy of nature, the two elements of form (the intelligible) and matter (the sensible) are distinguishable in the actual world. The intelligible is the basis of all being, whereas matter accounts only for the impoverishment of being; intelligent comprehension of form is sufficient for an understanding of that which exists in the world, whereas sense experience represents no addition to such understanding, only deficiency of it. Natural objects are artifacts (or analogous to artifacts) in this respect: they are nothing but an embodiment of form.

Pirrotta explained the (imperfect) intersection of the Boethian tripartition of music with

> the complex . . . tradition of . . . Platonism. . . . [M]usic is not merely the perceptible concord of sounds, but the deep inner relationship by which the poetic word reflects some fragment of the transcendent harmonious world of cosmic truths, and is thus an echo of the universal harmony[54] . . . . [T]he effects exerted by sounding music on . . . human beings . . . were but consequences of a superior truth, weakly reflected by the opaqueness of [*musica organica*].[55]

In Platonic terms, Boethius's celestial *musica mundana* was the universal, the formal, the intelligible: eternal and immutable. Terrestrial *musica organica*

---

[52]My sources for this section are several important works by Francis Oakley: *The Political Thought of Pierre d'Ailly: The Voluntarist Tradition*, (New Haven: Yale University Press, 1964); *Creation: The Impact of an Idea*, eds. Francis Oakley and Daniel O'Connor (New York: Charles Scribner's Sons, 1969); and *The Medieval Experience: Foundations of Western Cultural Singularity* (New York: Charles Scribner's Sons, 1974). See also David Knowles, *The Evolution of Medieval Thought* (New York: Vintage Books, 1962); Etienne Gilson, *History of Christian Philosophy in the Middle Ages* (New York: Random House, 1955); and Heiko Augustinus Oberman, *The Harvest of Medieval Theology. Gabriel Biel and Late Medieval Nominalism* (Grand Rapids, MI: Baker Book House, 1983). See especially Oakley, *The Political Thought of Pierre d'Ailly*, 18.

[53]I have borrowed liberally from M.B. Foster, "The Christian Doctrine of Creation and the Rise of Modern Natural Science," *Mind*, n.s., 43 (1934): 446–68.

[54]**1969**: *Music and Theatre*, 211.

[55]**1965**: "Dante *musicus*," 20.

was the individual, the sensible, the material: transient and to some extent illusory.

Early Christian philosophers had attempted "to Christianize the Platonic doctrine of . . . Ideas by locating them in the divine mind as exemplars in accordance with which God created the world and ruled it."[56] In 1277, however, several hundred philosophical propositions were condemned by the Bishop of Paris and the Archbishop of Canterbury. The condemnations reveal a concern that the absolute freedom and omnipotence of the Christian God were limited and thus endangered by such Hellenizing tendencies.[57]

Pirrotta's passing allusion to "nominalism" situates the music of the fourteenth century within its broadest philosophical context. In invoking it, he employs the terms of the

> recurrent dialectic between the Realist and Nominalist schools, between those philosophers who claimed that [the Platonic] universals possess something more than merely conceptual existence, and ascribed, therefore, some degree of extra-mental reality to them, and those who believed that only individuals truly exist and that universals corresponded to no extra-mental reality. Thus the radical difference between the philosophies of the thirteenth and fourteenth centuries, respectively, were seen to flow from the familiar realist-nominalist divide; the thirteenth century distinguished by the triumph of moderate realism, and the fourteenth by the recrudescence of nominalism in the philosophy of those who followed the so-called *via moderna*.[58]

Fourteenth-century philosophers, sensitive to the concerns that precipitated the condemnations of 1277, exemplify the "recrudescence of nominalism" that contrasts with the "moderate realism" of the thirteenth century. Universals—the Platonic Forms or Ideas—were now deemed mere conceptual abstractions, possessing no extra-mental reality; reality was considered to reside instead in the individual: the sensible and material.

The increased attention to musical notation in the fourteenth century suggests a "recrudescence of nominalism," because it elevates the status of *musica organica*: terrestrial music. In heightening the attention devoted to notation, the fourteenth century privileges the only music in the Boethian classification scheme that is ever reliant on notation for its existence. Formal, intelligible *musica mundana*, conversely, is free from such reliance for *its* existence. A preponderant weighting of notation is a sign of a shift in philosophical sensibility, an indication of the emerging preeminence of Nominalism as a philosophical tradition.

---

[56] Oakley, *Creation*, 63.
[57] Oakley, *The Political Thought of Pierre d'Ailly*, 17, 20, 22; *Creation*, 62–63; *The Medieval Experience*, 164–65.
[58] Oakley, *The Political Thought of Pierre d'Ailly*, 15.

In brief, Pirrotta's invocation of the terms of this late-medieval dialectic suggests the following: In the earlier article "On the Origin and History of the 'Caccia' and Fourteenth-Century 'Madrigal,' " he had proposed that before the fourteenth century, music had been understood as "a species of sonorous geometry, mirror of astral harmonies, '[*musica*] *mundana*' . . . made terrestrial and human." Fourteenth- and early-fifteenth-century composers who shared the prevailing Nominalist sympathies of contemporary philosophers metaphorically transferred the musical essence—relocated the reality of the music—from the celestial to the terrestrial, from the universal to the individual, from music for which notation is unnecessary, to sensible, material musical notation per se.[59] For the Realists, *musica organica* was mutable, perishable, and to some extent illusory; for the Nominalists, *musica organica*, entirely dependent on musical notation, was the only music that truly existed. Such a Realist/Nominalist opposition, and the fourteenth century's alignment with the latter, partly explains the more "sensual" character of the music of the *Ars subtilior*, as contrasted with the austere music of the so-called "school" of Nôtre Dame of the twelfth and thirteenth centuries, which represents the "high-medieval" triumph of *ars*.

By means of this almost nonchalant reference, which is elaborated no further, Pirrotta captures, and permits us to grasp, the elusive quiddity of the music of the *Ars subtilior*—its sensuality, its "fussiness," its bedevilingly complex notational representation—and in so doing illuminatingly contextualizes it.

*****

Let us summarize the principal themes and intellectual accomplishments of the writings of the Palermo years.

Pirrotta first advances the thesis that will become a signature component in his emerging vision of the entire development of Italian music in the medieval and early-modern periods: the existence of the unwritten musical tradition, which can be glimpsed, if at all, largely on the basis of nonmusical evidence—literary, iconographic—given that the music in question did not require notation for it to be preserved, transmitted, and performed.

This argument relates to another, which concerns the dependence of most varieties of polyphony on musical notation, the means of unambiguously specifying pitch and pitch duration. As a result of this dependence, the polyphonic tradition is the better known to us; and yet the musical culture accommodated many other varieties of musical practice that, *qua* actual

---

[59]See also **1965**: "Ars nova e stil novo," 27. And later still, in **1986**: "Problemi di una storia della musica," Pirrotta again makes this observation.

sounding music, are effectively lost because they were transmitted solely in oral form.

The article "Lirica monodica trecentesca" ("Fourteenth-Century Monophonic Song") introduces another signature Pirrotta thesis, concerning the contrasting aesthetics of melodic composition in polyphonic versus monophonic (or "monodic") composition. An individual melody embedded within a polyphonic complex is constructed so as to take account of the vertical requirements of the composition; its linear content is in part fashioned in accordance with the demands—not necessarily compatible—imposed by its simultaneously serving harmonic ends. In contrast, the melody of a monophonic composition is under no such additional constraints and can obey a different set of artistic considerations in melodic style and compositional aesthetic.

All of these arguments relate to yet another: in both the journalistic writings of the early to mid-1930s and the scholarly writings that soon follow, Pirrotta is intent on describing as precisely as possible the contrasting quiddities of late-medieval French and Italian music, a contrast drawn most sharply in "'Dulcedo' e 'subtitilas'" but alluded to elsewhere.

The relationship of this argument to the others is not easily explained, at least not in a nontrivial manner. It entails subtle, elusive matters of "cultural fashion,"[60] of a people's fundamental aesthetic sensibilities as central to their cultural and intellectual identity. Throughout the remainder of Pirrotta's career, he endeavors to describe the fragile, recurring dialectic in Italian musical life between the exogenous intellectualistic practice of polyphonic composition and native Italian responses (and even resistance) to it. In "Marchettus of Padua and the Italian Ars Nova," "Music and Cultural Tendencies in 15th-Century Italy," and " 'Maniera' polifonica e immediatezza recitativa," he traces the early-fourteenth-century importation into Italy of a French fashion for courtly, secular polyphonic musical composition and performance, which, significantly, was first supported on the Italian peninsula at the Angevin court of Naples ("Marchettus of Padua"). He examines the reaction of many fifteenth-century Italian Renaissance humanists, who disdained such practices as typifying the perceived inelegance of medieval scholasticism as an intellectual program ("Music and Cultural Tendencies"). He then considers developments in the sixteenth century, when polyphonic practice was momentarily reconciled with the continuing objectives in sensitive text expression of the sixteenth-century successors to the Quattrocento humanists ("'Maniera' polifonica").

Against this background, the theories concerning polyphonic practice, its reliance on musical notation as its means of preservation, and the attendant

---

[60]I am borrowing from the title of Mircea Eliade's *Occultism, Witchcraft, and Cultural Fashions: Essays in Comparative Religions* (Chicago: University of Chicago Press, 1976).

matter of the contrasting aesthetics of melodic style (depending on whether the melody is monophonic or embedded within a polyphonic context) relate to the larger matters of cultural fashion at any given moment in history and a people's cultural and intellectual identity. The choices a people make about fundamental musical-compositional practices and preferences in melodic style are expressions of identity. The Idealist, and Nationalist, concerns implicit in such matters are obvious.

Such Nationalist concerns relate, in turn, to Pirrotta's determination to achieve a proper balance in the collective scholarly imagination between competing claims on behalf of France and Italy, to correct imbalances in inherited views about the putative primacy of France with respect to European musico-cultural achievement in the Middle Ages. This particular theory therefore relates to all those advanced thus far, because claims concerning French supremacy within the musical culture of the Middle Ages depend to some extent on assumptions about the superiority of written polyphony as a compositional technique. If, on the other hand, one's fundamental assumptions—one's aesthetic "first principles"—allow for an appreciation for "open madrigalesque melodizing, in svelte melismatic sequences, which open like oases in the dense forest of stubborn syncopations," the balance in claims concerning French and Italian medieval musical cultures and the worth of their relative achievements will be recalibrated.

A more circumscribed theory first formulated during the Palermo years concerns the relationship of the limited diffusion of polyphony to the conditions of the Material *ambiente:* polyphony was confined to particular environments, populated by those who had had a certain kind of education; its composers—even when the musical repertory in question was secular—were frequently ecclesiastics, whose engagement with polyphonic musical compositions was the expression of particular moments in their lives and professional and personal activities.

Pirrotta had a Materialist's interest in describing the infrastructure of musical patronage. We note, for example, the careful account of the practices of the Avignonese papacy, or the view that the cultivation of polyphony in early-fifteenth-century Italy was due to the presence of musicians in the retinues of members of Councils called to resolve the Great Schism. The geographical universality of the medieval ecclesiastical orders was a factor of great consequence for the diffusion of polyphonic musical practice.

In the writings of the Palermo years, Pirrotta also first explores the relationship between the "learned" and "popular" traditions and the vestiges of the latter occasionally detected in the former, as the result of painstaking and imaginative analysis.

Finally, the early writings already reveal a professional's command of the macroscopic aesthetic and intellectual factors that inform microscopic developments in the musical culture: with the philosophers' realist–nominalist debate;[61] or the emergence of that new understanding of music, which previously had been understood in terms of its status as one of the Quadrivia, "a species of sonorous geometry, mirror of astral harmonies, '[*musica*] *mundana*' . . . made terrestrial and human"; or the "conquest" of the "tactile values" temporally coincident with the "clarity and melodic plasticity . . . at which the . . . Italian polyphonists who prepared the *ars nova* . . . arrived."

---

[61]In "Storia, filologia e gusto musicale: rileggendo i primi scritti di Pirrotta" (see "*Scena 3.ª*," n. 36), Fabrizio Della Seta speculates that Pirrotta's sensitivity to such philosophico-contextual matters—his use of the terms and concepts "*subtilitas*," "nominalism"—may be consequences of his friendship with Eugenio Garin.

Scena 5.ᵃ

The Conservatorio di Musica «S.ᵗᵃ Cecilia» di Roma (1948–56): *Opera Seicentesca*

DIRETTORE DELLE BIBLIOTECHE OF THE ACCADEMIA AND CONSERVATORIO «S.ᵀᴬ CECILIA» DI ROMA

THE INTERNATIONAL ASSOCIATION OF MUSIC LIBRARIES

THE *ENCICLOPEDIA DELLO SPETTACOLO*

THE MADRIGAL COMEDY AND DRAMATIC MADRIGAL

FLORENTINE ARISTOCRATIC OPERA

ANTONIO CESTI

"*COMMEDIA DELL'ARTE* AND OPERA"

In the "Relazione del Consiglio Accademico all'Assemblea Generale" of the Accademia di «S.ᵗᵃ Cecilia» of 21 November 1948, it was announced that

> Francesco Mantica, who for many years . . . has held the direction of the Biblioteca . . . , has left his post, having reached the age limit. . . . Professor Antoni[n]o Pirrotta was now called to direct the library.[1]

---

[1] Accademia di Santa Cecilia, *Annuario 1943–1949* (*CCCLIX–CCCLXV*) (n.d.): 192, 210–11. The vacancy in the library directorship at the «S.ᵗᵃ Cecilia» was actually occasioned by the conclusion of the tenure of Signorina Maddalena Pacifico as temporary regent. Signorina Pacifico's career was an expression in microcosm of the tragic macrocosmic history of Italy during the 1920s, '30s, and '40s: she had served as one of the *applicati* (clerical staff) during the directorship of *Bibliotecario* Mantica (1920–48) (see *REGIA ACCADEMIA DI SANTA CECILIA ANNUARIO 1935-1936* [*XIII–XIV*] [*CCCLI–CCCLII*] [1936]: 357), but during the Fascist era was dismissed from her post, a victim of anti-Semitic Fascist racial laws (see Walter H. Rubsamen, "Music Research in Italian Libraries: An Anecdotal Account of Obstacles and Discoveries," *Notes*, 2nd series, 6 [1949]: 220–33). With the American occupation of Rome, beginning in 1944, and the fall of the Fascist régime, Signorina Pacifico was returned to a post at the library and subsequently appointed temporary regent. To her, musicologists owe the discovery of the precious autograph manuscript one of Giovanni Pierluigi da Palestrina's liturgical compositions: see Palestrina, *Omnis pulchritudo Domini a 8 voci in 2 cori (da un manoscritto autografo inedito)*. Partitura in notazione moderna di GIANFRANCO MASELLI con nota di VIRGILIO MORTARI stampata in 1000 esemplari numerati (Rome: Edizioni DE SANTIS—Roma della Ditta Alberto De Santis, Roma, 1950), p. 3.

Nino Pirrotta's seniority within the Italian state educational system, his success in rapidly bringing the conservatory library in Palermo back to functioning order, and his growing stature as a scholar qualified him for advancement when the library directorships at the Accademia and Conservatorio di Musica «S.ᵗᵃ Cecilia» di Roma fell vacant. Because the «S.ᵗᵃ Cecilia» was one of those institutions not required by financial constraints to combine the responsibilities of *bibliotecario* and professor of music history, Pirrotta's Roman responsibilities were more circumscribed than his Palermitan ones.

The Roman years were extremely productive for Pirrotta's scholarship.[2] He continued his series of publications on the music of the Trecento and began his edition of that repertory.[3] His tenure at the «S.ᵗᵃ Cecilia» afforded him contact with European and American librarians and scholars and resulted in several reflections on the library as crucial to scholarship.[4] Most important, Rome had a wealth of sources for other phases of the history of Italian music, and Pirrotta took advantage of them to inaugurate his series of studies of the origins and early development of that most characteristic of Italian musical genres, the opera. Initially, he concentrated on the aristocratic Florentine phase of operatic history and the genre's development thereafter by one of its most colorful figures, Antonio Cesti.

*****

DIRETTORE DELLE BIBLIOTECHE OF THE ACCADEMIA AND CONSERVATORIO «S.ᵀᴬ CECILIA» DI ROMA

The Accademia di «S.ᵗᵃ Cecilia» is the descendant of an institution founded in the mid-sixteenth century, the informal "Compagnia di Roma," whose early history, interestingly, was studied by Pirrotta.[5] Following the unification of Italy, the Conservatory proper emerged from music schools supported by the Accademia. In 1915, M. Enrico Bossi was named director of the Conservatory. When Pirrotta was appointed *bibliotecario*, the director was Maestro Alessandro Bustini, appointed by the Allies as "Commissario straordinario per il Conservatorio," who served from 1947 to 1950. Bustini's successor was Maestro Guido Guerrini, who earlier had been director of the Conservatory in

---

[2] See Ziino's "Pirrotta between Cambridge and Rome," *Studi musicali* 28 (1999): 39–42.

[3] The plan of the edition of the *Trecento* repertory—the first volume of which was published in 1954—had earlier been described in the back matter of *Musica disciplina* 5 (1951).

[4] **1951**: "Fondi musicali non inventariati nè catalogati"; **1952**: "Le biblioteche musicali italiane"; and **1954**: "Compiti regionali, nazionali ed internazionali delle bilioteche musicali."

[5] See **1993**: *I musici di Roma e il madrigale*, especially XXXI. See also the opening paragraph of **1983**: "Un'altra congregazione di Santa Cecilia." On 1 May 1585, Pope Sixtus V issued the Bull *Rationi congruit*, which officially recognized a "Congregation of Roman musicians under the protection of the Blessed Virgin, Gregory the Great[,] and Saint Cecilia." Ibid.

Florence during the last of Pirrotta's four years there as student and served as director of the «S.ᵗᵃ Cecilia» throughout the remainder of Pirrotta's tenure.

A portion of the library of the Accademia, opened to the public in 1878, was administratively separated from the Academy in 1919 and annexed to the Conservatory;[6] today it is the "Biblioteca musicale governativa del Conservatorio di Musica «S.ᵗᵃ Cecilia»."[7] With the relocation of the capital of Italy to Rome, the Conservatory was assigned the Monastero delle Orsoline as its quarters, with space reserved for the associated Accademia di «S.ᵗᵃ Cecilia», and to this day the former convent in Via de' Greci houses the Conservatory and its associated "Biblioteca . . . governativa."[8]

Pirrotta first went to Rome alone, to be joined by his wife and four children once their apartment in Via Eustachio Manfredi was ready. The family settled into a routine. Pirrotta would work all morning at the «S.ᵗᵃ Cecilia». Some afternoons, he would sequester himself in his study (a space in the *salotto*, enclosed like a Renaissance *studiolo*), to devote quiet hours to his scholarship; on others, he would return to the «S.ᵗᵃ Cecilia».[9]

Pirrotta assumed his responsibilities as "Direttore delle Biblioteche dell'Accademia e del Conservatorio di «S.ᵗᵃ Cecilia»" in October 1948.[10] His nephew Agostino has provided a picture of his uncle's activities at the library.[11] In the ironic, almost whimsical tone that often enlivens his writings, Pirrotta wrote of "demands arising from one moment to the next, which need to be answered immediately,"

> such as requests from readers . . . , bureaucratic matters, problems connected with cataloguing, and—why not?—projects and programs intended to develop the library's structure and equipment in order to make the best use of the space [and]

---

[6] By the terms of law n. 1672 (22 August 1919).

[7] At the end of the twentieth century its collection numbered some 170,000 printed volumes and 7,000 manuscripts.

[8] The Accademia and its associated library have since been relocated to the Parco della Musica.

[9] It was a period in the history of Italian society (and European society more generally) when, supervised by a governess, the children of families of the Pirrottas' social status would often lead somewhat separate lives from their parents'; and, so, at night, the Pirrotta children would have supper without their mother and father, who would then take the evening meal alone.

[10] Pirrotta's official appointment as *direttore* ran from 1948–58, but he was away for the academic year 1954/55 and for the fall semester of the 1955/56 academic year, and his permanent appointment to the faculty at Harvard took effect in the fall semester of 1956. However, he did not formally resign his position at the «S.ᵗᵃ Cecilia» until 1958, at which time he was succeeded by Prof.ssa Emilia Zanetti. This circumstance explains the dates and references given in such sources as *Il Conservatorio di Musica "S. Cecilia . . . di Roma in occasione della cerimonia d'inaugurazione della rinnovata sede dell'Istituto nel restaurato ex Monastero delle Orsoline alla presenza del Presidente della Repubblica Italiana On.ᵗᵉ Prof. Antonio Segni* (n.p.: Repubblica Italiana, 1964), 61, and **1955**: "Cronologia e denominazione dell'ars nova italiana," a paper that evidently went to press after Pirrotta had accepted the appointment at Harvard but before he had formally resigned the post at the «S.ᵗᵃ Cecilia». See also Accademia di Santa Cecilia, *Annuario 1957–1958* (CCCLXXIII–CCCLXXIV) (n.d.): 491, and Accademia di Santa Cecilia, *Annuario 1960–1961* (CCCLXXVI-CCCLXXVII) (n.d.): 14.

[11] See Ziino, "Pirrotta between Cambridge and Rome."

render its headquarters more inviting and aesthetically suitable—projects and programs that the librarian cannot ignore, though he knows that he will inevitably encounter almost insurmountable difficulties in realizing them.[12]

He was initially assisted by a staff of six, including his immediate predecessor (Prof.ssa Maddalena Pacifico) and his immediate successor (Prof.ssa Emilia Zanetti).[13]

*****

THE INTERNATIONAL ASSOCIATION OF MUSIC LIBRARIES

Notwithstanding the riches of the primary sources at the «S.ta Cecilia» and Pirrotta's sense of how productive the Rome years were, he had only limited time for his own research because of his administrative responsibilities.

Nonetheless, his status as director of one of the major music libraries of Europe provided opportunities for productive scholarly activity. Pirrotta was among the first to examine the famous "Medici Codex," which has prompted much musicological debate. He began an association with the Florentine publisher Olschki and its journal *Collectanea Historiae Musicae*.[14] And he developed a close relationship with Armen Carapetyan, then living in Rome, who founded the American Institute of Musicology (AIM) during Pirrotta's Rome years.[15] The AIM was to be one of the most important vehicles for the dissemination of Pirrotta's scholarship: the Institute's journal (now *Music disciplina*) published no fewer than six of Pirrotta's articles, and his edition of the Trecento repertory appeared in the Institute's Corpus Mensurabilis Musicae.

At the «S.ta Cecilia», Pirrotta also had the opportunity to meet scholars from throughout the world who would visit the library to consult its materials. Among them was Oliver Strunk, Professor of Music at Princeton University,

---

[12]**1953:** "Nella biblioteca di Santa Cecilia: Cesti e Abbatini—'Opera,."

[13]Other colleagues are identified in Accademia di Santa Cecilia, *Annuario 1943–1949* (*CCCLIX–CCCLXV*) (n.d.): 780. For more on Pacifico and Zanetti, see Rubsamen, "Music Research in Italian Libraries." And on Zanetti, see now *Musicologia come pretesto: Scritti in memoria di Emilia Zanetti*, ed. Tiziana Affortunato (Rome: IISM, 2010).

[14]See Pirrotta, **1986:** "Historiae Musicae Cultores."

[15]For this information, I am grateful to James Haar, private interview at the annual national meeting of the American Musicological Society, 5–9 November 2008. Pirrotta suggests the importance of his friendship with Carapetyan in *Poesia e musica e altri saggi* (Florence: La Nuova Italia, 1994), VIII. For a glimpse of the activities of the American Institute of Musicology during these years, and Pirrotta's involvement, see, for example, Armen Carapetyan, "Editorial: In Reply to an Incorrect Statement," *Musica disciplina* 3 (1949): 45–54, especially 53, on the courses offered by the Institute, and Pirrotta, **1948:** "On the Problem of 'Sumer is icumen in,'" especially 209, on the courses.

whose colleagueship and friendship were among the most consequential of Pirrotta's career. There was rewarding interaction with other European and American librarians and scholars. And Pirrotta collaborated with Italian colleagues on an exhibition to mark the third centenary of Arcangelo Corelli's birth, and he coedited the accompanying catalog.[16]

*****

Soon after assuming his duties at the «S.ᵗᵃ Cecilia», Pirrotta also helped organize the first world congress of music librarians and museum curators, the "Premier Congrès des Bibliothèques Musicales," held in Florence in 1949. He was established thereby as one of the pioneers in the postwar effort to ensure that Europe's music librarians collaborate in the initiative to preserve and inventory the European manuscript and printed musical patrimony.[17]

The Accademia del Conservatorio «Luigi Cherubini», Pirrotta's alma mater, was the official host of the Congress, which opened with a ceremonial event in Florence's Palazzo Vecchio. The Congress was attended by some 60 participants from 12 countries, and among the urgent initiatives identified was the collaborative cataloguing of extant primary musical sources, to which Pirrotta made important conceptual and practical contributions. The project became the "Répertoire international des sources musicales" (RISM), fundamental to the scholarly activity of many musicologists.[18]

At the conclusion of the Florence congress, German musicologist Friedrich Blume advocated for a second gathering, to be held the following year in Lüneberg. At the second congress a proposal was drafted for the formation of a "Société Internationale des Bibliothécaires Musicaux." The Lüneberg congress also advanced the initiative launched a year earlier in Florence for the comprehensive inventory of source materials.

Finally, in 1951, the International Association of Music Libraries was officially founded, at the Maison de l'UNESCO in Paris.[19] Five attendees—among them founding members Nino Pirrotta and Friedrich Blume—spoke about the logistical challenges of cataloging the sources, an initiative that

---

[16]*1953: Catalogo della mostra corelliana.*

[17]See *Fontes Artis Musicae. Organe de l'Association International des Bibliothèques Musicales* 3 (1956): 187.

[18]On the initiative to launch RISM, and the role Pirrotta played, see "International Inventory of Musical Sources: The Joint Committee Meeting in Paris, January 1952," *Notes*, 2nd ser., 9 (1952): 213–25. For the developments recapitulated in this paragraph and the two following, see also Daniel Heartz, "The 'Répertoire International des Sources Musicales,'" *Journal of the American Musicological Society* 14 (1961): 268–73.

[19]For a photograph of Pirrotta at the Paris congress, see "Notes for *Notes*," *Notes*, 2nd ser., 9 (1951): 63–72. Attending the Paris congress was Kenneth Levy, then a graduate student at Princeton, who would play an important role in arranging Pirrotta's appointment as Visiting Professor of Music at Princeton and remain one of his lifelong friends. Levy was spending the academic year 1950/51 in Paris on research for his doctoral dissertation, and there he made the acquaintance of François Lesure, who invited Levy to participate at the 1951 congress. This information was provided by Professor Levy in an interview with A.M. Cummings.

Pirrotta now officially entitled the "Repertorio Internazionale delle fonti musicali."[20] As a member of the provisional commission and in preparation for his address, Pirrotta had circulated a questionnaire, and on the basis of the results he proposed that a universal cataloguing system be developed and that the financial and moral support of international organizations, governments, and public and private institutions be secured, as indispensable to completing the work.[21] And "thanks to Pirrotta, two contributions of 500,000.00 *lire* were made by the Ministry of Public Instruction."[22]

Among the more significant consequences of the 1951 congress were the launching of a journal—initially (in 1952 and '53) a modest *Bulletin d'information*, now *Fontes Artis Musicae*[23]—and Pirrotta's election to a three-year term as Vice President of the Association of Music Libraries and president of the Italian group. Pirrotta recalled that it was due to Fausto Torrefranca's advocacy that he began to assume an ever more visible role on the larger European scholarly stage: Torrefranca had nominated him to be the Italian representative on the United Nations Educational, Scientific and Cultural Organization's (UNESCO) Conseil International de la Musique, of which Torrefranca was vice president, and thus "opened the way ... to ampler fields of experience and encounters."[24]

*****

THE *ENCICLOPEDIA DELLO SPETTACOLO*

Pirrotta's engagement with the music of the Italian Renaissance theater and the beginnings of opera was the result of two developments: first, the commission for a series of articles for the *Enciclopedia dello Spettacolo*;[25] and second, the availability in Rome of relevant primary sources (among them a copy of the 1600 print of Jacopo Peri's *Euridice*, the earliest extant complete opera, and a manuscript copy of the complete score of Antonio Cesti's *Orontea*).

The encyclopedia was envisioned as early as 1944, not long after Rome's liberation by the Allies. In 1949, a new format for the publication was adopted:

---

[20]On Pirrotta's presentation, see Richard S. Hill, "*Association Internationale des Bibliothèques Musicales. Troisième Congrès International des Bibliothèques Musicales, Paris, 22–25 Juillet 1951*," Notes, 2nd ser., 10 (1953): 444–46.

[21]**1951**: "Fondi musicali non inventariati nè catalogati." RISM is also discussed in **1952**: "Le biblioteche musicali italiane [Italian Music Libraries]," and **1954**: "Compiti regionali, nazionali ed internazionali delle bilioteche musicali." For the report of the third congress, and Pirrotta's role, see also http://unesdoc.unesco.org/images/ 0017/001789/178950eb.pdf.

[22]See http://www.urfm.it/urfm-storia.html.

[23]Published by Bärenreiter Verlag in Kassel.

[24]**1983**: "Introduzione ai lavori," 11. But on Torrefranca's complex status with the discipline of musicology, see the references in my previous chapters.

[25]Sotto gli auspici della Fondazione Giorgio Cini, 9 vols. (Rome: Casa editrice Le Maschere, 1954–62).

The redaction was to be the responsibility of some 30 to 35 scholars, and among the "redattori" of the "sezione teatro musicale" was Nino Pirrotta.

Pirrotta was entrusted with responsibility for a long series of articles on subjects closely aligned with his own developing scholarly interests,[26] which made it possible for him to incorporate the results of his study of the primary sources. At the same time, the need for synthetic treatment of the material stimulated and directed his original research;[27] it yielded scholarly dividends from which he would profit for decades to come: in the encyclopedia entries, Pirrotta first adumbrates material and interpretations that he will elaborate greatly in future writings.

Apart from the continuing attention to the music of the Trecento, Pirrotta's scholarly interests of the Rome years may be classified as follows:

1. The musical elements of the comedies of Adriano Banchieri, treated in the entry on Banchieri for the *Enciclopedia* and a 1950 article for the Venice *biennale*.

2. The aristocratic Florentine origins of opera, illuminated as a result of his access to the 1600 print of Peri's *L'Euridice* and also described in encyclopedia entries on such subjects as Count Giovanni Bardi, the Caccini family, and the so-called Florentine Camerata. Concurrently, he was involved with a broadcast performance of *Euridice* over Italian radio in 1951, for which he prepared the edition. The entire project resulted in two important articles on differences of artistic temperament within the Camerata, in which he qualifies an earlier, simplistic understanding of the Camerata as a supposedly organic "institution" with a unity of purpose and perspective.

3. Cesti's early operatic activity, clarified as a result of his access to the manuscript score of *Orontea* and his encyclopedia entry on Cesti's supposed teacher Abbatini, which also resulted in a performance of the opera (in Siena, in 1953), as well as two substantial articles on Cesti.

Cesti's role in stabilizing a tradition of comic opera is a prominent theme in the articles on the composer. Pirrotta was thus able to synthesize his findings in the articles in the first of these categories (on the use of music in the theatrical comedies of the Italian Renaissance) with those in the third

---

[26] Among them "Abbatini, " "Apolloni," "Artusi," "Badoaro," "Banchieri," "Bardi," "Buffo," "Caccini," "Camerata fiorentina," "Cavalieri," "Cavalli," "Cesti," "Commedia dell'Arte," "Corsi," "Doni," "Ferrari," "Gagliano," "Galilei," "Intermezzo, I.1.," "Mei," "Peri," and "Rinuccini." With a few exceptions, I have not listed here the many other articles on sixteenth-century composers of music for theatrical performances, because I regard Pirrotta's more systematic and comprehensive engagement with music in the Italian Renaissance theater as belonging to a subsequent phase of his career.

[27] On the importance of the commissions from the *Enciclopedia* for inspiring the new directions in Pirrotta's scholarship, Pierluigi Petrobelli, "Nino Pirrotta e Diego Carpitella," especially 55 (see "*Scena 3.^{a},*" n. 14).

(the beginnings of comic opera), in an article that enjoys the status of a classic: "*Commedia dell'Arte* and Opera," in which the objective was to elucidate correspondences between "the two most typical forms of the Italian theater."

*****

THE MADRIGAL COMEDY AND DRAMATIC MADRIGAL

The articles on Banchieri are among the earliest published expressions of Pirrotta's abiding interest in the use of music in the Italian Renaissance theater, which culminated in his 1969, Kinkeldey Award-winning magnum opus, *Li due Orfei*.

Banchieri's music-theatrical works are indebted to those of Orazio Vecchi, which "started from a real aspiration to translate . . . the *vis comica* of the commedia dell'arte into madrigalesque language,"[28] to apply the compositional conventions of the madrigal tradition to theatrical comedies.

In his encyclopedia entry on Banchieri,[29] Pirrotta distinguishes between the "madrigal comedy" and "dramatic madrigal."[30] Among the stimuli for Banchieri's ventures in the former may have been the influence of his teacher Giuseppe Guami, who as organist in Munich and Venice had become familiar with attempts to incorporate music more fully into performances of comedies— such as those organized by Orlando di Lasso at the Bavarian court—and realize the performative possibilities inherent in the light Venetian musical genres of the giustiniane and mascherate.

As early as 1597, in *La Nobilissima, anzi asinissima compagnia delli briganti della Bastina* (Vicenza 1597 [1st ed.]), Banchieri had featured the familiar personages and distinguishing dialectical speech of the commedia dell'arte, and elsewhere he had used the characteristic parodies of well-known madrigal texts. But there was no dramatic action, and the decisive contribution in that respect came from Vecchi, whose *Amfiparnaso* of 1597 was promptly emulated by Banchieri in his *Pazzia senile*. Indeed, Banchieri's indebtedness to Vecchi is documented by his *Studio dilettevole . . . dal Amfiparnasso . . . del Horatio Vecchi* (Milan 1600; Cologne 1603), which is an arrangement of compositions by Vecchi for a vocal ensemble of three voices, his reduction of the five-voice madrigalian compositions in Vecchi's *Amfiparnaso*.[31]

---

[28] **1950**: "Il 'Festino' di Banchieri," especially 72.

[29] **1954**: "BANCHIERI, ADRIANO."

[30] In this respect, Pirrotta's understanding advanced since he wrote the earlier article, "Il 'Festino' di Banchieri," where, following Alfred Einstein, he seems to subsume all of Banchieri's theatrical works within a single generic category. In the later encyclopedia entry and the article on the *Commedia dell'Arte*, Pirrotta distinguishes between the two generic types of the madrigal comedy and dramatic madrigal, on the basis of the number of voices: three-voice compositions in the tradition of the *canzonetta* and *villanella alla napoletana* in the madrigal comedies, "proper" five-voice madrigals in the dramatic madrigal.

[31] On this matter, see also **1950**: "Il 'Festino.'"

Three of Banchieri's works are to be classified as "madrigal comedies" proper:

- the *Pazzia senile* (six editions between 1598 and 1621);
- *Il Metamorfosi musicale* (Venice 1600, 1608); and
- the *Virtuoso ridotto tra Signori e Dame entro il quale si concerta recitabilmente . . . una nuova comedia detta Proudenza giovanile* (Milan 1607, but perhaps composed before the *Metamorfosi*; the edition of 1628—identified as the "IV impressione"—bears the alternative title *Saviezza giovanile*).

Their plots (and that of Vecchi's *Amfiparnaso*) are essentially identical. They feature a time-honored comic/dramatic situation, familiar from innumerable Italian Renaissance comedies (Niccolò Machiavelli's *La mandragola* among them) and innumerable Italian and European comic operas (including Gioachino Rossini's *Il barbiere di Siviglia* and even the operas of W.S. Gilbert and Sir Arthur Sullivan): with the help of their servants, two attractive young lovers circumvent impediments to their union, which usually include the opposition of their elders and the unsolicited and unrequited overtures of other importunate, unattractive suitors. The comic types in such a dramatic situation ultimately derive from classical Latin exemplars, such as the comedies of Plautus and Terence.[32]

Pirrotta describes the principal musical elements of the madrigal comedies: they consisted of

> [1] extremely rapid and synthetic dialog, which tends toward a "talking" singability derived from various types of polyphonic canzonette or villanelle, though—compared to the contemporary monodic recitative—retaining a more musical accentuation; [2] pieces of local color, often interwoven with echoes of popular music, which end up assuming more or less openly the character of intermedii; [and 3] love scenes, which come closest to the serious madrigalesque style, whether for the sake of contrast or to parody certain musicians or works.[33]

The resources required for the polyphonic compositions are, without exception, limited to three voices.

The category of the "dramatic madrigal" includes such works as Banchieri's *Zabaione musicale, inventione boscareccia* (Milan 1603); *La Barca di Venezia per Padova* (Venice 1605, 1623); and *Il Festino nella sera del giovedì grasso* (Venice 1608). Here, the musical rendition of dialog is reduced to a minimum,

---

[32]See also my "*Scena 9.ª*," where I return to discuss the evocation of such archetypes of character and situation across time, genre, and national/cultural tradition.

[33]For an instance of dialog that "tends toward a 'talking' singability" "while conserving a more musical accentuation in contrast with the contemporary monodic recitative," see, for example, "O dalla casa" from the *Saviezza Giovanile*.

"supplanted in the presentation of the various episodes by the reading of purely literary 'captions,'" whereas "the pieces in the style of the intermedii, the jokes, and the musical parodies get greater development, even in the enlarged texture for five voices." "The 'mixtures' of pieces in various genres" were "held together . . . by the idea of a parlor or academy game (at that time, even comedy . . . was a characteristic academic manifestation)."

Thus the discrete "set pieces" are linked to one another by means of the imposition of the frame, in the venerable tradition of Boccaccio's *Decameron* or Chaucer's *Canterbury Tales*. As Pirrotta explained in "Il 'Festino' di Banchieri,"

> the preferred "frame" is that of a party, a banquet, [or] a series of meetings. But these works also reflect a custom going back to the sixteenth century, which replaced the story-telling of the earlier companies with music-making, by a soloist or in groups.

(This was a "sign of the influence exerted on the theater by stories.") Further,

> in the stories the framework was realistic, while the stories themselves [or, in the case of Vecchi's dramatic madrigals, the "pieces in the style of the intermedii, the jokes, and the musical parodies"] were removed from reality.[34]

Banchieri maintains the rigidly observed distinction between the two genres with respect to number of voices: his "madrigal comedies" are published in the series of books of his three-voice canzonette and villanelle, whereas the "dramatic madrigals" are published in the series of books of five-voice madrigals.[35]

*****

FLORENTINE ARISTOCRATIC OPERA

Musico-theatrical activity antedating the beginnings of opera was heterogeneous in nature, and the sensibilities underlying the Florentine aristocratic origins of the new genre were very different from those underlying Banchieri's madrigal comedies, notwithstanding the commonality of concern with the possible theatrical uses of music. In his publications on the subject, Pirrotta's

---

[34]**1969:** *Music and Theatre*, 127.
[35]See **1954:** "Commedia dell'Arte e Melodramma." This distinction is also clear from a rapid survey of the list of Banchieri's publications in the *Grove Music Online*, ed. L. Macy, http://www.grovemusic.com: the *Pazzia senile: ragionamenti vaghi, et dilettevoli...libro II*, 3 voices (Venice, 1598, rev. 2nd ed., 1599) is specifically identified as "*libro II*," and thus to be seen as a sequel to *Canzonette, novamente, sotto diversi capricci, composte . . . Hora prima di recreatione*, 3 voices (Venice, 1597); on the other hand, the *Zabaione musicale: inventione boscareccia, et 1 libro di madrigali*, 5 voices (Milan, 1604) is specifically identified as the "*1° libro di madrigali*."

presentation—his rhetorical devices—conveys the profound, though by no means easily describable, differences in the rarified "atmospherics."

Opera originated in a cultural ambience notable for its extraordinary intellectual refinement. Since the late fifteenth century, the Medici had surrounded themselves with humanist Neoplatonists, and one of the elements in the complex theoretical and practical activity that led to the beginnings of opera was a sophisticated Platonistic philosophizing. Pirrotta's principal objective in his various publications of the 1950s was to draw distinctions among the contrasting "temperaments and tendencies" in the profiles and activities of the creators of the new genre.

However, the original impetus for Pirrotta's engagement with the subject matter was practical.[36] He had been entrusted with preparing the edition for a performance of Jacopo Peri's *Euridice*, the earliest extant complete opera (premiered 6 October 1600 in Palazzo Pitti in Florence), which was to be recorded and broadcast over Italian radio—Radiotelevisione italiana (RAI)—in 1951.[37] The «S.ᵗᵃ Cecilia» library possessed a rare copy of the original 1600 print, and Pirrotta set about interpreting its late-Renaissance notation, rendering it understandable to modern performers, which involved expanding the many highly abbreviated elements of the original notation into an interpretable form (to "realize" them, in established musicological parlance).

Students of Baroque music know that one of the most potentially bedeviling challenges is the realization of the basso continuo, the bass line continuously underlying the texture throughout the composition and providing its foundation. Above this foundation, and in addition to the bass notes, the player of a plucked-string instrument (harpsichord, lute, chitarrone, theorbo) would improvise chords that were either suggested by the harmonic progression implicit in the bass line or schematically indicated by the composer by means of Arabic numerals, sharps, and flats placed intermittently above particular bass notes.

In 1951, musicologists—and performers—had much less collective experience in such matters than they do now, and Pirrotta's edition of *Euridice* was a pioneering attempt[38] to recover elusive improvisatory musical practices, which during their time had been the inheritance of accomplished musicians.

---

[36]For assistance with this section, I am grateful to Professor Tim Carter of the University of North Carolina, Chapel Hill.

[37]See Pirrotta's brief account of the enterprise in the Preface to *Music and Culture in Italy*, p. xi: "my operatic studies ... first started when I moved to Rome and, as a music librarian, had access to practically all the available sources for the initial phase of the new genre and its Roman developments. An unpublished edition of Peri's *Euridice*, which I prepared and commented on for a radio broadcast in 1951, was my first move to stress the importance that Peri, Caccini, and Cavalieri had achieved, each in his own way, on the positive side of competitive creativity."

[38]Though not *the* pioneering attempt, as Professor Carter reminds me: there were earlier editions of *Euridice*.

He consulted regularly with his brother-in-law Ottavio Ziino, composer and conductor, to check his own sense of what constituted a musically effective and satisfying realization of the basso continuo;[39] and he drew on his studies at the Conservatory in Florence, which had included training in figured-bass accompaniment.

There were other choices to be made: about instrumentation (very little is specified in the primary source[40]), about which modern singers' vocal ranges—and vocal apparatus and abilities—were most appropriate to the late-Renaissance aesthetic in Peri's writing for voice, about the division of the opera into discrete episodes or "scenes."

In addition to preparing the performing materials, Pirrotta also assumed responsibility for various details of the broadcast and commented on the opera and its performance. It was one in a series of performances dedicated to "Italian operas of the 1600s,"[41] inaugurated at the beginning of 1951. During

---

[39]As reported by Agostino Ziino in private conversation with A.M. Cummings.

[40]As Tim Carter reminds me, Peri does specify instrumentation at one point—Tirsi's "triflauto"—and the instruments that the basso continuo group comprised were known from Peri's preface.

[41]On the information in this paragraph, see above all Roberto Giuliani, "L'antica musica ridotta alla moderna prattica dell'etere. Quindici anni di committenze e recuperi (1946–1961), da Mantelli a Pirrotta, con una cauda sul linguaggio radiofonico," *"Et facciamo dolçi canti": Studi in onore di Agostino Ziino in occasione del suo 65° compleanno*, ed. Bianca Maria Antolini, Teresa M. Gialdroni, and Annunziato Pugliese, 2 vols. (Lucca: Libreria Musicale Italiana, 2003), 2:1311–55, especially 1327–29. There, Professor Giuliani revealed that Pirrotta's manuscript edition of *Euridice*, which had been assumed to be lost, has survived in the archives of the Radiotelevisione italiana, along with Pirrotta's manuscript editions of a concerto by Alessandro Scarlatti and Luzzasco Luzzaschi's madrigal *O primavera*. The tape of the performance, tape Rc 752, recorded 15 January 1951, was remastered on 10 December 1980, and on the page accompanying the tape is the annotation: "light noise in the background and some small rumblings, technical reconstruction." I am grateful to Professor Giuliani for additional information shared in private correspondence. See also Giuliani, "La diffusione dell'«alta cultura» musicale nella strategia radiofonica degli anni cinquanta. Il primo quinquennio del Terzo Programma delle Radio Audizioni Italia," *Nuova rivista musicale italiana* 35 (2001): 303–20, especially 307 and n. 25.

Professors Giuliani and Ziino have had occasion to consult Pirrotta's unpublished edition of *Euridice*, which is now housed at the RAI archive in Pomezia. The bibliographic information given in the on-line catalog of the archive reads as follows: "Identificativo Documento: 73633 / Autore Musica: Peri Jacopo / Autore Testo: Ottavi[a]no Rinuccini / Titolo: EURIDICE / Revisione o Strumentazione: Nino PIRROTTA / Organico: A / Genere: 1 / Posizione: OPERE / Numero: 108." "Identificativo Documento: 73625 / Autore Musica: Peri Jacopo / Titolo: EURIDICE / Revisione o Strumentazione: PIRROTTA / Posizione: SPARTITI / Numero: 440 / Sequenza del numero: 440." For assistance on this matter, I am grateful to Andrea Coen.

I have included Pirrotta's edition in my bibliography of his publications, because—although not published in the conventional sense of that term—it served as the basis for a broadcast performance and therefore as a vehicle for the dissemination (the "publication") of the results of his scholarship. Professor Giuliani and I have had correspondence about the possibility of his (or our) publishing Pirrotta's manuscript edition in facsimile, with a historical introduction.

In a report filed with the Office of the Dean of the Faculty of Arts and Sciences at Harvard, Pirrotta reports his own intention to publish an edition of the opera, with Ricordi: "3 copies to Dean's office / 3/27/61 . . . Work in progress: . . . An edition of Jacopo Peri's Euridice (1600), with a large introductory study, to be published by G. Ricordi & Co., Milan, in the series Istituzioni e Monumenti della Musica Italiana." It is possible, then, that another manuscript edition of the opera—either a copy of the one Pirrotta prepared in Rome for the 1951 broadcast, or another, (extensively) revised one—is preserved in the Ricordi archives. Professor Pierluigi Petrobelli informed me (in private correspondence) that he recalls being shown a score of *Euridice* prepared by Pirrotta, on the occasion of his periodic visits to the Pirrotta's Winchester home while a graduate student at Princeton. This would be exactly contemporary with the date of the document cited immediately above. For more on Pirrotta's projected published edition of *Euridice*, see Riccardo Allorto and Claudio Sartori, "La Musicologia italiana dal 1945 a oggi," *Acta Musicologica* 31, no. 1 (1959): 9–17.

Table 4 Musicians Performing in the 1951 Radio Broadcast of Peri's *Euridice*

La Tragedia [Tragedy]	[*mezzo*] *soprano:*	Adele Cezza
Euridice [Eurydice]	*soprano:*	Maria Vèrnole-Blazer
Orfeo [Orpheus]	*tenor:*	Africo Baldelli
Arcetro	*contratenor altus:*	Licia Cacciatori [*mezzo-soprano*]
Tirsi } shepherds Aminta	*tenor:*	Ottavio Plenizzio [*sic; recte:* Plenizio]
	tenor:	Walter Blazer
Shepherd	*bass:*	Walter Blazer
Nymph	*soprano:*	Rossana Zerbini
Dafne [Daphne]	*soprano:*	Luisa Ribacchi
Plutone [Pluto]	*bass:*	Plinio Clabassi
Proserpina [Persephone]	[*mezzo*] *soprano:*	Adele Cezza
Director:		Roberto Lupi
Chorus Master:		Roberto Benaglio
Orchestra e Coro di Milano della Radio Italiana		

Pirrotta's time in Rome, the larger series of broadcast performances also included Rossini's *Elisabetta, Regina d'Inghilterra* (1953), and he interpreted the entire enterprise as the manifestation of an interest in revisiting "minor" works as well as the most important operas, "inspired by a spirit analogous" to that which spawned the publication of composers' opera omnia.[42] He was only one of a number of Italian and European musicologists who participated in the initiative, furnishing learned introductions to the broadcasts.[43]

Euridice was recorded on 15 January 1951 and broadcast at 9:35 p.m. on 18 January, and again on 5 September of the same year. A recording of the performance has been recovered, thanks to the efforts of Dr. David Blazer, son of the singer—Signora Maria Vèrnole-Blazer—who performed the title role of Euridice (see Table 4). It is a fascinating document of the "early-music" movement, a historically sensitive realization of Peri's masterpiece. In my view, this is to be interpreted in part as the result of Pirrotta's musical and music-historical acumen and his success in communicating elusive matters of performance practice to the singers and instrumentalists, many of whom were accustomed to performing Verdi and Puccini.

Soon after the 1951 recording session, Maria Vèrnole-Blazer (born 12 August 1917) settled in the United States with her new husband and fellow cast member Walter Blazer (8 January 1918–10 March 2005). I have had the great pleasure of interviewing her on several occasions.

---

[42]**1993:** "Rossini eseguito ieri e oggi," especially 11.

[43]They included Higini Anglès, Edward J. Dent, Lorenz Feininger, Charles van den Borren, Fedele d'Amico, Guido M. Gatti, Gian Francesco Malipiero, Massimo Mila, Luigi Rognoni, Fausto Torrefranca, and Emilia Zanetti. Giuliani, "L'antica musica ridotta alla moderna prattica dell'etere," 1323 and n. 52.

Signora Vèrnole-Blazer recalls her experiences at RAI, and the recording of *Euridice* specifically. Both she and her husband had substantial professional résumés and expertise as performers in a wide repertorial range, including much "early" music (Monteverdi, Bach, Handel, Cimarosa); their voices were especially suited to Peri's *Euridice*. At the time of the 1951 broadcast they were living in Rome, just a few blocks from the RAI studios. They enjoyed regular employment there, in good part because of Maria's ability to sight-read rapidly and accurately.

RAI had several differently sized studios for performances, and *Euridice* was recorded in the large auditorium. The singers were seated behind recording microphones and at the appropriate moment would stand and sing. Typically, such performances would be preceded by at least one rehearsal, during which the conductor, Roberto Lupi would be assisted by an associate, who would also cue the performers. During the recording sessions and performances, Lupi himself would cue the singers.

Signora Vèrnole-Blazer remembers Lupi as a "distant" figure, although undeniably a good musician. And she recalls that the performance of *Euridice* was "a good performance," broadcast under the auspices of a special RAI program—from a separate radio station[44]—known as "Terzo programma": broadcast over regular frequencies, but intended for an audience with particular intellectual interests.[45]

As for Pirrotta, his involvement with Italian radio was in a sense an extension of his journalistic career, in that both reflect a concern for reaching a broader, nonscholarly audience.

*****

Many years later, there were resonances of Pirrotta's pioneering editorial work on Peri's *Euridice* in the analogous editorial work and accompanying scholarship of Howard Mayer Brown, who organized a performance of *Euridice* at the University of Chicago. Attendees were furnished with Brown's translation

---

[44]Professor Carter notes in private correspondence that "[a]ccording to http://www.radio3.rai.it/dl/radio3/ContentItem-e2889d98-867a-4c2b-a5e3-4d354fd7dba1.html?refresh_ce, the RAI 'terzo programma' first broadcast on 1 October 1950 and opened with a discussion of the Orpheus myth leading to a performance of Monteverdi's 'Orfeo' (and then other Orpheus works)[,] which puts the January 1951 'Euridice' in some kind of context. . . . [T]hese cultural radio stations employed and interacted with musicologists in the 1950s: the BBC Third Programme is another good example, with...Denis Stevens—another Monteverdi pioneer—as a producer from 1949–54." Carter describes it as a "very noticeable post-war phenomenon."

[45]Interviews with Maria Vèrnole-Blazer and her children Dr. David Blazer and Judith Blazer, 16 August 2008, 7 November 2008, and 8 March 2009, and e-mail correspondence with Signora Vèrnole-Blazer on 11 July 2009. I welcome this opportunity to express my gratitude to Signora Vèrnole-Blazer and her children for their kindness and generosity.

of the libretto, privately printed and published, in which he acknowledged Pirrotta's indispensable assistance. Brown then published an edition of the opera, where Pirrotta's assistance is acknowledged once more, and a classic paper on the beginnings of opera.[46]

*****

Peri's *Euridice* and the problems of interpretation it posed appealed as much to the musicologist in Pirrotta as the musician. When researching and drafting articles for volume 2 of the *Enciclopedia* (on Giovanni Bardi, Giulio Caccini, and the Florentine Camerata) and providing commentary on *Euridice* for the broadcast, he had occasion to clarify his thinking about the relative importance of the contrasting forces behind the beginnings of opera. The revisionist views expressed in the encyclopedia entries and the 1953 lectures for Paris[47] and the Accademia di «S.ᵗᵃ Cecilia»[48] have achieved classic status.

The "Florentine Camerata"—in the narrower sense—was a group of intellectuals who gathered at the home of Giovanni de' Bardi, Count of Vernio, around 1580. Their host, an aristocratic mathematician, philologist, and *letterato*, shared the convictions of his compatriots about the superiority of the Tuscan language. The principal document of the Camerata's music-theoretical "program"(its interests were not exclusively musical in nature) is Vincenzo Galilei's *Dialogo della Musica antica et della moderna* (Florence, 1581). Platonistic even in its form as dialog, Galilei's work presumably records his disquisitions on passages on music and citations from Plutarch, Aristoxenus, Euclid, and others, which he delivered at meetings of Bardi's *salon*.

Principal interlocutor in Galilei's dialog is Bardi, in the company of his contemporary Piero Strozzi. The singer Giulio Caccini reports that he, too, was among the members. Filippo Valori also attested the participation of Hellenist Girolamo Mei, who, however, could not have been a regular attendee, since he was then living in Rome. But there is no doubt that Mei was spiritually

---

[46]*Le musiche di Jacopo Peri, nobil fiorentino, sopra L'Euridice del Sig. Ottavio Rinuccini, rappresentate nello sponsalizio della cristianissima Maria Medici, regina di Francia e di Navarra* (n.p. [?Chicago], n.d. [1966]) ("This libretto for the first American performance of Jacopo Peri's *Euridice*, performed at The University of Chicago, January, 1967, was translated by Howard Mayer Brown...."); Jacopo Peri, *Euridice: An Opera in One Act, Five Scenes*, ed. Howard Mayer Brown (Madison, WI: A-R Editions, 1981); Brown, "How Opera Began: An Introduction to Jacopo Peri's *Euridice* (1600)," in *The Late Italian Renaissance, 1525–1630*, ed. Eric Cochrane (New York: Harper & Row, 1970), 401–43.

[47]1953: "Tragédie et comédie dans la Camerata fiorentina." On the lecture in Paris, see also *Renaissance News* 6, nos. 3–4 (1953): 41.

[48]1953: "Temperamenti e tendenze nella Camerata fiorentina." Agostino Ziino recalls Pirrotta's delivering his lecture on "Temperamenti e tendenze nella Camerata fiorentina"; see his "Pirrotta between Cambridge and Rome." See also Accademia di Santa Cecilia, *Annuario 1952–1953 (CCCLXVIII–CCCLXIX)* (n.d.): 203.

close to the Camerata; in fact, while drafting the *Dialogo*, between 1576 and 1581—the very years during which the Camerata was presumably at its most active—Galilei twice visited Mei in Rome to discuss his music-theoretical ideas, and they exchanged some 30 long letters on the subject.[49]

Pirrotta was later to acknowledge that he "may have been a bit too harsh on Galilei,"[50] and in "Temperamenti e tendenze nella Camerata fiorentina" and "Tragédie et comédie dans la Camerata fiorentina," he *is* sharply critical, which led D.P. Walker to challenge his characterization during the discussion following "Tragédie et comédie." A more positive subsequent reassessment resulted in part from Claude Palisca's researches and reappraisal, which Pirrotta was to find persuasive.[51] Galilei's theory manifests many affected appurtenances of philological erudition, however; pruned of them, it can be summarized as follows: to recapture the characteristics that had conferred such legendary power on ancient Greek music, it would be necessary to abandon polyphony—which compromises the intelligibility of the text and imposes its formal laws on the words, instead of subordinating itself to them and their affective content—and return to monody.

But Bardi's *Discorso mandato a Caccini sopra la musica antica e il cantar bene* reflects his skepticism that such a reform could soon take place. Indeed, Galilei's own musical experiments—perhaps the final concrete achievement of the Camerata true and proper, undertaken to translate his theorizing into practice—were so unsuccessful that the sumptuous 1589 Florentine intermedij, which Bardi designed for the Medici wedding of that year, renounced dialogic action and returned to pantomime, thus retrogressing to forms favored before the 1586 intermedio performances. Bardi's refined Neoplatonic sensibilities are revealed in the subject matter of the 1589 intermedij: *musica mundana* and *musica humana*, the cosmic and ethical aspects of music, represented by venerable allegorical figures. (The profound differences between the aesthetic sensibilities underlying the theatrical uses of music in late-Renaissance Florence and those underlying Banchieri's contemporary madrigal comedies are clear.)

Another figure responsible for the emergence of the new genre was the Roman aristocrat Emilio de' Cavalieri, who possessed an artistic temperament very different from that of Bardi (whom he replaced at the Medici court). First, Cavalieri's literary tastes contrasted starkly with those of Bardi and his

---

[49] In addition to Pirrotta's writings on these matters, see also Vincenzo Galilei, *Dialogue on Ancient and Modern Music*, trans. Claude V. Palisca (New Haven: Yale University Press, 2003), xx and n. 14 and xxv; and Girolamo Mei's 19 May 1582 letter to Giovan Vincenzo Pinelli, in Girolamo Mei, *Letters on Ancient and Modern Music to Vincenzo Galilei and Giovanni Bardi. A Study with Annotated Texts*, ed. Claude V. Palisca, 2nd corrected ed., with addenda (Neuhausen-Stuttgart: American Institute of Musicology, 1977), 184.

[50] "Temperaments and Tendencies in the Florentine Camerata," 419 n. 6 (see "*Intermedio I.^{mo}*, n. 144).

[51] Ibid.

followers, who had developed a program in which Tuscan linguistic purism was allied with classicizing, Platonizing tendencies. Cavalieri and his collaborator Laura Guidiccioni instead favored the pastoral strain in contemporary Italian literature, represented above all by Gianbattista Guarino and Torquato Tasso. Cavalieri and Guidiccioni were responsible for the staging of pastorals in music in Florence during the 1590s; they privileged a genre disdained by the exacting, late-Cinquecento Florentine humanists, because it had no known antecedent in antiquity.

Second, Cavalieri also had distinctive tastes in music. Unfortunately, it is now impossible to evaluate fully the accomplishment of Cavalieri and Guidiccioni, since their pastorals are no longer extant. But to judge from the critical reaction of Giovanni Battista Doni, the music deployed in them (and Cavalieri's theatrical music in general)—"ariette" and ballets—had "nothing to do with true, good theater music." Only one work survives that allows us to gauge the legitimacy of Doni's critique—Cavalieri's *Rappresentatione di Anima e di Corpo* (*The Representation of Body and Soul* [1600])—and the style of its music suggests that it was derived from the more elaborate canzonette and villanelle then being performed throughout Italy, typically by a solo voice accompanied by a string instrument. Above all, there were presumably many ballets. To the members of Bardi's Camerata, such light, almost inconsequential musical genres represented something of an aesthetic compromise, in view of the Camerata's more austere programmatic objectives.[52]

However, Cavalieri's claim to have been the first to stage theatrical works that consisted entirely of music was not disputed by the two remaining claimants, Giulio Caccini and Jacopo Peri. Their claims related instead to the matter of the *style* of the music and its deployment for dramatic purposes. Pirrotta acknowledges the legitimacy of Caccini's claims about the novelties of his compositional practices, among which was the nature of the instrumental accompaniment, which minimized polyphonic complexity and instead favored spare chords, to be strummed on an instrument that the vocalist himself would play. Thus accompanied, a vocalist could exploit the agogic freedom that permitted a performance characterized by spontaneity and "nonchalance."

More important still was the distinctive melodic style and execution of Caccini's vocal lines, which even Vincenzo Giustiniani—otherwise at pains

---

[52] One other document, though less substantial, permits us to draw some conclusions about Cavalieri's vision of theatrical music: see Warren Kirkendale, *Emilio de' Cavalieri, "Gentiluomo Romano": His Life and Letters, His Role as Superintendent of All the Arts at the Medici Court, and His Musical Compositions, With Addenda to L'Aria di Fiorenza and The Court Musicians in Florence* (Florence: L. S. Olschki, 2001), 196–98, and the accompanying discussion and footnotes. Interestingly, the setting of a text from Guarini's *Pastor Fido* suggests the same conclusion as in my main text, above: see Anthony Newcomb, *The Madrigal at Ferrara*, 2 vols. (Princeton, NJ: Princeton University Press, 1980), 1:42–46 and the edition of the work in Newcomb's vol. 2.

to minimize the achievements of the Florentines—was compelled to recognize. Giustiniani could not help but acknowledge that Caccini was "almost the inventor of a new way of singing."

The sources of that distinctive style were in the lighter vocal genres used in performances of theatrical comedies: compositions in the tradition of the villanella alla napolitana and the canzonetta, popular above all in Naples, where Caccini's teacher Scipione del Palla[53]—whose influence Caccini acknowledges in the preface to *Le nuove musiche*—had been active. In his own poetic choices, Caccini distances himself from the frivolous verse characteristic of such light genres, instead preferring more refined and substantial verse (the poetry of Chiabrera, Rinuccini, and Sannazzaro). But with respect to musical style, "Caccini, in order to realize his monodic ideal, [n]evertheless knows no other way than to ennoble the solo song of the villanella, while maintaining that freshness of execution in it."[54] This act of "ennoblement" rendered the style of Caccini's vocal writing more consequential than Cavalieri's, which was similarly indebted to the lighter genres of the villanella and canzonetta.

Finally, Peri's distinctive contribution lay in the appropriateness of his compositional style to dramatic performances. When Jacopo Corsi and Ottavio Rinuccini were seeking a composer to assist them in realizing their vision of restoring ancient tragedy,[55] they turned, not to Caccini—whose monodies were deemed too lyrical, too "musical"—but to Peri, who, in the preface to the printed edition of *L'Euridice*, described his musical style as an "imitation of speech in song," achieved by means of "a harmony surpassing that of ordinary speech but falling so far below the melody of songs as to take an intermediate form."[56]

Years after drafting these early articles on Florentine aristocratic opera, Pirrotta was again to describe the "differences in temperament" between the two men, "Caccini's more lyrical, Peri's more dramatic."[57] Some further evidence of the contrasting temperaments and tendencies among the Florentine creators of opera is suggested by the unjustified, polemicizing characterization of Peri by Caccini's disciples:

---

[53]See more recently the article by Howard Mayer Brown, "The Geography of Florentine Monody: Caccini at Home and Abroad," *Early Music* 9 (1981): 147–68. See also John Walter Hill's *Roman Monody, Cantata and Opera from the Circles around Cardinal Montalto*, 2 vols. (Oxford: Clarendon Press, 1998) and the review thereof by Dinko Fabris in *Journal of the Royal Musical Association* 125 (2000): 287–99, especially 290–91 and 294-95, and nn. 6, 11, and 21–22.

[54]**1954:** "Tragédie et comédie dans la Camerata fiorentina," 293.

[55]Although, as Pirrotta points out in his articles on Florentine aristocratic opera, the tradition's creators were very sensitive to matters of genre and its nomenclature and were careful to entitle their initial experiments, not *tragedie*, but *favole*, aware that in order to qualify as a tragedy a dramatic work had to embody certain time-honored characteristics not embodied in the first operas.

[56]**1969:** *Music and Theatre*, 252.

[57]**1969:** *Music and Theatre*, 252.

Temperamentally he was inclined ... to be melancholic, but he did not write in one style so monotonously as to deserve the epithet "lugubrious," which (not without a touch of malice) is what the pupils of the jealous Caccini called him.[58]

Pirrotta concludes with a masterful summation:

Doubts, uncertainties, no pre-established program, no practical realizations corresponding to the vague ideas of reform; such are the features of a general view of what strictly speaking was the *Camerata*, the one that met at Bardi's house. We cannot even be certain that its members continued their discussions about music beyond the year 1581 or 1582. Certainly the ideas that they debated were not wholly without influence; but now they began to be discussed and repeated in a less confined society. Only when opera was an accomplished fact did Caccini (a close friend of Bardi's), Severo Bonini (a pupil and admirer of Caccini's), Pietro de' Bardi, and others in their wake attempt, rather selfconsciously, to argue the importance of these discussions. Writers in our own time have been too quick to create the legend of a group of theorists and polemicists at whose meetings the theory of the new dramatic music was systematically evolved in the most minute detail before being put into practice.

*****

ANTONIO CESTI

Like those on the beginnings of opera, the pioneering publications on Antonio Cesti were prompted by the availability of crucial primary sources in various Roman libraries, including the «S.ᵗᵃ Cecilia». And they were likewise associated with the revival of an important seventeenth-century opera.

The opening salvo appeared in 1953 in the *Rivista dell'Accademia nazionale di Santa Cecilia*;[59] it brought to the attention of the musicological community—for the first time, to my knowledge—the existence of several complete scores of one of the greatest works in the entire Italian operatic repertory, Cesti's *Orontea*.[60] In his understated, matter-of-fact presentation, Pirrotta announced that there were, in fact, three complete manuscript scores of *Orontea*—one in Parma,[61] and two in Rome (at the Vatican library and the «S.ᵗᵃ Cecilia»).[62]

---

[58]1953: "Temperamenti e tendenze nella Camerata fiorentina," 232.

[59]1953: "Nella biblioteca di Santa Cecilia."

[60]As recent a publication as the entry on "Cesti" in *Die Musik in Geschichte und Gegenwart*, which had not even appeared in print at the time Pirrotta was drafting his article but was nonetheless known to him, had claimed—erroneously—that *Orontea* survived only as a fragment. For a recent explanation of *Orontea*'s importance in the "canon," see Jennifer Williams Brown, "'Innsbruck, ich muss dich lassen': Cesti, 'Orontea,' and the Gelone Problem," *Cambridge Opera Journal* 12, no. 3 (2000): 179–217.

[61]The score in Parma had been cited in the *Catalogo generale delle opere musicali, teoriche o pratiche, manoscritte o stampate, di autori vissuti sino ai primi decenni del XIX secolo esistenti nelle biblioteche e negli archivi d'Italia*, ser. 1, Città di Parma; Città di Reggio-Emilia (Parma: Tipografia Zerbini & Fresching, 1911), 266, but the citation had evidently escaped musicologists' notice until Pirrotta referred to it.

[62]We now know of a fourth, non-Italian score, at Cambridge: Cambridge University, Magdalene College, Pepysian Library, 2210. See Jennifer Williams Brown, "'Innsbruck, ich muss dich lassen.'"

There was now a basis for assessing the opera's artistic qualities, the reasons for its great contemporary success, and its extraordinary historical importance.

In the article, Pirrotta goes beyond simply reporting on the existence of the scores. He makes a preliminary attempt at identifying the textual tradition for the opera to which the Roman exemplars belong.[63] He situates Cesti culturally, qualifying received opinion that had erroneously identified him with the Venetian operatic tradition, suggesting affinities instead with the Roman "school" of opera and noting the Tuscan quality of Cesti's literary tastes. He observes that there is a network of interconnections between *Orontea* and the opera *Alessandro vincitor di sè stesso*, thus furnishing decisive empirical evidence to substantiate the earlier conjectures of Henri Prunières that *Alessandro*—raditionally attributed to Francesco Cavalli—was instead by Cesti.[64] He reveals that it was at his urging that *Orontea* was revived on the "occasione della «X Settimana Musicale Senese», 16–22 settembre 1953." And toward the conclusion of the article, he makes tantalizing, passing reference to the itinerant troupes of opera singers, so important in the dissemination of the new genre.[65] More than 20 years later, in the first of several Festschriften issued in Pirrotta's honor, Lorenzo Bianconi and Thomas Walker will offer a comprehensive account of the itinerant companies.[66]

*****

Pirrotta's old composition teacher at the Conservatory of Florence, Vito Frazzi, transcribed the music in the rediscovered scores of *Orontea*, which was performed at the Teatro de' Rinnuovati in Siena on 16 and 19 September

---

[63]On which see now Thomas Walker's introduction in Aurelio Aureli and Francesco Lucio, *Il Medoro*, ed. Thomas Walker and Giovanni Morelli (Milan: Ricordi, 1984). Pirrotta already observed in 1953 that the text of the prolog in all three scores corresponds neither to that of the libretto for the 1649 performance (a performance now thought to be, not of Cesti's setting of the libretto, but of Francesco Lucio's), nor to that of a Venetian revival of 1666, but instead to that of a libretto printed in 1656 in Innsbruck, a copy of which was at the Biblioteca Nazionale V.E. in Rome, and whose existence Pirrotta was also signaling for the first time.

[64]Prunières, *Cavalli et l'opéra vénitien au XVIIe siècle* (Paris: Rieder, 1931), 30 n. 1; Pirrotta will return to this matter in two further articles on Cesti. On the entire matter, see the discussion in Wolfgang Osthoff, "Antonio Cestis 'Alessandro Vincitor di se stesso,'" *Studien zur Musikwissenschaft* 24 (1960): 13–43, which makes repeated reference to Pirrotta's earlier studies.

[65]Pirrotta returns to a consideration of Abbatini's opera *La Comica* (see n. 66), and the itinerant performative traditions of which it is a mirror, in **1953**: "Tre capitoli su Cesti."

[66]"Dalla *Finta pazza* alla *Veremonda*: Storie di Febiarmonici," *Rivista italiana di musicologia* 10 (1975): 379–454; English translation forthcoming in *Drammaturgia musicale veneta* 1. One of the last articles Pirrotta will publish addresses itself to the itinerant companies: **1998**: "Storie di Febiarmonici." Finally, Pirrotta's article does something more: on the basis of a manuscript libretto at the «S.[ta] Cecilia», it identifies the composer—Antonio Maria Abbatini—of an otherwise unattributed opera, *La Comica del Cielo, ovvero La Baltasara*, whose manuscript score had been relocated at the Vatican library; on this matter, see also **1954**: "ABBATINI, Antonio Maria."

1953.[67] And on the occasion of the performances, the Accademia Musicale Chigiana and the Ente Autonomo per le Settimane Musicali Senesi published a volume of studies that included one of the longest essays of Pirrotta's entire career, his "Three Chapters on Cesti" ("Tre capitoli su Cesti").

If *Il Sacchetti* was Pirrotta's earliest substantial publication on the music of the Trecento (the first of his principal scholarly concerns), "Tre capitoli" was his first major publication on Italian opera of the seventeenth century (the second of his principal interests); the earlier works on seventeenth-century opera had either been encyclopedia entries or lectures, which had to be contained within a prescribed, concise format. In "Tre capitoli," he could afford to be more expansive, and he avails himself of this changed circumstance to offer a comprehensive statement similar to that in *Il Sacchetti:* a full-scale manifesto of his vision of the emergence of Italian opera, with many nuanced qualifications of received opinion.

First, Pirrotta announced additional forthcoming studies of Cesti—an entry in the *Enciclopedia dello spettacolo*, a contribution to the Festschrift in memory of Gino Marinuzzi—and he suggests that the "Three Chapters" on Cesti might one day become as many chapters in a book on the composer, which, alas, he would never write.

Whereas the earlier articles on the Trecento repertory had employed the vocabulary of Crocean Idealism in their effort to capture the contrast in medieval French and Italian musical aesthetics—"intellectualistic," "ratiocinative," etc., vs. "intuitive," "instinctive," etc.—the first of the "Three Chapters on Cesti" is laced with a nomenclature indebted to Materialism, which helps to correct misconceptions concerning the evolution of the genre in the first decades of its history. Matters of environment are all important here: material conditions and the political economy, embodied, for example, in the very question about whether "the opening of the public opera theaters had determined completely new and unique organizational and environmental conditions in Venice." And the Materialist approach adopted by Pirrotta will spawn impressive progeny: there are resonances not only in Bianconi and Walker's "Dalla *Finta pazza* alla *Veremonda:* Storie di Febiarmonici," but

---

[67]*Orontea. Dramma giocoso per musica di Giacinto Andrea Cicognini. Musica di Antonio Cesti. Trascrizione e realizzazione di Vito Frazzi* (see "Scena 2.ª," n. 31). For an account of the performances, and of Frazzi's editorial interventions, see Dyneley Hussey, "Cesti's 'Orontea' at Siena," *Musical Times* 94 (1953): 578–79. In Leonardo Pinzauti, *L'Accademia Musicale Chigiana da Boito a Boulez* (Milan: Electa, 1982), 267, there is documentation on the *Orontea* performance of 1953, including a list of the performers: Lucia Danieli, Augusto Romani, Marcella Pobbe, Gina Consolandi, Franco Calabrese, Licia Rossini Corsi, Luigi Pontiggia, Aureliana Beltrami, and Alessandro Ziliani. Orchestra dell'Accademia Chigiana. Franco Capuana, dir. Enrico Frigerio, "regista." Pinzauti (pp. 80, 141) also attests Pirrotta's contemporary pedagogical activities in Siena.

also in their "Production, Consumption, and Political Function of Seventeenth-Century Italian Opera" and in Giovanni Morelli and Walker's "Tre controversie intorno al San Cassiano."

The first of the chapters, "L'opera italiana prima di Cesti" ("Italian Opera before Cesti"), is a concise synopsis of the entire development of Italian opera in its immediate postaristocratic phase. The qualification offered earlier in the article in *Santa Cecilia*—concerning the traditional inclusion of Cesti in the Venetian operatic school—is the pretext for a larger assessment of the very thesis of the existence of a Venetian "school," at least in the early seventeenth century.

In a phrase emblematic of Pirrotta's fundamental scholarly methodology, he observes that "[t]he history of the first lyric companies . . . is a chapter that has not yet found official consecration in the history of music,"

> because it . . . is known only in an extremely fragmentary way: *indeed, it is necessary to divine it from sparse hints, casual references,* [and] *isolated municipal notices* [emphasis added].

Throughout his career, Pirrotta will press such fragmentary bits of elusive yet resonant evidence into service in an effort to recover lost musical traditions of particular interest to him. Among the kinds of documentation exploited here are the dedicatory prefaces to printed music and the forewords and dedications of period libretti. When Bianconi and Walker accept the challenge implicit in the passing reference to the itinerant companies, they will use precisely these kinds of evidence and assemble documentation impressive in its typological range.[68]

Beginning in 1637, Venice becomes a principal destination for the itinerant companies, and wherever they went, "they were encountering environmental and cultural conditions . . . analogous to those . . . characterizing the Venetian theaters."[69] (Herein is the foundation of Pirrotta's challenge to the traditional thesis about the existence of a distinctive Venetian school.) Pirrotta invokes the Materialists' species of explanation to illustrate how historical develop-

---

[68]One of my objectives in this biography is to identify important instances of what I shall term "intellectual patrimonies": examples of the inter-generational transfer of musicological achievement and learning from Pirrotta to his pupils, and to his pupils' pupils. In this context, mention must be made of Ellen Rosand's *Opera in Seventeenth-Century Venice: The Creation of a Genre* (Berkeley: University of California Press, 1991); the book coauthored by Beth L. Glixon (Rosand's pupil) and her husband, Jonathan E. Glixon (Lewis Lockwood's pupil), *Inventing the Business of Opera: The Impresario and his World in Seventeenth-Century Venice* (Oxford: Oxford University Press, 2006), which elaborates greatly upon the approaches exemplified by Bianconi, Morelli, and Walker's writings; and the dissertation and resulting book by Howard Mayer Brown's pupil Margaret Murata, which combines archival documentation and music analysis: *Operas for the Papal Court, 1631–1668* (Ann Arbor, MI: UMI Research Press, 1981).

[69]"[I]t would be erroneous to believe that the management of the theaters in Venice was being uniquely borne on the proceeds of the receipts...from paying spectators: instead, one has testimony that they constantly found an indispensable support in the backing of noble gentlemen."

ments may be shaped by economic factors, though his application of it is more circumscribed and restrained:

> limiting the number of components of the orchestra and progressively reducing the choral parts derive from the need for organizational leanness inherent in the structure of the itinerant companies.

The chamber character of seventeenth-century Italian opera in its postaristocratic phase is thus a consequence of the material conditions of its performance: the need for the itinerant companies to remain lean and mobile.

And the definition of the "material infrastructure" is broadened:[70]

> No less diffused and common throughout the entire peninsula was the spirit of political absolutism, in whose influence some German scholars have wished to locate one of the determining elements of the characteristics of the Venetian opera; ... in Venice, in fact, the republican constitution, although oligarchic, was entailing—more than elsewhere—a sense of control and limitation of the powers [that be], while flourishing commercial activities had created better conditions of life and culture, even for the lower classes, and, above all, the influence of the Inquisition—preponderant elsewhere—was more attenuated there.

Regarding the supposed "tendency toward historical realism" in the subject matter of the libretti of Venetian operas, Pirrotta argues that in fact "libretti on historical subjects are not prevalent in number in Venice, nor are they the exclusive prerogative of the Venetian opera," which is a further challenge to traditional assumptions about a Venetian school:

> Actually, except for some minor details, the Venetian genre of the libretto is no different from the Italian genre of the libretto in general. ... Its defects—offset by exceptional merits—are those of the contemporary theater of the time, then dominated by the activity of the "comici dell'arte."

Herein lies the kernel of a thesis that will soon receive systematic elaboration in one of the most representative articles of Pirrotta's career, "*Commedia dell'Arte* and Opera." In its preliminary exposition here, the article acknowledges an indebtedness to Henri Prunières for "having first hinted at a relationship between the Venetian genre of the libretto and the 'commedia dell'arte.'"

The second of the "Tre capitoli"—"*L'Orontea*"—opens with the observation that our incomplete knowledge of Cesti's art is based largely on the collection of manuscript scores at the Nationalbibliothek in Vienna, which comprises works from the final period of Cesti's life, the years of the second Tyrolean sojourn and the composer's imperial service. The operas of the first period

---

[70]Pirrotta returns to this matter in **1954**: "Le prime opere di Antonio Cesti," 166.

will be the subject of another essay on Cesti, the contribution to the Marinuzzi Festschrift. Some of the content of that article is anticipated, and one of the early operas is selected for particular comment here, the celebrated *Orontea*.

Pirrotta elaborates on his previous announcement of the existence of several manuscripts of the entire opera[71] and his earlier preliminary attempt to identify the textual tradition represented by the three Italian scores in Parma and Rome: There are correspondences between the prolog of the three and that of the libretto at the Biblioteca Naz. Centrale V.E. di Roma, which documents an Austrian performance of 1656.[72]

Bibliographical preliminaries concluded,[73] Pirrotta proceeds to more consequential considerations. Although *Orontea* is a document of the contemporary "affinity between comic theater and the opera theater," Cicognini's libretto represents an attempt to regularize the comic tradition, to supplant the orality of the "script" of the commedia dell' arte's with a fixed literary text.[74] Pirrotta provides an analysis of *Orontea*, its libretto, and its defining musical characteristics: "[w]ithin the limits in which that was possible in the theater of the time, the libretto of *Orontea* is essentially a psychological drama, in fact, a comedy." The male protagonist, Alidoro, is likened to da Ponte and Mozart's Cherubino, who "abandons himself to love—the impersonal love of women in general, and not of a particular woman." And a fuller enumeration of the roles suggests that the comic types exemplified by *Orontea*'s elderly nurse and the *buffone* Gelone have already become ritual presences in opera.

"But regarding the music, a fundamental difference in its organization immediately stands out from the preceding libretti of Tuscan dramaturgy, from [Baccio Baglioni and Niccolò Sapiti's] *Celio* and—even if to a lesser extent—from [Giacinto Andrea Cicognini and Francesco Cavalli's] *Giasone*":

---

[71]Pirrotta furthermore states that the majority of the arias are also contained in a manuscript at the Biblioteca del Conservatorio «S. Pietro a Majella» of Naples (which, moreover, possesses a manuscript score of the resetting of the libretto of *Orontea* by the Neapolitan composer Francesco Cirillo). On the relationship of Cirillo's setting to Cesti's, see Thomas Walker's introduction to Aurelio Aureli and Francesco Lucio, *Il Medoro*. Continuing with my inventory of instances of intellectual patrimonies, I here mention William C. Holmes' "Yet Another «*Orontea*»," in *Venezia e il Melodramma nel Seicento*, ed. Maria Teresa Muraro (Florence: L. S. Olschki, 1976), which takes Pirrotta's work on *Orontea* as its point of departures and considers Vismarri's setting.

[72]*L'Orontea . . . Di nuovo ristampata e rappresentata in Innsprugg nel Teatro di Sala l'anno 1656. Apresso Michael Wagner.*

[73]These preliminaries also include the statement that the *Orontea* performed in Venice in 1649 was Cesti's, whereas more recent scholarly opinion is that it was Francesco Lucio's; see Thomas Walker's introduction to Aurelio Aureli and Francesco Lucio, *Il Medoro*. In the Italian edition of his book on Don Giovanni, Pirrotta had revised his opinion to the extent that he says "musica, forse, di Antonio Cesti"; by the time of the English translation—**1994:** *Don Giovanni's Progress*—he identifies the composer as Lucio (p. 17 n. 5, which appears on p. 166).

[74]Pirrotta will later make a similar observation concerning the renowned Venetian comic playwright Goldoni; see **1994:** *Don Giovanni's Progress*, 50.

the concision of the parts to be translated musically into recitative compared to those from which the arias and ensemble pieces stem. In vain I searched the Florentine score of Baglioni and Sapiti's opera for some indication of the new balance . . . to characterize Cesti's opera four years later. . . . [I]t is . . . probable that the decisive shift in balance between dramatic and musical elements, which in *Orontea* occurs in favor of the latter, is the result of a conscious and direct influence of the musician upon the poet, proof of an already mature personality, perfectly aware of his means and needs.[75]

Cesti's artistic temperament, which was more lyrical than dramatic,[76] was served by his predilection for the comic: According to the theatrical conventions of the time, comic opera offered a more accepted rationale for lyric effusion and was more prepared to countenance it.[77]

For historians of Italian opera—of opera in general—this question is one of the most urgent: under what circumstances is an aria (or other species of "dramatically unrealistic" set piece) justified, and what musical means does the composer employ in crafting such lyrical effusions? It is related to a problem that Philip Gossett identified in a later phase of Italian opera: "The problem of the aria is to permit lyric expression to predominate without freezing the action."[78] Pirrotta's consideration of the question here is only one instance of his concern with it as implicitly raised by the early operatic repertory, and his conclusions concerning Cesti's solution are understood within the context of his larger assemblage of conclusions about seventeenth-century opera more generally.[79] "Never before could the hedonistic–musical

---

[75] And Cesti's refined literary sensibilities are reflected not only in his influence upon his librettists but also in his very selection of *libretti*, which, in their Tuscan quality, exemplify an interest in counteracting "Baroque" taste.

[76] In this matter, Pirrotta draws a revealing contrast with Cavalli's more dramatic than lyrical temperament, just as earlier he had drawn a similar revealing contrast between Cesti's more lyrical and Peri's more dramatic temperaments. See **1953**: "Tre capitoli," 52–53.

[77] "In the *Alessandro*, . . . in which [librettist] Sbarra undertook to transport the new conception of musical theater into the guise of serious opera, the need was felt of introducing a justification that had not appeared necessary in the preceding experiment in the comic genre. In fact, Sbarra—addressing himself to the audience—writes: 'I know that some people will consider the *ariette* sung by Alexander and Aristotle unfit for the dignity of such great characters; but I know also that it is not natural to speak in music, . . . and nevertheless it is not only permitted but even accepted with praise. For today this kind of poetry has only the aim of pleasure; and therefore we need to adapt ourselves to the usage of our time. If the recitative style were not intermingled with such a kind of *scherzi*, it would give more annoyance than pleasure.'" For the excerpt from the libretto of *Alessandro*, I have adopted Lewis Lockwood's translation in his translation of Pirrotta's **1954**: "*Commedia dell'Arte* and Opera." Pirrotta returns to this matter of the relationship between the use of closed pieces and the comic tradition in **1963**: "Monteverdi and the Problems of Opera," especially 249–50.

[78] Gossett then enumerates some of the specific compositional techniques Rossini employed. See Gossett. "Rossini, Gioachino," *Grove Music Online. Oxford Music Online*, http://0-www.oxfordmusiconline.com.libcat.lafayette.edu/subscriber/article/grove/music/23901 (accessed February 19, 2012).

[79] See the treatment of the problem in, for example, **1963**: "Monteverdi and the Problems of Opera."

conception of opera have been more clearly enunciated," writes Pirrotta (note the resonant Crocean term). At this point in the evolution of the new genre, earlier prejudices concerning the aria and other closed pieces having been largely overcome,[80] composer and audience alike surrendered to the "hedonistic" pleasure of lyrical effusion, if only as a means of achieving variety through an alternation of recitative and a more developed closed piece.

In addition, the second capitolo on Cesti offers suggestions concerning instrumental usage; observations on the performance history of the opera as documented by the extant libretti (and the consequences for the fluid "text" of the opera); a further elucidation of the elements that characterize the opera as "comic" in tone, among them the "parlante" style of melody employed in a dialog between Creonte and Orontea (which will later develop into the celebrated "patter" technique employed so successfully in Rossini's and Donizetti's comic operas, and even those of Sir Arthur Sullivan); and comment on the construction of the libretto and the cues it contains for musical realization, as then reflected in Cesti's setting.

The third of the three capitoli on Cesti—"Cesti nell'epistolario di Salvator Rosa ('Cesti in the Correspondence of Salvator Rosa')"—displays Pirrotta's concern with biography, about which Ellen Rosand has written eloquently. In this case, Pirrotta chose his subject skillfully: Cesti is one of Italian operatic history's most colorful figures, whose biography lends itself to evocative reconstruction, and Pirrotta portrays him vividly, his flaws as well as his virtues sharply outlined. The letters of Rosa are ideal sources for his project: gossipy, caustic epistolary exchanges, spiced with vituperative commentary on Cesti's ever-questionable behavior.

The third chapter also furnishes evidence of Pirrotta's tendency to specify not only what he had attempted to achieve, but also what he had not been able to achieve, so that future scholars could advance the program of research he had outlined. Pirrotta writes:

> At the moment of the death of his protector [Archduke Sigismund Francis], Cesti was in fact preparing the opera destined for the wedding festivities, *Semiramis*, on a libretto of Andrea Moniglia, this time commissioned by the Grand Duke of Tuscany. Meanwhile, he was conducting wearisome negotiations with the impresario Faustini for an opera (*Tito*) to be performed in Venice. A group of 16 letters from Cesti survives regarding these negotiations. Taddeo Wiel had pointed them out to

---

[80]See **1963**: "Monteverdi and the Problems of Opera."

Kretzschmar, who referred to some of them, but unfortunately in such an imprecise way that they can no longer be identified among the vast holdings of the Archivio di Stato di Venezia.[81]

Remo Giazotto and Carl B. Schmidt will later accept the challenge implicit in this passage.[82]

*****

The series of essays on Florentine aristocratic opera and the operas of Cesti, which established Pirrotta as an authority on Seicento opera, concludes with the article for the Marinuzzi Festschrift, which in good part elaborates material outlined in "Tre capitoli su Cesti."

In it, Pirrotta returns to the analogies between *Orontea* and *Alessandro vincitor di sè stesso* that substantiated Prunière's conjectures about Cesti's authorship of the latter. He focuses on the early operas to correct misapprehensions concerning Cesti's entire output, which had been characterized by Kretzschmar and Wellesz principally on the basis of manuscript scores in Vienna that document Cesti's activity while in imperial service. He surveys the work of Cicognini as librettist.[83] He returns to a discussion of the Tuscan quality of the literary text—intended to counteract Baroque taste—and the different balance between recitative and set-piece (the latter related, once more, to the composer's predilection for a comic aesthetic). He again questions if it is legitimate to associate Cesti with the Venetian tradition. He invokes a Materialist's explanation of the variety in instrumental usage in Cesti's operas as a corpus:

---

[81]In a footnote he continues: "The indication he gives of a 'Ratsarchiv' is too vague; Prunières, too, lamented the impossibility of identifying the very rich material Wiel pointed out to Kretzschmar (around 180 documents) and utilized by the latter in this and successive studies without adequate reference. Nor did I have any luck recently in a search that had to be cut short."

[82]In 1967, in the first issue of the revived [*Nuova*] *Rivista musicale italiana*, Giazotto published excerpts from Cesti's correspondence; and in 1973 and '78, Schmidt, in his doctoral dissertation—written under Pirrotta's direction—and in an article in the *Journal of the American Musicological Society*, used the same documents to reconstruct the circumstances behind the composition of Cesti's great opera *Tito*. See Schmidt, "Antonio Cesti's *Il pomo d'oro*: A Reexamination of a Famous Hapsburg Court Spectacle," *Journal of the American Musicological Society* 29 (1976): 381–412, especially 382 n. 6; Schmidt, "The Operas of Antonio Cesti," 2 vols. (Ph.D. dissertation, Harvard University, 1973); and Schmidt, "An Episode in the History of Venetian Opera: The *Tito* Commission," *Journal of the American Musicological Society* 31 (1978): 442–66, especially 443 n. 6.

[83]Pirrotta cites especially the earlier *Celio*, the subject of an article by Vittorio Ricci: "Un melodramma ignoto della prima metà del '600. «Celio» di Baccio Baglioni a di Niccolò Sapiti," *Rivista musicale italiana* 32 (1925): 51–79.

[h]is instrumental preludes, the *ritornellos* of the arias ... show a range and variety of writing ... that naturally is accentuated in the final period spent at the imperial court, through the greater availability of orchestral resources.

And he offers a concisely stated assessment of Cesti's music-historical importance.

Pirrotta concludes with an appendix of excerpts from *Orontea*, in his recognizable musical calligraphy.

*****

"*'COMMEDIA DELL'ARTE'* AND OPERA"

Throughout his career, Pirrotta was discerning in his choice of the kind of "publication" (in the sense of "making public") best suited to effective dissemination of the subject matter at hand. Among his earliest public lectures is "*Commedia dell'Arte* and Opera,"[84] one of the most important papers of his career[85] and an effective illustration of his distinctive method and voice. Aware that a live audience required a clearly articulated presentation, Pirrotta chose the rhetorical device of contrasting two music-theatrical genres and thereby elucidated his thesis more effectively.

The lecture also afforded him an opportunity to synthesize the findings of his earlier articles on Banchieri's "madrigal comedies" and the later ones on Cesti's comic operas, which allowed him to identify correspondences between the two music-theatrical traditions. The correspondences must have occurred to him precisely as a result of his research on Banchieri and Cesti.

If the writings from the Palermo years on the music of the Trecento may be considered exercises in intellectual history, drawing on the findings of historians of art, literature, and philosophy, and the writings of the Rome years exercises in economic history, indebted to the methodologies of the Economic Materialists, then "*Commedia dell'Arte* and Opera" is an exercise in social history, drawing on the kinds of approaches later adopted by historian

---

[84]**1954**: "Commedia dell'Arte e Melodramma." In the Preface to *Music and Culture in Italy from the Middle Ages to the Baroque* (see "Intermedio I.$^{\underline{mo}}$," n. 144), Pirrotta recalls that the paper was first written in French for Brussels and Charles van den Borren, and then translated into Italian for delivery in Rome. On the delivery in Brussels, see also *Scelte poetiche di musicisti. Teatro, poesia e musica da Willaert a Malapiero* (Venice: Marsilio, 1987), 147, the first note (preceding n. 1); on the delivery in Rome, see also Accademia di Santa Cecilia, *Annuario 1953–1954* (CCCLXIX–CCCLXX) (n.d.): 218.

[85]Pirrotta was particularly attached to this paper; see the introduction to the collection of essays *Music and Culture in Italy from the Middle Ages to the Baroque* (see "Intermedio I.$^{\underline{mo}}$, n. 144).

Natalie Zemon Davis, for example. J.H. Elliott has said of Davis that "[n]o historian of our time has a more immediate and vital sense of the past than Dr. Davis, and none has been more resourceful in putting the smallest piece of evidence to work in order to recover the sights, . . . sounds, and . . . sensations of a world we have lost."[86] Elliott might have been writing about Pirrotta, and specifically about "*Commedia dell'Arte* and Opera."

The objective in the first part of the paper is to reconstruct (if only imaginatively) the lost musical elements of performances by the *comici dell'arte*: "professional players . . . often of rustic origin and. . . . low condition."[87] The comici's social status thus immediately distinguishes the article's subject matter from that of most of the earlier papers, in that the creative artists in question—"composers" and performers—represented a different socioeconomic stratum of European society. It is in this sense that "*Commedia dell'Arte* and Opera" is an exercise in social history.

There are further distinctions of this kind. The repertory of the comici dell'arte was "essentially popular . . . , often in dialect, in which the dialogue is completely left to the player's capacity for improvisation, only a plot outline . . . having been decided upon in advance." As such, it contrasts with the "literary comedies of the Renaissance, . . . a kind of work in which, according to its learned humanistic end, the written text imposed its rules."[88]

"[T]he comici had no other aim than the pleasure of their public"; and

> they had the advantage over the authors and players of regular comedies of long experience as to the most suitable means for arousing the approbation of the audience. Among these means music certainly did not take the last place. But it often happens in the history of music that *the more widely diffused and popular are the facts the historian wishes to examine, the fewer precise elements of knowledge are available to him.* For, in this case, at the time of its performance every one knew the music performed and the ways and means of its execution; but *time has swallowed and buried this direct knowledge and has left us only scattered and second- or thirdhand documents. We need to gather them together and laboriously interpret them to recover a pale image of a reality that in its own time must have imposed itself with the most obvious power of suggestion* [emphases added].

This last observation captures effectively what is distinctive in Pirrotta's music-historical sensibility and scholarly tastes, and he avails himself of a

---

[86] See the excerpt from Elliott's review published in Davis's *Society and Culture in Early Modern France* (Stanford, CA: Stanford University Press, 1965).

[87] Throughout, I am quoting from Lewis Lockwood's translation, as published in *Musical Quarterly* 41 (1955).

[88] Here, one already detects resonances of the essays on Cesti. See the beginning of the second of Pirrotta's "Tre capitoli," as translated above, where he is characterizing the work of Cicognini as librettist.

range of evidence in his own Crocean attempt to "recover" that "pale image of a reality." Among the sources used are "[p]ictorial documents," which "give us evidence of the frequent presence of music" (notably an engraving by Giacomo Franco[89] and Jacques Callot's *Balli di Sfessania*[90]); "documents referring to the coincidence of musical and theatrical activities in the same people";[91] and other such nonmusical sources, which are not always so profitably exploited by the music historian.

The observation that courtesans "were very frequent characters in the comedy . . . and, at the time of [organist Girolamo] Parabosco, almost its only feminine public" affords the first of several conjectures as to what vestiges of the music of the *commedia* there may be in the extant repertory:

> a series of instrumental versions of . . . songs . . . bearing the title of "Arie" accompanied by . . . feminine names. . . . [T]his indicates that each courtesan generally had a personal, favorite song—a custom that the corresponding . . . character probably reproduced on . . . stage.[92]

The scene now shifts from Venice to Naples and the Bavarian court in Munich, where performances of comedies also took place. A 1568 performance in Munich is well known to music historians, since composer Orlando di Lasso was among the players. We have an imaginative visual record of the event: the frescos of commedia dell'arte characters decorating Duke Wilhelm V's bedroom and the walls of the "fool's staircase" in the Castle of Trausnitz, favorite ducal residence, where the 1568 performance took place.[93]

However, "[w]ith this performance at the Bavarian court" "and with the Neapolitan comedies mentioned earlier, we are no longer dealing with the authentic commedia dell'arte, but with its imitation." All the same,

> [w]e shall not be able to avoid using this reflecting mirror in order to approach at last some musical documents. We can find them in those works by Orazio Vecchi

---

[89]*Habiti d'hvomeni et donne venetiane: con la processione della Ser.*^{ma} *Signoria et altri particolari cioè. Trionfi feste et ceremonie pvbliche della nobilissima città di Venetia* (n.p. [Venice]: Giacomo Franco, 1610). But as Iain Fenlon reported to me, the date of 1610 customarily given for the Franco collection is misleading, since the individual images were prepared and first printed at different times, and only collected into an anthology when there was a call to do so, at which time the publication date of "1610" was given to the collection. For particulars, see Fenlon's *The Ceremonial City: History, Memory and Myth in Renaissance Venice* (New Haven: Yale University Press, 2007).

[90]*Balli di sfessania*, ed. Victor Manheimer, 2 vols. (Potsdam: Verlag G. Kiepenheuer, 1921).

[91]Among them the play *Stephanium* by musician Giovanni Armonio, on which see Walther Ludwig, ed., Ioannis Harmonii Marsi, *Comoedia Stephanium* (Munich: W. Fink, 1971).

[92]The repertory Pirrotta identifies was the subject of an article by Willi Apel, "Tänze und Arien für Klavier aus dem Jahre 1588," *Archiv für Musikwissenschaft* 17 (1960): 51–60, and of Apel's edition of Marco Facoli, *Collected Works* (n.p.: American Institute of Musicology, 1963).

[93]See n. 14 of Lockwood's translation of Pirrotta's "*Commedia dell'Arte* and Opera" in *Musical Quarterly* 41 (1955).

and Adriano Banchieri ... generally known as dramatic madrigals or madrigal comedies.

But "if we examine [the] text [of Vecchi's *Anfiparnaso*] as a comedy ..., we will easily perceive that the action and ... development of the play are far below the minimum of coherent and logical succession we should expect from the most mediocre comedy":

> There is in fact only a juxtaposition of scenes and episodes, for the greater part static or accessory from the theatrical point of view. Their connection and integration into a real comedy plot is left in great measure to the listener's imagination; in other words, these episodes are only allusions to an ensemble of situations and developments well known to the listener from the spectacles of the *commedia dell'arte*.... *Such pseudo-comedies, such reflected images of the* commedia dell'arte *allow us, however, to reach at least the knowledge of the most suitable occasions for the use of music in the course of the comedies* [emphasis added].[94]

Vecchi's and Banchieri's comedies—"reflected images of the commedia dell'arte"—are indeed amply provided with actual musical elements. Exercising due sensitivity, we can interpret them as second- or third-order echoes of the lost music of the commedia dell'arte proper to arrive at an imagined reconstruction of that elusive tradition. Serving the attempt is iconographic and musical evidence, which is mutually reinforcing. The evidence furnished by Banchieri's practices and the visual record suggests that the music of the commedia exemplified a venerable tradition: solo singing to the accompaniment of a plucked or strummed string instrument, which the characters themselves played. The melodic style of the vocal line of such music was characterized by the kind of tunefulness typical of the light genres of the canzonetta and villanella alla napoletana.[95] And confirmation is found in the iconographic evidence, in that the engravings of Franco and Callot and the frescos at Trausnitz castle depict music making of precisely this sort: solo singing to the accompaniment of the singer's playing of a plucked-string instrument.

But the extant musico-repertorial evidence is even more decisive testimony to the validity of such conjectures: among the compositions in Banchieri's madrigal comedy *La pazzia senile* is a parody of Palestrina's madrigal *Vestiva i colli*, where the three singers sing the nonsense syllables "Trinc tin, tin, tin, tin, tin, tronc, tin, tin, tin, tin, ti, ti tronc," thus imitating the sounds of

---

[94]Those "occasions for the use of music" had earlier been identified and are here recapitulated.

[95]These are genres and repertories subsequently elucidated in the writings of Donna G. Cardamone-Jackson (see, for a sampling, the essays collected in Cardamone-Jackson's *The Canzone Villanesca alla Napolitana* [Aldershot, Hants: Ashgate Variorum, 2008]) and Ruth I. DeFord (see, for example, DeFord's edition of Vecchi's *canzonette*: *The Four-Voice Canzonettas*, 2 vols. [Madison, WI: A-R Editions, 1993]).

a plucked-string instrument. Passages of music setting the nonsense syllables recur throughout the composition at regular intervals, thus fulfilling the function served by an instrumental ritornello in compositions for vocal solo and string accompaniment. Such a technique substantiates the earlier observation[96] that Vecchi's aim had been to apply the resources of the madrigal tradition to theatrical comedies, which Banchieri manifestly does, because the musical elements of his madrigal comedies are vocal polyphony. At the same time, he attempts to preserve the character of the original commedia dell'arte tradition in the vocal evocations of the sound of the lute.

We have thus been transported into a world of pedlars and mountebanks, of local and regional languages ("dialects") and local and regional musical genres (bergamasche, villanelle alla napoletana), of oral tradition, of "professional players ... of rustic origin and ... low condition," of popular song, of courtesans, of solo singing to the accompaniment of a strummed or plucked-string instrument. It is a world unlike any that Pirrotta had previously portrayed, and he does so evocatively, armed with a range of evidentiary "ammunition"—musical, literary, visual—and capturing the elusive atmospherics.

So much for the commedia dell'arte and its music. But what of its affinities with opera? Even "before the rise of opera[,] the commedia dell'arte had already created many of the conditions necessary for its acceptance by the public"; it resulted in a competition between the itinerant comic and lyric troupes, which closely resembled each other. Correspondences of character type in the two traditions are also important: the comic, often inebriated male servant; the nurse or old matron.

"But such discussion of the comic characters ... is not the most important argument in our comparison of commedia dell'arte and opera":

> [W]ith more telling effect, the comedy exercised its influence on the whole of opera, especially on its musical form. The first Venetian operas...are still dominated by the recitative style.... Only about the middle of the 17th century does that tendency appear which will give to opera its definitive form: a form in which the rules of music will supersede the literary text in a manner that no subsequent reform has been able to temper.... From now on the aria ... will become the basic element of the operatic structure, while the recitatives will be considered only ... connective.... *Orontea is ... tone of the first operas to which we can give the name of a real comic opera, and ... this quality allowed the new musical form to be attempted in it without opposition and even with the most considerable success* [emphasis added].

This last observation—the most important in a series in the second part of the paper—had been anticipated in the articles on Cesti, but here Pirrotta

---

[96]In the 1950 article on Banchieri.

observes further that the term "scherzi"—given by librettist Sbarra to the "ariette" of opera[97]—

> is only too similar to that of *lazzi*, employed by the *comici dell'arte*. . . . [L]*azzi* were not only the jokes and grimaces springing *extempore* from the . . . imagination of the players, but also some form of speech previously agreed upon. . . . And this name was also given to some preestablished scheme of monologue or dialogue which resembles actual "closed pieces". . . . I do not intend to state that the musical forms were inspired by these "closed" monologues or dialogues; but I believe that their practice in the *commedia dell'arte* had already prepared the public for the acceptance of the closed musical forms in the opera. . . . So in the performance of the *commedia del'arte* the rules of free invention and preestablished form, of realism and stylization, must have alternated in sharp contrast, and with sudden transition, much in the manner of the operatic alternation of recitatives and arias. On the other hand it will often happen in the history of opera that some given formal elements—as, for instance, the duets and the ensemble pieces, in which everyone is singing and nobody but the public is listening—are accepted in the serious opera only after having been used and generalized in the comic opera.[98]

Performances of the commedia dell'arte had thus habituated audiences to the use of set-pieces, interspersed among passages of narrative dialog: "lazzi," which are paralleled in early opera (especially early comic opera) by the new genre's "ariette" (or "scherzi," to use the term invoked by opera librettist Sbarra, which is semantically almost identical to "lazzi").[99] The operatic ariette derived their appeal, similarly, from the "hedonistic" variety they lent as alternatives to the potential monotony of unrelieved recitative.

Pirrotta concludes by identifying one last affinity between the two traditions, the audience's delight in the performance per se: "they liked to recognize behind the most disparate camouflages, the voice, the figure, the particular way of acting and gesturing of the players."[100]

---

[97]See the excerpt from "Tre capitoli su Cesti," above.

[98]Historians of opera will attest the validity of this final observation: Philip Gossett has written of the *bel canto* repertory that, "18th-century *opera seria* tended to minimize ensembles. Under the influence of *opera buffa*, ensembles gradually infiltrated the grand Metastasian design, until by 1800 ensembles within the act and lengthy finales were the norm." See Gossett, "Gioachino Rossini," in Philip Gossett, William Ashbrook, Julian Budden, Friedrich Lippmann, Andrew Porter, Mosco Carner, *The New Grove Masters of Italian Opera: Rossini, Donizetti, Bellini, Verdi, Puccini* (London: W.W. Norton, 1983).

[99]But on this entire matter, see more recently the abstract of John Walter Hill's paper at http://www.oudemuziek.nl/stimu/abstracts06.htm. There are also oblique resonances of Pirrotta's early observation in Emily Wilbourne's "*Lo Schiavetto* (1612): Travestied Sound, Ethnic Performance, and the Eloquence of the Body," *Journal of the American Musicological Society* 63 (2010): 1–43, as Beth Glixon reminds me.

[100]Continuing with my enumeration of instances of intellectual patrimonies and lineages, I mention here the scholarship of Anne MacNeil, especially her emphasis on the celebrated *comici* who performed the *commedie*. And MacNeil was a pupil of Howard Mayer Brown. For reminding me of this chain of intellectual relationships, I am grateful to Beth Glixon.

*****

MUSIC OF THE *"TRECENTO"*

When Pirrotta pursued new directions in his scholarship, he did not cease work on subjects that had engaged him before. When we turn from the writings of the Rome years on seventeenth-century opera to those on fourteenth-century music, we have the sensation of returning to familiar intellectual terrain: to familiar themes, expressed in familiar terms.

There are evocations of the by now recognizable "musicological Nationalism."[101] And "Italian Polyphonic Schools during the Fourteenth Century"[102] invokes a typically Crocean opposition, expressed in typically Crocean terms: in the two basic forms of parody procedure in Antonio Zacara's music, "both are, ... based upon a tenor, in which the nexus with the model is *wholly abstract: constructive and never intuitive* [emphasis added]." Pirrotta develops this observation—in similar Crocean language—in the article on the Faenza codex.[103]

Throughout his scholarly career, Pirrotta demonstrates a proclivity for observations that are simultaneously profound and simple, and this is one of them: there are at least two different techniques of using borrowed material, one of them sensible, perceptible, and "intuitive," in that the relationship of antecedent material to derived composition is audible, and the other abstract, constructive, and "ratiocinative," in that the borrowed material is embedded deeply within the derived composition, thus rendering the derived composition's nexus with its model "wholly abstract."[104]

The only paper of the Rome years on music of the Trecento that I wish to analyze in detail is the lecture on Marchettus of Padua, which is of particular importance within the entire corpus of Pirrotta's writings. It is the first of three synthetic papers that describe the oft-ambivalent posture of Italians toward the intellectualistic enterprise of polyphonic composition. "Marchettus of Padua" seeks to explain the origins of the Italian polyphonic tradition of

---

[101]In the entry on the ballata for *Die Musik in Geschichte und Gegenwart* (**1949–51**: "Ballata," especially 1163) and the articles on the earliest examples of parody procedure (**1950**: "Considerazioni sui primi esempi di Missa parodia"; on the delivery of this paper, see *Renaissance News* 3 (1950): 59–60, and for further on the origins of the cyclic mass and its relationship to so-called "parody" procedure, see also **1973**: "Bartholomaeus de Bononia") and "Italian Polyphonic Schools during the Fourteenth Century."

[102]This article—entitled **1951**: "Scuole polifoniche italiane durante il sec. XIV: di una pretesa scuola napoletana"—was a "Communicazione letta nella seduta del 24 luglio 1951 alla Société Française de Musicologie" and was published in *Collectanea historiæ musicæ* 1 (Florence: L. S. Olschki, 1953): 11–18. See also "Séances de la Société," *Revue de Musicologie* 33 (1951): 152–53.

[103]**1954**: "Note su un codice di antiche musiche per tastiera."

[104]"Chronology and Denomination of the Italian Ars Nova" documents more clearly still the Idealist origins of this general discourse.

the fourteenth century, "Music and Cultural Tendencies in 15th-Century Italy" the seeming absence of a robust polyphonic tradition during the fifteenth, and "'Maniera' polifonica e immediatezza recitativa" the momentary rapprochement during the sixteenth century between lingering period skepticism regarding polyphonic practice and wholehearted acceptance thereof.

Pirrotta begins the first of these by identifying what is, for him, a conundrum: it is ironic that the "secret of the Quattrocento" is thought to demand explanation, whereas the "secret of the Duecento" is not. His argument—which is fully appreciated only when "Marchettus" is read as the first title in the series of three—is that it is not the secret of the Quattrocento that requires explanation, nor the secret of the Duecento, but, rather, the appearance of the polyphonic tradition of the Trecento.

The anomaly to be explained, that is, is not the seeming *absence* of a robust polyphonic tradition in the thirteenth and fifteenth centuries, but, rather, the *presence* of one in the fourteenth century. The erroneous historiographic assumption is that the emergence of a polyphonic tradition in the fourteenth century was inevitable and "natural," not demanding explication. So conditioned have we become to privileging the written polyphonic tradition, because of our assumptions and prejudices concerning its supposed stature, prestige, inevitability, and ubiquity, that we often do not appreciate that it is its presence rather than its absence that demands explanation.

"Marchettus of Padua" represents both a culmination of earlier research and an anticipation of what Pirrotta will argue in his second study. Elsewhere, he will suggest that the "default position" in medieval Italian musical life, so to speak, ordinarily entailed oral practice, with all the "negative" implications such a practice could have for the cultivation of polyphony.[105] His task in "Marchettus of Padua" is to explain that anomalous "sudden blooming" of fourteenth-century polyphonic practice.

We have thus returned to that elusive phenomenon of "cultural fashion": the sudden emergence of a polyphonic tradition in fourteenth-century Italy requires careful explanation not only in terms "of historical or social conditions of a general sort, but also of particular and special factors." The original benefactors were royal and aristocratic figures: King Robert of Naples (a Frenchman who imported a taste for French polyphonic practice to the Italian peninsula) and the aristocratic figures elsewhere in Italy (specifically in the north) who were anxious to emulate him.[106] From there, a chain of dates, names, events, and musical documents leads without interruption to the appearance of the three Italian masters who represent the earliest known

---

[105] **1973**: "Novelty and Renewal in Italy, 1300-1600"; **1980**: "Italy."
[106] **1985**: "Introduzione ai lavori."

generation of Italian Ars nova composers: Giovanni da Cascia, Jacopo da Bologna, and Fra Piero.

*****

Several general observations can be made about Pirrotta's scholarly achievements of the Rome years. First, we see him availing himself yet again of various opportunities, in this case not only with respect to professional appointments but also scholarly problems open to exploration on the basis of available primary materials: the 1600 printed edition of Peri's *Euridice* and the rediscovered manuscript scores of Cesti's great *Orontea*, which support the revivals and scholarly papers seeking to clarify the operas' historical contexts.

Second, the corpus of Pirrotta's writings was by then substantial enough that we begin to see instances of what I shall term "intellectual/programmatic trajectories": an article on a particular subject suggests related problems to be explored systematically in future papers. Thus the article on the Lucca manuscript spawns further research and writing on Paolo *tenorista*, the article on the Modena manuscript leads to further research and writing on parody as a compositional procedure and on the possible existence of a Neapolitan school of composition, the articles on Banchieri and Cesti suggest the lecture on the correspondences between commedia dell'arte and opera.

Finally, it is significant that almost half of the publications of the Rome years originated in lectures and conference presentations, a consequence of Pirrotta's growing stature as a scholar and lecturer. The importance of these papers is that they reveal a different, more accessible *style of presentation*, reflecting his awareness of the needs of his "live" audience.

But the style of presentation is only one distinguishing feature of these papers, related to yet another: the fact that, almost without exception, the lectures and conference presentations of the Rome years also had a different *intellectual purpose* and, accordingly, a different explanatory power. They are more synthetic in character, more motivated by an intention to advance an overarching argument concerning the material under discussion.

"Temperamenti e tendenze nella Camerata fiorentina," "Tragédie e comédie dans la Camerata fiorentina," "Commedia dell'Arte e Melodramma," and "Marchettus of Padua and the Italian Ars Nova"—lectures all—are nothing less than statements of fundamental theses concerning such consequential matters as the beginnings of opera, the fragile nature of the historical enterprise when the subject matter (the commedia dell'arte) exemplifies oral tradition, and—in the final case—the continuing dialectic in Italian musical life between written and unwritten practices and the consequences it had for the origins of the Italian Ars nova.

In his lectures, Pirrotta exploits the opportunity to clarify his thinking at a particular moment in his scholarly life about such transcendent phenomena and to advance an organic thesis that seeks, above all, to explain and elucidate. Throughout his career, he will capitalize on such opportunities and periodically publish comprehensive, synthetic papers, characterized by their explanatory force.

Scena 6.^a

Princeton, California, and Columbia (1954–55)

As director of the «Santa Cecilia» library, Pirrotta often had the opportunity to meet scholars from throughout the world. In 1950, he made the acquaintance of Oliver Strunk, Professor of Music at Princeton University, the fourth of those individuals destined to play an especially important role in his career.[1]

W. Oliver Strunk (22 March 1901–24 February 1980) was the son of William O. Strunk Jr., coauthor of the book known to thousands of Americans simply as "Strunk and White."[2] Strunk had studied at Cornell, which was his father's university, and at the University of Rochester before departing for Europe to complete his formal musicological training at the University of Berlin under the tutelage of legendary figures in the German musicological world: Friedrich Blume, Curt Sachs, Johannes Wolf.[3] When he returned to the States, he joined the staff of the Library of Congress in 1928[4] and in 1934 succeeded Carl Engel as head of its music division. Three years later he was appointed to the faculty at Princeton, where in 1950 he became Professor of Music. During Strunk's tenure at the Library of Congress, he had helped found the American Musicological Society.[5] It is generally agreed that Strunk is one of the seminal figures in American musicology.

Oliver Strunk and Nino Pirrotta met in 1950, when Strunk was visiting the Badia Greca, a Basilian monastery in Grottaferrata, a small town in the Alban

---

[1] Strunk is the only American musicologist whom Pirrotta memorialized in an obituary or other encomium; see **1981**: "OBITUARIES. William Oliver Strunk."

[2] Available in numerous editions; see, for example, *The Elements of Style*, by William Strunk, Jr., with Revisions, An Introduction, and a Chapter on Writing by E.B. White; foreword by Roger Angell, 4th ed. (Boston: Allyn and Bacon, 2000).

[3] For Strunk's account of his career, see his letter to Carl Engel in Robert Bailey, "Wagner, Verdi, and Oliver Strunk," in *Remembering Oliver Strunk. Teacher and Scholar*, eds. Christina Huemer and Pierluigi Petrobelli (Hillsdale, NY: Pendragon Press, 2005), 107–18, especially 107–09.

[4] **1981**: "OBITUARIES. William Oliver Strunk."

[5] **1981**: "OBITUARIES. William Oliver Strunk."

hills south of Rome.⁶ In the spring of that year, Pirrotta and Strunk attended the "Congresso internazionale di musica sacra" organized by the Pontificio Istituto di Musica Sacra and the Commissione di Musica Sacra per l'Anno Santo, which was held at the Palazzo della Cancelleria in Rome from 25–30 May. Both men delivered papers that were later published.⁷ While in Rome, Strunk took the opportunity to call on Pirrotta in his office at the «Santa Cecilia», and their first meeting was memorable. Carolyn Gianturco wrote that "[i]n the first encounters in the library in Rome, Strunk was impressed with the culture of the young Italian scholar, be it humanistic or musical."⁸

It is not difficult to determine the reasons for the profound friendship that ensued. There were important commonalities in the personal and professional identities of the two men. Pierluigi Petrobelli attributed their friendship to the breadth of their cultural formation.⁹ Moreover, both had come of age professionally at a time when there were limited career possibilities for aspiring music historians, and they had therefore begun as music librarians.¹⁰ Such experience helps to explain a distinguishing characteristic of both men's scholarship: their reliance on examination of the primary sources, and their command of such materials.

Moreover, one of the reasons for their eclecticism—the breadth of their scholarly interests—was precisely their experience as librarians, which required them (within resource constraints) to maintain comprehensive collections and become familiar with a broad range of the scholarly literature in music and scholarly problems in music history.

They also shared intellectual interests: Strunk was to publish an article on the dating of the treatises of Marchettus of Padua, which was crucial for establishing the independence of the Italian theoretical tradition from that of the Frenchmen Jean de Muris and Philippe de Vitry. Their common interest would serve Pirrotta in his ongoing project of ensuring a proper balance in the collective music-historical understanding of the relative significance of French and Italian achievements. His esteem for Strunk's article is clear from his own on Marchettus, where he reviews the scholarly controversy concerning

---

⁶Owing to its collection of manuscript materials, the monastery was an important center of Byzantine studies. For the information that Strunk was visiting the monastery in 1950, I am grateful to Professor Kenneth Levy.

⁷Pirrotta, **1950**: "Considerazioni sui primi esempi di Missa parodia"; Strunk, "The Classification and Development of the Early Byzantine Notations," in *Essays on Music in the Byzantine World*, foreword by Kenneth Levy (New York: W.W. Norton, 1977), 40–44. On the Rome conference, and Pirrotta's presentation, see also "Conferences," *Renaissance News* 3 (1950): 59–60.

⁸Gianturco, "Nino Pirrotta" (see "Scena 3.ᵃ," n. 13).

⁹Interview with Petrobelli, 16 December 2007.

¹⁰Like Pirrotta, Strunk reflected on the absence of opportunities in his own country to study music history scientifically, and the attractions, therefore, of a position as a music librarian; see Bailey, "Wagner, Verdi, and Oliver Strunk," 108.

the dating of the theoretical treatises and suggests that "[o]nly recently... Oliver Strunk has dealt with this problem in an absolutely definitive manner."[11] And Pirrotta had also written on Byzantine music, the abiding interest of Strunk's professional life, which Pirrotta described as "a major pole of attraction in Strunk's richly motivated career."[12]

But the commonalities extended well beyond matters of intellectual and professional profile. The two men shared personal attributes. Both had a good measure of humility and reserve. Both were, or could be, taciturn. Both exemplified an uncommon integrity, as Pierluigi Petrobelli observed.[13]

Furthermore, both were completely absorbed in their musicological scholarship. Upon Strunk's retirement, his pupil Harold S. Powers wrote that "the teacher, the scholar, and the man are indivisible: musical insight, intellectual *virtuosismo*, immense learning, generous tolerance, and courtesy are permeated with humane sensibility and moral responsibility." Powers might have been writing about Pirrotta. Earlier, Powers had observed that Strunk's "remarkable intellectual and personal capacities are activated by a love of music and an insatiable curiosity about its phenomena." This characteristic also—this oneness of the human being with the scholar, with the music historian—was common to both men. And one of Pirrotta's Italian pupils similarly made reference to Pirrotta's absorption in his musicological work, almost to the point of finding anything else distracting.[14] For both Nino Pirrotta and Oliver Strunk, being a musicologist was not what they did; it was who they were.

But there were also differences between Strunk and Pirrotta, principally in matters of intellectual style and sensibility. Strunk is featured prominently in Joseph Kerman's portrayal of the different intellectual sensibilities that characterized musicology in postwar America, where he figures as emblem of "German positivistic historiography." Although Pirrotta was demonstrably more Positivist than Idealist in his *forma mentis*, anyone familiar with his intellectual style, as reflected in his scholarly writings, will immediately perceive how different it is from that of Oliver Strunk.[15]

---

[11]**1955**: "Marchettus de Padua and the Italian Ars Nova," 60. See also **1951**: "Scuole polifoniche italiane durante il sec. XIV."

[12]**1938**: review of Ottavio Tiby, *La musica bizantina*. Pirrotta's characterization of the place of scholarship on Byzantine music in Strunk's career is in **1981**: "OBITUARIES."

[13]A.M. Cummings interview with Professor Petrobelli, 16 December 2007. This quality in Pirrotta is attested by all who knew him well, among them Frank D'Accone, who emphasized it in an interview with A.M. Cummings at the 2009 annual national meeting of the American Musicological Society in Philadelphia.

[14]A.M. Cummings interview with Professor Franco Piperno of the University of Rome, 20 December 2007.

[15]On Strunk, see also *Remembering Oliver Strunk, Teacher and Scholar*, passim. I also found the following title especially revealing, in particular for its portrayal of Strunk's intellectual style and its indebtedness to philology (and the possible relationships to Pirrotta's intellectual profile, therefore): Charles Rosen, "The Discipline of Philology: Oliver Strunk," in Rosen, *Critical Entertainments: Music Old and New* (Cambridge, MA: Harvard University Press, 2000), 12–22.

These differences did not mitigate the strength of their friendship. Strunk's papers were left to the American Academy in Rome, and among them are many offprints of Pirrotta's articles, each inscribed—in Pirrotta's elegant handwriting—with a few playful words reflective of their friendship: "Scelte poetiche di Monteverdi" is inscribed "Do I write too much? Affectionately / Nino"; "Ars nova e stil novo," "To Oliver, 'musicologo non arcigno' ['a non-sullen musicologist'] / Nino"; "Ars musica," "A dull dedication for a dull paper, to a brightest critic and friend / Nino"; both "Novelty and Renewal in Italy" and "On Text Forms from Ciconia to Dufay," "To Oliver, affectionately / Nino"; and "Dante *musicus*," "To Oliver musicus from Nino." The facsimile edition of the Paolo *tenorista* fragment is inscribed: "To Oliver: another abbot's portrait. Do you like it better? / Nino."

*****

Strunk's pupil Kenneth Levy met Pirrotta a few months after Pirrotta's first encounter with Strunk, toward the end of 1950 or the beginning of 1951. Levy was in Paris for the academic year 1950/51, engaged in research for his dissertation. There, Madame the Comtesse de Chambure, Geneviève Thibault, hosted Wednesday-afternoon musicological salons, with François Lesure serving as her unofficial adjutant. Pirrotta was also an occasional attendee, when he would play the organ, and he impressed Levy deeply as a "wonderfully genial" participant in the gatherings.[16]

In the summer of 1951, at the conclusion of Levy's year in Paris, Strunk was again in Rome, where he and Levy met and called on Pirrotta at the «Santa Cecilia». The return visit reinforced Strunk's already positive impression of his new Italian friend.

*****

During the academic year 1954/55, Strunk was eligible for a sabbatical, and the Department of Music at Princeton was given approval to appoint a visitor to cover his courses. Strunk, who had played a significant role in assisting other European musicologists secure appointments in the United States,[17]

---

[16]Interview with Professor Kenneth Levy. Pirrotta visited Paris in connection with his responsibilities as vice president of the International Association of Music Libraries (see my "*Scena 5.ª*," above, as well as **1951**: "Fondi musicali non inventariati nè catalogati," 46–47), and also because of professional opportunities—invitations to lecture—resulting from his growing stature as a scholar: see, for example, **1951**: "Scuole polifoniche italiane durante il sec. XIV"; **1953**: "Tragédie et comédie dans la Camerata fiorentina" (see also *Renaissance News* 6 [1953]: 41); and **1955**: "Cronologia e denominazione dell'ars nova italiana"; on the delivery of the first of these, see also "Séances de la Société" (see "*Scena 5.ª*," n. 102).

[17]Gianturco, "Nino Pirrotta" (see "*Scena 3.ª*," n. 13).

recommended Pirrotta, whose expertise in seventeenth-century opera, a subject on which Strunk had taught a course in 1948, was an additional impetus. Kenneth Levy heartily endorsed the recommendation.

There followed sensitive communications with Pirrotta concerning the plausibility of his taking a leave of absence from the «Santa Cecilia» for the academic year.

On 25 May 1954, the tenured and tenure-track faculty members in Princeton's Department of Music voted unanimously to recommend Pirrotta's appointment to the administration. On 4 June 1954 Department chairman Arthur Mendel, Professor of Music, communicated their recommendation to the university's dean of the faculty. It received the remaining required approvals from the university president and the Curriculum Committee of the Board of Trustees.

Thus was Antonino Pirrotta, *Licenziato, Diplomato di Magistero*, and *Dottore in Lettere*, Direttore delle Biblioteche of the Accademia and Conservatorio di Musica «Santa Cecilia» di Roma—characterized in the materials submitted to Princeton's Trustees as "[p]robably the ablest of the Italian musicologists"—appointed Visiting Professor of Music at Princeton University for the period September 1954–June 1955. He was to receive the princely sum of $9,000. On 18 August, the *New York Times* published a special that reported "Italian to Teach at Princeton."

> PRINCETON, N.J., Aug. 18—Dr. Nino Pirrotta, director of the music library for the St. Cecilia Conservatory and National Academy at Rome, has been named visiting professor in Princeton University's department of music for the academic 1954–55. He is an authority on fourteenth century Italian music.[18]

*****

The Pirrottas and their four young children embarked from Naples on the ocean liner *Saturnia*, which after a two-week voyage docked in Halifax, Nova Scotia, where Professor and Mrs. Strunk met them. Because of Canadian and American postwar anxieties about immigration, the Pirrottas were briefly detained before being permitted to disembark, a situation to which both Pirrotta and Strunk later made ironic reference.[19] The Pirrottas arrived in New York City in mid-September 1954.

---

[18] *New York Times (1857–Current file)*; Aug 19, 1954; ProQuest Historical Newspapers, The New York Times (1851–2004), 19.

[19] Strunk, "A Letter from a Friend," *Rivista italiana di musicologia* 10, "In onore di Nino Pirrotta" (1975): 8–9, esp. p. 8. In his inscription on the copy given to Strunk [copy in the American Academy of Rome] of vol. 1 of **1954:** *The Music of Fourteenth-Century Italy*, Pirrotta wrote: "Al Prof. Oliver Strunk / in ricordo di un incontro nelle acque di / Halifax." After being detained, the family went ashore, and then reboarded and continued to New York that same day. I am grateful to Dr. Sergio Pirrotta for his clarification.

For Pirrotta, the time at Princeton was of exceptional importance. Many years later, he dedicated an anthology of his essays to "dearest and unforgettable friends: . . . Oliver Strunk and Arthur Mendel, who, favoring my relocation to their country, opened the way for me to precious new experiences of life and study. With a profoundly grateful spirit, Rome, June 1984."[20] In Mendel's negotiations with the Office of the Dean of the Faculty concerning the possibility of Pirrotta's appointment, Mendel had "spoken enthusiastically of that prospect."

The Pirrottas immersed themselves in informal American academic culture, even attending Princeton football games, an experience that prompted Pirrotta's whimsical inscription to Strunk on volume I of his edition of the *Trecento* repertory: "in remembrance of an introduction to the 'Ars nova' in Palmer Stadium / Nino Pirrotta / Princeton, 9 October 1954."[21]

Pirrotta taught two courses, both at the graduate level, given that his command of English was still too uncertain for undergraduate teaching. On the other hand, as Mendel's supporting documentation suggested, "he speaks and writes a fluent and idiomatic French, which all our students understand," and, so, Pirrotta's instruction was initially in French, although by the end of his year at Princeton his English had improved to the point where he was offering some instruction in that language.

Pirrotta's two, three-hour-long graduate seminars—one taught each semester—were Music 510 and Music 515, "Music of the Ars Nova / Studies in the musical style of fourteenth-century France and Italy and its literary background," and "Problems in the history of the Opera / Studies in the development of the serious, comic, and romantic opera in Italy, France, and Germany during the 17th, 18th, and 19th centuries."[22] Music 510 was a survey of the major composers of Trecento polyphony, and Pirrotta's principal pedagogical method was to distribute his own transcriptions of representative compositions in the repertory and have performances of them. His students thus gained an intimate sense of the musical characteristics of works in the Trecento repertoire. Harold Powers was among those enrolled in Music 515; Powers had been away from Princeton during academic years 1952/53 and 1953/54. Pirrotta's teaching sparked an interest in Powers that would later be reflected in three splendid articles on Seicento opera.[23]

---

[20]*Musica tra Medioevo e Rinascimento* (Turin: Einaudi, 1984), x.

[21]Strunk papers, American Academy in Rome: "Al Prof. Oliver Strunk / in ricordo di . . . una introduzione all'"ars nova, / nel Palmer Stadium / Nino Pirrotta / Princeton 9 ottobre 1954."

[22]This information is drawn from the Princeton University *Graduate School Announcement* for academic year 1954/55, which I consulted in the Princeton University Archives.

[23]"*Il* Serse trasformato – I," *Musical Quarterly* 47 (1961): 481–92, and 48 (1962): 73–92; "*L'*Erismena travestita," in *Studies in Music History: Essays for Oliver Strunk* (Princeton, NJ: Princeton University Press, 1968), 259–324; "*Il* «Mutio» tramutato" (see "Intermedio I.^{mo}," n. 146). In the first and third of these, Powers explicitly acknowledges his indebtedness to Pirrotta.

Another of Strunk's Princeton pupils with whom Pirrotta established a lasting friendship was Lewis Lockwood. During the Princeton year, Lockwood translated Pirrotta's "Commedia dell'Arte e Melodramma,"[24] which had originally been written in French and delivered in Brussels, after which it was translated into Italian and delivered at the «Santa Cecilia» in January of 1954. Lockwood's translation, which appeared in the *Musical Quarterly* for 1955, helped to secure a wider American and English readership for Pirrotta.[25]

The academic year offered other opportunities for Pirrotta to gain exposure to a larger American audience. On 5 March 1955, he addressed the Greater New York Chapter of the American Musicological Society, at the Fifth Avenue branch of the New York Public Library.[26]

The Princeton year came to an end, but not the Pirrottas' inaugural American experience. The family drove to Los Angeles, where Pirrotta taught at the University of California for the summer.[27]

At the conclusion of the summer term, the Pirrottas returned to New York and departed from there at the beginning of August. But the rewarding professional and personal relationships established with their new American friends during the 1954/55 academic year did not end. Lewis Lockwood and his wife, Doris, were in Rome in August of 1955. Kenneth Levy spent the 1955/56 academic year in Rome and had many chances to see the Pirrottas during the second half of the year.

Indeed, thanks to the professional opportunities of the Princeton year, Pirrotta would very soon return to the United States—this time without his family—to teach at Columbia University during the fall semester of 1955/56 (29 September 1955–31 January 1956), an opportunity occasioned by Columbia Professor Erich Hertzmann's sabbatical and offered under the auspices of the Department of State's Exchange-Visitor Program, whose "purpose . . . is to simplify the exchange of scholars between the United States and the free nations of the world."[28]

---

[24]**1954**: "Commedia dell'Arte e Melodramma."

[25]I am grateful to Lewis Lockwood for his recollections about translating Pirrotta's article; private e-mail communication, 18 July 2008.

[26]Announcement in the *New York Times* (5 March 1955).

[27]Frank D'Accone suggested to me (private interview) that Walter Rubsamen was the crucial player in arranging Pirrotta's summer-term appointment at U.C.L.A. When the Pirrottas arrived in Los Angeles, they were hosted for dinner and as overnight guests by Professor W. Thomas Marrocco, one of Pirrotta's fellow specialists in the music of the Italian Trecento, and a friend as well as a colleague. In January of 1955, Marrocco had published a complimentary review of the first volume of Pirrotta's edition of the *Trecento* repertory in *Musical Quarterly*. Moreover, the second edition of Marrocco's edition of *Trecento cacce* is dedicated to Pirrotta.

[28]Unless otherwise noted, the information in this paragraph is from documents in the Columbia University Archives and Columbiana Library, "Central Files / Box 225" and "Appointment Records." For assistance in procuring copies, I am grateful to Farris G. Wahbeh, Project Archivist for the Meyer M. Schapiro Papers at Columbia's Rare Book & Manuscript Library. Professor Frank D'Accone suggested to me (private interview) that Paul Henry Lang was the critical player in arranging Pirrotta's fall-term appointment at Columbia.

Pirrotta consulted with Maestro Guido Guerrini, director of the «Santa Cecilia», and obtained permission to extend his leave of absence. On 29 August, he wrote to composer Douglas Moore, chairman of Columbia's Department of Music, to report that he was able to accept the invitation to teach at Columbia as Visiting Professor of Music, for which the University compensated him $3,500.

This time, Pirrotta flew rather than sailed to the United States and arrived in New York City at the end of September. During the Columbia semester, he reported to Frank D'Accone, whom he had met the previous spring in Princeton, that he was finding New York City "fascinating" and was pleased with his seminar on Italian opera.[29] In turn, his Columbia students developed a sincere affection for him, and when Pirrotta finished the semester they honored him with a mock Festschrift, a playful document of their warm rapport with him.[30] And just as Pirrotta's teaching at Princeton inspired Harold Powers's later scholarship on *opera seicentesca*, so the teaching at Columbia had similar consequences: One of the students in the seminar on opera, William C. Holmes, was to write his doctoral dissertation on Cesti's *Orontea* and publish the first scholarly edition of the work.[31] At the end of the semester Pirrotta departed from New York (on 19 January) and returned to Italy.

*****

On 24 October 1955, while at Columbia, Pirrotta had received a telephone call from Randall Thompson, Professor of Music and Chairman of the Department of Music at Harvard University, which was to have life-altering consequences for him and his family.

---

[29]D'Accone saw Pirrotta in Princeton in the spring of 1955, and at Columbia in the fall of that year; A.M. Cummings interview with D'Accone, 2009 annual national meeting of the American Musicological Society, Philadelphia.

[30]See D'Accone's contribution to the essays in Pirrotta's memory published in *Musica disciplina* 50 (1996); also, A.M. Cummings interview with D'Accone, 2009 annual national meeting of the American Musicological Society, Philadelphia.

[31]D'Accone, *Musica disciplina* 50 (1996). Holmes's writings referenced are the following: "*Orontea:* A Study of Changes and Development in the Libretto and Music of Mid-Seventeenth Century Italian Opera" (Ph.D. diss., Columbia Univ., 1968); and Holmes, ed., Antonio Cesti (1623–1669), *Orontea* (n.p.: Wellesley College, 1973). In Frank D'Accone's introduction to the volume of essays for Holmes—*Music Observed: Studies in Memory of William C. Holmes* (Warren, MI: Harmonie Park Press, 2004)—he recounts that Holmes had studied with Pirrotta during the semester when Pirrotta served as Visiting Professor at Columbia University. Holmes's edition has now been revised by another of Pirrotta's American pupils, Alejandro Planchart, Ph.D. Harvard University 1971: Antonio Cesti (1623–1669), *Orontea. Opera in Three Acts and a Prologue. Libretto by Giacinto Andrea Cicognini. Version of the Italian Manuscripts*, ed. William Holmes, rev. Alejandro Enrique Planchart (Santa Barbara, CA: Marisol Press, 2002).

Intermedio II.^{ndo}
["apparente"]

Images

Figure 2 Nino Pirrotta's grandfather, Antonino. (Antonino was married to Giulia Pirandello, whose first cousin Stefano was the father of Nobel Laureate Luigi Pirandello; Nino Pirrotta was thus the Nobel Laureate's second cousin once removed.)

Figure 3 Nino Pirrotta's father, Vincenzo.

Figure 4 Nino Pirrotta's mother, Adele Restivo-Pirrotta.

Figure 5 A painting by Pirrotta's mother.

Figure 6 A painting by Pirrotta's mother.

Figure 7 A painting by Pirrotta's mother.

Figure 8 Pirrotta later in life, in his apartment in the Parioli district of Rome, with pieces of the family collection of majolica displayed behind him.

Figure 9 Nino Pirrotta (*left*) with his mother and sister Giulia.

Figure 10 Nino and Giulia Pirrotta.

Figure 11 Pirrotta at around 18 years of age.

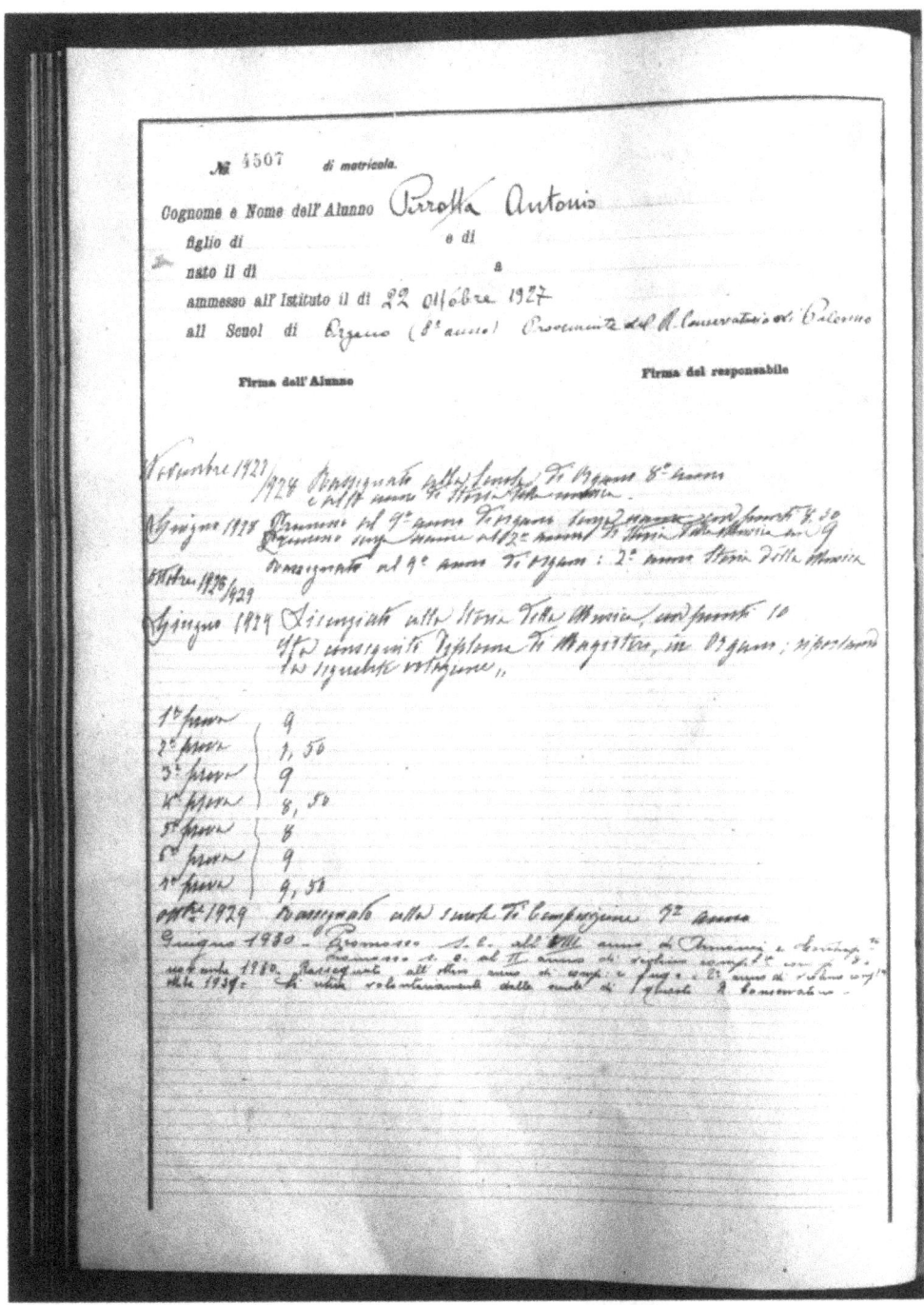

Figure 12 The entry on Pirrotta in the register of the Regio Conservatorio di Musica «Luigi Cherubini» di Firenze.

Figure 13 Gaetano Salvemini, adherent of the Idealist and Materialist schools of history and professor of history at the Regia Università degli Studi di Firenze in the years immediately before Pirrotta enrolled. (Pictured with Salvemini is Francesco Cantarella, whose sister Nelda Cantarella-Ferace held an important administrative post at Villa I Tatti, The Harvard University Center for Italian Renaissance Studies, where Pirrotta served as a member of the Advisory Committee.)

Figure 14 Pirrotta playing volleyball on the beach, identified by a "+" in the original photograph.

Figure 15 Lea Paternostro-Pirrotta.

Figure 16 Lea Pirrotta on horseback.

Figure 17 Pirrotta on his wedding day, with his father.

Figure 18 Nino and Lea Pirrotta on their wedding day.

Figure 19 Lea Pirrotta on her wedding day.

Figure 20 Nino's mother, Nino, Lea, Lea's mother, and Nino's father on Nino and Lea's wedding day. (The photograph visible between Lea's mother and Nino's father is of Lea's father, Angelo Paternostro.)

Figure 21 Lea Pirrotta later in life.

Figure 22 Dilli, Lea, and Vincenzo Pirrotta.

Figure 23 Dilli, Nino, and Silvia Pirrotta.

Figure 24 Nino and Lea Pirrotta and their son.

Figure 25 Sergio and Nino Pirrotta.

PAGINA 27

TERZO PROGRAMMA

Stazioni a modulazione di frequenza di BOLOGNA - FIRENZE - GENOVA - MILANO - NAPOLI
ROMA - TORINO - VENEZIA e onde corte su m. 47,90; 48,10; 50,2 e m. 75.6

21 — L'avvenimento della settimana

21,15 Musiche di danza del XVI e XVII secolo

21,35 Opere italiane del Seicento
EURIDICE
di Ottavio Rinuccini
Trascrizione e rielaborazione di Nino Pirrotta delle musiche di
Jacopo Peri

La Tragedia	Adele Cezza	Dafne	Luisa Ribacchi
Euridice	Maria Vèrnole		
Orfeo	Africo Baldelli	Ninfa	Rossana Zerbini
Arcetro	Licia Cacciatori		
Tirsi	Ottavio Plenizzio	Plutone	Plinio Clabassi
Aminta	Walter Blazer		
Pastore		Proserpina	Adele Cezza

Direttore Roberto Lupi
Istruttore del coro Roberto Benaglio
Orchestra e coro di Milano della Radio Italiana
Presentazione a cura di Nino Pirrotta

22,35 Luigi Dallapiccola
Piccolo concerto per Muriel Couvreux
per pianoforte e orchestra
Pastorale, girotondo, ripresa - Cadenza, notturno e finale
Solista Armando Renzi
Orchestra dell'Associazione «A. Scarlatti» di Napoli
Direttore Franco Caracciolo

Autonome

TRIESTE

7,15 Calendario e ginnastica da camera. 7,30 Segnale orario, Giornale radio. 7,45-8,30 Musica del mattino. 11,30 La Radio per le scuole. 12 Ritmi moderni. 12,15 Per ciascuno qualcosa. 12,45 Oggi alla radio. 12,46 Spettacoli e ritrovi. 12,55 Calendario Antonetto. 13 Segnale orario, Giornale radio. 13,27 Orchestra diretta da Pino Vatta. 14 Terza pagina. 14,20 Musica var.a. 14,30-15 Programmi dalla BBC, Listino borsa. 17.30 La voce dell'America. 18 Suoni

Estere

ALGERIA
ALGERI

18,30 Trasmissione culturale. 19,15 I bei testi. 19,30 Notiziario. 19,40 Musica leggera. 20 Organista Marie-Antoinette Gard. 20,15 Varietà. 20,30 Rassegna artistico-letteraria. 20,45 Sul vivo. 21 Notiziario. 21,20 D.ssi. 21,30 Rivista. 21,50 Concerto diretto da Victor Clovez. 23,20 Musica notturna. 23,45-24 Notiziario.

AUSTRIA
SALISBURGO - LINZ

18,45 Trasmissione della B.B.C. 19 «Pronto New York: qui Vienna!». 19,15 Notizie sportive.

Figures 26 and 27 Newspaper notices of the 1951 RAI broadcast performance of Jacopo Peri's *Euridice* (1600), attesting the participation of Maria Vèrnole, Walter Blazer, and Nino Pirrotta. (The author of the second notice is Emilia Zanetti, Nino's colleague in the library at the Conservatorio di Musica «S.ta Cecilia» di Roma.)

Figures 26 and 27 (continued).

IMAGES 229

Figures 28 and 29 Maria Vèrnole-Blazer, 1951's Euridice, ca. 1951 and today.

Figures 28 and 29 *(continued).*

Figure 30 Pirrotta's 1954 passport photograph.

Figure 31 Silvia, Dilli, Vincenzo, Sergio, Lea, and Nino Pirrotta aboard ship *en route* to New York in 1954.

Figure 32 Lea Pirrotta at the mailbox in the Dutch Neck neighborhood outside Princeton, N.J., 1954/55.

Figure 33 Lea and the Pirrotta family automobile, 1954/55.

Figure 34 Mildred Strunk, Dilli, and Oliver Strunk on their way to the Princeton football stadium, 1954.

Figure 35 Nino, Mildred Strunk, Dilli, Lea, Vincenzo, and Oliver Strunk, at Erich Hertzmann's apartment in New York City.

Figure 36 Pirrotta at Harvard.

Figure 37 Pirrotta on the occasion of his receiving the degree of Doctor of Fine Arts, *Honoris causa*, from the College of the Holy Cross (1970).

Figure 38 Pirrotta receiving the degree of Doctor of Humane Letters, *Honoris causa*, from Princeton University (1988).

Figure 39 Nino and Lea Pirrotta later in life.

Atto III.^{tio}

Professore

Scena 7.[a]

Harvard University (1956–71): *Rinascimento* (or: "Rome Fumbles, and Harvard Recovers")

My chapter on the Cambridge years is subtitled "Rinascimento" for two reasons—one literal, the other metaphoric. First, it was during his Harvard years that Pirrotta began to make substantial contributions to the scholarly literature on the music of the Italian Renaissance, complementing the earlier publications on the music of the Trecento and seventeenth-century opera. Second, Pirrotta regarded his relocation to the United States as inaugurating a personal intellectual Renaissance, made clear by his words of gratitude to Oliver Strunk and Arthur Mendel, "who, favoring [his] transfer to their country, opened the way for [him] to precious new experiences of life and study."

*****

The Department of Music at Harvard had witnessed tragic fluctuations in its staffing as a result of the deaths of two gifted appointees: the Hungarian musicologist Ottó János Gombosi[1] († 17 February 1955), Professor of Music, who had been called to Harvard from the University of Chicago little more than three years before (1 February 1952[2]); and the promising young musicologist

---

[1] Dr.phil. Universität Berlin 1925. See John M. Ward, "Otto John Gombosi (1902–55)," *Acta Musicologica* 28 (1956): 57–59.

[2] "MUSIC AIDE JOINS HARVARD. Dr. O.J. Gombosi, Renaissance Expert, Named Professor. Special to THE NEW YORK TIMES.," *New York Times* (2 December 1951). Gombosi had been a visiting faculty member at Harvard as of the fall semester of the 1951/52 academic year, with the expectation that he would be appointed professor in the spring of that year. In reconstructing Gombosi's complicated career, I found indispensable Laurence Libin's "Otto Gombosi's Correspondence at the University of Chicago," *Historical Musicology: Sources, Methods, Interpretations*, ed. Stephen A. Crist and Roberta Montemorra Marvin (Rochester, NY: University of Rochester Press, 2004), 388–413.

Stephen Davidson Tuttle[3] († 9 April 1954), Associate Professor of Music, who had been called to Harvard from the University of Virginia less than two years earlier (1 July 1952).[4]

Therefore, in academic years 1954/55 and 1955/56, the Department was seeking to make several appointments. It first replaced Tuttle with Gombosi's former pupil John Milton Ward III,[5] who was named Associate Professor of Music, with tenure, effective 1 July 1955 (the semester following Gombosi's death). Although Ward had been a pupil of Gombosi, his scholarly interests corresponded more to those of Tuttle,[6] so that he is indeed to be understood in some sense as Tuttle's successor. He would become one of Pirrotta's closest colleagues and friends during the years they taught at Harvard.

Then, knowing of the "sad events" in the Harvard department, an acquaintance of the department chairman reported during the spring of 1955 that he had become aware of Pirrotta's interest in remaining in the United States.[7]

---

[3] A.M. Harvard '31, Ph.D. Harvard '41. On Tuttle, see http://www.thecrimson.com/article.aspx?ref=487321 and the obituary by Harvard University professors Archibald T. Davison, John H. Finley, Jr., Kenneth B. Murdock, and Randall Thompson in *Harvard University Gazette* 50 (15 January 1955), reprinted in the *Denison Alumnus* (June 1956): 11, 14–15. For information on Tuttle (A.B. Denison University 1929), I am grateful to Denison alumna Nancy Ball, and her friends and colleagues at Denison, who located important data in the Denison archives. Owen Jander's 1962 Harvard doctoral dissertation is "dedicated" "[w]ith respect and . . . gratitude" "to the memory of STEPHEN D. TUTTLE"; see Jander, "Alessandro Stradella and His Minor Dramatic Works," 2 vols. (Ph.D. dissertation, Harvard University, 1962), vol. 1.

[4] See Harvard University, *Report of the President of Harvard College and Reports of Departments* for academic year 1951/52, available online at http://pds.lib.harvard.edu/pds/view/2582287?n=1165&s=4&printThumbnails=no. See also the *New York Times* for 17 March 1952.

[5] Mus. M. University of Washington 1942; PhD. New York University 1953. See Harvard University, *Report of the President of Harvard College and Reports of Departments* for academic year 1954/55, available online at http://pds.lib.harvard.edu/pds/view/2582287?n=3365&s=4&printThumbnails=no, pp. 37–38. On Ward, see, most recently, *John Ward and His Magnificent Collection*, ed. Gordon Hollis (Beverly Hills, CA: Golden Legend, 2010); on the circumstances surrounding his appointment—the deaths of Gombosi and Tuttle, and other such circumstances—see Carl B. Schmidt's contribution to the volume, "A Personal Recollection. 'Give What You Have'—John Milton Ward as Educator," 42–52, especially 43 and 52 n. 2. On Ward's relationship to Gombosi, and the intergenerational transfer of musicological learning—from Gombosi, to Ward, to Arthur J. Ness (A.M. Harvard 1961)—see an interesting footnote in Gombosi, "In Search of Renaissance Form: Francesco da Milano," *Journal of the Lute Society of America* 41 (2008): 57–66, especially 57 n. 1.

[6] Tudor–Stuart instrumental music and related subjects. Tuttle's scholarly specialization is documented by his principal monographic publications: William Byrd, *Forty-Five Pieces for Keyboard Instruments*, ed. Stephen Davidson Tuttle (Paris: Éditions de l'Oiseau-Lyre, 1939); and Thomas Tomkins, *Keyboard Music*, ed. Stephen D. Tuttle, 2nd rev. ed. (London: Stainer and Bell, 1973).

[7] "POMONA COLLEGE / CLAREMONT, CALIFORNIA / DEPARTMENT OF MUSIC / May 26, 1955 / Mr. Randall Thompson, Chairman / Department of Music / Harvard University / Cambridge 38, Massachusetts / . . . / William F. Russell / Chairman" Pirrotta file, Department of Music, Harvard University. See also the *The Harvard Crimson*'s account, 27 May 1955, where Department chairman Randall Thompson was quoted as saying that "the department is finally emerging from 'the valley of the shadow of death'" and announces the appointment of one unidentified new professor for the following year, who must be John M. Ward; http://www.thecrimson.com/article/1955/5/27/the-department-of-music-general-education.

If Ward was in some sense Tuttle's successor, Pirrotta can be understood as Gombosi's.[8] And Pirrotta's seniority relative to Ward justified a different initial status (as Professor of Music), the consequence of a fuller scholarly record that was also more like Gombosi's than Tuttle's in its breadth.

Harvard's interest in Pirrotta would have been multidimensional.[9] Like Gombosi, he enjoyed an international reputation, by virtue of the quantity and quality of his writings (which complemented Arthur Tillman Merritt's and Ward's in subject matter) and the fact that they were becoming increasingly well known to an English-speaking audience, owing partly to the Nigel Fortune and Lewis Lockwood translations in the *Musical Quarterly* for 1954 and '55.

Furthermore, as director of one of Europe's great music libraries, visited by many distinguished foreign scholars, Pirrotta had often had contact with European and American music librarians, who convened repeatedly in Europe in the early 1950s to advance the objectives of the newly established International Association of Music Libraries. He had thereby acquired a professional's thorough conversance with the challenges and opportunities that libraries were then facing. The Harvard University Library had undertaken to consolidate its scattered holdings in music in a single building, whose construction was nearing completion,[10] and the library system was seeking an experienced professional like Pirrotta who could serve as inaugural head of the new Eda Kuhn Loeb Music Library. The importance of this latter consideration is not to be underestimated.

Finally, the presence of Gombosi—however brief—had sensitized the Department (and the University) to the virtues of diversifying its otherwise Crimson-hued faculty.[11]

Pirrotta had many witnesses who could testify on his behalf: not only Oliver Strunk and Arthur Mendel (A.B. Harvard '25) but also another member of the Princeton music faculty, Elliott Forbes (A.B. '41, A.M. '47 Harvard), who taught at Princeton from 1947 until 1958, when he returned to Harvard. Forbes was in a position to observe Pirrotta's success at Princeton closely

---

[8]This was both Pirrotta's and Christoph Wolff's own understanding of the character of the successive appointments at Harvard, and Pirrotta once joked to Wolff that that particular faculty "line" should always remain in European hands, and that the German who succeeded the Italian who succeeded the Hungarian should in turn be succeeded by another "exotic," in Wolff's words; see Wolff's "*In Memoriam* Nino Pirrotta," *Studi musicali* 28 (1999): 36–67, see 37.

[9]My understanding of the circumstances surrounding Pirrotta's Harvard appointment was greatly enhanced through conversation with James Haar, whose assistance I gratefully acknowledge.

[10]**1958:** "The Eda Kuhn Loeb Music Library." The Harvard Corporation gave approval to proceed in 1954, and in the spring of 1955 construction commenced; the library was completed during the summer of 1956, in time for the collections to be consolidated before the beginning of the 1956/57 academic year, Pirrotta's first. For more on the construction and functioning of the music library, see Schmidt, "A Personal Recollection," especially 48 and 52 n. 7.

[11]On this matter, see the Festschrift for A. Tillman Merritt: *Words and Music: The Scholar's View*, ed. Laurence Berman (n.p. [Cambridge, MA]: Department of Music, Harvard University, 1971), xii.

during the 1954/55 academic year, and report on it to old colleagues and friends at Harvard.

On 24 October 1955, composer Randall Thompson[12]—professor and chairman, Department of Music at Harvard, and an unreconstructed Italophile, who had been a Fellow at the American Academy in Rome[13]—telephoned Pirrotta at Columbia and inquired about his interest in a permanent appointment at Harvard, to begin the following year (1 July 1956).[14] Pirrotta immediately penned a courteous response to Thompson:

Home address: Butler Hall
400 W. 119th St.
New York 27, N.Y.
Tel.: University 40200 ext. 15 U
Columbia University in the City of New York [NEW YORK 27, N.Y.]
DEPARTMENT OF MUSIC
October 24, 1955

Dear Professor Thompson,

I hope you did realize how embarrassed I was speaking with you this morning. First because the telephone makes me always very uncomfortable, my English still not being as fluent as it should be. Then because I did not expect at all what your calling was about. A very pleasant and exciting surprise, indeed, but troubling too, since it could mean quite a considerable change not only in my own life but in that of my family. I would like very much to know more about [it] as soon as possible. . . . I'll be very glad to visit you at Harvard. It could be very easy for me . . . [any] week you prefer on Friday, since I am busy the . . . [preceding] days with my duties at Columbia. . . . I beg your pardon, once more, for my English and my handwriting.

With best regards

Very gratefully yours,[15]

---

[12]Thompson had also been a faculty member at Princeton, during academic years 1946/47 and 1947/48, immediately after which he returned to his *Alma Mater* to teach. Note the network of interrelationships between Princeton and Harvard, embodied in the profiles of the relevant personnel: Mendel, Forbes, Thompson; there would have been ample testimony on Pirrotta's behalf. Interestingly, Thompson had also been a faculty member at the University of Virginia during Stephen Tuttle's tenure there, and his acquaintanceship with Tuttle had to have been a factor in Tuttle's going to Harvard in 1952; it was an era when such personal relationships were instrumental in academic appointments.

[13]Thompson had been fellow in musical composition at the Academy for three years.

[14]Professor Frank D'Accone suggested to me (private interview) that A. Tillman Merritt was the active agent in arranging Pirrotta's appointment at Harvard.

[15]Pirrotta file, Department of Music, Harvard University. This letter is also excerpted in Christoph Wolff, "*In Memoriam* Nino Pirrotta."

Thus began the delicate conversations leading to Pirrotta's tenure at Harvard, that all-important phase of his career described as the "memorable Cambridge years."[16]

From Pirrotta's perspective, the advantages of a long-term appointment in the United States were obvious. As early as the Princeton year (and perhaps earlier), he had come to the conclusion that prospects for a career of the type to which he aspired were more promising elsewhere, since Italian academic life was then characterized by the almost complete absence of regular positions in music history in the faculties of letters and philosophy[17] and hence of a robust institutional infrastructure that provided for the *academic* study of music. In the words of the citation issued on his receiving the 1983 Premio "Antonio Feltrinelli" from the Accademia Nazionale dei Lincei, "Pirrotta was induced to accept [Harvard's offer] because a university career in Italy appeared impossible to him at that time."[18]

As one of the obituaries published in 1998 suggested, there was another professional factor, quite apart from the absence of positions in music history in the Italian faculties of letters and philosophy: Whatever the talents and achievements of the aspiring entrant, it has often been difficult to enter the Italian university system. Thus Alfredo Gasponi could write in *Il Messaggero* on 24 January 1998 that "Pirrotta's story is like that of numerous talented scholars who, unable to find work in Italy, were forced to go abroad."

Of course, there were also the advantages associated with an appointment at Harvard specifically: the international stature of the institution, the excellence of its library holdings and the support of Pirrotta's scholarship resulting therefrom, and other such considerations.

Finally, the United States occupied an enviable place in Italian collective consciousness in the postwar era, a consequence in part of the recent American presence in Italy and the American role in liberating Italy from Fascism and the German occupation. Pirrotta's nephew Agostino Ziino testified to these perceptions on the part of many Italians.[19]

---

[16]See the foreword by Lewis Lockwood and Christoph Wolff to the anthology of Pirrotta's essays published by Harvard University Press: *Music and Culture in Italy from the Middle Ages to the Baroque* (see "*Intermedio I.mo*," n. 144).

[17]What American universities term the "college" or "faculty of the liberal arts," or "the arts and sciences."

[18]See also **1954:** "Compiti regionali, nazionali ed internazionali delle biliotleche musicali," where Pirrotta observes that research and teaching in the field of history of music were then [1954] practically nonexistent in Italy.

[19]Ziino, "Pirrotta between Cambridge and Rome" (see "*Scena 5.ª*," n. 2).

Pirrotta thus entered into the negotiations, although tentatively, and visited Cambridge not long after his first exchange with Randall Thompson. Thompson had asked Frank D'Accone if he would host Pirrotta at D'Accone's parents' Cambridge home, to ensure that the visit was handled with the requisite discretion. Thompson explained the potential for embarrassment for all concerned were the conversations not to yield the intended outcome. D'Accone—who had met Pirrotta the previous spring in Princeton—happily obliged, accompanying Pirrotta while he surveyed the holdings of the University's Widener Library and hosting him at a reception with the Department's graduate students at D'Accone's Winthrop House residence.

After his return to New York, Pirrotta wrote a note to Thompson, expressing pleasure with his visit to Harvard.[20] The date of the note[21] is revealing, because it documents, first, how soon after Thompson's initial contact[22] the visit to Cambridge took place, and, second, the speed with which the Department then acted.

In mid-November, Randall Thompson wrote to the Dean of the Faculty of Arts and Sciences to report that Pirrotta was the Department's first choice, urging expeditious handling of its request for his appointment.[23] Some months later Thompson reported that the choice had been influenced by the

> recommendation of a committee of six experts widely familiar with the whole field of music scholarship. He was appointed because in their estimation no other man,

---

[20]"Columbia University in the City of New York / [NEW YORK 27, N.Y.] / DEPARTMENT OF MUSIC / November 3, 1955...." Pirrotta file, Department of Music, Harvard University.

[21]3 November 1955.

[22]24 October.

[23]"November 15, 1955 / Dean McGeorge Bundy / University Hall 5 / Dear Dean Bundy: / During the past six weeks, the senior members of the Music Department have met frequently to discuss filling the vacancy caused by the death of Professor Gombosi. These discussions resulted in two important decisions: / First, that the new appointee should be, like Professor Gombosi, primarily a musicologist, a creative scholar of distinction; and / Second, that *he should be appointed to serve as Librarian of the new Music Library, and to teach on a half-time basis* [emphasis added; note, however, that Pirrotta taught a full schedule of classes subsequent to his first year at Harvard]. / In our opinion, two highly qualified candidates meet both of these specifications: 1) Dr. Nino Pirrotta, visiting lecturer at Columbia University during this term, a brilliant scholar and the Music Librarian of the Accademia Santa Cecilia in Rome; and / 2) Dr. Donald J. Grout, visiting lecturer at Carleton College during this term, Professor of Music at Cornell, also an outstanding scholar and exceptionally well versed in Library matters. Dr. Pirrotta's age is exactly right from the point of view of the chart: he is approximately ten years older than Associate Professor Ward and six years younger than Professors Merritt and Woodworth. On the other hand, Dr. Grout is almost the exact contemporary of Professors Merritt and Woodworth. By vote, therefore, Dr. Pirrotta is our first choice. It is only proper to state, however, that Professor Woodworth, though not opposed to Dr. Pirrotta, is so strongly in favor of Dr. Grout that he feels that the chart should not be the determining factor. And it is only fair to add [that] the only point raised against Dr. Grout was his age. In view of the fact that there are pressing decisions to be made about the new Music Library, we hope that this appointment may be made as soon as it can be conveniently. I am informed that Dr. Pirrotta is returning to Rome in February 1956, but that he would, in all probability, not be averse to accepting a permanent position in this country. Although Professor Piston is on leave of absence, he has been kept informed of our decisions and is in accord with the contents of this letter. / Sincerely yours, / _____ / Chairman" Pirrotta file, Department of Music, Harvard University.

either in America or in Europe, could compare with him either as a scholar or as a Librarian.[24]

Only after the Department had concluded its deliberations did Thompson feel that he could respond informatively to Pirrotta's postvisit letter.[25] And the efficiency of the decision-making process thereafter remained impressive: as of 17 January 1956, Pirrotta could write, "Dear Randall, Many thanks, to you and to Dean Bundy, for the letter.... I am extremely happy... that I am coming to such ... [a] University as Harvard."[26]

There remained only the matter of ratification by the University's venerable governing boards, the ancient Corporation—"The President and Fellows of Harvard College"—and the even more ancient "Honorable and Reverend the Board of Overseers," established by the "Great and General Court of the Massachusetts Bay Colony."[27] For his pains, Pirrotta was to be compensated $12,000 annually, a figure that elicits a smile in the early twenty-first century, though in the mid-twentieth century it was respectable compensation.[28]

In the meantime, Pirrotta had returned to Rome and resumed his responsibilities at the «S. Cecilia»—temporarily, as it developed—after an absence of a year and a half. On 29 April 1956 the *New York Times* reported that "Nino Pirrotta, director of the music library of Rome's St. Cecilia Academy, has been named the librarian of the new Eda K. Loeb music library at Harvard,"[29] neglecting to mention one of the truly consequential terms of the

---

[24] 24 May 1956 memorandum from Randall Thompson. Pirrotta file, Department of Music, Harvard University. There can be little question that Oliver Strunk played a critical role in Pirrotta's appointment at Harvard.

[25] "December 9, 1955 / Dear Dr. Pirrotta: ... / Very sincerely yours, / _____ / Chairman." Pirrotta file, Department of Music, Harvard University.

[26] The letter continues: "This is my last letter from New York, since I am leaving the day after tomorrow. I'll be in Rome on January 27;.... Your, extremely pleased to be called colleague and friend, Nino Pirrotta." Pirrotta file, Department of Music, Harvard University.

[27] "At a meeting of the / President and Fellows of Harvard College / in Cambridge, March 5, 1956 / ... / David W. Bailey / Secretary / Professor Randall Thompson" Pirrotta file, Department of Music, Harvard University.

[28] Randall Thompson 7 June 1956 letter to the Immigration and Naturalization Service, Boston. Pirrotta file, Department of Music, Harvard University.

[29] Ross Parmentier, "World of Music: May Festivals in U.S.," the *New York Times. New York Times (1857–Current file)*; Apr[.] 29, 1956; ProQuest Historical Newspapers The New York Times (1851–2004), 138.

Pirrotta was to serve as head of the music library until the beginning of the 1969/70 academic year. See David A. Wood, *Music in Harvard Libraries. A Catalogue of Early Printed Music and Books on Music in the Houghton Library and the Eda Kuhn Loeb Music Library* (Cambridge, MA: Houghton Library of the Harvard College Library, 1980), xii. However, an official Harvard publication clarifies that the appointment as Librarian of Mary Lou Little, who had initially served as Pirrotta's Assistant Librarian, was effective as of the 1969/70 academic year (*REPORT OF THE PRESIDENT OF HARVARD COLLEGE AND REPORTS OF DEPARTMENTS 1969–1970*, OFFICIAL REGISTER OF HARVARD UNIVERSITY LXVIII, NO. 12 [AUGUST 12, 1971]). This chronology is logical given that Pirrotta was on sabbatical during the fall semester of the 1969/70 academic year, and it would thus have been appropriate for him to relinquish the Library headship (although he did not relinquish it during the 1962/63 sabbatical year; see his correspondence with Harvard president Nathan Pusey on the interim arrangements made at that time).

Pirrotta thus served simultaneously for a time as Professor of Music, Chairman of the Department of Music, *and* Head of the Eda Kuhn Loeb Music Library ("Music Dept[.]'s Library Will Be Expanded," *Harvard Crimson* [December 2, 1965] [http://www.thecrimson.com/article/ 1965/12/2/music-depts-library-will-be-expanded].

appointment: the status as tenured Professor of Music in Harvard's Faculty of Arts and Sciences.[30]

*****

I had occasion to ask Pirrotta[31] how it happened that much of his career was spent at Harvard rather than in his own country, and his response was characteristic. He responded matter-of-factly, with the faintest trace of a smile, "They offered me a job."

Pirrotta's modesty notwithstanding, the significance of the offer, and of his decision to accept a professional opportunity outside Italy, cannot be exaggerated. In the early twenty-first century, scholarship has become considerably more internationalized, but in the immediate post-World War II world, the process of academic internationalization had scarcely begun, and Pirrotta's case is one of the earliest examples of it in the discipline of musicology.[32]

A consequence of Pirrotta's Harvard appointment was a notable internationalization of the musicological discipline in a different sense. There are certainly other instances of such internationalization, even in the 1950s: we find it in other disciplines, such as history, and between national traditions of scholarship other than the Italian and the American. But I have long been impressed by the extent and character of the interconnections between American and Italian musicology, and although it would be an exaggeration to suggest that Nino Pirrotta was single-handedly responsible for that phenomenon, it would not be an exaggeration to identify his role as foundational. Even today, many aspiring Italian musicologists undertake graduate training in the United States, after which some remain here to teach, others return to Italy. And many American musicologists enjoy friendly and professionally rewarding relationships with their Italian colleagues. For me, Pirrotta's role in creating such a situation is clear. I believe it grew out of his personal experience and was a consequence of his personal and professional comportment, in which he actualized the possibilities for such scholarly internationalization.[33] At the same time, Pirrotta's Harvard years loom so large in the collective American musicological consciousness that the risk is that they will assume inordinate importance. It is essential to appreciate that the time at Harvard represents only one phase of Pirrotta's career.

---

[30]There was also an announcement in the local Boston paper [*Boston Herald* (28 April 1956)].

[31]During academic years 1988/89 and 1989/90.

[32]I am excluding the instances of German and eastern European musicologists who fled to the United States during the Nazi era. See *Driven into Paradise: The Musical Migration from Nazi Germany to the United States*, ed. Reinhold Brinkmann and Christoph Wolff (Berkeley, CA: University of California Press, 1999).

[33]On the trans-Atlantic effects and importance of Pirrotta's career, see Pierluigi Petrobelli, "Nino Pirrotta e Diego Carpitella," especially 57 (see "*Scena 3.ª*," n. 14).

*****

Among Pirrotta's first formal obligations at Harvard, as Head of the Eda Kuhn Loeb Music Library, was to speak at the library dedication ceremony, which occurred within days of his arrival (7–9 December 1956). His fellow speakers included members of the University community.[34] The new library consolidated the previously distributed holdings in music in a new wing of the music building, and the completion of the construction occasioned an article in the *Harvard Library Bulletin* where Pirrotta reflected on the purposes of the music library at an institution like Harvard and recounted the history that had led to the construction of the new building.

Pirrotta was initially assisted by a staff of five.[35] Many years later, Pirrotta's colleague John Ward wrote that

> [o]nce the music books and recordings had been moved from their various Harvard locations to the Eda Kuhn Loeb Music Library and Nino Pir[r]otta appointed music librarian, gaps in what was already a major collection of scores and books about music began to be filled.[36]

And during that first year (1956/57), the President and Fellows of Harvard College awarded Antonino Pirrotta—*Licenza in Storia della Musica* and *Diploma in Organo e Composizione Organistica*, Regio Conservatorio della Musica «Luigi Cherubini» di Firenze; *Dottore in Lettere*, Regia Università degli Studi di Firenze—the Harvard degree of *Artium Magister*, thus ensuring that he—like Harvard faculty members before and after him—was a Harvard alumnus and therefore qualified to teach Harvard students, as no other certification or pedigree could possibly have qualified him or anyone else.[37]

---

[34]Thompson had written to Pirrotta [29 October 1956]: "Paul Buck, Librarian of the Harvard College Library . . . agreed to say a few words on December 8th at the time of the celebration in honor of the opening of the Music Library on December 7th, 8th, and 9th. We do most earnestly hope that you will be here by that time!"

[35]See Pirrotta, **1957**: "Dedication of the Loeb Music Library"; "History—Loeb Music Library—Harvard College Library," http://hcl.harvard.edu/libraries/loebmusic/history.html; Pirrotta, **1958**: "The Eda Kuhn Loeb Music Library"; and Elliot Forbes, *A History of Music at Harvard to 1972* (n.p. [Cambridge, MA]: Department of Music, Harvard University, 1988), 124–56 and n. 62. On the library generally, and Pirrotta's role in its administration, see John B. Howard, "The Eda Kuhn Loeb Music Library at Harvard University," *Library Quarterly* 64 (1994): 163–76.

[36]John M. Ward, "Music Librariana," *Golden Muse: The Loeb Music Library at 50*, ed. Sarah Adams, Virginia Danielson, Robert J. Dennis, *Harvard Library Bulletin* 18, no. 1–2 (2007): 21–24, especially 23.

[37]This was not an honorary degree as customarily understood. Nor was it a vestige of Harvard's seventeenth-century origins: in the early-modern world, an alumnus of a particular university was deemed a member of the international community of scholars and could thus petition another university to be awarded its comparable degree, assuming that the institution where he had completed his own formal studies were recognized. See Samuel Eliot Morison, *The Founding of Harvard College* (Cambridge, MA: Harvard University Press, 1963), 349 and n. 2; and Morison, *Harvard College in the Seventeenth Century*, 2 vols. (Cambridge, MA: Harvard University Press, 1936), 299 and nn. 3–4, and 300 and n. 1. See also http://pds.lib.harvard.edu/pds/view/2573358?n=5506&s=4, pp. 327–28.

*****

In an exquisite irony of timing, professorships of music history in the faculties of letters and philosophy in the Italian universities were established almost immediately after Pirrotta assumed his posts at Harvard.[38] Before the end of his first semester there, he learned the results of the *concorso* (competitive application process) organized to identify the first incumbents of the new chairs (*cattedre*). Pirrotta placed second to Luigi Ronga, who as Professore di Storia della Musica at the Conservatory of Rome had been Pirrotta's colleague for eight years; simultaneously, Ronga had been serving as *Libero docente di Storia della Musica* at the University of Rome, and he was elected to the professorship at Rome.

Pirrotta's success in the *concorso* precipitated a minor professional and personal crisis, because it unexpectedly afforded the possibility of an immediate return to Italy. He wrote to Giulia:

Cambridge, 3 January 1957

My dear little sister,

. . . [A] letter from [Mario] Salmi has now reached me, which tells me of his having learned the result from [Lionello] Venturi (to whom he says he has spoken of me, evidently with no success), and he adds that the *Dir*[*ettore*] *Gen*[*erale*] has already read the report and found everything in order, and that there shouldn't be any difficulty in its approval, therefore. Naturally, there could be recourse, but I hope not (for Ronga).

I am perfectly aware that all this is the beginning of a new difficult period. If this *concorso* had happened a year before, it would probably have closed the American "parenthesis," limiting it to a happy recollection of an interesting experience. Now it is difficult to nullify all the efforts and expense of time, energy, and money, asked of more or less everyone in the family, in order to come here; the decision to turn back could be taken only if something weren't going well here, so serious as to cause giving up the undeniable advantages that the children could have in the future. It is probable, therefore, that I shall forego a possible position in Italy; however, I should like to delay renouncing it as long as possible in order to be as sure as possible of the perfect adjustment of the entire family to the new conditions of life. And being in second place is, in this regard, inconvenient, because each delay of mine in reaching a decision will affect the third [Luigi

---

[38]On the history of the establishment of such positions, see Carolyn Gianturco's contribution ("2. Italy") to Vincent Duckles, et al., "Musicology," *Grove Music Online. Oxford Music Online*, http://0-www.oxfordmusiconline.com.libcat.lafayette.edu/subscriber/article/grove/music/46710pg3 (accessed 2 September 2011).

Rognoni], who cannot be called until I'm either placed or eliminated. . . . To you, little sister, all the affection of

Nino[39]

Had an Italian opportunity materialized before the Pirrottas' departure for Cambridge, he might well have declined Harvard's invitation in order to remain in Italy, notwithstanding the advantages. As it was, the opportunity did *not* materialize in time, and Italy's (momentary) loss was America's (momentary) gain.

"Rome fumbles, and Harvard recovers." Nino Pirrotta will remain at Harvard until 31 December 1971, and among his A.M. and Ph.D. advisees will be some of the most accomplished American musicologists of their generation. His influence on the development of American musicology as a university discipline and formal intellectual enterprise will be almost immeasurable.

UNIVERSITY AND DEPARTMENTAL LIFE

During Pirrotta's first few years at Harvard, his colleagues among the Department's musicologists were Professors Merritt (academic years 1932/33 and thereafter), whose scholarly specialization was early-modern French music,[40] and Forbes (academic years 1958/59 and thereafter), an authority on Beethoven's life and music; Associate Professor Ward (academic years 1955/56 and

---

[39] "Cambridge, 3 genn. 1957 / Sorellina mia cara, . . . Ora mi è giunta una lettera di Salmi che mi dice di avere appreso il risultato da Venturi (al quale dice di avere parlato di me, evidentemente con nessun successo) e aggiungere che il Dir. Gen. ha già letto la relazione a [sic; recte: "e"] trovato tutto in ordine, e che quindi non ci dovrebbe essere nessuna difficoltà nell'approvazione. Ci potrebbero, naturalmente, essere dei ricorsi, ma speriamo di no (per Ronga). Non mi nascondo che tutto questo è l'inizio di un nuovo periodo difficile. Se questo concorso fosse venuto un anno prima, avrebbe probabilmente chiuso la parentesi americana, limitandola ad un felice ricordo di una esperienza interessante. Ora è difficile annullare tutti gli sforzi e il dispendio di tempo, energie, e denaro, richiesto più o meno a tutti in famiglia per venire qui; soltanto se qualche cosa non andasse bene qui, tanto grave da far rinunziare agli indiscutibili vantaggi che i ragazzi potrebbero avere in avvenire. È probabile dunque che rinunzierò ad una eventuale sistemazione italiana; vorrei però ritardare quanto più è possibile la rinunzia per essere meglio sicuro del perfetto adattarsi di tutta la famiglia alle nuove condizioni di vita. E l'essere al secondo posto è, sotto questo riguardo, un inconveniente, perchè ogni mio ritardo nel prendere una decisione si rifletterà sul terzo, che non può essere chiamato finchè io non sia collocato o eliminato. . . . A te, sorellina, tutto l'affetto di / Nino" For providing me with a copy of this letter, and permitting me to quote from it, I·am grateful to Professor Agostino Ziino. Pirrotta's initial uncertainty as to the correctness of the decision to accept the position at Harvard explains the fact that he did not officially resign the position as librarian at the «Santa Cecilia» until 1958.

[40] On Merritt, see http://www.news.harvard.edu/gazette/1998/10.29/ATMerrittRenais.html; http://www.nytimes.com/1998/10/29/arts/arthur-merritt-96-renaissance-music-expert.html; http://www.news.harvard. edu/gazette/1999/06.03/merritt.html; *Harvard University. Quinquennial Catalogue of the Officers and Graduates 1636-1930* (Cambridge, MA: Published by the University. . . . 1930), 775, 777; and *Historical Register of Harvard University, 1636–1936* (Cambridge, MA: Harvard University, 1937).

thereafter), who specialized in early-modern English and Spanish music;[41] and Assistant Professors David G. Hughes (academic years 1956/57 and thereafter), a specialist in liturgical chant, medieval monophonic accretions to the liturgy (tropes, liturgical drama), and early polyphony; and Harold Powers (academic years 1958/59–1958/60), a comparative and historical musicologist, a South Asianist and Europeanist.

Soon after Pirrotta's tenure at Harvard commenced, the Department was joined by Rulan Chao Pian (academic years 1961/62 and thereafter), a comparative musicologist and East Asianist, who was appointed Visiting Lecturer in Music in 1961 and Professor of Music and of East Asian Languages and Civilizations in 1974.[42] Another eminent colleague was composer and theorist Walter H. Piston, whose retirement created a vacancy in the Walter W. Naumburg '89 Professorship, to which Pirrotta was named in 1961, a sign of the ever growing esteem in which he was held by Departmental and University colleagues.[43]

Apart from his teaching, Pirrotta's principal official role in the Department was as Head of the Eda Kuhn Loeb Music Library. But he also served part of a term as Chairman of the Department, succeeding Randall Thompson (1952/53–1956/57), John Ward (1957/58–1960/61), and David Hughes (1961/62–1964/65).[44] One of the most notable developments of Pirrotta's tenure as chairman was the establishment of the A.M. and Ph.D. programs in composition, advocated by his colleague, composer Leon Kirchner.[45]

The customary term as chairman was four years, and Pirrotta assumed the chairmanship in 1965/66 with that expectation. However, the Department had entered a period when fund-raising was to be all-important. There was to be a further expansion in the Department's physical plant,[46] and Harvard

---

[41]On Ward see http://hul.harvard.edu/publications/letters_fall08.pdf.

[42]For a bibliography of Pian's scholarly publications, see http://rulanchaopian.lib.cuhk.edu.hk/byrulan.htm. On her training and career, see the pertinent issues of the publication (available online) *Harvard University. Report of the President of Harvard College and Reports of Departments* for 1961/62 and 1963/64, and the comparable reports for Radcliffe College, available at http://pds.lib.harvard. edu/pds/view/2573641.

[43]Ross Parmenter, "Music World: State Helps Foot the Bill," *New York Times* (*1857–Current file*); Jun[.] 4, 1961; ProQuest Historical Newspapers The New York Times (1851– 2004).

[44]On Pirrotta's appointment as chairman, see the report in the *Harvard Crimson*: http://www.thecrimson.com/article.aspx?ref=248686, and http://www.thecrimson.com/article/1964/11/13/faculty-names-three-to-head-departments: "Faculty Names Three To Head Departments," *Harvard Crimson* (November 13, 1964). See also the Pirrotta file in the Department of Music, Harvard University: "October 30, 1964 / Dear Mr. Pirrotta: / The President has approved your appointment as Chairman of the Department . . . from July 1, 1965. . . . Franklin L. Ford."

[45]See Forbes, *A History of Music at Harvard*, 153–54, where Forbes recounts that at an October 1966 faculty meeting, a committee comprising Kirchner, Tillman Merritt, and Pirrotta was formed and charged with responsibility for discussing Kirchner's proposal and reporting back to the department. See also Robert Riggs, *Leon Kirchner: Composer, Performer, and Teacher*, (Rochester, NY: University of Rochester Press, 2010), a title brought to my attention by Curtis P. Cacioppo. Indeed, I am grateful more generally to Professor Cacioppo (A.M. Harvard University, composition, 1979; Ph.D. Harvard University, composition, 1980) for informative discussion on this entire matter.

[46]"Music Dept[.]'s Library Will Be Expanded," *Harvard Crimson* (December 2, 1965) [http://www.thecrimson.com/article/1965/12/2/music-depts-library-will-be-expanded].

Department chairmen had historically played a critical role in securing the funds necessary for any such enhancement. One of the most successful fund-raisers in the Department's history was Tillman Merritt.

It is perhaps to be expected that a reserved, scholarly Sicilian, the representative of a fundamentally different cultural tradition, where institutions of higher education were state-supported, would not possess the inherent aptitude for fund-raising of someone like Tillman Merritt, more conversant with the vital American capitalist tradition of private philanthropy. Pirrotta therefore resigned the department chairmanship before the end of his third year, on 4 March 1968. Harvard president Nathan Pusey asked Merritt to complete Pirrotta's term, and despite Merritt's misgivings, he became chairman for a second time, serving until the end of academic year 1971/72, when he retired altogether from teaching and administrative service at Harvard.[47]

Pirrotta was able to understand and interpret his experience as chairman in ironic terms. Many years later, he wrote to one of his successors in the chairmanship, Reinhold Brinkmann:

> May 16, 1991 / Dear Reinhold, . . . Best wishes for your work. I am often reminded of my short chairmanship[,] when I took to a painting which I used to have hanging in my chairman['s] office: it represents Hercules' Labors. Maybe the trouble was that I didn't have a properly Herculean constitution.[48]

TEACHING AND ADVISING

Pirrotta's principal contribution as a departmental citizen was as a teacher and adviser, in both cases especially at the graduate level. He discharged his obligations creditably, contributing to the undergraduate General Education program with courses on "Comedy and Opera: 1500–1700" (Humanities 103) and "Music and Poetry in Dante's Time" (Humanities 104),[49] which had an appropriately transdisciplinary character.[50]

The two General Education courses prompt a further observation. The course on Dante is an elegant demonstration of the relationship of Pirrotta's teaching to his scholarship.[51] As rationale for the offering, the course description explained that it was then the seventh centennial of Dante's birth.[52]

---

[47]Elliot Forbes, *A History of Music at Harvard*, 160, 194. On the occurrences recounted here, I am also grateful for information provided by Frank D'Accone: A.M. Cummings interview with D'Accone, 2009 annual national meeting of the American Musicological Society, Philadelphia.

[48]Department of Music, Harvard University, Pirrotta file.

[49]The relevant information is accessible in Forbes and relevant various issues of the publication *OFFICIAL REGISTER OF / HARVARD UNIVERSITY . . . . COURSES OF INSTRUCTION / OFFERED BY THE / FACULTY OF ARTS AND SCIENCES*.

[50]The precursor to Harvard's later "core curriculum," or what other institutions term the "common course of study."

[51]See the preface to his anthology *Music and Culture in Italy from the Middle Ages to the Baroque*.

[52]See Forbes, *A History of Music at Harvard*.

During precisely that period, Pirrotta delivered two of his most celebrated lectures (later published), occasioned by the same event: "Ars nova e stil novo,"[53] and "Dante *musicus:* Gothicism, Scholasticism, and Music."[54] Teaching nourished scholarship; and scholarship, teaching.

Pirrotta also twice taught a course for both advanced undergraduates and beginning graduate students, Music 124, "The History and Literature of Music: 1600–1900."

But the preponderance of his teaching was at the graduate level, where the students would have been especially prepared to benefit from his learning, his reflections on the history of music, and his scholarly sensibilities. Every year he was at Harvard but one, Pirrotta taught Music 203, "Seminar in Music History"; he repeatedly taught Music 205, "Notation"; and other graduate courses were taught once or twice. And he was regularly listed as a prospective adviser under the rubrics "Individual Research and Advanced Work," "Direction of Doctoral Dissertation(s)," and "Reading and Research."

What of Pirrotta's pedagogical methods in the formal graduate courses? Frank D'Accone and James Haar retain vivid recollections of his teaching, half a century later.

Haar had been away during Pirrotta's first year at Harvard, and on returning audited a graduate seminar on the frottola, in which some ten students were enrolled. Pirrotta did not lecture. Rather each student was asked to analyze, inventory, and comment on one of the ten surviving books of frottole published by Ottaviano Petrucci in the early Cinquecento. Pirrotta would then respond, and his responses often ran longer than the student's presentation. He spoke extemporaneously and would discuss not only the music but also the texts, and especially such matters as the means of expanding the abbreviated presentation of the formal scheme into a fully realized musical composition.

D'Accone recalls the regularity of his meetings with Pirrotta while writing his dissertation: once weekly during academic year 1959/60, and often twice, for some 30 minutes each time, they would review what D'Accone had accomplished since the previous meeting. Above all, D'Accone attests encouragement given generously.

*****

If one index of a teacher's success is the distinction of his pupils, Pirrotta could look back on the Harvard years with great satisfaction and pride. Table

---

[53] **1966:** "Ars nova e stil novo." A variant was also delivered at Harvard; see the *Harvard Crimson* for March 2, 1965, "Septecentennial."

[54] **1965:** "Dante *musicus.*" On the initial delivery of "Dante *musicus,*" see also "Eighty-Fourth: Annual Report of the Dante Society of America," *Dante Studies, with the Annual Report of the Dante Society* 84 (1966): 115–31.

5 lists those awarded the Ph.D. in musicology at Harvard during Pirrotta's years there (and shortly thereafter) and the titles of the doctoral dissertations.

Those familiar with American musicology will recognize the names of these scholars and know of their achievement,[55] and especially of the extent to which their aggregate record attests the fulfillment of Harvard's institutional mission as a research university: Their studies and editions have advanced collective understanding of European music history. In addition, many of these pupils secured positions at the nation's major colleges and universities, where they "gave birth to," or "sired," Pirrotta's "intellectual grandchildren": their own pupils, who represent the next generation in the intergenerational transfer of musicological learning.[56]

One notes the extent to which the subject matter of the theses and dissertations written under Pirrotta's direction capitalizes on his expertise; there is (perhaps predictably) an Italianist, early-modernist cast to the material.

The sense of indebtedness toward Pirrotta that these scholars felt is expressed time and again, and the mutual esteem similarly documented by reciprocal expressions of regard on Pirrotta's part.

*****

By Pirrotta's own account, his relocation to the United States entailed "not-easy problems of adaptation,"[57] so that his scholarly productivity was not initially what it had been during more settled periods of his life, nor what it was to be again when the "problems of adaptation" had been met. With few exceptions, the earliest Cambridge years witnessed little other publication than encyclopedia entries, commissioned long before.[58] But by the end of his third academic year at Harvard, he was fully active once more.

Previously, Pirrotta's scholarship had been concentrated on either the music of the Trecento or seventeenth-century opera. There were only a few papers on the music of fifteenth- and sixteenth-century Italy.[59] But during the Harvard

---

[55] Ellen Rosand is a special case. Although she earned the A.M. at Harvard, where she studied with Pirrotta, her Ph.D. was completed at New York University. All the same, she is one of the Harvard graduate alumni most closely identified with Pirrotta.

[56] Many of these "intellectual grandchildren"—and I consider myself one of them—contributed to one of the Festschriften issued in Pirrotta's honor (in this case, regrettably, in his memory, since it appeared after his death): *Musica disciplina* 50 (1996).

[57] **1972:** "Studi corelliani." In his characteristically modest, self-effacing manner, Pirrotta himself identifies one of the consequences of his "itinerancy": **1985:** "Back to Ars Nova Themes," 167 n. 4.

[58] Though he continued as a member of the editorial boards of various series of monographic publications, such as (as of 1956) "the second series (Facsimiles of Manuscripts) of 'Documenta Musicologica,' whose distinguished committee includes Hans Albrecht, Higinio Angles, Jacques Handschin, Nino Pir[r]otta, Bertram Schofield[,] and Karl Votterle."

[59] **1937:** review of Federico Mompellio, *Pietro Vinci madrigalista siciliano*; **1950:** "Il 'Festino' di Banchieri"; **1954:** "Commedia dell'Arte e Melodramma; and **1954:** "Attaingnant, Pierre"; "Banchieri, Adriano"; and "Bati, Luca."

Table 7 Ph.D. Degrees in Musicology Awarded by Harvard
During Pirrotta's Years and Thereafter

1956/57	**Heartz, Daniel,** "Sources and Forms of the French Instrumental Dance in the Sixteenth Century" **Velimirovic, Milos,** "The Byzantine Elements in Early Slavic Chant" **Yellin, Victor,** "The Life and Operatic Works of George Whitefield Chadwick"
1957/58	*****Downes, Edward,** "The Operas of Johann Christian Bach as a Reflection of the Dominant Trends in *Opera Seria*, 1750-1780" **Keller, Walter,** "The Italian Organ Hymn from Cavazzoni to Aresti: A Study of the Interrelation of Roman Plainchant and Liturgical Keyboard Music in the Sixteenth and Seventeenth Centuries"
1958/59	**Brown, Howard M.,** "The *Chanson* in the French Theater of the Fifteenth and Early Sixteenth Centuries: Moralities, *Farces*, *Sotties*, and Monologues" **Wicks, John,** "The Motets of Pierre de Manchicourt, *ca.* 1510-1564"
1959/60	*****D'Accone, Frank,** "A Documentary History of Music at the Florentine Cathedral and Baptistry During the Fifteenth Century" **Kaufmann, Henry W.,** "The Life and Works of Nicola Vicentino" *****Layton, Billy Jim,** "Italian Music for the Ordinary of the Mass, 1300-1450" **Pian, Rulan Chao,** "Musical Sources of the Sung Dynasty (960-1279)"
1960/61	*****Haar, James,** "*Musica Mundana:* Variations on a Pythagorean Theme" *****Slim, H. Colin,** "The Keyboard *Ricercar* and *Fantasia* in Italy, *c.*1500-1550, with Reference to Parallel Forms in European Lute Music of the Same Period"
1961/62	*****Jander, Owen,** "Alessandro Stradella and His Minor Dramatic Works"
1962/63	*****Churgin, Bathia,** "The Symphonies of G.B. Sammartini" **Crawford, John,** "The Relationship of Text and Music in the Vocal Works of Schönberg, 1908-1924"
1963/64	*****Bonta, Stephen,** "The Church Sonatas of Giovanni Legrenzi" *****Chapman, Catherine Weeks,** "Andrea Antico" **Waldbauer, Ivan,** "The Cittern in the Sixteenth Century and Its Music in France and the Low Countries" [also *****Rosand, Ellen,** A.M. '64]
1964/65	**Archibald, Bruce,** "Harmony in the Early Works of Alban Berg" **Berman, Laurence,** "The Evolution of Tonal Thinking in the Works of Claude Debussy" **Culley, Thomas D., S.J.,** "A Documentary History of the Liturgical Music at the German College in Rome, 1573-1674" **Fuller, David,** "Eighteenth-Century French Harpsichord Music"

continued

Table 7 *(continued)*

1965/66	Bonvalot, Anthony, "The Round of Shakespeare's Age in England and Scotland: Three Collectors and Their Store, 1580-1612" *Gallucci, Joseph, "Festival Music in Florence, ca. 1480-ca. 1520: *Canti Carnascialeschi*, *Trionfi*, and Related Forms" *Kanazawa, Masakata, "Polyphonic Music for Vespers in the Fifteenth Century" Peterson, Floyd, "Johann Hermann Schein's *Cymbalum Sinoium*: A Liturgico-Musical study"
1966/67	[no recipients]
1967/68	England, Nicholas, "Music Among the *zu wa-si* of South West Africa and Botswana"
1968/69	*Armstrong, James, "The Vesper Psalms and Magnificats of Maurizio Cazzati (ca. 1620-78)"
1969/70	Schwager, Myron, "Beethoven's Arrangements: the Chamber Works"
1970/71	Planchart, Alejandro, "The Repertory of Tropes at Winchester"
1971/72	*Cardamone, Donna G., "The *Canzone Villanesca alla Napolitana* and Related Italian Vocal Part-Music: 1537-70" Connolly, Thomas H., "The Old Roman Introits" *Hill, John Walter, "The Life and Works of Francesco Maria Veracini" *Lindgren, Lowell E., "A Bibliographic Scrutiny of Dramatic Works Set by Giovanni and His Brother Antonio Maria Bononcini" *Troy, Charles E., "The Comic *Intermezzo* in Eighteenth-Century Italian *Opera Seria*" Wright, Craig M., "Music at the Court of Burgundy, 1364-1419"
1972/73	Adams, F. John, "The Place of the Piano Concerto in the Career of Mozart: Vienna, 1782-86" Kelly, Thomas Forrest, "Responsory Tropes" Kovarik Jr., Edward G., "Mid Fifteenth-Century Polyphonic Elaborations of the Plainchant *Ordinarium missae*" *Schmidt, Carl B., "The Operas of Antonio Cesti"
1973/74	Price, Curtis A., "Musical Practices in Restoration Plays, With a Catalogue of Instrumental Music in the Plays, 1665-1713" Tawa, Nicholas Edward, "The Parlor Song in America, 1790-1860" Wiley, Roland J., "Tchaikovsky's *Swan Lake*: the First Productions in Moscow and St. Petersburg"
1974/75	*DeFord, Ruth I., "Ruggiero Giovannelli and the Madrigal in Rome, 1572-99" Shapiro, Anne Dhu, "The Tune-Family Concept in British-American Folk-Song Scholarship" Vennum, Jr., Thomas, "Southwestern Ojibwa Music" Youens, Susan, "Music and Religion in the French Reformation and Counter-Reformation"

*Asterisks indicate Ph.D. recipients who are especially identified with Pirrotta.

years, Pirrotta launched a series of studies of the music of the Italian Renaissance, several of which were to achieve classic status. Among them is the Kinkeldey Award-winning monograph *Li due Orfei* and the paper "Music and Cultural Tendencies in 15th-Century Italy." Before considering the papers on the music of the Italian Renaissance we briefly review several publications in the continuing series devoted to the music of the Italian and European Middle Ages and then proceed to studies of Seicento opera.

*****

In "Dante *musicus*," Pirrotta identifies his objective as "showing that the . . . development of . . . [twelfth- and thirteenth-century Parisian] polyphony" was "under the powerful cultural influence of the newly institutionalized University of Paris," as articulating "the *spiritual congruity* and cultural continuity *that must have existed between those expressions of a single society*": "a Gothic cathedral, *a scholastic approach to knowledge and faith*, and the then new style of music now variously labeled Nôtre-Dame polyphony, or *Ars antiqua* [emphases added]."

Pirrotta acknowledges that his model was Erwin Panofsky's earlier attempt to explain the characteristics of Gothic architecture as a reflection of the scholastic method; the crucial manifestation of the scholastic mentality in the music of the time was as follows:

> Leoninus' work was a product of *Ars musica*. . . . [T]he plan of the musical cathedral opens with the season of Nativity and encompasses the year according to the cycle of the liturgical, not merely seasonal, calendar. Newer, however, than this attunement to the rhythm of macrocosm is the introduction of rhythmic "modes" to give an "order" to the succession of musical sounds. Musicologists agree, though they may disagree on details, that the plainchant had what we describe as a free rhythm. A regularity of rhythm may have existed in some forms of popular song or dance music. But whoever first thought of casting polyphony into *ordines* determined by certain *modi* had in mind no secular or popular tastes but the desire, characteristic of his time, to introduce *ars*, that is, rationality, into whatever had to do with serious subjects.

Thus it was the distinguishing characteristic of contemporary Parisian intellectual life—a passion for order and rationality, expressed quantitatively (assuming a liberal definition of that term)—that explains the definitive solution to the bedeviling problem of notating rhythm, indispensable to most polyphonic composition.[60]

There are also references to the traditional Boethian tripartition of music into *musica mundana, humana,* and *instrumentalis* (or *organica*), as reflected

---

[60]For a further statement of Pirrotta's understanding of the relationship between the solution to the problem of notating musical rhythm and the intellectual context for that solution as typified by the University of Paris, see **1993**: "Natura e problemi del testo musicale."

in Dante's epic *Commedia*. *Inferno* is a "cattivo coro"; "*Purgatory* is full of sounding music—*musica instrumentalis*, according to the Boethian distinction already mentioned"; and

> the higher level of music, *musica mundana*, makes its appearance from the very beginning of the heavenly journey, for Dante's "trasumanar," his experience, in the first canto of *Paradiso*, of a transcending beyond humanity that "cannot be expressed in words," has as its first connotation the perception of the divine illumination and of the harmony that rules the world.[61]

*****

Pirrotta also continues his studies of the music of the Trecento. The remaining volumes of the edition of the Trecento repertory to appear are published during the Harvard years. And Paolo *tenorista*, whose life and work Pirrotta had already investigated in several publications,[62] is now afforded culminating treatment in the facsimile edition of a manuscript fragment transmitting his work, which is accompanied by a substantial historical introduction.[63]

Two of the papers from the Cambridge years on the music of Trecento receive particular comment here, for reasons of the distinctive contribution they make. "An Archaic Fourteenth-Century Description of the Madrigal"[64] is notable for the thesis it advances concerning the origins of the Trecento madrigal, which represents a further refinement and even emendation of earlier arguments.[65] Here we find Pirrotta again using a Materialist causal explanation for a musical phenomenon, interpreting the defining characteristics of the early-Trecento madrigal as an expression of the status of the earliest composers of Trecento polyphony as organists, who applied their understanding of musical form (conditioned by their professional circumstances) to their composition of vocal polyphony.[66]

---

[61] On this entire discourse, see now Francesco Ciabattoni, *Dante's Journey to Polyphony*, (Toronto: University of Toronto Press, 2010). For this reference, I am grateful to Professor Christopher Celenza.

[62] **1949–51**: "Il codice di Lucca"; **1952**: "Paolo Tenorista, fiorentino 'extra moenia'"; and **1956**: "Paolo da Firenze in un nuovo frammento dell'"Ars Nova.'"

[63] **1961**: *Paolo Tenorista in a New Fragment of the Italian Ars Nova*. For Pirrotta's account of his earliest knowledge of the manuscript fragment, see **1986**: "Historiae Musicae Cultores." The fragment is now housed at the Newberry Library in Chicago, and stored with it are photographs of the original manuscript, two letters from Pirrotta to the manuscript's previous owner—Edward E. Lowinsky—and other documents in typescript relating to the manuscript. But see now David Fallows, "Paolo da Firenze," Grove Music Online. Oxford Music Online, http://0-www.oxfordmusiconline.com.libcat.lafayette.edu/subscriber/article/grove/music/20842 (accessed May 5, 2010), and the revisionist literature that Fallows cites.

[64] **1961**: "Una arcaica descrizione trecentesca del madrigale."

[65] **1946 and 1947**: "Per l'origine e la storia della «caccia» e del «madrigale» trecentesco," summarized in my "Scena 4.ª." **1960**: "Madrigal." Pirrotta specifically suggests that the space limitations imposed by the nature of the genre—an encyclopedia entry—prohibited him from the full exposition he will now offer.

[66] For an evocation of Pirrotta's thesis, see James Haar, *Essays on Italian Poetry and Music in the Renaissance, 1350–1600* (Berkeley and Los Angeles: University of California Press, 1986), 17 and following and especially n. 43. See also **1954**: "Note su un codice di antiche musiche per tastiera," and **1972**: "Novelty and Renewal in Italy, 1300–1600."

The importance of "Polyphonic Music for a Text Attributed to Frederick II"[67] is perhaps more the result of the methodology it exemplifies and the questions it poses than of its specific findings. Many years later, Pirrotta will reminisce that

> I ... have ... contemplated music, but a good part of my career as a musicologist has also been characterized by a particular interest in the contemplation of *absent music* [emphasis added] and the attempt to recoup some glimmer of it: [1] in the contemplation of the "cicliane," for example, already known in Florence and the Veneto from the middle of the 14th century; [2] in that of the "viniziane" and "giustiniane," which flourished amply in all of northern Italy in one century, the fifteenth, which is substantially deprived of music written by Italian authors; [3] or in that of the "napoletane," having suddenly surfaced in 1537 in a brief vogue of polyphonic elaborations that took the name of "canzoni villanesche alla napoletana." They are all researches that, in a certain sense, have made of me an ethnomusicologist of the past, a researcher of music whose absence is due to the fact that ... the indispensable support of notation was missing, or ... only occasional and sporadic.[68]

The article on the polyphonic setting of Emperor Frederick's verse is one of the earliest examples of this ongoing intellectual program of identifying vestiges of oral practice in the written tradition and thus recapturing whatever possible of lost oral tradition.[69] There is also an element of regional "dialectical" tradition in the enterprise, given that the three examples cited exemplify Sicilian, Venetian, and Neapolitan oral and "popular" practices, which are subsequently refashioned—regularized according to the practices of "art" music—and then preserved in the written tradition. Further products of this ongoing enterprise are the articles in the Festschrift for Tillman Merritt (on the siciliana)[70] and in *Studi musicali* (on the almost mythic fifteenth-century quasi-giustiniana *O rosa bella*[71] and the polyphonic refashionings by Adrian Willaert and others of the canzona villanesca alla napolitana[72]).

---

[67]**1968**: "Musica polifonica per un testo attribuito a Federico II."

[68]**1992**: "Contemplando la musa assente."

[69]For a consideration of Pirrotta's ethnomusicological sensibilities, see also Giovanni Giuriati, "Italian Ethnomusicology," *Yearbook for Traditional Music* 27 (1995): 104–31. For further reflections on the ethnomusicological character of much of Pirrotta's writing, see also Agostino Ziino, "Aurelio Roncaglia, Nino Pirrotta e Diego Carpitella: ricordi e riflessioni," *L'eredità di Diego Carpitella: etnomusicologia, antropologia e ricerca storica nel Salento e nell'area mediterranea: atti del convegno, Galatina, 21, 22 e 23 giugno 2002*, ed. Maurizio Agamennone and Gino Leonardo Di Mitri (Nardò: BESA, 2003), 65–75, especially 70, where Ziino writes: "Tutti sappiamo quante volte Pirrotta ha toccato temi tangenziali con l'Etnomusicologia, dal concetto di 'musica non scritta' o di 'tradizione [musicale] non scritta' fino all'individuazione '[. . .]in alcuni documenti musicali scritti di riflessi di pratiche musicali 'etniche.'"

[70]**1972**: "New Glimpses of an Unwritten Tradition."

[71]**1972**: "Ricercari e variazioni su 'O rosa bella.'" See also **1984**: "Echi di arie veneziane del primo Quattrocento?"

[72]**1980**: "Willaert and the *Canzone Villanesca*."

In all cases, Pirrotta is careful to note that the written reflections necessarily alter the character of the orally transmitted original. Nonetheless, they represent the historian's sole available means of gaining any truly substantive access to the lost oral tradition.[73]

*****

The Cambridge years witness the publication in Olschki's *Collectanea* of two important articles on early-seventeenth-century opera: "Falsirena and the Earliest Cavatina,"[74] and "The Lame Horse and the Coachman: News of the Operatic Parnassus in 1642,"[75] in the second of which Pirrotta reports that Francesco Cavalli functioned as impresario at the Venetian theater of S. Moisè in 1642, information contained in a kind of literary document not always consulted by musicologists: Francesco Melosio's *Poesie e prose*.[76] Pirrotta's conversance with this type of primary source says something about the "multi-disciplinarity" of his habits of reading, because only by reading systematically through the host haystack would one have found this needle.

Pirrotta's enlivens his two encyclopedia entries on Stradella with the sorts of suggestions not typical of the genre. The earlier of the two[77] offers a conjecture concerning Stradella's operatic output, later substantiated by empirical evidence.[78] The later one[79] offers observations about the oratorios—which, though "[l]ittle studied," "are probably the compositions that should better give the measure of the personality of Stradella"—and about the operas, about the crystallization of form, according to "the rules of the Theater, not of Poetics": such "hedonistic" blandishments as scene-ending da capo arias, or—in the comic episodes—the adoption of a style that "tends to be simplified in order to adapt itself to the intrusiveness of the verbal comicality and the quick rhythm of the action, such that recitative and aria are often leveled in a common style of arietta."

*****

More than once, Lewis Lockwood urged me to pay particular attention to Pirrotta's encyclopedia entries. Many of them are brief, their length dictated by the nature of the publication. But occasionally, when the subject matter warrants, Pirrotta offers a comprehensive statement, rich in impressionistic

---

[73]See my "*Scena 4.$^{\underline{a}}$ The Conservatorio di Palermo (1936–48): Il Trecento*."
[74]**1956**: "Falsirena and the Earliest *Cavatina*."
[75]**1966**: "Il caval zoppo e il vetturino."
[76]*Poesie e prose. In questa nuova impressione diligentemente corrette* (Venice: A. Poletti, 1704).
[77]**1962**: "STRADELLA, Alessandro."
[78]Harold S. Powers, "*Il «Mutio» tramutato*" (see "*Intermedio I.$^{\underline{mo}}$*," n.146).
[79]**1966**: "Alessandro STRADELLA."

suggestions that could not be developed because of space limitations. In fact, the suggestions are so rich that they afforded, and afford, other scholars opportunities for research for decades.

During the Harvard years, two such encyclopedia entries appear, in *Die Musik in Geschichte und Gegenwart* (*M.G.G.*): "Italien B. 14.–16. Jahrhundert" (1957) and "Rom. C. Spätmittelalter und Renaissance" (1963). Both—but especially "Italien"—first adumbrate themes that Pirrotta will elaborate for the remainder of his career.

The later article in *M.G.G.* —"Rom. C. Spätmittelalter und Renaissance" (1963)—opens with a consideration of the "continuous and final new establishment of the papal chapel" in the early fifteenth century. There follow observations concerning the centrality of the organ to the musical practices of the principal Roman basilicas, the introduction of polyphonic practices at various ecclesiastical institutions, lay brotherhoods' practice of lauda singing, public processionals, and music for banqueting.

I wish to focus on the last two topics, not only because Pirrotta's interest in such ephemeral practices was relatively unusual for the time (at least among American musicologists), but also because his treatment of them—characterized by a Crocean narrative means of presentation—is revealing and atmospheric. The article leaves one with an enhanced understanding of the "texture" of actual musical life, the actual uses of music and its role in the actual quotidian experiences of contemporary aristocratic and ecclesiastical figures. Once more, Pirrotta has recourse to sources not often consulted by musicologists, in particular literary sources that describe musical performances whose specific musical elements are usually no longer extant. The resulting picture of the musical culture is altered and enriched, since such sources furnish evidence that actual notated music manuscripts (and, later, prints) do not often provide.

The second half of the article is devoted to the sixteenth century: to the singers of the Sistine Chapel, to the chapel at St. Peter's Basilica and other Roman churches, to the private, secular musical practices of aristocratic and ecclesiastical figures, and to Andrea Antico's printed collections of secular music. Pirrotta's consideration of the last occasions an additional observation concerning the origins of the Cinquecento madrigal.[80]

Readers familiar with Pirrotta's publications would have been reasonably well prepared for the first section of the earlier *M.G.G.* article ("Italien B. 14.–16. Jahrhundert"), because it covers material—the music of the Trecento—about which he had been writing since 1935. However, given the

---

[80]"The collections by Antico indicate an emphatic Petrarchism, even for Rome at the time of Leo X. In contrast to the recitative tendencies that dominated in Northern Italy, in Rome it came to an elaborate polyphony in the *Musica ... sopra le canzone del Petrarca* by B. Pisano (1520)."

absence before the mid-1950s of his comparable coverage of the music of the Italian Renaissance, it would have been impossible to be as well prepared for the panoramic richness of the account of Quattrocento and Cinquecento music. I regard "Italien" as an elegant demonstration of the Crocean/Gentilean philosophy of history: in its adherence to the narrative rhetorical mode, in its focus on the evocative particular, in its intuitive apprehension and imaginative "representation" (to invoke another Crocean term) of the underlying historical data. It is a highly distilled, yet comprehensive history of the music of the Italian Renaissance, which remains provocative half a century after it appeared.

The opening paragraph of the second section identifies the anomaly to be explored more systematically six years later in the paper for the American Musicological Society on music and cultural tendencies in fifteenth-century Italy: the "interruption in Italian polyphonic composition from 1420/30 onwards for approximately half a century." In various allusions to the Material infrastructure, we first encounter the germ of the thesis later advanced in explaining that anomaly.

The subsequent text is rich in passing references, any one of which could be amplified; but it was inevitable that they remained brief.[81] All the same, the roster of names of preeminent Quattrocento humanists—Giorgio Anselmi, Francesco Filelfo, Marsilio Ficino, "Panormita" (Antonio Beccadelli), Giovanni Gioviano Pontano, Tommaso Tebaldi, Giovanni Aurispa—and the mention of their musical proclivities—"the singing of Latin odes to the lute . . . or . . . the accompaniment of the . . . *psalterium*," the singing of "graceful verses to the lute"—constitute a first enumeration of the primary data underlying the thesis of "Music and Cultural Tendencies in 15th-Century Italy." Not all will be deployed in "Music and Cultural Tendencies," and in assessing the persuasiveness of Pirrotta's thesis advanced there, the data presented must be supplemented with those assembled in *M.G.G.*; the substantiating evidence becomes more compelling still.

If the opening passage of the section suggests possibilities for further research that Pirrotta himself will not fully pursue, subsequent passages suggest possibilities that are, in fact, developed in his own future publications. He follows up on a reference to Giannozzo Manetti, identifying reflections in written tradition of oral, "popular" Sicilian musical practice;[82] he will often deploy the evidence of Simone Prodenzani's text;[83] more than once, he will

---

[81] I intend to follow up, with a full study, on the promising suggestions now only implicit in this passage, a study to be based on a comprehensive assembling of complete bibliographic references for the titles cited and substantial excerpts from them.
[82] **1972**: "New Glimpses of an Unwritten Tradition."
[83] For example, ibid.

return to references in Filippo Scarlatti's notebooks;[84] and Ambrogio Traversari's encomium of Leonardo Giustinian—and Giustinian's compositional and performative practices (as imaginatively reconstructed, given that no written musical evidence of them survives)—are crucial to the later article on *O rosa bella*.[85]

We already find a statement of his view that the published frottola repertory of the early Cinquecento reflects—though imperfectly—mid-Quattrocento oral tradition. And Pirrotta also offers observations on the "[m]usic for . . . masques (not only for carnival, but also those . . . inserted at festivals or banquets or . . . used as *intermedii* during the performance of comedies)," the polyphonic lauda, and the sacra rappresentatione.

In two additional passages of the article, Pirrotta adumbrates themes developed more fully in his later scholarship. In the first, he considers the complex historiographic "problem of the Renaissance" and the potential role that the evidence of music history can play in solving it, which in some sense is the fundamental objective of the article on "Musical and Cultural Tendencies in 15th-Century Italy." Furthermore, he suggests illuminating analogies with the history of art and makes specific reference to Josquin Desprez, who will figure prominently in "Music and Cultural Tendencies" and in writings resulting from it. The second passage concerns the origins of that most characteristic of Italian musical genres of the early-modern era, the Cinquecento madrigal, and offers nothing less than a thesis about its emergence, which Pirrotta will elaborate in a continuing series of papers, one of which appears only a few years before his death.[86]

Pirrotta concludes with a survey of the effects of music printing, the instrumental tradition, regional schools of composition and performance (the Venetian, the Roman), and reflections on "the transition from a constructive view of music to a new attitude, in which the main accent lies on the expression of affects." The entire article merits the closest possible reading.

*****

The polyphonic "production gap" of the fifteenth century—the "segreto del Quattrocento"—had thus been identified as a presumed anomaly inviting explanation. Having taught at Harvard for six years, Pirrotta was eligible for

---

[84]For example, **1973**: "Su alcuni testi italiani di composizioni polifoniche quattrocentesche."
[85]**1972**: "Ricercari e variazioni su 'O rosa bella.'"
[86]See **1961**: contributions to the panel discussion "From Frottola to Madrigal"; **1994**: "Before the Madrigal"; and **1996**: "Florence from Barzelletta to Madrigal" and even the chapter "Temporal Perspective and Music" in **1969**: *Music and Theatre*.

a sabbatical during academic year 1962/63,[87] and as his project he chose to explore Italian Renaissance humanist attitudes toward what I have termed "the exogenous intellectualistic enterprise of polyphonic composition."[88] Pirrotta reported in a paper at the 1963 annual meeting of the American Musicological Society that it "sums up the results of a negative—yet useful and necessary—search for musical information in humanistic sources."[89]

The paper Pirrotta delivered is "Music and Cultural Tendencies in 15th-Century Italy,"[90] and I believe it to be one of the most important papers ever published in the discipline of historical musicology.[91]

When I was an undergraduate history major, one of my teachers—the medievalist Francis Oakley—introduced me to the vast literature on the historiographic problem of the Renaissance. I subsequently read "Music and Cultural Tendencies" (together with the contributions of Lowinsky and Schrade) against the backdrop of the larger historiographic debate. It immediately became clear to me that Pirrotta was especially sensitive to the findings of the leading historians of the Renaissance. Of all the studies by musicologists whose objective was to apply the evidence of music history to the historiographic "problem of the Renaissance," I believe Pirrotta's to be the one that most satisfactorily addresses the question of whether there was a "Renaissance" in music and explains what the "Renaissance" elements are in "Renais-

---

[87]He negotiated the terms with Harvard President Nathan Pusey, and reported that he was confident that "[a]s far as the ... Library is concerned, I am sure that my excellent Assistant Librarian, Miss Little, can carry on the work without me." See the Pirrotta file, Department of Music, Harvard University.

[88]1985: "Musica e Umanesimo." See also "Antonino Pirrotta," *Premi "Antonio Feltrinelli" 1983*, Accademia Nazionale dei Lincei, 69–74, especially 72.

[89]"... a search made possible by a Fellowship granted to the author by the American Council of Learned Societies." See the announcement in the *Harvard Crimson* of Pirrotta's receipt of the A.C.L.S. grant: http://www.thecrimson.com/article/1962/2/14/council-gives-funds-to-harvard-professors.

[90]The paper was also read at a chapter meeting of the American Musicological Society at Yale University, 24–25 April 1965, where it was entitled, interestingly, "Cultural Tides in Music of the Fifteenth Century."

[91]I am not alone in this belief; see, for example, James Haar's review of Pirrotta's *Music and Culture in Italy from the Middle Ages to the Baroque: A Collection of Essays* and his *Musica tra Medioevo e Rinascimento* in *Early Music History* 5 (1985): 269–74, and Iain Fenlon's "Italian Insights," another review of *Music and Culture in Italy from the Middle Ages to the Baroque*, in *Musical Times* 126 (1985): 411.

sance" music, and most compellingly articulates a justification for characterizing a musical repertory as "Renaissance."[92]

"Music and Cultural Tendencies" is best read as part of a trilogy of related titles, which also includes "Marchettus of Padua and the Italian *Ars Nova*" and "'Maniera' polifonica e immediatezza recitativa." The problem addressed by the three is essentially the same: the ambivalent posture in Italian musical aesthetics toward polyphonic practice. The first ("Marchettus of Padua") considers the "anomalous" adoption of a polyphonic "maniera" in the Trecento; the second ("Music and Cultural Tendencies"), the seemingly anomalous, but in fact explicable, "polyphonic production gap" of the Quattrocento; and the third ("'Maniera' polifonica"), "the entire development of Italian sacred and secular music during the" Cinquecento as exemplifying the "deliberate adoption of a polyphonic 'maniera.'"[93]

I summarize Pirrotta's argument in "Music and Cultural Tendencies" in his own words. His objective "is ... to draw attention to the ... factor of *environment*" and consider "the degree to which *the atmosphere of the Italian courts and towns during the second half of the 15th century* was actually favorable to the ... development of a ... composer of polyphonic music [emphases added]." Although "Italy did not produce any active polyphonist of renown after the second or third decade of the 15th century," "the first part of that century was a time of intense ... polyphonic activity, reflected in a number of well-known sources ... of primary importance for our knowledge of the music of this period," now distributed geographically "along the valley of the river Po and the vast arc of the Alps."

---

[92] No more than a handful of other musicological papers make similarly important contributions to this scholarly conversation; most fail to elucidate the problem sufficiently, and very few are as useful as "Music and Cultural Tendencies." Of course, we must mention Edward Lowinsky's "Music in the Culture of the Renaissance," *Journal of the History of Ideas* 15 (1954): 509–53; but Lowinsky's terminology reveals that his thesis is decisively colored by a Burkhardtian conception of the Renaissance, as has been observed by Lewis Lockwood in "Renaissance," *Grove Music Online. Oxford Music Online*, http://0-www.oxfordmusiconline.com.libcat.lafayette.edu/subscriber/ article/grove/music/23192 (accessed June 25, 2011). In addition to Lockwood's article, I would cite Charles van den Borren's "Quelques reflexions a propos du style imitatif syntaxique," *Revue belge de Musicologie* 1 (1946): 14–20; like Pirrotta's "Music and Cultural Tendencies," van den Borren's identifies stylistic characteristics in the music that justify classifying a particular musical repertory as "Renaissance," based upon a persuasively articulated congruence between those stylistic characteristics and the distinguishing features of the Renaissance as a cultural phenomenon in European history. Gary Tomlinson's recent "Renaissance Humanism and Music," in *European Music, 1520–1640*, ed. James Haar (Woodbridge: Boydell Press, 2006), 1–19, is a clear and cogent survey of the various music-historiographic explanations attempted. I also have found the following two studies to present much more persuasive interpretations of the primary texts they explicate than other attempts to explicate the same texts: Rob C. Wegman, "Johannes Tinctoris and the 'New Art,'" *Music & Letters* 84, no. 2 (2003): 171–88; and Wegman, "New Music for a World Grown Old: Martin Le Franc and the 'Contenance Angloise,'" *Acta Musicologica* 75, no. 2 (2003): 201–41. In my opinion, few, if any, other attempts to contribute to the scholarly meta-discourse are worthy of attention, with the exception of papers to be cited presently, whose objective is to refute or qualify the thesis of Pirrotta's "Music and Cultural Tendencies." These revisionist statements are serious and consequential and demand most careful consideration, whatever conclusion is ultimately reached concerning their validity.

[93] **1995**: "'Maniera' polifonica e immediatezza recitativa."

However, "[w]hat we know of such major centers as Milan, Padua, and Florence does not seem to justify so extensive a repertory." On the contrary, the relevant Material infrastructure that supported its creation and performance was largely foreign in origin:

> [T]he crisis inaugurated by the Great Schism and unresolved even by its conclusion called for . . . the Councils of Pisa, Cividale, Constance, Pavia-Siena, Basel, Ferrara, and finally Florence, which brought . . . an unusual concentration of the leading figures of the Church. . . . [T]hese dignitaries had musicians in their *familiae*. . . . [T]he greater and better part of the polyphonists of this time, either singers or composers, . . . had received academic training, and combined their musical skills and gifts with many other talents, capacities, and ambitions. . . . They belong to a broad cultural type, the product of an educational pattern especially designed to prepare for an ecclesiastical career, and represented at its best by the curriculum of the University of Paris.

"[T]he sharp decline of polyphonic practice in Italy after 1437" is thus partly to be related "to the diminished influx of foreign prelates," certainly. But "[a]n even more important factor . . . was . . . the process by which the representatives of the old cultural type"—"which we may define as scholastic[,] using the term in its broader acceptance"—

> were being replaced, in the Curia as in the executive ranks of every Italian court or town government, by the followers of the *studia humanitatis*. By this process those who had practiced polyphony as a creative, liberal activity, as well as those who could best appreciate it, were being eliminated. . . . Younger humanists gave definite evidence of their distrust of a technical tradition of music that was too closely associated in their minds with medieval Latin and the French vernacular. . . . The most usual attitude of a humanist, however, seems . . . to have been not one of distrust or contempt toward the most technical aspects of music, but simply one of ignorance for lack of exposure. His musical experience is chiefly empirical, concentrating on the most immediate aspects of this art, on soloistic singing, dance tunes, flourishes of trumpets, lulling sounds of harps and flutes, and perhaps some display of instrumental virtuosity on the lute or on a keyboard instrument.

Pirrotta's argument is carefully qualified. It is not his contention

> that *artistic polyphony was never or seldom performed in Italy. It may have been performed even rather frequently, but as one kind of music among many*, without any special attention paid to what we consider its special merits and importance in view of future developments [emphasis added].

Our understandable interest in the written tradition, and especially in polyphonic practices, may have led us to exaggerate the importance of those practices for fifteenth-century Italy, to lavish "special attention" on them, when, in fact, for Quattrocento humanists, polyphony was merely "one kind of music among many."

This is only one of several careful qualifications:

> It is true that the difference between the old, scholastic and the new, humanistic type of culture was not a basic one. Much of the old curriculum was maintained or even expanded. Differences existed, however, derived in part from the less speculative and more pragmatist tradition of the Italian communal universities; in part from the emphasis put on classical models as a necessary approach to the art of composing all types of documents, letters, and speeches, and, even further, as an ideal guidance to every aspect of human life.[94]

The virtue of this particular qualification is that it aligns Pirrotta's presentation with that of one of the premier students of Italian Renaissance humanism, Paul Oskar Kristeller, who suggested that "much of the humanist polemic against medieval science was not even intended as a criticism of the contents or methods of that science, but merely represents a phase in the 'battle of the arts,'" "a noisy advertisement for the field of learning advocated by the humanists, in order to neutralize and overcome the claims of other, rivaling sciences": "the humanistic attack was as much a matter of departmental rivalry as . . . a clash of opposite ideas or philosophies."[95]

Pirrotta's objective is a subtle one: to articulate carefully a people's fundamental "cultural tendencies" at a particular moment in history, elusive temporary shifts in the balance among such tendencies, and what they portend for attendant practices, including the aesthetics of musical composition and performance.[96]

To state this differently: Pirrotta's aim was to contrast (though not too starkly) two concurrent, peacefully coexisting, yet also competing educational programs and their underlying intellectual sensibilities and to relate the "polyphonic production gap" of the fifteenth century to the rise of the Italian Renaissance humanists, many of whom associated polyphonic composition with contrasting sensibilities, characteristic—in their view—of the ages that came in the middle between the fall of Rome and their own era. Consonant

---

[94]**1963**: "Music and Cultural Tendencies in 15th Century Italy."

[95]Kristeller, *Renaissance Thought. The Classic, Scholastic, and Humanist Strains* (New York: Harper & Row, 1961), 43, 102, 113, and 162 n. 68. Kristeller continues: "Bruni is even hinting at one point that he is not speaking quite in earnest. . . . After having joked about the Barbaric names of the English logicians, Bruni continues: 'Et quid Colucci ut haec ioca omittam quid est inquam in dialectica quod non Britannicis sophismatibus conturbatum sit?'" See also James Hankins, "Two Twentieth-Century Interpreters" (see "*Scena 2.ª*," n. 85), where Hankins writes that "the struggle between humanism and scholasticism (a central episode in the history of thought for European historians of philosophy) was for Kristeller no more than a series of 'interdepartmental rivalries,'" and Hankins, "Garin and Paul Oskar Kristeller" (see "*Scena 2.ª*," n. 84), where Hankins writes that "[f]or Kristeller, scholasticism as an intellectual tradition was not replaced by humanism, but the two flourished side by side throughout the Renaissance and beyond as separate departments of culture."

[96]See also the qualification in **1963**: "Music and Cultural Tendencies," 139 n. 44.

with the fundamental objective of the Renaissance, they were seeking to "correct" such "medieval" sensibilities through the restoration of classical standards and accomplishments.

Such a rebirth had the potential to affect many areas of human achievement, including the visual arts and neo-Latin literature as well as music. The evocation of classical exemplars—as manifested in Bramante's celebrated "Tempietto," for example, or in the neo-Ciceronian Latin cultivated by the humanists—could also have resonances in the musical practices of Renaissance Italy.

One of the virtues of Pirrotta's argument is its fidelity to the Italian Renaissance humanists' own perspectives. Unlike attempts by other historical musicologists to decode the Renaissance, Pirrotta's is grounded specifically in an Italian Quattrocento humanist's understanding of the matter. His approach is consistent with the findings of Wallace K. Ferguson's classic essay on the historiographic interpretation of the Renaissance:

> It has become a commonplace to say that the traditional conception of the Renaissance as a new age in the history of Western civilization... arose during the Renaissance itself; and it is more or less true.... [T]he humanists furnished the materials for such an interpretation of the course of European history and for the scheme of periodization adopted by later generations.[97]

Like Ferguson, Pirrotta refrains from implicitly defining the Renaissance—in his case, the musical Renaissance—in arbitrarily selected terms: through abstract, more generalized notions of newness not necessarily pertinent to the Quattrocento context, for example, or through an inadequate chronological scheme. (Dufay and Ockeghem are Renaissance composers because they lived during the fifteenth century, and their music is thus to be analyzed for the insights it affords as to what constitutes the Renaissance in music.) Pirrotta's is an historicist's approach, which contextualizes the various data pertinent to a solution of the problem. He articulates his thesis in terms derived from—and substantiated by—authoritative period texts.

Given that "the traditional conception of the Renaissance as a new age in the history of Western civilization... arose during the Renaissance itself," and that "the humanists furnished the materials for... the scheme of periodization adopted by later generations," we ask how Italian Quattrocento humanists themselves understood music and how we might analyze particular period

---

[97]Ferguson, *The Renaissance in Historical Thought. Five Centuries of Interpretation* (Boston: Houghton Mifflin Co., 1948), 1. See also Theodore E. Mommsen, "Petrarch's Conception of the 'Dark Ages,'" *The Italian Renaissance. The Essential Readings*, ed. Paula Findlen (Malden, MA: Blackwell, 2002), 219–36. I consider it axiomatic that any music historian who wishes to attempt a truly serious contribution to the solution of the historiographic problem of the Renaissance must first carefully and fully absorb the findings of Mommsen's and Ferguson's classic essays. To proceed otherwise is to do so in the absence of a full command of the relevant scholarly literature.

musical repertories—northern and Italian, written and unwritten—in terms of that understanding.

Further: what does the analysis yield when we classify those repertories as Renaissance, as contrasted with medieval repertories, a fundamental contrast of the humanists' own making? Is there justification for the periodization assumed in many—most—histories of European music, where northern composers of the fifteenth century are identified as Renaissance composers, evidently because of the chronological coincidence of their biographies with the period of the (Italian) Renaissance, thus legitimizing an uncritical understanding of the Renaissance as a period in history, rather than a circumscribed development or movement, the expression of an intellectual and social elite, with limited effects? In what sense can Dufay and Ockeghem be considered Renaissance composers? And if we accept such an identification, how does our understanding of their musical style as Renaissance perhaps contaminate—inadvertently—our definition of the Renaissance character of Renaissance music?

In other words, rather than arbitrarily (re)defining the Renaissance to accommodate composers like Dufay and Ockeghem—rather than seeking some contrivance that makes it possible for us to include such composers in the Renaissance, because for some untested reason we wish to do so—perhaps we ought instead to define it first in historiographically authoritative terms, and then (and only then) analyze composers and repertories to determine the extent to which they exemplify the concept of the Renaissance.

"Music and Cultural Tendencies" does not consider all these matters in the aforesaid way. Nonetheless, in this article Pirrotta succeeds, where most other musicologists do not, in providing the means to treat them persuasively.

For example, the value of his argument lies in providing a conceptual scheme and vocabulary for characterizing so fundamental an element of music as constructional technique, a scheme and vocabulary that respect the relevant terms in his underlying thesis about "cultural tendency." The habit of reflexively including Dufay and Ockeghem in the European musical Renaissance—based presumably on the superficial chronological coincidence—is unjustified. Much of their sacred music can instead be analyzed in terms that underscore the indebtedness of their aesthetic to high-medieval compositional tradition, to practices that originated with the beginnings of European polyphony: the more-or-less verbatim quotation of a *prius factus* element in the tenor, which is often borrowed from the chant repertory. In this respect, Dufay and Ockeghem in the fifteenth century are no different from Leoninus and Perotinus in the twelfth (and, before them, Guido of Arezzo in the tenth and Hucbald and the authors of the two *Enchiriadis* treatises in the ninth). In their fundamental compositional technique, Dufay and Ockeghem more convincingly exemplify Huizinga's "waning of the Middle Ages" than Burckhardt's

"Renaissance." Ironically, this is as true—even truer—when the *cantus prius factus* is secular in origin, since in Dufay's and Ockeghem's music such a practice is congruent with the vital, "messy" heterogeneity of the high-medieval motet, with its haphazardly polytextual, even polylingual character.

Further, the compositional use of a *cantus prius factus* element in the tenor is emblematic of the larger, characteristically medieval tendency to appeal to *auctoritas*, to ground the creative act in the use of authoritative antecedent material. Such a compositional technique is not unlike the practices of the medieval glossators, who commented on authoritative antecedent texts. Their marginal commentaries surrounding the central authoritative text are analogous to the medieval composer's newly composed voice(s) written in counterpoint to the Gregorian melody embedded at the center of the polyphonic texture.

This view of Dufay's artistic personality is consistent with non music-historical evidence. Craig Wright suggested that, "Dufay was cast in the mold of a composer of the Middle Ages, not the Renaissance. His education in a cathedral school, his training in canon law, and his library of theological works point to a life much in the traditions of Philippe de Vitry, bishop of Meaux, and Guillaume de Machaut, canon of Rheims," a portrait substantiated by the evidence of the composer's habits in book collecting: although "[h]e must have been a bibliophile of at least moderate passion, for according to a list in the execution of his testament he owned thirty-four volumes, a sizable collection for a single individual in the late Middle Ages," "newer, more humanistic works are poorly represented," the sole classical text of the thirty-four being a copy of Virgil ("Item pour j Vergile en papier, 1").[98]

The compositional aesthetic and constructional technique exemplified by the music of the northerners Leoninus, Perotinus, Dufay, and Ockeghem contrast with those favored by Italian humanists of the fifteenth century.[99] The data substantiating Pirrotta's thesis are more extensive than those cited in "Music and Cultural Tendencies," and any informed assessment of the validity of his thesis demands conversance with the larger evidential basis. Initially at least, the classicizing tendencies of Italian Renaissance music are exemplified by the iconic, pan-Mediterranean practice of solo-singing to the singer's playing of a plucked-, strummed-, or bowed-string instrument.[100] The

---

[98] Craig Wright, "Dufay at Cambrai: Discoveries and Revisions," *Journal of the American Musicological Society* 28 (1975): 175–229.

[99] On the other hand, Dufay (unlike Ockeghem) spent considerable time in Italy, and Pirrotta himself suggests that there are distinctive features of Dufay's music that might be characterized generally as exemplifying a "Renaissance" character: see **1957**: "Italien B. 14.–16. Jahrhundert."

[100] As Joshua Rifkin reminds me, however, the north also had its accompanied solo song, though—as Professor Rifkin reminds me once more—it may not have been understood or valued in quite the same way as in fifteenth-century Italy.

musical rebirth is thus a restoration of ancient mythological (Orphic) and historical practices. The following statements—each substantiated by period documentation—are illustrative. Among them, the reference in Filelfo is especially emblematic of the correspondence between a Quattrocento humanist's classicizing impulses and their musical expression:[101]

> Filelfo's *Convivia* [1443] show how, through the acquaintance with Greek texts, the desire for historical knowledge about classical music already spread, and how one liked to link musical practice—... the singing of Latin odes to the lute (lyra) or ... the accompaniment of the monochord (*psalterium*) ... —with scholarly discussions, as a necessary and natural complement of every human activity.[102]

> The *Epistolæ gallicæ* by Panormita (Pavia 1430–33) often praise the skill of the young Ergotele (T[ommaso]. Tebaldi, later one of the participants at the *Convivia* of Filelfo) in singing graceful verses to the lute.

> Characteristic of this tendency was the Venetian patrician and humanist Leonardo Giustiniani (ca. 1388–1446), who before 1428 wrote love poems in Venetian dialect ... in a demonstratively folk-like tone; he composed the music himself for the poems and performed it to a lute. ... A[mbrogio]. Traversari (†1439) wrote to him: "I have known for some time that your agile and golden ingenuity ... [has achieved] skill in singing the sweetest songs with accompaniment" ["So da tempo che quel tuo ingegno agile e aureo ... ha conseguito) la perizia nel cantare con accompagnamento soavissimi canti"].

> Around 1470, F[ilippo]. Scarlatti transcribed into one of his notebooks, after "rispetti da cantare in sul liuto" and "stanze," which "si dicono in sulla viuola la sera per serenata," Neapolitan, Sicilian, and Calabrese songs.

> From the title of a series of eleven volumes ... published by O. Petrucci between 1504 and 1514 derives the custom generally to use the term "Frottola" to designate the entire production. ... The starting point for this production was the creation—which clearly fed from humanistic sources—of the "cantori a liuto," "alla lira," or "alla viola"..... Although it had the tendency to become a real and independent profession, the activity of these singers was initially essentially carried out by men of letters, who held positions of some importance at the courts of Florence, Naples, Rome, and Milan (cf., e.g., B. Gareth, called il Cariteo; A. Tebaldi, called Tebaldeo; V. Calmeta, et al.). Even if they were not always such in the true sense, they

---

[101] All of these quotations are from **1957**: "Italien B. 14.–16. Jahrhundert."

[102] Filelfo's text is so important to an understanding of the correspondence of generalized Quattrocento classicizing tendencies and that century's specific musical practices that I quote it here in English translation: "'But so as not to seem to have ignored entirely the normal customs of a symposium, it may perhaps be timely to hear how capable your boys are, Rembaldo, in playing and singing, both of whom I see ready, the one with the lyre, the other with the psaltery.' 'You admonish correctly,' Rembaldo said, and—having turned to his boys—he ordered them to fulfill their tasks. And thus touching and gently strumming the strings, they—taking turns—accommodated the rhythms to these words: 'Whoever wishes to see the beauty of the stars and the splendid unifications of the one who thunders, come here, happy, to rich meals under a benevolent star.'" For the translation of the original Latin, I am grateful to Claudia Wiener of the University of Munich and my colleague Professor Markus Dubischar of Lafayette College.

performed as improvisers of Italian, Latin, and Greek verses and accompanied them on one of the above mentioned instruments. B. Castiglione probably alludes later to their manner of recitation in his *Cortegiano* (begun 1508), when he points out that it befits a nobleman more than anything else to "sing to the viola in order to recite ['cantar alla viola per recitare,']" which "adds much of grace and efficacy to the words, which is a great marvel ['tanto di venustà e di efficacia aggiunge alle parole, che è gran meraviglia']."

The "aeri per cantar versi latini" and those for sonnets, strambotti, capitoli, etc., that were later included in several frottola collections of Petrucci are four-voiced, but it is more probable that for the singing voice the improvisers used only two accompanying voices: tenor and contrabass. Petrucci did indeed print the frottole intabulated for the lute in this three-voiced form.[103]

We can now return to some of Pirrotta's formulations in articles predating "Music and Cultural Tendencies" and understand them in a new way. His characterizations of late-medieval French polyphony enhance our understanding of its relationship to the macroscopic sensibilities—the "cultural tendencies"—underlying it. He identifies

[w]hat is evident above all in French polyphony of the Gothic period, in which the worship of construction—well-ordered by means of an industrious craftsmanship of technique and the liveliness of the ratiocination—finally gives way to an intellectualism and ... geometricizing and symbolizing abstraction.[104]

Writing of de Vitry's artistic personality and his *ars nova*, he argues that

they carry technical procedures to extreme consequences, developing them above all in the sense of abstract intellectualism and in a certain way indifferent to the reality of auditory perception.... Through ... its primitive destination toward pure delight ..., the Italian *ars nova* ... interrupted a tradition of subordination of musical intuition to the intellectual faculties.[105]

On the specific matter of the deployment of antecedent material—and *how* it is deployed—Pirrotta writes that

parody is a mode of derivation from a 'res prius facta' that rests upon the effect of the sensible perception of the relationship with the model (in contrast with ratiocinative or constructive procedures, of which the classic example is composition on a given tenor).[106]

---

[103]Because of the format of encyclopedia entries, Pirrotta had to forgo all annotations, as well as complete period documentation substantiating his summary statement. I intend to provide such in my follow-up study. Pirrotta's excerpts from and references to Filelfo and Manetti in particular substantiate their authors' Renaissance-humanist, Neoplatonist intentionality, since the authors employ the term "convivium" and "symposium" to characterize the events at which the music-making that they describe occurred; this can only be regarded, I believe, as an explicit act of homage to the *Symposium* of Plato.

[104]**1948:** "'Dulcedo' e 'subtilitas' nella pratica polifonica franco-italiana al principio del '400."

[105]**1955:** "Cronologia e denominazione dell'ars nova italiana."

[106]**1950:** "Considerazioni sui primi esempi di Missa parodia."

The effect of this final quotation is to suggest that the *cantus prius factus* element embedded within the sacred polyphony of Leoninus, Perotinus, Dufay, and Ockeghem is inaudible: its deployment "ratiocinative" or "constructive," as contrasted with "sensible."[107]

However, whatever equivocation there may have been concerning the efficacy of polyphony as a means of furthering humanism's fundamental cultural objectives, it was momentary. The prestige of that aesthetic and the talent and vision of gifted northern polyphonists like Josquin Desprez, who spent much of his career in the company of Italian Renaissance humanists, were such that a reframing of the polyphonic tradition—its purification (to load my language), undertaken specifically to make it more responsive to humanistic ideals—was not only possible but perhaps even predictable.[108]

One of the distinguishing characteristics of Josquin's fundamental aesthetic is what Charles van den Borren termed the *"style imitatif syntaxtique,"* a compositional procedure—a "genre of imitation"—that "consists in the treatment of a text, in prose or poetry, by means of a series of themes presented in the form of free imitations," "corresponding respectively to the phrase-members of which the text is composed."[109] Note the emphasis on text generally, and specifically on the component of language that linguists term its syntax (as contrasted with its semantics and phonology); such was a vital

---

[107]Pirrotta's general understanding of the character of polyphony as a compositional technique, as expressed here—and of "default" Italian convictions concerning it—also inform his **1992**: "The Music."

[108]One of the most revealing early documents of that transformation is Josquin's extraordinary *motet Huc me sydereo*. The text and music of its tenor, like the tenors of countless "high-medieval" and "late-medieval" compositions, are liturgical in origin, a *prius factus* element derived from the Gregorian repertory. However, the text of the four other voices is (like their music) newly composed, the work of a fifteenth-century Milanese humanist, Maffeo Vegio. It is a remarkable text in which Jesus describes his descent "from starry Olympus"; Vegio has transformed Jesus into a Greco-Roman god, and the Christian heaven is now identical with the Olympus of classical mythology.

More important for purposes of the argument advanced here, Josquin has demonstrated the potential responsiveness of the polyphonic tradition to humanistic ideals: his *motet* is a moving musical reading of the entire text as an organic statement, and is replete as well with exquisite instances of local text-painting, such as at the word "Descendere," which is illustrated not only by the descending melodic motion of the individual voice parts, but also by a systematic exploration—from top to bottom—of the tonal space occupied by the composition. I know of few more powerful early illustrations of the potential for reconciling northern polyphonic practice with the literary concerns of the Italian humanists.

[109]"Quelques reflexions a propos du style imitatif syntaxique," especially 14.

concern of the Quattrocento humanists. In this instance, textual-syntactic form generates musical-syntactic form.[110]

The purification of the polyphonic tradition under the influence of humanistic ideals might therefore be construed as the yielding of a "ratiocinative," "intellectualistic," "constructive" deployment of the antecedent material—typical of the Middle Ages—to an aurally perceptible deployment of the material, paralleling the momentary displacement of the Aristotelian ratiocinative procedures of the scholastics by the humanists' neo-Ciceronian concern for grammar and rhetoric. The transition from an aesthetic grounded in the use of a *prius factus* element—quoted verbatim, though inaudibly, in the tenor—to one that instead makes audible use of antecedent material in a manner responsive to the text—to its phonology, its semantics, and above all its syntactic organization (this last producing what musicians and musicologists call imitative polyphony)—was the response of the northern polyphonists to Italian-humanist literary concerns.

There is a substantial scholarly literature relevant to Pirrotta's thesis in "Music and Cultural Tendencies" that, to my knowledge, has yet to be duly considered in the ongoing assessment of the validity of his argument: a generation of historians of science produced findings congruent with his. Although they do not employ such terminology, historians of science identified their own "segreto del Quattrocento"—parallel to that identified by historians of music (Torrefranca, Pirrotta, and others)—and they attributed it to the same factors.[111]

---

[110]Lewis Lockwood offers a view of the same developments in constructional technique that is similar to van den Borren's in its broad outlines and emphasis on the importance of the text as motivating factor: "Characteristic of . . . the fifteenth century—both chansons and motets—is a normal setting for three voices, in which, quite frequently, the Discant and Tenor form an essential pair of voices. To this basic two-part complex is added a Contratenor, and sometimes a Contratenor bassus, the fourth part often being 'si placet'. . . . Significant in the fifteenth-century chanson style is the conception of the composition as superimposing several linear levels, each level being formed as an integral line possessing a considerable degree of melodic independence. . . . [M]usical procedures motivated directly by text are relatively rare. The contrasting features of the newer motet are equally familiar: a change to four voices as the norm; the gradual abandonment of the successive and horizontal conception in favor of a more nearly simultaneous and certainly vertical conception . . . ; the virtual end of the Discant-Tenor pair as the axis of musical organization and its replacement by a four-part complex in which all voices participate more or less equally in the motivic development. The rise of imitation as a thoroughly developed technique is usually attributed to the late fifteenth and earlier sixteenth century, but perhaps more decisive is that even though motivic imitation may not be exact or may not embrace all voices of a motet, the principle of alternate voice-grouping and rhythmic complementation is fully established. *The result is that no single voice is any longer a self-contained linear totality.*" The implications for sixteenth-century "parody procedure" of this change in the constructional technique of the antecedent material are obvious: "the essential element is no longer the total line but the individual motive." Lockwood, "A View of the Early Sixteenth-Century Parody Mass," *Twenty-Fifth Anniversary Festschrift (1937–1962), Queens College of The City University of New York. Department of Music* (n.p. [New York]: Queens College of The City University of New York, 1964), 53–77.

[111]But for a more recent reconsideration of the relationship between humanism and science, see Ann Blair and Anthony Grafton, "Reassessing Humanism and Science," *Journal of the History of Ideas* 53, no. 4 (1992): 535–40, and the titles it cites, among them, importantly, Eric Cochrane, "Science and Humanism in the Italian Renaissance," *American Historical Review* 81 (1976): 1037–59.

Historian of philosophy Daniel O'Connor has written of "the empirical science already emerging in the fourteenth and fifteenth centuries," which was "definitively established only in the seventeenth" "because of a recession during which humanist literary and ethical interests dominated."[112] Musicologist Richard Hoppin quoted historian of science A.C. Crombie to the effect that "15th-century humanism, which arose in Italy and spread northwards, was an interruption in the development of science."[113] In a classic paper on "Tradition and Innovation in Fifteenth Century Italy,"[114] historian of science Dana B. Durand,—summarizing findings given more systematic exposition in his monograph on cartography[115]—undertook to

> test in a single instance the validity of the opinion, commonly held since Burckhardt, that the Quattrocento marks a radical break with the Middle Ages and institutes the era of Modern Europe.... [B]y tradition one may understand the persistence of ... categories of speculative thought, in this case ... the scholastic method, ... - science, etc.... The composite balance sheet of the departments of Quattrocento science ... does not appear to present a clear and uniform Italian advantage.... The chief increments of knowledge ... must be classed as internal elaboration of traditional material, ... Some historians who have admitted a partial continuity of subject-matter between medieval and Quattrocento thought have credited the latter with a new approach or spirit, a greater strenuousness, consistency, rigor, a revolutionary insight which amounted to a creation *ex nihilo*, a decisive jump in the course of progress. Claims of originality based upon an intangible spirit are not, of course, subject to absolute proof or disproof. Yet such would seem to be the basis for much of the case for a comprehensive Quattrocento "primato".... [T]he balance of tradition and innovation in fifteenth-century Italy was not so decisively favorable as to distinguish that century radically from those that preceded it, nor to constitute the Quattrocento a unique and unrivaled moment in the history of western thought.

Now, there is much in these formulations that a current generation of historians of science would no longer find acceptable. The presentation of O'Connor and Crombie in particular rests on now discredited Whiggish historiographic assumptions, which viewed fourteenth-century scholastics as precursors to Galileo. Nor would many historians of science any longer consider fourteenth and early-fifteenth century scholastics to be empiricists in the modern sense

---

[112]O'Connor, "Introduction: Two Philosophies of Nature," in O'Connor and Francis Oakley, eds., *Creation*, 15–28, especially 20–21 (see "*Scena 4.ª*," n. 52).

[113]Hoppin, "Tonal Organization in Music Before the Renaissance," *Paul A. Pisk. Essays in His Honor*, ed. John M. Glowacki (Austin, TX: College of Fine Arts, University of Texas, 1966), 25–37, especially 31 and 37, n. 15.

[114]Dana B. Durand, "Tradition and Innovation in Fifteenth Century Italy: 'Il primato dell'Italia" in the Field of Science," *Journal of the History of Ideas* 4 (1943): 1–20.

[115]Durand, *The Vienna-Klosterneuburg Map Corpus of the Fifteenth Century. A Study in the Transition from Medieval to Modern Science* (Leiden: E.J. Brill, 1952).

of that word.[116] Moreover, as Pirrotta suggested, scholasticism as an intellectual program continued to enjoy considerable prestige throughout the fifteenth century, especially within the Italian university system. (The humanist movement, conversely, first flourished outside the Italian university and only later secured a place within.) Under no circumstances ought one to exaggerate the extent to which humanism as an intellectual program fully eclipsed the scholastic tradition, even momentarily.

All the same, there are elements of the more general findings summarized here that are pertinent and remain valid. For purposes of the relevance of this literature to Pirrotta's thesis, the critical observation in Durand's paper is the characterization of the "scholastic method" as a component in an organic category "of speculative thought." That "category of speculative thought"—that "cultural tendency," in Pirrotta's formulation—subsumed both the "scholastic method" and polyphonic composition, and during the fifteenth century the temporary dominance of a competing category of thought—Renaissance humanism—served temporarily to challenge the status of rival categories.

Pirrotta argued repeatedly that the cultivation of polyphonic composition assumed particular sensibilities and an audience of representatives of a particular educational tradition, which he termed "scholastic." His relating of polyphony to scholasticism is congruent with Durand's invocation of a "category of speculative thought," which embraces a number of subsidiary expressions of human activity,[117] all of them characterized, broadly speaking, by a shared sensibility: a generalized grounding in Aristotelian logic and rigorous quantitative reasoning (the kind of reasoning indispensable to the composition and performance of complex polyphony intended for a vocal ensemble, for example—which assumes the precise quantitative calibration of pitch and rhythm, of the frequency and duration of pitch—as contrasted with the flexible soloistic performance of orally transmitted settings of classicistic neo-Latin odes to the accompaniment of the lute).

The commonality in intellectual style and temperament between the scholastic method and polyphonic composition contrasts with the literary and ethical concerns of the Quattrocento humanists, and the momentary shift in

---

[116]See, for example, John E. Murdoch, "The Analytic Character of Late Medieval Learning: Natural Philosophy without Nature," in *Approaches to Nature in the Middle Ages: Papers of the Tenth Annual Conference of the Center for Medieval & Early Renaissance Studies*, ed. Lawrence D. Roberts (Binghamton, NY: Center for Medieval & Early Renaissance Studies, 1982), 171–213. For this reference, I am grateful to Craig Martin, Associate Professor of History at Oakland University, to whom, indeed, I am grateful more generally for useful discussion on the entire matter addressed in these paragraphs.

[117]For an evocation of the relationship of music and medicine, for example, consistent with Pirrotta's own, see the study by historian of medicine Nancy G. Siraisi, "The Music of Pulse in the Writings of Italian Academic Physicians (Fourteenth and Fifteenth Centuries)," *Speculum* 50, no. 4 (1975): 689–710.

emphasis in Italian intellectual life is said (by Pirrotta) to explain the polyphonic production gap of the fifteenth century.

Thus historians of science and historians of music—independently of one another—have identified and assembled mutually substantiating primary evidence of a tendency in fifteenth-century Italian thought and of its consequences for fifteenth-century Italian intellectual achievement in discrete yet related spheres of activity.

Once again, these are subtle arguments, based on the identification of an elusive, oblique rebalancing in Italians' intellectual sensibilities.

I offer here a brief account of the entire historical development that "Music and Cultural Tendencies" permits, an account indebted to Pirrotta's, which I regard as essentially correct. In broad strokes:

Rather than construing the Renaissance as a discrete period in European history, I am persuaded by the findings of the medievalists who revolted[118] against the traditional periodization of European history, and I therefore construe the Renaissance, rather than as a *period*, as a limited *movement*, which developed to differing degrees in different European countries at different times, first and most powerfully in Italy, around 1400, and only later in the north. These chronological and geographical asymmetries have important implications for our understanding of the history of European music, in that northern European music continues to reveal the effects of medieval ideals throughout much of the fifteenth century. Dunstaple, Dufay, and Ockeghem more nearly exemplify Huizinga's "waning of the Middle Ages" than the Renaissance, and they are more legitimately characterized as late-medieval artists.

To state this differently: abandoning the conception of the Renaissance as a unitary period obviates the need to find some means of accommodating all fifteenth-century developments within it, such as the written polyphony of Dunstaple, Dufay, and Ockeghem. If we instead define the Renaissance as a movement, whose effects were felt in different parts of Europe at different times, our collective argument need not be contorted so that Dunstaple, Dufay, and Ockeghem can be located within the musical Renaissance, when, in fact, they may simply not belong there. Rather, a Renaissance sensibility in music ought to be defined a priori, in such a way as to be respectful of Quattrocento humanists (who, after all, essentially invented the notion of a Renaissance); such tastes were literary and ethical in character and radiated outward from Italy and thereafter affected cultural productivity in many of its manifestations in different places at different times.

---

[118] I am adopting Wallace Ferguson's terminology; see *The Renaissance in Historical Thought*.

One manifestation of the Italian iteration of the Renaissance movement was a momentary equivocation about written polyphony and a corresponding preference for classicistic musical practices, such as the soloistic, neo-Orphic singing of orally transmitted compositions to the accompaniment of the singer's playing of a stringed instrument.

Simultaneously, however, the polyphonic practices of northern European composers continued to be in vogue in Quattrocento Italy, though as only one kind of (unprivileged) practice among many. The presence in Italy of gifted northern polyphonists like Josquin Desprez created circumstances favorable to a transformation of the polyphonic tradition, which made it more responsive to the tastes of the Italian humanist patrons of expatriate northern polyphonists. As a result, the sacred polyphonic tradition in particular underwent a fundamental change in technique, in which the antecedent material was now treated in a way sensitive to the syntactic organization of the text, and the musical setting aimed to express the semantic content and phonological characteristics of the text in ways responsive to humanistic ideals. Such an aesthetic contrasts with the intellectualistic, ratiocinative, constructional techniques of late-medieval polyphony, to which fifteenth-century humanist Italy took some exception, and only from this moment—from the time of Josquin Desprez—can one speak of Renaissance polyphony, in ways congruent with an historiographically legitimate understanding of the Renaissance as a phenomenon.

Recently, Pirrotta's thesis has elicited negative critical response.[119] Because of the place of Pirrotta's findings in the collective understanding of the problem

---

[119]See, for example, Margaret Bent, "Humanists and Music, Music and Humanities," *Tendenze e metodi nella ricerca musicologica: atti del Convegno internazionale: Latina, 27–29 settembre 1990* (Florence: L.S. Olschki, 1995), 29–38; Reinhard Strohm, *The Rise of European Music, 1380–1500* (Cambridge: Cambridge University Press, 1993); James Haar, review of Strohm, *The Rise of European Music*, *Renaissance Quarterly* 50 (1997): 647–48; Bent, "Music and the Early Veneto Humanists," *Proceedings of the British Academy; 1998 Lectures and Memoirs* (1999): 101–30; Bent, "Singers of Polyphony in Padua and Vicenza around Pietro Emiliani and Francesco Malipiero," *Beyond 50 Years of Ars Nova Studies at Certaldo. 1959–2009. Atti del Convegno internazionale di Studi. Certaldo, 12–14 giugno 2009*, ed. Francesco Zimei and Agostino Ziino (Lucca: Libreria Musicale Italiana, forthcoming); Reinhard Strohm, "Neue Aspekte von Musik und Humanismus im 15. Jahrhundert," *Acta Musicologica* 76, no. 2 (2004): 135–57; Strohm, *Guillaume du Fay, Martin le Franc und die humanistische Legende der Musik*, (Winterthur: Amadeus, 2007); and Strohm, "Music, Humanism, and the Idea of a 'Rebirth' of the Arts," *Music as Concept and Practice in the Late Middle Ages*, ed. Strohm and Bonnie J. Blackburn (Oxford: Oxford University Press, 2001), 346–88. For a summation of the scholarly conversation, see Giovanni Zanovello, "Les humanistes florentins et la polyphonie liturgique," *Poétiques de la Renaissance. Le modèle italien, le monde franco-bourguignon et leur héritage en France au XVIe siècle*, ed. Perrine Galand-Hallyn and Fernand Hallyn (Geneva: Librairie Droz, 2001), 625–38 and 667–73, especially 625–26 and nn. 197–99 and the secondary literature cited there. Another important contribution to the scholarly discussion is Rob C. Wegman, *The Crisis of Music in Early Modern Europe, 1470–1530* (New York: Routledge, 2005). I myself shall contribute to the scholarly debate on the musico-historiographic problem of the Renaissance in a forthcoming article entitled "The Renaissance in Music-Historical Thought: A Century of Interpretation," a title borrowed, respectfully, from Wallace Ferguson's classic study.

he addresses, and also because his article is—to my knowledge—one of his few publications to provoke credible challenge, the critical reception demands most respectful consideration.

In my view, Pirrotta's thesis is more persuasive than the critique of it, and to say so does not imply that I do not have the greatest respect for the seriousness of the critique. It is merely that I find it less convincing than Pirrotta's original argument.

Various elements of the challenge—in particular the terminology employed in framing the argument—suggest something of a misalignment of the presentation of Pirrotta's thesis with his own. A careful decoding of the language of the critique and a juxtaposition of it with Pirrotta's presentation—a careful consideration of the extent to which the critical characterization of his thesis is actually supported by the texts and word usage of his own publications—suggests (to me, at least) that the presentation of his argument in the critque thereof is not fully consistent with his.

There are more up-to-date contributions to this scholarly conversation, therefore. But in matters of interpretation, more up-to-date does not necessarily mean more correct or more persuasive; it may simply mean more recent. There are numerous instances in the history of scholarship in which the initial formulation of a problem is then challenged by a new generation of scholars; later still, a systematic reconsideration of the matter suggests that the initial formulation was likelier to be correct: more informed, more successful in sensitively interpreting the underlying primary data, more authoritative.

My own independent review of the primary sources—and of the musicological literature interpreting them, and of the scholarly literature on the historiographic problem of the Renaissance more generally—suggests to me that this is the situation in this instance: Pirrotta's original thesis is likelier—indeed, far likelier—to be correct. To say so is not necessarily to be unresponsive to new interpretations; it may be nothing other than a difference of scholarly opinion.

*****

"Music and Cultural Tendencies" also establishes a framework for an understanding of the achievement of Josquin Desprez, the subject of one of Pirrotta's encyclopedia entries, written simultaneously with "Music and Cultural Tendencies." In contrast with the image of Josquin in American or German scholarship, that which emerges from Pirrotta's article is distinctive; we might characterize it as an Italianate image, in that the presentation of the composer's profile is determined by the perspectives of a writer conversant with the Italian context for much of Josquin's career.

The Josquin Masses are said to exemplify an aesthetic in which the voices maintain the character of continuous flux, scarcely interrupted by pauses, regulated by a preestablished order given to the tenor or some other *prius-factus* element, but all concentrated on the linear unfolding of the *superius* voice, delicate, elegant[,] and majestic, but little observant of the dialectic of the text beyond the assertion of a general ethos.

When we read this passage against the background of many cited earlier, where Pirrotta sought to capture the characteristics of the early-fifteenth-century "parody" mass, for example, their shared references to the role of the tenor as *prius factus* element make it clear that, in Pirrotta's view, Josquin's contributions to the Mass literature are faithful to practices established in the High Middle Ages.

He has a very different understanding of Josquin's contributions to the motet literature, which are characterized as the "manifestations of a personality in which completely acquired technical mastery is now ... subordinated to the exigencies of a superior poetic sense."[120]

As Pirrotta suggested in "Musical and Cultural Tendencies," Josquin Desprez thus transformed the basis of polyphonic composition, tempering reflections in it of a medieval "culture of technicality" and minimizing a dependence on the tradition of the *trobar clus*, thus rendering it more expressive of the text. In short, Josquin's innovative aesthetic represents a rapprochement between the architectonic practices of the medieval polyphonists and the literary concerns of the Italian Renaissance humanists.

*****

During his years at Harvard, Pirrotta published additional important papers on the music of the Italian Renaissance. One, "On Text Forms from Ciconia to Dufay,"[121] again reveals his conversance with an understanding of poetic form. Another, "Two Anglo-Italian Pieces in the Manuscript Porto 714,"[122] is a further demonstration of his familiarity with literary history.

---

[120]"Asserting with his works (and perhaps also with his teaching) the intrinsic expressive capacity of music, D[esprez]. opened the way to a consideration of the text that is humanistic, not in the sense of a rigorous observance of accents and quantities but in the sense of ... the expressive integration of word and music. ... In great part, the stylistic transformation also depends on the poetic conception of the music. For the continuous flow of fifteenth-century polyphony, ruled by a preestablished order (under the form of the tenor or some other *prius-factus* element), and—even in the variety of the particulars—by a stasis of expression, is substituted a succession and differentiation of expressive moments, a dialectic ... articulated in the transitions and contrasts between chordal and contrapuntal episodes, and which tend in these last towards accentuating the elaboration of each episode's characteristic themes. ... [H]is having given an example of a new relationship counts even more, which on the one hand modified the traditional attitude of the polyphonists—often embroiled in the culture of technicality and the *trobar clus* of musical allusions and citations – and on the other ... succeeded in making a breach in the literary prejudices of humanistic culture, still reflected by Cortese, notwithstanding his praise of Despres." **1966:** "Despres, Josquin (Després, Desprez, Des Prez, ecc.; Josquinus o Jodocus Pratensis, a Prato, ecc.; Juschino, Josse, ecc.)."

[121]**1966:** "On Text Forms from Ciconia to Dufay."

[122]**1970:** "Two Anglo-Italian Pieces in the Manuscript Porto 714."

The second also illustrates that oft-attested ability to exploit the tiniest bit of evidence and that oft-attested command of the primary material that permit such tiny bits of evidence to catch the eye in the first place. In this case, the evidence is the use of two quatrains of an obscure multistrophic poem (one the opening quatrain, one an interior quatrain) by the obscure Ferrarese poet Girolamo Nigrisoli ("Hyeronimus Nigrisolius edidit. Ferraria condolens de recessu inlustrissime Isotte, nymphe estensis") in polyphonic settings by the obscure English composer Galfridus ("Galfridus de Anglia").

The identification of the poem as Nigrisoli's, his very obscurity, his status as Ferrarese, and the further identification of the subject matter as an homage to Isotta d'Este—Niccolò III d'Este's daughter and Leonello and Borso d'Este's sister—permit Pirrotta to posit that "the Porto manuscript ... originated in Ferrara about the middle of the fifteenth century," thus for the first time suggesting a provenance and approximate date for the manuscript. This in turn becomes the basis for a preliminary reconstruction of Ferrarese musical life of the mid-fifteenth century, a subject to receive comprehensive treatment in the Kinkeldey Award-winning study by Lewis Lockwood, who dedicated his book to Pirrotta.

*****

The understanding of poetic form (and of poetics more fundamentally) also characterizes further reflections on the origins of the Italian madrigal of the sixteenth century[123]—already anticipated in the *M.G.G.* article "Italien"—and a series of important papers on the poetic choices of celebrated Italian madrigalists of the late Cinquecento—Gesualdo, Marenzio, and Monteverdi—which begin to appear during the Harvard years.

The first of these—"Gesualdo da Venosa nel IV centenario della nascita"—merits particular attention for a number of reasons. First, it prompts an additional comment on Pirrotta's absorption in his lifework as a musicologist, as well as an observation about the work ethic that such absorption assumed. How so?

Living in Winchester in 1957 and thereafter, Pirrotta would rise well before dawn so that he might devote uninterrupted time to his work. Pierluigi Petrobelli reported to me that one of the products of that predawn activity

---

[123] **1961**: Contributions to the panel discussion, "From Frottola to Madrigal: The Changing Pattern of Secular Italian Vocal Music," 72–87; see also 123–38 and Example 48 [254–55]. I consider Pirrotta's contributions to the panel discussion following Rubsamen's paper among the most important statements one can read on the origins of the Cinquecento madrigal.

was a substantial body of transcriptions of Cinquecento madrigals that had not yet been transcribed into modern notation and put into score. These transcriptions served Pirrotta in the analyses offered in the papers on Gesualdo,[124] Marenzio, and Monteverdi.

One of the happy consequences of Pirrotta's appointment at Harvard was his access to the riches of the University's library collections. The Houghton Library and Loeb Music Library house early printed editions of compositions by Scipione Cerreto, Alfonso Fontanelli, Carlo Gesualdo, Luca Marenzio, Pomponio Nenna, and other pertinent figures, which served Pirrotta well in his ongoing study of the Cinquecento madrigal.[125]

The early paper on Gesualdo (1961) is notable for other reasons. It is one of Pirrotta's earliest substantial contributions to the literature on the music of the Italian Renaissance, other than encyclopedia entries on Italy and the *intermedio*. It is important, too, because it is yet another document of his continuing involvement with Italian radio, because it was, according to Pirrotta, originally "written and read as a comment to the casting of about 30 pieces, mainly by Gesualdo."[126] Anthony Newcomb has characterized it as "richly informative." It is one of Pirrotta's most significant papers, one of the few that is among his finest and yet has never been translated into English (and, moreover, was published in a relatively inaccessible publication, thus limiting its circulation, whatever the readership's mother tongue[127]).

Finally, it demonstrates a deep conversance with poetic sensibilities in late-Cinquecento Italy, since—as Pirrotta describes them—Gesualdo's poetic choices (and Marenzio's and Monteverdi's) are expressions of personal responses by the composer to the verse he chose to set.

The activity demanded to produce the commentary spawned two further publications, including an encyclopedia entry. Many years later, Pirrotta will

---

[124]In the archives of the Italian state radio system [RAI], there is an unpublished transcription, in Pirrotta's handwriting, of the Luzzasco Luzzaschi madrigali *O primavera*, which may be one of the products of that predawn scholarly activity in the second-floor study at 6 Fells Road in Winchester, Massachusetts. See Roberto Giuliani, "L'antica musica ridotta alla moderna prattica dell'etere" (see "*Scena 5.ª*," n. 41).

[125]David A. Wood, *Music in Harvard Libraries*. Some holdings of note are the following: Allacci, Leone, pp. 8–9; Artusi, Giovanni Maria, p. 18; Boethius, p. 39; Cerreto, Scipione, p. 54; Croce, Giovanni, p. 70; Desprez, Josquin, pp. 77–78; Doni, Antonio Francesco, p. 81; Doni, Giovanni Battista, pp. 81–82; Fontanelli, Alfonso, p. 95; Gaffurio, Franchino, p. 98; Gagliano, Marco da, pp. 98–99; Galilei, Vincenzo, p. 99; Gasparini, Francesco, p. 101; Gesualdo, Carlo, Principe da Venosa, pp. 103–04; Marenzio, pp. 158–59; Nenna, Pomponio, pp. 183–84; Palestrina, Giovanni Pierluigi da, pp. 188–89; Salieri, Antonio, p. 236; Vecchi, Orazio, p. 266. In addition, the substantial resources of the Isham Memorial Library are to be considered as well, as Iain Fenlon reminded me.

[126]We read in the subsequent publication that "[a]ll the texts published in the present *Quaderno* were broadcast by the 'Terzo Programma' in the first trimester of 1961." **1961:** "Gesualdo da Venosa nel IV centenario della nascita," "MUSICA," 199–216.

[127]I shall shortly publish a translation, to increase its accessibility.

consolidate—in his words, "conflate"—the findings in these several papers into a single study.[128]

As the published, tripartite version of the paper suggests, the broadcast was in three installments: on 2 January, 8 January, and 22 January 1961. Pirrotta's commentary ran to some 60 minutes, the musical performances to almost 80. The commentary is an analysis of the composer's poetics and his entire development as madrigalist, and as a composer more generally. The first installment is entitled—*nota bene*—"The Temptations of Monody." After some preliminaries, Pirrotta observes that

> [i]f the letters of Fontanella [*sic; recte:* "Fontanelli"] help us bring to life the faded image of the Prince of Venosa still to be seen in a painted altarpiece in the Church of Gesualdo, they are even more important for understanding the musician's activity, as it was then emerging.

Pirrotta's objective of recovering the lost human actuality behind the ephemeral vestiges is thus served yet again by contemporary correspondence, evidence that he fully exploits. Within two years, he will produce revised transcriptions of these letters of Alfonso Fontanelli[129] (as will Anthony Newcomb, who will also provide English translations and a commentary). They yield a vivid portrait of Gesualdo the man: the complex, flawed, yet immensely talented human being who made such important contributions to the Cinquecento madrigal.

The first illustration of Gesualdo's poetic sensibilities and their reflection in his music—which, from a musicologist's perspective, is one of the principal objectives—occurs in an analysis of *Baci soavi e cari*, on a text by Guarini. It is emblematic of the entire collection it introduces, dominated by the pastoral tone characteristic of Guarini's contemporary poetic output, which was expressive of Ferrarese court culture more generally. Typically, Gesualdo's response to the gently feigned elegance, softness, and veiled sensuality of Guarini's verse is to renounce contrapuntal artifice and abandon himself instead to an airy melodicity, located above all in the superius voice.[130] The sources of that melodic style are principally Neapolitan: in the compositions of the southerner Pomponio Nenna and also the Modenese composer Orazio Vecchi, whose work furnishes us with examples of the kind of "airy melodicity" Gesualdo invokes.

---

[128]On the broadcast, others' participation in it and their independent framing of the various components (the delivery of Pirrotta's text, the performances), and the complicated history of the various published reflections of Pirrotta's scholarly activity relating to Gesualdo, see Giuliani, "L'antica musica ridotta alla moderna prattica dell'etere," especially 1344–55 (see "Scena 5.ª," n. 41); on 1351–52 n. 155, Giuliani lists the performers involved in the broadcast and furnishes bibliographic information on the extant tapes of the performances. Guiliani's account is indispensable to one's understanding of Pirrotta's involvement with the entire initiative. Pirrotta also furnishes some details on p. VIII of his anthology *Poesia e musica e altri saggi* (see "Scena 5.ª," n. 15).

[129]**1963:** "Gesualdo, Ferrara e Venezia."

[130]Here and in what follows, I am quoting Pirrotta almost verbatim, though in translation.

Fontanelli's letters also provide evidence of Gesualdo as performer on the lute and of an interest on the part of Gesualdo the polyphonist in a practice that was later to develop into a revolutionary style, which music historians call "accompanied monody." That a monodic mode of performance of polyphonic madrigals was always an option is suggested by *Sì gioioso mi fanno*, distinguished by its arioso character and the expressive prevalence of the superius voice. But for various reasons, neither the airy melodicity of the Neapolitan villanella nor the melodic style of the monodies of Giulio Caccini helped Gesualdo realize his artistic objectives. There is an "intensity of accent" in his aesthetic that is rarely encountered in the madrigal, one of the few parallels being that of Giaches de Wert. But neither will Gesualdo be able to model his own madrigals on those of Wert: he abstains from a reliance on the recitative-like arias used by solo singers for the delivery of the *ottave* of epic poetry and finds unacceptable Wert's practice of delegating responsibility to the *performer* for the desired dramatic effect, achieved through an expansion of the music's schematic simplicity. "The Prince of Venosa was aspiring to more artistic solutions to the problem of expressive intensity . . . to solutions that were those of the composer" rather than the performer.

> [T]he Prince...did not share with the most radical of his contemporaries the distrust in the possibilities of the polyphonic language.[131]

The second installment describes the compositional output of Gesualdo's Ferrarese years and identifies the sources of his style during that phase of his activity, which include—on the positive side, first—reflections in a number of Gesualdo's madrigals of the renowned Ferrarese "concerto delle dame."

On the negative side, although the composer's admiration for Luzzasco Luzzaschi is a matter of record, there are stark differences between Luzzaschi's aesthetic and Gesualdo's, which complicate an attempt to relate Gesualdo's style to Luzzaschi's. Luzzaschi exemplified the aesthetic then current at the Ferrarese court: the "hedonism" of Guarino (note Pirrotta's Crocean *linguaggio*) rather than the pathos exemplified by Tasso's verse, the expression of a contrasting aesthetic that proved more attractive to the Prince of Venosa. The dominant tone of Luzzaschi's music is that of a late classicism—of sleeping passions, of beauty regretted—and an example drawn from Gesualdo's third book of madrigals («*Non t'amo*» - *o voce ingrata!*) immediately establishes the contrast in attitudes.

But if the relationship of Gesualdo's art to Luzzaschi's remains unclear, stylistic derivations from another of Cipriano de Rore's pupils, who in the preceding decade had had frequent, intense relations with the Este court—that same Giaches de Wert—are more plausible. Unlike Wert, Gesualdo rarely

---

[131] On this point, Anthony Newcomb concurs with Pirrotta: see "Carlo Gesualdo and a Musical Correspondence of 1594," *Musical Quarterly* 54 (1968): 409-36, especially 417.

set narrative texts; but among the compositions of the Ferrarese period—those of books III and IV—is a "narrative essay," a setting of the text *Spargea la morte*, whose "recitative insistence" manifests affinities with Wert's style.

In the third installment, the scene shifts from Ferrara to Gesualdo's Neapolitan dominions. His mission there was to renew a specifically Neapolitan musical tradition, and it seems likely that during gatherings of his informal salon, the prince would regularly pontificate on a theme of great concern to him and others: the past, present, and future of the musical art. We might identify the essence of Gesualdo's opinions—as they were surely emphatically expressed—in the words *Musica vaga e artificiosa*, the title of an anthology later published by one of the musicians in his employ, the Roman Romano Micheli. The meaning of the adjectives "vaga" and "artificiosa" is clarified by the contemporary Roman gentleman Vincenzo Giustiniani: "Prince Gesualdo of Venosa," Giustiniani wrote,

> began to compose madrigals full of many artifices and exquisite counterpoint, with difficult, beautiful canonic subjects.... And because this refinement of the rules was wont sometimes to make composition hard and difficult, it was necessary to make every effort to choose the subject carefully, for even though there might be difficulties in its composition, the music should be melodious and emerge sweet and fluent.[132]

One of the compositions that most clearly exemplifies Giustiniani's description is *Ardita zanzaretta* of Gesualdo's book VI.

Yet again in this phase of Gesualdo's career we encounter the challenge of articulating affinities with contemporary masters. And yet again we cite Luzzaschi, whose *Seconda scelta* (*Second Selection*) of madrigals was published by Gesualdo's printer, Giangiacomo Carlino, in 1613. An example suggests how much the tone had changed from that of the music Luzzaschi had earlier composed for the duke of Ferrara and his concerto delle dame: analogies with Gesualdo's style are notable in the madrigal *Itene mie querele*. And a relationship with Pomponio Nenna is clearer still.

But the characteristic of this phase of Gesualdo's career that most demands explanation is the composer's disinclination to adopt practices that his great contemporary Monteverdi had by 1605 completely absorbed and regularly deployed: the use of that flexible element of harmonic accompaniment, the *basso continuo*. Pirrotta conjectures that Gesualdo's disinclination is attributable to neither the absence of audacity nor an ostentatious traditionalism. Rather, it was probably a consequence of the composer's habit of mentally "reading" his own music:

---

[132]I have used the translation of MacClintock: 1. Hercole Bottrigari, *Il Desiderio or Concerning the Playing Together of Various Musical Instruments*. 2. Vincenzo Giustiniani, *Discorso sopra la musica*, trans. Carol MacClintock (n.p.: American Institute of Musicology, 1962), 70.

the internal hearing—mental, more intense, sharper, more perfect for the musician than any performance whatsoever—can have attributed psychological resonances ... that to him appeared to obviate the need for the physical resonance of...accompaniment by the *basso continuo*.

*****

Having developed a fruitful methodology—the examination of a composer's poetic choices, as determinative of his aesthetic development writ large—Pirrotta was to apply it to other subsets of the Cinquecento madrigal literature: Marenzio's settings of Tasso's verse, and the corpus of Monteverdi's madrigalistic compositions.

The study of this latter—one of Pirrotta's longest articles—has been translated into English and thus attracted a substantial readership. It contains stimulating observations, at both the microscopic and macroscopic levels: analyses of individual madrigals as well as observations on large-scale developments in general compositional practice and more specifically Monteverdian practice in the madrigal literature.

Among the latter is the qualification of the importance once attributed to the introduction, in the *Quinto Libro*, of the *basso continuo*: a correction of the error of perceiving in it the advent of "a new Monteverdi," monodist and cantata composer, who succeeds the polyphonist and madrigalist of the preceding period. The contraposition, Pirrotta argues, can only seem absurd to anyone who sees in the polyphony and monody of the time, as he does, *parallel* rather than *contrasting* expressions of analogous needs. More absurd still is to attribute a causal value to a development such as the adoption of the *continuo*, which at most was symptomatic of an inner change. Even the outward signs of such a change suggest that it was not a radical renunciation of the past, but, rather, the gradual addition of new interests, needs, and methods.

*****

The Cambridge years also witnessed the publication of Pirrotta's *magnum opus*, the book on the varied uses of music in the Italian Renaissance theater.[133]

---

[133]There was initially some interest on the part of Princeton University Press in publishing the translation, and soon after the appearance of the original Italian edition; moreover, the translation was to be the work of Pirrotta and his son Vincenzo. See Pirrotta's letter to Lewis Lockwood: "[20 May 1971] ... as for the translation of Li due Orfei, the three chapters were available in March (without footnotes), but lately Vincent has been too busy and myself too tired to do anything more. We shall go back to it, some time, but I do not know when." I am grateful to Professor Lockwood for providing me access to this correspondence. The translation was ultimately published by Cambridge University Press almost a decade and a half after the Italian edition appeared. Two letters sent to Iain Fenlon document the phases in the production of the book for Cambridge (I am grateful to Professor Fenlon for sharing these letters and permitting me to quote them): "1st May 1980. ... I had ... started this letter when a parcel arrived from Cambridge U.P., including a list of bibliographical suggestions coming from you, ... I certainly will accept your suggestions, ... I shall be at Princeton from September to January, which will not make the exchange of correspondence and proofs with CUP any easier. Anyway, the end result is what counts and I am encouraged by your good omens"; and "20 March 1981. ... Thank you for your invitation to Cambridge, which we are delighted to accept. We had planned to come Sunday night if Rosemary Dooley thought this could help the preparations for Li due Orfei."

Li due Orfei originated in an invitation from Remo Giazotto to Pirrotta and his coauthor, Elena Povoledo, to prepare a book for E.R.I.—the Edizioni Radiotelevisione Italiana (R.A.I.)—on the so-called Florentine *camerata*. But Pirrotta was skeptical about assigning unusual significance to the *camerata*, and he and his coauthor made a counterproposal: that they instead situate the achievements of the *camerata* within a much broader and deeper context. The book thus became the comprehensive study of the theatrical uses of music in Italy from the very beginnings of the restitution of a tradition of vernacular theater in the late fifteenth century to the beginnings of opera in the early seventeenth.

Pirrotta was eligible for a sabbatical during the fall semester of academic year 1969/70.[134] He and Povoledo had been engaged in research before the beginning of the sabbatical year, as documented by the publication of the chapter on early opera in the Festschrift for Donald Grout in 1968. During much of calendar year 1969 (from the end of academic year 1968/69 until the end of the first semester of academic year 1969/70), Pirrotta was once more in Rome, where he devoted himself to work on *Li due Orfei*.[135]

Only when we read *Li due Orfei* against the background of Pirrotta's entire scholarly record predating 1969 do we appreciate the extent to which it represents an instance of the "scholarship of synthesis,"[136] for which Pirrotta had been preparing for almost two decades. Much of the substance of chapters 1, 2, and 4 is new; but chapter 3 synthesizes and redeploys material from the encyclopedia entry on Banchieri, the paper on the commedia dell'arte and opera, and so recent a study as the entry for *M.G.G.* on the *greghesca*; chapter 5 develops material from two encyclopedia entries on the Renaissance *intermedium* (for the *Enciclopedia dello spettacolo* and *M.G.G.*); and chapter 6 develops and presents material that had been treated in the lectures on Florentine aristocratic opera, the 1963 lecture at the Fondazione Cini on correspondences between Peri's *Euridice* and Monteverdi's *Orfeo*, and the many encyclopedia entries for the *Enciclopedia dello spettacolo* on subjects related to the content of the chapter, among other writings.[137]

---

[134]During the spring semester of that year, Pirrotta resumed his regular teaching schedule at Harvard. In a 19 March 1969 memorandum, Dean of the Faculty of Arts and Sciences Franklin L. Ford approves Pirrotta's request for a leave of absence for fall 1969/70. Pirrotta files, Department of Music, Harvard University.

[135]See Ziino, "Pirrotta between Cambridge and Rome" (see "*Scena 5.ª*," n. 2), especially 41. But Pirrotta was also in Palermo during part of that time: his department chairman writes to him concerning the spring 1970 course schedule on 31 July 1969 and asks if Pirrotta would assume responsibility for Music 215, Studies in Baroque Music, which would necessitate his relinquishing Music 206a, "Secular Works of Josquin." On 14 August 1969, Pirrotta writes to agree, and he in fact taught Music 215 during the spring of 1970. Pirrotta files, Department of Music, Harvard University.

[136]Ernest L. Boyer, *Scholarship Reconsidered: Priorities of the Professoriate* (Princeton, NJ: Carnegie Foundation for the Advancement of Teaching, 1990).

[137]Another of Pirrotta's publications that synthesizes and summarizes the material first presented in the titles cited here is an encyclopedia entry, which is a concise statement: **1966**: "Monodia."

Li due Orfei is also of interest because it is one of Pirrotta's rare authored (rather than edited) monographic publications, in which he sustains the presentation of a thesis over many pages of text, as contrasted with his essays, which are typically concentrated in design and scope. The comprehensiveness of *Li due Orfei* is one of its distinguishing characteristics.

In no other of Pirrotta's publications does the interdisciplinarity of his methodology reveal itself so clearly, largely because it is a document of the scholarship of synthesis. I cite only two examples: the considerations in chapter 6 of the terms and concepts "aria" and "sprezzatura": elusive terms, susceptible to misinterpretation at the hands of a less skilled and knowledgeable critic.

Pirrotta characterizes aria[138] as exemplifying the quality that "any musical entity (although preferably . . . a melodic one) . . . appears to possess as being . . . precisely determined and inflected on an unavoidable course—no matter whether such unavoidability stems from tradition, repetition, and habit or from an inner sense of coherence and finality," and, further, as "the unrestricted and undiverted naturalness of the melody . . . , its 'air' of being entirely self-determined or self-propelled."[139] Numerous contemporary texts, such as those of the "Renaissance" dancing masters—who define "aiere" as "a generally graceful carriage"—are cited to substantiate and illuminate Pirrotta's definition.[140]

More recently, Martha Feldman—like Pirrotta before her—interpreted the concept of the "most esteemed, elusive, and mystical appellation of 'aria'" as ultimately Platonistic in origin, as possessing "an ineffable expressive power endowed with the Neoplatonic force located in the realm of the suprasensual."[141] In Pirrotta's words, "for each melody" there was stipulated "the necessity of a course determined by a model in the world of Platonic ideas."

Such observations occur in the context of a discussion about the efficacy of the *basso continuo* in Florentine aristocratic opera, the minimalist, largely improvised instrumental accompaniment designed expressly so as to be

---

[138]See also my discussion of Pirrotta's article "Fourteenth-Century Monophonic Song" in my "Scena 4.*a*," above, and the sources cited there.

[139]Elsewhere his definition is as follows: "a somewhat indefinable quality . . . alluding to the sense one had, listening to certain compositions, that they were taking place, phrase after phrase, with a coherent sense of direction, with a determination that was seeming to launch inevitably towards a precise objective with a will that was seeming to be more properly of the sonorous material than the composer." See **1994:** "Maniera e riforme nella musica italiana del '500," especially 123; and my "Musical References in Brucioli's *Dialogi* and Their Classical and Medieval Antecedents," *Journal of the History of Ideas* 71 (2010): 169–90, especially n. 50 and the accompanying text.

[140]See Otto Gombosi, "About Dance and Dance Music in the Late Middle Ages," *Musical Quarterly* 27 (1941): 289–305, especially 298.

[141]Feldman, "The Courtesan's Voice: Petrarchan Lovers, Pop Philosophy, and Oral Traditions," in *The Courtesan's Arts: Cross-Cultural Perspectives*, ed. Feldman and Bonnie Gordon (New York: Oxford University Press, 2006), 105–23, especially 114.

"entirely subservient to the 'aria' of the vocal part." The quality of aria, in turn, is contrasted with the melodic properties of the "many lines of a polyphonic composition," which "usually lacked an aria." Girolamo Mei, whom Pirrotta characterizes as "the real mentor of the so-called camerata,"

> perceived that no ethos was possible ... for each one of the single lines as long as they were determined by the polyphonist's combinatory criteria and not by their inner coherence to a mode.[142] We have only to replace the word "mode" by "air" ... to go back to our starting point.

The discussion thus represents a comprehensive treatment of matters first addressed a decade and a half earlier, in the series of lectures and encyclopedia entries on the camerata.[143] An aria is a melodic entity with a "countenance," "features that give ... individual physiognomy," "behaviour ... determined by ... intrinsic nature and acquired habits."

The concept of "sprezzatura"—similarly quintessentially Italianate in character—is related to that of aria. In contemporary texts, it, too, is invoked to suggest a distinctive kind of comportment, marked by "the apparently inborn spontaneity and relaxed self-confidence that must characterize the performance of the perfect courtier, no matter how difficult his task," "the self-assurance of the accomplished performer," thus revealing a Platonistic influence. Applied to music, the term came to signify "the intangible elements of rhythmic buoyancy and dynamic flexibility of the performance."

The discussion of these terms is yet another instance of that phenomenon in Pirrotta's writings, where his absorption and deployment of Crocean Idealist sensibilities and nomenclature were seen to operate at two different levels: the one "methodological" or "epistemological," where he feels free to indulge in a more intuitive and less Positivistic apprehension of the factual material, the other "substantive," where an Italianate, Crocean sensibility informs his analysis of the music per se and inflects his articulation of its defining properties. In this case, his analysis leaves us with an appreciation for the fundamentally Italianate and Crocean character of the concepts of aria and *sprezzatura*, especially as contrasted with the properties of the melodies of vocal polyphony. When so deployed, to characterize melodic style and performativity, such terms as "unavoidability," "naturalness," "buoyancy," "countenance," "individual physiognomy," "inborn spontaneity," and "flexibility" are redolent of Crocean philosophy, when juxtaposed with the terms invoked to characterize the inevitable effects on melodic style of the "polyphonist's combinatory criteria." An Italian musicologist invokes the speech

---

[142]Pirrotta recapitulates this important observation in **1986**: "Problemi di una storia della musica."
[143]See my "*Scena 5.ª*," above.

of Italian Idealist philosophers to capture the defining properties of a quintessentially Italianate musical repertory.

*****

On 6 November 1970, at the annual national meeting of the American Musicological Society in Toronto, Pirrotta was awarded the Society's Otto Kinkeldey Memorial Prize for *Li due Orfei*, identified as "the most distinguished book by a member of the Society published in 1969,"[144] which was announced at the 7 December 1970 meeting of the music department faculty at Harvard.[145]

Just over a year later, on 31 December 1971, Pirrotta will retire from teaching at Harvard and return to Italy.

---

[144]*AMS Newsletter. American Musicological Society* 1 (January 15, 1971): 3.
[145]Forbes, *A History of Music at Harvard*, 173 n. 110.

Scena 8.ᵃ

The Università degli Studi di Roma, «La Sapienza» (1972–78)

In 1971, Pirrotta was not insensitive to the call of his homeland and the possibility that was being presented to him of assuming the chair in the Faculty of Letters and Philosophy at the University of Rome, held until then by the illustrious Professor Ronga.[1]

These words—written when Nino Pirrotta was awarded the Premio "Antonio Feltrinelli"—give his reasons for resigning from Harvard on 31 December 1971 and returning to his native land as Professore Ordinario di Storia della Musica at the University of Rome. Pirrotta was indeed "not insensitive to the call of his homeland." Before retiring from teaching altogether, he wished to have Italian as well as American pupils and to play a greater role in Italian musicological life. And in 1971, there was a greater institutional commitment to the musicological enterprise in Italy than in 1956 and a more substantial Italian musicological tradition. Pirrotta rightly aspired to playing a significant part in making that enterprise and tradition even more robust.

There were more mundane considerations in the decision as well. American academic practices being what they then were, Pirrotta—who would have

---

[1]"Antonino Pirrotta," *Premi "Antonio Feltrinelli" 1983* (Accademia Nazionale dei Lincei), 69. On the return to Rome, see also "Laurea 'honoris causa' a Nino Pirrotta," 10 (see "*Prologo*," n. 36), and *Dizionario enciclopedico universale della musica e dei musicisti* (see "Scena 1.ᵃ," n. 35).

been 65 in 1973—would soon have reached retirement age and left Harvard in any event, whereas Italian practice permitted him to teach until age 70 (1978).²

Thus Pirrotta, a dedicated teacher, availed himself of the opportunity created by Luigi Ronga's retirement. The vacancy in the chair, Pirrotta's success in the 1956 *concorso*, his availability: all these eliminated the need for a new selection procedure, and he was readily confirmed as Ronga's successor.³

Pirrotta's Harvard departmental colleagues were anxious to explore the possibility with the University administration that he be permitted to teach there until he was 70, but Pirrotta declined, on grounds that the negotiations with the «Sapienza» had by then progressed to the point where he was "already too far committed."⁴

Therefore, as of 1 January 1972, Antonino Pirrotta became Professore Ordinario di Storia della Musica in the Facoltà di Lettere e Filosofia at the Università degli Studi di Roma, «La Sapienza», although due to a bureaucratic complication he did not actually begin teaching there until the fall semester of academic year 1972/73.⁵

---

²For informing me of these considerations, I am grateful to Professor D'Accone: A.M. Cummings interview with D'Accone, 2009 annual national meeting of the American Musicological Society, Philadelphia. Also, see some correspondence between Pirrotta and Lewis Lockwood: "[28 September 1971]...I had in Rome the visit of Frau [Ursula] Guenther and worked with her [on] a Paolo da Firenze volume for my Ars nova edition.... [T]here is a possibility that I am called to take Ronga's succession in Rome. Although I have mixed feelings about this.... I'll go if they ask me, since I am nearing retirement here. But this might mean that I will be faced with the move at mid year." I am grateful to Professor Lockwood for the use of the letter.

Note the reference to a projected sixth volume of the edition of the *Trecento* repertory, to contain the music of Paolo *tenorista* and be coedited with Ursula Günther, which, alas, was never to appear. In a 1993 reprint of vol. 3 of Pirrotta's edition of that repertory, he expresses his regret at "never reaching beyond vol. V of CMM 8" and reports that "[t]wo more volumes were at one time near completion." He concludes with a touching reminiscence of Armen Carapetyan.

For a brief history of the music department at the «Sapienza» and the effect of Pirrotta's arrival there after his tenure at Harvard, see Pierluigi Petrobelli, http://rmcisadu.let.uniroma1.it/glotto/archivio/testi/Petrobelli-Grandi Scuole.html

³On 30 October 1971, Pirrotta wrote to Lewis Lockwood: "The 'facoltà' in Rome has unanimously voted that they want me there."

⁴See the following memoranda in the Pirrotta folder in the Department of Music, Harvard University; in reverse chronological order:

"HARVARD UNIVERSITY / FACULTY OF ARTS AND SCIENCES / OFFICE OF THE DEAN.... June 23, 1972 / Professor Nino Pirrotta / ... / John T. Dunlop"

"HARVARD UNIVERSITY / FACULTY OF ARTS AND SCIENCES / OFFICE OF THE DEAN.... January 24, 1972 / Dear Tillman: / ... / John T. Dunlop"

"November 9, 1971 / Dean John T. Dunlop / .../ David G. Hughes...."

"November 2, 1971 / Faculty Memorandum—... A. Tillman Merritt / Chairman"

⁵For clarification of the chronology of Pirrotta's "re-entry" into the Italian academic world, I am grateful to his daughter Dott.ssa Silvia Pirrotta-Giuffré and her son Dott. Mario Giuffré.

*****

The larger musicological community is the unintended beneficiary of Italian pedagogical practices of the time: Italian university professors typically prepared "textbooks"—*dispense*—for their students, which were inexpensively photocopied. One of Pirrotta's textbooks for Rome developed into his book on Don Giovanni,[6] and two others were devoted to the Italian madrigal[7] and the beginnings of opera.[8] As Pirrotta noted,[9] he was principally an essayist, even a miniaturist, not ordinarily inclined—with the notable exception of *Li due Orfei*—toward comprehensive published statements concerning the large-scale scholarly problems that engaged him. We are fortunate, therefore, to have his narratives on the madrigal and early opera, which are expressed in an accessible style, synthetic in character, their objective being to state—for Italian "undergraduates"—their author's fundamental theses concerning these two quintessential manifestations of Italian musical culture. They are valuable, too, because in them we catch glimpses of Pirrotta the teacher: of what his courses entailed, of their intellectual emphases and his pedagogical priorities.[10]

*****

The reminiscences of his Italian pupils are also valuable in attempting to understand Pirrotta's pedagogical practices at the «Sapienza». Two laureates in letters who are especially closely identified with him—Fabrizio Della Seta[11] and Franco Piperno[12]—recall his techniques and methods as teacher.

Piperno characterized Pirrotta's teaching. At one end of a continuum were the large classes for "undergraduates," who need not have had any particular professional interest in the study of music. Such courses enrolled some 30 to 40 students and were taught in the lecture hall at the «Sapienza» now known as the Aula «Nino Pirrotta»; they addressed the subjects of Pirrotta's *dispense*: the madrigal, the beginnings of opera, musical treatments of the Don Juan legend.

Then there were seminars on more specialized topics, which typically enrolled some four to six students. They focused on some of the same topics

---

[6]**1974**: *Don Giovanni in Musica;* **1994**: *Don Giovanni's Progress.*
[7]**1972**: *Introduzione al Madrigale.*
[8]**1973**: *Storia dell'Opera dalle Origini al 1645.*
[9]See Pirrotta's foreword to *Music and Culture in Italy from the Middle Ages to the Baroque* (see "*Intermedio I.$\underline{mo}$*," n. 144).
[10]These two textbooks are understandably quite inaccessible, and I am grateful to Professor Agostino Ziino and Dott.ssa Paola Granata-Ziino for furnishing me with access to the copies in their possession.
[11]*Dottore in Lettere*, 1975, University of Rome; see http://musicologia.unipv.it/organizzazione/personale/curricula/dellaseta.html.
[12]On Piperno, see http://www.disas.unifi.it/CMpro-v-p-480.html.

treated in the large lectures (the madrigal, the operas of Cavalli, Landi, and Marazzoli), as well as musical paleography and fifteenth- and sixteenth-century music.

Finally, there were the formal exercises for students pursuing the laurea in music, both qualifying examinations and the handicraft tutoring for students writing the *tesi*. During the tutoring sessions, Pirrotta would refer to the relevant bibliography, check the aspiring laureate's transcriptions into modern notation, discuss specific problems in the subject area (such as the realization of the *basso continuo*), and address other such matters.

In bearing, Pirrotta tended to be professorial, especially in the large lecture courses. His presentation was enlivened with atmospheric illustrations, suggestive of his learning and historical imagination. In the examinations for the laurea, he could appear serious, even stern. Above all, he appeared to his Italian pupils to be utterly absorbed in his musicological ruminations.

Piperno recounts that, due in great part to Pirrotta's presence, there was a notable increase in musicological activity in Italy and a corresponding enhancement of Italy's place within the international musicological enterprise. Pirrotta's intellectual sensibilities and professional methodologies contrasted with those of his predecessor, Luigi Ronga, a Crocean Idealist who practiced aesthetic interpretation and critical judgment. Pirrotta, on the other hand, emphasized not only the page of music and the theory that could be employed to elucidate it, but also such signature concerns as the unwritten tradition and the utility of interdisciplinary approaches, which revealed the effects of his training in art history as thereafter applied to the history of music. And during Pirrotta's time at the «Sapienza», medieval, Renaissance, and seventeenth-century music became *the* topics of musicological investigation.

However, notwithstanding the nature of his training in art history, Pirrotta's approach to the act of transcription was always "more musical than philological," in Piperno's judgment; the music that Pirrotta studied was a "living thing." He possessed refined and developed musical abilities, acumen, and sensitivities.

*****

Pirrotta's publications from the period of his tenure at the University of Rome are notable for three principal defining characteristics:

1. A return to themes addressed earlier, which are now subjected to more detailed and systematic treatment ("Ars musica," "Su alcuni testi italiani di composizioni polifoniche quattrocentesche");
2. the extension of several "intellectual/programmatic trajectories" established earlier ("Ricercari e variazioni su 'O rosa bella,'" "Note su Marenzio e il Tasso"); and

3. an expansion of the range of interests to include seventeenth-century Italian instrumental music ("Studi corelliani") and Ottocento opera[13] ("Semiramis e Amneris, Un anagramma o quasi," the first in a noteworthy series).

*****

"Ars musica"[14] afforded Pirrotta occasion to return to material treated in "Dante *musicus*" and treat it more fully. As was characteristic of his method, he situated the music within the broadest possible intellectual context, which provided him with the terms for its explication.

Pirrotta's theme—inspired by the contributions of colleagues at the conference where he originally delivered "Ars musica"—was the significant role numerical proportions played in both music and architecture. It thus seemed appropriate to him to return to the source that had initially inspired this "cult of proportions": *ars musica*, the expression with which the Middle Ages indicated, not the practical activity of making music, nor its aesthetic values, but a theoretical discipline. The exposition of *ars musica* began by recalling its inventors and the paradigmatic sources identified with them: the classical and patristic texts of Pythagoras and Tubalcain, where the discipline was first systematically elaborated. Pythagoras and Tubalcain were the inventors, not of *sounding* music, of course, but of the philosophical consideration thereof, of the intellectual reflection on it. Thus the discourse immediately leads—not to the playing, singing, or composition of music, nor to dancing—but to findings resulting from that distinctive mode of engagement.

In this sense, music is one of the Quadrivia, an interpretation consistent with a tradition that goes back for the most part to Boethius. Music is a discipline in the Quadrivium inasmuch as it is one of the mathematical arts. It is therefore accompanied by arithmetic, which is the science of number per se, and geometry and astronomy, which are instead the sciences of the "multitudo ad aliquid": of number *applied* to "something." The *aliquid* ("something") of music is of immense scale, so immense, in fact, that music could almost have claimed to have been first among the disciplines of its category, given that it embraces essentially the entire universe. The recognition of the existence of precise numeric relationships and correspondences underlying the sonorous fact—of "coaptatio"—seemed to furnish the key to explaining the universe, the harmony of the entire cosmos. Such relationships articulated

---

[13]During his years as a journalist, however, Pirrotta had authored any number of music-critical pieces on Ottocento opera; see Cummings and Eiche, "Nino Pirrotta's Early Music-Critical Writings"(see "*Scena 1.ª*," n. 69).

[14]**1973:** "Ars musica." Some of the same material treated in the article is also treated in **1993:** *O tu chara sciença*.

the distances between planets, and analogous concepts were applied to the succession of the seasons and the union and coexistence of body and soul.

It was natural that the concept would then be applied to musical composition, but it was also transferred to architecture. And it was in the twelfth century that those revolutionary developments occurred that most clearly illustrate the relationship between music and architecture, in their common indebtedness to numerical proportion. For it was the twelfth century that witnessed that "application of number not only to the various sounds and dimensions of the bodies that produce them, but also their duration in time":

> at a certain point polyphony proper began to abandon the free, flexible, oratorical rhythm of the liturgical chant and instead adopt a rhythm based on regularity.

In the terms of the modern musician's lexicon, number began to be applied to rhythm (pitch duration) as well as to pitch, and both were now unambiguously quantified.

The relationship of *ars musica* to scholasticism is already evident in music's status as one of the Quadrivia. But in the second part of his paper, Pirrotta returns to a relationship earlier explored in "Dante *musicus*" and now considered more systematically: the relationship of "Gothicism" as an aesthetic ideal to scholasticism. Pirrotta relates the "harnessing of a strong and joyous rhythmic thrust within a system regulated by insistent symmetries and repetitions" "to the conquest and discipline of space ... in Gothic architecture." In both processes, although "the steps are gradual" (there are discrete "phases of the rhythmic conquest of time," just as in the conquest of space), the correspondences between them are profound, in that Magister Leoninus's

> *Magnus liber organi* composed for Nôtre-Dame of Paris is like *a sonorous cathedral, which one wished to create in parallel to the cathedral of stone* [emphasis added].[15]

Pirrotta concludes his paper with ruminations that remind his readers of his coming of age at the moment when the debate between Italian Positivism and spiritualist reactions thereto was at its most urgent: He contrasts his own varied personal responses to the Gregorian chant, the one more "mystical" and susceptible to the chant's "expressivity" counterposed against the other, deriving from an intellectual understanding of the chant's centonate construction. And he acknowledges the satisfactions and validity of both, of entrusting oneself to a "mystical" experience of the chant as well as "analyzing and clarifying [it] philologically."

---

[15]See also **1993**: "Natura e problemi del testo musicale."

*****

If "Music and Cultural Tendencies in 15th-Century Italy" had sought to explain the "polyphonic production gap" of the mid-Quattrocento, Pirrotta now seeks—in "Su alcuni testi italiani di composizioni polifoniche quattrocentesche"[16]—to describe the full-scale revival of a tradition of Italian secular polyphony toward the end of the fifteenth century.

However, his more immediate objective is to classify the 23 Italian-texted polyphonic compositions in the north-Italian[17] manuscript Escorial IV.a.24:

> [B]ut only a series of careful and minute stylistic examinations could give us the opportunity of distinguishing—among the compositions on Italian texts—those that conform to general tendencies of international polyphony, and those others—if indeed there are any of them—that suggest some more specifically Italian characteristic.

The manuscript is in three repertorial layers, and the Italian-texted compositions of the first indeed manifest a "retrospective direction" (the "general tendencies of international polyphony"); but "the eight compositions of the third . . . do not betray the expectation of novelty" ("some more specifically Italian characteristic"). Two of them, *Hora may che fora sono* and *Fate darera* are—text and music—"authentic ballate, but of a popular tone and style and dramatic immediacy that stand in decided contrast with the amorous sentimentalities of the majority of the ballate of the first group."

Pirrotta's conversance with Italian poetic tradition permits him to make such discriminations, and his distinctions among repertorial layers afford the principal conclusion to be drawn from his study: that

> the decade 1470–80 was probably the time of the decisive turning point, subsequent to which international polyphony—which for several decades had dominated in Italian musical codices[,] almost without opposition . . . —began to recede and make way for decidedly national forms.[18]

What typified those "decidedly national forms"?

> The reprise of Italian polyphonic activity was not determined by *ars-novistic* restitutions (present during the entire preceding period, and—they, too—destined to fade), but by suggestions of a different musical practice, which it would be equivocal to define as popular, because it was welcomed and accepted in every social stratum.

---

[16]**1973**: "Su alcuni testi italiani. . . ."

[17]But for an argument that the manuscript is Neapolitan rather than northern, see Allan W. Atlas, *Music at the Aragonese Court of Naples* (Cambridge: Cambridge University Press, 1985), 118–19 n. 12.

[18]Pirrotta returns synoptically to this formulation in **1989**: "Un intermedio campestre."

It would also be too simplistic to identify with one person, Leonardo Giustinian, that "different musical practice," which Pirrotta loved to call the unwritten tradition of music, and which, until that moment, had not been reflected in the polyphonic codices. For there were other renowned practitioners of the tradition, several of whom are represented in Escorial. There is a setting of verse (*Hora cridar oymè*) by the Veronese poet Leonardo Montagna,[19] who was "sensibly younger" than Giustinian, and of *Morte o mercé* by the Spaniard Johannes Cornago, who was associated with the Aragonese court of Naples. And the Florentine Filippo Scarlatti copied the texts of *Hora may che fora sono* and *Fate darera* into his notebook.

Up to this point, Pirrotta has restricted himself to a consideration of the texts, but he wished to undertake a rapid examination of the musical settings in Escorial of these two last compositions to determine whether they could have been the very ones that Filippo Scarlatti included in his own musical repertory. The answer is uncertain with respect to *Hora may che fora sono*: first, the superius part (the only one provided with text) has too high a tessitura for a man's voice (even if we accept that there were not then, and were not to be for some time, precise norms regarding pitch); nor would it have been possible to transpose the composition downward without compelling the contratenor bassus to descend to an unusual register for the time. Moreover, the execution on an accompanying instrument of the three lower voices of the customary four would have been unthinkable.[20]

However, all such difficulties are eliminated if the singer accompanying himself on the lute were restricted to the cantus and tenor parts alone, which form the necessary and sufficient nucleus of the composition. The hypothesis that a version for two voices was accepted by lutenist singers in practice finds confirmation in *Fate darera*, which is for two voices; otherwise, it is stylistically very close to *Hora may*.

Pirrotta has thus recovered two precious vestiges of the unwritten tradition, instances of the retrospective inclusion of such compositions in late-fifteenth-century manuscripts of secular polyphony. Moreover, he has described the earliest stages of the rapprochement forged between Quattrocento humanists and the polyphonic tradition of the European Middle Ages, a subject to which he will return in "'Maniera' polifonica e immediatezza recitativa."[21]

---

[19]G. Biadego, "Leonardo di Agostino Montagna letterato veronese del secolo XV," *Il Propugnatore*, n.s., 6, no. 1 (1893): 295–350, and 6, no. 2, 39–111. See **1973**: "Su alcuni testi italiani di composizioni polifoniche quattrocentesche," Pirrotta's n. 20, for justification of the attribution of the text to «Dni Leonardi Montanæ Veronensis»; the musical setting is unattributed.

[20]On *Hora may*, see now the detailed treatment and edition in Atlas, 119 and n. 13, 144–46, 220–21, and 236.

[21]**1995**: "'Maniera' polifonica e immediatezza recitativa."

*****

Two other articles of the «Sapienza» years continue established "intellectual/ programmatic trajectories." They invoke a methodology pioneered previously and now applied to a new and different "data set."

"Ricercari e variazioni su 'O rosa bella'"[22] is another installment in the series dedicated to recapturing elusive oral, "dialectic" musical practices: the siciliana, the viniziana (or giustiniana), the napoletana.[23] It also relates to "Su alcuni testi italiani di composizioni polifoniche quattrocentesche" and even to "Ars musica," as is evident in the opening sentences, where Pirrotta describes the fifteenth-century humanist's conviction that in order to restore that fabled ancient situation in which every man practiced singing and instrumental playing, it would be necessary to rely—not on the Quadrivium's *ars musica*—but on natural gifts and instinctive resources, as expressed in the popular musical tradition.

O rosa bella—only the most famous example of a kind of poetry celebrated as giustiniane, which need not have been by Leonardo Giustinian himself— and other verse like it was set polyphonically by trans-Alpine composers, which raises the question of whether such non-Italian composers sought to record their impressions in polyphonic language of soloistic performance of those texts characteristic of "unlearned" musicians.

If so, the settings had to reflect two different types of performance: (1) one in which the greater length of the text dictated rapid recitation; and (2) another in which the text's brevity permitted vocal effusion.

In the case of the longer poems, the music functioned as the text's formal vehicle, which, however, neither excluded the possibility of a distinct melodic individuality nor prevented it from adding to the expressive result, provided only that it unfolded rapidly. This, of course, minimized the possibility of indulging in effusions.[24]

Representative of the second category were strambotti, which presumably had tunes in a sober rhythm and arioso design, alternating recitative and extended vocalization; the principal emphasis must have been on fully developed melody rather than a recitative-like setting of the text.

---

[22]1972: "Ricercari e variazioni su 'O rosa bella.'"

[23]In addition to the installments identified in the previous chapter, the series also includes **1994:** "Echi di arie veneziane del primo Quattrocento?"

[24]This distinction is echoed in David Fallows, "Leonardo Giustinian and Quattrocento Polyphonic Song," in *L'edizione critica tra testo musicale e testo lettarario. Atti del Convegno internazionale, Cremona, 4–8 ottobre 1992* (Lucca: Libreria Musicale Italiana, 1995), 247–60, especially 255, but without reference to Pirrotta's article, which Fallows certainly knew.

O rosa bella exemplifies the second of these categories, which may have reflected the singing of short lyrical ballate, or even strambotti. In the fifteenth century, *O rosa bella* itself was widely celebrated as a well-known "ayre": at a banquet given in Rome in 1473 by Cardinal Pietro Riario it "was sung to a small guitar" ("cantosse in uno chitarino 'o rosa bella'").[25] Thus to the usual elements of the "contenance angloise," *O rosa bella*'s English composer (whether Bedyngham or Dunstable) may have added—always consistent with the rules of art polyphony, of course—an emulation of the expressive effectiveness achieved in less "regular" ways by performers of the "Giustinian type." The composition's memorable melodic properties may thus be understood as a possible response to Italianate influences.

*****

Similarly, in "Note su Marenzio e il Tasso,"[26] Pirrotta applies to a new data set—Marenzio's madrigals—the technique pioneered in the 1961 article on Gesualdo and developed in the 1968 article on Monteverdi's poetic choices, in both of which he describes the composers' poetic sensibilities as documented in their selection of contemporary verse set polyphonically.

*****

In two of Pirrotta's articles from the years at the «Sapienza», we observe him in a different scholarly guise: as a student of Seicento instrumental music (his published scholarly writings are principally on vocal music) and of post-Seicento opera.

"Studi corelliani"[27] is a critical evaluation of the proceedings of a conference on the music of virtuoso violinist and composer Arcangelo Corelli. Its principal interest is twofold. First, it contains one of the most explicit discussions of methodology yet seen in Pirrotta's work, since he was not given to extended public ruminations on contrasting scholarly methodologies, especially—as here—when there is a difference between Italian and non-Italian sensibilities. His classification of the proceedings reveals the effects of his absorption—decades earlier—in a Crocean, Italianate philosophy of history, in which historical developments are to be fully contextualized and abstract constructions derived therefrom (such as "classicity") are somewhat suspect. Pirrotta writes:

> Two of the presentations delivered at the congress not only hinted at, but even insisted upon, a generally-accepted concept, that of the classicity of Corelli. Now,

---

[25] See also the entry **1963**: "Rom. C. Spätmittelalter und Renaissance."
[26] **1973**: "Note su Marenzio e il Tasso."
[27] **1972**: "Studi corelliani."

in a certain sense this is a legitimate concept, but also a dangerous one, because it tends just a bit to create a "portrait medallion," to place particular attention upon the "classic," upon the model, and *from it make a figure uprooted from the terrain and detached from all that . . . surrounds him* [emphasis added]. . . . But beyond this objective function of model, there is also an intentionality in the term "classic," a more fixed projection,. . . . I do not intend to polemicize, nor to deny how much positive there can be in such ideas; but I reference an impression related while reading the *Studi corelliani* . . . : the impression of a duality in the attitude toward Corelli. In general, *in the Italian presentations, there is an effort to insert Corelli into his time, into instrumental and musical tradition, as a point in a flux of continuous development, but which also has antecedents and consequents* [emphasis added]. Pincherle and Finscher are [instead] led from the themes chosen by them to consider him—the same Corelli—from the point of view of foreign tastes . . . placed in juxtaposition—not with a tradition—but with the final effect or consequence of a tradition, to which some are opposed while others react sympathetically. *From this comes the tendency to consider the figure of the representative more than the entire movement represented by him* [emphasis added].[28]

Second, there is an instance of that oft-attested ability to view "local" musical developments from a macroscopic viewpoint, to situate them within larger developments and identify relationships between music and the other arts. In this instance, Pirrotta draws the same analogy drawn virtually simultaneously in "Ars music," the analogy of music and architecture:

From an era that I should still like to call "madrigalesque," in which the music would pass from one attitude to another, principally on the thrust of the suggestions of a text, one passes to a moment—let us thus say—of "spatial conquest," in which the dynamic of various dispositions in space is also added to the textual element: separate groups or choruses are positioned in various places, such that there are responses and echoes from one part of the venue where the performance unfolds to another, at times also with reference to the text or situation that one wishes to illustrate with the music. . . . *Bit by bit, the music tends to be given architectonic systematization* [emphasis added]. Here, naturally, it now deals with architecture in *time*, no longer with architecture in *space*; of thematic elements and tonal plans . . . organized—just as the architect disposes his masses and architectonic elements—in desired symmetries or asymmetries. . . . *The novelty of the Corellian moment is precisely this: the end of a phase during which the composition had rested upon those extrinsic elements, and the beginning of another in which one tends toward formal organization on purely musical bases. There it accompanies the definitive conquest of what one is accustomed to calling modern tonality* (by now anything other than modern, but still called modern tonality by custom) [emphases added].[29]

---

[28]1972: "Studi corelliani."
[29]1972: "Studi corelliani." Pirrotta's reference, clearly, is to Baroque "ritornello" form, with its recurring statements of the theme by the "ripieno" group in a variety of related keys, interspersed with soloistic passages executed by the "concertino."

His metaphor concerns nothing less consequential than the evolution of tonality, that revolutionary means of organizing the large-scale pitch content of an entire composition according to a macro-level architectural plan, or "blueprint," which emerges during precisely the period in question. In place of such tonal planning as is evident in the Renaissance madrigal, where the tonal architecture may operate on no grander a level than the individual musical phrase (typically corresponding to a text phrase), the seventeenth century witnesses the emergence of an intention to organize the pitch content according to a plan that governs the tonal design of the entire composition.[30] Just as an architectural blueprint predetermines the layout of *physical*space, so the precompositional tonal scheme developed by composers of Baroque instrumental music, operating within the conventions of *ritornello* form, predetermines the exploration of autonomous levels of *tonal* space—"keys"—in a carefully articulated sequence.

*****

Whereas Seicento opera had previously been the almost exclusive focus of Pirrotta's interests as an opera historian, "Semiramis e Amneris, Un anagramma o quasi" inaugurates a series of scholarly articles on post-Seicento opera.[31] His expertise in the earlier stages of the genre's history serves him well, because he is able to situate Verdi's *Aida* within the long tradition of Italian opera, of which it is only one (late) representative. We now see *Aida* in a new light, the legatee of operatic developments over two and a half centuries; and several distinguishing features of Verdi's masterpiece are related to venerable elements of the tradition and elucidated in such terms.

Pirrotta's immediate objective is to demonstrate a "typological relationship" between Verdi's *Aida* and Rossini's *Semiramide*, evident in the "Orientalizing archaeology" that characterizes both, in "the disposition of the three principal figures of the plot of *Aida* according to the traditional Metastasian scheme of amorous attraction and repulsion," which is "no less anachronistic," and in other such "archaicizing characteristics" "that associated it with *Semiramide*." To Verdi, *Semiramide* must have appeared rich in "ambient suggestions," "much richer . . . than to us."

---

[30]See my review of Bernhard Meier, *The Modes of Classical Vocal Polyphony*, trans. Ellen S. Beebe (New York: Broude Brothers, 1988), in *Music and Letters* 72 (1991): 79–84, especially 82–84, and the titles cited there; and also Lewis Lockwood, ed., Giovanni Pierluigi da Palestrina, *Pope Marcellus Mass. An Authoritative Score, Backgrounds and Sources, History and Analysis, Views and Comments* (New York: W.W. Norton, 1975), 90.

[31]Although I observe, once more, that during Pirrotta's journalistic career, he had written extensively on post-*Seicento* opera; it was instead during his academic career that he had focused on the early stages of operatic history.

No music in the opera serves more effectively to characterize Amneris than her music in the first scene of Act II, which—though not a *cavatina* (it is reduced realistically to a Verdian *"parola scenica"*)—

> fulfills the task of psychological auto-definition that the operatic tradition for a long time had specifically assigned to the *cavatinas*, not infrequently locating them in a *boudoir*, with the female personage physically and psychologically in front of a mirror.

Pirrotta had written about one of the earliest *cavatinas* in the operatic repertory, and his invocation of the tradition in describing Amneris's Act II music situates it within that tradition. (He need not have made explicit reference in "Semiramis e Amneris" to Rosina's celebrated *cavatina* in *Il barbiere di Siviglia* for that notable precedent to come immediately to mind.)

Correspondences between the characters of Semiramide and Amneris are "not casual"; nor do they

> issue exclusively from the scenario . . . or . . . the modifications carried out by Verdi and Du Locle during the week, or a little less, that they spent on such an enterprise in Sant'Agata between 18 and 26 June 1870. Instead, they are born of a further modification—neither the only one nor the last—desired entirely by Verdi.[32]

However, the analogies between Semiramide and Amneris should not permit us to overlook the differences between them, should not obscure Verdi's "ambivalence toward the Rossinian model," expressed in a 25 July 1871 letter to Opprandino Arrivabene, in which "we hear the echo of reflections made during the composition of *Aida*."[33] Among the elements of that ambivalence is Verdi's critical posture toward coloratura, a hallmark of the Rossinian aesthetic. Pirrotta, however, does not hesitate to champion that aesthetic, and in his view "Semiramide's *cavatina* is efficacious not only in the passages in which the melody—as Verdi wanted it—expresses amorous ardor":

> the impetuosity and imperiousness represented by the passages of coloratura are also part of the personage, according to a *topos* whose semantic value is not invalidated by one's recollection of the cavatina in *Barbiere*. . . . On a more general plane, it is inexact that coloratura signifies negation of melody.

For Pirrotta's readers in 1977, the difficulty was largely due to the negative perception of coloratura "derived from the acrobatic volatility of the light

---

[32]Pirrotta offers evidence for such an assertion in **1977**: "Semiramis e Amneris, Un anagramma o quasi."
[33]In that letter, Verdi explicitly references *Il barbiere di Siviglia*, *La gazza ladra*, and *Semiramide*.

sopranos, who today are the only ones to practice it systematically." In an era before the professional successes of coloratura mezzo-sopranos Agnes Baltsa, Cecilia Bartoli, Marilyn Horne, Jennifer Larmore, and numerous others, one's experience of this element of the Rossinian aesthetic was indeed limited by virtue of the circumstance that Pirrotta had identified:

> almost completely lacking for us is the experience of the easy agility in fullness of sound and sameness of tone for which the voice of Isabella Colbran, among many others, was celebrated.

Pirrotta concludes with a measured call for renewed assessment of judgments of Rossini, "separate from the temptation of every impossible comparison... between Rossini and Verdi." Verdi's "ambivalence toward the Rossinian model" is counterbalanced by the evidence of a possible relationship between *Aida* and *Semiramide*.

*****

Notwithstanding the brevity of the bibliography of the «Sapienza» years, the range is notable: from the late antique theoretical apparatus underlying the high medieval application of number to the polyphony of the "school" of Nôtre Dame, to the possible evocation of the vocal practices of representatives of the "unwritten tradition" in polyphonic settings of Italian texts by trans-Alpine composers of the fifteenth century, to the recovery of vestigial remains of that unwritten tradition, to the poetic sensibilities of a celebrated Cinquecento madrigalist, to the foundational change in compositional aesthetic in the seventeenth century (from a creative principle based on text to one in which the composer is instead concerned with the spatial elements of the tonal architecture), to the continuing development of that quintessential manifestation of Italian musical culture—opera—and the indebtedness of late examples of the genre to developments first traceable centuries before.

The article on *Aida* in particular foreshadows an important series of articles from Pirrotta's retirement years, in which he extends his scholarly involvement with the history of Italian music to complement the earlier studies on the music of the Trecento and Italian Renaissance and on Seicento opera with a substantial series devoted to Beaumarchais, Goldoni, Martello, and—above all—Metastasio.

Scena 9.ᵃ

Il Principe (1978–98):
Opera Settecentesca ed Ottocentesca[1]

In April of 1978, Nino Pirrotta wrote to Ellen Rosand that he would be expected to administer examinations in June and October of that year, but that "as of October 31," "I'll be a free man." On Pirrotta's retirement, the chair he had held at the University of Rome passed to Fedele d'Amico, Dottore in Giurisprudenza, who was as much critic as musicologist.[2]

Although no longer on the «Sapienza»'s *elenco principale* (official roster of tenured/tenure-track faculty members) after academic year 1977/78, Pirrotta remained active "fuori ruolo" for three more years. As professor emeritus, he was compensated for his activity *fuori ruolo* and therefore did not receive his full retirement pension until such status had terminated.[3]

*****

Pirrotta's professional achievements had been formally recognized by learned societies and institutions of higher education beginning in 1956.[4] After his retirement, the pace at which such recognitions were conferred accelerated.

---

[1] For invaluable assistance on this chapter, I gratefully acknowledge Daniel Heartz, Professor *Emeritus* of Music at the University of California, Berkeley. Throughout this chapter, I shall be quoting periodically from Heartz's essay "Goldoni, *Opera Buffa*, and Mozart's Advent in Vienna," Opera Buffa *in Mozart's Vienna*, ed. Mary Hunter and James Webster (Cambridge: Cambridge University Press, 1999), 25–49. Professor Heartz also reminded me of John A. Rice's *Mozart on the Stage* (Cambridge: Cambridge University Press, 2009) and suggested that it might prove useful to me in drafting this chapter.

[2] D'Amico occupied the *cattedra* at Rome for only a short time, after which he was succeeded by Pierluigi Petrobelli, *Dottore in Lettere* University of Rome, M.F.A. Princeton University.

[3] A professor "fuori ruolo" may not offer regular courses, but may sit on commissions for *concorsi*, place students as the result of *concorsi*, chair the department, and offer incidental lectures. Responsibility for the regular courses for the degrees rests with the faculty on the "elenco principale," however. For clarification, I am grateful to Pirrotta's daughter Dott.ssa Silvia Pirrotta-Giuffré and her son Dott. Mario Giuffré.

[4] He was named a member of the Accademia "Santa Cecilia" on 15 January 1956 and a member of the American Academy of Arts and Sciences on 10 May 1967 ["Class IV, 'Humanities'/Section 3, 'Philology and Criticism.'"] and was awarded the degree of Doctor of Fine Arts *Honoris Causa* by the College of the Holy Cross in Worcester, Massachusetts (1970), even before the conclusion of his tenure at Harvard.

Pirrotta was named an honorary member of the Royal Musical Association (1978), American Musicological Society (1980)[5] and International Musicological Society (1987); and in 1984 he was elected vice president of the Consiglio Accademico of the Accademia «S. Cecilia»

Additional honorary doctorates followed, awarded by some of the world's most venerable universities: the degree of *Musicae doctor* (Cantab.) from the University of Cambridge (13 June 1985);[6] the degree of *Litterarum humanarum doctor* (Doctor of Humane Letters) from both the University of Chicago[7] and Princeton University, in 1975 and 1988; the *Laurea «Ad Honorem»* from the University of Urbino in 1996.[8]

In recognition of his achievements as an essayist, Pirrotta also received the Premio "Viareggio" (1987),[9] awarded annually since 1929, and in the company of Federico Mompellio the prestigious Premio "Antonio Feltrinelli," from the Accademia Nazionale dei Lincei (1983).[10] That same year the "Nino Pirrotta Research Fund" at Harvard was "[e]stablished in honor of Nino Pirrotta, Walter W. Naumburg Professor of Music, Emeritus, on the occasion of his seventy-fifth birthday, June 13, 1983, by his colleagues and friends, the income of which is to provide grants-in-aid towards research projects of doctoral students in the Department of Music," a fund to which Pirrotta directed the royalties from sales of his anthology of essays published by Harvard University Press in 1984.[11]

---

[5]Pirrotta had been a dedicated member and officer of the A.M.S. during his Harvard years; see *The American Musicological Society. An Anniversary Essay by Richard Crawford* (Philadelphia, PA: The American Musicological Society, 1984), available online at http://books.google.com/books?id=0_5jfG0cTr4C&printsec=frontcover& source=gbs_ge_summary_r&cad=0#v=onepage&q&f=false

[6]The awarding of the degree at Cambridge is illuminated in various letters from Pirrotta to Iain Fenlon, who advocated for the honor (I thank Professor Fenlon for permission to quote): "14.3.85.... You spoke in your last letter of a visit which we might have made to Cambridge in the not-too-distant future; and I think I correctly understood what you meant, but was under advice to keep silent. Now I am told by your Vice-Chancellor that the University has approved the conferment of a honorary degree on me next June 13, and want to express my gratitude, for I suspect that you had some part in it and I have it dear as a new mark of our good friendship. Now I need also your advice, for I am required to write whom do I want to have invited to the Congregation.... [D]o you think my good friends the [Denis] Arnolds and the [Frederick] Sternfelds would expect one, or would it be too much of an imposition to ask them to come to Cambridge? And what about Rose Mary Dooley?... I apologize for burdening you with so many questions, but otherwise I would be completely helpless; I have not yet mastered the art of receiving honorary degrees!" and "3 July 1985.... Our stay in Cambridge was most pleasant, only too short, the official ceremony very exciting and rewarding, and I am most grateful to the one, whomever he was, who thought of me for such a distinction."

[7]Pirrotta wrote to Lewis Lockwood on 29 May 1975: "We'll ... go to Chicago, w[h]ere I am to get a degree—my 'Incoronatione', as Oliver [Strunk] calls it."

[8]See the formal invitation: "Università degli Studi di Urbino / Il giorno 23 agosto 1996 / alle ore 11,30 / nell'Aula Magna dell'Università (Via Saffi, n. 2) / verrà conferita / la laurea in Lettere / ad honorem / al Professor / Nino Pirrotta. / Sarà molto gradita / la presenza / della Signoria Vostra. / Urbino, 20 luglio 1996 / Il Preside / della Facoltà di Lettere e Filosofia / Raffaele Molinelli / Il Rettore / Carlo Bo." For providing me with a copy of this document, I am grateful to Lewis Lockwood.

[9]Leonardo Pinzauti, "La morte di Pirrotta, maestro della musicologia italiana," *La Nazione* (Saturday, 24 January 1998).

[10]On the awarding of the Feltrinelli, see http://www.lincei.it/modules.php?name=Content&pa=showpage&pid =97.

[11]See Christoph Wolff's contribution to a volume of essays in Pirrotta's memory, "*In Memoriam* Nino Pirrotta," 37-38 (see "Scena 7.ª," n. 8).

Yet another kind of tribute were the numerous Festschriften in Pirrotta's honor, the first of which was an issue of the *Rivista italiana di musicologia* (vol. 10, 1975). Pirrotta was lured to Florence[12] for the presentation on the pretext that there were to be discussions of summer activities at Certaldo, which for several decades had hosted conferences on the music of the Trecento. Instead, "a nice ceremony took place at Palazzo Medici-Riccardi, in which I was presented with this fine volume."[13] For Pirrotta, the homage was entirely unexpected, and he was visibly moved when he became aware of the intention of honoring him.[14]

Finally, there were the collections of his essays, of which the Harvard anthology was only one.[15]

*****

Retirement also made it possible for Pirrotta to travel extensively and in particular to accept invitations to visit at several American universities: Harvard for a semester during academic year 1978/79, Princeton in the fall of 1980, the University of North Carolina at Chapel Hill in the fall of 1983.[16]

Pirrotta's visit to Harvard was as "Lauro de Bosis Lecturer on the History of Italian Civilization." He taught a graduate seminar on medieval music and an undergraduate course on Monteverdi, team-taught with Christoph Wolff,

---

[12]On 11 January 1976.

[13]See Ellen Rosand's contribution to the volume of essays in Pirrotta's memory, *Studi musicali* 28 (1999): 32. See also a letter from Pirrotta to Lewis Lockwood—"[5 February 1975] I went to Florence convinced I was to attend a meeting about summer courses at Certaldo, and found myself surrounded by a number of old and young friends honoring me with a handsome and handsomely bound Volume X of the Rivista.... I do not know how much ... I deserve such honor, but can not deny that I was deeply affected by such an indication that there is not, after all, a big generation gap ... between my younger Italian and American colleagues and my poor self"—and the formal invitation—"*Domenica 11 gennaio 1971 alle ore 11,30 in Palazzo Medici-Riccardi, Sala delle Quattro Stagioni, Alberto Basso, presidente della Società italiana di Musicologia, presenterà il Volume X (1975) della* Rivista italiana di musicologia, *dedicato agli studi in onore di Nino Pirrotta, fondatore del Centro di studi sull'Ars Nova.*" For both of these documents, I am grateful to Professor Lockwood.

For a listing of the Festschriften issued in Pirrotta's honor and memory, see Teresa M. Gialdroni, "Bibliografia di Nino Pirrotta," *Studi musicali* 28 (1999): 43–63.

[14] For this account, I am grateful to Iain Fenlon, who was present on the occasion. A.M. Cummings conversation with Professor Fenlon, 14 November 2010. On the presentation of another Festschrift in Pirrotta's honor, see his letter to Iain Fenlon (I am grateful to Professor Fenlon for permission to quote): "2 March, 1989.... Sunday afternoon a jolly party was offered to us by the [Fabrizio] Dellasetas, on which occasion the volume In cantu et in sermone was presented to me.... I say a jolly party, but it was very touching for me[,] and the gift, an elegant book ..., brought near to my heart all its kind contributors. Do I really deserve that much? How tempting to think so!"

[15]Correspondence preserved in the Pirrotta file, Department of Music, Harvard University, contains interesting details concerning the Harvard anthology. A letter of 2 August 1981 to Harvard professor and volume coeditor Christoph Wolff reports on Pirrotta's having heard from the Press that the Board of Syndics had approved the publication; he negotiates the contents of the volume with Wolff, and evidently had originally envisioned including "On Text Forms from Ciconia to Dufay" and jettisoning "Il luogo dell'orchestra" instead. In a letter of 18 May 1984 to Peg Fulton of Harvard University Press, Pirrotta signals his desire to have the royalties dedicated to the Pirrotta Research Fund. For full bibliographic information on the anthologies of essays, see my Bibliography.

[16]Rosand, *Studi musicali* 28 (1999): 32. On the visiting appointment at Chapel Hill, see a 30 January 1983 letter from Pirrotta to Harvard music professor Christoph Wolff, in which Pirrotta announced that he would be in Chapel Hill from late August to December 1983, as replacement for James Haar, who would be visiting at the University of California, Berkeley. Pirrotta file, Department of Music, Harvard University.

in which some fifteen undergraduate concentrators and a few graduate students were enrolled.[17]

The visit to Princeton (1 September 1980-31 January 1981) was arranged during the spring semester of the 1979/80 academic year by Lewis Lockwood, who wrote to Pirrotta in January of 1980 to remind him that he had "mentioned as a possibility the idea of a course[18] dealing with the antecedents of Mozart's Don Giovanni. . . . That would . . . be . . . splendid." The course replicated one at the «Sapienza», and, once again, teaching nourished scholarship—and scholarship, teaching—since Pirrotta was to produce both an article on the subject for the *Proceedings of the Royal Musical Association* (the published version of a lecture) and his book-length treatment, a developed version of his *dispensa* for the «Sapienza».

In his response of 31 January 1980, Pirrotta takes the opportunity to report on the condition of his old friend Oliver Strunk, whose health was then rapidly declining:

> Dear Lewis, . . . I gratefully accept your formal offer. . . . I have already started to collect whatever materials I may need, mainly microfilms of scores and libretti, for the course on Don Giovanni before Mozart; . . . I went this morning to see Oliver. His conditions were not very different from the last time I had been there, this last Sunday. He's very weak, often sleepy, unwilling to speak and barely audible when he has something to say. Today I had the impression that he had some physical pain, which I hadn't noticed before; but when I asked him he didn't complain of anything. It's a pity to see him in such conditions and so lonely. . . . Warmest wishes to Doris and to you. As ever, Nino[19]

Soon thereafter, Strunk died, and the Pirrottas were inexpressibly saddened when the traffic in Rome made it impossible for them to attend the memorial service.[20]

*****

The Pirrottas now had more time to host numerous visiting musicologists, who in many cases visited them in Rome specifically to honor one of their discipline's celebrated figures and his wife.[21] The freedom from regular professional obligations also gave Pirrotta ample opportunity to participate at conferences. Together with Lea, he would regularly travel to Cortina with his colleague Michelangelo Muraro and Muraro's wife, and after the vacation in

---

[17] Wolff, "*In Memoriam* Nino Pirrotta," 35 (see "Scena 7.ª," n. 8). Correspondence and other documents in the Pirrotta file, Department of Music, Harvard University, contain important details about the visiting appointment at Harvard. Pirrotta and his wife planned "to arrive Jan 15th [1979]" and his compensation was to be "per six months" (1 January–6 June 1979). As of 1 July 1978, the understanding was that the Pirrottas were to live in Harvard's Leverett House.

[18] The course was eventually offered under the rubric Music 515, "Problems in the History of the Opera."

[19] Pirrotta faculty file, Princeton University Archives.

[20] Private conversation, the Pirrottas and A.M. Cummings, academic years 1988/89 and 1989/90.

[21] Agostino Ziino, "Pirrotta between Cambridge and Rome," 41 (see "Scena 5.ª," n. 2).

Cortina there would often be a conference at the Fondazione Cini in Venice, where Pirrotta would lecture.[22] Indeed, in most cases his attendance at such conferences entailed delivering papers, any number of which was then published.

Pirrotta was impressively active as a scholar until the very end of his life. In attempting to capture the general character of his writings in these years, I would identify, first, the quality of "summing up" that distinguishes writings like the general pieces on the great figures Landino[23] and Monteverdi,[24] the essay "'Maniera' polifonica e immediatezza recitative," and the introductory essays in the facsimile editions of the Trecento manuscripts Florence, Biblioteca Laurenziana, 87 (the famous Squarcialupi codex)[25] and Vatican Rossi 215.[26] As an elder statesman, at an age when opportunities for summary statements would inevitably be decreasing rather than increasing, Pirrotta was interested in reflecting on transcendent scholarly questions with the insight accumulated during a lifetime of involvement with them.

Moreover, we find, for the first time, a willingness to reflect publicly—in a considerable corpus of writings—on matters of methodology: "Contemplando la musa assente," "Malipiero e il filo d'Arianna," "Problemi di una storia della musica," and "Natura e problemi del testo musicale."

However, Pirrotta also returned to subjects that had engaged his interest for decades. There is an extension of the earlier series on the Italian madrigal to consider the Roman madrigal of the late sixteenth century,[27] a subject worthy even now of considerable further investigation;[28] and there is the treatment of Andrea Gabrieli's choruses for Sophocles' *Oedipus*, one of the relatively few instances in which an Italian Renaissance composer furnishes musical *intermedij* for a tragedy.[29]

---

[22] A.M. Cummings interview with Dr. Adelaide M. Pirrotta-Bahr; see also Rosand, *Studi musicali* 28 (1999): 33. Pirrotta's relationship with Muraro was especially important to both men, founded on a close congruence in their visions of scholarship and decided intellectual and aesthetic positions in common, as Iain Fenlon reminded me. On Muraro, see David Rosand, "Michelangelo Muraro (1913–1991)," *Burlington Magazine* 133 (1991): 517-18.

[23] **1997**: "Francesco Landini: i lumi della mente."

[24] **1994**: "Claudio Monteverdi, veneziano di adozione"; **1995**: "Opera: Da Monteverdi a Monteverdi."

[25] **1992**: "The Music ['Le musiche']."

[26] **1992**: ed., *Il codice Rossi 215*, which summarizes arguments presented in more detail in the contemporary articles 1985: "'Arte' e 'non arte' nel frammento Greggiati," 1995: "A Sommacampagna Codex of the Italian Ars Nova?", and **2007**: "La notazione del Codice Rossi 215."

[27] **1985**: "'Dolci Affetti'"; **1993**: coed. with Giuliana Gialdroni, *I musici di Roma e il madrigale*.

[28] On this point, see Anthony Newcomb, "II. Italy, 16th century. 7. The 1570s: hybrid styles," in Kurt von Fischer, et al., "Madrigal," *Grove Music Online*. Oxford Music Online, http://0-www.oxfordmusiconline.com.-libcat. lafayette.edu/subscriber/article/grove/music/40075 (accessed January 30, 2012): "*Il quarto libro delle muse* (RISM 1574⁴), the most important Roman anthology of the 1570s, contains the first published madrigals of a new generation of Roman composers (e.g., G.A. Dragoni, Francesco Soriano, G.M. Nanino and Macque), whose production is just beginning to be investigated (Pirrotta, 1985, 1993)." Newcomb himself is preparing a complete edition of the madrigals of Nanino.

[29] **1985**: "I cori per l'"Edipo Tiranno'"; **1995**: ed., *Chori in musica composti sopra li chori della tragedia di Edippo Tiranno*.

*****

Nearly six decades before the publication of "Rileggendo *Il Pirata* di Bellini" (1993), Pirrotta had reviewed, in the Palermitan daily *L'Ora*, a production of Bellini's opera at the Teatro Massimo di Palermo, on the centennial of the composer's death in 1935. In 1993, he recalls having done so but having no memory of what he then wrote. Pirrotta's journalistic writings are once again accessible,[30] and the relationship of his later vision of that work to the earlier one—the commonalities and differences—is revealing.

He opens with a characterization of Bellini's masterpiece consistent with that offered 60 years before, which is "[c]ontrary to the widely-diffused idea of a Bellini, supreme melodist above all." There are expressions of Pirrotta's and Bellini's shared "sicilianità"—"Bellini truly has echoed melodies *of his land*"—and an analysis of the coda to the Act I finale that recapitulates formulations in the music-critical piece of 1935, which, however, are now more benignly expressed, the rhetoric of an octogenarian: "It is an admirable—and admired—page, which reveals a Bellini to us [who was] not only a melodist but [also] a skilled contrapuntist and harmonist."

Pirrotta's analysis of the opera's overture is similarly reminiscent of the 1935 piece, in its assessment of the "Austro/Germanic" quality of the work: its "eminently quartetistic writing" and

> a sonata form complete with exposition and recapitulation, but with the development supplanted—as would then be customary in Italian operatic overtures—by a few hesitant chords that lead back to the principal tonality.

But the most notable features of "Rileggendo" are the Idealist and Materialist formulations that occur toward the conclusion. Pirrotta refers explicitly to Immanuel Kant, the German Idealist to whom Croce, Gentile, Carabellese, and Fazio-Allmayer were indebted:

> For the musician—as also for the poet, certainly—composing is no less arduous, gradual, and tiring than is the labor for the sculptor of drafting a figure bit-by-bit and defining its desired forms and gestures with correctness. Inspiration is not the striking vision but the sense of beauty, *the Kantian judgment*, which guides and sustains the search—receives or rejects the ideas—and it refinishes and leads those received to perfection. The "long, long" melodies of Bellini (to cite only one characteristic of his art) were certainly not born entirely in a stream; it suffices to examine one—Imogen's . . . —in the *stretta* of *Finale* I . . . to see how they had to have been the fruit of successive additions, supported by an infallible *instinct* in *judging* what could be added to that already-made, with *naturalness* and *apparent spontaneity*, and to extend it and intensify it [emphases added].

---

[30]Cummings and Eiche, "Nino Pirrotta's Early Music-Critical Writings" (see "*Scena 1.ª*," n. 69).

And the indebtedness of the following to Labriolan Materialism is equally clear:

> For an operatic composer like Bellini, the composing also then comes to be *conditioned* by infinite *practical considerations*, beginning with the so-called formal "conventions" to which the expectations of the public were linked.... And then there were all those involved... in *the practical realization of the opera*.... All that corresponds to a condition that was still decidedly (even if superbly) *artisanal*, as a result of which neither Rossini, nor Donizetti, nor Bellini, nor the early Verdi conceived their operas in the way in which we now see them: as definitive and immutable creations. On the contrary, they were ready to modify and retouch them in order to adapt them to new *circumstances* of performance, or partly re-utilize the elements in other contexts, if one were aware that that for which they had originally been conceived no longer had any hope of remaining in the current repertory [emphases added].

*****

The first of Pirrotta's essays of the retirement years to receive detailed comment here is "'Maniera' polifonica e immediatezza recitativa,"[31] which originated in a 1995 lecture at the Accademia Nazionale dei Lincei.[32] The importance of "'Maniera' polifonica e immediatezza recitativa" lies in the fact that it completes a narrative begun in 1955 with "Marchettus of Padua and the Italian Ars Nova." In "'Maniera' polifonica," we also find revealed that keenness, manifested periodically throughout Pirrotta's career, to synthesize his findings, to take a macroscopic view and distill his thoughts to their concentrated essence, so that we may "see the forest." He furthermore evokes the phenomenon of cultural fashion, the cultural tendencies characteristic of a people's experience at any given moment in their history. The practical and theoretical activities of Italian composers reveal an ongoing, ever-changing dialectic with respect to their sympathy for the northern polyphonic tradition, which expresses itself in the Italian musical repertory in different ways at different times.

In his opening paragraph, Pirrotta acknowledges that he has "already spoken about 'maniera' other times in past years, suggesting that the entire development of Italian sacred and secular music during the sixteenth century was to be considered a deliberate adoption of a polyphonic 'maniera.'"[33]

---

[31] **1995:** "'Maniera' polifonica e immediatezza recitativa."

[32]*Corriere della Sera* (9 March 1995): 52. "'Maniera'"—along with **1948:** "'Dulcedo' e 'subtilitas' nella pratica polifonica franco-italiana al principio del '400," **1985:** "Musica e Umanesimo," **1973:** "Su alcuni testi italiani di composizioni polifoniche quattrocentesche," and **1961:** "Gesualdo da Venosa nel IV centenario della nascita"—is among those articles of Pirrotta's that have remained solely in the Italian original. A coauthor and I intend to translate the five into English and publish them, either within a single volume or as a series of independent translations, expressly so as to increase their accessibility for English-speaking audiences.

[33]See, for example, **1973:** "Novelty and Renewal in Italy, 1300–1600."

However, not having yet had an opportunity to deepen one's understanding of such a proposition, he is induced to take it up once more, precisely in order to clarify it "above all to myself."[34]

Pirrotta begins by recapitulating the essential argument of "Music and Cultural Tendencies": the decline in musical activity during the Quattrocento was limited to music of a particular type—polyphonic composition—which, because of its transmission by written means, is the sole type to come down to us abundantly represented in musical documents. There *were* Italian polyphonists at the time, and the Italian manuscripts preserving polyphonic compositions are not few in number. At the same time, such compositions were for the most part composed, and even more often imported, by *foreign*musicians, recruited from north of the Alps to staff the musical chapels of Italian ecclesiastical institutions and seigneurial courts. To explain such a seemingly anomalous historical development, Pirrotta summarizes the argument of the earlier article:

> [t]he new humanistic generations . . . privileged—even exalted—more immediate and spontaneous expressions of musicality: music . . . by singers who, by virtue of their self-accompaniment on a stringed instrument—small guitar, viola, or lute— seem to belong among the ancient lyrists.

Thereafter, notated compositions by Italian composers on Italian poetic texts— above all frottole and barzellette—appear in abundance at the end of the fifteenth century and the beginning of the sixteenth, first in manuscript, then also in print. They retain fundamental characteristics of Quattrocento unwritten tradition: a vocal solo supported by two or three instrumental parts or the chords of a single instrument like the lute.

The transition from this so-called "frottolistic" phase of musical production to the most typical form of Italian sixteenth-century secular music, the madrigal, was the result of two processes, one literary, the other musical. Regarding the literary process, there was a tendency to liberate lyric expression from predetermined metrical constraints. This lessened the internal symmetries of the stanzas of ballate or canzoni, for example, and permitted a freedom and variety of meter that excluded appropriating music composed for one given poetic text for another. These are the characteristics that distinguish madrigalian texts, together with an epigrammatic vein that often found its culmination in the distich, the rhyming couplet that frequently concludes brief texts in the new (or newly resuscitated) madrigal genre.

With respect to the *musical* process, the novel element is the transition from the "frottolistic" practice of a vocal melody supported by instrumental

---

[34]In what follows, I am essentially excerpting directly from Pirrotta's text, though rendered in English.

accompaniment, largely chordal, to a greater complexity in which the prevalence of the upper voice is attenuated relative to the oft-accentuated contrapuntal independence of the lower voices, to which a text is now added. We can only conjecture what motivated such a transition, which occurred above all in the Florentine–Roman ambience, encouraged by the tastes of the Medici popes Leo X and Clement VII and members of their circles. Pirrotta's opinion had always been that behind the transition was the desire to create an "artistic" Italian equivalent (he underscores the adjective "artistic") to two genres that had long been central to the Franco–Flemish polyphonic tradition: the chanson and the motet, above all the latter, a composition on a nonstrophic text in which the "search" for "artistic" effects was more accentuated. In support of such a conjecture, we note, on the one hand, that motets and madrigals are often transmitted together in the primary sources, and, on the other, that the term "canzone," which predates what will soon become the canonical Italian term for the new Italian genre ("madrigal"), is etymologically related to the French term "chanson."

For some time, many of the most important composers of the new genre were non-Italians. Therefore, the new genre was born not of the development of artistic modes already characteristic of Italian tradition, but from the deliberate adoption of a polyphonic "maniera," which since the end of the Trecento had not been widely employed by Italian composers in setting Italian poetry to music.

In the first few years of the development, the music remains faithful to the exposition of the poetic text, often setting it with chords that alternate with brief contrapuntal episodes. Soon enough, however, such respect for the text begins to be attenuated, so that contrapuntal play might be accentuated instead, in which the "excellence" of the "most perfect musicians"—Pirrotta is deliberately using expressions from the title of one of the printed sources of the new genre—tended increasingly to be affirmed. As a result, it is difficult for Pirrotta to subscribe to the notion that the music of the madrigal has as its primary scope emphasizing and underlining the poetic senses of the text.

Of course, the text's syntactic articulations were respected, by cadences that were sometimes more conclusive, sometimes less so, or of musical pauses corresponding to the completion of a textual phrase or period, which were now more audible, now less so. But such textual cues were valuable above all as suggestions to the composer concerning the formal design of his creation.

It is debatable, therefore, whether the listener, even if at times already cognizant of the poetic text, could fully follow its reflection in the musical episodes motivated by it.

And thus we are led to consider the various modes of performance in the madrigal literature and to question whether an entirely vocal chamber performance, and the experience of the madrigal "from outside," as a member of an audience—modes of performance to which we have become habituated—may not have alternated with others.

Not widely diffused, perhaps, yet not entirely exceptional, was the ability among members of the cultivated classes to perform madrigals themselves.[35] More common was the instrumental execution of polyphonic compositions, including—although we lack extensive and decisive proof of it—the madrigal.

Therefore, in madrigalian polyphony—whether performed by voices, instruments, or both together—it was not so much *the poetic sense*, from which the composer drew the textual cues stimulating his creative act, that a discerning listener perceived and accepted, as it was instead *the resultant sonority* for itself, which was variously colored by the confluence of voices and instruments.

Three developments coexisted with central developments in the "canonic" iteration of the genre, which illuminate its distinguishing character and define it more clearly:

1. The polemic of those who wished the Council of Trent to banish polyphony from sacred services was predicated on the matter of the intelligibility of the text, and in the secular tradition a document expressive of the same concern appears as early as 1536: a collection of madrigals by Verdelot, arranged by Willaert so that only the superius voice is provided with text and, further, is rendered in mensural notation, while the other voices are intabulated for lute performance.

2. Not so much a polemical reaction to the increasingly well-established madrigal, but, rather, the expression of other tendencies and the fulfillment of other tastes was the vogue of the canzone villanesca alla napoletana, inaugurated almost simultaneously (1537) with Willaert's intabulation of Verdelot's madrigals, which exemplified the taste for melodic spontaneity and rhythmic vivacity, a freedom unimpeded by technical rules.

3. A number of anthologies of madrigals from the midpoint of the production of the genre are entitled "madrigali ariosi," a reference to a quality not always achieved in the "canonic" madrigalian output, in which the contrapuntal "search" produced outcomes often lacking an "aria."[36]

These three developments and the general historical narrative of which they are elements suggest that despite the "deliberate adoption of a polyphonic

---

[35] This concurs with Anthony Newcomb's characterization of the early *Cinquecento* madrigal, in contrast with its late *Cinquecento* counterpart, as an art form intended to be experienced by amateur performers, rather than by members of an audience who would listen to professionals' execution of the virtuosic late sixteenth-century variant of the genre: *The Madrigal at Ferrara, 1579–1597*, 2 vols. (Princeton, NJ: Princeton University Press, 1980), vol. 1.

[36] On the meaning of the term *"aria,"* see the conclusion of my chapter on Pirrotta's Harvard years.

'maniera'" in Cinquecento secular polyphony, the rapprochement between polyphonic practice and vestigial humanistic suspicions thereof was not complete.[37] And nowhere is that equivocation more illuminatingly expressed than at the end of the Cinquecento and the beginning of the Seicento. As emblematic of the "secunda prattica," Monteverdi and his brother will identify tendencies that will be more decisively affirmed at the beginning of the Seicento: the various manifestations of accompanied monody, which feature the predominance of a single solo voice, now the sole bearer of the poetic text, supported by instrumental harmonies that either enhanced its "arioso" melodic course or underlined its textual elements with the musical richness and emotive contribution of unexpected chromaticisms.

Monteverdi was not among the original monodic reformers who emerged during the eleven years of silence between his *Terzo Libro de Madrigali* in 1592 and his *Quarto Libro* in 1603, a pause presumably explained by the demands of court life. But already in the *Terzo Libro*, the orientation of Monteverdi's poetic choices toward dramatic passages of the *Gerusalemme liberata*, which lend themselves to recitative-like musical treatment, had aligned him with artists who, like Marenzio, Gesualdo, and Wert, were by no means renouncing the resources of polyphony. In Monteverdi's *Quarto Libro* of 1603, and even more in the *Quinto* of 1606, a conception of the madrigal is affirmed as almost a "vocal symphonic poem,"[38] in which all the resources of the five voices—those of counterpoint included, though not more determinative than other such resources, and not an end in itself—concur to determine light and shade, tensions and distensions in the acoustical frame.

We now have Pirrotta's completed, comprehensive account of Italian composers' shifting posture, during three centuries (1300–1600), toward secular polyphonic composition: from the somewhat anomalous adoption of a polyphonic "maniera" in the fourteenth century, which produced the riches of the Trecento tradition, nonetheless circumscribed in scope; to the rise to momentary dominance of the Quattrocento humanists, many of whom preferred classicizing musical practices—typified by solo-singing to string accompaniment—to polyphony of the type favored by their Trecento predecessors; to the Cinquecento's adoption of a polyphonic "maniera," which, however, was delimited as the result of the lingering equivocation about polyphony that produced such documents as Willaert's arrangements for solo voice and lute

---

[37]Pirrotta here quotes a revealing text of Zarlino's that offers a damning critique of polyphony. At the same time, an earlier passage in Zarlino, which Pirrotta also quotes, suggests that Zarlino is admiring of some polyphonic settings of Italian secular poetry. Thus my reference to equivocation. Pirrotta suggests that the polyphonic madrigals especially successful with respect to expressive effect profile the superius voice, which features a "recitative accentuation."

[38]For a similar characterization of the late-sixteenth-century madrigal, see Newcomb, *The Madrigal at Ferrara*, 1:62.

accompaniment of Verdelot's polyphonic madrigals and the "madrigale arioso" of mid-century.

*****

Pirrotta's tendency, late in his career, to "sum up" is also manifest in several of the articles on Seicento opera. "Claudio Monteverdi, veneziano," moreover, considers the problems of the chronology of and venue for the first performances of Monteverdi's *Il ritorno d'Ulisse in patria*, problems that had long interested Pirrotta and involved him in an amicable "virtual" debate with his friend and colleague Wolfgang Osthoff, with whom he ultimately disagrees.[39] In "Opera: da Monteverdi a Monteverdi," Pirrotta returns to such specific matters as the alternative finales of *Orfeo* (for which he offers a classic Materialist explanation, concerning the physical constraints imposed by the various spaces where the several performances took place) and the likelihood of Striggio and Monteverdi's conversance with Jacopo Peri's treatment of the same material. "Forse Nerone cantò da tenore" posits that in Monteverdi's original conception of *L'incoronazione di Poppaea*, the role of the Emperor Nero was intended, not for a castrato, but for a tenor, and Pirrotta marshals evidence from period sources.[40] "Note su Minato" is a consideration of Conte Nicolò Minato's achievement as librettist, in which Pirrotta offers observations concerning the conditions necessary for the emergence of a comic operatic tradition and for the familiar aria/recitative distinction.[41] Finally, "Invito al recitativo," in considering that same all-important distinction of recitative and elaborate set piece, returns to the justification for its emergence offered earlier in "Monteverdi and the Problems of Opera."[42]

*****

However, there are also new directions in Pirrotta's scholarship, and remarkably so, considering that they date from the 1980s or even '90s. Indeed, the particular achievement of the retirement years was a series of articles on eighteenth- and nineteenth-century Italian opera. What is notable about these writings is the broad and deep contextualization of important developments in operatic history. One had assumed that one was reasonably familiar with Beaumarchais's spoken comedies *Le mariage de Figaro* and *Le barbier de Séville* and Mozart's and Rossini's operatic masterpieces based on them, but

---

[39] See **1994**: "Claudio Monteverdi, veneziano. . . . ." The Osthoff study to which Pirrotta took some exception is "Zur Bologneser Aufführung von Monteverdis Ritorno d'Ulisse im Jahre 1641," *Anzeiger der phil.-hist. Klasse der österreichischen Akademie der Wissenschaften* (1958): 155–60.

[40] But see his postscript to the version published as "Forse Nerone cantò da tenore," in *Poesia e musica e altri saggi*, 179-93 (see "Scena 5.^{a}," n. 15).

[41] **1990**: "Note su Minato."

[42] See my synopsis of the matter of justification in my "Scena 5.ª, The Conservatorio di . . . Roma (1948–56)."

Pirrotta's article on Beaumarchais situates various elements of the plots and music of both musical masterpieces within the long history of Italian comic opera, illuminating their composers' use of compositional convention and providing fresh understanding of age-old practices in the comic tradition. We now apprehend Mozart's *Figaro* and Rossini's *Barbiere* not only as singular masterpieces but also as the products of decades—even centuries—of operatic compositional practice.

Four of the seven articles on the Italian opera of the Settecento are linked through their focus on librettist Pietro Metastasio; the remaining three, to which we turn first, are devoted to Beaumarchais, Goldoni, and Pier Jacopo Martello.

The legendary French man-of-letters Pierre-Augustin Caron de Beaumarchais (1732–99) had been a *faiseur* of *parades* and *vaudevilles*, and indeed, the first incarnation of *Le barbier de Séville* belongs to the tradition of the *parade*.[43] In his role as *faiseur* of works in such genres, Beaumarchais would have found the guitar indispensable to the full realization of his conception, given its status as an assumed feature of the tradition.[44] That instrument's celebrated appearance in both Mozart's *Le nozze di Figaro* and Rossini's *Il barbiere di Siviglia* is thus contextualized historically, permitting us now to understand Cherubino's and Count Almaviva's songs and serenades to guitar accompaniment in a more historically informed way.

A noteworthy counterexample is the *séguedille* that Figaro sings to the guitar in Act II/23, which Beaumarchais calls an *air noté*, a term distinguishing pieces composed according to the rules of art ("en musique") from those that are part of "oral tradition." Pirrotta relates the distinction assumed in Beaumarchais's comedy to a time-honored distinction to which he and Howard Mayer Brown[45] had made reference innumerable times before: The distinction between compositions fashioned according to the practices of the *ars musica*—whose features had been regularized according to the precepts of that tradition—and those exemplifying the more "unruly" practices of the unwritten tradition.

Pirrotta further contextualizes the appearance of guitar-playing characters: the greater number of their compositions—and the use of the guitar in accompanying them—are part of the action, are performed—song and instrumental accompaniment alike—by the actors themselves, during the scene. They

---

[43]As Professor Heartz reminds me in a summation of Beaumarchais' importance to operatic history (private communication), the librettist furnished source material that was a stimulus, first, to Paisiello, whose achievement was in turn helpful to Da Ponte and Mozart when they were creating *Le nozze di Figaro*; the success of *Figaro*, in turn, was critical to the further collaboration on *Don Giovanni* and *Così fan tutte*.

[44]Professor Heartz informs me that guitar serenades sung and played by actors appearing on stage were commonplace in the offerings of the Comédie Italienne throughout the eighteenth century and even earlier.

[45]This distinction is invoked for example, in Brown, *Music in the French Secular Theater, 1400–1550* (Cambridge, MA: Harvard University Press, 1963), 107–08, 130–31, and echoed by Pirrotta in **1969:** *Music and Theatre*.

thus exemplify what he elsewhere described as the "realistic use of music in comedy."[46]

There are further echoes of theatrical tradition. In *Le mariage de Figaro*, the kiss and slap intended for the Countess and Cherubino and received instead by the Count and Figaro (V/6–7) eventually drive the characters to caricatural behavior: established routines ultimately derived from the commedia dell'arte. The elaborate, comic stage action involving the Count, Cherubino, and the large chair in Act I/7–8 is in the same tradition.

We are no longer able to view a performance of Mozart's or Rossini's comic masterpieces in quite the same way. Our experience of them has become more resonant and allusive, and various mythic moments are now understood as evocations of time-honored convention.

*****

"Divagazioni su Goldoni" is a further demonstration of the virtues of such contextualization. But the original impetus for the article was different.

Throughout his career, Pirrotta was concerned with questions of genre, specifically period understanding of genre and of distinctions in genre. That Mozart's *Don Giovanni* is termed—seemingly ambiguously—a "dramma giocoso" has prompted much hypothesizing about its interpretation, and unwarranted hypothesizing, too: the same nomenclature, Pirrotta documents, was also applied to the composer's *La finta semplice* and *Così fan tutte*, the latter undiluted comedy.[47] In fact, the term "dramma giocoso" has an even more venerable lineage: it appeared in Venetian libretti as early as 1744, associated especially with operas by composers of the Neapolitan "school."

And there are other respects in which the seeming ambiguity of the Mozartian usage may be no ambiguity at all. Although the evidently uncontested distinction between serious and "buffo" roles, which in turn highlights the supposed ambivalence of the mixed term "dramma giocoso," is characteristic of Goldonian libretti, it seems to have been the particular preference of Goldoni's printer Modesto Fenzo. Therefore, we ought not to be troubled by the period nomenclature, either that which suggests a sharp distinction between the serious and the "buffo," or nomenclature like "dramma giocoso" that suggests an ambivalence.[48]

Indeed, Pirrotta reveals that in the sixteenth-century commedia dell'arte tradition there was already a depicting of contrasting character types within

---

[46] See the chapter so entitled in **1969**: *Music and Theatre*. Less susceptible to convincing classification and interpretation is the "ariette dans le goût espagnol" that Rosina is to sing during the famous singing-lesson scene (III/4) in *Le barbier de Séville*.

[47] On the matter of genre in eighteenth-century opera, see the relevant chapter in Rice, *Mozart on the Stage*.

[48] On this matter generally, see Heartz, "Goldoni, *Opera Buffa*," 37–39, especially 39.

the same work: both the "innamorati"—more-or-less serious and dramatic character types—and the buffoonish, jocular "maschere." Such ambiguity was a conventional given of the comic theatrical genre: implicit and accepted, even if not specified.[49]

Similarly, that celebrated feature of comic opera—the tumultuous, concerted, act-ending finales, in which most of the characters participate—also seems by custom to have been a traditional element, the conventional culmination of the action in the comic theatrical genre.[50]

These observations lead in turn to an analysis of specific musical procedures in the two genres, serious and comic, and the distinctions between them. A "precipitous recitation"—the celebrated comic "patter"—produces "effects of accentuated comicity."[51] In opera seria—a genre whose principal attraction was instead the solo arias of celebrated singers—monologic and dialogic recitatives give way to scene-ending exit arias. In opera comica (Pirrotta's preferred term, rather than "opera buffa")—although there, too, we find solo arias—choruses, duets, and ensembles predominate, the last being especially suited to the celebrated finales.[52]

These are not entirely unfamiliar matters; and yet, Pirrotta's handling of them, and above all his historical contextualization, permits us to understand them in a more ramified way.

*****

---

[49]On this critically important matter of character types and their appearance across genres, time periods, and national traditions, see Rice, *Mozart on the Stage*, 34–35; there, Rice—quoting Northrup Frye's classic "The Mythos of Spring: Comedy" in his *Anatomy of Criticism* (Princeton, NJ: Princeton University Press, 1957), 163–86—introduces the notion of the "dramatic archetype" of the "obstructing character"; he further cites Mary Hunter's identification of the dramatic situation of the "triumph of young love over rigidity, lust, or greed in the form of a father, uncle, or guardian [Rice' 'obstructing character'] who tries to prevent his daughter, niece, or ward from marrying the young man of her choice." The recurrence of this device in such diverse works as Machiavelli's *Mandragola*, Rossini's *Barber of Seville*, and the Gilbert and Sullivan operas makes manifest the profundity of the tradition. See my *Scena 5.ª* on the "madrigal comedies" of the Renaissance, where such types and situations occur.

[50]Lorenzo da Ponte's famous injunction concerning act-ending finales thus expresses long-standing tradition, and the finale to Act II of Mozart's *Le nozze di Figaro* serves as a brilliant case in point. The operettas of Gilbert and Sullivan, which in so many other ways reveal an adherence to pan-European tradition in comic opera, also do so with respect to the structure and character of act-ending finales. On the all-important question of the *buffo finale*, see also Heartz, "Goldoni, *Opera Buffa*," 28 and n. 3; Heartz, "The Creation of the Buffo Finale in Italian Opera," *Proceedings of the Royal Musical Association* 104 (1977–78): 67–78; Heartz, "Goldoni, Don Giovanni and the Dramma Giocoso," *Musical Times* 120 (1979): 993–95, 997–98; and John Platoff, "Musical and Dramatic Structure in the Opera Buffa Finale," *Journal of Musicology* 7 (1989): 191–230.

[51]This is yet another feature of the pan-European comic-operatic tradition that is also invoked in the Gilbert and Sullivan operas.

[52]Pirrotta also offers observations about the poetic and metrical distinctions between recitative and aria verse in Italian opera, distinctions that are echoed in surveys by Lorenzo Bianconi ("Italy 3. Drama and Form: A Historical Outline," in *The New Grove Dictionary of Opera*, ed. Stanley Sadie [London: Macmillan; New York: Grove's Dictionaries of Music, 1992]) and Thomas Walker (*Il Medoro* [see "Scena 5.ª," n. 63]).

The article on Martello is an *explication de texte*, a decoding of the *Quinta sessione* of Martello's *Dialogo sopra la tragedia antica e moderna*.[53] Martello reveals an awareness of the blistering critique of opera then ripening among the Arcadians, who often associated the genre with that other quintessentially Italian form of theater, the commedia dell'arte. In the words of Ludovico Antonio Muratori, Martello and his great contemporary and fellow librettist Apostolo Zeno "must suffer in having such ignorance forced upon them," for no other reason than "to serve the taste of our times";[54] and, in fact, Martello acknowledges his ambivalence concerning the conflict between the classicistic tendencies to which he as *letterato* subscribed and the professional and financial exigencies that he and his peers typically encountered. Indeed, Pirrotta cites Martello's "realism," his "indulgence," his greater "humor," and his recognition of the "absurdity" of attempting to impose literary standards on a genre like opera, in which the literary element is only one of many, and not the first in importance.[55]

Martello's dialog thus highlights the opposition then emerging between the Arcadians' austere views on music and those attributed to the interlocutor whom Martello calls the "Imposter" (Aristotle). Muratori, Arcadian par excellence, disparages the music of his time, in established parlance, which—in its invocation of arguments about the potential negative effects of music on the "well-ruled City" and the "customs of the people"—can be traced back to Plato.[56] Martello's Imposter, on the contrary, exalts contemporary music, proclaims that "[t]he musical composition is the very substance of operas, and all the other parts are incidental, poetry among them," and asserts that "this music . . . is one of the most marvelous and perfect arts in the world. Pasquini, . . . the two Scarlattis, . . . Bononcini, . . . Pollaroli, . . . and so many others . . . shall live on in their works to the end of time."[57]

---

[53]See now Pier Jacopo Martello, from "On Ancient and Modern Tragedy (1715)," in *The Baroque Era*, ed. Margaret Murata, *Source Readings in Music History*, ed. Oliver Strunk, rev. ed. (New York: W.W. Norton, 1998), 4:178–83, and Piero Weiss "Pier Jacopo Martello on Opera (1715): An Annotated Translation," *Musical Quarterly* 66 (1980): 378–403.

[54]My translation is taken from **1982**: "Metastasio and the Demands of his Literary Environment."

[55]**1982**: "Metastasio and the Demands of His Literary Environment," **1982**: "Metastasio e i teatri romani."

[56]See my compilation of related texts from Plato, to Cicero, to the Renaissance educators, and to the Arcadians, in *The Maecenas and the Madrigalist: Patrons, Patronage, and the Origins of the Italian Madrigal* (Philadelphia, PA: American Philosophical Society, 2004), chapt. 1. The Platonic lineage of Muratori's critique is referenced in **1993**: "Metastasio e il terminare le scene con spirito e vivezza," where Pirrotta cites the "distant critiques" of Plato.

[57]See **1993**: "Metastasio e il terminare le scene con spirito e vivezza." I am quoting the translation of Weiss, "Pier Jacopo Martello on Opera."

*****

The articles on Metastasio, occasioned by the 1982 bicentennial of the librettist's death, are appropriately considered as a group.[58] Although Pirrotta would not have so characterized them, they are effectively an exposition of the emergence and distinguishing features of what opera historian Philip Gossett has called "Metastasian traditions": that "grand Metastasian design"[59] that influenced the course of operatic history for many decades. Such traditions were decisively supplanted only at the beginning of the nineteenth century, when a new set of operatic conventions emerged: the "Code Rossini," to which Gossett has devoted such careful scholarship; it in turn influenced Italian operatic composition for much of the remainder of the Ottocento.[60]

However, Metastasio initially had other professional aspirations and did not necessarily envision a career for himself as librettist.[61] But during the early Neapolitan phase of his activity,[62] he was commissioned to provide verse

---

[58]In a sense, the series on Metastasio is anticipated as early as **1962**: contributions to the panel discussions "The Concept of the New in Music from the *Ars Nova* to the Present Day" and "The Neapolitan Tradition in Opera." For a subsequent consideration of the entire series, see Friedrich Lippmann, "Rileggendo i lavori di Nino Pirrotta su Metastasio," *Il melodramma di Pietro Metastasio: la poesia, la musica, la messa in scena e l'opera italiana del Settecento*, ed. Elena Sala Di Felice and Rossana Caira Lumetti, (Rome: Aracne, 2001), 805–22. Writing of Pirrotta's four articles, Lippmann suggests (806) that "Questi . . . trovano posto tra le più importanti pubblicazioni metastasiane degli ultimi decenni, e la loro rilettura è estremamente proficua." Pirrotta's original treatment is enriched with Lippmann's references to subsequent scholarship, and although he offers some alternative interpretations (e.g., 818), he concludes (821–22)—signaling some of the same characteristics of Pirrotta's scholarly discourse that innumerable others have signaled—that "la musicologia ha presentato lavori significativi, ma moltissimo rimane ancora da fare. Mancano, con poche eccezioni, accurate ricerche stilistiche sui compositori che hanno musicato i drammi di Metastasio. . . . Gli argomenti non mancano. Per il loro trattamento ci possono essere di guida gli scritti di Nino Pirrotta, con la loro lungimiranza, il loro intuito per l'essenziale[,] e la loro impostazione interdisciplinare."

[59]Gossett, "The 'Candeur Virginale' of 'Tancredi,'" *Musical Times* 112 (1971): 326–29, 326: "Metastasian traditions"; Gossett, "Rossini, Gioachino," *Grove Music Online. Oxford Music Online*, http://0-www.oxfordmusiconline.com.libcat.lafayette.edu/subscriber/article/grove/music/23901 (accessed 13 June 2010): "the conventional world of Metastasian *opera seria*"; "the grand Metastasian design."

[60]However, I offer the following qualification, for which I am grateful to Professor Heartz: the "grand Metastasian design" was, in fact, disintegrating well before the beginning of the nineteenth century. Among the factors affecting that development were substantial interpolations of ballet music, and a predilection for French models (see, for example, Mozart's magisterial *Idomeneo*). As Heartz suggested to me, in setting the libretto of *La clemenza di Tito*, Mozart had his librettist Mazzolà trim and alter the original text drastically: three acts were reduced to two, and choruses, other ensembles, and finales were added. And when entering the reference to the work in his thematic catalog, Mozart characterized the work, revealingly, as "Opera seria ridotta à vera opera." Metastasio continued to be admired for the refined quality of his verse, but the grand design associated with his name had long since disintegrated.

[61]In what follows, I am summarizing Pirrotta's arguments closely, and often in his own words, which I have translated into English.

[62]See not only the four articles on Metastasio, but also **1994**: *Don Giovanni's Progress*, 9.

for three "theatrical actions" performed at private aristocratic venues, which were the occasion for decisive and congenial encounters with new leading operatic composers of the Neapolitan school: Feo, Porpora, Sarro, and perhaps also Vinci, who were just then emerging on the national and international scenes, and whose style was marked by a new composure and expressive "cantabilità." Step by step, the future librettist was drawn into a professional association with opera composers. And with respect to his personal preferences in the musical elaboration of his texts, he remained forevermore partial to those "good professors" of the Neapolitan school who set his earliest libretti.

Metastasio's initial formation was thus completed, around 1725, within a setting populated by composers who best represent the transition from "the Baroque" to a new style period, for which—in Pirrotta's estimation—there was not yet an adequate designation: neither "Rococo"; nor "Stil Galant" (both of which are derived from other arts and cultures and capture the sense of lightness and precious fineness, but not the more substantial clarity, equilibrium, and plastic relief that characterize Italian vocal and instrumental music of this period); nor "preclassical" (predicated on the equivocal bundling together of the three great Viennese masters Haydn, Mozart, and Beethoven). In fact, the style of the music in question evinces a full-blown "classicism," parallel to that advocated by the Arcadians (who nonetheless manifested very little regard for it), yet different from their classicism in its greater spontaneity and freedom from abstract theorizing.

Pirrotta also suggests that it is not yet appropriate to speak of "Neapolitan" or "Metastasian" opera, given that both designations suggest a substantial difference in stylistic direction from other traditions of Italian operatic composition, when, in fact, such designations are warranted principally on the basis of the greater excellence of the Metastasian and Neapolitan achievement rather than its distinctiveness.

The Neapolitan phase of Metastasio's career also reveals the *letterato*'s professionalism, which was counterbalancing his purely literary preoccupations. The ambivalence that was thenceforth to define Metastasio's entire career—the conflict between the *letterato* on the one hand, who would always refer to his operatic libretti as "mine" ("'my' *Ezio*," "'my' *Demetrio*"), and, on the other, the realist, sensitive to professional exigencies—emerges as early as the Neapolitan years.[63]

A return to Rome and a renewed, cordial association with the Arcadians permitted Metastasio to surrender to the more purely literary side of his

---

[63]See above for my recapitulation of Pirrotta's article on Martello, where this same ambivalence is identified, in both Martello and Muratori.

artistic personality. The last twenty years of the seventeenth century witnessed a new naturalism and rationalism, a reaction to Seicentismo and what the Arcadians regarded as its "Baroque" bombast and bizarreness. There was a longing for a new Renaissance, whose tastes and standards would be consonant with those of the Quattrocento and Cinquecento Renaissance, and, through it, with the achievement of the classical world. Francesco Redi, a Florentine physician, was a paradigmatic figure in the Arcadian movement: His scientific sensibilities suggested a taste for precision of thought and clarity of expression believed to be transferable to literary practice.

In general terms, the Arcadian "reform" resulted in the elimination of the comic elements of dramatic works;[64] in a classicizing, neo-Aristotelian simplification of the plot; in a better characterization of the personages by means of the dialog; and in a purification of the poetic language, the highest expressions of which were the translucence and "musicality" of Metastasian literary style.

Concerning the first outcome of the reform, Pirrotta observes that the abolition of all comicality—embodied above all in the inclusion of comic character types (servants, nurses, and other "lowly" characters)—although it undeniably eliminated abuses, also eliminated a cherished element of variety in the musico-dramatic conception, which was promptly re-established in the new independent genre of comic opera.[65]

Maintaining fidelity to the rules of theatrical poetry suggests an identification of opera with tragedy. A much-needed reconciliation of the literary content of the opera libretto with the traditions of tragedy was attained. However, there was the enduring problem that the librettist had to balance such austere theoretical considerations with the inconsistent claims of the musical element and its composers and performers.

For Metastasio, the critical development was a commission that permitted him to contribute to the restoration of tragedy: "his" *Catone in Utica*. In various libretti, "his" *Didone abbandonata* had already been designated a "tragedy for music," consistent with the protagonist's tragic end; however, it was not so designated in the 1727 Roman libretto, Metastasio surely doubting that such a designation was appropriate to an opera so permeated with the

---

[64]On this matter, which was understood by period observers such as Goldoni himself, see Heartz, "Goldoni, *Opera Buffa*," 37–38.

[65]Pirrotta also observes that the variety, flexibility, and dramatic impact of seventeenth-century opera were gradually lost, replaced by a new inflexible structure that asserted the rigid alternation of dialogic recitative and *da capo* exit aria; note his obvious love for seventeenth-century opera and his celebration of its virtues. On this set of developments, see Heartz, "Goldoni, *Opera Buffa*," 37–38, which documents Goldoni's own conversance with them.

sweetness of amorous sentiments. It was justified, instead, in the *Catone* by the conflicts of strong passions and exaltation of Roman virtue, not to mention the catastrophic plot elements.

For librettists and composers, the most urgent matter raised by the Arcadians was that of the theatrical uses of music: the justification for such uses, in what quantities, and of what sort.[66]

As of the Lenten season of 1730, Metastasio was imperial poet at the Viennese court. There was a reformist character to his activity there, although only in a restricted and personal sense. His experiences and achievements were governed by the character of the Material infrastructure at that particular court, where the sovereign—sympathetic to the objectives of the Arcadian reformers—had the authority to regulate all courtly artistic enterprises.

Metastasio was by no means entirely freed from the strictures imposed by the usual practical requirements of operatic activity. But given the nature of imperial court life, he was relatively shielded from their effects and able to produce literary work that was more mediated (exemplifying dramatic action and dialog more fully in harmony with Arcadian artistic criteria) and characterized by fuller use of the chorus and a greater number of roles than customary.

Initially, Metastasio was not entirely satisfied with the specific musical possibilities represented by the composers of the imperial court: Caldara's music, for example, was thought too antiquated, too contrapuntal. Later, Metastasio was to develop greater sympathy for the talents of Jommelli and Hasse; the enduring effects of the librettist's early experiences in Naples are revealed once more.[67]

Most notable—even surprising, in retrospect—is Metastasio's disdain for Gluck, whom the librettist dismissed as "that arch-Vandal."[68] Charles Burney provided an illuminating glimpse of the rival schools of operatic composition in Vienna in mid-century and the aesthetic sensibilities underlying each. Heading one school were Metastasio and Hasse, who regarded all operatic innovation as the practices of charlatans; they instead adhered to an antiquated vision of music drama, in which the librettist and composer claimed equal attention from the opera-going public: the librettist in the dialogic recitatives,

---

[66]In **1994**: "Poesia e musica," Pirrotta reflects on the ancient hostility toward every form of poetry destined to be associated with music, a prejudice that more modern criticism has perhaps inherited from the bitter polemic of the founders of the Arcadian movement and their disciples—Gravina, Crescimbeni, Muratori—which was aroused against the corrupt prevailing vogue of the music drama (the 18th-century *opera seria libretto*). In **1992**: "Contemplando la musa assente," he, similarly, reflects on the tradition of a "poetry for music," toward which there is a diffidence in our literary culture that perhaps goes back to the aversion of the Arcadians toward the union of word and music, which for them culminated in the "forced ignorance" of those poets who were nonetheless constrained to write "dramas for music." See the synopsis of Pirrotta's article on Martello, above, and the quotation from Muratori contained therein.

[67]On these preferences, in addition to the articles on Metastasio, see also **1994**: *Don Giovanni's Progress*, 9.

[68]**1994**: *Don Giovanni's Progress*, 36.

the composer in the arias and ensembles. Heading the other school were Gluck and his librettist Calzabigi.[69]

Metastasio's mature aesthetic precepts and practices were thus forged from these varied experiences. Codified and emulated by his contemporaries, they constitute his putative contribution to the operatic reform associated with his name.

But throughout his career, Pirrotta was given to qualifying received opinion, whenever such qualification was demanded. And it was demanded in this case. As he suggested, the concept of "Metastasian opera" is linked to that related, yet ill-understood, concept of a "Metastasian *reform* of opera." Indeed, there is a tendency to narrate the entire history of eighteenth-century opera as the history of its reforms: Furgoni and Traetta's; above all Calzabigi and Gluck's in 1770s Vienna. But despite the unquestionable artistic and historical interest of such episodes, they were isolated phenomena: "greenhouse flowers," associated with the tastes of one court or another, not necessarily having immediate repercussions for the principal European operatic practices of the time.

Pirrotta's argument here is not unlike that advanced earlier in his career, in reference to the character of medieval and early-modern European music, which featured written polyphonic music but also other musical practices that are not extensively documented by notated sources, ordinarily "the coin of the realm" for the music historian. Our fixation on the written document and understandable interest in polyphony, on artistic and historical grounds, misleads us. It was one option, though perhaps an isolated one, not necessarily broadly characteristic of the musical culture writ large.

So, too, in the case of eighteenth-century opera, the reform movements are important and interesting, but the predominant operatic culture of the time ought to be understood in other terms, rather than as the result of a privileging of the achievements of the reformers.

Pirrotta invokes a revealing visual metaphor: of the history of opera as a river, with principal and crosscurrents. We are inclined to assume that Metastasian opera was the principal current when, in fact, the crosscurrents played a preponderant role and reduced truly Metastasian opera to a trickle: crystalline in its exemplarity, yet nonetheless meagre. The principal current was formed instead by the multiform activity of the many opera theaters of Europe,

---

[69]Pirrotta provides a fuller synopsis of Burney's report on his encounter with Metastasian operatic practices in mid-century Vienna, which is extremely revealing of the librettist's tastes and artistic proclivities. He regarded the music of the preceding era to be too full of fugal writing and other such artifices to be apprehended, except by the privileged initiate among members of the audience, and he regarded contemporary musical composition as exemplifying an undeniably great "scientific" character, with respect to counterpoint, the conversance with the instruments, and the singers' vocal powers, but there is an element of wistfulness in Metastasio's observations.

which often compromised the artistic qualities of Metastasio's libretti (or those of Metastasian character) as the result of their being transplanted: of the adjustments dictated by local conditions and the demands of local fashion and taste. Metastasio's very success precipitated a situation in which his dramas were immediately reprised elsewhere and replicated numerous times, often with new music by different composers; as a result, each Metastasian text was subject to modifications: adapted to those contingencies from which Metastasio the *letterato* had attempted to shield it.

Therefore, the changes in the conventions of operatic composition occurring during the first three decades of the eighteenth century are not especially attributable to Metastasio (nor to his great contemporary Apostolo Zeno). Rather, they were gradual, the result of both: (1) generic Arcadian influences on the one hand; and, on the other, (2) the claims of the composers and performers of the music per se.

1. With respect to the first: Metastasio (and Zeno) must have felt conflicted about the inconsistency between their aspirations as *letterati* and the demands governing their literary activity as librettists, which resulted from their status as professionals in the service of powerful benefactors. Therefore, Metastasio's true contribution to a reform of opera was that of *letterato*, who, although accepting the practical necessities associated with the musical elaboration of his texts and the entire operatic spectacle, was nonetheless aiming to transform opera into a genre possessing autonomous literary value. His reform, like all those that form part of the narrative of eighteenth-century operatic history, was associated with the ambitus of a particular setting: it could be actuated only within the context of the imperial court.

In 1732 begins Metastasio's vast correspondence with Bettinelli concerning the printing of the first of numerous collections of his works, which were thus made available to a wider audience than the opera-going public: the silent audience of readers. It is the expression of a novel concept of drama, capable of possessing independent literary value, and it is only in this sense—and it is not an insignificant one—that we can speak of a true "Metastasian reform," where the librettist's literary output was freed of the tyranny imposed by the requirements of "theatrical convenience."[70]

In contrast, Eximeno's 1776 plan to publish a selection of the musical settings of Metastasio's texts is among the earliest expressions of a new, "post-Arcadian" sympathy for theatrical music per se, not theatrical music as intended for immediate consumption but as an enduring product of human creativity, meritorious of lasting appreciation, no less than a poet's verses or a painter's paintings.

---

[70] Goldoni's libretti were subject to the same treatment: see Heartz, "Goldoni, *Opera Buffa*," 29.

All the same, a recognition of the full artistic validity of the musical elaboration of his texts remained extraneous to Metastasio's fundamentally Arcadian mentality. Although he appreciated that opera was a grand, "artisanal," collective enterprise, he believed that, nonetheless, the sole elements susceptible to attaining artistic stature were the literary element of the dramatic plot and its realization in verse.

2. With respect to the second: from a musicologist's perspective, the developments that are of particular interest are the more purely "artisanal" musical developments emerging concurrently with the rationalistic philosophizing of the Arcadians to produce what we now celebrate as "the grand Metastasian design."

Differences among the multiple settings of a single libretto illuminate changes over time in operatic composition. According to Robert Freeman's findings,[71] which assist in isolating some of the principal elements of the late-Seicento/early-Settecento reform, comic scenes are reduced in number, or eliminated altogether;[72] a progressive diminution in the number of arias results in the individual aria's attaining an ampler and more complex design, typified by the da capo procedure; the musical distinction between aria and recitative is ever more sharply drawn; and the position of the aria in the dramatic context is redefined, leading to a decline in the number of entrance, medial, and medial-exit arias, and a corresponding increase in the number of exit arias.

This last development is reported on by none other than Pier Jacopo Martello:

> Exit arias must close every scene, and no singer may exit without first warbling a canzonetta. Whether 'tis verisimilar is not material. It is much too pleasant to hear a scene end with spirit and vivacity ("con spirito e vivezza").[73]

Pirrotta thus draws a contrast between seventeenth- and eighteenth-century operatic designs: the reduction in the number of arias and the increase in their scale make their insertion into the dialog considerably more difficult. During the seventeenth century, the aria had been a dynamic element in the dialog and action; the Settecento design makes this deployment of the aria—its seamless, inextricable embedding within the dialog—almost impossible.

But if the aria's increasing scale made it difficult for Metastasio (and other librettists) to adjust it to the course of the dialog and action, it increased the

---

[71]In addition to Freeman's findings cited by Pirrotta, those in three articles by Harold S. Powers are illuminating: "*Il* Serse *trasformato* —I" (see "Scena 6.ª," n. 23), and "*Il* Serse *trasformato*— II," *Musical Quarterly* 48 (1962): 73–92; "*L'*Erismena *travestita*" (see "Scena 6.ª," n. 23); and "*Il* «Mutio» *tramutato*" (see "*Intermedio I.*ᵐᵒ," n. 146).

[72]Heartz, "Goldoni, *Opera Buffa*," 37–38.

[73]See the translation by Weiss, "Pier Jacopo Martello on Opera," 394. Note the final phrase in the translation, which furnishes Pirrotta with the title of one of his articles on Metastasio.

sense of exaltation that the aria was now assuming: as peroration, as final pronouncement serving as conclusion to an episode, or as announcement of developments yet to come.

The ampler scope of the aria—the "sense of monumentality"—is often also attributed to the growing influence of bel canto, virtuoso singers. Pirrotta attributes it as well to a tendency among period composers toward broader musical forms, parallel to developments in instrumental music.[74] Opera composers, increasingly concerned with formal organization, wrote longer da capo arias, featuring an elaborate interplay of voice and orchestra that recalls the contemporary instrumental solo concerto and concerto grosso, with their glittering orchestral ritornelli.

Indeed, the analogy of the alternating of orchestral ritornelli (the "tutti") with the vocal "solos" is undeniable, as are other elements of the correspondence with the contemporary concerto and concerto grosso: the orchestral accompaniment is lightened at the moment when the vocal solo emerges, and the "B" section of the canonical ABA' da capo aria design is characterized by a more extended adventurous conception (tonally if not vocally), while our sense of the tonal design of the entire composition is stabilized and reinforced through the return to the tonic key at the repeat of A (A'). The aria is thus constructed as an alternation of soloistic vocal episodes framed by orchestral ritornelli, in which the central soloistic vocal episode (B) plays a critical role in the structural and tonal design:[75]

ritornello [instrumental "tutti"] | **A** [vocal solo] | ritornello | **B** | ritornello | **A'** | ritornello

The correspondences with the structural and tonal design of ritornello form in the contemporary concerto and concerto grosso are obvious. Pirrotta's analysis furnishes an additional data set relevant to an understanding of "Baroque" "monothematicism" and its distinction from the "polythematicism" of the "Classic" era.[76]

To characterize another factor in the increase in scale of the aria and the ever growing distinction between it and the recitative, Pirrotta invokes classic Materialist understanding of causality: the social aspects of the operatic "rite," which transformed the entire spectacle into an occasion for socializing,

---

[74] This observation is made not only in the articles on Metastasio but also in **1994**: *Don Giovanni's Progress*, 10.

[75] This is another example of a programmatic trajectory in Pirrotta's writings, since these observations are very reminiscent of those in **1972**: "Studi corelliani" (summarized in my "*Scena 8.ª*"), where Pirrotta makes extended reference to the structure and tonal architecture of Baroque *ritornello* procedure.

[76] On this matter, see Edward T. Cone's essay *Musical Form and Musical Performance* (New York: W.W. Norton, 1968) and Giorgio Pestelli's *The Age of Mozart and Beethoven* (Cambridge: Cambridge University Press, 1984).

conversation, and—ultimately—card-playing, so that the listener's attention was diverted from all moments other than those that best showcased the most admired singers and their virtuosity. It reinforced the already existing tendency to place the aria at the culmination of each discrete phase of the dramatic situation, which had been developed by the recitative. And given that the dramatic situations were often known to the audience because of the frequent resetting of the same libretti, the audience's curiosity, inevitably, was piqued by those moments of greater musical novelty.

In sum, although Metastasio would certainly not have regarded poetry as mere "accident," he undoubtedly shared some of the esteem for music, assuming that the list of appropriate composers was up-to-date. Contrary to every criterion of verisimilitude invoked by rationalist critics, he could not judge his arias to be additions existing outside the time and logic of the action. They had a proper dimension whose differentness was accepted (indeed, on the whole forgotten) once the curtain was raised and the opening notes of the overture played. In such dimension and difference, the aria did not have the function of static comment, but was a source of excitement that underscored the tragic pathos.

Until the end, however, Metastasio remained faithful to a polarized conception of musical drama as the regular alternation of recitative and aria. This conception of opera had been attained in the first few decades of the eighteenth century, under contrasting but ultimately converging impulses: of the rigorous aesthetic and unilaterally literary reformism of the Arcadians,[77] from the one side; and, from the other, the exigency of more extended and articulate formal structures inherent in the development of the musical language, whether vocal or instrumental.

In the seclusion of a closed ambience, Metastasio perhaps made too much of that conception, accepting music as the vehicle of poetic expression in the recitative and admitting reluctantly that the poetry served the expressive expansion of the music in the static moment of the aria. Extraneous and incomprehensible to him was every attempt to supplant the dialectic and verisimilitude of the *poetic* with the dialectic (less precisely semantic but still efficacious and coherent) and improbable verisimilitude of the *musical expression*.

*****

Although Pirrotta would never give the development of Italian opera per se the kind of systematic monographic treatment that he lavished on the preoperatic

---

[77]Metastasio's essential fidelity to the Arcadians' aesthetic principles is suggested by a letter, which Pirrotta summarizes (**1983**: "I musicisti nell'epistolario . . . " 250–51).

theatrical uses of music in *Li due Orfei*, the many articles on post-1600 opera, when read as a group, furnish a panoramic account of the evolution of the genre from its beginnings until 1800, and even beyond: from the Florentine and Mantuan aristocratic phases and the early Monteverdi; to Roman hagiographic opera and related genres, the brothers Mazzocchi, and the earliest example of the *cavatina*; to the genre's Venetian commercial phase, its librettists, the late Monteverdi, and Cavalli; to Antonio Cesti; to Alessandro Stradella; to the Arcadian "reform" of the late Seicento and the establishment of the "code Metastasio";[78] to the comic traditions of the mid- to late eighteenth century; and, finally, to the establishment and development of the "great tradition" of the Ottocento (Rossini, Bellini, and Verdi).

*****

Like many elderly people, Pirrotta experienced some depression during his retirement, specifically during the late 1980s. Such a psychological response to retirement is understandable when the person has led a rich, full life, abundant in professional responsibilities and accomplishments. Now, there was the absence of an established "infrastructure," not to mention the absence of responsibilities associated with regular professional activity. Pirrotta's depression was momentarily debilitating, and it prevented him from pursuing his musicological scholarship. But he recovered, and was professionally active once more.

All the same, the physical effects of aging were sadly unalterable and the consequences sadly predictable. On 18 February 1996, Pirrotta's wife, who had left their apartment in the Parioli district to attend to errands, collapsed on the sidewalk at the bottom of the stairs.

There can be little doubt that Pirrotta never recovered from his wife's death. But he sought refuge in his scholarship, and several important studies appeared during the period following Lea's death; some were published posthumously.

In 1997, Pirrotta fractured a vertebra, and the resulting pain prevented further scholarly work. Moreover, the fracture and a concurrent heart arrhythmia made it inadvisable for him to remain alone. In November 1997 he moved to Palermo to live with his daughter Silvia.

*****

Antonino Pirrotta died at Silvia's home in Palermo on 22 January 1998, at 89 years of age. His remains—and Lea's—were interred in Palermo. The Italian daily *Il Messaggero* wrote of Pirrotta:[79]

---

[78] I am adapting the terminology of Julian Budden, who wrote illuminatingly of the "Code Rossini."

[79] Alfredo Gasponi, "E morto a Palermo, a 89 anni, il grande studioso. La sua lezione: rigore e passione. Addio Nino Pirrotta, padre della musicologia moderna," *Il Messaggero* (24 January 1998). For providing me with copies of the obituaries in Italian dailies, I am grateful to Professor Agostino Ziino and Paolo Granata-Ziino.

> He was a shy and modest man and would never put himself at the head of the line, but if, for this reason, his name is not celebrated, his prestige in the world of music at the highest levels was immense. Because Nino Pirrotta, who died the day before yesterday in his native Palermo at the age of 89, was the father of modern musicology. A man from a by-gone era, sensitive and with an aristocratic manner, he brought new and rigorous methods of inquiry to a discipline that had become sclerotic by the middle of the century: methods that after him were made their own by the principal students of music that is distant in time, shrouded in mystery because of the scarcity of the sources. Pirrotta's story is like that of numerous talented scholars who, unable to find work in Italy, were forced to go abroad. In the mid-1950s, he won a *concorso* for a university professorship in the history of music, but the chairs were entirely occupied. In 1956 he therefore accepted an invitation from Harvard University.... From his "school" issued many of the most brilliant American and Italian musicologists of the last few generations.... [H]e directed the library of the Conservatory of Palermo and then that of the Conservatory of Santa Cecilia in Rome. There, he had occasion to view hundreds of prints and manuscripts, in great part unknown, and he realized that they overturned many theses in traditional musicology, which often proceeded by means of hypothesis, and without troubling to check the sources or find new ones.[80] Above all, he developed the idea that the history of music cannot be separated from the history of culture: literature, philosophy, history of art. In these disciplines could be retraced testimony and hints of missing links, of music that has not come down to us, either because the sources are lost or because it was entrusted to oral tradition.... This great scholar did not consider philological rigor a "totem".... He thought that introducing music into the schools was more important than achieving perfection in the musicological field. His modernity lies in his refusal to consider research as an ivory tower.

La Nazione styled him "the dean of Italian musicologists and the most famous of them at an international level," "the greatest of the Italian musicologists of the twentieth century."

> To the end, he preserved a fidelity and love for his roots as a musician, but also a scientific rigor.

However, his studies were "never drily 'philological,'" but were

> rather always guided by an interest in the aesthetic facts and customs that in his scholarship united the medieval masters with the theatre of Malipiero, the Florentine musical Camerata, and Monteverdi, Dufay, and the Venetian eighteenth century.

In the United States, obituaries appeared in the *New York Times* (3 February 1998) and the Pittsburgh *Post-Gazette* (4 February 1998). Harvard University memorialized Pirrotta with a notice in the *Harvard Magazine* (May/June 1998). One of the most epigrammatically concise yet also illuminating characterizations of Pirrotta's authorial style and profile was provided by the Harvard

---

[80]Note the implicit reference to Pirrotta's fidelity to the Positivistic enterprise of controlling the primary sources, and the implicit refutation of Idealism.

Faculty Memorial Minute, which attests some of those same qualities of intellect and character identified in the Italian obituaries:

> The so-called gap between the "positivistic" and the "critical" did not exist for him, ... [H]e provided a model of how to fuse historically justified exegeses of specific problems, works, and situations with a highly individual and personal viewpoint.[81]

Fuller, more formal reflections by Italian musicologists—Nicoletta Guidobaldi,[82] Pierluigi Petrobelli,[83] Franco Piperno[84]—were also published. Piperno identified Pirrotta as "the principal—if not the sole—Italian musicologist of international scope," and suggested that

> [t]he name of Nino Pirrotta is indissolubly linked to moments and personages of our musical past ... several of which, without his illuminating studies, would have remained arid material for lexicographical compilations rather than becoming objects of loving investigation. ... Pirrotta was unique in the ability to coordinate a concrete interest for the musical page (Pirrotta loved Landini's *ballate* as he loved Monteverdi's madrigals, Cavalli's operas, and Bellini's *Il pirata*) with the exigencies of scientific rigor of research, turned toward responding to its various "why"s (cultural motivations, philological problems, origins and tradition), and in the ability to develop it well beyond the anxieties of the documentary or bibliographical type, in order to make of them an occasion for real intellectual deepening and conceptual verification on an interdisciplinary basis.

The Italian obituaries refer to that elusive quality that has long been perceived in Pirrotta's writings and his scholarly persona, but never fully satisfactorily described: that disinclination to surrender entirely to either uncritical Positivistic reverence for "philological rigor," or sclerotic hypothesizing "without troubling to check the sources or find new ones"; to either the "drily 'philological,'" or the aesthetic; to either "arid ... lexicographical compilations," "the exigencies of scientific rigor," and "the anxieties of the documentary or bibliographical type," or "loving investigation," "a concrete interest in the musical page," and "intellectual deepening and conceptual verification."

---

[81]The full text of the "Faculty of Arts and Sciences Memorial Minute," written by Reinhold Brinkmann, Elliott Forbes, Lewis Lockwood, Christoph Wolff, was printed in the *Harvard University Gazette* for 9 July 1998.

[82]*Early Music* 26 (1998): 531–32.

[83]Petrobelli's obituary deserves the closest possible reading: *Acta musicologica* 70 (1998): XIII–XV.

[84]Piperno, "Omaggio a Nino Pirrotta" (see "Scena 3.ª," n. 43).

Epilogo

Pirrotta's Narrative of the History of Italian Music: Music and "Cultural Fashion"

Given the Mediterranean's status as a complex organic cultural system and Italy's prominent place within it, as repository, ancient pan-Mediterranean traditions were destined to influence Italy's artistic expression, including its "ethnophonic patrimony."[1] The primeval Hellenic, Theocritan, "pagan" mythological elements underlying Mediterranean (and specifically Sicilian) experience have left their traces in the arts of the Mediterranean world[2]—music among them—throughout its long history and vast geographic reaches. As "recently" as the sixteenth century emerged the *greghesca*, a musical genre setting texts in the patois of the "Orientalized," Venetian lingua franca of the Mediterranean ports, which evoked the linguistic practices of the *stradioti*, Greek mercenaries in the service of Venice.[3]

But there was also the converse, similarly attributable to the antiquity of Mediterranean cultures: their gradual emergence at a time when most inhabitants of that world could not enjoy ease of transportation and communication beyond their own local community. Existing concurrently with pan-Mediterranean sensibilities, therefore, were circumscribed local traditions: linguistic, musical, and artistic "dialects," with characteristics that readily distinguished them as Sicilian,[4] Neapolitan,[5] Bergamasque, Paduan, Venetian.[6] Linguistically, the regional languages associated with each of the different geopolitical entities were direct, parallel descendants of Latin; the musical traditions associated with those regional entities were also distinctive and identifiable.

Yet another characteristic that defined the artistic productivity of the Mediterranean world was its continuing dialectic—its tension—between popular and learned traditions, and between orality and literacy. Elusive vestiges of popular tradition that we can occasionally identify in the learned constitute what little evidence there is of widespread practices that are otherwise irretrievable, a musico-anthropological undertaking of great importance, subtlety, and complexity.[7]

These various characteristics of the culture of the Mediterranean world bequeathed to its music such features as "a delicate and graceful polymodality

---

[1] **1938:** review of Tiby, *La musica bizantina*.
[2] **1933–35:** 26–27 February 1934 "IL CONCERTO MULE AL TEATRO MASSIMO"; **1936–37:** review of Mompellio, *Pietro Vinci madrigalista siciliano*.
[3] **1956:** "Greghesca."
[4] **1968:** "Musica polifo5nica per un testo attribuito a Federico II"; **1972:** "New Glimpses of an Unwritten Tradition."
[5] **1980:** "Willaert and the *Canzone Villanesca*."
[6] **1972:** "Ricercari e variazioni su 'O rosa bella'"; **1984:** "Echi di arie veneziane del primo Quattrocento?"
[7] **1933–35:** 19–20 April 1934 "'Baronessa di Carini, di G. Mulè e 'Galatea, di A. Savasta al TEATRO MASSIMO"; **1968:** "Musica polifonica per un testo attribuito a Federico II"; **1972:** "New Glimpses of an Unwritten Tradition"; **1972:** "Ricercari e variazioni su 'O rosa bella,'"; **1980:** "Willaert and the *Canzone Villanesca*"; **1984:** "Echi di arie veneziane del primo Quattrocento?"

that gives the music an archaic flavor"[8] and such distinctive performance practices as the pan-Mediterranean predilection for solo-singing to the accompaniment of a bowed, strummed, or plucked string instrument.

But these are developments that predate our narrative, which begins instead around A.D. 1150.

*****

With the European "Renaissance of the twelfth century,"[9] powerful aesthetic and intellectual sensibilities emerged in northern Europe, associated above all with an educational program that might be termed "scholastic," and with the emergence late in the century of the University of Paris. The recovery of Aristotle's writings and the triumph of Aristotelian logic as an intellectual system or style, and the resultant emergence of a passion for intellectual order, were developments that were sufficiently robust and honored to influence many manifestations of elite culture: the prevailing architectural style (the "Gothic"), musico-compositional technique (complex polyrhythmic polyphony, which necessitated a musical notation that unambiguously specified pitch and pitch-duration, or rhythm).[10]

It is not a coincidence that the earliest decisive European solution to the problem of notating rhythm precisely is associated with Paris, medieval university-city par excellence.[11] And that same association with university cities of polyphonic practice and its customary supporting "technology" (the unambiguous notation of pitch and rhythm), which characterized the musical culture of medieval France, was typical of medieval Italy as well. Some of the major centers of polyphonic practice in fourteenth-century Italy were also university cities: Bologna and Padua, among others. It was perhaps natural that there should have been a congruence between an interest in musical notation on the one hand and the intellectual interests of the notaries, grammarians, and, above all, physicians on the other; and, indeed, one of the oldest known examples of Italian secular polyphony sets a text on a medical topic, which was sent to Accursino, physician of Boniface VIII. Among the guests depicted in the *Paradiso degli'Alberti* as attending a banquet hosted by Coluccio Salutati are the physician Marsilio di Santa Sofia and the natural philosopher Biagio Pelacani, who was the teacher of Giorgio Anselmi, son and grandson of physicians and author of a celebrated music-theoretical

---

[8]**1936–37**: review of Mompellio, *Pietro Vinci madrigalista siciliano*.

[9]My phrase is borrowed from the title of Charles Homer Haskins's classic volume: (Cambridge, MA: Harvard University Press, 1927).

[10]Erwin Panofsky, *Gothic Architecture and Scholasticism* (see "Prologo," n. 29); and Pirrotta **1965**: "Dante musicus"; **1972**: "Ars musica"; **1993**: notes to *O tu chara sciença*.

[11]**1993**: "Natura e problemi del testo musicale."

treatise, the *Dialogi de harmonia* (1434).[12] There was a commonality of intellectual sensibility among those who practiced the distinct yet related professions of medicine, natural philosophy, and polyphonic musical composition.[13]

The original impetus for the establishment of a vital, though circumscribed, Italian tradition of secular polyphonic composition may have been the taste for secular polyphony imported to early fourteenth-century Naples by its king, Robert d'Anjou[14] (a Frenchman, nota bene). In fact, Neapolitan practices proved repeatedly influential in Italian musical culture throughout the centuries that followed, for understandable reasons: as the seat of the sole royal court on the entire Italian peninsula, Naples commanded considerable interest throughout it, and ruling figures at other Italian aristocratic courts sought models in the political and cultural practices and achievements of the royal Neapolitans. Among them were the Visconti of Milan and the Scaligeri of Verona, the benefactors of the earliest known Italian polyphonists whose compositions have come down to us in any quantity: Johannes de Florentia and Jacobus de Bononia.[15]

From the aristocratic courts of northern Italy in the fourteenth century, the scene changes to Florence, whose status as a republic assumed a different Material basis to musical activity and polyphonic composition and performance. Many of the composers were ecclesiastics who composed and performed polyphony for their own delectation, rather than for aristocratic patrons. The primary sources documenting both northern and Florentine manifestations of the development suggest that polyphonic settings of madrigal and caccia verse precede those of ballata verse. And Giosuè Carducci's assumption to the contrary notwithstanding, the polyphonic madrigal and caccia—rather than being expressions of Carducci's "mondo elegante" of Trecento Florence— were far likelier to have been cultivated in the ecclesiastical *ambiente*, where there was an audience appreciative of the austere, objective tone of madrigalian verse and its correspondingly complex polyphonic treatment. Many of the Florentine composers were organists by profession (a status consistent with their identity as ecclesiastics), which may explain the distinctive musical characteristics of the madrigal as a compositional genre.[16]

Carducci's "mondo elegante," conversely, was initially likelier to have favored the monophonic ballata and only subsequently its polyphonic manifestation, documented in the compositional output of Andreas de Florentia and

---

[12]**1958–61:** "Due sonetti musicali del secolo XIV."

[13]For an evocation of this relationship of music and medicine, consistent with Pirrotta's own, see the study by historian of medicine Nancy G. Siraisi, "The Music of Pulse in the Writings of Italian Academic Physicians" (see "Scena 7.ª," n. 117).

[14]**1985:** "Introduzione ai lavori."

[15]**1955:** "Marchettus of Padua and the Italian Ars Nova."

[16]**1961:** "Una arcaica descrizione trecentesca del madrigale."

Francesco Landino in particular.[17] Thus the few extant monophonic ballate—transmitted in the rhythmically unambiguous musical notation ordinarily reserved for polyphonic music—are precious vestiges of a vast repertory now almost irretrievably lost.

The individual pitches of the single melody of a monophonic ballata were not required to concord harmonically with pitches occurring simultaneously in a vertical context, as in polyphony. As a result, monophony's melodic character was governed less by "artificial" harmonic considerations than by an intrinsic linear naturalness and spontaneity (or "sprezzatura"): an "aria." That is, such a melody was not compelled, in its linear motion, to favor untoward pitches in order that the composition's vertical requirements be met, as a result of which the arc or shape of the melody of a monophonic composition was less contrived and artificial, more naturalistically and instinctively "tonal."[18]

Yet even after the application of a polyphonic technique to ballata texts, there always remained the Italianate option of soloistic vocal performance of the topmost line in the complex, with instrumental execution of the one or two lower voices.

Toward the end of the fourteenth century, two forces combined to subject native Italian compositional practices to the powerful influences of the French compositional aesthetic, "impregnated with scholastic doctrines," characterized by its "conceptual symbolistic":[19] (1) the Material conditions resulting from the transnational status of the ecclesiastical orders, which were conducive to the dissemination of French aesthetic ideals in Italy, especially where native Italian traditions were less strongly rooted;[20] and (2) the encounter between native Italian composers and northern musicians in the retinues of the simultaneously reigning popes and schismatic anti-popes and of the high-ranking Church officials who assembled in Italy in an effort to end the Great Schism. Some of these Italian composers (for example, Zacara[21]) partly surrendered to the compositional fashion of the French "ars subtilior" and sought to compose in accordance with its bedeviling melodic and rhythmic complexities, as well as continuing in the sparer, indigenous Italian style. They favored both the intuitive "dulcedo" of their native tradition and the

---

[17] **1935**: *Il Sacchetti;* **1960**: "Landini (Landino) Francesco"; **1973**: "Andreas de Florentia"; **1997**: "Francesco Landini: i lumi della mente"; † **1999**: "'*Franciscus peregre canens.*'"

[18] **1936**: "Lirica monodica trecentesca."

[19] **1935**: *Il Sacchetti.*

[20] **1946–47**: "Per l'origine e la storia della 'caccia' e del 'madrigale' trecentesco"; **1948**: "'*Dulcedo*' e '*subtilitas*'."

[21] **1971**: "Zacharus Musicus."

cultivated, intellectualistic "subtilitas" of their French colleagues;[22] the Lucca and Modena manuscripts are documents of both aesthetics.[23] But where a native Italianate tradition was more firmly established, as in Florence, there was less of a tendency to surrender to French compositional fashion, the native tradition exemplifying the "ready ductility of Italian musical language" rather than an understanding of music as "a species of sonorous geometry, mirror of astral harmonies, '[musica] mundana'.... being made terrestrial and human."

In fact, there is no justification for generalizing unduly from the repertory of the Modena manuscript and concluding that most or even many Italian composers of the late Trecento and early Quattrocento succumbed uncritically to the allure of the French "ars subtilior." The influence was also bidirectional. Just as some Italian composers of the late Trecento sought to master "[t]hat which is evident above all in French polyphony of the Gothic period, in which the worship of construction—well ordered by means of an industrious craftsmanship of technique and the liveliness of the ratiocination—finally gives way to an intellectualism and... geometricizing and symbolizing abstraction"[24] (a characteristic typified above all by the genre of the motet, "the most refined and intellectualistically-complex among those created by French polyphonic art"[25]), so some of their French contemporaries were seduced by the "hedonistic pleasure... connected to the satisfaction of the secret exigencies of musical instinct and above all... those of a melodic sensibility unwittingly governed by latent harmonic laws." Indeed, a fundamental desideratum of the entire musicological enterprise is to achieve an accurate balance in collective music-historical thinking about the relative importance, prestige, and influence of French and Italian compositional aesthetics and accomplishments of the late Middle Ages.[26]

Medieval Italian polyphonic practice was a circumscribed development, the expression of a tiny elite. After the resolution of the Great Schism, there was a diminished presence of foreign prelates in Italy and a resultant diminished presence of northern polyphonists. And with the rise of humanism, and the humanists' temporary success in wresting a position of preeminence in their society from representatives of other intellectual traditions (such as

---

[22]**1948:** "'Dulcedo' e 'subtilitas'"; **1950:** "Considerazioni sui primi esempi di Missa parodia."
[23]**1944/45:** "Il codice estense lat. 568 e la musica francese in Italia al principio del '400"; **1948/49–51:** with Ettore Li Gotti, "Il codice di Lucca."
[24]**1948:** "'Dulcedo' e 'subtitilas'."
[25]**1944/45:** "Il codice estense lat. 568 e la musica francese in Italia al principio del '400."
[26]**1949–51:** "Ballata"; **1950:** "Considerazioni sui primi esempi di Missa parodia"; **1951:** "Scuole polifoniche italiane durante il sec. XIV."

scholasticism), there was arguably a concomitant slowing in developments in natural science[27] and a concomitant equivocation about the composition and performance of secular polyphony. Natural philosophers, physicians, theologians trained in the scholastic method of inquiry, adherents of polyphonic musical practice: all shared an intellectual sensibility, and the momentary challenge represented by the humanist movement had implications for all manifestations of cultural and intellectual activity, music included.

The interests of the humanists were largely ethical and literary, for which they sought models in the classics, and their vision for music thus entailed a return to the musical practices of the antique world, above all a neo-Orphic tradition of solo-singing to the accompaniment of a bowed, plucked , or strummed string instrument. As a result, there was a "polyphonic production gap" of some 50 years, during which polyphonic settings of Italian secular texts by Italian composers are fewer in number, as contrasted with both the secular polyphonic productivity of the north and the secular polyphonic productivity of Trecento Italy.[28]

But because of the prestige of the northern polyphonic tradition and the success of northern composers resident in Italy, such as Josquin Desprez, in demonstrating the adaptability of polyphonic practice to the humanists' objective of sensitive and moving text expression, there was a rapprochement between the architectonic compositional practices of the northern polyphonists and the literary concerns of the Italian humanists. Josquin's later motets offer moving polyphonic readings of their texts, in ways that proved satisfactory to the literary objectives of his Italian humanist colleagues and their patrons.[29]

A vital tradition of notated polyphonic settings of secular Italian verse by native Italian composers is resumed toward the end of the fifteenth century.[30] However, there were vestiges of an equivocation about the "exogenous intellectualistic enterprise" of polyphonic composition, and in evaluating the musical culture of late-fifteenth- and early-sixteenth-century Italy, there remains the necessity of achieving a proper balance in the music-historical imagination about the achievements of the Italians and their French contemporaries:

> the frottola ... was often considered ... a minor genre, an opinion supported by sixteenth-century French judgments of it as "très commun," and so on.

---

[27]Daniel O'Connor, "Introduction: Two Philosophies of Nature," 15–28 (see "*Scena 7.ª*," n. 112); Richard Hoppin, "Tonal Organization in Music Before the Renaissance," 25–37 (see "*Scena 7.ª*," n. 113); Dana B. Durand, "Tradition and Innovation in Fifteenth Century Italy" (see "*Scena 7.ª*," n. 114); Durand, *The Vienna–Klosterneuburg Map Corpus of the Fifteenth Century* (see "*Scena 7.ª*," n. 115). But see the qualifications in my chapter on Pirrotta's Harvard years.

[28]**1957**: "Italien B. 14.–16. Jahrhundert"; **1963**: "Music and Cultural Tendencies in 15th Century Italy."

[29]**1966**: "Despres, Josquin (Després, Desprez, Des Prez, ecc.; Josquinus o Jodocus Pratensis, a Prato, ecc.; Juschino, Josse, ecc.)."

[30]**1957**: "Italien B. 14.–16. Jahrhundert"; **1973**: "Su alcuni testi italiani di composizioni polifoniche quattrocentesche."

But there is a legitimate question whether such an assessment "is fair":

> There are frottole which are poor music; but there are some which[,] while simple[,] are highly refined, of a cultivated simplicity; here the frottola takes advantage, as did Italian music of the fourteenth century, of its very provinciality in order to obtain an individual flavor.[31]

All the same, the entire Cinquecento may in some respects be understood as manifesting the application of a northern polyphonic "maniera" to texts set to music.[32] One of the principal documents of such is the Cinquecento madrigal, which, after an initial phase dominated by northerners resident in Italy—Verdelot, Arcadelt, Willaert—is appropriated by native Italian composers, who apply the technique of polyphonic composition to Italian secular verse in sensitive readings of the text. Luca Marenzio,[33] Luzzasco Luzzaschi and Carlo Gesualdo,[34] Claudio Monteverdi[35] all demonstrate the native Italian composer's talent for polyphonic treatment of Italian secular verse, as well as varied tastes in the verse they chose to set: the sweeter, more "hedonistic" verse of Giovanni Battista Guarini, favored by Luzzaschi and others; and more "psychologically probing" verse, such as that of Torquato Tasso, favored by Gesualdo and others. Such poetic choices had implications for the stylistic characteristics of the attendant musical setting.

However, throughout the sixteenth century there were continuing manifestations of the equivocation about the entire practice of polyphonic treatment of Italian secular verse: in the phenomenon of the madrigals by Verdelot arranged by Willaert so that only the superius voice is provided with text and, further, rendered in mensural notation, while the other voices are intabulated for lute performance; in the vogue of the *canzone villanesca alla napoletana*, inaugurated almost simultaneously (1537) with Willaert's intabulation of Verdelot's madrigals; in the madrigals adorned with the title "madrigali ariosi," a reference to a quality not always achieved in the "canonic" madrigalian output, in which the contrapuntal "search" produced outcomes that often lacked an "aria." The second of these developments is only one instance of a phenomenon whereby indigenous dialectical traditions—the Neapolitan, the Sicilian, even the "pan-Mediterranean"—are episodically, obliquely expressed and reflected in the art tradition and document the persistence of

---

[31]**1961**: contributions to the panel discussion, "From Frottola to Madrigal: The Changing Pattern of Secular Italian Vocal Music."
[32]**1973**: "Novelty and Renewal in Italy, 1300-1600"; **1995**: "'Maniera' polifonica e immediatezza recitativa."
[33]**1973**: "Note su Marenzio e il Tasso."
[34]**1961**: "Gesualdo da Venosa nel IV centenario della nascita"; **1963**: "Gesualdo, Ferrara e Venezia"; **1966**: "Carlo Gesualdo di Venosa. Sommario: I. La vita. – II. Caratteristiche dell'opera."
[35]**1968**: "Scelte poetiche di Monteverdi."

musical practices that always lay just beneath the surface, to be recaptured only by means of a sensitive and imaginative reading of the elusive historical evidence, which requires one to be "an ethnomusicologist of the past."[36]

*****

Throughout the late fifteenth and sixteenth centuries, the musical genres described here also furnished theatrical performances with musical elements, which enhanced and intensified the entire dramatic effect of the theatrical experience: Madrigalian polyphony employed as *entr'acte* entertainment ("intermedij"), or the venerable practice of solo-singing to the accompaniment of a string instrument.[37] Such developments are not only important per se, but also as background to the emergence of that most characteristic of Italian musical genres and most thorough-going integration of music and drama: opera.

One especially notable use of solo-singing to string accompaniment was in the commedia dell'arte and madrigal comedy.[38] The evidence of musical practice in the commedia is fragmentary and elusive, difficult to interpret. What evidence remains is essentially nonmusical—it is iconographic (visual representations of commedia performances), and literary (ex post facto prose accounts of such performances)—but it is internally consistent: both kinds of historical document suggest that solo-song to string accompaniment typified the musical component of the commedia.

Banchieri's and Vecchi's madrigal comedies and dramatic madrigals aim to deploy the full compositional resources of the polyphonic madrigal (and related, lighter genres) in comic theatrical performances. Even here, however, there was an effort to respect the time-honored association of solo-song to string accompaniment with the comic theater.

There was also a faithful restitution of classical tragedy, in translation, complete with newly composed polyphonic choruses by Andrea Gabrieli,[39] designed to serve the same function of commentary as in the ancient Greek original.

Contemporaneously with the madrigal comedy and dramatic madrigal, Florentine humanists and musicians of the late Cinquecento were feeling their way—fitfully, hesitatingly, anything but systematically or consciously—

---

[36] **1992:** "Contemplando la musa assente." For a consideration of Pirrotta's ethnomusicological sensibilities, see also Giovanni Giuriati, "Italian Ethnomusicology" (see "*Scena 7.ª*," n. 69).

[37] **1969:** *Li due Orfei.*

[38] **1950:** "Il 'Festino' di Banchieri"; **1954:** "Commedia dell'Arte e Melodramma"; **1954:** "Banchieri, Adriano"; **1956:** "Commedia dell'Arte [Part IV]."

[39] **1985:** "I cori per l'"Edipo Tiranno'"; **1995:** ed., *Chori in musica composti sopra li chori della tragedia di Edippo Tiranno.*

toward the creation of that magisterial new genre, opera.[40] Vincenzo Galilei—the astronomer's father—maintained that any effort to recapture the power of ancient Greek music would necessitate a return to monody. But his benefactor, Giovanni de' Bardi, concluded that it was unlikely that such a reform could be effected, skepticism substantiated by musical developments contemporary with the meetings of Bardi's *camerata*. And by no means was there a consistency of vision among the Florentine cultural and intellectual figures. One of the most important of them, Emilio de' Cavalieri, favored dramaturgical practices and a compositional style in his musico-dramatic works that would not have met the exacting standards of fin-de-siècle Florentine humanists.

Another relevant figure, Giulio Caccini, did not dispute Cavalieri's chronological primacy in setting the entire text of a dramatic work to music; his claims turned instead on the ideal compositional style to be adopted in setting text to music.

Caccini's claims to the contrary notwithstanding, when Jacopo Corsi and Ottavio Rinuccini were seeking a musician-collaborator to assist in bringing a newly composed narrative rendering of the Orpheus myth to the stage, set entirely to music (the *Euridice* of 1600), they turned—not to Caccini, whose style was judged too lyrical—but to Jacopo Peri, who pioneered in a revolutionary style, an "imitation of speech in song," the recitative. As instrumental substructure underlying the voice—one ideally suited to providing unobtrusive, schematic, flexible accompaniment, so that the solo voice would be intelligibly projected—Peri and his contemporaries developed what is known as the "basso continuo," essential to the entire earlier conception of the recitative style.

But only when the developments leading to the beginnings of opera are situated within the deep and broad context of theatrical uses of music in Italy—from the restoration of a secular theatrical tradition at the end of the fifteenth century to 1600—do we appreciate that the beginnings of the new genre were the culmination of trends that had been developing for more than a century.[41]

After its inaugural, aristocratic phase, in Florence (represented by Caccini and Peri), Mantua (by the younger Monteverdi[42]), and Rome (by Cornacchioli,[43] the brothers Mazzocchi,[44] and others)—which witnessed the establishment of

---

[40]**1951**: unpublished edition of Jacopo Peri, *Euridice;* **1953**: "Temperamenti e tendenze nella Camerata fiorentina"; **1953**: "Tragédie et comédie dans la Camerata fiorentina"; **1954**: "Bardi, Giovanni, conte di Vernio"; "Caccini (famiglia)"; "Camerata fiorentina."

[41]**1969**: *Li due Orfei.*

[42]**1963**: "Monteverdi e i problemi dell'opera"; **1968**: "Teatro, scene[,] e musica nelle opere di Monteverdi"; **1994**: "Claudio Monteverdi, veneziano di adozione"; **1995**: "Opera: Da Monteverdi a Monteverdi."

[43]**1956**: "Cornacchioli, Giacinto."

[44]**1964**: "I fratelli Mazzocchi."

such signature characteristics of the new genre as the "cavatina," or entrance aria, in which a character's defining personal characteristics are revealed to the audience in a soliloquy[45]—the Material conditions underlying the development of opera changed, from exclusive noble patronage to commercial enterprise,[46] supported not only by the benefactions of noble or high-bourgeois sponsors but also proceeds from ticket sales, conditions in which the itinerant lyric troupes (the "Febiarmonici") were critical in establishing a taste for the genre. Wherever the troupes went, "they were encountering environmental and cultural conditions . . . analogous to those . . . characterizing the Venetian theaters," which witnessed the offerings of the older Monteverdi[47] and Francesco Cavalli.[48] However,

> . . . it would be erroneous to believe that the management of the theaters in Venice was being uniquely borne on the proceeds of the receipts . . . from paying spectators: instead, . . . they constantly found an indispensable support in the backing of noble gentlemen.[49]

And despite the thesis of a supposed "tendency toward historical realism" in the subject matter of the libretti of Venetian operas, "libretti on historical subjects are not prevalent in number in Venice, nor are they the exclusive prerogative of the Venetian opera."

> In reality, the Venetian genre of the libretto, other than in minimal particulars, is not differentiated from the Italian genre of the libretto in general. . . . Its defects—compensated for by rare merits—are those of the Italian theater of the time, then dominated by the preponderant activity of the "comici dell'arte."

Thus the evidence substantiates a conjecture of Henri Prunières, who had the merit of "having first hinted at a relationship between the Venetian genre of the libretto and the 'commedia dell'arte.'"

One of the first great "comic operas," Antonio Cesti's *Orontea*,[50] establishes (or at least popularizes) some of the defining characteristics of the comic tradition. Although a document of the "affinity between comic theater and the opera theater," *Orontea* sets a libretto that attempts to regularize the literary basis of the comic theatrical tradition, to replace the orality of the

---

[45] **1956**: "Falsirena e la più antica delle cavatine."
[46] **1953**: "Tre capitoli su Cesti."
[47] **1963**: "Monteverdi e i problemi dell'opera"; **1968**: "Teatro, scene[,] e musica nelle opere di Monteverdi"; **1994**: "Claudio Monteverdi, veneziano di adozione"; **1995**: "Opera: Da Monteverdi a Monteverdi."
[48] **1956**: "Cavalli, Pier Francesco"; **1966**: "Il caval zoppo e il vetturino."
[49] **1953**: "Tre capitoli su Cesti"; see also **1966**: "Il caval zoppo e il vetturino," which documents Francesco Cavalli's rôle as impresario, a status that conditioned his thinking about the relationship of artistic factors to the need for commercial viability.
[50] **1953**: "Nella biblioteca di Santa Cecilia: Cesti e Abbatini–'Opera,"; **1953**: "Tre capitoli su Cesti"; **1954**: "Le prime opere di Antonio Cesti"; **1954**: "Commedia dell'Arte e Melodramma."

commedia dell' arte with a complete literary text, which is also more Tuscan in its linguistic character (and therefore less susceptible to the charge of "Baroque" extravagance). "Within the limits in which that was possible in the theater of the time, the libretto of *Orontea* is essentially a psychological drama, in fact, a comedy"; and the comic character types exemplified by the nurse and the drunken *buffone* Gelone are already established presences.

"[C]onsidering the music," however, "a fundamental difference in its organization immediately stands out from the preceding libretti of Tuscan dramaturgy . . . and . . . [Giacinto Andrew Cicognini and Francesco Cavalli's celebrated] *Giasone*": "the concision of the parts destined to be translated musically into recitative with respect to those from which the arias and ensemble pieces draw their origin," a "new . . . equilibrium between dramatic and musical elements, which occurs in *Orontea* in favor of these latter."

For historians of Italian opera, it is a question of some urgency as to what circumstances justify an aria or other species of "dramatically unrealistic" set piece. And the importance of the comic tradition in permitting such set pieces is undeniable, a development in which the earlier practices of the *comici dell'arte* were critical in habituating Italian audiences to such a design: the arias of the new comic opera parallel the established comic routines and "lazzi"—"set pieces"—of the *comici*.[51] According to the theatrical conventions of the time, lyrical effusion was more compatible with a comic than tragic aesthetic: comic opera offered a rationale for such effusion. Thus by this moment in the development of the genre, earlier prejudices concerning the aria and other closed pieces were largely overcome, and devotees of opera surrendered to the "hedonistic" pleasure of lyrical effusion, partly as a means of achieving variety through an alternation of recitative with set piece.

Among the further elements marking an opera as "comic" is the "parlante" style of melody, employed, for example, in a dialog between Creonte and the title character in *Orontea*; later in the seventeenth century, in the operas of Alessandro Stradella, the comic episodes reveal a related style that "tends to be simplified in order to adapt itself to the intrusiveness of the verbal comicality and the quick rhythm of the action, such that recitative and aria are often leveled in a common style of arietta."[52]

Seicentesca opera was characterized not only by a free mixing of comic and serious character types but also a design in which the aria was a dynamic element in the dialog and action. Because it was embedded within the dialog, there is often a seamless transition from recitative, to aria accompanied solely by the *basso continuo*, to recitative once more, to *arioso*, to instrumental *ritornello*; the eighteenth-century's sharp distinction of recitative and aria,

---

[51] **1954:** "Commedia dell'Arte e Melodramma."
[52] **1966:** "Alessandro STRADELLA."

and the canonical sequencing of secco recitative and scene-ending da capo exit aria, did not yet characterize the genre.

The Arcadian reforms of the late *Seicento*, and the concomitant emergence of the "grand Metastasian design," profoundly altered both defining characteristics of seventeenth-century opera.[53] Comicality (expressed principally in the established character types) was expunged; there was a classicizing simplification of the plot and purification of the poetic language. But because of the audience's taste for the comedic element, it was almost immediately resuscitated and featured in the independent genre of comic opera. And for the seventeenth century's seamlessness of design, the early eighteenth century substituted an ever sharper distinction between recitative and aria; arias manifesting an ampler and more complex structure (the celebrated *da capo*), so that the number of arias was reduced; and a relocation of the aria within the dramatic structure, a decline in the number of scene-opening and medial arias and a corresponding increase in the number of scene-ending arias.

But the expanding scale of arias is attributable not only to the reduction in their number. There was a general tendency among period composers toward broader forms, not only in vocal genres but also instrumental. Thus the early-eighteenth-century aria is, like ritornello form in the contemporary solo concerto and concerto grosso, a juxtaposition of vocal or instrumental soloist and orchestral accompaniment, where soloistic episodes alternate with orchestral ritornelli, and recurring statements of the theme by the "ripieno" group in a variety of related keys are interspersed with passages executed by the instrumental "concertino" or a solo voice:

> [T]he music tends to be given architectonic systematization.....[I]t ... deals with ... thematic elements and tonal plans ... organized ... in desired symmetries or asymmetries.... The novelty of the Corellian moment is precisely this: the end of a phase during which the composition had rested upon ... extrinsic elements, and the beginning of another in which one tends toward formal organization on purely musical bases. There it accompanies the definitive conquest of what one is accustomed to calling modern tonality.[54]

Thus both the da capo aria in the vocal literature and ritornello form in the instrumental literature reveal an increasing concern with large-scale tonal organization: a precompositional tonal plan adopted by composers of Baroque vocal and instrumental music, operating according to the conventions of the da capo aria or ritornello form, governs the exploration of various keys in a logical sequence.

---

[53] **1982:** "Metastasio and the Demands of his Literary Environment"; **1982:** "Metastasio e i teatri romani"; **1983:** "I musicisti nell'epistolario di Metastasio"; **1993:** "Metastasio e il terminare le scene con spirito e vivezza"; **1995:** "Pier Jacopo Martello."

[54] **1972:** "Studi corelliani."

An understanding of the entire history of a particular genre—in this case, Italian opera—makes it possible to contextualize any given development within that history and assess its supposed novelty. For example, the iconic appearance of the guitar as accompaniment to the solo voice in both Mozart's *Le nozze di Figaro* and Rossini's *Il barbiere di Siviglia* is attributable to the origins of both works in the celebrated comedic trilogy of Beaumarchais, who as *faiseur* of *parades* and *vaudevilles* would have been conversant with the venerable practice of featuring that instrument in such theatrical works.[55] In both operatic masterpieces, moreover, the arias accompanied by the characters' own playing of the guitar are instances of the "realistic use of music in comedy" and thus conform to time-honored Italian theatrical tradition,[56] as do the comic routines and "bits" in *Le nozze di Figaro*, which ultimately derive from the commedia dell'arte.

Further, the alleged ambivalence of the term and concept "dramma giocoso," as invoked in Mozart's *Don Giovanni*,[57] is not, in fact, ambivalence, when understood contextually: as early as the commedia dell'arte tradition of the sixteenth century, the practice was established of including contrasting character types in the same work, both the serious "innamorati" and the buffoonish "maschere." The act-ending ensembles of the comic operatic tradition were also an established feature of the larger theatrical tradition.

Thus each genre—whether the iteration in question were within the spoken theatrical tradition, or the sung (opera)—manifested certain traditional procedures. In opera, the comic genre employed the celebrated "precipitous recitation" and ensembles, especially those concerted, end-of-act ensembles, in parallel with their spoken comic counterpart; in the serious operatic genre, solo arias were featured, canonically sequenced with monologic and dialogic secco recitative that give way to scene-ending, "da capo" exit arias.

Even the distinguishing elements of so mature and singular a document of the Italian operatic tradition as Giuseppe Verdi's *Aida* can be contextualized historically.[58] The three main characters are disposed "according to the traditional Metastasian scheme of amorous attraction and repulsion"; Amneris's music in Act II/scene i "fulfills the task of psychological self-definition that the operatic tradition had for a long time specifically assigned to the *cavatinas*," an aria type that emerges as early as the first few decades of operatic history; and there are illuminating correspondences between *Aida* and Gioacchino Rossini's *Semiramide* in the "Orientalizing archaeology" of both.

A quintessential feature of Italian music (whether of the fourteenth century or the nineteenth) has been its emphasis on melody—"[n]ot just today are

---

[55]**1981**: "Causerie su Beaumarchais e la musica teatrale."
[56]**1969**: *Music and Theatre.*
[57]**1996**: "Divagazioni su Goldoni e il dramma giocoso."
[58]**1977**: "Semiramis e Amneris, Un anagramma o quasi."

we pleased to admire ... a tremulous lyric vein that gave ... Italian art the most limpid melodic gems"[59]—and in no other manifestation of Italian musical art is it more effectively revealed than in the "Great Tradition" of Italian opera, represented above all by the masterpieces of Verdi and the bel canto repertory of Gioachino Rossini, Vincenzo Bellini, and Gaetano Donizetti. For Bellini, a Sicilian who "truly ... echoed melodies of his land," it was

> neither an easy nor a tranquil task, ... liberating from the slag those melodies whose apparent facility ... enchants us. That the task was undertaken was the result of a spiritual necessity that drives Bellini to self-renewal, so that the bubbling fountain of lyric expression not be obfuscated.[60]

One of *Pirata*'s features is notable,

> and it is the refinement and finesse of the instrumental expression. ... [T]he overture is of a classical design and proportions, on a par with a Mozartian overture. Nourished on German instrumental music more ... than any other Italian composer, Bellini aspires to a completeness of instrumental expression. ... The same refinement of construction is in the quintet, in which the counterpoint of the tenor, bass, and chorus—even if it does not add anything to the beauty of the melody of the upper part—is disposed with a ... mastery that suffices to belie the accusations made of Bellini several times: of not knowing how to construct, nor harmonize, nor orchestrate his pieces. If such technical assurance appears in the opera of the 26-year-old composer, it is evident, more than ever, that the renunciation of the resources of counterpoint and orchestration in subsequent operas was not determined by a lack of capability, but was a voluntary and coherent act of the eminently lyric nature of Bellini, which—in the almost naked simplicity of the melody ... typical of the unforgettable pages of *Norma* and *La sonnambula*—found more concentrated and intense expression.[61]

Indeed, "[h]is having voluntarily renounced it ... shows that[,] within himself, Bellini ... felt the baggage and apparatus of learned elaborations not only unnecessary ... but an obstruction of his musical nature."[62]

Here once again, we are compelled to seek an accurate balance—in music-historical understanding writ large—of the achievements of the Italians and their northern colleagues. Bellini's renunciation of "the resources of counterpoint" and "baggage ... of learned elaborations" was "voluntary," the result of aesthetic preference rather than compositional incompetence or creative

---

[59]**1933–35:** 28–29 March 1934 "'LA SONNAMBULA, AL TEATRO MASSIMO."
[60]**1933–35:** 10–11 April 1935 "L'inaugurazione della stagione lirica al Massimo: La commemorazione belliniana."
[61]**1933–35:** 24 April 1935 "Al Teatro Massimo 'Il Pirata, di Bellini."
[62]**1933–35:** 10–11 April 1935 "L'inaugurazione della stagione lirica al Massimo: La commemorazione belliniana."

deficiency; he simply favored and privileged "lyric expression," "those melodies whose ... facility ... enchants us." He was *capable* of a completeness of instrumental expression and refinement of construction; he simply chose to expend his compositional energies elsewhere, consistent with his essential Italian-ness. Notwithstanding the contributions of a Corelli to the complex tonal architecture of Baroque ritornello form,[63] or the undeniable indebtedness of a Haydn or Mozart to a Clementi or a Sammartini,[64] and notwithstanding the contribution of Italian composers to the celebrated European symphonic literature, an account of the masterpieces of that literature is an account of the accomplishments of composers named Haydn, and Mozart, and Beethoven, and Schubert, and Schumann, and Brahms, of the complexities of the sonata-allegro principle and other such abstract formal procedures and instrumental genres not dependent for their effect on text. In the nineteenth century, as in the fifteenth, there was instead an Italianate predisposition to rely on "the power of words."[65]

*****

Idealism's understanding of the artistic creative act reserved space for the artist's (and the historian's) "instinct" and "Kantian judgment," which yielded works of art distinguished by a "naturalness" and "apparent spontaneity":

> For the musician ... composing is no less arduous, gradual, and tiring than is the labor for the sculptor of drafting a figure bit-by-bit and defining its desired forms and gestures with correctness. Inspiration is ... the sense of beauty, the Kantian judgment, which guides and sustains the search—receives or rejects the ideas—and refinishes and leads those received to perfection. The "long, long" melodies of Bellini ... were certainly not born entirely in a stream; ... they had to have been the fruit of successive additions, supported by an infallible instinct in judging what could be added to that already-made, with naturalness and apparent spontaneity, ... to extend it and intensify it.[66]

Such was Nino Pirrotta's vision of the Italian musical past and of the exacting music-historical activity demanded in the never-ending effort to understand and describe it.

---

[63] **1972:** "Studi corelliani."
[64] **1933–35:** 17–18 April 1935 "Teatri e Concerti."
[65] **1963:** "Music and Cultural Tendencies in 15th Century Italy."
[66] **1993:** "Rileggendo *Il Pirata* di Bellini."

Appendix

Documents of Pirrotta's Formal Education

REGIO LICEO «GIUSEPPE GARIBALDI» DI PALERMO (1922–24[1])

ANNO SCOLASTICO 19<u>24</u>–19<u>25</u> / RISULTATO CONSEGUITO DA <u>PIRROTTA ANTONINO</u> / NELL'ESAME DI MATURITÀ CLASSICA /

MATERIE D'ESAME	SESSIONE DI PRIMO ESAME[1]
Lettere italiane	<u>sette</u>
Lettere latine	<u>sei</u>
Lettere greche	<u>sette</u>
Storia	<u>sette</u>
Filosofia ed economia politica	<u>sette</u>
Matematica e fisica	<u>sei</u>
Scienze naturali, chimica e geografica	<u>otto</u>
Storia dell'arte	<u>sei</u>.... /

<u>Palermo</u> addì <u>26 gennaio</u> 19<u>26</u> / IL PRESIDENTE DELLA COMMISSIONE / [signature] /[1]
I voti debbono essere scritti in lettere.

*****

REGNO D[']ITALIA / MINISTERO _ DELLA / PVBBLICA _ ISTRVZIONE / DIPLOMA / DI _ MATURITA / CLASSICA _/ conferito a <u>l Signor Pirrotta Antonino</u> / figli<u>o</u> di <u>Vincenzo</u> e di <u>Restivo Adele</u> / nat <u>o</u> a <u>Palermo</u> (prov. di –) / il giorno <u>13 giugno</u> 19<u>08</u> / <u>Palermo</u> addì <u>26 gennaio</u> 19<u>26</u> / IL PRESIDENTE DELLA COMMISSIONE / [signature]

---

[1] As explained in my "*Scena 1.ª Famiglia* (1908–24)," Pirrotta was not enrolled at the *liceo* during academic year 1924–25, although, as the document clarifies, that was the year he sat for the examinations for the *licenza liceale*. He was tutored privately at home during that year, since he was already enrolled at the Conservatory of Palermo.

REGIO CONSERVATORIO DI MUSICA «LUIGI CHERUBINI DI FIRENZE» (1927–29)

N°. 4507 di matricola.

Cognome e Nome dell'Alunno Pirrotta Antonio [sic]

figlio di _____ *e di* _____

nato il dì _____ *a* _____

ammesso all'Istituto il dì 22 ottobre 1927

all _____ *Scuol* _____ *di* Organo (8° anno) Proveniente dal R. Conservatorio di Palermo

Firma dell'Alunno   Firma del responsabile

Novembre 1927/928 Rassegnato alla Scuola di Organo 8° Anno e al 1° anno di Storia della musica.
Giugno 1928 Promosso al 9° anno di organo senza esame con punti 8,50
Promosso senza esame al 2° anno di Storia della musica con 9

Ottobre 1928/929 Rassegnato al 9° anno di organo: 2° anno Storia della Musica
Giugno 1929 Licenziato alla Storia della Musica, con punti 10
Ha conseguito Diploma di Magistero, in Organo; riportando la seguente votazione:

1ª prova		9
2ª prova		7,50
3ª prova		9
4ª prova		8,50
5ª prova		8
6ª prova		9
7ª prova		9,50

ott[o]b^{re} 1929 Rassegnato alla scuola di Composizione 7° Anno Giugno 1930 – Promosso s.[enza] e.[same] all'VIII anno di Armonia e Contrap[pun].^{to} Promosso s.e. al II anno di violino compl[ementa]^{re} con p: 8.

novembre 1930. Rassegnato all'ottavo anno di comp[osizione]: e fuga: 2° di violino compl^{re}

ottobre 1931: Si ritira volontariamente dalle scuole di questo R. Conservatorio.

APPENDIX

REGIA UNIVERSITA DEGLI STUDI DI FIRENZE (1927–1930)

Anno Scolastico 19____ – 19____

N. <u>11</u> del Registro ____   Num. di Matricola <u>9164</u>

R. UNIVERSITA DEGLI STUDI
DI FIRENZE

Firenze, addì <u>3 XII 19 27</u>

<u>Antonino Pirrotta</u>

figlio di <u>Vincenzo</u>
e di <u>Adele Restivo</u>
nato nel Comune di <u>Palermo</u>   Provincia di ____
il giorno <u>13 giugno 1908</u> nazionalità
____

Professione e condizione del Padre o di chi ne fa le veci	possidente
Abitazione e nome della persona presso la quale dimora in Firenze	presso Tito Travaglia Via di Pepoli 224
Comune ove la famiglia risiede (via e numero)	Piazza Giuseppe Verdi 6 – Palermo
Studente o Uditore	studente
Facoltà ed anno di Corso a cui s'inscrive	Facoltà di Lettere sezione Filosofia 3° anno
Stabilimenti di istruzione secondaria nei quali fece gli studi	R. Ginnasio-Liceo G. Garibaldi, Palermo
Stabilimenti di istruzione superiore cui ha appartenuto	R. Università di Palermo
Titolo di Studi presentato per la immatricolazione	Diploma di maturità classica
Se usufruisce di Borse di Studio o è impiegato in un'Amministrazione pubblica o privata	=

Firma
Nino Pirrotta

R. UNIVERSITA DEGLI STUDI— FIRENZE

Cognome e Nome <u>Pirrotta Antonino</u> Numero della filza <u>155</u>
di <u>Vincenzo</u> e della <u>Adele Restivo</u>
Nato il <u>13 Giugno 1908</u> a <u>Palermo</u> N. Inserto <u>3018</u>
Immatricolato il <u>30 November 1927</u>
Facoltà <u>Lettere e Filosofia</u>
Titolo di Studi per l'ammissione <u>Diploma di Maturità Classica</u>
   Matricola N. <u>9164</u>
Laureato il <u>13 Novembre 1930</u>, Diploma N° <u>1931</u>
Titolo della tesi di laurea "<u>Fonti iconografiche e stilistiche della pittu=</u>
   Registro N. <u>XIV</u> Pag. N. <u>11</u>
<u>ra su maioliche umbro-marchigiana durante il Rinascimento,,</u>.
Congedato il _____
per _____
Fuori corso dal _____ Numero della filza <u>155</u> Facoltà <u>Lettere e Filosofia</u>

Bibliography

The Publications of Nino Pirrotta[1]

FLORENCE

Facoltà di Lettere e Filosofia, Regia Università degli Studi di Firenze

1931

Pirrotta, Antonino. *Fonti iconografiche e stilistiche della pittura su maioliche del Rinascimento*, 2 vols. (*Tesi di Laurea* [*Dottore in Lettere*], Facoltà di Lettere e Filosofia, Regia Università degli Studi di Firenze, ["Presentata il 31–X."] 1931).[2]

PALERMO

1933–35

Music-critical/journalistic writings for the Palermitan daily *L'Ora*:[3]

22–23 December 1933	"Commemorazione di J. Brahms," a[ntonino].p[irrotta].r[estivo].
23–24 January 1934	"MARIO PILATI AGLI «AMICI DELLA MUSICA»," unsigned.
26–27 February 1934	"IL CONCERTO MULE AL TEATRO MASSIMO," n[ino].p[irrotta].r[estivo].

---

[1]My bibliography is based in great part on that compiled by my friend Teresa M. Gialdroni, "Bibliografia di Nino Pirrotta," *Studi musicali* 28 (1999): 43–63. Prof.ssa Gialdroni's bibliography—which she graciously made available to me in electronic form—is the indispensable basis for accessing Pirrotta's corpus of published work.

[2]The University of Florence copy of the doctoral thesis was lost in the 1966 flood; to the best of my knowledge, the sole remaining copy is in the possession of Pirrotta's children. I am very grateful to them for the opportunity to consult it.

[3]These journalistic writings, long out of circulation, have now been republished in Cummings and Eiche, "Nino Pirrotta's Early Music-Critical Writings" (see "*Scena 1.ᵃ*," n. 69).

19–20 March 1934	"Il concerto Feu[e]rmann," *n.p.r.*
21–22 March 1934	"Il Concerto Buranello," *n.p.r.*
28–29 March 1934	"'LA SONNAMBULA, AL TEATRO MASSIMO," *n.p.r.*
6–7 April 1934	"'La Fanciulla del West, al Massimo," *n.p.r.*
16–17 April 1934	"Il 'Ballo in maschera, al Massimo," *n.p.r.*
19–20 April 1934	"'Baronessa di Carini, di G. Mulè e 'Galatea, di A. Savasta al TEATRO MASSIMO," *n.p.r.*
23–24 April 1934	"«Maria Egiziaca» di Respighi al Massimo," *n.p.r.*
28–29 June 1934	"Il concerto di musiche contemporanee," *n.p.r.*
14–25 September 1934	"LE CELEBRAZIONI MARCHIGIANE: Due profili di Rossini," *n.p.r.*
29–30 November 1934	"*IL DECENNALE DELLA MORTE DI PUCCINI*: Rivendicazione," *n.p.r.*
13–14 February 1935	"Il pensiero dell'on. Lualdi sulla musica italiana contemporanea," *n.p.r.*
25–26 February 1935	"Vecsey e Agosti agli 'Amici della Musica," *n.p.r.*
9–10 March 1935	"Yoshiko Fausta Beltramelli agli Amici della Musica," *n.p.r.*
19–20 March 1935	"Il pianista Orloff agli 'Amici della Musica," *n.p.r.*
10–11 April 1935	"L'inaugurazione della stagione lirica al Massimo: La commemorazione belliniana," *n.p.r.*
12–13 April 1935	"La stagione lirica al Massimo: 'ANDREA CHÉNIER, con Giglio e Montesanto," *n.p.r.*
17–18 April 1935	"Teatri e Concerti," *n.p.r.*
18–19 April 1935	"La prima di 'Manon, al Massimo," *n.p.r.*
24 April 1935	"Al Teatro Massimo 'Il Pirata, di Bellini," *n.p.r.*
30 April 1935	"Il pianista Gimpel al Massimo," *n.p.r.*
5 June 1935	"La commemorazione di Donaudy al Circolo della Stampa," *n.p.r.*
9 June 1935	"Il Quintetto femminile alla Mostra d'Arte," *n.p.r.*
13 October 1935	"Il Concerto Marinuzzi al Teatro Massimo," *n.p.r.*

1934–35

Taucci, P. Raffaele M. "Fra Andrea dei Servi, organista e compositore del trecento," *Studi storici dell'Ordine dei servi di Maria* 2, no. 2 (Rome: Istituto storico O.S.M., 1934–35): 73–108, especially 104–08: "Trascrizione del M.° Nino Pirrotta."

1935

With Ettore Li Gotti, *Il Sacchetti e la tecnica musicale del Trecento italiano* (Florence: Sansoni, 1935).

Regio Conservatorio di Musica «Vincenzo Bellini» di Palermo
Bibliotecario and *Docente in Storia della Musica*

1936

"Lirica monodica trecentesca," in *Poesia e musica e altri saggi*, Discanto/ Contrappunti 33 (Florence: La Nuova Italia, 1994), 35–45 [originally in *La rassegna musicale* 9 (1936)].

1936–37

Review of Federico Mompellio, *Pietro Vinci madrigalista siciliano*, Vie nuove della storia musicale (Milan: Hoepli, 1937), in *Archivio storico per la Sicilia* 2–3 (1936–37): 489–93.

Bibliotecario and *Professore di Storia della Musica* [*titolare di cattedra*]

1938

Review of Ottavio Tiby, *La musica bizantina.—Teoria e storia* (Milan: Fratelli Bocca, 1938), in *Archivio storico per la Sicilia* 4 (1938): 604–08.

1944/45

"Il codice estense lat. 568 e la musica francese in Italia al principio del '400," estratto [1946] dagli *Atti della Reale Accademia di Scienze Lettere e Arti di Palermo*, ser. 4, vol. 5, pt. 2 (Palermo: presso la Reale Accademia di Scienze Lettere e Arti, 1944/45): 1–59.

1945

N. P., "Note ad "Anna,, o dei dispetti amorosi," *Accademia. Rivista italiana di lettere, arti, scienze* 1, no. 2 (1945): 7.

1946–47

"Per l'origine e la storia della 'caccia' e del 'madrigale' trecentesco," *Rivista musicale italiana* 48 (1946): 305–23, and 49 (1947): 121–42.

1948

("Palermo"), "'Dulcedo' e 'subtilitas' nella pratica polifonica franco–italiana al principio del '400," in *Musica tra Medioevo e Rinascimento*, Saggi 670

(Turin: Einaudi, 1984), 130–41 [originally in *Revue belge de musicologie* 2 (1948)].

1948/49–51

With Ettore Li Gotti, "Il codice di Lucca," *Musica disciplina* 3–5 (1949–51), vol. 3 [I: "Descrizione e Inventario," Nino Pirrotta], 119–38; vol. 4 [II: "Testi letterari," Ettore Li Gotti (Palermo), and "Appendice ai testi," N. P. Palermo], 111–47, and 148–52; and vol. 5 [III.: "Il repertorio musicale," Nino Pirrotta (Roma)], 115–42.[4]

ROME

Accademia and Conservatorio di Musica «Santa Cecilia» di Roma
Direttore delle Biblioteche

1948

("Rome"), "On the Problem of 'Sumer is icumen in,'" *Musica disciplina* 2 (1948): 205–16.

1949

("Roma, gennaio 1949"), with Ettore Li Gotti, "Paolo Tenorista, fiorentino 'extra moenia,'" in *Estudios dedicados a [D. Ramón] Menéndez Pidal*, 7 vols. (Madrid: Consejo Superior de Divestigaciones Cientificos, 1950–62), tirada aparte– tomo 3 [1952], 577–87.

1949–51

"Ballata," in *Die Musik in Geschichte und Gegenwart* (Kassel: Bärenreiter Verlag, 1949–73), vol. 1 [1949–51].

1950

"Considerazioni sui primi esempi di Missa parodia," in *Atti del congresso internazionale di musica sacra organizzato dal Pontificio Istituto di Musica Sacra e dalla Commissione di Musica Sacra per l'Anno Santo*, Rome, 25–30 May 1950, ed. Mons. Iginio Anglès (Tournai: Desclée, 1952), 315–18.

---

[4] Although this article appeared in 1949–51, part of Pirrotta's contribution is signed "N.P. Palermo," which documents that it was drafted before 1948 and the relocation to Rome.

"Il 'Festino' di Banchieri," in *Biennale di Venezia. XIII° Festival internazionale di musica contemporanea, IV Autunno Musicale Veneziano, 4–24 settembre 1950. Programma ufficiale* (n.p. [Venice]: no publisher [A. Giuriola], n.d. [1950]), 72–74.

1951

Unpublished edition of Jacopo Peri, *Euridice;* prepared for 18 January and 5 September 1951 radio broadcasts.[5]

"Fondi musicali non inventariati nè catalogati," in *Troisième congrès international des bibliothèques musicales Paris, 22–25 juillet 1951, Actes du congrès*, ed. V. Fedorov, Association internationale des bibliothèques musicales/Internationale Vereinigung der Musikbibliotheken/International Association of Music Libraries (Kassel: Bärenreiter Verlag, 1953), 46–47.

"Scuole polifoniche italiane durante il sec. XIV: di una pretesa scuola napoletana (Communicazione letta nella seduta del 24 luglio 1951 alla Société Française de Musicologie)," *Collectanea historiae musicae* 1 (Florence: L. S. Olschki, 1953): 11–18.

1952

"Le biblioteche musicali italiane," *Rassegna musicale* 22 (1952): 123–29.

1953

Antonino Pirrotta, "Temperamenti e tendenze nella Camerata fiorentina. Conferenza tenuta dal Prof. Nino Pirrotta il 30 aprile 1953," *Manifestazioni di attività culturali. Supplemento alla rivista "Santa Cecilia,,* (Rome: Accademia Nazionale di Santa Cecilia, July 1953): 35–45; trans. Nigel Fortune as "Temperaments and Tendencies in the Florentine Camerata," now in *Music and Culture in Italy from the Middle Ages to the Baroque. A Collection of Essays*, Studies in the History of Music 1 (Cambridge, MA: Harvard University Press, 1984).

("Directeur de la Bibliothèque Santa Cecilia à Rome"), "Tragédie et comédie dans la Camerata fiorentina," in *Musique et poésie au XVIe siècle, Colloque*

---

[5] See Roberto Giuliani, "L'antica musica ridotta alla moderna prattica dell'etere, " especially 2:1327–29 (see *"Scena 5.ª,"* n. 41). See also my *"Scena 5.ª"* for more on this manuscript edition of *Euridice*. There are also manuscript editions of a concerto by Alessandro Scarlatti and Luzzasco Luzzaschi's madrigal *O primavera*, which I have not listed among the titles in Pirrotta's bibliography, given their relative "insubstantiality." On the current location of the unpublished edition of *Euridice*, and plans to publish it in facsimile, see my *"Scena 5.ª"*

international, Paris, 30 juin–4 juillet 1953, Colloques internationaux du Centre national de la recherche scientifique, Sciences Humaines 5 (Paris: Centre nationale de la recherche scientifique, 1954), 287–97.

Nella biblioteca di Santa Cecilia: Cesti e Abbatini—'Opera," *Santa Cecilia: Rivista dell'Accademia Nazionale di Santa Cecilia* 2, no. 3 (1953): 31–34.

"Tre capitoli su Cesti: I. L'opera italiana prima di Cesti, II. L''Orontea,' III. Cesti nell'epistolario di Salvator Rosa," in *La scuola romana: G. Carissimi—A. Cesti—M. Marazzoli . . . , pubblicati in occasione della "X Settimana Musicale Senese," 16–22 settembre 1953*, Accademia Musicale Chigiana. Ente Autonomo per le Settimane Musicali Senesi (Siena: Ticci, 1953), 27–79.

Coed. with Luisa Cervelli and Adelmo Damerini, *Catalogo della mostra corelliana. Manoscritti—Documenti—Edizioni antiche e rare—Iconografia—Strumenti musicali–Stampe ed incisioni—Edizioni moderne. Roma, Palazzo Braschi, dicembre 1953–gennaio 1954*, ed. Comitato Nazionale per la Celebrazione del III Centenario della Nascita di Arcangelo Corelli sotto l'alto Patronato del Presidente della Repubblica. Comitato organizzatore: Conte Dr. Francesco Pellati, M.º Dr. Giovanni Penta, Dr. Ennio Colucci, Prof. Dr. Antonino Pirrotta, Prof. Adelmo Damerini, Dr. Luisa Cervelli, M.º Dr. Cesare Valabrega, Arch. Umberto Piazzo, Dr. Italo Faldi, Rag. Felice Cerreto (Rome: Fratelli Palombi, 1953).

1954

"Commedia dell'Arte e Melodramma, Conferenza del Prof. Antonino Pirrotta. 21 gennaio 1954. Sala dell'Accademia," in *Accademia Nazionale di Santa Cecilia. Manifestazioni culturali predisposte d'intesa con l'Accademia Nazionale dei Lincei e con l'Insigne Accademia Nazionale di San Luca* (Rome: Studio Tipografico B.S., n.d. [1954]), 3–17; translated by Lewis Lockwood as "Commedia dell'Arte and Opera," now in *Music and Culture in Italy from the Middle Ages to the Baroque.*

"Compiti regionali, nazionali ed internazionali delle bilioteche musicali," in *Atti del Congresso internazionale di musiche popolari mediterranee e del Convegno dei bibliotecari musicali* [Palermo, 26–30 giugno 1954] (Palermo: F.lli De Magistris, n.d. [1959]), 333–38.

Ed., *The Music of Fourteenth-Century Italy*, 5 vols., Corpus Mensurabilis Musicae 8/I–V (Amsterdam: American Institute of Musicology, 1954–64), vol. 1.

"Note su un codice di antiche musiche per tastiera," *Rivista musicale italiana* 56 (1954), "Le ricerche d'archivio," 333–39.

Pirrotta, Antonino. "Le prime opere di Antonio Cesti," in *L'Orchestra*, ed. Pietro Castiglia (Florence: G. Barbera, 1954), 153–79.

Entries in vols. 1 and 2 of the *Enciclopedia dello Spettacolo*, Sotto gli auspici della Fondazione Giorgio Cini, 9 vols. (Rome: Le Maschere, 1954–62):
"Abbatini, Antonio Maria."
"Adam de La Halle."
"Agazzari, Agostino."
"Allegri, Lorenzo"
"Ammerbach, Elias Nikolaus."
"Antifonario."
"Apolloni, Giovanni o Giovanni Filippo."
"Artusi, Giovanni Maria."
"Astorga, Emanuele Rincon barone d.'"
"Attaingnant, Pierre."
"Badoaro (o Badoer), Giacomo."
"Ballata."
"Banchieri, Adriano."
"Bardi, Giovanni, conte di Vernio."
"Bati, Luca."
"Belli, Domenico."
"Buffo, Buffi."
"Burla."
"Caccini (famiglia)."
"Camerata fiorentina."
"Campra, Andrè."
"Canzone, Canzonetta."
"Cappellini, Carlo."
"Caprioli (or Caproli), Carlo detto del Violino."

Entry in vol. 3 of *Die Musik in Geschichte und Gegenwart*:
"Donatus de Florentia."

1955

Pirrotta, M. N. (Rome–Cambridge, MA; "Bibliothécaire du Conservatoire S. Cecilia de Rome et professeur à l'université de Harvard"), "Cronologia e denominazione dell'ars nova italiana," in *L'ars nova: Recueil d'études sur la musique du XIVe siècle*, Les colloques de Wégimont II—1955, Bibliothèque de la Faculté de Philosophie et Lettres de l'Université de Liège–Fascicule 149 (Paris: Société d'Édition «Les Belles Lettres», 1959), 93–104.

"Marchettus de Padua and the Italian Ars Nova," *Musica disciplina* 9 (1955): 57–71.

Entries in vol. 4 of *Die Musik in Geschichte und Gegenwart*:
"Florence [...] Codex Palatino Panciatichiano 26."
"Garzoni, Tommaso."

CAMBRIDGE, MASSACHUSETTS

Faculty of Arts and Sciences, Harvard University
Professor of Music and Head of the Eda Kuhn Loeb Music Library

1956

"Falsirena e la più antica delle cavatine," in *Music and Culture in Italy from the Middle Ages to the Baroque*, 335–42 and 459–65 [originally in *Collectanea Historiae Musicae* 2 (Florence, 1956)].

"Paolo da Firenze in un nuovo frammento dell'"Ars Nova,'" *Musica disciplina* 10 (1956): 61–66.

Entries in vol. 3 of the *Enciclopedia dello Spettacolo*:
"Cavalieri, Emilio de.'"
"Cavalli, Pier Francesco."
"Cesti, Antonio o Marco Antonio (Pietro C., detto)."
"Cesti, don Remigio."
"Commedia dell'Arte [Part IV]."
"Cornacchioli, Giacinto."
"Corsi, Jacopo."
"Corteccia, Francesco."
"Costa, Margherita."
"Coussemaker, Charles-Edmond-Henri de."
"Cristina di Svezia."
"Croce, Giovanni."

Entries in vol. 5 of *Die Musik in Geschichte und Gegenwart*:
"Gherardellus de Florentia."
"Ghivizzani (Guivizzani), Alessandro."

"Giustiniani, Vincenzo."
"Gratiosus de Padua."
"Greghesca."

1957

"Dedication of the Loeb Music Library," *Harvard Library Bulletin* 11 (1957): 141.[6]

Entries in vol. 4 of the *Enciclopedia dello Spettacolo*:
"Della Valle, Pietro."
"Della Viola, Alfonso."
"Direzione e concertazione."
"Doni, Giovanni Battista."

Entries in vol. 6 of *Die Musik in Geschichte und Gegenwart*:
"Intermedium."
"Italien B. 14.–16. Jahrhundert."
"Jacobus de Bononia."

1958

"Due sonetti musicali del secolo XIV," in *Musica tra Medioevo e Rinascimento*, Saggi 670 (Turin: Einaudi, 1984), 52–62 [originally in *Miscelánea en homenaje a Monsnor Higinio Anglés*, 2 vols. (Barcelona: Consejo Superior de Investigaciones Cientificas, 1958–61), vol. 2].

"The Eda Kuhn Loeb Music Library," *Harvard Library Bulletin* 12 (1958): 410–17.

Entries in vol. 5 of the *Enciclopedia dello Spettacolo*:
"Ferrari, Benedetto."
"Gagliano, Marco da."
"Galilei, Vincenzo."
"Gasparini, Francesco."

Entry in vol. 7 of *Die Musik in Geschichte und Gegenwart*:
"Johannes de Florentia."

---

[6]According to Elliot Forbes, *A History of Music at Harvard to 1972*, 126 n. 62 (see "*Scena 7.ª*," n. 35), this short notice was authored by Pirrotta.

1959

"Piero e l'impressionismo musicale del secolo XIV," in *Musica tra Medioevo e Rinascimento*, 103–14 [read at the first Convegno Internazionale di Studi sull'Ars Nova, Certaldo, 23–26 July 1959; subsequently published in *L'Ars Nova Italiana del Trecento* 1, ed. Bianca Becherini (Certaldo: Centro di Studi sull'Ars Nova Italiana del Trecento, 1962)].

1960

Entries in vols. 6 and 7 of the *Enciclopedia dello Spettacolo*:
"Intermezzo, I.1." [contributions for the musical part only: the entry is by Elena Povoledo].
"Mei, Girolamo."

"L'Ars Nova italienne," in *Encyclopedie de la Pleiade. Histoire de la musique* 1 (Paris: Gallimard, 1960), 781–801.

Entries in vol. 8 of *Die Musik in Geschichte und Gegenwart*:
"Landini (Landino) Francesco."
"Laurentius de Florentia."
"Madrigal. A. Das Madrigal der Ars Nova. Etymologie, formale Gestaltung und Geschichte."

Vol. 2 of *The Music of Fourteenth-Century Italy*.

Walter W. Naumburg '89 Professor of Music and Head of the Eda Kuhn Loeb Music Library

1961

Ed., *Paolo Tenorista in a New Fragment of the Italian Ars Nova. A Facsimile Edition of an Early Fifteenth-Century Manuscript Now in the Library of Professor Edward E. Lowinsky, Berkeley, California* (Palm Springs: Ernest E. Gottlieb, 1961).

"Una arcaica descrizione trecentesca del madrigale," in *Musica tra Medioevo e Rinascimento*, 80–89 [originally in *Festschift Heinrich Besseler zum sechzigsten Geburtstag*, ed. Eberhardt Klemm (Leipzig: Deutscher Verlag für Musik, 1961)].

"Gesualdo da Venosa nel IV centenario della nascita. 1. Le tentazioni della monodia 2. Gli anni di Ferrara 3. La pastorale dell'io," *Terzo programma*.

Quaderni trimestrali 2 (Rome and Turin: ERI. Edizioni della Radiotelevisione italiana [RAI], 1961), "Musica," 199–216 ["Tutti i testi pubblicati nel presente Quaderno sono stati trasmessi dal Terzo Programma nel primo trimestre del 1961"].

Entries in vol. 8 of the *Enciclopedia dello Spettacolo*:
"Peri, Jacopo."
"Rinuccini, Ottavio."

Contributions to the panel discussion "From Frottola to Madrigal: The Changing Pattern of Secular Italian Vocal Music," in Walter H. Rubsamen, *Chanson & Madrigal, 1480–1530. Studies in Comparison and Contrast. A Conference at Isham Memorial Library, September 13–14, 1961*, ed. James Haar (Cambridge, MA: Harvard University Press, 1964), 72–87; see also 123–38 and Example 48 [254–55].

Contributions to the panel discussions "The Concept of the New in Music from the *Ars Nova* to the Present Day" and "The Neapolitan Tradition in Opera," in *Report of the Eighth Congress of the International Musicological Society* (Kassel: Bärenreiter Verlag, 1962), vol. 2: "Reports," 112–17 and 132–34.

1962

"Ballate e «soni» secondo un grammatico del Trecento," in *Musica tra Medioevo e Rinascimento*, 90–102 [originally in *Saggi e ricerche in memoria di Ettore Li Gotti*, 3 vols., Centro di studi filologici e linguistici siciliani. Bollettino 6–8 (Palermo: G. Mori, 1962), vol. 3].

Entries in vol. 9 of the *Enciclopedia dello Spettacolo*:
"Stradella, Alessandro."
"Striggio, Alessandro, Sr. e Jr."

Vol. 3 of *The Music of Fourteenth-Century Italy*.

1963

"Gesualdo, Ferrara e Venezia," in *Studi sul teatro veneto fra Rinascimento ed età barocca*, ed. Maria Teresa Muraro (Florence: L. S. Olschki, 1971), 305–19 [read 30 March 1963 at the Fondazione Giorgio Cini, Venice].

"Monteverdi e i problemi dell'opera," in *Music and Culture in Italy from the Middle Ages to the Baroque*, 235–53 and 421–22 [originally delivered at the Fondazione Giorgio Cini, Venice, 6 April 1963; subsequently published in *Studi sul teatro veneto fra Rinascimento ed Età barocca*, ed. Maria Teresa Muraro (Florence: L. S. Olschki, 1971)].

"Music and Cultural Tendencies in 15th Century Italy," in *Music and Culture in Italy from the Middle Ages to the Baroque* [read 27 December 1963 at the annual national meeting of the American Musicological Society; subsequently published in the *Journal of the American Musicological Society* 19 (1966)].

Entries in vol. 1 of the *Enciclopedia della musica* (n.p. [Milan]: Ricordi, n.d. [1963–65)]):
"Ballata."
"Bartolino da Padova."
"Bartolomeo da Bologna."
"Caccia."

Entries in vol. 9 of *Die Musik in Geschichte und Gegenwart*:
"Rom. C. Spätmittelalter und Renaissance."

Vol. 4 of *The Music of Fourteenth-Century Italy*.

1964

Entries in vol. 3 of the *Enciclopedia della musica*:
"I fratelli Mazzocchi."
"Revisione."

Vol. 5 of *The Music of Fourteenth-Century Italy*.

1965

"Ars nova e stil novo," in *Music and Culture in Italy from the Middle Ages to the Baroque*, 26–38 and 373–75 [originally delivered 7 January 1965 at The Johns Hopkins University, Baltimore; subsequently published in *Rivista italiana di musicologia* 1 (1966)].

"Dante *musicus:* Gothicism, Scholasticism, and Music," in *Music and Culture in Italy from the Middle Ages to the Baroque*, 13–25 [read 25 May 1965 in Cambridge, MA.; subsequently published in *Speculum* 43, no. 2 (1968)].

1966

"Il caval zoppo e il vetturino. Cronache di Parnaso 1642," in *Music and Culture in Italy from the Middle Ages to the Baroque*, 325–34 and 455–59 [originally in *Studi di musicologia in onore di Guglielmo Barblan*, Collectanea Historiae Musicae 4 (1966)].

"On Text Forms from Ciconia to Dufay," in *Aspects of Medieval and Renaissance Music: A Birthday Offering to Gustave Reese*, ed. Jan LaRue (New York: W. W. Norton, 1966), 673–82.

Entries in the encyclopedia *La Musica*, under the direction of Guido M. Gatti, ed. Alberto Basso, first part: "Enciclopedia storica," (Turin: UTET, n.d. [1966–71]):
"Ars Nova," vol. 1.
"Despres, Josquin (Després, Desprez, Des Prez, ecc.; Josquinus o Jodocus Pratensis, a Prato, ecc.; Juschino, Josse, ecc.)," vol. 2.
"Carlo Gesualdo di Venosa. Sommario: I. La vita.— II. Caratteristiche dell'opera.," vol. 2.
"Monodia," vol. 3.
"Alessandro Stradella," vol. 4 [see "Stradella, Alessandro," with Carolyn Gianturco, *Dizionario Enciclopedico Universale della Musica e dei Musicisti*, directed by Alberto Basso, "Il Lessico" (Turin: UTET, 1983–); *Dizionario Enciclopedico Universale della Musica e dei Musicisti*, directed by Alberto Basso, "Le Biografie" (Turin: UTET, 1985–88), vol. 7 (1988), 486–89].

1968

"Church Polyphony Apropos of a New Fragment at Foligno," in *Music and Culture in Italy from the Middle Ages to the Baroque*, 113–25 and 391–95 [originally in *Studies in Music History: Essays for Oliver Strunk*, ed. Harold S. Powers (Princeton, NJ: Princeton University Press, 1968)].

"Musica polifonica per un testo attribuito a Federico II," in *Music and Culture in Italy from the Middle Ages to the Baroque*, 39–50 and 375–77 [originally in *L'Ars Nova Italiana del Trecento* 2, ed. F. Alberto Gallo, Convegni di studio 1961–67 (Certaldo: Centro di Studi sull'Ars Nova Italiana del Trecento, 1968)].

"Scelte poetiche di Monteverdi," in *Music and Culture in Italy from the Middle Ages to the Baroque*, 271–316 and 428–52 [originally in *Nuova rivista musicale italiana* 2 [1968]).

"Teatro, scene e musica nelle opere di Monteverdi," in *Music and Culture in Italy from the Middle Ages to the Baroque*, 254–70 and 422–28 [originally in Comitato per le celebrazioni nazionali del IV centenario della nascita di Claudio Monteverdi, *Congresso internazionale sul tema Claudio Monteverdi e il suo tempo. Relazioni e comunicazioni* (Venice/Mantua/Cremona, 3–7 May 1968), ed. Raffaello Monterosso (Verona: Stamperia Valdonega, 1969)].

Walter W. Naumburg '89 Professor of Music

1969

Music and Theatre from Poliziano to Monteverdi, trans. Karen Eales, Cambridge Studies in Music (Cambridge: Cambridge University Press, 1982) [originally *Le due Orfei da Poliziano a Monteverdi*, con un saggio critico sulla scenografia di Elena Povoledo (Turin: ERI—Edizioni RAI Radiotelevisione Italiana, 1969); Chapter 6 originally appeared as "Early Opera and Aria," in *New Looks at Italian Opera. Essays in Honor of Donald J. Grout* (Ithaca, NY: Cornell University Press, 1968)].

"Early Venetian Libretti at Los Angeles," in *Music and Culture in Italy from the Middle Ages to the Baroque*, 317–24 and 452–55 [originally in *Essays in Musicology in Honor of Dragan Plamenac*, ed. Gustave Reese and Robert J. Snow (Pittsburgh, PA: University of Pittsburg Press, 1969)].

"Tradizione orale e tradizione scritta della musica," in *Music and Culture in Italy from the Middle Ages to the Baroque*, 72–79 and 380–82 [originally read at the second "Convegno Internazionale" on the fourteenth-century Ars nova, Certaldo, 17–22 July 1969; subsequently published in *L'Ars Nova Italiana del Trecento* 3, ed. F. Alberto Gallo (Certaldo: Centro di Studi sull'Ars Nova Musicale Italiana del Trecento, 1970)].

1970

"Two Anglo-Italian Pieces in the Manuscript Porto 714," in *Speculum Musicae Artis. Festgabe für Heinrich Husmann zum 60. Geburtstag*, eds. Heinz Becker and Reinhard Gerlach (Munich: W. Fink Verlag, 1970), 253–61.

1971

"Zacharus Musicus," in *Music and Culture in Italy from the Middle Ages to the Baroque*, 126–44 and 395–401 [originally in *Memorie e contributi alla musica dal Medioevo all'Età moderna offerti a Federico Ghisi*, Quadrivium 12, no. 1 (1971)].

Contributions to the panel discussion, "Problems in Editing the Music of Josquin des Prez: A Critique of the First Edition and Proposals for the Second Edition," in *Josquin des Prez. Proceedings of the International Josquin Festival—Conference held at The Juilliard School at Lincon Center in New York City, 21–25 June 1971*, ed. Edward E. Lowinsky, in collaboration with Bonnie J. Blackburn (London: Oxford University Press, 1976), 723–54.

ROME

**Facoltà di Lettere e Filosofia,
Università degli Studi di Roma, «La Sapienza»
Professore Ordinario di Storia della Musica**

1972

"Ricercari e variazioni su 'O rosa bella,'" in *Music and Culture in Italy from the Middle Ages to the Baroque*, 144–58 and 401–06 [originally in *Studi musicali* 1 (1972)].

"New Glimpses of an Unwritten Tradition," in *Music and Culture in Italy from the Middle Ages to the Baroque*, 51–71 and 377–80 [originally in *Words and Music: The Scholar's View. A Medley of Problems and Solutions Compiled in Honor of A. Tillman Merritt by Sundry Hands*, ed. Laurence Berman (n.p. [Cambridge, MA]: Harvard University, Department of Music, 1972)].

Introduzione al Madrigale (Dalle lezioni di Storia della Musica tenute nell'Università di Roma), Anno Accademico 1971–72 (Città Universitaria—Rome: Laboratorio Multigrafico de "La Goliardica" Società Coop. a.r.l./Centro Grafico Editoriale, Opera Universitaria, Università di Roma, 1972).

"Ars musica," in *Musica e arte figurativa nei secoli X–XII, 15–18 ottobre 1972*, Convegni del Centro di Studi sulla Spiritualità Medievale 13 (Todi: Accademia Tudertina, 1973), 225–40 [originally read at the *convegno*].

"Studi corelliani," *Lo spettatore musicale. Rivista bimestrale*, diretta da Mario Bortolotto –Duilio Courir, 7, no. 6 (Bologna: *Distribuzione* a cura della Soc. ed. «Il Mulino»/Imola: *Stampa* Grafiche Galeati, novembre–dicembre 1972): 4–8.

1973

"Novelty and Renewal in Italy, 1300–1600," in *Music and Culture in Italy from the Middle Ages to the Baroque*, 159–74 and 406–08 [originally in *Studien zur Tradition in der Musik: Kurt von Fischer zum 60. Geburtstag*, eds. Hans Heinrich Eggebrecht and Max Lütolf (Munich: Katzbichler, 1973)].

"Su alcuni testi italiani di composizioni polifoniche quattrocentesche," in *Testimonianze, studi e ricerche in onore di Guido M. Gatti (1892–1973)*, Quadrivium 14 (Bologna: A.M.I.S., 1973), 133–57.

"Note su Marenzio e il Tasso," in *Music and Culture in Italy from the Middle Ages to the Baroque*, 198–209 and 412–17 [originally in *Scritti in onore di Luigi Ronga*, ed. Raffaello Monterosso (Milan: R. Ricciardi, 1973)].

Storia dell'Opera dalle Origini al 1645 (Dalle lezioni di Storia della Musica tenute nell'Università di Roma). Anno Accademico 1972–1973 (Città Universitaria, Rome: "La Goliardica" Società Coop. A.R.L./Centro Grafico Editoriale Opera Universitaria, Università di Roma, 1973).

Entries in vol. 15 of *Die Musik in Geschichte und Gegenwart*:
"Andreas de Florentia."
"Bartholomaeus de Bononia."

1974

Don Giovanni in Musica (Dalle lezioni di Storia della Musica tenute nell'Università di Roma) (n.p. [Rome]: "La Goliardica," n.d. [1974]); see **1994**: *Don Giovanni's Progress: A Rake Goes to the Opera*.

1975

"The Orchestra and Stage in Renaissance *Intermedi* and Early Opera," in *Music and Culture in Italy from the Middle Ages to the Baroque*, 210–16 and 417–18 [originally in *Illusione e pratica teatrale. Proposte per una lettura dello spazio scenico dagli Intermedi fiorentini all'Opera comica veneziana*, catalog of the exhibition, eds. Franco Mancini, Maria Teresa Muraro, and Elena Povoledo (Vicenza: Neri Pozza, 1975)].

"Le tre corone e la musica," in *Poesia e musica e altri saggi*, 23-34 [originally read as the opening lecture at the Congresso Internazionale on the theme "La musica al tempo del Boccaccio e i suoi rapporti con la letteratura italiana,"

Siena/Certaldo, 19–22 July 1975; subsequently published in *L'Ars Nova Italiana del Trecento* 4, ed. Agostino Ziino (Certaldo: Centro di Studi sull'Ars Nova Musicale Italiana del Trecento, 1978)].

"Dalla musica di tradizione non scritta al madrigale: spigolature e postille," in *La letteratura, la rappresentazione, la musica al tempo e nei luoghi di Giorgione*, Atti del Convegno Internazionale di Studi, Castelfranco Veneto, 1975, ed. Michelangelo Muraro (Rome: Jouvence, 1987), 227–31.

1976

"'Musica de sono humano' and the Musical Poetics of Guido of Arezzo," in *Music and Culture in Italy from the Middle Ages to the Baroque*, 1–12 and 363–68 [originally in *Medievalia et Humanistica*, Studies in Medieval and Renaissance Culture, n.s., 7 (1976)].

"Musiche intorno a Tiziano," in *Poesia e musica e altri saggi*, 137–47 [originally in *Tiziano e Venezia. Convegno internazionale di studi, Venezia, 1976* (Vicenza: Neri Pozza, 1980)].

Contribution to the program notes for *Celebrazioni per il IV centenario della morte di Tiziano Vecellio: concerto di musiche rinascimentali . . . , Venezia . . . venerdì 27 a sabato 28 agosto 1976 . . . , Pieve di Cadore . . . .domenica 29 agosto 1976* (Pieve di Cadore: Comune di Pieve di Cadore, 1976/Venice: Comune di Venezia, 1976).

Contributions to the panel discussions following several papers in *Venezia e il Melodramma nel Seicento*, eds. Maria Teresa Muraro, Fondazione Giorgio Cini, Centro di cultura e civiltà, Studi di musica veneta 5 (Florence: L. S. Olschki, 1976).

"Conclusioni," in *L'etnomusicologia in Italia*, ed. Diego Carpitella (Palermo: Flaccovio, 1975), 295–300.

1977

"Ricordo di Laurence Feininger (1909–1975)," *Nuova rivista musicale italiana* 11 (1977): 71–79.

"Semiramis e Amneris, Un anagramma o quasi," in *Scelte poetiche di musicisti. Teatro, poesia e musica da Willaert a Malapiero*, Musica critica (Venice: Marsilio, 1987), 339–48 [originally in *Il melodramma italiano dell'Ottocento. Studi e ricerche per Massimo Mila* (Turin: Einaudi, 1977)].

"Introduction," "Humanism and Music," in *International Musicological Society. Report of the Twelfth Congress, Berkeley 1977*, eds. Daniel Heartz and Bonnie C. Wade (Kassel: Bärenreiter Verlag, 1981), 870.

1978

"Antonio Vivaldi, il prete rosso. Il musicista veneziano a trecento anni dalla nascita," *Corriere della sera* (mercoledì 1 marzo 1978).

"Musiche intorno a Giorgione," in *Poesia e musica e altri saggi*, 129–35 [originally in *Giorgione: atti del Convegno Internazionale di Studio per il 5° centenario della nascita, 29–31 maggio 1978* (Venice: Comitato per le celebrazioni giorgionesche, Comune di Castelfranco Veneto, 1979)].

Retirement

1979

"I poeti della scuola siciliana e la musica," in *Poesia e musica e altri saggi*, 13–21 [originally read at Harvard University, 2–3 April 1979; subsequently published in *Yearbook of Italian Studies* 4 (1980)].

1980

"The Traditions of Don Juan Plays and Comic Operas," *Proceedings of the Royal Musical Association* 107 (1980 [but 1981]): 60–70.

"Willaert and the *Canzone Villanesca*," in *Music and Culture in Italy from the Middle Ages to the Baroque*, 175–97 and 409–12 [originally in *Studi musicali* 9 (1980)].

Entries in *The New Grove Dictionary of Music and Musicians*, ed. Stanley Sadie (London: Macmillan Publishers/Washington, D.C.: Grove's Dictionaries of Music, 1980); *The New Grove Dictionary of Music and Musicians*, ed. Stanley Sadie (New York: Grove, 2001 [2nd ed.]); *Grove Music Online* [electronic resource] ([Oxford/New York]: Oxford University Press).
"Cortese, Paolo."
"Italy."
"Medieval."
"Rome."

1981

"Causerie su Beaumarchais e la musica teatrale," in *Scelte poetiche di musicisti*, 309–21 [originally in *Letterature comparate. Problemi e metodo. Studi in onore di Ettore Paratore* (Bologna: Pàtron, 1981), vol. 3].

"Maniera e riforme nella musica italiana del '500," in *Poesia e musica e altri saggi*, 107–28 [read September 1981, XXIII Corso Internazionale d'Alta Cultura, Fondazione Giorgio Cini, Venice].

"La siciliana trecentesca," in Paolo Emilio Carapezza, Fabio Carboni, Giuseppe Donato, Alberto Gallo, Nino Pirrotta, T[h]om[as] Walker, Agostino Ziino, *Musica Popolare e Musica d'Arte nel Tardo Medioevo. Testi della I Giornata di Studi sulla Musica Medievale, Palermo, maggio 1981*, Schede medievali n. 3, Contributi (Palermo: Officina di Studi Medievali, 1982), 297–308.

"OBITUARIES. William Oliver Strunk," *AMS Newsletter. The American Musicological Society. Constituent Member of the American Council of Learned Societies* 11, no. 1 (February, 1981): 8.

1982

"Discorso inaugurale," *Chigiana* 39, n.s. 19 (1982 [but 1988–89]): 11–15 [read on the occasion of the Convegno Internazionale di Studi on the theme *Alessandro Stradella e il suo tempo*, Siena, 8–12 September 1982].

"Metastasio and the Demands of his Literary Environment," in *Crosscurrents and the Mainstream of Italian Serious Opera, 1730–1790: A Symposium, February 11–13, 1982*, 2 vols., special issue to Studies in Music from the University of Western Ontario 7, nos. 1–2 (1982) (London, Ontario: Department of Music History, Faculty of Music, University of Western Ontario, 1983), 2:10–27, and "Final Licenza," 2:197–203.

"Metastasio e i teatri romani," in *Scelte poetiche di musicisti*, 291-307 [read at the international conference on "Roma e il teatro nel Settecento," Rome, 15–20 November 1982; subsequently published in *Le Muse galanti. La musica a Roma nel Settecento*, ed. Bruno Cagli (Rome: Istituto della Enciclopedia Italiana, 1985)].

"Malipiero e il filo d'Arianna," in *Scelte poetiche di musicisti*, 349-61 [read at the international conference, 24–25 September 1982, Asolo/Fondazione

Giorgio Cini, Venice; subsequently published in *Malipiero. Scrittura e Critica*, ed. Maria Teresa Muraro, Studi musica veneta [Florence: L. S. Olschki, 1984]).

1983

"Un'altra congregazione di Santa Cecilia," *Studi musicali* 12 (1983): 221–38.

"Introduzione ai lavori," in *Fausto Torrefranca: l'uomo, il suo tempo, la sua opera*, Atti del Convegno internazionale di Studi, Vibo Valentia, 15–17 dicembre 1983, eds. Giuseppe Ferraro and Annunziato Pugliese (Vibo Valentia: Istituto di Bibliografia Musicale Calabrese, 1993), 11–12.

"Istituzioni musicali nella Firenze dei Medici," in *Firenze e la Toscana dei Medici nell'Europa del '500* (Florence: L. S. Olschki, 1983), vol. 1, "Strumenti e veicoli della cultura. Relazioni politiche ed economiche," 37–54.

"I musicisti nell'epistolario di Metastasio," in *Convegno indetto in occasione del II centenario della morte di Metastasio d'intesa con Arcadia, Accademia Letteraria Italiana, Istituto di Studi Romani, Società Italiana di Studi sul Sec. XVIII (Roma, 25–27 maggio 1983)*, Accademia Nazionale dei Lincei, Atti dei convegni lincei 65 (Rome: Accademia Nazionale dei Lincei, 1985), 245–55.

"Rhapsodic Elements in North-Italian Polyphony of the 14th Century," *Musica disciplina* 37 (1983) [volume dedicated to Armen Carapetyan], 83–99.

"Il sorriso di Mozart," in *Scritti in onore di Giovanni Macchia* (Milan: Mondadori, 1983), 497–509.

1984

"Echi di arie veneziane del primo Quattrocento?" in *Poesia e musica e altri saggi*, 47–64 [originally in *Interpretazioni veneziane. Studi di Storia dell'arte in onore di Michelangelo Muraro*, ed. David Rosand (Venice: Arsenale, 1984)].

"Problemi musicali di una rappresentazione dell'*Orfeo* di Poliziano," in *Origini del Dramma Pastorale in Europa*, eds. Maria Chiabò and Federico Doglio, acts of the VIII Convegno del Centro di Studi sul Teatro Medioevale e Rinascimentale, Viterbo, 31 May–3 June 1984 (Viterbo: Union Printing, 1985), 119–31.

"Prefazione di Nino Pir[r]otta" to Remo Giazotto, in *Le due patrie di Giulio Caccini, musico mediceo, 1551–1618: nuovi contributi anagrafici e d'archivio sulla sua vita e la sua famiglia,* Biblioteca Historiae Musicae Cultores 38 (Florence: L.S. Olschki, 1984).

1985

"'Arte' e 'non arte' nel frammento Greggiati," in *L'Ars Nova Italiana del Trecento* 5, ed. Agostino Ziino (Palermo: Enchiridion, 1985), 200–17.

"Back to Ars Nova Themes," in *Music and Context. Essays for John M. Ward,* ed. Anne Dhu Shapiro (Cambridge, MA: Harvard University, Department of Music, 1985), 166–82.

"I cori per l'"Edipo Tiranno,"" in *Andrea Gabrieli e il suo tempo,* Atti del Convegno Internazionale, Venezia, 16–18 settembre 1985, ed. Francesco Degrada (Florence: L. S. Olschki, 1987), 273–92.

"Dal manoscritto alla stampa musicale," in *L'Europa musicale, un nuovo Rinascimento, la civiltà dell'ascolto,* eds. Anna Laura Bellina and Giovanni Morelli (Florence: Vallecchi, 1988), 145–61 [read in 1985 within the ambitus of Corsi di Alta Cultura della Fondazione Giorgio Cini, Venice].

"'Dolci Affetti': i Musici di Roma e il madrigale," *Studi musicali* 14 (1985): 59–104.

"Introduzione ai lavori," in *La musica a Napoli durante il Seicento,* Atti del Convegno Internazionale di Studi, Napoli, 11–14 aprile 1985, eds. Domenico Antonio D'Alessandro and Agostino Ziino (Rome: Edizioni Torre d'Orfeo, 1987), 3–6.

"Musica e Umanesimo," in *Poesia e musica e altri saggi,* 89–106 [read at the XXVII Corso Internazionale d'Alta Cultura organized by the Fondazione Giorgio Cini, August/September 1985; subsequently published in *Lettere italiane* (1985)].

"Umanesimo e Rinascimento," in *Cinque secoli di stampa musicale in Europa. Catalogo della mostra,* Rome, Palazzo Venezia (Naples: Electa, 1985), 21–22.

1986

Coed. with Danilo Curti, *I codici musicali trentini a cento anni dalla loro riscoperta: atti del Convegno Laurence Feininger: la musicologia come missione: a Trento, Castello del Buonconsiglio, 6–7 settembre 1985* (Trent: Provincia Autonoma di Trento, Servizio Beni Culturali, Museo provinciale d'Arte, 1986).

"Poesia e musica," in *Poesia e musica e altri saggi*, 1–11 [originally read in Ravenna on 14 September 1986 (the 665th anniversary of the death of Dante) at the conclusion of the international conference "La musica al tempo di Dante"; subsequently published in *Letture classensi* 16 (Ravenna: A. Longo, 1987)].

"Problemi di una storia della musica," estratto from *Convegno Internazionale sul tema: Problema e problemi della storia letteraria (Roma, 25–27 novembre 1986)*, Accademia Nazionale dei Lincei, Atti dei convegni lincei 86 (Rome: Accademia Nazionale dei Lincei, 1990), 113–21.

"Historiae Musicae Cultores," in *La casa editrice Leo S. Olschki (1946–1986). Testimonianze di Francesco Adorno, Vittore Branca, Nino Pirrotta*, ed. Stefano De Rosa, Olschki: Un secolo di editoria (1886–1986) 2 (n.p.: L. S. Olschki, 1986), 23–25.

1987

"Dalla musica di tradizione non scritta al madrigale: spigolature e postille," in *La letteratura, la rappresentazione, la musica al tempo e nei luoghi di Giorgione*, ed. Michelangelo Muraro (Rome: Jouvence, 1987), 227–31.

Coed. with Agostino Ziino, *Händel e gli Scarlatti a Roma. Atti del convegno internazionale di studi (Roma, 12–14 giugno 1985)*, Anno europeo della musica, Accademia Nazionale di Santa Cecilia (Florence: L. S. Olschki, 1987).

1989

"Un intermedio campestre," in *Miscellanea di studi in onore di Aurelio Roncaglia a cinquant'anni dalla sua laurea* (Modena: Mucchi, 1989), 1057–73.

1990

"Note su Minato," in *L'opera italiana a Vienna prima di Metastasio*, ed. Maria Teresa Muraro (Florence: L. S. Olschki, 1990), 127–63.

1991

"Forse Nerone cantò da tenore," in *Poesia e musica e altri saggi*, 179–93 [originally in *Musica senza aggettivi. Studi per Fedele d'Amico*, ed. Agostino Ziino (Florence: L. S. Olschki, 1991)].

1992

Ed., *Il codice Rossi 215. The Rossi Codex 215. Roma, Biblioteca Apostolica Vaticana. Ostiglia, Fondazione Opera Pia don Giuseppe Greggiati. Studio introduttivo ed edizione in facsimile. Introductory Study and Facsimile Edition,* Centro di Studi sull'Ars nova musicale italiana del Trecento, Ars nova 2 (Lucca: Libreria Musicale Italiana, 1992).

"Contemplando la musa assente. Minima personalia," *Belfagor* 47 (1992), "Noterelle e schermaglie," 717–24.

"Introduzione," in *La musica a Roma attraverso le fonti d'archivio*, Atti del Convegno Internazionale, Roma, 4–7 giugno 1992, ed. Bianca Maria Antolini, Arnaldo Morelli, and Vera Vita Spagnuolo (Lucca: Libreria Musicale Italiana, 1994), 1–4.

"The Music ['Le musiche']," trans. Hugh Ward Perkins, in F. Alberto Gallo, ed., *Il codice Squarcialupi: Ms. Mediceo Palatino 87, Biblioteca laurenziana di Firenze*, 2 vols., Ars nova (Florence: Giunti Barbèra/Lucca: Libreria Musicale Italiana, 1992), 1:195–221.

1993

Coed. with Giuliana Gialdroni, *I musici di Roma e il madrigale: Dolci Affetti (1582)*. Introduction and transcription by Nino Pirrotta. *Le Gioie (1589)*. Introduction and transcription by Giuliana Gialdroni, L'Arte Armonica. Collana di facsimili, studi e testi musicali della Accademia Nazionale di Santa Cecilia, Serie 2: Musica Palatina 1. Accademia Nazionale di Santa Cecilia (Lucca: Libreria Musicale Italiana, 1993).

"Metastasio e il terminare le scene con spirito e vivezza," in *Poesia e musica e altri saggi*, 231–40 [originally in *Omaggio a Gianfranco Folena* (Padua: Editoriale Programma, 1993)].

Antonino Pirrotta, "Natura e problemi del testo musicale," *estratto* from *Convegno internazionale sul tema: La filologia testuale e le scienze umane organizzato in collaborazione con l'Associazione Internazionale per gli Studi di Lingua e Letteratura Italiana (Roma, 19–22 aprile 1993)*, Accademia Nazionale dei Lincei, Atti dei convegni lincei 111 (Rome: Accademia Nazionale dei Lincei, 1994), 127–35.

Notes to *O tu chara sciença. La Musique dans la Pensée Médiévale*, trans. John Millerchip. La Reverdie. Arcana 332 (Nantes: Michel Bernstein Éditeur à Nantes, 1993/2006).

"Rileggendo *Il Pirata* di Bellini," in *Napoli e il teatro musicale in Europa tra sette e ottocento. Studi in onore di Friedrich Lippmann*, eds. Bianca Maria Antolini and Wolfgang Witzenmann (Florence: L. S. Olschki, 1993), 407–16.

"Rossini eseguito ieri e oggi," estratto, *La recenzione di Rossini ieri e oggi. Convegno organizzato con la collaborazione della Accademia Nazionale di Santa Cecilia, Fondazione Giorgio Cini, Fondazione Gioacchino Rossini, Società Italiana di Musicologia (Rome, 18–20 febbraio 1993)*, Atti dei convegni lincei 110 (Rome: Accademia Nazionale dei Lincei, 1994), 3–13.

1994

"Before the Madrigal," *Journal of Musicology* 22 (1994): 237–52.

"Claudio Monteverdi, veneziano di adozione," *Studi musicali* 23 (1994): 73–86 [originally read at the instance of the "Comitato Nazionale per le Celebrazioni del 350° anniversario della morte di Claudio Monteverdi," at the Palazzo Ducale of Venice, the Biblioteca Vallicelliana of Rome, and the Biblioteca Statale of Cremona, on 27 November, 1st, and 6 December 1993, respectively].

Don Giovanni's Progress: A Rake Goes to the Opera, trans. Harris S. Saunders, Jr. (New York: Marsilio, 1994).

1995

Ed., *Chori in musica composti sopra li chori della tragedia di Edippo Tiranno. Recitati in Vicenza l'anno M.D.lxxxv. Con solenissimo apparto*. Venezia, Angelo Gardano 1588, Edizione nazionale delle opere di Andrea Gabrieli [1533]–1585, Edizione critica, Opere postume 12. Fondazione Giorgio Cini, Istituto per la Musica (Milan: Ricordi, 1995).

"Federico II e la musica," in *Federico II e l'Italia. Catalogo della Mostra, Palazzo Venezia, dicembre 1995–aprile 1996* (Rome: De Luca, 1995), 145–47.

"'Maniera' polifonica e immediatezza recitativa," in *Giornata lincea dedicata a Claudio Monteverdi: Monteverdi. Recitativo in monodia e polifonia*, Atti dei convegni lincei 124 [acts of the study day, Rome, 9 March 1995] (Rome: Accademia Nazionale dei Lincei, 1996), 9–20.[7]

"Opera: Da Monteverdi a Monteverdi," in *Attualità di Monteverdi. Conferenza di Nino Pirrotta* (Cremona: Comitato nazionale per le celebrazioni del 350°

---

[7]See *Corriere della Sera* (9 marzo 1995), 52.

anniversario della morte di Claudio Monteverdi, in collaborazione con il Ministero per i beni culturali e ambientali, Ufficio centrale per i beni librari, Gli Istituti culturali e l'editoria, 1995), 7–20.

"Pier Jacopo Martello: 'Et in Arcadia ego,' ma 'cum modo,'" in *Le parole della musica: Studi sulla lingua della letteratura musicale in onore di Gianfranco Folena*, ed. Maria Teresa Muraro (Florence: L. S. Olschki, 1995), 2:33–46.

"A Sommacampagna Codex of the Italian Ars Nova?" in *Essays on Mediaeval Music in Honor of David G. Hughes*, ed. Graeme M. Boone (Cambridge, MA: Harvard University Press, 1995), 317–31.

"Per Diego Carpitella," in *Tendenze e metodi nella ricerca musicologica: Atti del convegno internazionale*, ed. Raffaele Pozzi, Historae musicae cultores biblioteca 71 (Florence: L. S. Olschki, 1995).

1996

"Divagazioni su Goldoni e il dramma giocoso. A Tom Walker," *Rivista italiana di musicologia* 32 (Florence: L.S. Olschki, 1997): 99–108 [read 4 September 1996 on the occasion of a conference on the theme "Metrica e canto," announced by the Fondazione Giorgio Cini di Venezia and dedicated to Thomas Walker].

"Florence from Barzelletta to Madrigal," in *Musica Franca. Essays in Honor of Frank A. D'Accone*, eds. Irene Alm, Alyson McLamore, and Colleen Reardon, Festschrift Series No. 18, Pendragon Press Musicological Series (Stuyvesant, NY: Pendragon Press, 1996), 7–18.

Lezione tenuta il 23 agosto 1996 all'Università degli Studi di Urbino in occasione del conferimento della Laurea *honoris causa*, in *Studi Urbinati B, Scienze umane e sociali* 68 (1997–98): 11–16.

"Parole di chiusura," in *Convegno internazionale Cristina di Svezia e la musica: Roma, 5–6 dicembre 1996*, Atti dei convegni lincei 138 (Rome: Accademia Nazionale dei Lincei, 1998).

1997

"Dalla favola pastorale all'opera," *Avidi lumi: quadrimestrale di culture musicali del Teatro Massimo di Palermo*, 1, no. 1 (Palermo: E.A. Teatro Massimo, 1997): 7–9.

"Francesco Landini: i lumi della mente," in *Dolcissime armonie. Nel sesto centenario della morte di Francesco Landini*, ed. Piero Gargiulo (Fiesole [Florence]: Cadmo, 1997), 3–11.

"Musiche profane di Domenico Massenzio," in *Tullio Cima, Domenico Massenzio e la musica del loro tempo*, Atti del Convegno internazionale, Ronciglione, 30 ottobre–1 novembre 1997 (Rome: IBIMUS, 2003), 321–24.

"La 'nascita' dell'opera," *Studi musicali* 27 (1998): 3–5 [read to inaugurate the Convegno Internazionale di Studi on the theme *I primi decenni dello stile rappresentativo*, Rome, Palazzo della Cancelleria, 30 September 1997].

Rome, "On Landini and Ser Lorenzo," *Musica disciplina. A Yearbook of the History of Music* 48, eds. Frank A. D'Accone and Gilbert Reaney (n.p.: American Institute of Musicology/Hänssler-Verlag, 1994 ["Though the present volume of *Musica Disciplina*, 48, bears the date 1994, it is ... appearing in 1997"]), 5–13.

† 1998

"Invito al recitativo," *Studien zur italienischen Musikgeschichte* 15, ed. Friedrich Lippmann, Analecta Musicologica 30/1–2 (Regensburg: Laaber-Verlag, 1998): 145–65.

"Storie di Febiarmonici," *Avidi lumi: Quadrimestrale di culture musicali del Teatro massimo di Palermo* (Palermo: E.A. Teatro Massimo, 1997–), 1, no. 2 (1998): 19–22.

† 1999

"'*Franciscus peregre canens*,'" in *Col dolce suon che da te piove. Studi su Francesco Landini e la musica del suo tempo in memoria di Nino Pirrotta*, La tradizione musicale 4 SPFM 2 (Florence: SISMEL/Edizioni del Galluzzo, 1999), 7–13.

† 2007

"La notazione del Codice Rossi 215," in *Antologia. Parte prima, secoli IX–XIV*, Le Notazioni della Polifonia Vocale dei Secoli IX–XVII, 1, eds. Stefano Aresi, Maria Caraci Vela, and Daniele Sabaino, Università di Pavia. Dipartimento di Scienze Musicologiche e Paleografico-Filologiche. Centro di Musicologia Walter Stauffer (Pisa: ETS, 2007–), 247–50.

Index

A

Accademia Nazionale dei Lincei, 10, 247, 295, 311
Adler, Guido, 83–85
Aida, Verdi, 18, 306
AIM. *See* American Institute of Musicology
Amadio, Luigi, 18–20, 22–24, 28–29, 31, 36–37
American Institute of Musicology, 158, 170, 184, 288
American Musicological Society, 107, 110, 120, 158, 193, 195, 199–200, 255, 265, 267, 273, 293, 296, 310–311
Anselmi, Giorgio, 265, 340
Ardigò, Roberto, 88–89, 95
Aristotle, 15, 27, 179, 325, 340
Aristoxenus, 169
Arrivabene, Opprandino, 307
Aurispa, Giovanni, 265

B

Baccelli, Alfredo, 15–16
Ballata, monophonic, 129, 342
Baltsa, Agnes, 308
Banchieri, Adriano, 161–164, 170, 182, 185–186, 190, 257, 290, 346
Bardi, Giovanni, 15, 29, 161, 169–171, 173, 347
Baron, Hans, 50
Bartoli, Cecilia, 308
Beccadelli, Antonio, 265
Bellini, Vincenzo, 19, 23–24, 28, 31, 56, 65, 71, 122, 128, 137, 143, 187, 315–316, 335, 337, 352–353
Benvenuti, Giacomo, 84
Berchet, Giovanni, 59, 61, 133
Berenson, Bernard, 9, 17, 37
Bergson, Henri, 89–90
Berkeley, George, 15, 176, 250, 261, 310, 312
Bertoni, Giulio, 57–63, 67, 69, 92–93, 100, 130–135, 141
Besseler, Heinrich, 61, 63, 83, 85, 135
Biagi, Luigi, 8–9
Bianconi, Lorenzo, 174–176, 324
Biardeau, Madeleine, 118
Bobbio, Norberto, 46, 86–88, 91–92, 99, 102, 104, 107
Boccaccio, 16, 64, 66, 138
Boethian tripartition of music, 260
Boethius, 147–148, 285, 299
Bonaventura, Arnaldo, 30–31, 45
Bonini, Severo, 173

Bossi, Enrico, 18–19, 36, 156
Boyer, Ernest L., 290
Brentano, Robert, 138
Brown, Howard Mayer, 66, 105, 138, 168–169, 172–173, 176, 187, 258, 321
Burney, Charles, 328–330

C

Caccini, Giulio, 161, 165, 169–173, 287, 347
Calderoni, Mario, 101
Callot, Jacques, 184–185
Camerata, Florentine, 72, 77, 116, 144, 161, 169–173, 190, 196, 290, 292, 336, 347
Carabellese, Pantaleo, 27, 91, 315
Carapetyan, Armen, 158, 296
Cavalli, Francesco, 161, 174, 178–179, 263, 298, 335, 337, 348–349
Celenza, Christopher, 91, 96–97, 99, 261
Center for Italian Renaissance Studies, Harvard University (Villa I Tatti), 9, 17, 37, 214
Cerreto, Scipione, 285
Cesareo, Giovanni Alfredo, 25–26, 59, 61, 63, 131, 135
Cesti, Antonio, 24, 30, 84–85, 120–121, 123, 155–156, 158, 160–161, 173–183, 186–187, 190, 200, 259, 335, 348
Chilesotti, Oscar, 84
Churchill, Winston, 135
Cicognini, Giacinto Andrea, 30, 175, 178, 181, 183, 200, 349
Clement VII, Pope, 317–318
Collins, Randall, 86, 92, 96, 98, 100
Columbia University, 38, 193–200, 246, 248
Comedy, madrigal, 162–164
Conant, James Bryant, 12–13
Conservatorio «Luigi Cherubini» di Firenze, 24, 28–37, 41, 174
Conservatorio «Vincenzo Bellini» di Palermo, 7, 9–10, 18, 22–24, 31, 56, 58, 69, 91, 127–153, 336
Conservatorio di Musica «S.ta Cecilia» di Roma
Corelli, Arcangelo, 31, 159, 304–305, 353
Cornago, Johannes, 302
Corsi, Jacopo, 161, 172, 175, 347
Council of Trent, 318–319
Croce, Benedetto, 16, 46, 59–60, 75, 90–98, 100–101, 114, 116–119, 285
Crocean Idealism, 59, 93–94, 131, 175

D

D'Accone, Frank, 30, 195, 199–200, 246, 248, 255–256, 258, 296
Dallapiccola, Luigi, 30
Damerini, Adelmo, 19, 28, 31, 69
D'Anjou, Robert, King of Naples, 341
D'Annunzio, Gabriele, 69, 71–72, 143–144
Dante, 14, 16, 99, 255–256, 261, 299, 340
Darwin, Charles, 86–88
Davidsohn, Robert, 65, 67, 139
Davis, Natalie Zemon, 183
Debenedetti, Santorre, 140
The Decameron, Boccaccio, 16, 66, 138
Desprez, Josquin, 121, 266, 276, 281–283, 285, 344
Doni, Giovanni Battista, 161, 171, 285
Donizetti, Gaetano, 180, 187, 316, 352
Dramatic madrigal, 162–164
Durand, Dana B., 278–279, 344

E

Economic materialism, 103–106, 182
  influences of on Pirrotta, 122–124
Eda Kuhn Loeb Music Library, Harvard University, 78, 245, 249, 251, 254
Elliott, J.H., 183
Enciclopedia dello Spettacolo, 160–162

INDEX

Ercole, Francesco, 17, 25

F
Faenza codex, 188
Fara, Giulio, 111
Fascism, Italian, and its possible influences on Pirrotta, 50, 68, 70–71, 142–143, 247
Fascist regime, Italian, 7, 97
Fazio-Allmayer, Vito, 27, 315
Feldman, Martha, 291
Fenzo, Modesto, 322–323
Ficino, Marsilio, 265
Filelfo, Francesco, 265, 274–275
Fite, Warner, 97, 114–115
Florentine aristocratic opera of the early seventeenth century, 164–173
Fontanelli, Alfonso, 285–287
Franchetti, Alberto, 28–29
Franck, Cesar, 19
Franco, Giacomo, 184–185
Frazzi, Vito, 29–31, 174–175

G
Galilei, Vincenzo, 27, 161, 169–170, 285, 347
Gardner, Edmund G., 59, 61, 133
Garin, Eugenio, 50, 103, 270
Gaunt, Simon, 58, 60, 132
Gentile, Giovanni, 15–16, 27, 39, 46, 60, 75, 88, 90–92, 95–101, 111, 114–116, 132, 315
Gentilean Idealism, 59, 93, 97–98, 123, 131
Gentilean educational reforms, 16–17, 98
Gesualdo, Carlo, 78–79, 119, 132, 284–288, 304, 320, 345
Ghisi, Federico, 31, 70, 72, 84, 144
Gianturco, Carolyn, 57, 65, 113, 129, 137, 194, 252
Giazotto, Remo, 181, 290
Gilbert, W.S., 163, 324
Giustinian, Leonardo, 266, 302–304
Giustiniani, Vincenzo, 171–172, 274, 288
Goldschmidt, Hugo, 84
Gombosi, Otto, 243–245, 248, 291
Grafton, Anthony, 13, 82, 277
Great Schism, 139, 269, 342–343
Guami, Giuseppe, 162
Guarini, Giovanni Battista, 286, 345
Guarino, Gianbattista, 119, 171, 287
Guerrini, Maestro Guido, 29, 156, 200
Guidiccioni, Laura, 171
Gurlitt, Willibald, 85

H
Haar, James, 51, 70, 142, 158, 245, 256, 258, 267–268, 281, 312
Haberl, Franz Xaver, 83–84
Haeckel, Ernst, 86–87
Hall, Robert A., 58, 60–62, 132–134, 246, 297
Harvard University, 9, 13–14, 17, 21, 37, 48, 50, 78, 83, 86, 110, 157, 166, 181, 195, 200, 214, 237, 243–293, 295–296, 310–313, 319, 322, 336, 340, 344
Hempel, Carl G., 108
Hertzmann, Erich, 199, 236
Holmes, William C., 100, 178, 200
Hoppin, Richard, 116, 278, 344
Horne, Marilyn, 308

I
Idealism, 16, 27, 40, 46–47, 50, 59–62, 75–76, 79–80, 86, 90–95, 97–102, 107, 110, 113–115, 117, 121–123, 131–134, 175, 336, 353
    Crocean, 59, 93–94, 131, 175
    European, 27
    Gentilean, 59, 93, 97–98, 123, 131
    German, 314–315
    Kantian-Hegelian, 86
Idealist philosophy, 16, 100, 120
Ignazio, Alfano, 20

International Association of Music Libraries, 158–160, 245
International Musicological Society, 107, 310–311
Italian spiritualist philosophies, influences of on Pirrotta, 114–124

J
Jaja, Donato, 97
James, William, 100–101
John XXIII, Pope, 139

K
Kant, Immanuel, 27, 97–98, 114, 314–315
Kantian-Hegelian idealism, 86
Kerman, Joseph, 81, 84, 106–108, 195
Kernan, Alvin, 105
Kinkeldey Award, American Musicological Society, 162, 260, 284
Kirchner, Leon, 254
Kretzschmar, Hermann, 84, 181
Kristeller, Paul Oskar, 50, 141, 270
Kunsthistorisches Institut, Florence, 37

L
Labriola, Antonio, 46, 75, 86, 91–92, 103–105
Larmore, Jennifer, 308
Leo X, Pope, 25, 264, 317–318
Levy, Kenneth, 159, 194, 196–197, 199
Liuzzi, Fernando, 64, 66, 138
Lockwood, Lewis, 70, 76, 78, 81, 112, 142, 176, 179, 183–184, 199, 245, 247, 263, 268, 277, 284, 289, 296, 306, 311–313, 337
Lovarini, Emilio, 83, 140
Ludwig, Friedrich, 83, 184
Luzzaschi, Luzzasco, 166, 285, 287–288, 345

M
Machiavelli, Niccolò, 15, 163, 324
Madrigal comedy, 162–164
Madrigals, Italian, of the fourteenth and sixteenth centuries, 15, 63–68, 81, 83, 119, 122–123, 135–140, 155, 162–164, 170, 182, 185–186, 259, 261, 266, 284–289, 297–298, 304, 306, 314, 317–321, 324–325, 337, 341, 345–346
  relation of the sixteenth-century madrigal to the "chanson," 317
Maggio Musicale,Florence, 69, 71, 143
Mantegna, Andrea, 76–77
Mantica, Francesco, 155
Mantua, San Giogio, Gonzaga castle, 76
Marenzio, Luca, 132, 284–285, 289, 298, 304, 320, 345
Marinuzzi, Gino, 23–24, 175, 178, 181
Martello, Pier Jacopo, 308, 321–322, 324–325, 327, 329, 332, 350
Materialism
  economic, 103–106, 182
  scientific, 86
Mauro, Antonino, 19
Mei, Girolamo, 161, 169–170, 292
Meier, Bernhard, 306
Melosio, Francesco, 263
Mendel, Arthur, 107–108, 197–198, 243, 245–246
Merritt, Tillman, 112, 245–246, 248, 253–255, 262, 296
Ministry of Public Instruction, Italian, 47, 160
Modena Codex, 123
Mompellio, Federico, 19, 21, 59, 131, 257, 311, 339–340
Moniglia, Andrea, 180
Monody, late-sixteenth-century Florentine, 72, 144, 170, 172, 286–287, 289, 320, 347
Monophonic ballata, 129, 342
Montagna, Leonardo, 302
Monteverdi, Claudio, 38, 71–72, 76, 80–81, 115–116, 132, 143–144, 168, 180, 196, 284–285, 288–290, 304, 312, 314, 320–321, 335–337, 345, 347–348
Moore, Douglas, 87, 200
Morelli, Giovanni, 174, 176
Municipal Gallery of Modern Art, Palermo, 7

Index

Muraro, Michelangelo, 118, 178, 312–314
Muratori, Ludovico Antonio, 324–325, 327, 329
Mussolini, Benito, 15, 70–71, 142–143

N

Nationalism, Italian, and its influences on Pirrotta, 100–101, 121–122
Nenna, Pomponio, 285–286, 288
Newcomb, Anthony, 79, 171, 285–287, 314, 319
Nietzsche, Friedrich, 69, 71, 143
Nigrisolius, Hyeronimus, 284
Nominalist school, Realist school, dialectic between, 149
Novati, Francesco, 83

O

Oakeshott, Michael, 108
Oakley, Francis, 267, 278
O'Connor, Daniel, 278, 344
Oedipus, Andrea Gabrieli's choruses for, 313–314
Orontea, 24, 30, 84–85, 120–121, 123, 155–156, 158, 160–161, 173–183, 186–187, 190, 200, 259, 335, 348–349
Osthoff, Wolfgang, 174, 320–321
Otto Kindeldey Memorial Prize, 293

P

Pacifico, Maddalena, 155, 158
Palermo, 53–71
Palisca, Claude, 170
Papini, Giovanni, 38, 75, 86–88, 102–103, 105
Parsifal, Wagner, 18
Peri, Jacopo, 79, 160–161, 165–169, 171–172, 179, 190, 227, 290, 321, 347
Petrarch, 16, 64, 66, 138, 271
Petrobelli, Pierluigi, 24, 29–30, 56–57, 63–64, 73, 120, 128–129, 135–136, 145, 161, 166, 193–195, 250, 284, 296, 310, 337
Philosophical trends, twentieth-century Italy, 85–106

Piero, Fra, 30, 169, 190, 325
Pirandello family, and its relationship to the Pirrottas, 3–5, 22, 203
Piston, Walter H., 248, 254
Plato, 15, 108, 275, 325
Platonic forms, ideas, 149
Plautus, 163
Plutarch, 169
Pontano, Giovano Giovanni, 265
Pontificio Istituto di Musica Sacra, Rome, 194
Pope, Isabel, 59
Positivism, 27, 46, 75–76, 85–92, 97–99, 101–104, 106–107, 110–111, 113–114, 300
  influences of on Pirrotta, 113–114
  scientific, 89, 98
Positivistic historiography, German, 195
Povoledo, Elena, 290
Pragmatism, Italian, 101–102
Prezzolini, Giuseppe, 38, 75, 102–103, 111
Princeton University, 21, 46, 82, 108–109, 158, 171, 193–200, 239, 248, 289, 310–311, 313, 319, 324
Prodenzani, Simone, 265
Pusey, Nathan, Harvard president, 249, 255, 267

Q

Quadrivia, 299–300
Quattrocento humanists, 265, 270–271, 277, 279–280, 302, 320
Quattrocento, Italian music of, 265
Quattrocento Renaissance, 327

R

Raccuglia, Filippo Ernesto, 136
Realist school, Nominalist school, dialectic between, 149
Redi, Francesco, 327–328
Reforms, Gentilean, 16–17, 98
Restivo family, 6–9, 18, 47, 55, 57–58, 127–130, 167, 205
Riario, Cardinal Pietro, 304
Riemann, Hugo, 84
Rinaldi, Giacomo, 86, 91–92, 99–100

Rinuccini, Ottavio, 161, 166, 169, 172, 347
Ronga, Luigi, 65, 137, 252–253, 295–296, 298
Rosa, Salvator, 25, 80, 180, 262, 266, 298, 303–304, 339
Rosand, Ellen, 48, 77, 110, 114, 123, 133, 176, 180, 257–258, 309–310, 312, 314
Rossini, Gioacchino, 111, 122, 163, 167, 175, 179–180, 187, 306, 308, 316, 321–324, 326, 335, 351–352
Royal Musical Association, 310–311, 313

S

Sacchetti, Franco, 15, 17, 55, 57, 62–70, 73, 80, 83, 119, 122, 129, 134–142, 145, 175, 342
Sachs, Curt, 193
Salmi, Mario, 8, 40–41, 44, 47–48, 60, 62, 134, 138, 252–253
Salutati, Coluccio, 340
Salvemini, Gaetano, 39, 46–47, 214
San Giogio, Mantua, Gonzaga castle, 76
Sangiorgi-Paternostro, Francesca, 133
Sapegno, Natalino, 83
Savasta, Antonio, 24, 128, 339
Scarlatti, Filippo, 166, 266, 274, 302
Schiaparelli, Luigi, 39
Schmidt, Carl B., 181, 244–245, 259
Selvaggi, Rito, 136
Seneca, 15, 76
Socialism, Marxist, 87
Soldanieri, Niccolò, 130
Sophocles, 12
Spaventa, Bernardo, 15
Spencer, Herbert, 88
Spiritualist philosophies, influences of on Pirrotta, 114–124
Squarcialupi codex, 62
Strozzi, Piero, 169
Strunk, Oliver, 193-200
Sullivan, Sir Arthur, 163

T

Tacitus, 12
Taine, Hippolyte, 105–106
Tasso, Torquato, 15
Taucci, Raffaele M., 60
Tebaldi, Tommaso, 265
Tebaldini, Giovanni, 19
Tenorista, Paolo, 14
Terence, 21
Thompson, Randall, 200
Toesca, Pietro, 39
Torrefranca, Fausto, 113
Toscanini, Arturo, 81
Traversari, Ambrogio, 266
Tuttle, Stephen Davidson, 244
Twentieth-century Italy, philosophical trends, 85–106

U

United Nations Educational Scientific and Cultural Organization, 160
University of Florence, 37–51
University of Palermo, 24–28

V

Vailati, Giovanni, 75, 101–102
Valori, Filippo, 169
Vecchi, Orazio, 30
Venetian opera of the seventeenth century, 177
Venturi, Adolfo, 8
Verdelot, Philippe, 81
Verdi, Giuseppe, 18
Vinci, Pietro, 131–133
Virgil, 12

W

Wagner, Richard, 18
Walker, Thomas, 9
Warburg, Aby, 31
Ward III, John Milton, 243–245
Weiss, Julian, 58
Wiel, Taddeo, 180

Index

Wilhelm V, Duke, 184
Wolf, Friedrich August, 63, 82
Wood, David A., 249

X
Xenophon, 12

Z
Zacara, Antonio, 188
Zanetti, Emilia, 133
Zeno, Apostolo, 324
Ziino, Ottavio, 4, 6, 56, 59, 128, 131, 166–167, 169, 172, 195, 347
Zuelli, Guglielmo, 23

www.ingramcontent.com/pod-product-compliance
Lightning Source LLC
Chambersburg PA
CBHW081113160426
42814CB00035B/298